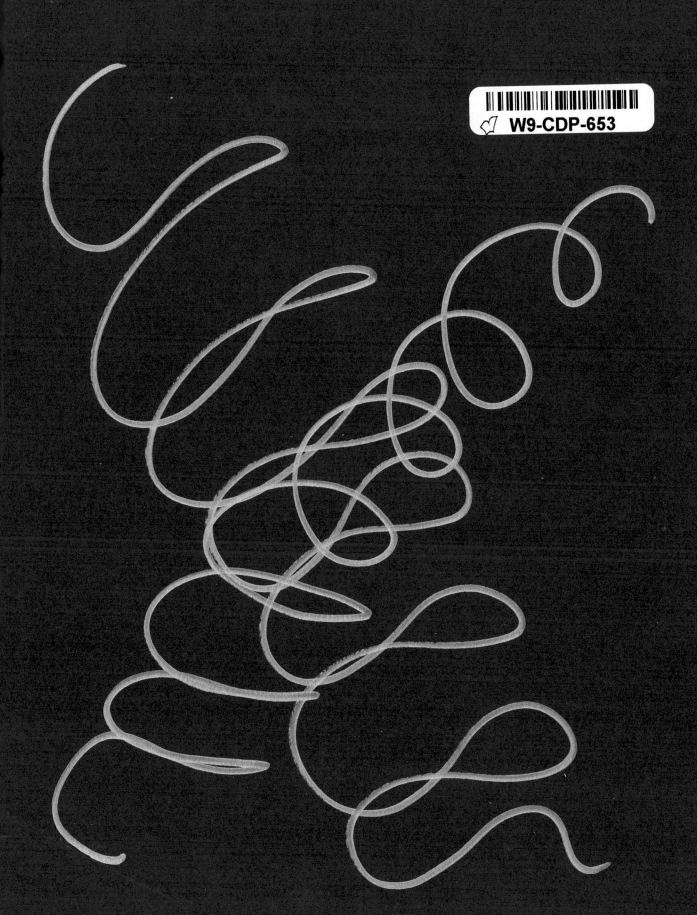

CONTEMPORARY MARKETING

Fifth Edition

CONTEMPORARY MARKETING

Fifth Edition

Louis E. Boone

Ernest G. Cleverdon Chair
of Business and Management
University of South Alabama

David L. Kurtz

The University Professor of Marketing
Seattle University

The Dryden Press

Chicago   New York   Philadelphia
San Francisco   Montreal   Toronto
London   Sydney   Tokyo   Mexico City
Rio de Janeiro   Madrid

To our families,
Pat, Barry, and Christopher
Diane, Jennifer, and Tom

Acquisitions Editor: Mary Glacken
Developmental Editor: Rob Zwettler
Project Editor: Jan Doty
Managing Editor: Jane Perkins
Design Director: Alan Wendt
Production Manager: Mary Jarvis
Permissions Editor: Doris Milligan

Library of Congress Cataloging in Publication Data

Boone, Louis E.
  Contemporary marketing.

  Includes bibliographies and index.
  1. Marketing.   I. Kurtz, David L.   II. Title.
HF5415.B53   1986   658.8   85-4458
ISBN 0-03-003189-3

Printed in the United States of America
678-039-98765432

Address orders:
383 Madison Avenue
New York, NY 10017

Address editorial correspondence:
One Salt Creek Lane
Hinsdale, IL 60521

THE DRYDEN PRESS
HOLT, RINEHART AND WINSTON
SAUNDERS COLLEGE PUBLISHING

About the Authors

Louis E. Boone (Ph.D.) holds the Ernest G. Cleverdon Chair of Business and Management at the University of South Alabama. He formerly chaired the Division of Management and Marketing at the University of Tulsa and has taught marketing in Australia, Greece, and the United Kingdom.

Dr. Boone has been active in applying computer technology to marketing education. His research on marketing information systems has been published in the *Proceedings of the American Marketing Association, Business Horizons,* and the *Journal of Business Strategy*. His marketing simulations include *Marketing Strategy* (Charles E. Merrill Publishing Company, 1971 and 1975) and *The Sales Management Game* (PennWell Books, 1978). His research has also been published in such journals as the *Journal of Marketing, Journal of Retailing, Journal of Business of the University of Chicago, Business, Journal of Business Research,* and *Journal of Psychology*. He has served as president of the Southwestern Marketing Association and vice-president of the Southern Marketing Association.

David L. Kurtz (Ph.D.) is the University Professor of Marketing at Seattle University. Dr. Kurtz has also taught at Eastern Michigan University, the University of Arkansas, and Chisholm Institute of Technology in Melbourne, Australia.

Dr. Kurtz has authored or coauthored fourteen books and more than 40 articles, monographs, cases, book reviews, and computer simulations. His text *Foundations of Marketing* (Louis E. Boone and Dale M. Beckman, coauthors) is used as the introductory marketing text by over 50 percent of all Canadian colleges and universities. Dr. Kurtz serves as president of the Western Marketing Educators Association and vice-president of the Academy of Marketing Science. He has also served as editor and associate editor of two academic journals and has been the president of a small corporation.

The Dryden Press Series in Marketing

Kurtz and Boone
Marketing
Second Edition

Marquardt, Makens, and Roe
Retail Management: Satisfaction of Consumer Needs
Third Edition

Rachman
Marketing Today

Rosenbloom
Marketing Channels: A Management View
Second Edition

Schary
Logistic Decisions: Text and Cases

Schnaars
MICROSIM
A marketing simulation available for IBM PC® and Apple®

Sciglimpaglia
Applied Marketing Research

Shimp and DeLozier
Promotion Management and Marketing Communication

Talarzyk
Cases for Analysis in Marketing
Third Edition

Talarzyk
Contemporary Cases in Marketing
Third Edition

Terpstra
International Marketing
Third Edition

Young and Mondy
Personal Selling: Function, Theory, and Practice
Second Edition

Zikmund
Exploring Marketing Research
Second Edition

Zikmund, Lundstrom, and Sciglimpaglia
Cases in Marketing Research

Preface

In the 12 years since the first edition was published, two-thirds of a million students have begun the study of marketing with *Contemporary Marketing*. What has made the text such a common fixture in the marketing programs of the nation's colleges and universities? User feedback has identified several factors that collectively explain the success of the text. *Contemporary Marketing* is comprehensive, systematic, and rigorous. It is also decidedly shorter than other texts, and it is both practical and written in a lively, engaging style that avoids tedious, boring prose. Readily identifiable cases and real-world examples are included to illustrate the application of fundamental marketing concepts discussed in the text. To reinforce student learning, examples follow the explanation of each concept. End-of-chapter discussion questions and cases require application of this knowledge.

Contemporary Marketing has served as a model for marketing texts written during the past 12 years. It has introduced a number of "firsts" that have been incorporated in every marketing textbook introduced since then. For example, the text has stressed pedagogical soundness by identifying specific learning objectives for each chapter. Each chapter has opened with an example of an actual individual or firm attempting to apply the concepts discussed in the chapter. Boxed items were used within chapters to show additional applications—often in novel settings. Such features are now included in each of the eight to ten basic marketing textbooks published every year.

Time for a Change

While sweeping changes in text materials in such disciplines as finance, accounting, management, and statistics have occurred to reflect the major changes in their fields, marketing texts have shown little similar evolution. (The most widely used textbook in the nation's colleges and universities was first published over a quarter-century ago.) In fact, the only substantial difference between the current basic marketing textbooks and those of the 1950s and 1960s is the inclusion of coverage on services marketing and marketing in nonprofit organizations. Whereas courses and texts in other disciplines have incorporated analytical techniques and computer technology, basic marketing texts have remained highly descriptive, offering only end-of-chapter cases as a vehicle for marketing analysis.

Although the nature of the marketing discipline requires that subjective judgments be complemented by analytical techniques, the fact remains that the typical principles of marketing text provides little or no integration of decision-oriented marketing tools. In disciplines such as finance and accounting, students in introductory courses are required to utilize sophisticated techniques and computer technology to solve problems. In a basic marketing course, however, the typical student assignment is to read a chapter. Instructors seeking more analytical homework assignments have the limited options of either a short case problem or a study guide assignment.

Both students and professors recognize the shortcomings of the basic marketing textbook. In a recent AMA publication, Bentley College senior Valerie B. Ross stated:

In looking to the future, I've found one shortcoming to existing marketing texts. Many refer to the "Computer Age," yet there is no defined way of applying computers to marketing in the texts. Other subjects' texts usually have projects or exercises that involve the computer. I would like to see some computer exercises in my marketing texts. After all, when I start my career, I'll be surrounded by computers. Therefore, the preparation is necessary now to see how computers fit in with the marketing principles.*

Computer Applications

The new fifth edition of *Contemporary Marketing* accomplishes the dual objectives of increasing the student's level of analytical thinking in the basic marketing course and integrating the use of microcomputers in the marketing curriculum. At the end of each chapter, a special *Computer Applications* section describes the use of a technique or marketing concept that can be adapted to the microcomputer. Each section contains at least five marketing problems that focus specifically on marketing concepts discussed in the chapter. Techniques used in solving marketing problems include such basic models as breakeven analysis, return on investment, inventory turnover, the EOQ model, Engel's laws, the exchange process, markups and markdowns, and sales forecasting. A total of 110 computer problems are included in the text; another 100 problems are contained in the *Study Guide*. Each computer problem is identified by this symbol: ■

The Boone & Kurtz Marketing Disk

The computer problems in *Contemporary Marketing* can be solved with the use of a new and unique software supplement available free to adopters for use with the IBM PC and the Apple II systems. The *Boone & Kurtz Marketing Disk* includes the following 16 programs, presented in a user-friendly, menu-driven format, for use in solving marketing problems:

1.	Exchange Process	9.	Inventory Turnover
2.	Decision Tree Analysis	10.	Markups
3.	Sales Forecasting	11.	Markdowns
4.	Sales Analysis	12.	Economic Order Quantity (EOQ)
5.	Engel's Laws	13.	Promotional Budget Allocations
6.	Evaluation of Alternatives	14.	Advertising Evaluations
7.	Competitive Bidding	15.	Sales Force Size Determination
8.	Return on Investment (ROI)	16.	Breakeven Analysis

*Valerie B. Ross, "Boring Books Out; Mind-Teasing Texts In; But They Need More Computer Exercises," *Marketing Educator* (Winter 1985), p. 3.

Each menu item on the disk includes page references to the text discussion of the technique being applied.

Since full descriptions of each technique and sample worked-out problems are included in the text, the instructor can use these computer problems in a variety of formats. If students have ready access to microcomputers, problem assignments can be used as daily homework. If students do not have easy access to computers, the problems can be solved by using a hand calculator. When microcomputer access is difficult, instructors can integrate computer usage in their classes by making one or two assignments during the term and/or by spacing computer assignments for different groups of students throughout the course to relieve demand for computer access in the microcomputer lab. Each of these alternatives will succeed in providing homework assignments involving quantitative problems for every chapter in the textbook.

Stop-Action Cases

The first edition of *Contemporary Marketing* pioneered the use of chapter-opening vignettes, in which an individual or firm was faced with a problem relating to concepts discussed in the chapter. In addition, highlighted boxed items were interspersed throughout each chapter to provide additional examples of concept application. Over the past decade, opening vignettes and boxed items have become standard features of almost every basic marketing textbook.

However, user feedback has revealed dissatisfaction with these two features. Many professors have reported that their students dislike the interruptive nature of long boxed examples interspersed throughout the text. This is particularly true of some textbooks in which different types of boxed inserts make it difficult to separate conceptual materials from peripheral examples. In addition, professors have indicated that the opening vignettes were poorly used. Many have felt that authors had neglected the opportunity to make more effective use of these examples by failing to refer to them throughout the chapter.

In *Contemporary Marketing* the boxes and the opening vignettes have been replaced by *stop-action cases*. These real-life cases emphasize the application of marketing concepts presented in each chapter. Each chapter begins with a description of a firm experiencing a marketing problem. Students are given background information, a statement of the problem, and a request to use material in the chapter to assist the firm's decision makers in solving the problem. In the middle of the chapter a *Return to the Stop-Action Case* provides additional information about the firm and creates a stronger linkage to specific chapter concepts. In *Solving the Stop-Action Case* at the end of the chapter the students learn how the firm's decision makers resolved their problem.

Examples of stop-action cases in the text include the following:

- NutraSweet Brand Sweetener
- Team Xerox
- The Porsche Distribution System
- Kent State University
- Federal Express

Additional Cases

For instructors who prefer the case-study approach, an additional real-life case, along with questions designed to stimulate students' integration of chapter concepts, is included at the end of each chapter. Examples of these cases include:

- Trivial Pursuit
- The Collapse of the Diesel Car Market
- Prudential's New Approach to Advertising Life Insurance
- Women in Selling

The *Integrated Resource Manual* contains an additional short case for each chapter as well as longer, more comprehensive cases for each part of the textbook. The availability of these additional cases and the varying length and complexity of each provides added flexibility for the instructor who makes extensive use of cases.

Chapter Overviews

Although most introductory marketing texts follow the same general table of contents, in all too many instances little effort is made to integrate materials within individual chapters or to relate the subject matter of one chapter with concepts discussed in previous chapters. The result is that such texts resemble "fleshed-out" outlines. By contrast, each *Contemporary Marketing* chapter begins with an overview that relates the material to be studied to concepts discussed in preceding chapters. This enables students to view marketing in a complete and unified context.

Strategic Orientation

Contemporary Marketing is written with a strong marketing planning/strategy orientation. As a number of reviewers have pointed out, planning occurs at the beginning of the marketing effort, not at the end. Consequently, coverage of marketing planning and forecasting begins in Chapter 3. The chapter has been revised extensively to provide a strong, logical treatment of both the *why* and *how* of marketing planning. Chapter 5 provides detailed coverage of major segmentation bases in both consumer and industrial markets. The treatment of retailing in Chapter 12 has been thoroughly reworked to replace descriptive materials with more strategic-oriented information. All of the chapters in Part Six have been rewritten to emphasize a more analytic, decision-oriented approach to promotional strategy. The merits and limitations of global marketing strategies are discussed in Chapter 19. The new edition of *Contemporary Marketing* also presents an analysis of marketing in nonprofit organizations as well as person and idea marketing in Chapter 20.

While almost every basic marketing textbook includes an appendix on marketing arithmetic or financial analysis in marketing, these materials are always placed at the end of the book. In *Contemporary Marketing* these marketing analysis subjects are integrated at appropriate locations throughout the text in the form of computer applications.

Emphasis on Buyer Behavior and Marketing Mix Elements _____

Contemporary Marketing is designed to meet instructor demands for a thorough treatment of the core topics of market segmentation, buyer behavior, and the elements of the marketing mix. Part Three devotes three chapters to these topics. Chapter 5 analyzes the concept of market segmentation and describes segmentation techniques used in both consumer and industrial markets. Coverage of consumer behavior in Chapter 6 has been thoroughly revised and improved. The chapter on industrial marketing has been broadened at the suggestion of reviewers to focus on *organizational* buying behavior by including concise, comprehensive treatment of buyer behavior in the producer, trade industries, institutional, and government markets.

At least two chapters focus on each of the elements of the marketing mix. Unlike some recent texts, *Contemporary Marketing* does not neglect the vital roles of marketing institutions and physical distribution. Separate chapters are devoted to the subjects of retailing, wholesaling, and the management of physical distribution.

Services, Organizational Marketing, and International Marketing _____

A broadened view of marketing, beginning with the definition of marketing in Chapter 1, is integrated throughout the text. This expanded concept of marketing incorporates nonprofit organizations, persons, and causes as well as tangible goods. A number of stop-action cases, such as St. Joseph Hospital and Kent State University, are devoted to nonprofit application. Chapter 20 presents an in-depth treatment of the subject.

Contemporary Marketing also extends its coverage to the vital yet often neglected area of service strategy. Part Four in the new edition is expanded to Product/Service Strategy in order to thoroughly treat both tangible and intangible products. In addition, unique aspects of the marketing of services are discussed at appropriate locations throughout the text. For instance, Chapter 10 contains a section entitled "Marketing Channels for Services."

Chapter 19, "Global Dimensions of Marketing," has been extensively revised and strengthened to produce a more analytical, decision-oriented treatment of a subject whose coverage is highly descriptive in most marketing texts. The added information stresses the importance of world marketing and is in accordance with AACSB requirements.

Other Content Changes _____

Contemporary Marketing is written to help students learn about marketing. Students are challenged to apply marketing concepts rather than just memorize lists and definitions. The following features are designed to make the new fifth edition of the text even more effective as a teaching/learning tool:

A Completely New Full-Color Art Program

Perhaps the most visible indicator of the significantly improved fifth edition of *Contemporary Marketing* is the use of a full-color design. Every figure and table is new and has been designed by a team of artists based upon the authors' instructions. The result is a state-of-the-art book using color photographs and illustrations to emphasize text concepts.

Stressing Vocabulary Building

Vocabulary building is an important learning objective in a basic marketing course. In *Contemporary Marketing,* each chapter begins with a list of key terms. Then, throughout the chapter these key terms and concepts are defined in a running glossary adjacent to their introduction and discussion in the text. For reference, all terms are listed and defined in an alphabetical glossary at the end of the book.

Pedagogical Changes

Feedback from teachers of basic marketing courses was utilized in making a number of specific changes. To meet demands of professors and students, the following suggestions have been implemented:

- The new edition uses the official definition of marketing introduced recently by the American Marketing Association. This broader definition incorporates the profit-seeking and nonprofit sectors, tangible goods and intangible services, and marketing activities for persons, organizations, and ideas in addition to consumer and industrial products.

- The marketing environment is erroneously treated as a totally uncontrollable variable in some basic marketing textbooks. The concept of environmental management is discussed in Chapter 2 of *Contemporary Marketing.*

- A number of recently developed concepts have been included in the new edition. These include:

just-in-time inventory systems	strategic window concept
direct response retailing	teleshopping
marketing opportunity analysis	advocacy advertising
environmental management	idea marketing

- The new edition contains more detailed coverage of the consumer and organizational purchase decision processes. The classification of consumer behavior as routinized response behavior, limited problem solving, or extended problem solving is utilized in Chapter 6, while the description of organizational buying situations in Chapter 7 is based upon the parallel classifications of straight rebuy, modified rebuy, and new task buying.

- The word *middleman*—a "dinosaur" term from the 1920s—has been replaced by the term *marketing intermediary.*

Marketing Telecourse

We are honored that *Contemporary Marketing* was selected as the basis for the only college-level marketing telecourse available in North America. The 26-tape telecourse presents basic marketing concepts by utilizing real-world case studies, on-location footage, animations, special effects, and state-of-the-art electronic graphics. Each tape segment is related to a *Contemporary Marketing* chapter. The telecourse format can be used in a regular classroom setting or in learning centers and libraries; it can also be used as broadcast/cablecast programming material. Instructors interested in utilizing the telecourse format can obtain specific details by contacting Coast Telecourses, 11460 Warner Avenue, Fountain Valley, CA 92708, (714) 241–6109. All 26 tapes are available for viewing.

Instructional Resource Package

The fifth edition of *Contemporary Marketing* is a comprehensive teaching/learning package unparalleled in its completeness. The textbook is undoubtedly the most critical element in the package, but it is only one part. Because of extensive research and careful coordination, the complete package is uniquely suited to the needs of marketing professors. Since both authors of *Contemporary Marketing* teach introductory marketing, we are well aware of the challenges facing the instructor. The *Instructional Resource Package* is designed to assist the basic marketing professor, who so often has large classes and a heavy teaching load.

The *Instructional Resource Package* consists of the supplementary teaching aids described next.

Integrated Resource Manuals

The eight bound volumes, one for each part of the textbook, contain the following sections for each chapter:

- Slide/Lecture Series Description
- Changes from Fourth Edition
- Annotated Learning Goals
- Key Terms
- Stop-Action Case
- Lecture Outline
- Description of Transparencies
- Lecture Illustration File
- Answers to Discussion Questions
- Answers to Chapter Case Questions
- Solutions to Computer Applications Problems
- Supplemental Case
- Experiential Exercises
- Enrichment Items (including guest speaker suggestions)
- Annotated Film Guide

Each *Integrated Resource Manual* also contains longer, more comprehensive cases for those instructors desiring to rely more heavily on cases in their courses.

Test Bank

The completely revised 2,300-question *Test Bank* is available in both a printed and a computerized format. The *Test Bank* has been designed to aid the classroom learning experience with a wide range of testing alternatives. The three major areas of multiple choice, true/false, and more difficult multiple choice questions also contain subtopical elements in the areas of application, theoretical foundations, definitional matching, quantitative calculations, and situational analysis. All learning goals and key terms in each chapter are thoroughly covered by several types of questions. The more difficult multiple choice questions are designed to give the person being tested a mini-case type problem situation that requires a more thorough analysis and synthesis of information than the typical multiple choice question. Each question is keyed to specific text page numbers and level of difficulty. The *Test Bank* was prepared by Professor William E. Rice of California State University, Fresno.

Study Guide

The *Study Guide* is a learning supplement designed to further students' understanding and to provide them with additional practice in applying concepts presented in the text. It includes a summary of learning objectives for each chapter, experiential exercises, a self-quiz, conceptual applications, cases, and computer problems. The *Study Guide* was prepared by Professor Stephen K. Keiser of the University of Delaware, Robert E. Stevens of Oral Roberts University, and Lynn J. Loudenback of New Mexico State University.

Marketing Simulation Games

Two alternative simulation games are available for marketing instructors. MICROSIM, written by Professor Steven Schnaars of Baruch College, enables students to assume the role of a marketing manager for a microwave oven company and manipulate fundamental marketing variables to maximize profits. *M.A.R.S.*, the second simulation game, involves competition among student teams who vie for sales, profits, and market shares in the microcomputer industry. It was written by Professors Linda Swayne and Christie H. Paksoy of the University of North Carolina at Charlotte. Both simulation games are designed for use with Apple II or IBM PC microcomputers.

The Boone & Kurtz Marketing Disk

The *Boone & Kurtz Marketing Disk* contains complete programs for the computer applications problems in the textbook and *Study Guide*. It is available free to adopters for use with Apple II or IBM PC microcomputers.

Full-Color Overhead Transparencies

This innovative component includes a set of 100 original full-color acetates. Without duplicating the presentation of material in the text, each transparency is a striking graphic illustration of a concept discussed in *Contemporary Marketing*.

Computerized Test Bank

This test generator is available for IBM PC or Apple II microcomputers. It contains the entire bank of 2,300 questions from the printed *Test Bank*. The program is designed to allow the user to preview questions on a terminal or printer, generate and store up to ten tests with random or manual selection of questions, print tests with optional separate answer sheets and alternative versions, add questions to the test pool, and change questions in the test pool. This flexibility permits the instructor to personalize the test bank by including questions based entirely on class lecture materials and by replacing problem examples with examples of local individuals, business firms, and nonprofit organizations.

Slide/Lecture Series

The series consists of three 50-minute lecture modules, each illustrated by approximately 55 full-color slides and accompanied by a written commentary for instructors. The entire series contains 165 slides and covers the following marketing subjects:

- Marketing planning and segmentation
- International marketing
- Marketing for small business

The lectures present fundamental marketing concepts, applications, and examples keyed to material in *Contemporary Marketing,* but with new materials, examples, and illustrations not contained in the text.

Acknowledgments

Every successful textbook is the product of many people's work. First, we would like to acknowledge the many scholars whose works are cited in *Contemporary Marketing* for their contributions to the marketing discipline. Textbooks are, after all, merely a reflection of contemporary thought in a discipline. In this respect, marketing is blessed with a strong cadre of academicians and practitioners who are constantly seeking to improve and advance the discipline.

The authors gratefully acknowledge the following academic colleagues who reviewed all or part of the manuscripts for earlier editions:

Keith Absher	Don L. James	Arthur E. Prell
Dub Ashton	David Johnson	Gary Edward Reiman
Wayne Bascom	Eugene M. Johnson	Arnold M. Rieger
Richard D. Becherer	Bernard Katz	C. Richard Roberts
Howard B. Cox	Charles Keuthan	Patrick J. Robinson
Gordon Di Paolo	Donald L. Knight	William C. Rodgers
Jeffrey T. Doutt	Philip Kotler	William H. Ronald
Sid Dudley	Paul I. Londrigan	Carol Rowey
John W. Ernest	Dorothy Maass	Jack Seitz
Gary T. Ford	James McCormick	Bruce Seaton
Ralph M. Gaedeke	James McHugh	Howard Seigelman
James Gould	Robert D. Miller	Steven L. Shapiro
Donald Granbois	J. Dale Molander	A. Edward Spitz
Paul E. Green	John F. Monoky	William Staples
Blaine Greenfield	James R. Moore	Howard A. Thompson
Matthew Gross	Carl McDaniel	Dennis H. Tootelian
John H. Hallaq	Colin Neuhaus	Dinoo T. Vanier
Cary Hawthorn	Robert T. Newcomb	Robert J. Williams
Sanford B. Helman	Constantine Petrides	Julian Yudelson
Nathan Himelstein	Barbara Piasta	
Ray S. House	Barbara Pletcher	

Our work in preparing the fifth edition was enhanced greatly by the following reviewers who made numerous suggestions. In preparing the fifth edition, we sought out the advice of marketing specialists who reviewed text components that matched their specialized research and teaching areas. The new edition is greatly improved as a result of the dozens of suggestions offered by the following individuals:

Richard F. Beltramini
Arizona State University

Michael R. Czinkota
Georgetown University

Kathy Daruty
Pierce College

Phillip E. Egdorf
Tarleton State University

Gerry P. Gallo
Long Island University

Robert D. Hisrich
University of Tulsa

Michael D. Hutt
Arizona State University

James C. Johnson
St. Cloud State University

Harold H. Kassarjian
University of California, Los Angeles

James H. Kennedy
Navarro College

Francis J. Leary, Jr.
Northern Essex Community College

David L. Loudon
Northeast Louisiana University

James C. Makens
Wake Forest University

Lou Mansfield
Kankakee Community College

Dennis D. Pappas
Columbus Technical Institute

Dennis Pitta
University of Baltimore

Bert Rosenbloom
Drexel University

Ronald S. Rubin
University of Central Florida

Robert E. Stevens
Oral Roberts University

Vern Terpstra
University of Michigan

John E. Timmerman
Abilene Christian University

Fred Trawick
University of Alabama, Birmingham

Fred Weinthal
Rockland County Community
   College

Robert J. Zimmer
California State University, Fullerton

We are especially indebted to Stephen K. Keiser of the University of Delaware, Robert E. Stevens of Oral Roberts University, and Lynn J. Loudenback of New Mexico State University for preparing the *Study Guide*. Our special thanks go to Steven Schnaars of Baruch College for creating the marketing simulation game MICROSIM and to Linda E. Swayne and Christie H. Paksoy of the University of North Carolina at Charlotte for developing the *M.A.R.S.* marketing simulation game. We also wish to thank William E. Rice of California State University at Fresno for his preparation of the *Test Bank*. Appreciation is also expressed to Jerry Funk and Andy Smith of Brazosport College for developing *The Boone & Kurtz Marketing Disk*. We are also appreciative of the suggestions made by colleagues Tom Becker, Julius M. Blum, Janice Bowers, Don Gibson, James Grant, John D. Milewicz, and Lynn B. Robinson of the University of South Alabama and Gerald M. Hampton and Rex Toh of Seattle University. We especially thank our capable secretaries Jeanne Monk and Linda Troup for their invaluable assistance in typing the manuscript.

Finally, we gratefully acknowledge the many contributions of the professionals at The Dryden Press. We would particularly like to thank our publisher Bill Schoof and our editor Mary Glacken for their insights and suggestions for the new edition. Our developmental editor Rob Zwettler was a continuing source of good advice. Jan Doty, Mary Jarvis, Doris Milligan, Nancy Moudry, Jane Perkins, and Alan Wendt proved on numerous occasions their ability to eliminate seemingly insurmountable obstacles. And our senior marketing manager Marie Schappert was a constant source of creative suggestions for improving the new edition. The revision was truly a team effort, and we are in their debt.

Louis E. Boone
Mobile, Alabama
October 1985

David L. Kurtz
Seattle, Washington
October 1985

Brief Contents

Contents

PART THREE
MARKET SEGMENTATION AND
BUYER BEHAVIOR   120

Chapter 5
Market Segmentation   122

Chapter 6
Consumer Behavior   148

PART FOUR
PRODUCT/SERVICE STRATEGY   208

Chapter 9
Elements of Product / Service Strategy 238

Chapter 13
Physical Distribution 350

PART SIX
PROMOTIONAL STRATEGY 374

Chapter 14
Introduction to Promotion 376

PART SEVEN
PRICING STRATEGY   460

Chapter 17
Introduction to Pricing   462

Chapter 20
Societal Issues and Nonprofit Applications   546

PARTONE

The Contemporary Marketing Environment

The Marketing Process: An Overview

Key Terms

utility
marketing
exchange process
production orientation
sales orientation
seller's market
buyer's market
consumer orientation
marketing concept
marketing myopia
product strategy
distribution strategy
marketing channels
promotional strategy
pricing strategy
marketing mix

Learning Goals

1. To explain the types of utility and the role played by marketing in their creation
2. To relate the definition of marketing to the concept of the exchange process
3. To contrast marketing activities in each of the three eras in the history of marketing
4. To explain the concept of marketing myopia
5. To identify the variables involved in marketing decision making and the environmental factors that affect these decisions
6. To explain each of the universal functions of marketing
7. To identify three reasons for studying marketing

Stop-Action Case

Perdue Farms, Inc.

How do you take an unbranded, unglamorous agricultural commodity like chicken and turn it into a familiar, recognizable, and sought-after branded product? How does one become the Coca-Cola of the chicken industry? A chicken farmer from Maryland's Eastern Shore faced such a challenge in 1968 when he decided to change the way that chickens were marketed to the American public.

Frank Perdue understood that beef—not chickens—was what most U.S. consumers thought of when they wanted meat on their dinner plates. To succeed, he would have to change the basic diets of millions of Americans. He also realized that almost no brand loyalty existed among those shoppers who preferred chicken to other meats. Few consumers knew or cared which company produced or packed the poultry they ate.

When Frank Perdue assumed control of his family's chicken business in 1950, his primary goal was quality. "I want to grow the best chickens in America," said Perdue. "That's my thing." Eighteen years later, Perdue Farms made a significant move when it purchased its own processing plant in Salisbury, Maryland. By so doing, the firm could control at least part of the production–marketing system by extending its quality programs from chicken raising to chicken processing.

But the firm's horizons continued to be limited. "In the beginning," said Perdue, "we just sold to butcher shops. I'd run my production meeting Monday morning and a sales meeting Monday afternoon, jump on a plane about five o'clock, eat dinner in the Baltimore airport, and go to work the next morning calling on meat buyers. All of them."

Marketing a quality product to butchers brought Perdue success—but not the kind of growth he wanted. His approach of direct contact with marketing intermediaries rather than focusing upon the ultimate food purchaser also meant that he was unable to secure brand-name recognition for his chicken products. Perdue needed a dramatic new way of thinking and a different marketing focus if his chickens were to become a household name. "I wanted . . . the company to grow to the maximum extent possible without sacrificing quality," said Perdue. "I wouldn't be satisfied with Number Two."

Assignment: Use the materials in Chapter 1 to recommend a course of action for Frank Perdue.

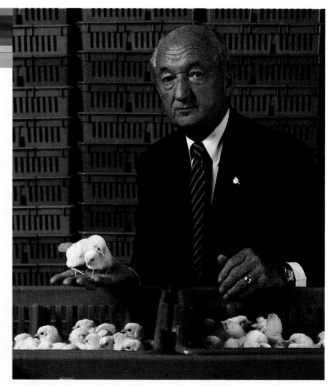

Photo Source: Courtesy of Perdue Farms Incorporated.

Source: Quotation in paragraph two is from Grover Heiman, "Fainthearted? Not 'Mr. Chicken'," *Nation's Business* (August 1982), p. 42. Quotations in paragraphs three and four are from "Face to Face: Frank Perdue," *Inc.* (February 1984), p. 22.

Chapter Overview _____

All organizations perform two basic functions—they produce a good, a service, or an idea, and they market it. This is true of all firms—from giant manufacturers such as Boeing Aircraft and Apple Computer to the neighborhood convenience store. It is true of profit-seeking firms and nonprofit organizations. Production and marketing are the essence of economic life in any society.

Through the production and marketing of goods, services, and ideas, organizations satisfy a commitment to society, to their customers, and to their owners. They create what economists call **utility**, which may be defined as the want-satisfying power of a product or service. There are four basic kinds of utility—form, time, place, and ownership.

Form utility is created when the firm converts raw materials and component inputs into finished products and services. Glass, steel, fabrics, rubber, and other components are combined to form a new Camaro or Fiero. Cotton, thread, and buttons are converted into Ocean Pacific shirts. Sheet music, musical instruments, musicians, a conductor, and the facilities of Carnegie Hall are converted into a performance by the New York Philharmonic. Although marketing inputs may be important in specifying consumer and audience preferences, the actual creation of form utility is the responsibility of the production function of the organization.

Time, place, and ownership utility are created by marketing. Time and place utility are created when products and services are available to the consumer when and where the person wants to purchase them. Ownership utility is created when title to the product or service may be transferred at the time of purchase.

The four types of utility are shown in Figure 1.1. Whereas time, place, and ownership utility are created by marketing, form utility is the primary responsibility of production. However, the contributions of marketing in supplying information concerning consumer preferences and expectations are also of critical importance in creating products and services designed to match actual consumer needs.

Chapter 1 sets the stage for the entire text by examining the meaning of marketing and by describing the importance of marketing to organizations—both profit-seeking and nonprofit. The chapter examines the development of marketing in our society and its contributions. The marketing variables utilized in a marketing strategy are also introduced.

Utility
Want-satisfying power of a product or service.

What Is Marketing? _____

All organizations must create utility if they are to survive. The designing and marketing of want-satisfying products, services, and ideas is the foundation for the creation of utility. However, the role of marketing in the success of an organization has only recently been recognized. Management author Peter F. Drucker emphasized the importance of marketing in his book, *The Practice of Management:*

If we want to know what a business is, we have to start with its purpose. And its purpose must lie outside the business itself. In fact, it must lie in society since a business enterprise is an organ of society. There is one valid definition of business purpose: to create a customer.[1]

How does an organization "create" a customer? As Professors Guiltinan and Paul explain:

Figure 1.1
Four Types of Utility

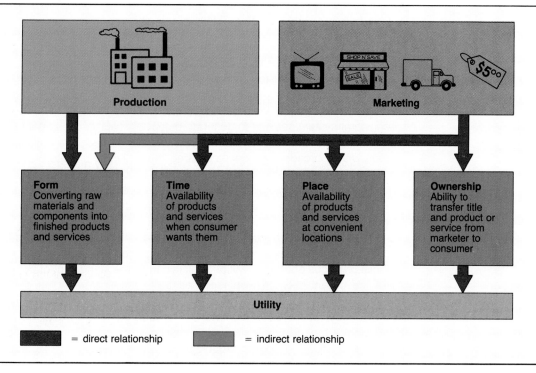

Essentially, "creating" a customer means identifying needs in the marketplace, finding out which needs the organization can profitably serve, and developing an offering to convert potential buyers into customers. Marketing managers are responsible for most of the activities necessary to create the customers the organization wants. These activities include:

- Identifying customer needs
- Designing products and services that meet those needs
- Communicating information about those products and services to prospective buyers
- Making the products or services available at times and places that meet customers' needs
- Pricing the products to reflect costs, competition, and customers' ability to buy
- Providing for the necessary service and follow-up to ensure customer satisfaction after the purchase.[2]

Marketing: A Definition

Ask five persons to define marketing, and five definitions are likely to follow. Due to the continuing exposure to advertising and personal selling, most respondents are likely to link marketing and selling. Over a quarter-century ago the American Marketing Association, the international professional association in the marketing discipline, attempted to standardize marketing terminology by defining marketing as "the performance of business activities that direct the flow of goods and services from producer to consumer or user."

But the old definition proved much too narrow. It also conjured up visions of marketing beginning at the end of a producer's loading dock by emphasizing the flow of products and services that have already been produced. It failed to recognize marketing's crucial role in analyzing consumer needs and securing information designed to make certain that the products or services created by the firm's production facilities would match buyer expectations. In addition, the old definition ignored the thousands of nonprofit organizations currently engaged in marketing activities. A broader and more descriptive view was needed—one that would describe the firm or enterprise as an organized behavioral system seeking to generate output of value to consumers.

In 1985 the American Marketing Association replaced its antiquated definition with a broader one encompassing the activities of both profit-seeking and nonprofit organizations. Marketing is the process of planning and executing the conception, pricing, promotion, and distribution of ideas, goods, and services to create exchanges that satisfy individual and organizational objectives.[3]

Marketing
Process of planning and executing the conception, pricing, promotion, and distribution of ideas, goods, and services to create exchanges that satisfy individual and organizational objectives.

The expanded concept of marketing activities permeates all organizational functions. It assumes that the marketing effort will be in accordance with ethical practices and that it will be effective from the standpoint of both society and the organization. It also identifies the marketing variables of product, price, promotion, and distribution that are used to provide consumer satisfaction. In addition, it assumes that the consumer segments to be satisfied through the organization's production and marketing activities have been selected and analyzed prior to production. In other words, the customer, client, or public determines the marketing program. Finally, it recognizes that marketing concepts and techniques are applicable to nonprofit organizations as well as to profit-oriented businesses.

Figure 1.2 illustrates this expanded concept of marketing by demonstrating marketing activities in a variety of organizations and for a number of different products and services. The advertisements for BankAmerica Travelers Cheques and the Chicago Cubs contrast marketing activities for tangible products (travelers checks) and intangible services (entertainment in the form of baseball). The AT&T telephone system for offices and other small businesses is illustrative of marketing activities aimed at satisfying business users in addition to those focusing upon the ultimate consumer. Finally, the U.S. Air Force advertisement is an effective reminder of how marketing concepts apply to nonprofit organizations as well as to profit-seeking enterprises.

The Origins of Marketing

Exchange Process
Process by which two or more parties give something of value to one another to satisfy felt needs.

The essence of marketing is the exchange process. This is the process by which two or more parties give something of value to one another to satisfy felt needs. In many cases, the item is a tangible good, such as a newspaper, a hand calculator, or a pair of shoes. In other cases, intangible services, such as a car wash, transportation, or a concert performance, are exchanged for money. In still other instances, funds or time donations may be offered to political candidates, a Red Cross office, or a church or synagogue.

The marketing function is both simple and direct in subsistence-level economies. For example, assume that a primitive society consists solely of Person A and Person B. Assume also that the only elements of their standard of living are food, clothing, and shelter. The two live in adjoining caves on a mountainside. They weave their own clothes and tend their own fields inde-

Figure 1.2
Applying Marketing Concepts in a Variety of Organizations

Money that knows no bounds.

When you cross over into another country, carrying ordinary money can present certain obstacles. That's why you're better off carrying BankAmerica Travelers Cheques wherever you go.

They're welcome in 160 countries, from the Great Wall to the Wailing Wall. And if somewhere in between they're ever lost or stolen, you can get them promptly refunded in more than 40,000 places worldwide.

So next time you're planning a trip along international lines, avoid some of the barriers by converting to BankAmerica Travelers Cheques.

Because today the only real obstacles to international travel are time and money. And legend has it if you carry BankAmerica Travelers Cheques far enough, one day you may actually gain a day in return.

BankAmerica Travelers Cheques. Accepted and refunded all over the world.

BankAmerica Corporation

Can your business afford one of these?

Call 1 800 247-7000 for AT&T's Small Business Connection. And make sure your phone system will never go sour.

Because today's AT&T equipment undergoes up to 4 weeks of the most rigorous testing ever. That's why every phone can withstand up to 20 years-worth of professional bumps, bangs, hang-ups and slamdowns.

But if your equipment should ever succumb to the pressures of business, you're protected by a unique nationwide service network—the "Circle of Service."

For 100 years, AT&T has believed there's just one way to produce a business phone—the right way.

Call 1 800 247-7000 for AT&T Information Systems. When you've got to be right.

AT&T

In the Air Force no idea is too far out.

Air Force engineers are designing tomorrow's technology today. It takes imagination to dream new dreams and skills to bring those dreams to life.

If you're an electrical or aerospace engineer, or plan to be, the Air Force gives you a chance to push your skills to the limit and learn new ones. And while you're growing,

you'll be helping your country grow stronger, too.

For more detailed information, call us toll-free at 1-800-423-USAF (in Calif. 1-800-232-USAF). Better yet, send your resume to HRS/RSAANK, Randolph AFB, TX 78150. We're waiting for your ideas.

AIM HIGH AIR FORCE

One Of Our Subsidiaries Just Posted A Particularly Successful Year.

At Tribune Company, we couldn't be any happier.

Like Cubs fans everywhere, we're thrilled to see the team win its division championship.

Unlike many fans, though, we're not all that surprised by it.

Because ever since we bought the Cubs three years ago, we've been working to make it happen. We had to.

You see, we want to be leaders in every business we're in.

From newspapers and newsprint production to broadcasting and cable TV.

And now we can add baseball to the list.

At Tribune Company, we're known for a long time what millions of Cub fans are now finding out. It's great to be with a winning team.

Tribune Company.
Holy cow.

pendently. They are able to subsist even though their standard of living is minimal.

Person A is an excellent weaver but a poor farmer, whereas Person B is an excellent farmer but a poor weaver. In this situation, it would be wise for each to specialize in the line of work that he or she does best. The net result would then be a greater total production of both clothing and food. In other words, specialization and division of labor would lead to a production surplus. But neither Person A nor Person B is any better off until each trades the product of his or her individual labor, thereby creating the exchange process.

Exchange is the origin of marketing activity. In fact, marketing has been described as the process of creating and resolving exchange relationships. When there is a need to exchange goods, the natural result is a marketing effort on the part of the people involved.

Wroe Alderson, a leading marketing theorist, said, "It seems altogether reasonable to describe the development of exchange as a great invention which helped to start primitive man on the road to civilization."[4]

While the cave dweller example is simplistic, it does reveal the essence of the marketing function. Complex industrial society has a more complicated exchange process, but the basic concept is the same. Production is not meaningful until a system of marketing has been established. Perhaps publisher Red Motley's adage sums it up best: "Nothing happens until somebody sells something."

Three Eras in the History of Marketing

Although marketing has always existed in business, its importance has varied greatly. Three historical eras can be identified: (1) the production era, (2) the sales era, and (3) the marketing era.

The Production Era

One hundred years ago, most firms were production oriented. Manufacturers stressed production of quality products and then looked for people to purchase them. The Pillsbury Company is an excellent example of a production-oriented company. Here is how the company's board chairman, the late Robert J. Keith, described Pillsbury during its early years:

We are professional flour millers. Blessed with a supply of the finest North American wheat, plenty of water power, and excellent milling machinery, we produce flour of the highest quality. Our basic function is to mill high-quality flour, and, of course (and almost incidentally), we must hire salesmen to sell it, just as we hire accountants to keep our books.[5]

Production Orientation
Business philosophy stressing efficiency in producing a quality product; attitude toward marketing is "a good product will sell itself."

The prevailing attitude of this era was that a good product (defined in terms of physical quality) would sell itself. This production orientation dominated business philosophy for decades. Indeed, business success was often defined in terms of production victories.

Although marketing had emerged as a functional activity within the business organization prior to the twentieth century, management's orientation remained with production for quite some time. In fact, what might be called industry's production era did not reach its peak until the early part of this century. The apostle of this approach to business operations was Frederick

W. Taylor, whose *Principles of Scientific Management* was widely read and accepted. Taylor's approach reflected his engineering background by emphasizing efficiency in the production process. Later writers, such as Frank and Lillian Gilbreth, the originators of motion analysis, expanded on Taylor's basic concepts.

Henry Ford's mass production line serves as a good example of this orientation. Ford's slogan, "They [customers] can have any color they want, as long as it's black," reflected a prevalent attitude toward marketing. Production shortages and intense consumer demand were the rule of the day. It is no wonder that production activities took precedence.

The "Better Mousetrap" Fallacy   The essence of the production era is reflected in a statement made over 100 years ago by the philosopher Ralph Waldo Emerson:

If a man writes a better book, preaches a better sermon, or makes a better mousetrap than his neighbor, though he builds his house in the woods, the world will make a beaten path to his door.

But Chester M. Woolworth knows better. Woolworth, who is president of the nation's largest mousetrap producer, once designed a new mousetrap based on thorough research on the type of trap that would be most "appealing" to mice. The new model had a modern, black plastic design, was completely sanitary, and was priced only a few cents more than the commonplace wooden type of trap. Also, it never missed!

But the better mousetrap failed as a new product venture. While Woolworth's designers had created a quality product, they had forgotten the customer and the environment in which the purchase decision is made. The postmortem analysis of this marketing disaster went something like this: Men bought the majority of the newly designed plastic mousetraps. In most instances, it was also the responsibility of the male member of the household to set the trap before the family retired for the night. But the problem occurred the next morning when he failed to check the trap before leaving for work. Women were most likely to check the trap—during the morning in the case of wives not employed outside the home and, in the case of working women, in the afternoon when they returned from work.

With the conventional wooden trap, they would simply sweep both trap and mouse onto a dustpan, minimizing the effort and time involved with this undesirable task. However, the new trap looked too expensive to throw away, even though it cost only a few cents more. Consequently, the wife was faced with first ejecting the mouse and then cleaning the instrument. In a short time, the new, improved mousetrap was replaced with the wooden version.

The moral of the mousetrap story is obvious: A quality product is not successful until it is effectively marketed. Mr. Woolworth expressed it most eloquently when he said, "Fortunately, Mr. Emerson made his living as a philosopher, not a company president."[6]

The Sales Era

As production techniques became more sophisticated and output grew, manufacturers began to increase the emphasis on an effective sales force to find customers for their output. In this era firms attempted to match their output to

Sales Orientation
Business philosophy assuming that consumers will resist purchasing nonessential products and services; attitude toward marketing is that creative advertising and personal selling are required to overcome consumer resistance and to convince them to buy.

customers. A sales orientation assumes that customers will resist purchasing products and services not deemed essential and that the task of personal selling and advertising is to convince them to buy. Marketing efforts were also aimed at wholesalers and retailers in an attempt to motivate them to stock greater quantities of the manufacturer's output.

Although marketing departments began to emerge during the sales era, they tended to remain in a subordinate position to production, finance, and engineering. Many chief marketing executives held the title of sales manager. Here is how Pillsbury described itself during the sales era:

We are a flour-milling company, manufacturing a number of products for the consumer market. We must have a first-rate sales organization which can dispose of all the products we can make at a favorable price. We must back up this sales force with consumer advertising and market intelligence. We want our sales representatives and our dealers to have all the tools they need for moving the output of our plants to the consumer.[7]

But selling is only one component of marketing. As Theodore Levitt has pointed out: ". . . marketing is as different from selling as chemistry is from alchemy, astronomy from astrology, chess from checkers."[8]

The Marketing Era

As personal income and consumer demand for goods and services dropped rapidly during the Great Depression of the 1930s, marketing was thrust into a more important role. Organizational survival dictated that managers pay closer attention to the markets for their products. This trend was halted by the outbreak of World War II, when rationing and shortages of consumer goods became commonplace. The war years, however, were an atypical pause in an emerging trend that resumed almost immediately after the hostilities ceased. The marketing concept was about to emerge.

Emergence of the Marketing Concept _____

Seller's Market
Marketplace characterized by a shortage of goods and/or services.

Buyer's Market
Marketplace characterized by an abundance of goods and/or services in relation to level of consumer demand.

Consumer Orientation
Business philosophy incorporating the marketing concept of first determining unmet consumer needs and then designing a system for satisfying those needs.

What was the setting for the crucial change in management philosophy? Perhaps it can best be explained by the shift from a seller's market—one with a shortage of goods and services—to a buyer's market—one with an abundance of goods and services. When World War II ended, factories stopped manufacturing tanks and jeeps and started turning out consumer goods again—an activity that had, for all practical purposes, stopped in early 1942.

The advent of a strong buyer's market occasioned the need for consumer orientation on the part of U.S. business. Goods had to be sold, not just produced. This realization has been identified as the emergence of the marketing concept. The recognition of this concept and its dominant role in business can be dated from 1952, when General Electric's *Annual Report* heralded a new management philosophy:

(The concept) introduces the marketing man at the beginning rather than at the end of the production cycle and integrates marketing into each phase of the business. Thus, marketing, through its studies and research, will establish for the engineer, the design and manufacturing man, what the customer wants in a given product, what price he is willing to pay, and where and when it will be wanted. Marketing will have authority in product planning, production scheduling, and inventory control, as well as in sales, distribution, and servicing of the product.[9]

Marketing would no longer be regarded as a supplemental activity performed after the production process had been completed. The marketer would, for instance, now play the lead role in product planning. Marketing and selling would no longer be synonymous.

Marketing Concept
Company-wide consumer orientation with the objective of achieving long-run success.

The marketing concept can be defined as a company-wide consumer orientation with the objective of achieving long-run success. The key words are company-wide consumer orientation. All facets of the organization must be involved with assessing, and then satisfying, customer wants and needs. The effort is not something to be left only to the marketers. Accountants working in the credit office and engineers employed in product design also play important roles.

The words "with the objective of achieving long-run success" are used to differentiate the concept from the policies of short-run profit maximization. The marketing concept is a modern philosophy for dynamic organizational growth. Since the continuity of the firm is an assumed component of the marketing concept, company-wide consumer orientation will lead to greater long-run profits than will managerial philosophies geared to reaching short-run goals.

Converting Needs to Wants

Every consumer must acquire goods and services on a continuing basis to fill certain needs. The fundamental needs for food, clothing, a home or apartment, and transportation must be satisfied through purchase or, in some instances, temporary use in the form of rented property or hired or leased transportation. By focusing upon the *benefits* resulting from these products and services, effective marketing converts needs to wants. A need for clothing may be translated into a desire (or want) for designer clothes. The need for transportation may become a consumer's desire for a new Honda Accord. The need for liquid refreshment may be satisfied by a product as basic as water or as expensive as Perrier. As the Heineken advertisement shown in Figure 1.3 illustrates, marketing focuses on basic needs and converts them into wants for specific products and brands.

Avoiding Marketing Myopia _____

Marketing Myopia
Term coined by Theodore Levitt in his argument that executives in many industries fail to recognize the broad scope of their business. According to Levitt, future growth is endangered because these executives lack a marketing orientation.

The emergence of the marketing concept has not been devoid of setbacks. One troublesome situation has been what Theodore Levitt called "marketing myopia."[10] According to Levitt, marketing myopia is the failure of management to recognize the scope of its business. Future growth is endangered when management is product oriented rather than customer oriented. Levitt cited many service industries—dry cleaning, electric utilities, movies, and railroads—as examples of marketing myopia.

Organizational goals must be broadly defined and oriented toward consumer needs. Trans World Airlines, for example, has redefined its business as travel rather than just air transportation. The firm now offers complete travel services, such as hotel accommodations, credit, and ground transportation, in addition to air travel.

Figure 1.3
Marketing: Converting Needs to Wants

Source: Copyright Heineken Brouwerijen B.V., Amsterdam, Holland. Reprinted by permission.

Revlon Cosmetics founder and president Charles Revson understood that a broader focus upon benefits rather than products was required to avoid marketing myopia. As Revson described it, "In the factory we make perfume; in the store we sell hope." Figure 1.4 illustrates how firms in a number of other industries have overcome myopic thinking with a marketing-oriented description of their businesses that focuses upon consumer need satisfaction.

Broadening the Marketing Concept for the 21st Century

Industry has been responsive to the marketing concept as an improved method of doing business. Since consideration of the consumer is now well accepted in most organizations, the relevant question has become, "What should be the nature and extent of the concept's parameters?"

Most marketers agree that the concept should be substantially broadened to include many areas not formerly associated with marketing efforts. Recent experience, for instance, has shown that many nonprofit organizations have adopted the marketing concept. The U.S. armed forces use advertising to recruit volunteers; the United Fund and other charitable groups have developed considerable marketing expertise; and some police departments have used marketing-inspired strategies to improve their public image. Marketing

Figure 1.4

Avoiding Marketing Myopia by Focusing upon Benefits Provided by the Organization

Company	Myopic Description of the Firm's Business	Marketing-Oriented Description of the Firm's Business
Walt Disney Enterprises 	"We are in the animated film business."	"We are in the entertainment business."
Burlington Northern Railroad 	"We are in the railroad business."	"We are in the transportation business."
Exxon 	"We are in the petroleum business."	"We are in the energy business."
Nynex 	"We are a telephone company."	"We are a communications company."

Disney Graphic Source: © Walt Disney Productions

efforts are, of course, necessary in political campaigns. A comprehensive discussion of marketing in nonprofit settings appears in Chapter 20.

It would be difficult to envision business returning to an era when engineering genius prevailed at the expense of consumer needs. It would be equally difficult to envision nonprofit organizations returning to a time when they lacked the marketing skills necessary to present their messages to the public. Marketing is a dynamic function, and it will no doubt be subject to continuous change. In one form or another, however, it is playing a more important role in all organizations and in people's daily lives.

Introduction to the Marketing Variables

Product Strategy
Element of marketing decision making comprising activities involved in developing the right product or service for the firm's customers.

Distribution Strategy
Element of marketing decision making comprising activities and marketing institutions involved in getting the right product or service to the firm's customers.

The starting place for effective marketing is the consumer. Part Three of this book is devoted to a thorough treatment of consumer behavior. This extensive coverage indicates the importance of consumer analysis in the development of effective marketing programs. After a particular consumer group has been identified and analyzed, the marketing manager can direct company activities to profitably satisfy that segment.

Although thousands of variables are involved, marketing decision making can be conveniently divided into four strategies: (1) product, (2) pricing, (3) distribution, and (4) promotion.

Return to the Stop-Action Case

Perdue Farms, Inc.

While Frank Perdue recognized that all four elements of his marketing mix were vital to the success of his plan to achieve marketplace success with his branded products, none was more important than the product itself. As Perdue points out, "In advertising, you have to have a product that's better than most—if possible, the best in your field. . . . Too many people advertise a mediocre product and fail. Eighty percent of all newly advertised products fail. Some manufacturers think the consumer is ignorant. That's why the product fails. People mistakenly think advertising is a cure-all."

Perdue uses computers to calculate the least expensive method of turning the smallest amount of feed into the most poultry. Company geneticists work at breeding bigger-breasted fowl, and veterinarians concentrate on producing healthy birds. "I'm a firm believer in putting money into research," says Perdue. "Without research I can't maintain my position in the industry."

Quality control is also a key element in Perdue's marketing strategy. "I have probably six or seven times more quality control personnel than anyone else," says Perdue. What does this accomplish? "Consistency," he says. "That is what quality is all about." Perdue is so confident of his chickens that he backs them with a money-back guarantee. "It costs me $1 million to give my chickens their healthy, yellow color. If I'm going to spend that much money to get a bird that looks healthy, you know I'm going to work hard to make it healthy, too."

Perdue Farms also works with members of its marketing channel to ensure freshness. Recently the firm invested several hundred thousand dollars for a machine that maintains the chickens' freshness for an extra day. "One day's shelf life!" Perdue exclaims. "Well, that's important to me because we lose a certain amount of control when the chicken leaves our trailer. The woman picks one out of a meat case which was not cold enough. . . . It smelled when she got it, let alone when she took it out of the refrigerator three days later. So she writes a letter: 'Perdue Chicken smells! I want my money back!' And we gave it back. We wrote her a letter thanking her for her attention to detail. So I've got to get that extra day [of shelf life]. I don't waste my time thinking about something like that. It might be the difference between an odor or no odor."

Sources: Quotations in paragraphs one and four are from "Face to Face: Frank Perdue," *Inc.* (February 1984), p. 22. Quotation in paragraph two is from Phil Patton, "Fowl Play: The Great Chicken War," *New York Times* (November 19, 1979), p. 54. Quotation in paragraph three is from Grover Heiman, "Fainthearted? Not 'Mr. Chicken'," *Nation's Business* (August 1982), pp. 42–43.

Marketing Channels
Steps a good or service follows from producer to final consumer.

Promotional Strategy
Element of marketing decision making that involves appropriate blending of personal selling, advertising, and sales promotion for use in communicating with and seeking to persuade potential customers.

Pricing Strategy
Element of marketing decision making that deals with the methods of setting profitable and justified exchange values for goods and services.

Product strategy comprises decisions about package design, branding, trademarks, warranties, guarantees, product life cycles, and the development of new products. The marketer's concept of product strategy involves more than the physical product: It also considers the satisfaction of all consumer needs in relation to the good or service. **Distribution strategy** deals with the physical distribution of goods and the selection of marketing channels. **Marketing channels** are the steps a good or service follows from producer to final consumer. Channel decision making deals with establishing and maintaining the institutional structure in marketing channels. It involves retailers, wholesalers, and other channel intermediaries. **Promotional strategy** involves personal selling, advertising, and sales promotion tools. The various aspects of promotional strategy must be blended together for the organization to communicate effectively with the marketplace. **Pricing strategy**, one of the most difficult areas of marketing decision making, deals with the methods of setting profitable and justified prices. It is closely regulated and subject to considerable public scrutiny.

Figure 1.5
Blending the Elements of the Marketing Mix

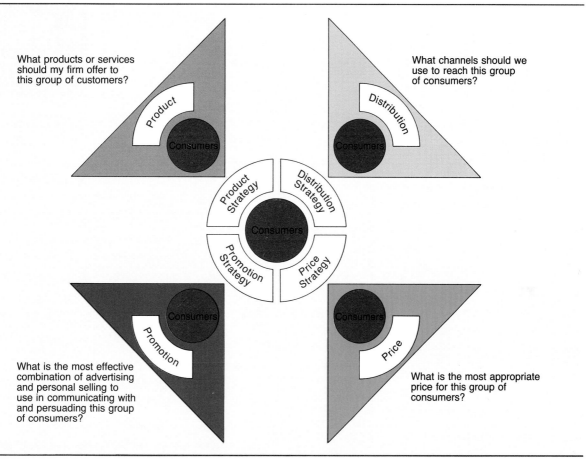

Marketing Mix
Blending the four strategy elements of marketing decision making—product, distribution, promotion, and pricing—to satisfy chosen consumer segments.

The total package forms the marketing mix—the blending of the four strategy elements of marketing decision making to satisfy chosen consumer segments. As Figure 1.5 shows, each of the strategies is a variable in the mix. While this fourfold classification is useful in study and analysis, the total package, or mix, determines the degree of marketing success.

Riunite: Developing an Effective Marketing Mix

Riunite wines provide an excellent example of an effective marketing mix.[11] The popular brand is the nation's leading imported table wine, with a 23 percent share of the market. Riunite outsells the second-place import by a three-to-one margin. Villa Banfi, Riunite's importer and marketer, developed the following marketing mix:

Consumer Target (covered in Chapters 3–7)
- The mass market consisted of many first-time wine consumers.

Product Strategy (covered in Chapters 8 and 9)
- Riunite is a Lambrusco wine—sweeter, fruitier, fizzier, and with a lower alcohol content than its competitors. It also does not require aging.

- The Villa Banfi product strategy is based on the premise that Americans prefer sweeter and colder drinks.

- The company has also produced a 6.3-ounce bottle in an attempt to reach markets like airlines, fast-food franchises, and sporting events.

- Villa Banfi is also marketing other brands. Bell 'Agio is similar to Riunite and carries a comparable price. A higher-priced vintage label is also being introduced.

Distribution Strategy (covered in Chapters 10–13)

- The marketing channel for Riunite leads from an Italian grape cooperative to Villa Banfi to wine dealers to the consumer.

- Villa Banfi is soliciting other sales outlets such as airlines, fast-food franchises, sporting events, and restaurant salad bars via the 6.3-ounce bottle.

- The 6.3-ounce bottle is also being promoted through supermarkets, a traditional outlet.

Promotional Strategy (covered in Chapters 14–16)

- Villa Banfi's promotional strategy is based primarily on an extensive advertising budget equal to more than 6 percent of annual sales.

- Approximately two-thirds of the advertising budget is allocated to television.

- Riunite is now being promoted as a competitor for all drinks, not just wine. Villa Banfi has targeted some of its promotional efforts at soft drinks, beer, and other beverages, in addition to competitive brands of wine.

Pricing Strategy (covered in Chapters 17 and 18)

- Because Riunite does not require aging, Villa Banfi was able to introduce the wine at $1.99 per bottle. It now sells for $3.00—still low by wine industry standards.

- Villa Banfi's Bell 'Agio is priced close to Riunite. The importer's vintage wines are priced higher than Riunite.

The Marketing Environment

Marketing decisions are not made in a vacuum. Marketers cannot experiment with single variables while holding other factors constant. Instead, marketing decisions are made on the basis of the constant changes in the mix variables and the dynamic nature of environmental forces. To be successful, these decisions must take into account the five environments—competitive, political and legal, economic, technological, and societal and cultural—in which they operate.

In recent years, the U.S. Postal Service has found itself in an unfamiliar position involving direct competition from profit-seeking private enterprises in many of its markets. In addition to competitors such as United Parcel Service, the Postal Service saw such firms as Federal Express, Airborne, and Purolator Courier make serious inroads into its profitable small-package service by offering overnight deliveries. This competition resulted in the creation of Express Mail, by which the Postal Service offers similar service at lower rates and a money-back guarantee.

Consider also the case of Riunite. Villa Banfi's competition originally came from Cella and Giacobazzi. Later, Coca-Cola's acquisition of Taylor Wines added a new dimension to Riunite's competitive environment. Villa Banfi's political and legal environment is characterized by import regulations and by state and local laws dealing with alcoholic beverages. All of these factors influence the company's marketing decisions.

The economic environment affects all marketers. So Villa Banfi diversified into other wine ventures—two in Italy and one in California. The technological environment is illustrated by package design and product aging requirements. The societal environment has also played a major role in the marketing of Riunite. For example, many of the brand's customers were first-time wine buyers. The American preference for sweeter, colder drinks is another societal factor that figured in Riunite's marketing strategy. Environmental influences are discussed in Chapter 2. Consideration of these factors is critical to effective marketing.

Marketing Costs and Marketing Functions

Creation of time, place, and ownership utility costs money. Numerous attempts have been made to determine marketing costs in relationship to overall product and service costs, and most estimates have ranged between 40 and 60 percent. On the average, one-half of the costs involved in a product such as a Domino's pizza, an ounce of *L'Air du Temps* perfume, a pair of Gloria Vanderbilt jeans, or even a Honda Elite scooter can be traced directly to marketing. These costs are not associated with fabrics, raw materials and other ingredients, baking, sewing, or any of the other production functions necessary to create form utility. What, then, does the consumer receive in return for this 50 percent marketing cost? What functions are performed by marketing?

As Figure 1.6 reveals, marketing is responsible for the performance of eight universal functions: buying, selling, transporting, storing, standardization and grading, financing, risk taking, and securing market information. Some functions are performed by manufacturers, others by retailers, and still others by marketing intermediaries called wholesalers.

Buying and *selling*, the first two functions shown in Figure 1.6, represent exchange functions. Buying is important to marketing on several levels. Mar-

Figure 1.6
Eight Essential Marketing Functions

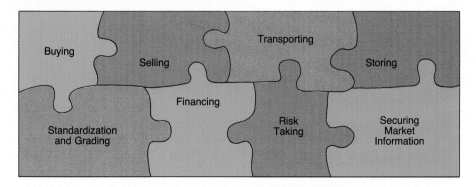

keters must determine how and why consumers buy certain products and services. To be successful, they must seek to understand consumer behavior. In addition, retailers and other intermediaries must seek out products that will appeal to their customers. Since they are generating time, place, and ownership utility through these purchases, they must make decisions concerning likely consumer preferences that will be expressed through purchases several months after the time the orders are placed. Selling is the second half of the exchange process. It involves advertising, personal selling, and sales promotion in an attempt to match the firm's products and services to consumer needs.

Transporting and *storing* are physical distribution functions. Transporting involves the physical movement of the product from the seller to the purchaser. Storing involves the warehousing of goods until they are needed for sale. These functions frequently involve manufacturers, wholesalers, and retailers.

The final four marketing functions—*standardization and grading, financing, risk taking,* and *securing market information*—are often called facilitating functions because they assist the marketer in performing the exchange and physical distribution functions. Quality and quantity control standards and grades, frequently set by federal or state governments, reduce the need for purchasers to inspect each item. Specific tire sizes, for example, permit buyers to request a needed size and to know that they will receive a uniform size. Financing is another marketing function because funds are often required to finance inventories prior to their sales. In many instances, manufacturers may provide financing for their wholesale and retail customers. In other instances, some types of wholesalers perform similar functions for their retail customers. And retailers frequently permit their customers to make credit purchases.

The seventh function, risk taking, is a part of most ventures. Manufacturers create products and services based upon their belief (and research studies) that a consumer need exists for them. Wholesalers and retailers acquire inventory based upon similar expectations of future consumer demand. These uncertainties about future consumer behavior must be assumed by entrepreneurial risk takers when they market products and services.

The final marketing function involves securing market information. Marketers gather information about their markets to determine decision-oriented input about their customers—who they are, what they buy, where they buy, and how they buy. By collecting and analyzing market information, marketers also seek to understand why consumers purchase some product offerings and reject others.

The Study of Marketing

Marketing is a pervasive element in contemporary life. In one form or another, it is close to every person. Three of its most important concerns for students are discussed below.

1. Marketing costs may be the largest item in the personal budget. As pointed out earlier, marketing costs account for approximately 50 percent of the total costs for the average product. Based upon costs alone, marketing is undeniably a key item in any consumer's budget.

Cost alone, however, does not indicate the value of marketing. If someone says that marketing costs are too high, that person should be asked, "Relative to what?" The standard of living in the United States is in large part a function of the country's efficient marketing system. When considered in this perspective, the costs of the system seem reasonable. For example, marketing expands sales, thereby spreading fixed production costs over more units of output and reducing total output costs. Reduced production costs offset many marketing costs.

2. There is a good chance that many students will become marketers. Marketing-related occupations account for 25 to 33 percent of the nation's jobs. Indeed, marketing opportunities remained strong even during recent periods when one out of four graduates could not find a job. History has shown that the demand for effective marketers is not affected by cyclical economic fluctuations.

3. Marketing provides an opportunity to contribute to society as well as to an individual company. Marketing decisions affect everyone's welfare. Furthermore, opportunities to advance to decision-making positions come sooner in marketing than in most occupations. (Societal aspects of marketing are covered in detail in later chapters.)

Why study marketing? The answer is simple: Marketing impacts numerous facets of daily life as well as future careers and economic well-being. The study of marketing is important because it is relevant to students today and tomorrow. It is little wonder that marketing is now one of the most popular fields of academic study.

Summary

The two primary functions of any organization are production and marketing. Traditionally, industry has emphasized production efficiency often at the expense of marketing. After World War II, however, the marketing concept became the accepted business philosophy. The change was caused by the economy shifting from a seller's market to a buyer's market.

Marketing is the process of planning and executing the conception, pricing, promotion, and distribution of ideas, goods, and services to create exchanges that satisfy individual and organizational objectives. It is applicable to both profit-oriented and nonprofit organizations. Marketing decision making can be classified into four strategies: (1) product, (2) pricing, (3) distribution, and (4) promotion. These four variables together form the total marketing mix. Marketing decisions must be made in a dynamic environment determined by competitive, legal, economic, technological, and societal functions.

Marketing costs represent approximately 50 percent of total costs of a typical product. These costs result from the performance of eight essential marketing functions that result in the creation of time, place, and ownership utility. These functions include two exchange functions (buying and selling); two physical distribution functions (transporting and storing); and four facilitating functions (standardization and grading, financing, risk taking, and securing market information).

Three basic reasons for studying marketing are (1) marketing costs may be the largest item in the personal budget; (2) there is a good chance many students will become marketers; and (3) marketing provides an opportunity to contribute to society as well as to an individual organization.

Solving the Stop-Action Case

Perdue Farms, Inc.

In 1968, 400 people worked for Perdue Farms. By 1984, that number had grown to over 9,000. And over this time period, Perdue Farms' chicken sales skyrocketed by 525 percent. "We have already grown four or five times as fast as other companies," said company president Frank Perdue. "We have 43 percent of the market share in New York, 36 percent in Boston, 41 percent in Hartford, and 28 percent . . . in Philadelphia."

How did Frank Perdue bring about this marketing success? The firm's marketing strategy was designed to build consumer awareness and acceptance of a superior chicken. Through exacting production techniques, rigid quality control, and a creative marketing campaign coupled with delivery of a consistently top-quality product, Perdue Farms developed a high degree of customer loyalty, even at premium prices.

Even though Perdue Farms' efforts at producing a high-quality product were successful, Frank Perdue understood that marketplace success would not come unless the firm's market target knew about his product. Consequently, each year he allocated millions of dollars—one cent for every pound of chicken sold—to advertising. Since 1972, Perdue has not only paid these advertising bills, he has also become famous as the firm's spokesperson. Aided by the ingenious advertising slogan, "It takes a tough man to make a tender chicken," Perdue has become a recognizable celebrity in the Northeast and Mid-Atlantic states, where most of his chickens are marketed. His folksy style and Chesapeake Bay accent have helped convince consumers to pay a premium for Perdue Farms' chickens. His money-back guarantee also contributes to the quality image.

Perdue's message has reached nearly all targeted consumers. When asked to name a brand of chicken, 97 out of 100 people in one survey said, "Perdue." He has made a special effort to reach the Spanish-speaking market. His characteristic voice and pronunciation are unmistakable when he translates his well-known product slogan: *Le necisita un hombre fuerte para hacer un pollo tierno.*

Part of Perdue Farms' marketing success can be traced to the fact that it gives consumers more poultry

Photo Source: Courtesy of Perdue Farms Incorporated.

choices than its competitors do. In addition to branded broilers, Perdue's first market entry, the company now offers its market target such products as "prime parts," the "Oven Stuffer" roaster, fresh Cornish game hens, and deboned chicken breasts. The "Oven Stuffer" roaster, for example, satisfies consumer needs for a chicken large enough to feed the average household and small enough to avoid leftover problems. Perdue recently moved into further processed foods, with chicken franks and chicken bologna. Years of research and testing preceded their introductions.

To make certain that his market offerings are well received, Perdue's marketing strategy also includes personal calls on ten distributors and retailers who purchase the five million broilers, roasters, and game hens that he markets each week. He and his field marketing representatives openly solicit complaints about Perdue chickens and act on them to improve overall quality. He also works closely with the firm's production personnel to make sure that market demand is met. An executive at Perdue's advertising agency summarized Perdue's marketing style in this way: "Frank Perdue is the antithesis of the company president. Most guys talk a lot, but whom do they talk to? Frank talks to butchers in a Boston ghetto at 7:30 in the morning. He knows the territory and he fights like hell to keep it."

Sources: Quotation in paragraph one is from Constance Y. Bramson, "Frank Perdue: America's No. 1 Chicken Salesman," *The Harrisburg, Pa. Evening News* (October 12, 1983), p. C1. Quotation in paragraph six is from Phil Patton, "Fowl Play: The Great Chicken War," *New York Times* (November 19, 1979), p. 54.

Questions for Discussion _____

1.   What are the four types of utility? With which is marketing concerned?

2.   What types of utility are being created in the following examples?
     a.   One-hour cleaners
     b.   7-Eleven convenience food store
     c.   Nissan truck assembly plant in Smyrna, Tennessee
     d.   Annual boat and sports equipment show in local city auditorium
     e.   Regional shopping mall

3.   How does this text's definition of marketing differ from the older definition proposed by the American Marketing Association in 1960?

4.   Relate the definition of marketing to the concept of the exchange process.

5.   Contrast the production era and the sales era.

6.   In what ways does the marketing era differ from the previous eras?

7.   Give two examples of firms you feel are in the following eras and defend your answers:
     a.   Production era
     b.   Sales era
     c.   Marketing era

8.   Explain the concept of marketing myopia. Why is it likely to occur? What steps can be taken to reduce the likelihood of its occurrence?

9.   Suggest methods by which the following organizations might avoid marketing myopia by correctly defining their industries:
     a.   AT&T
     b.   United Artists (motion picture company)
     c.   Illinois Central Railroad
     d.   Gulf Oil
     e.   Bank of America

10. What did the General Electric *Annual Report* mean when it said it was introducing the marketer at the beginning rather than at the end of the production cycle?

11. Identify the product and the consumer market in each of the following:
     a.   Local cable television firm
     b.   Milwaukee Brewers baseball club
     c.   Planned Parenthood
     d.   Dr. Pepper

12. How would you explain marketing and its importance in the U.S. economy to someone not familiar with the subject?

13. What should be the parameters of the marketing concept?

14. Identify the major variables of the marketing mix.

15. What are the components of the marketing environment? Why are these factors not included as part of the marketing mix?

16. Evaluate the marketing strategy devised for Riunite.

17. Identify two or three products that have failed recently because of poor marketing? What went wrong?

18. Jennifer Shannon is a recreation major at Center City College. She hopes eventually to direct a community recreation program involving sports leagues, youth camps, adult education classes, cultural programs, and other leisure-time activities. What does she need to know about marketing?

19. Assume that a recent series of traffic tragedies involving drunk drivers has led to a public protest in your community. You have been asked to explain how marketing can help a group crusading against drinking drivers. What will you say?

20. Categorize the following marketing functions as either an exchange function, a physical distribution function, or a facilitating function. Choose a local retail store and give an example of how this store performs each of the eight functions.

a.	Buying	e.	Selling
b.	Financing	f.	Standardization and grading
c.	Securing marketing information	g.	Storing
d.	Risk taking	h.	Transporting

Case: Trivial Pursuit

To those few people who are still unfamiliar with Trivial Pursuit, it is a board game that tests the mental capacity of participants to remember such miscellaneous minutiae as the names of Howdy Doody's sister (Heidi Doody) and Rhoda's doorman (Carlton). Created by Scott Abbott and brothers Chris and John Haney, Trivial Pursuit has participants moving plastic pieces around a playing board shaped in the pattern of a spoked wheel. By continuing to answer questions correctly, players make their way up the spoke toward the wheel hub. The first to reach the hub (after depositing each of his or her colored triangles in appropriate slots) wins. Some 6,000 questions, many of which are answerable only by a 12-year-old who spent his or her formative years watching TV reruns, in six different categories keep most players guessing for hours on end.

Although the original Trivial Pursuit concept was created in 1979 in less than an hour, it took the three inventor/partners two years to create the game's 6,000 questions, finance the project with money from friends and acquaintances, and distribute the games to retail stores. Initial sales, which began in Canada in November 1981, far outpaced the trio's projections despite the fact that no advertising was used. When Selchow & Righter Company, producers of Scrabble, acquired the U.S. rights in 1982, even the firm's most optimistic executives could not have dreamed that sales of $400 million would be possible within 18 months. In 1983, Trivial Pursuit sold one million copies in the United States.

Unlike many products that rely on heavy advertising to maintain sales, Trivial Pursuit's early success was tied mainly to word-of-mouth advertising. The Trivial Pursuit craze spread like wildfire on college campuses and from there to homes where students' parents and younger siblings picked up the fever. Restaurants and lounges began to sponsor Trivial Pursuit contests. The ensuing demand created a scarcity of games, and Selchow & Righter responded by running the two-page ad shown on the right.

With 1984 retail sales forecasted as high as $700 million, Selchow & Righter marketers began producing games in five different factories, at one point reaching one million games a week. The original Genus Edition is now only one of several Trivial Pursuit games: others are All-Star Sports, Silver Screen, and Baby Boomer Editions. Who's Who, popular music, and young

Sources: McDermott and Nason quotations from Frederick Rose, "If You Don't Like 20 Questions, Maybe 6,000 Will Grab You," *The Wall Street Journal* (April 12, 1983), p. 1. Moore quotation from Julie Liesse Erickson, "Trend Setters Play Winning Games," *Advertising Age* (July 19, 1984), p. 47. 1985 update courtesy of John Nason, Selchow & Righter Company.

Photo Source: Courtesy of Selchow & Righter Company.

players' editions are also in the works. Special versions of the game are being released in England, Australia, France, Holland, Germany, and Japan. In addition, several special merchandising products are fueling the craze, including a Trivial Pursuit calendar, cartoon books, and desk accessories. An ABC-TV Trivial Pursuit special is also planned.

Not surprisingly, Trivial Pursuit's phenomenal success has produced dozens of imitators. Magazines no less prestigious than *Time, People,* and *TV Guide* have their own versions, and some 37 other trivia board games are crowding the market. Thus far, none of these games has succeeded in unseating Trivial Pursuit. Moreover, their likelihood of success is slim as long as Haney, Haney, and Abbott keep dreaming up the kinds of questions that tickle the fancy of trivia buffs.

Several skeptics question just how long Trivial Pursuit will last. Some, like Ian McDermott, senior buyer at the New York toy store chain F.A.O. Schwarz, have already proven wrong. In 1983, McDermott predicted that Trivial Pursuit would be the board game of the year the next year, but, "like Rubik's Cube (it will) come to a sudden halt." However, its ability to achieve classic status like games such as Monopoly or Scrabble, is still unknown. Even John Nason, Selchow & Righter's marketing vice-president, admits that Trivial Pursuit may not have the winning formula—offering players the infinite number of actions they need to keep coming back for more. To be a classic, says Nason, "the game should be new every time you play it."

Interestingly, Trivial Pursuit is similar to Coleco's Cabbage Patch Kids product success of 1985 in that both succeeded at a time when technologically based video games were the rage. Some observers feel that part of Trivial Pursuit's success is due to the fact that people are tired of playing games by themselves. "Trivial Pursuit is a party in a box," said John Moore, vice-president at Selchow & Righter's public relations agency. "It's a $30 guarantee of a good time. Even if you don't get a single question right, you have a ball." Moore believes that video games helped Trivial Pursuit in another way. "Trivial Pursuit might never have made it if video games hadn't broken the price barrier. No one had ever tried to sell a $30 to $35 board game before Trivial Pursuit."

Questions

1. Relate the marketing of Trivial Pursuit to the concept of the consumer and the elements of the marketing mix. Describe the product's target purchaser. Discuss how each of the marketing mix elements is employed by the firm.

2. Relate the material in this case to each of the environmental factors affecting marketing decisions.

3. Which of the marketing functions are performed by Trivial Pursuit's marketers?

4. Recommend a course of action designed to extend the success of the product.

Computer Applications

Earlier in the chapter, the origin of marketing activity was traced to the exchange process. Two of the eight fundamental marketing functions—buying and selling—are performed when suppliers exchange surplus products or services for other items or money.

Figure 1 illustrates the most primitive form of exchange in which producers contact one another directly to exchange surplus output. In this example of what might be termed *decentralized exchange,* the small barter economy consists of eight families living within a few miles of one another on a small island named Nandina. At one time in the past, each family was completely self-sufficient. Over time, however, they began to realize that they could increase their standards of living by specializing in the production of a limited number of products and then by exchanging their surplus production for other products being produced by other families. Although they were uncomfortable at first with the prospect of being dependent on others for products necessary for their own comfort and enjoyment, they gradually accepted this new approach to production and trade due to its ability to provide them with more goods and services than they could produce under the previous system of total self-sufficiency.

Although specialization produced benefits for the eight families of Nandina, the decentralized exchange proved time-consuming since each family had to make direct contact with each of the other seven families to complete the exchange. In addition, complaints were frequently voiced when one family representative seeking to make an exchange with another family discovered that the second family had travelled to the residence of still another family to make an exchange, leaving no one at home.

Figure 1 illustrates the inefficiency of decentralized exchange by showing all of the connecting lines necessary to complete the transactions among the eight families. A total of 28 connecting lines are drawn on the figure.

Instead of resorting to drawing all the lines that connect each of the families and then counting the lines, the following formula can be used to determine the number of transactions required to carry out decentralized exchange:

$$T = \frac{n(n-1)}{2}$$

where T is the number of transactions and n is the number of producer families. In this case:

$$T = \frac{8(8-1)}{2} = \frac{8(7)}{2} = \frac{56}{2} = 28.$$

But what happens if the decentralized exchange economy is converted to a *centralized exchange system* through the introduction of some form of marketing intermediary such as a central market? The results are shown in Figure 2.

The exchange process becomes much more efficient when a central market is created because each family can contact the manager of the market directly to exchange surplus production for other needed products. The need to make direct contact with the other families to facilitate exchange no longer exists. Instead of the 28 transactions required for decentralized exchange, only 8 transactions are needed when a marketing intermediary is introduced. The result is increased efficiency, since the

Figure 1
Decentralized Exchange among Eight Families

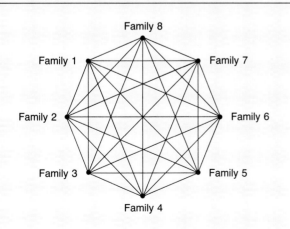

Figure 2
Centralized Exchange among Eight Families

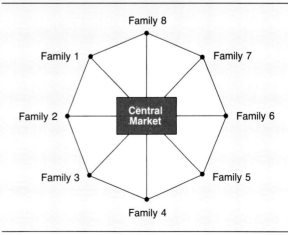

marketing intermediary reduces the amount of work that must be done.

How much more efficient is centralized exchange than the former system of decentralized exchange?[1] The following calculation provides the answer to this question:

$$\text{Percentage of Increased Efficiency} = \frac{\text{Number of Transactions with Decentralized Exchange}}{\text{Number of Transactions with Centralized Exchange}}$$

$$= \frac{28}{8}$$

$$= 350\%.$$

[1] The concepts of decentralized exchange and centralized exchange are discussed in Wroe Alderson, *Marketing Behavior and Executive Action* (Homewood, Ill: Richard D. Irwin, 1957), pp. 213–214. Alderson discusses the percentage of increased efficiency in terms of a *ratio of advantage*.

Directions: Use menu item 1 titled "Exchange Process" to solve each of the following problems.

Problem 1 A small community of 80 farmers residing in a rural area of western Pennsylvania were considering the development of a central farmers' market for their exclusive use in trading with one another. How many transactions are currently necessary to conduct decentralized exchange among the 80 farmers? How many transactions will be necessary if the farmers' market is constructed and utilized by each of the farmers? What effect will the farmers' market have on efficiency?

Problem 2 A group of 10 families located in an isolated region near Fairbanks, Alaska, have been engaged in decentralized exchange of surplus products for several years. They are considering opening a central market that would operate every Saturday in a conveniently located meeting place.

a. How many transactions are involved under the present decentralized exchange system?
b. How many transactions would be involved if the families decide to establish the central market?
c. What effect would the central market have on efficiency?

Problem 3 Eight years ago, 25 families immigrated to a small Pacific island located 800 miles north of Auckland, New Zealand. Since they are completely dependent upon trading surplus goods with one another, they have been actively engaged in a decentralized exchange system since the late 1970s. Due to the problems involved in their current informal system of trade, they are considering a proposal to establish a central market.

a. How many transactions are involved under the present system?
b. How many transactions will be involved if the central market is established?
c. Specify the impact of the central market in terms of increases in efficiency.

Problem 4 Six small manufacturers were operating in close proximity. Each manufacturer made purchases from and, in turn, sold products to the other five manufacturers. A marketing intermediary offered to serve as a linkage among the firms to reduce the time and costs involved in the old system of decentralized exchange. However, one of the manufacturers argued that the small number of firms was insufficient to justify a marketing intermediary. How much will efficiency increase if the intermediary is used?

Problem 5 Nine families currently reside on the small Caribbean island of Anta. Another seven families live on Benzille, another island three miles from Anta. At the present time, the nine families on Anta are engaged in decentralized exchange but do not trade with the residents of Benzille. Decentralized exchange is also in effect on Benzille. During recent trade discussions between a Benzille representative and a resident of Anta, two proposals were presented in an attempt to increase efficiency:

a.   Establish two central markets, one located on Anta and the second on Benzille. Although a centralized exchange system would replace the previous system on both islands, no inter-island trade would be involved.

b.   Establish one large central market on the currently uninhabited island of Centar, located midway between Anta and Benzille. Residents of both Anta and Benzille would utilize this market, and their original decentralized exchange systems would be eliminated.

Compare the current decentralized exchange systems on Anta and Benzille with the first proposal. How much will efficiency increase on Anta if the first proposal is implemented? On Benzille? How many transactions will be involved if the second proposal is implemented?

The Environment for Marketing Decisions

Key Terms

environmental management
competitive environment
political and legal
  environment
corrective advertising
economic environment
inflation
stagflation
technological environment
demarketing
societal/cultural
  environment

Learning Goals

1. To identify the five components of the marketing environment
2. To explain the types of competition faced by marketers and the steps involved in developing a competitive strategy
3. To identify the three phases of government regulation in the United States
4. To explain the methods used by the Federal Trade Commission in protecting consumers
5. To outline the economic factors that affect marketing decisions
6. To explain the impact of the technological environment on a firm's marketing activities
7. To explain how the societal/cultural environment influences marketing

Waste Management, Inc.

In 1968, Dean L. Buntrock, H. Wayne Huizenga, and Lawrence Beck, owners of three separate carting companies in Chicago and Ft. Lauderdale, decided to combine their efforts into a single operation. They formed Waste Management, Inc., a company that quickly became a giant in the waste disposal industry. During the 1970s, Waste Management followed a path of rapid expansion. After raising funds through a public stock sale in 1971, the company began an aggressive growth program by buying other companies and purchasing landfill sites. Within 12 years, it had added approximately 100 dumping companies and landfills to its operation. By the early 1980s, Waste Management was picking up garbage in about 170 U.S. cities and in foreign countries such as Saudi Arabia and Argentina. The ability of the firm to match its product/service offerings to specific customer needs is illustrated by the accompanying photograph taken in Jeddah, Saudi Arabia. In the narrow, winding streets leading to Jeddah's traditional markets, the firm uses a mini-rearloader instead of the familiar large garbage trucks to collect and haul trash and garbage.

Although hauling garbage proved extremely profitable for Waste Management, Inc., it did not possess the enormous growth potential of the chemical waste disposal market. With the lid in sight on the $10 billion-a-year U.S. solid waste disposal market and with foreign operations being squeezed by tough competition, Waste Management executives turned their sights to the disposal market for toxic industrial byproducts such as PCBs, low-level nuclear wastes, dioxins, and DDT.

A new subsidiary, Chemical Waste Management, was formed, and a network of treatment and disposal centers was set up throughout the United States. The landfill sites acquired earlier gave the company an important edge over its competitors. "Chemical Waste Management was ahead of its time" in securing large, hazardous waste landfill capacity, said Robert Fletcher, president of the chemical division of competitor SCA. "We can't compete with their landfills."

The formation of Chemical Waste Management coincided with a federal government crackdown on corporate producers of toxic waste. A new series of stringent federal regulations created major new business from such corporate giants as Union Carbide, Monsanto, and W. R. Grace. Additional growth came from the federal Environmental Protection Agency's Superfund clean-up project, from individual plant clean-ups, and from the handling of plant accidents.

Photo Source: Courtesy of Chemical Waste Management, Inc.

Ironically, although government regulations brought major new business for the company, they also limited the company's vision. "There has been a lot of responding by natural instinct," said Chemical Waste Management president Lawrence Beck. Seeking to break loose from its profitable but confining attitudes, the firm's management took a new stance in 1980. "We don't want to be in a position of being a slave to regulation or letting regulations dictate what our future business will be," said Raymond Bock, the firm's marketing director. "We have made the determination that we are, in fact, going out there and making investments (in technology) and betting on the outcome."

Perhaps the riskiest of Chemical Waste Management's expansion moves was the decision to apply for a permit to burn toxic chemical wastes on its incinerator ships Vulcanus I and II. Although company executives knew that a tremendous demand could be satisfied through the use of this disposal method and that its safe operation had been demonstrated in Europe, they realized that they faced a stiff fight before a permit would be granted and even stiffer opposition from environmentalists who feared the ecological impact of chemical incineration at sea.

Assignment: Use the materials in Chapter 2 to recommend courses of action to insure future growth of Waste Management's disposal operations.

Source: Fletcher, Beck, and Bock quotations from "Waste Disposal's Aggressive No. 1," *Chemical Week* (August 12, 1981), pp. 40–41.

Chapter Overview _____

The tragic Tylenol poisonings of the early 1980s reveal the importance of environmental factors to the success of any organization. Although most marketers will never face the life-and-death issues dealt with by Johnson & Johnson managers, forces outside the control of the decision maker will continue to affect the operations of any firm. These forces must be identified and analyzed; then the marketing decision makers must determine the nature of their impact upon a particular marketing decision. Although they frequently cannot be controlled by the marketing manager, they must be considered together with the controllable variables of the marketing mix in the development of marketing strategies.

Chapter 1 introduced marketing and the elements of the marketing mix used to satisfy chosen market targets. But the blending of a successful marketing mix must be based upon thorough analysis of environmental factors. The marketer's product, distribution, promotion, and pricing strategies must filter through these environmental forces before they reach their goal—the consumers who represent the firm's market target. In this chapter we examine how each of the environmental variables can affect a firm's marketing strategy.

As Figure 2.1 indicates, the environment for marketing decisions actually consists of five elements: (1) the competitive environment, (2) the political and legal environment, (3) the economic environment, (4) the technological environment, and (5) the societal/cultural environment. These forces are important because they provide the frame of reference within which marketing decisions are made. However, since they represent outside factors, they are *not* marketing mix components.

Figure 2.1 _____
Elements of the Marketing Mix as They Operate
within an Environmental Framework

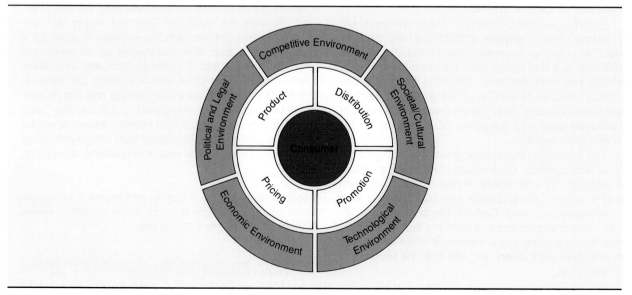

The Marketing Environment: Not Always Uncontrollable _____

Although some marketing writers argue that the marketing environment is completely beyond the control of marketing management, this is not always the case.[1] In some instances, marketers can influence the environment in which the firm operates.

Environmental Management
Accomplishment of organizational objectives by predicting and influencing the competitive, political and legal, economic, technological, and societal/cultural environments.

Environmental management is the accomplishment of organizational objectives by predicting and influencing the competitive, political and legal, economic, technological, and societal/cultural environments.[2] This influence can result from a number of activities by the firm's management. Political power in the form of lobbying among legislative groups and contributions by political action committees (PACs) may result in modifications of regulations, laws, or tariff restrictions. The competitive environment can be affected by new-product developments, joint ventures, and mergers. For example, a firm with a limited product line may strengthen its competitive position through a joint venture or a merger with another company whose products complement those of the acquiring corporation. Southland Corporation's decision to acquire the refineries of Cities Service Company assured the firm's chain of 7-Eleven convenience food stores of a predictable supply of gasoline at a known cost.

Successful research and development efforts may result in changes in the technological environment. A research breakthrough may lead to reduced production costs or a technologically superior new product. While the marketing environment may exist outside the confines of the firm and its marketing mix components, effective marketers continually seek to predict its impact upon marketing decisions and to modify it whenever possible.

In addition to their importance in affecting current marketing decisions, the dynamic nature of the marketing environment means that management at every level must continually reevaluate marketing decisions in response to changing conditions. Even modest environmental shifts can alter the results of marketing decisions. RCA's failure to recognize the flexibility, ease of use, and rapidly declining prices of video cassette cameras and recorders contributed to the market failure of their SelectaVision videodisc player. RCA's product offered very high visual quality programs but lacked the recording features of the video cassette competition.

The Competitive Environment _____

Competitive Environment
Interactive process that occurs in the marketplace among marketers of directly competitive products, marketers of products that can be substituted for one another, and marketers competing for the consumer purchase dollar.

The interactive process that occurs in the marketplace as competing organizations seek to satisfy markets is known as the competitive environment Marketing decisions by an individual firm influence consumer responses in the marketplace; they also affect the marketing strategies of competitors. As a consequence, marketers must continually monitor the marketing activities of competitors—their products, channels, prices, and promotional efforts.

In a few instances, organizations enjoy a monopoly position in the marketplace. Utilities, such as natural gas, electricity, water, and cable television service, accept considerable regulation from local authorities in such marketing-related activities as rates, service levels, and geographic coverage in exchange for exclusive rights to serve a particular group of consumers. However, such instances are rare. In addition, traditional monopoly industries such as telephone service have been deregulated in recent years, and American Telephone & Telegraph and the newly formed spinoff companies resulting from the AT&T breakup currently face competition in such areas as the sale of telephone receivers, long-distance telephone service, and installation and maintenance of telephone systems in larger commercial and industrial firms.

Sporting goods provide an illustration of the importance of the competitive environment. Sports and recreation fads result in boom periods for the manufacturers of the equipment involved, and dozens of new competitors enter the market. Bowling boomed in the early 1960s, snowmobiles in 1971, skiing in 1973, tennis in 1975, and aerobic dancing and exercise during the 1980s. Each of these periods has been followed by a terrific expansion of the related segment of the sporting goods industry. Excess supply soon develops regardless of optimistic predictions in the sport. The net result is that some firms try to compete by cutting prices. Other firms are then forced to make similar reductions to remain competitive. Tensor sold its metal tennis racquets for $25 in 1968 and for $9 by the mid-1970s. Eventually, many of the marginal competitors are forced out of the industry, and production and marketing resume normal patterns.

Jogging and racquetball are among the sports fads today that have given rise to industries serving the participants. Many companies now make running shoes or "training flats" for joggers. Racquetball courts dot the landscape of most suburban areas and smaller cities. Today, supplying racquetball equipment and accessories is a major industry. But there are signs of change: joggers can choose from more than a hundred different models of running shoes, and racquetball courts face increased competition in many major metropolitan areas. The competitive environment is a fact of life even in recreation and leisure activities.

Types of Competition

Marketers actually face three types of competition. The most direct form of competition occurs between marketers of similar products. Xerox photocopiers compete with models offered by Canon, Sharp, and Olivetti. Kubota tractors face competition from Ford Motor Company's farm equipment division, Case, and John Deere.

As Union Oil Company pointed out in the advertisement shown in Figure 2.2, it does not enjoy a monopoly position, as some critics have claimed. It actually competes with 72 leading oil companies, none of which has larger than an 8.5 percent market share.

A second type of competition involves products that can be substituted for one another. In the construction industry and in manufacturing, steel products by Bethlehem Steel may compete with similar products made of aluminum by Alcoa or Reynolds Aluminum. In many industries, cast-iron pipes compete with pipes made of such synthetic materials as polyvinyl chloride (PVC). In instances where a change such as a price increase or an improvement in the strength of a product occurs, demand for substitute products is directly affected.

The final type of competition occurs among all organizations that compete for the consumer's purchases. Traditional economic analysis views competition as a battle among companies in the same industry or among substitutable products and services. Marketers, however, accept the argument that all firms are competing for a limited amount of discretionary buying power. Delco batteries directly compete with Sears DieHard. U.S. Steel competes with Alcoa with substitutable products. The Honda Accord competes with a vacation in Europe, and Asylum/Electra Records competes with a Dan Akroyd movie for the consumer's entertainment dollars.

Figure 2.2
Direct Competition: The U.S. Petroleum Industry

Because the competitive environment often determines the success or failure of a product, marketers must continually assess marketing strategies of competitors. New product offerings with technological advances, price reductions, special promotions, or other competitive actions must be monitored to adjust the firm's marketing mix in light of such changes. Among the first purchasers of any new product are the product's competitors. Careful analysis of its components—physical components, performance attributes, packaging, retail price, service requirements, and estimated production and marketing costs—allows the marketer to forecast its likely competitive impact. If necessary, adjustments to one or more marketing mix components may take place as a result of the new market entry.

Developing a Competitive Strategy

All marketers must develop an effective strategy for dealing with the competitive environment. Some will compete in a broad range of product markets in many areas of the world. Others prefer to specialize in particular market segments, such as those determined by geographical, age, or income factors. Essentially, the determination of a competitive strategy involves three questions:

1. Should we compete?
2. If so, in what markets should we compete?
3. How should we compete?

The answer to the first question—should we compete?—must be based on the resources and objectives of the firm and expected profit potential for the firm. In some instances, potentially successful ventures are not considered due to the lack of a match between the venture and the overall organizational objectives. RCA's sale of its CIT division to Manufacturers Hanover Corporation was based upon a poor match between the technologically oriented parent firm and its financial services subsidiary. Atari sold its Pizza Time Theater outlets due to a perceived mismatch.

The other critical issue in deciding whether to compete is expected profit potential. If the expected profits are insufficient to pay an adequate return on the required investment, then the firm should consider moving into other lines of business. Many organizations have accomplished this switch quite efficiently. This decision should be subject to continual reevaluation so that the firm avoids being tied to traditional markets with declining profit margins. It is also important to anticipate competitive responses.

The second question concerns the markets in which to compete. This decision acknowledges that the marketer has limited resources (sales personnel, advertising budgets, product development capability, and the like) and that these resources must be allocated to the areas of greatest opportunity. Too many marketers have taken a "shotgun" approach to market selection and thus do an ineffective job in many markets rather than a good one in selected markets.

Answering the third question—how should we compete?—requires that the marketer make the tactical decisions involved in setting up a comprehensive marketing strategy. Product, pricing, distribution, and promotion decisions, of course, are the major elements of this strategy.

The Political and Legal Environment

Political and Legal Environment Component of the marketing environment consisting of laws and interpretation of laws that require firms to operate under competitive conditions and to protect consumer rights.

Before you play the game, learn the rules! It would be absurd to start playing a new game without first understanding the rules, yet some businesspeople exhibit a remarkable lack of knowledge about marketing's political and legal environment—the laws and interpretation of laws that require firms to operate under competitive conditions and to protect consumer rights. Ignorance of laws, ordinances, and regulations could result in fines, embarrassing negative publicity, and possibly expensive civil damage suits.

Considerable diligence is required to develop an understanding of the legal framework for marketing decisions. Numerous laws and regulations, often vague and legislated by a multitude of different authorities, characterize the political and legal environment for marketing decisions. Regulations affecting marketing have been enacted at the federal, state, and local levels, as well as by independent regulatory agencies. Our existing legal framework was constructed on a piecemeal basis, often in response to concerns over current issues.

The United States has tended to follow a public policy of promoting a competitive marketing system. To maintain such a system, competitive practices within the system have been regulated. Traditionally, the pricing and promotion variables have received the most legislative attention.

The Impact of Societal Expectations upon the Political and Legal Framework

We live in and desire a free enterprise society—or do we? The concept of free enterprise is not clear and has been gradually changing. At the turn of the century the prevalent attitude was to let business act quite freely. As a result, it was expected that new products and jobs would be created and the economy would continue to develop and prosper.

This provided great freedom for both the scrupulous and unscrupulous. Although most marketers sought to serve their market targets in an equitable fashion, abuses did occur. Figure 2.3 is an example of questionable marketing practices. Such advertisements were not unusual in the late 1800s and the early years of the twentieth century.

In addition, advancing technology resulted in a multitude of products. Considerable expertise was sometimes needed just to choose among them.

Figure 2.3
1896 Advertisement Containing Questionable Health Claims

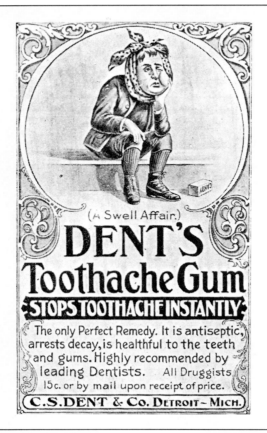

Source: *Those Were the Good Old Days,* (New York: A Fireside Book published by Simon and Schuster, 1959), p. 86.

With the increasing complexity of products, growth of big, impersonal business, and unfair or careless treatment of consumers by a few, the values of society changed. Government should regulate business more closely, we said. Over time, governments at the federal, state, and local levels have responded, and many laws have been passed to protect consumers and to help maintain a competitive environment for business. Large bureaucracies have been established to accomplish this.

The history of governmental regulation in the United States can be divided into three phases. The first phase was the antimonopoly period of the early twentieth century, when major laws such as the Sherman Act, Clayton Act, and the Federal Trade Commission Act were passed to protect competition by reducing the trend toward increasing concentration of industry power in the hands of a small number of competitors. The second phase was aimed at protecting competitors. This phase developed during the depression era of the 1930s, as independent merchants felt the need for legal protection against competition from larger chain stores. Federal legislation enacted during this era included the Robinson-Patman Act and the Miller-Tydings Resale Price Maintenance Act. The third phase of governmental regulations focused upon protection of consumers. Although consumer protection is an underlying objective of most laws—the Sherman Act, FTC Act, Federal Food and Drug Act, and Meat Inspection Act are good examples—many of the major pro-consumer laws have been enacted during the past 25 years.

The following sections briefly describe the major federal laws affecting marketing. Many of them are referred to throughout the text. In addition, legislation affecting specific marketing practices, such as product warranties or franchise agreements, are discussed in chapters dealing with these subjects.

Antitrust Legislation

The Sherman Antitrust Act (1890) prohibits restraint of trade and monopolization. It subjects violators to civil suits and to criminal prosecution. Although the practices covered by the act were unlawful under common law and under several state acts passed in the previous decade, the Sherman Act was the first piece of federal legislation to clearly delineate the maintenance of a competitive marketing system as national policy.

However, antitrust legislation has not been completely effective in eliminating abuses. A Department of Justice official once estimated that antitrust violations cost U.S. consumers between 3 and 12 percent of the nation's gross national product each year.[3]

The economic philosophy of the Sherman Act contrasts sharply with the philosophies of many foreign countries where monopolies are openly encouraged by the government. In such cases, governments usually attempt to foster productive efficiency that might be injured by excessive competition. Few nations have antitrust legislation even remotely comparable to that of the United States. As a result, foreign cartels (monopolies) at one time had a distinct advantage over U.S. companies operating independently in international markets.

Because of this situation, the Webb-Pomerene Export Trade Act (1918) exempted voluntary export trade associations from the Sherman Act restrictions—but only in their foreign trade dealings. Exemptions of a similar nature have since been granted on the domestic front for the merger of the National and American Football Leagues and for pollution control research carried out by automobile manufacturers.

The Clayton Act (1914) strengthened antitrust legislation by restricting such practices as price discrimination, exclusive dealing, tying contracts, and interlocking boards of directors where the effect "may be to substantially lessen competition or tend to create a monopoly." Later, the Celler-Kefauver Antimerger Act (1950) amended the Clayton Act to include the purchase of assets where such purchases would reduce competition.

Another important aspect of the regulation of competition is the Federal Trade Commission Act, which also became law in 1914. This act prohibited unfair methods of competition and established the Federal Trade Commission (FTC) as an administrative agency to oversee the various laws dealing with business.

Since its early days, the FTC has assumed a large workload that continues to grow each year. Under the original act, the FTC had to demonstrate injury to competition before a court would declare a marketing practice unfair. The Wheeler-Lea Act (1938), however, amended the Federal Trade Commission Act so as to ban deceptive or unfair business practices per se.

FTC Activities in Protecting Consumers

Armed with the Wheeler-Lea requirements, the FTC has assumed an activist role in consumer protection. It uses three procedures to carry out its duties:

1. Conferences with the individuals or industries involved to secure voluntary compliance with its rules.

2. The consent method, under which the FTC secures the agreements of the firm or industry to abandon a practice the FTC deems unfair.

3. Formal legal action. (All FTC decisions can be appealed through the courts.)

The consent order is an FTC favorite for remedying what the agency believes is an undesirable business practice. A few years ago, the commission decided that AMF advertising had depicted children in unsafe bicycling situations. The resulting consent agreement banned AMF from using commercials showing a variety of dangerous situations, such as children performing bicycling stunts. AMF was also required to produce two safety messages and distribute them to television stations for use as public service announcements. The consent order specifically required that 5,963,000 children from 6 to 11 years old see the safety message or AMF would have to distribute the commercials to a second group of television stations.[4]

Corrective Advertising
Policy of the Federal Trade Commission, under which companies found to have used deceptive promotional messages are required to correct their earlier claims with new messages.

Another technique adopted by the FTC during the past two decades is corrective advertising.[5] This approach requires firms found to have used deceptive advertising to correct their earlier claims with new promotional messages. During the mid-1970s, STP Corporation advertised that its oil treatment would reduce oil consumption by 20 percent. The FTC ruled that the tests used by the company to base its claims were unreliable, fined the firm $500,000, and required it to spend another $200,000 on corrective advertising in newspapers and magazines. The STP corrective advertisement is shown in Figure 2.4.

Figure 2.4
An Example of Corrective Advertising

ADVERTISEMENT

FTC NOTICE

As a result of an investigation by the
Federal Trade Commission into certain allegedly
inaccurate past advertisements
for STP's oil additive, STP Corporation
has agreed to a $700,000 settlement.
With regard to that settlement,
STP is making the following statement:

It is the policy of STP to support its advertising with objective information and test data. In 1974 and 1975 an independent laboratory ran tests of the company's oil additive which led to claims of reduced oil consumption. However, these tests cannot be relied on to support the oil consumption reduction claim made by STP.

The FTC has taken the position that, in making that claim, the company violated the terms of a consent order. When STP learned that the test data did not support the claim, it stopped advertising containing that claim. New tests have been undertaken to determine the extent to which the oil additive affects oil consumption. Agreement to this settlement does not constitute an admission by STP that the law has been violated. Rather, STP has agreed to resolve the dispute with the FTC to avoid protracted and prohibitively expensive litigation.

February 13, 1978

Legislation Designed to Regulate Competitors

The Robinson-Patman Act (1936) was typical of depression-era legislation. Known in some circles as the Anti-A&P Act, it was inspired by price competition from the developing grocery-store chains. In fact, the law was originally prepared by the United States Wholesale Grocers Association. The country was in the midst of the depression, and legislative interest was directed toward saving jobs. The developing chain stores were seen as a threat to traditional retailers and to employment. The Robinson-Patman Act was a government effort to reduce this threat.

The act, which was technically an amendment to the Clayton Act, prohibited price discrimination in sales to wholesalers, retailers, or other producers that was not based on a cost differential. It also disallowed selling at an unreasonably low price to eliminate competition. The Clayton Act had applied only to price discrimination by geographic area that injured local sellers. The supporting rationale for the Robinson-Patman legislation was that the chain stores might be able to secure supplier discounts that were not available to the small, independent stores. The major defenses against charges of price discrimination are that it has been used in an attempt to meet competitors' prices and that it is justified by cost differences.

When a firm asserts that price differentials are used in good faith to meet competition, the logical question is: What constitutes good-faith pricing behavior? The answer depends on the circumstances of each situation.

When cost differentials are claimed as a defense, the price differences must not exceed the cost differences resulting from selling to different classes of buyers. A major difficulty of the defense is justifying the differences. Indeed, many authorities consider this area one of the most confusing in the Robinson-Patman Act.

The varying interpretations of the act certainly qualify it as one of the vaguest of marketing laws. For the most part, charges brought under the act are handled on an individual basis. Marketers must therefore continually evaluate their pricing actions to avoid potential Robinson-Patman violations.

Unfair Trade Laws   Enacted in the 1930s, unfair trade laws are state laws requiring sellers to maintain minimum prices for comparable merchandise. These laws were intended to protect small specialty shops, such as dairy stores, from the loss-leader pricing of similar products offered by chain stores. Typically, the retail price floor was set at cost plus some modest markup. Although most of these laws remain on the books, they have become less important in the more prosperous years since the 1930s and are seldom enforced.

Removing Barriers to Competition   Fair trade is a concept that affected regulation of competitive activities for decades. In 1931, California became the first state to enact fair trade legislation. Most other states soon followed suit; only Missouri, the District of Columbia, Vermont, and Texas failed to adopt such laws. *Fair trade laws* permitted manufacturers to stipulate a minimum retail price for a product and to require their retail dealers to sign contracts stating that they would abide by such prices.[6]

The basic argument behind the legislation was that a product's image, implied by its price, was a property right of the manufacturer who should have the authority to protect the asset by requiring retailers to maintain a minimum price. Fair trade legislation can be traced to lobbying by organizations of independent retailers who feared chain-store growth. The economic mania of the depression years was clearly evident in these statutes.

A U.S. Supreme Court decision holding fair trade contracts illegal in interstate commerce led to the passage of the Miller-Tydings Resale Price Maintenance Act (1937). This law exempted interstate fair trade contracts from compliance with antitrust requirements. The states were thus authorized to keep these laws on their books if they so desired.

Over the years, fair trade declined in importance as price competition became a more important marketing strategy. These laws became invalid with the passage of the Consumer Goods Pricing Act (1975). This act halted all interstate use of resale price maintenance, an objective long sought by consumer groups.

Consumer Protection: A Changing Legal Environment

The first activist legislation dealing with a specific marketing practice was the Pure Food and Drug Act (1906), which prohibited the adulteration and mis-branding of foods and drugs involved in interstate commerce. The bill was enacted because of the unsanitary meat-packing practices of Chicago stock-yards. It was strengthened in 1938 by the Food, Drug, and Cosmetic Act and in 1962 by the Kefauver-Harris Drug Amendments (the latter legislation was a response to the thalidomide tragedies). Since that time, the Food and Drug Administration (FDA) has held increased regulatory authority in such matters as product development, branding, and advertising.

Rules governing advertising and labeling constitute another sphere of marketing's legal environment. The Wool Products Labeling Act of 1939 (re-quiring that the kind and percentage of wool in a product be identified), the Fur Products Labeling Act of 1951 (requiring identification of the animal from which the fur was derived), and the Flammable Fabrics Act of 1953 (prohibit-ing the interstate sale of flammable fabrics) formed the original legislation in this area. A more recent law—the Fair Packaging and Labeling Act, passed in 1967—requires the disclosure of product identity, the name and address of the manufacturer or distributor, and information concerning the quality of the contents. In 1971, the Public Health Cigarette Smoking Act prohibited tobacco advertising on radio and television.

The truth-in-lending law deserves special attention. Formally known as Title I of the Consumer Credit Protection Act (1968), the statute requires dis-closure of the annual interest rates on loans and credit purchases. The basic premise is that this information will make it easier for consumers to compare sources of credit. Various assessments of the law, however, suggest that many consumers pay relatively little attention to interest rates; furthermore, they often have limited alternative credit sources.

Other laws that may influence marketing practices are the Fair Credit Reporting Act and the Environmental Protection Act, both of which became law in 1970. The Fair Credit Reporting Act gives individuals access to credit reports prepared about them and permits them to change incorrect informa-tion. The Environmental Protection Act established the Environmental Protec-tion Agency (EPA) and gave it the power to deal with major types of pollution. EPA actions, of course, have a profound effect on the marketing system.

The Consumer Product Safety Act (1972) also has far-reaching influence on marketing strategy and on the marketing environment. This legislation cre-ated the Consumer Product Safety Commission, which has the authority to specify safety standards for most consumer products.

The Equal Credit Opportunity Act (1975–1977) banned discrimination in lending practices based on sex, marital status, race, national origin, religion, age, or receipt of payments from public assistance programs. The sex and marital status portions of the act went into effect in 1975, and the remaining portions became effective in 1977.

The Fair Debt Collection Practices Act (1978) prohibited harassing, de-ceptive, or unfair collection practices by debt-collecting agencies. In-house debt collectors, such as banks, retailers, and attorneys, are exempt, however. Misrepresentation of the consumer's legal rights is an example of a specific practice that was banned by the act.

Several laws have been passed within the past ten years in an attempt to deregulate the U.S. transportation industry. Air transportation was the sub-ject of the Airline Deregulation Act of 1978, while the Motor Carrier Act and

Return to the Stop-Action Case

Waste Management, Inc.

Although Chemical Waste Management's landfill operations had always been subject to the stringent regulations of federal and state environmental protection agencies, the company's attempt to begin incinerating toxic substances at sea put it in a struggle with state and federal authorities it had never before experienced.

From the beginning, the federal Environmental Protection Agency required sophisticated automatic monitoring devices to provide a permanent record of the incineration. The agency also required test burns to determine the effectiveness of the system. The results of such a test in the Gulf of Mexico were so successful that the firm's management grew confident that a permit would soon be granted. According to company spokesperson Bob Reincke, EPA officials monitoring the test "were able to confirm that the Vulcanus I successfully destroys wastes that contain PCBs and does it with no environmental impact."

The design of both Vulcanus I and II was aimed at ensuring the effectiveness of the system. Both ships were built with double-thick hulls, bottoms, and tank walls. Each waste storage tank (there are 15 on Vulcanus I and 8 on Vulcanus II) has a segregated air system and pumps; absorbent materials are also built into the ships to contain any chemical leak. In addition, highly sophisticated monitoring systems ensure that temperature levels remain high enough during incineration to meet government specifications. Rigid annual inspections and prevoyage and postvoyage maintenance and safety checks are designed to guarantee continuing compliance with EPA regulations.

Source: Reincke quotation from Susan Fass, "Ships to Burn Hazardous Waste," *Journal of Commerce* (August 5, 1983), p. 12A.

the Staggers Rail Act were both enacted in 1980 to deregulate the trucking and railroad industries. These acts are discussed in detail in Chapter 13.

Figure 2.5 summarizes the major legislative acts affecting marketing and indicates whether a particular law was primarily intended to promote a competitive environment, to assist in regulating competitors, or to regulate marketing practices affecting consumers. The figure also lists the elements of marketing strategy affected by the legislation.

Many of the pieces of legislation introduced in this section are referred to throughout the text. In summary, the legal framework for marketing decisions is basically a positive environment; it attempts to encourage a competitive marketing system employing fair business practices. What marketing's legal future will be, of course, is open to debate. It appears, however, that future marketing legislation will be more directly concerned with protecting consumer interests and will probably come from three sources: (1) state and local governments, (2) court decisions, and (3) regulations by administrative agencies such as the Federal Trade Commission and the Food and Drug Administration. These sources, closely tied to consumer affairs, are likely to assume an active role in marketing legislation.

Figure 2.5

Major Marketing Legislation and Its Impact on Marketing Decisions

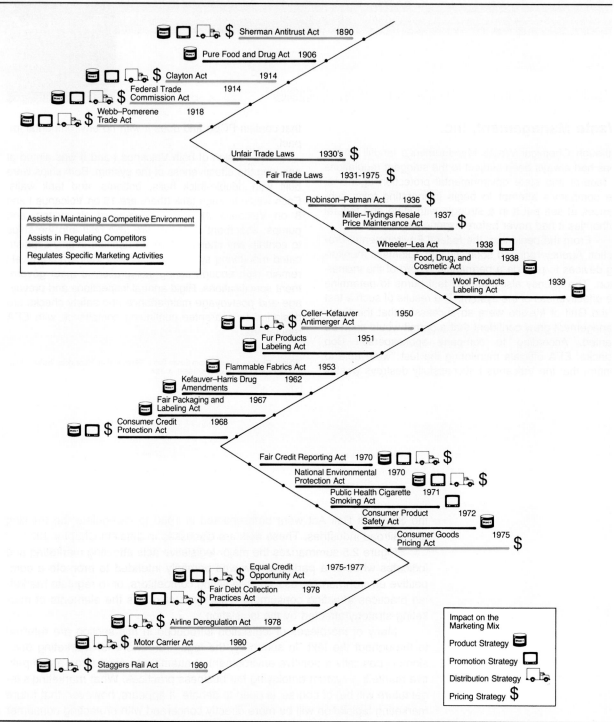

The Economic Environment _____

Economic Environment
Component of the marketing environment consisting of a setting of complex and dynamic business fluctuations that historically tend to follow a four-stage pattern: recession, depression, recovery, and prosperity.

In addition to the competitive and the political and legal environments, marketers must understand the economic environment and its impact upon their organizations. Three economic subjects of major concern to marketers in recent years have been recession, unemployment, and inflation.

A deteriorating economic environment adversely affects most marketers. However, for some companies, the recent recession was good news. As inflation continues and production declines with corresponding growth in the level of unemployment, consumer buying patterns shift. Flour millers note that flour sales increase. Automobile repairs and home improvements also increase. Greeting card firms report that consumers buy fewer gifts, but more expensive cards. Hardware stores show higher sales. Decline is, of course, experienced by many other firms. Clearly, the economic environment has a sizable influence on the way marketers operate.

Stages of the Business Cycle

The economic environment is extremely complex. Operating within it are dynamic business fluctuations that tend to follow a cyclical pattern composed of four stages:

1. Prosperity
2. Recession
3. Depression
4. Recovery

It should be noted that many economists argue that society is capable of preventing future depressions through intelligent use of various economic policies. Thus a recession would be followed by a period of recovery.

No marketer can disregard the economic climate in which a business functions, for the type, direction, and intensity of a firm's marketing strategy depend upon it. The marketer must also be aware of the economy's relative position in the business cycle and how it will affect the forecasts of future economic activity.

Of necessity, marketing activity differs with each stage of the business cycle. During prosperous times, consumers are usually more willing to buy than when they feel economically threatened. For example, during the recent recession, personal savings climbed to high levels as consumers (fearing possible layoffs and other work-force reductions) cut back their expenditures for many products in the nonessential category. Marketers must pay close attention to the consumer's relative willingness to buy. The aggressiveness of one's marketing strategy and tactics is often dependent upon current buying intentions. More aggressive marketing may be called for in periods of lessened buying interest, such as when automakers use cash rebate schemes to move inventories.

Inflation
Rising price level that results in reduced purchasing power for the consumer.

Inflation Inflation has been a major economic concern to marketers in recent years. Inflation, which can occur during any stage of the business cycle, is defined as a rising price level resulting in reduced purchasing power for the consumer. A person's money is devalued in terms of what it can buy. Traditionally, this phenomenon has been more prevalent in countries outside North America. However, during the late 1970s and early 1980s, the United States experienced double-digit inflation. Although the rate of inflation declined considerably during the mid-1980s, the recent experiences led to widespread concern over public policy designed to stabilize price levels and over ways to adjust personally to reductions in the dollar's spending power.

Stagflation
Situation in which an economy has both high unemployment and a rising price level.

Stagflation is a word that has been coined to describe a peculiar brand of inflation that characterized some recent economic experiences. It is a situation in which an economy has high unemployment and a rising price level at the same time. Formulation of effective strategies is particularly difficult under these circumstances.

Unemployment   As the rate of inflation slowed in the mid-1980s, public concern turned to a second economic problem: *unemployment*. Unemployment—officially defined as people actively looking for work who do not have jobs—results from a number of factors. In some instances, workers in the process of leaving old jobs and finding new ones, or students leaving school and looking for jobs, are unemployed for short periods of time. The estimated 2 to 3 percent of the labor force who are likely to be in the job search phase of their careers are termed *frictionally unemployed*. Still other workers are *structurally unemployed* because they either lack the necessary skills required by available jobs or the skills they possess are not demanded by potential employers. Many workers in Minnesota became jobless when the iron ore deposits in the Mesabi Range were exhausted.

Cyclical unemployment results from disruptions in overall economic activity. The severe recession of the early 1980s contributed greatly to the ranks of the unemployed. As production slowed and many factories ceased operation entirely, millions of workers found themselves out of work. The consequences of reduced income and uncertainty about future income were reflected in the marketplace.

Both unemployment and inflation affect marketing by modifying consumer behavior. Unless unemployment insurance, personal savings, and union supplementary unemployment benefits are sufficient to offset lost earnings, the unemployed individual has less income to spend in the marketplace. Even if the individual is completely compensated for lost earnings, his or her buying behavior is likely to be affected. As consumers become more conscious of inflation, they are likely to become more price conscious in general. This can lead to three possible outcomes, all important to marketers. Consumers can (1) elect to buy now, in the belief that prices will be higher later (automobile dealers often use this argument in their commercial messages), (2) decide to alter their purchasing patterns, or (3) postpone certain purchases.

The Technological Environment

Technological Environment
Applications to marketing of knowledge based upon discoveries in science, inventions, and innovations.

The **technological environment** consists of the applications to marketing of knowledge based upon discoveries in science, inventions, and innovations. It results in new products for consumers and improves existing products. It is a frequent source of price reductions through the development of new production methods or new materials. It also can make existing products obsolete virtually overnight—as slide rule manufacturers would attest. Technological innovations are exemplified in the container industry, where glass and tinplate containers have faced intense competition from such innovations as aluminum, fiberfoil, and plastics.

Marketing decision makers must closely monitor the technological environment for a number of reasons. New technology may be the means by which they remain competitive in their industries. It may also be the vehicle for the creation of entirely new industries. Computers, lasers, and xerography all resulted in the development of major industries during the past 30 years.

In addition, marketers must anticipate the effect such technological innovations are likely to have upon the life-styles of consumers, the products of competitors, the demands of industrial users, and the regulatory actions of government. The advent of video cassette recorders, video cassette rental shops, and lower cost satellite receiving stations may adversely affect concert attendance and movie ticket sales. A longer-lasting engine may reduce industrial purchases. A new process may result in reduction of pollution and produce changes in local ordinances.

A major source of technological innovations from government research has been the space program. Hundreds of industrial applications of space technology have been made, and the federal government has encouraged private enterprise to make use of these innovations. Figure 2.6 reveals some applications that have already been implemented.

The Energy Crisis

The term *energy crisis* refers to the general realization that our energy resources are not limitless. This realization was first brought on by the 1973–1974 Arab oil embargo. Threatened by the cutbacks, much of the industrialized world scrambled for ways of conserving energy. Conservation measures are widespread—for example, reduced speed limits and inducements to increase insulation usage. In Canada, a division of Nashua Corporation even began labeling its promotional material "Printed in U.S.A. to conserve Canadian raw material and energy."

Several facts have now become evident about the energy crisis of the 1970s. First, the crisis has forced business and society to rethink the current allocation of energy resources. Existing sources are being expanded. Traditional resources like coal are being rediscovered. New resources are being sought. Perhaps the most important fact is that attempts are being made to cut waste in energy utilization. The oil embargo of the 1970s forced the industrialized free world to take the necessary steps for self-preservation.

Marketing has also been affected by the energy crisis. For example, the U.S. tire industry has had to deal with three energy-related setbacks:

1.   Reduced levels of driving, causing a reduction in sales;
2.   Lower new car sales, reducing the original equipment market (OEM) for tires; and
3.   Increased costs of petroleum-based raw materials.

Other markets have faced similar problems; the toy industry, for example, depends on a petroleum derivative—plastic. Some plastics have increased substantially in price within a very short time.

As shortages began to appear in many critical industrial areas, marketers were faced with a relatively strange phenomenon: How should limited supplies be allocated to customers whose demands exceed the quantities available for distribution? Many marketers were not prepared to cope with such a

Figure 2.6
Technological Products Resulting from the U.S. Space Program

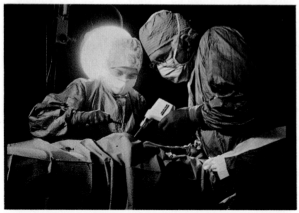

Battery-powered, cordless surgical instruments give surgeons optimum freedom and versatility in the operating room.

Mobile firefighting modules, mounted on trailers and pulled by pickups, draw water from hydrants or open bodies of water to suppress ship or waterfront fires.

Shock-absorbing Temper Foam is used in seat cushions for transportation vehicles, padding for burn patients, and special mattresses for the bedridden.

Fire-resistant suits protect firefighters when they move directly into flames and when they combat fires involving highly flammable products.

Protective face masks prevent head and facial injuries incurred by cerebral palsy victims and other physically impaired patients while they are learning to walk.

Computerized police communication systems incorporating display consoles provide maximum efficiency in coordinating telephone and radio dispatches and interoffice transmissions.

Source: Courtesy of NASA.

situation. The energy crisis and other shortages have forced marketing to devise a fuller range of strategy alternatives.

Demarketing—Dealing with Shortages

Shortages—temporary or permanent—can be caused by several factors. A brisk demand may exceed manufacturing capacity or outpace the response time required to gear up a production line. Shortages may also be caused by a lack of raw materials, component parts, energy, or labor. Regardless of the cause, shortages require marketers to reorient their thinking.

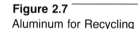

Demarketing
Process of reducing consumer demand for a product or service to a level that can be supplied by the firm.

Demarketing, a term that has come into general use in recent years, refers to the process of cutting consumer demand for a product back to a level that can reasonably be supplied by the firm. Some oil companies, for example, have publicized tips on how to cut gasoline consumption. Utility companies have encouraged homeowners to install more insulation to lower heating bills. Many cities have discouraged central business district traffic by raising parking fees and violation penalties.

Shortages present marketers with a unique set of marketing problems. In some instances, they force marketers to be allocators of limited supplies. This is in sharp contrast to marketing's traditional objective of expanding sales volume. Shortages require marketers to decide whether to spread a limited supply over all customers so that none are satisfied or to limit purchases by some customers so that others may be completely supplied.

One method of addressing the dwindling supply of raw materials such as aluminum is through recycling. Reynolds Aluminum has been actively involved in recycling programs for waste aluminum, as pictured in Figure 2.7, for more than a decade. Its most recent approach is a cash-paying vending

Figure 2.7
Aluminum for Recycling

Source: Courtesy of Reynolds Metals Company.

machine. Such reverse vending machines allow recyclers to insert empty cans and receive money, stamps, and/or discount coupons for merchandise or services.

The Societal/Cultural Environment

The Chevalline Meat Company knows that the societal/cultural environment works against them. When you try to get someone to eat somebody's pony, you've got trouble. Chevalline is trying to induce North Americans to eat more horsemeat, despite an environment that views horses as pets and companions, not livestock for slaughter. U.S. and Canadian consumers eat virtually no horsemeat, although in France and other European countries the meat is well liked.

Chevalline even had some difficulty obtaining a license to open a horsemeat market. Whether the firm will ever change consumer opinion is debatable, but its problems dramatize the importance of understanding and assessing the societal/cultural environment when making marketing decisions.

Societal/Cultural Environment
Component of the marketing environment consisting of the relationship between the marketer and society and its culture.

The societal/cultural environment is the marketer's relationship with society and/or its culture. Obviously, there are many different facets of significance. One important category is the general readiness of society to accept a marketing idea, as discussed above.

Another important category is the trust and confidence of the public in business as a whole. Such confidence has been on the decline since the mid-1960s. Opinion polls suggest that people have lost confidence in major companies (although they maintain faith in the private enterprise system). These declines should, however, be viewed in perspective. All institutions have lost public confidence to some degree. In fact, some would argue that government and labor unions are even less popular than business.

The societal/cultural environment for marketing decisions has both expanded in scope and increased in importance. Today no marketer can initiate a strategy without taking the societal/cultural environment into account. Marketers must develop an awareness of the manner in which it affects their decisions. The constant flux of societal issues requires that marketing managers place more emphasis on addressing these questions instead of merely concerning themselves with the standard marketing tools. Some firms have created a new position—manager of public policy research—to study the changing societal environment's future impact on the company.

Importance in International Marketing Decisions

The cultural context for marketing decision making is often more important in the international sphere than in the domestic arena. Marketers must be cognizant of cultural differences in the way that business affairs are conducted abroad. Consider the following case:

The stereotype of the American male—hail-fellow-well-met, cordial, friendly, outgoing, and gregarious—does not mesh with the discomfort he feels and often shows in his contacts with Latin Americans and Middle Easterners. These people crowd close to him, and in Latin America his host is likely to greet him with a warm *abrazo*, suggesting unfamiliar intimacy. Anyone who has ever attended a party or a reception in Latin America must surely have observed the self-consciousness of the uninitiated stateside visitor who keeps backing away from his native host, to whom it is natural to carry on a

Figure 2.8
Advertisement Portraying a Woman in a Contemporary Role

Source: Courtesy of The Travelers Insurance Companies.

conversation separated by inches. Last year at a businessmen's club in Brazil, where many receptions are held for newly arrived executives, the railings on the terrace had to be reinforced because so many businessmen fell into the gardens as they backed away.[7]

Consumer behavior and tastes also differ from place to place, as is suggested by these situations.

1. An American marketer blundered in West Germany by basing a promotional campaign on the theme "The $1 Billion Coin Giveaway." Since the symbol DM denotes money in Germany, the dollar sign was interpreted as indicating pompous U.S. attitudes of superiority.

2. Nestlé, a Swiss multinational company, now brews more than 40 varieties of instant coffee to satisfy different national tastes.

3. General Foods Corporation entered the British market with its standard powdered Jell-O only to find that British cooks prefer the solid wafer or cake form, even if it takes more time to prepare. After several frustrating years, the company gave up and pulled out of the market.

4. In Italy a company that set up a corn processing plant found that its marketing effort failed because Italians think of corn as pig food.

Importance in Domestic Marketing Decisions

Many marketers recognize societal differences among countries but assume that a homogeneous societal environment exists domestically. Nothing could be further from the truth! The United States is a mixed society composed of varied submarkets. These submarkets can be classified by age, ethnic group, place of residence, sex, and numerous other determinants.

Sex is an increasingly important societal factor. The feminist movement has had a decided effect on marketing and particularly on promotion. Figure 2.8 (shown on preceding page) is a good example of how today's advertising aims at the "new" woman by featuring women in nonstereotyped roles.

Since societal variables change constantly, marketers must continually monitor their dynamic environment. What appears to be out of bounds today may be tomorrow's greatest market opportunity. Consider the way subjects that were previously taboo, such as feminine hygiene products, are now commonly advertised.

The societal variables must be recognized by modern business executives because they affect the way consumers react to different products and marketing practices. One of the most tragic—and avoidable—of all marketing mistakes is the failure to appreciate societal differences within our own domestic market.

The rise of consumerism can be partially traced to the growing public concern with making business more responsible to its constituents. Consumerism, which is discussed in detail in Chapter 20, is an evolving aspect of marketing's societal environment. Certainly the advent of this movement has influenced the move toward more direct protection of consumer rights in such areas as product safety. This concern will undoubtedly be amplified and expanded in the years ahead.

As a conclusion to this look at the marketing environment, Figure 2.9 illustrates how the marketing manager focuses upon a chosen market target by controlling marketing elements in relationship to the forces bearing on a firm's marketing mix. In light of the opportunities and constraints perceived in the environmental framework, as well as the firm's objectives and resources, the manager develops a marketing program (marketing strategy) designed to satisfy customer needs. The elements or tools of the marketing strategy are product, pricing, distribution, and promotion strategies. These are blended together in a unique manner to make up the marketing mix. The result wins customers, sales, and profits for the firm.

While this concept seems simple and straightforward, it is complicated in practice and difficult to execute. The remainder of this text elaborates on the process. The next chapters focus upon marketing planning and forecasting as starting points for the ultimate determination of market segments and the designing of effective marketing mixes.

Figure 2.9

Development of a Marketing Program Designed to
Satisfy Chosen Market Target

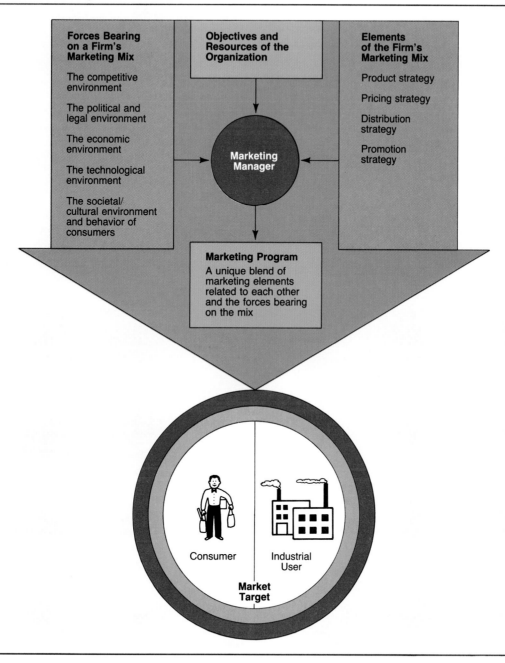

Summary

The environment for marketing decisions is the theme of this chapter. Five specific environments are considered: competitive, political and legal, economic, technological, and societal/cultural. These are important to the study of marketing because they provide a framework within which marketing strategies are formulated. Environmental factors are among the most dynamic aspects of contemporary business. While they are frequently uncontrollable, they can sometimes be changed through such means as political lobbying, mergers and joint ventures, and research and development activities.

The competitive environment is the interactive process that occurs in the marketplace. Marketing decisions influence the market and are in turn affected by the counterstrategies of competition. The legal segment attempts to maintain a competitive environment and to regulate specific marketing practices. The economic environment often influences the manner in which consumers will behave toward varying marketing appeals. The technological environment generates new and improved products but may render currently profitable products and services obsolete. Societal aspects, however, may become the most important to marketers. Concern with adapting to a changing societal environment, both domestically and internationally, has advanced to the forefront of marketing thought.

Photo Source: Courtesy of Chemical Waste Management, Inc.

Solving the Stop-Action Case

Waste Management, Inc.

The solution for Waste Management has proven to be far from simple. Despite positive test results and tentative EPA approval, the firm has continued to encounter barriers preventing the issuance of a permit to burn hazardous wastes in U.S. waters.

Clearly, the firm should have given the political and legal environment and the societal/cultural environment greater weight before choosing the controversial, emotion-laden route of ocean incineration. Among the most vocal critics are residents of Alabama, Texas, and other Gulf Coast states who fear pollution from the ships as they operate in neighboring waters. Many of the Alabama protesters have expressed anger at the firm's practice of bringing in hazardous wastes from other states for disposal at a huge landfill at Emelle, Alabama, and the planned overland movement along Alabama highways of the materials to be incinerated at sea. Company representatives justified the choice of the Gulf of Mexico as the ship's base of operations by pointing to the large amount of toxic wastes produced by area petrochemical plants.

Residents' fears persist despite promises—and demonstrations—by Chemical Waste Management that the toxic wastes would be burned at a safe distance and in a safe manner. A *Wall Street Journal* reporter summarized these fears:

In operation, the vessel—which some have called a leper ship—puts on a show befitting its name, taken from the Roman god of fire. "The noise from the burners and the fire shooting up is quite something to see," says [Gert] Heineman [general manager of Chemical Waste Management's ocean incineration operation], who thinks the eerie glow emitted during night burning adds to people's apprehension.

Another factor contributing to residents' lack of trust that the burns will go according to plans stems from recent reports of illegal dumping at landfill sites in Vickery, Ohio, and Emelle, Alabama. Waste Management paid

Sources: Norton and *The Wall Street Journal* quotations from Hal Lancaster, "Waste Management Still Hits Snags in Bid to Operate Incinerator Ship," *The Wall Street Journal* (November 17, 1983), p. 33.

hefty fines for these violations, and, as a result, its credibility is a sticking point. "There's no one out there to watch them," said Larry Norton, a spokesperson for the Gulf Coast Coalition for Public Health. "The possibility of abuse is there."

EPA action to grant limited testing permits to Chemical Waste Management is dependent, in part, on whether or not the state of Alabama allows the shipment of chemical wastes through the Port of Mobile. This decision is opposed by many who do not want the port used as a storage and loading facility.

Pressure on the EPA to reject Chemical Waste Management's applications extended from the Gulf states to Congress. Congressional critics demanded that clear-cut guidelines governing ocean incineration be written and approved before any permits be granted. Some want the EPA to require pollution-cleansing scrubbers similar to those used on land-based incinerators. These antipollution devices would substantially reduce the ship's expected profits and competitive edge.

Clearly, the environment for Chemical Waste Management's marketing decision to pursue at-sea incineration as another "product" offering has been more hostile than hospitable. The firm has already lost money on Vulcanus I and II and will return to more traditional means of waste disposal if the EPA permits are not granted. Even if the EPA relents and grants the permits, Chemical Waste Management has lost a considerable marketing edge due to the delay. Two competing firms have already filed similar ocean incineration applications with the FDA.

Questions for Discussion

1. Identify and briefly describe the five components of the marketing environment.

2. Give an example of how each of the environmental variables discussed in this chapter might affect the following firms:
   a. Delta Airlines
   b. Local aerobics exercise center
   c. Pizza Hut
   d. Avon Products
   e. Sears catalog department
   f. Local CATV franchise

3. Explain the types of competition faced by marketers.

4. What are the steps involved in developing a competitive strategy?

5. Can the consumerism movement be viewed as a rejection of the competitive marketing system? Defend your answer.

6. Comment on the following statement: The legal framework for marketing decisions is basically a positive one.

7. Government regulation in the United States has evolved in three general phases. Identify each of these phases and give an example of laws enacted during each phase.

8. How did the Great Depression influence marketing legislation?

9. Classify the following laws as either:
   a. Assisting in maintaining a competitive environment
   b. Assisting in regulating competitors
   c. Regulating specific marketing activities
   List more than one if applicable.
   _____ Airline Deregulation Act
   _____ Fair trade laws
   _____ Fair Packaging and Labeling Act
   _____ Clayton Act

10. Give an example of a federal law affecting:
    a. Product strategy
    b. Distribution strategy
    c. Promotion strategy
    d. Pricing strategy

11. Explain the methods used by the Federal Trade Commission to protect consumers.

12. Distinguish between fair trade laws and unfair trade laws.

13. As a consumer, do you favor laws permitting resale price maintenance agreements? Would your answer vary if you were the producer of Zenith television sets? If you were the retailer of Zenith television sets? Why or why not?

14. What are the major defenses firms might use if accused of a Robinson-Patman Act violation? Evaluate each defense.

15. What are the major economic factors affecting marketing decisions?

16. Distinguish between inflation and stagflation. In what ways do they affect marketing?

17. Cite several recent examples of demarketing.

18. Identify the ways in which the technological environment affects marketing activities.

19. Cite two examples of instances where the technological environment produced positive benefits for marketers. Give two instances of the harmful impact of the technological environment on a firm's marketing operations.

20. Explain how the societal/cultural environment influences marketing.

Case: The Collapse of the Diesel Car Market

Back in the energy conscious late 1970s, diesel engines looked like a boom waiting to happen. Analysts predicted that by 1985 as much as 25 percent of the U.S. passenger-car market would be diesel powered.

So Robert F. Humrick expanded his Fresno, California, machine shop that built diesel fuel injectors. He also hired new mechanics and opened a fourth retail outlet. But instead of booming, the diesel market sputtered. Sagging diesel sales in a generally weak car market caused about $190,000 of losses for Mr. Humrick in the past two years.

A lot of other people who bet on the diesel boom have suffered, too. From manufacturers of specialized diesel parts to engine mechanics, thousands of people geared up for the predicted diesel market explosion, only to see the market implode instead.

The shock waves from the diesel engine's failure hit especially hard because there had seemed to be so many reasons to think diesels would be popular. Viewed from a 1979 gasoline line, with oil prices soaring and Americans held hostage in Iran, energy conservation seemed the watchword of the future. Backed by the immense spending and savvy marketing expertise of General Motors Corporation, there seemed to be little question that the diesel would enjoy a rosy future.

But in the 1980s, gasoline prices fell. In many parts of the country, diesel fuel became more expensive than gasoline, while gasoline-powered cars were becoming more fuel efficient. At the same time, GM suffered a heavy dose of bad publicity about defects in its diesel engines. After peaking at 6.1 percent of the new-car market in 1981, diesels sank to 4.4 percent in 1982, to 2.2 percent in 1983, and to a scant 1.5 percent in the first five months [of 1984].

Source: Frederick A. Brodie, "Collapse of Diesel Car Market Leaves Many Firms Sputtering in Its Wake," *The Wall Street Journal* (July 11, 1984), p. 17. Reprinted by permission of *The Wall Street Journal*, © Dow Jones & Company, Inc. 1984. All rights reserved.

"Diesels," says David Healy, an auto analyst at Drexel Burnham Lambert, Inc., "are an idea whose time has passed."

The evidence of the diesel engine's boom and bust is scattered throughout America. As goes the diesel, so goes the glow plug, a pocket-sized device that provides the initial heat that helps start diesel-car engines. In 1980, glow plugs seemed a promising business opportunity to Walter Genthe, president of three-year-old Hella North America, Inc., a subsidiary of the West German company, Westfaelische Metal Industries KG. Hella obtained a license and invested $500,000 in a Flora, Illinois, manufacturing line for glow plugs and other diesel components.

Mr. Genthe anticipated supplying a burgeoning diesel auto market with two million units a year of glow plugs and other parts. Now, he says, business is "miserable"—Hella's diesel parts sales are "down to a trickle" of under 100,000 units a year. "We've tied up $500,000 and it just sits there," he says.

Stanadyne, Inc., Windsor, Connecticut, projected in its *1980 Annual Report* that more than 40 percent of all American passenger cars would have diesel engines by 1990. To supply that booming demand, Stanadyne's diesel systems division opened two new plants in North Carolina to produce fuel injection devices for GM's diesel cars.

The plants still are operating, but the company has laid off more than 200 workers. Since 1981, the diesel division's sales have plunged 25 percent, and operating profit sank 35 percent. "We don't design the car, we don't design the engine, so we're a little bit at the mercy of the consumer and the builder of the car," says George J. Michel, Jr., Stanadyne's vice-chairman and chief financial officer.

Questions

1. Relate the material in this case to each of the marketing environments described in Chapter 2.

2. Suggest methods by which firms facing similar uncertainties may be able to limit market and financial losses.

3. Recommend possible courses of action for Hella North America and Stanadyne.

Computer Applications

While the environmental factors discussed in this chapter are frequently beyond the control of the marketing decision maker, it is often possible to minimize their adverse effect on operations by predicting their occurrence and taking actions designed to maximize possible benefits resulting from their occurrence. In some cases, the marketer may be able to engage in environmental management and actually influence occurrences in the competitive, political and legal, economic, technological, and societal/cultural environments.

A useful method for making decisions in an uncertain marketing environment is *decision tree analysis*. This is a quantitative technique used in identifying alternative courses of action, assigning probability estimates for the profits or sales associated with each alternative, and indicating the course of action with the highest profit or sales. The marketer must be able to estimate the likelihood of occurrence of each alternative. In addition, he or she must assign financial payoffs (sales, profits, or losses) for the various alternative courses of action.[1]

The following example illustrates how decision tree analysis works. The vice-president of marketing of a major bicycle manufacturer estimates that a 60 percent likelihood exists that the federal government's Consumer Product Safety Commission will require added safety features on bicycles beginning in 1987. If the new safety fea-

---

[1]See Barry Shore, *Quantitative Methods for Business Decisions* (New York: Mc-Graw-Hill, 1979), pp. 118–119; and Louis E. Boone and David L. Kurtz, *Principles of Management* (New York: Random House, 1984), pp. 198–200.

tures are included as a part of the basic designs now, they will add $10 to the cost of each bicycle produced. On the other hand, if they are not included and if the new safety requirements are enacted next year, the cost of adding them to the finished product will be $15 per bicycle. In addition, the inclusion of these features would involve additional time and would delay the shipment of finished bicycles from the manufacturer to its dealers. This would reduce 1987 sales from current estimates of 800,000 units to 600,000 units. Per-unit profits with no changes in product design are estimated at $20. If the new features are built into product design at this time, per-unit profits are estimated to be $10, as compared with $5 if they have to be added to the finished product next year as a result of new government regulations.

The problem can be illustrated as a type of decision tree lying on its side. Each branch represents a different possible course of action. In this example, the expected profits from a decision to add the new safety features now are $8 million. This determination is made by first multiplying expected total profits ($10 per unit times the 800,000 units) by the .6 probability that the new regulations will be enacted. Next the expected total profits ($10 per unit times the 800,000 units) are multiplied by the .4 probability that no new safety regulations will be enacted. Finally, the expected values of the two possible outcomes are combined for a total of $8 million.

In this example, the decision to defer installation of additonal safety features produces a slightly larger net expected value of profits. Unless the firm's marketers are greatly concerned that the shipment delays would generate ill will among their retail dealers and customers should the proposed regulations be enacted, they should choose the second option.

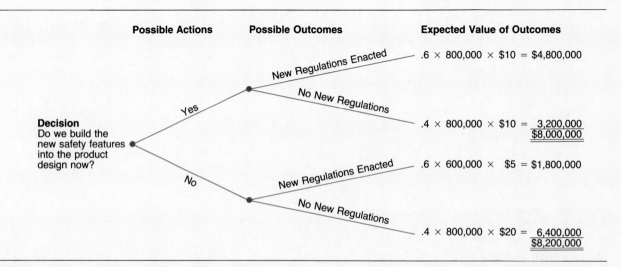

Directions: Use menu item 2 titled "Decision Tree Analysis" to solve each of the following problems.

Problem 1 Jack Thompson, vice-president of marketing at Houston Industries, is confident that next year's sales will reach $36 million. However, he is worried about the impact of increased costs on his firm's profits during the coming year. Thompson estimates that a 70 percent likelihood exists of a major price increase in one of the petroleum-based raw materials used in the production of his firm's products. Since his industry is highly price competitive, Thompson feels that he would be unable to raise prices to cover these cost increases. His major competitors have recently switched to a new, blended process that uses a small percentage of petroleum in combination with synthetic materials. Thompson projects next year's earnings at 10 percent of sales. If he converts to the new process, earnings are expected to be reduced to 7 percent of sales as a result of the changeover expenses. On the other hand, if he does not make the change and the price increase occurs, Thompson feels that his earnings will be reduced to 2 percent of sales as a result of the price–cost squeeze. Recommend a course of action for Houston Industries.

Problem 2 Nashville WaterMania manager Bruce Bennett is pleased with next year's $800,000 revenue forecast and his projected earnings of 12 percent of sales. However, he is concerned about reports of a new waterslide park opening. In fact, he estimates the likelihood of the new competitor being open for business in time for the next year's season at 50 percent. If the new park opens at the location under consideration and Nashville WaterMania takes no competitive moves at this time, Bennett estimates that total revenues will plummet to $300,000 and his earnings could drop to only 2 percent of sales. If the competing park fails to materialize and he reduces admission prices by 25 percent to match admission prices charged in other cities by the potential Nashville competitor, Bennett believes that overall sales revenues would increase to $900,000 and earnings would be 8 percent of sales. If he lowers prices and the new park is opened, Bennett feels that his competitive prices would be sufficient to generate $600,000 in revenues and earn profits of 6 percent of sales. He would prefer to postpone his decision until he is certain of the plans of his potential competitor, but the need for a huge new sign and the preparation of tickets, coupons, and advertising materials require him to make the decision now. Recommend a course of action for Bennett.

Problem 3 Vince Jacobs, director of marketing for Tampa-based FloridaFruit, recognizes more than most people the difficulty involved in producing time, place, and ownership utility during winters when the citrus industry is devastated by unpredictable, killing freezes. Smudge pots and water spraying—the current methods of reducing the impact of low temperatures—are of little help when the temperatures dip below the 25°F mark. After carefully analyzing the test results of a newly developed citrus grove heating system, Jacobs was viewing his firm's technological environment in a most positive way. Not only did the new system appear to work, it could be leased on a year-to-year basis, thereby avoiding huge outlays for equipment. Jacobs estimates the likelihood of a severe freeze at 20 percent for the upcoming season. He expects total revenues from next year's crop to reach $700,000 and earnings to amount to 9 percent of sales—as long as no severe freeze occurs. Should a severe freeze occur, Jacobs estimates that sales would fall to $200,000 and profits would be zero. If FloridaFruit decides to lease the new system, Jacobs's calculations show that the added leasing costs would trim profits to 5 percent of sales. However, should a freeze occur after the system is in place at FloridaFruit citrus groves, the increased price resulting from the reduced overall industry output would increase the firm's revenues from $700,000 to $850,000. Recommend a course of action for FloridaFruit.

Problem 4 The political and legal environment has been on Ralph Knight's mind lately. Knight is vice-president of marketing of Carolina Industries, an Asheville furniture manufacturer. Although the firm's sales projections are a healthy $14 million for next year with profits estimated at 8 percent of sales, Knight is concerned about rumors that the federal government will ban the use of the filler material used by Carolina Industries in its furniture cushions. Although substitute filler materials are available (and, in fact, are used by many of the firm's major competitors), they are more expensive. Knight estimates that a switch to the alternative filler material would reduce profits to 4 percent of sales. On the other hand, if he decides not to switch now and the ban is enacted, the time involved in converting to the new materials next year is likely to represent a loss of $8 million in projected sales and a corresponding profit decline to 2 percent of sales. Knight feels there is a 30 percent chance that the ban will be enacted.

a.   Recommend a course of action for Carolina Industries.

b.   Would your recommendation change if Knight reduces his estimate of the likelihood of the ban being enacted to 20 percent?

Problem 5 Marcia Stanaland, manager of the Femme chain of fashion clothing stores headquartered in Miami, realizes that the success of her operations depends upon the ability to monitor—and predict—changes in consumer tastes. Sales projections for next year total $4.2 million with expected profits of 5 percent of sales. Several of Stanaland's managers, who make up Femme's merchandise buying committee, have recommended a significant purchase of a radical new line of clothing that is enjoying huge sales in Europe. Although Stanaland is always concerned about significant investments in inventory of unproven lines, she is also aware of the consequences of missing major changes in shopper tastes. Stanaland makes the following notes as she listens to the presentation about the new line:

My guess is that the chances of a major consumer taste switch to the new line are 60 percent. If we don't get in on the bandwagon now, our sales could fall next year to $3 million and—at that level—Femme would only earn 2 percent on sales. On the other hand, if we place the orders and our inventory matches a change in buyer tastes, we could generate as much as $6 million in sales. If this happens, our profits should rise to 7 percent of sales. Even if we place the orders and no radical changes in consumer tastes occur, I think we could still push sales up to $5 million next year. Unfortunately, if tastes don't change as much as those in Europe, the extra inventory and sale merchandise that would result would depress earnings to 2 percent.

a.   Recommend a course of action for Stanaland.
b.   Would your recommendation change if Stanaland decreases the likelihood of consumer taste changes to 30 percent?

PARTTWO

Marketing Planning and Information

3 Marketing Planning and Forecasting

Key Terms

planning
marketing planning
strategic planning
tactical planning
strategic window
marketing strategy
undifferentiated marketing
differentiated marketing
concentrated marketing
strategic business units (SBUs)
market share/market growth matrix
marketing audit
sales forecast
jury of executive opinion
sales force composite
survey of buyer intentions
market test
trend analysis
input-output models
environmental forecasting

Learning Goals

1. To distinguish between strategic planning and tactical planning
2. To explain how marketing plans differ at different levels of the organization
3. To identify the steps in the marketing planning process
4. To compare the three basic strategies for matching markets with product/service offerings
5. To explain the portfolio and the market growth/market share matrix approaches to marketing planning
6. To identify the major types of forecasting methods
7. To explain the steps involved in the forecasting process

Stop-Action Case

Kent State University

Over the first 60 years of its existence, Kent State University had evolved from an obscure teachers college into a multipurpose university of 21,000 students pursuing bachelor, master, and doctoral degrees in dozens of subjects. By 1970 it ranked as the second largest university in Ohio, trailing only Ohio State University. The attractive campus with an array of modern buildings is located in Kent, a town of about 30,000 and within easy commuting distance of Akron and Cleveland.

But on May 4, 1970, Kent State became a bloodstained symbol of student resistance to intervention in Cambodia during the Vietnam War when Ohio National Guardsmen fired into a group of KSU students, killing four and wounding ten more. Kent State became a household word that carried an image worldwide, indelibly linked to horrifying photographs such as the one shown here.

Life goes on, however, and, after having been closed one quarter, the campus reopened. The next 15 years saw slight reductions in total enrollment as significant declines in the traditional pool of college students occurred in Ohio and other surrounding states. Dr. William E. Shelton, who joined Kent State as vice-president for institutional advancement in 1983, realized that steps had to be taken along two paths: (1) to develop a more positive image for the university, and (2) to assist the university in attracting additional qualified students. As Jan Zima, manager of communications services at KSU, remarked, "Kent State has great name recognition. But it is high time the university's true excellence be known."

Assignment: Use the materials in this chapter to recommend a method for improving the Kent State University image and attracting additional students.

Source: Zima quotation from *News from Kent* press release, June 5, 1984.

May 18, 1970 / 50 cents

Newsweek

NIXON'S HOME FRONT

Photo Source: Courtesy of *Newsweek*. Copyright 1970 by Newsweek, Inc. All rights reserved.

Chapter Overview _____

"Should we grant a license for our new liquid-crystal watch display to a Japanese firm or simply export our models to Japan?"

"Will changing the performance time and date affect concert attendance?"

"Should we utilize company sales personnel or independent agents in the new territory?"

"Should discounts be offered to cash customers? What impact would such a policy have on our credit customers?"

These questions are examples of the thousands of major and minor decisions the marketing manager regularly faces. Continual changes in the marketplace resulting from changing consumer expectations, technological improvements, competitive actions, economic trends, political and legal changes, as well as product innovations or pressures from distribution channel members, are likely to have substantial impact on the operations of any organization. Although these changes are often beyond the control of the marketing manager, effective planning can help the manager anticipate many changes and focus upon possible actions to take. Effective planning is often a major factor in distinguishing between success and failure.

The two chapters in this part provide a foundation for all subsequent chapters in the text by demonstrating the necessity of effective planning and reliable information in providing a structure within which a firm can take advantage of its unique strengths. The choice of specific market targets and the most appropriate marketing mix both result from marketing planning. Marketing planning is examined in detail in this chapter. Chapter 4 is devoted to the subject of marketing research and how decision-oriented information is used to plan and implement marketing strategies.

What Is Marketing Planning? _____

Planning
Process of anticipating the future and determining the courses of action necessary to achieve organizational objectives.

Planning is the process of anticipating the future and determining the courses of action to achieve organizational objectives. As the definition indicates, planning is a continuous process that includes specifying objectives and the actions required to achieve them. The planning process creates a blueprint that not only specifies the means of achieving organizational objectives, but also includes checkpoints where actual performance can be compared with expectations to determine whether the organizational activities are moving the organization toward its objectives.

Marketing Planning
Implementation of planning activity as it relates to the achievement of marketing objectives.

Marketing planning—the implementation of planning activities as they relate to the achievement of marketing objectives—is the basis for all marketing strategies. Product lines, pricing decisions, selection of appropriate distribution channels, and decisions relating to promotional campaigns all depend upon plans formulated within the marketing organization.

Strategic Planning versus Tactical Planning

Planning is often classified on the basis of scope or breadth. Some plans are quite broad and long range, focusing on certain organizational objectives with major impact on the organization for a time period of five or more years. Such

Strategic Planning
Process of determining an organization's primary objectives and allocating funds and proceeding on a course of action designed to achieve those objectives.

plans are typically called strategic plans. Strategic planning can be defined as the process of determining the primary objectives of an organization and the adoption of courses of action and the allocation of resources necessary to achieve those objectives.[1] Atlantic Richfield's decision to convert many of its Arco gas stations to convenience food store locations offering self-service gasoline represents strategic planning.

The word *strategy* is derived from a Greek term meaning "the general's art." Strategic planning has a critical impact on the destiny of the organization because it provides long-term direction for decision makers. At Kmart, the nation's second largest retailer, the strategic plan calls for marketers to use relatively low prices on commodity-type items and some highly recognized, brand-name clothing items, such as Levi's, to attract customers who may also buy merchandise with higher profit margins. In addition, the plan calls for a store location density in urban markets: Each Kmart store should be located within three miles of another store to reach a larger proportion of the market and to maximize the benefits of local advertising and store image.

Tactical Planning
Implementation of activities specified by the strategic plan that are necessary in the achievement of a firm's objectives.

By contrast, tactical planning focuses on the implementation of those activities specified by the strategic plan. Tactical plans are typically more short-term than strategic plans, focusing more on current and near-term activities that must be completed to implement overall strategies. Resource allocation is a common decision area for tactical planning. The decisions by Keebler and Frito-Lay to counter the crispy, fresh-baked style of Duncan-Hines cookies with chewy centers by offering their own competing brands were the result of tactical planning.

Planning at Different Levels in the Organization

Planning is a major responsibility for every manager. Although managers at all levels devote some of their work days to planning, the relative proportion of time spent in planning activities and the types of planning vary at different organizational levels.

Top management of a corporation—the board of directors, president, and functional vice-presidents, such as the chief marketing officer—spend greater proportions of their time engaged in planning than middle- and supervisory-level managers. In fact, one company president recommends that 30 to 50 percent of a chief executive's time should be spent on strategic planning.[2]

Also, top management is more likely to devote more of its planning activities to longer-range strategic planning, whereas middle-level managers (such as the director of the advertising department, regional sales managers, or the physical distribution manager) tend to focus on narrower, tactical plans for their departments, and supervisory personnel are more likely to engage in developing specific programs to meet the goals for their responsibility areas. Figure 3.1 indicates the types of planning involved at various organizational levels.

The Marketing Planning Process

The basic objectives of the organization are the starting point for marketing planning. They serve as the guideposts from which marketing objectives and plans are derived. As Figure 3.2 shows, these objectives provide direction for all phases of the organization and serve as standards in evaluating perfor-

Figure 3.1
Types of Plans Prepared by Different Levels of Management

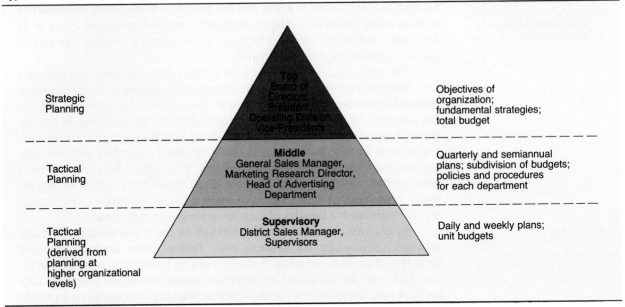

Source: Adapted from William F. Glueck, *Management*, 2nd ed. (Hinsdale, Ill.: The Dryden Press, 1980), p. 246. Copyright
1980 by The Dryden Press. Reprinted by permission of CBS College Publishing.

Figure 3.2
Steps in the Marketing Planning Process

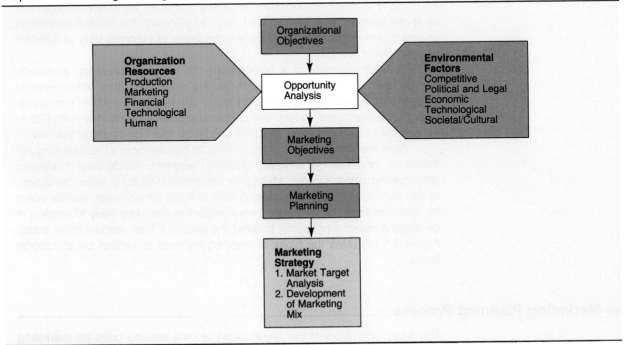

Figure 3.3

A Marketing Opportunity Resulting in Increased Sales, Broadened Market
Exposure, and Improved Name Recognition

Source: Copyright © by Universal Pictures, a Division of Universal City Studios, Inc.
Courtesy of MCA Publishing, a Division of MCA, Inc.

mance. For Nike, Inc., the overall objective is to be the leading firm in the $1.5
billion, quality athletic-shoe market in the United States. Nike's marketing
plans—both strategic and tactical—are based on this objective.

Opportunity Analysis

Marketing opportunities arise from a number of sources. After Universal Films
decided to use Reese's Pieces candy in their film about a tiny traveler from
another galaxy, they contacted Hershey Foods Corporation about a possible
promotional tie-in with the film. After considerable deliberation, Hershey marketers agreed and committed $1 million to a strategy that centered on the
giveaway of free premium items with proofs of purchase. For example, five
proofs of purchase from a one-pound bag of Reese's Pieces could be exchanged for a free $E.T.$ t-shirt. The offers were communicated through 30-
second television commercials, in-store displays, and displays in over 800 the-
atres nationwide.

The movie, as depicted by the photograph in Figure 3.3, proved to be a
major hit, breaking all previous attendance records. The Pieces promotion was
also a huge success, resulting in a sales increase of about 65 percent in the
weeks following the film's release. Equally important to Hershey marketers
was the tremendous exposure and increased name recognition for their
product.

The environmental forces described in Chapter 2—competitive, political
and legal, economic, technological, and societal/cultural—are forces impacting

Figure 3.4
The Pontiac Fiero Sport Coupe: Targeting a Strategic Window

Source: Courtesy of General Motors Corporation.

upon marketing opportunities. For example, environmental factors have adversely affected the market for afternoon papers. These papers, frequently called PMs, were very popular when people went to work in the predawn hours and returned home sometime in the afternoon. But the PM environment has changed in recent times. The white-collar labor force now reports for work at 9 a.m. rather than 6 a.m. Because approximately 60 percent of all married women now work, families are more likely to shop during the evening hours when they used to read PMs. Furthermore, television is rapidly becoming the most popular source of news. The PMs are attempting to counter this trend by improving their suburban, entertainment, and special-interest sections. Some are even beginning to offer morning editions.

Another major influence on a firm's decision to take advantage of marketing opportunities is the resources of the organization. Resources include marketing strengths, production strengths, financial position, research and development capability, and quality of management. Bic, a French manufacturer of inexpensive ballpoint pens, decided to enter the U.S. market but recognized the problems caused by its lack of an effective distribution system. It decided to purchase Waterman, a U.S. firm that manufactured and marketed refillable fountain pens. Although Bic discontinued the Waterman pen line four years later, it had acquired the distribution system it previously lacked.

The Strategic Window

Strategic Window
Limited periods during which the "fit" between the key requirements of a market and the particular competencies of a firm is at an optimum.

Environmental factors and resource constraints have different impacts upon the organization at different times. Derek Abell has suggested the term strategic window to define the limited periods during which the key requirements of a market and the particular competencies of a firm best fit together.[3] Pontiac's decision in 1983 to develop and market the Fiero, the first U.S.-built sports car in more than two decades, as shown in Figure 3.4, was in response to its marketers' decision that organizational and environmental factors resulted in a strategic window.

Return to the Stop-Action Case

Kent State University

Although the objectives of the unfolding Kent State University marketing plan were dual, they were not mutually exclusive. The two focal points of the plan—achieving the objectives of image development and admissions support—are linked, since stronger, more positive images are likely prerequisites to increased enrollments by northeast Ohio students who have more than a dozen university alternatives in that region of the state.

Like many other universities, Kent State University marketers were limited by a relatively small marketing budget. The available marketing dollars were stretched through the generosity of Diversa, Inc., a Kent, Ohio, agency offering a full range of services in sales presentation materials, advertising, and marketing research. Because the agency is largely staffed by KSU alumni with a genuine interest in the future of their alma mater, the firm's services were donated to the cause. As Gene Petrus, president of Diversa, stated, "This is a labor of love. Every one of us at Diversa is a Kent State graduate. So we all try especially hard to make Kent State known as the quality institution it is."

In 1984, Angeles Entertainment Group decided not to compete that summer with movie blockbusters such as *Indiana Jones and the Temple of Doom, Star Trek III: The Search for Spock, Ghostbusters, Gremlins*, and *The Natural*. Instead it saw a strategic window in a September release after the spring–summer films and prior to the end-of-the-year holiday releases. Its film, *Irreconcilable Differences*, also benefitted from the extra market exposure of its star Shelley Long, whose television series "Cheers" also began a new television season in early September.

Marketing Objectives, Marketing Planning, and Marketing Strategy

The net result of opportunity analysis is the formulation of marketing objectives designed to achieve overall organizational objectives and the development of a marketing plan. Marketing planning efforts must be directed toward establishing marketing strategies that are resource-efficient, flexible, and adaptable. The term marketing strategy describes the overall company program for selecting a particular market segment and then satisfying consumers in that segment through careful use of the elements of the marketing mix. The components of the marketing mix—product planning, distribution, promotion, and pricing—represent subsets of the overall marketing strategy.

Marketing Strategy
Overall company program for selecting a particular market target and then satisfying those target consumers through a blending of the elements of the marketing mix.

Alternative Marketing Strategies

Much of the strategic planning effort is dedicated to the development of marketing strategies that best match product offerings to the needs of particular market targets. A successful match is vital to the market success of the firm.

Three basic strategies for achieving consumer satisfaction are available. Firms that produce only one product and market it to all customers with a

Figure 3.5
Alternative Market Matching Strategies

Market Segment	Product Offerings			
	Ford Motor Company		Audi/Volkswagen/Porsche	
	1908 Undifferentiated Marketing	1986 Differentiated Marketing	1956 Concentrated Marketing	1986 Differentiated Marketing
General Purpose Cars				
Small-Sized	Model T	Escort Lynx	Beetle	Golf Jetta
Medium-Sized	Model T	Taurus Tempo Topaz	—	—
Large-Sized	—	LTD Crown Victoria Sable	—	—
Sports Cars				
Low-Priced	—	EXP	—	—
Medium-priced	—	Mustang Capri	—	Scirocco
High-Priced	—	Thunderbird Cougar	—	Porsche 911 Porsche 928 Porsche 944
Luxury Cars				
Medium-Priced	—	Lincoln	—	Audi Quattro Audi 4000
High-Priced	—	Continental	—	Audi 5000
Trucks				
Small-Sized	Model T (truck)	Ford Ranger	—	Vanagon
Medium-Sized	—	Ford F-150	—	—

Source: Adapted from M. Dale Beckman, David L. Kurtz, and Louis E. Boone, *Foundations of Marketing*
(Toronto: Holt, Rinehart and Winston of Canada, Ltd., 1985), p. 120.

Undifferentiated Marketing
Marketing strategy employed by some organizations that produce only one product or service and market it to all customers using a single marketing mix.

Differentiated Marketing
Marketing strategy employed by organizations that produce numerous products or services with different marketing mixes designed to satisfy numerous market segments.

Concentrated Marketing
Marketing strategy that directs all of a firm's marketing resources toward serving a small segment of the total market.

single marketing mix practice undifferentiated marketing.[4] This strategy is sometimes called mass marketing. Firms that produce numerous products with different marketing mixes designed to satisfy smaller segments practice differentiated marketing. Firms that concentrate all marketing resources on small segments of the total market practice concentrated marketing. These market matching strategies are illustrated in Figure 3.5.

Undifferentiated Marketing

The policy of undifferentiated marketing was much more common in the past than it is today. Ignoring the luxury market, Henry Ford built the Model T and sold it for one price to everyone. He agreed to paint the car any color that consumers wanted "as long as it is black." Ford's only concession to more specific customer needs was to add a truck body for those Model T purchasers who needed more hauling capacity.

Although marketing managers using an undifferentiated marketing strategy recognize the existence of numerous segments in the total market, they generally ignore minor differences and focus on the broad market. To reach the general market, they use mass advertising, mass distribution, and broad themes. One immediate gain from the strategy of undifferentiated marketing is the efficiency resulting from longer production runs. This strategy allowed Henry Ford to mass produce and market a simple, well-designed product. The undifferentiated marketing strategy simplified Ford's production operations. It also minimized inventories, since neither Ford nor its affiliated automobile dealers had to contend with optional equipment and numerous color combinations.

However, there are dangers inherent in the strategy of undifferentiated marketing. A firm that attempts to satisfy everyone in the market faces the threat of competitors who offer specialized products to smaller segments of the total market and better satisfy each of these segments. Indeed, firms implementing a strategy of differentiated marketing or concentrated marketing may enter the market and capture sufficient small segments to make the strategy of undifferentiated marketing unworkable for the competition.

A firm that uses undifferentiated marketing may also encounter problems in foreign markets. The Campbell Soup Company suffered heavy losses in marketing tomato soup in the United Kingdom before the company discovered that the British prefer a more bitter taste. Another U.S. firm, Corn Products Company, discovered real differences in U.S. and European soup preferences when it failed in an attempt to market Knorr dry soups in the United States. Although dry soups are commonly purchased by Europeans, the U.S. homemaker prefers liquid soups, apparently because they require shorter cooking time.

Differentiated Marketing

The company employing a strategy of differentiated marketing is still attempting to satisfy a large part of the total market. Instead of marketing one product with a single marketing program, it markets a number of products designed to appeal to individual parts of the total market. As Figure 3.5 indicates, Ford now offers Lincoln Town Cars, Mustangs, and Escorts to various segments of the new car market. The various automobile products under the Volkswagen parent company compete for a much broader number of market segments than did the Beetle. The objectives of both firms are to generate a great number of total sales and to develop more product loyalty in each of the submarkets. They seek to accomplish this by providing a marketing mix designed to serve the needs of each market target rather than by inducing each of the consumer segments to purchase one product designed for everyone. Similarly, Cadillac planners noted that import owners tended to trade up to BMWs and Audis, not to traditional Cadillac models. To counteract this the Cimarron was introduced to appeal to younger, affluent buyers.

Most firms practice differentiated marketing. Procter & Gamble markets Bold, Bonus, Cheer, Dash, Duz, Gain, Oxydol, Tide, and other detergents to appeal to detergent buyers. Lever Brothers offers two brands of complexion soap, Dove and Lux, and two brands of deodorant soap, Lifebuoy and Phase III.

By providing increased satisfaction for each of numerous market targets, the company with a differentiated marketing strategy can produce more sales than are possible with undifferentiated marketing. In general, however, the costs of a differentiated marketing strategy are greater than those of an undifferentiated marketing strategy. Production costs usually rise because additional products mean shorter production runs and increased set-up time. Inventory costs rise because of added space needs for the products and increases in the necessary record-keeping. Promotional costs also increase because unique promotional mixes are required for each market segment.

Even though the costs of doing business are typically greater under a differentiated marketing strategy, consumers are usually better served because products offered are specifically designed to meet the needs of smaller segments. Also, a firm that wants to employ a single marketing strategy for an entire market may be forced to choose a strategy of differentiated marketing instead. If competitors appeal to each market target in the total market, the firm must also use this approach to remain competitive.

Concentrated Marketing

Rather than attempting to market its product offerings to the entire market, a firm may choose to focus its effort on profitably satisfying a smaller market target. This strategy of concentrated marketing is particularly appealing to new, small firms that lack the financial resources of their competitors.

Perhaps the most famous example of a firm practicing the concentrated marketing strategy is Volkswagen of America. For 20 years, the Volkswagen Beetle was symbolic of a product specifically designed and marketed to buyers wanting economy and practical performance in their transportation. Volkswagen of America concentrated on selling to this segment despite the fact that they sold many other models in Europe. Similarly, Rolls-Royce is known for producing and marketing the ultimate in expensive, luxury automobiles.

Although Saab-Scania had sold approximately 10,000 of its moderately priced "Swedish Tinkertoys" annually in the U.S. for several years, it decided to undertake a serious attempt to occupy a small but profitable market niche. It targeted the 30 to 40-year-old, well-educated, professional male with a household income of $50,000 to $80,000. Many of them are part of dual-income households. Saab avoided the compact-car market and instead aimed at the luxury/sport segment with its 900S and 900 Turbo models. And the strategy worked, as Saab sales increased 42 percent between 1982 and 1983.[5]

Concentration on a segment of the total market often allows a firm to maintain profitable operation. Fisher-Price has developed an enviable image in the toy industry because of its reputation as a high-quality manufacturer and marketer of children's toys.

Concentrated marketing, however, poses dangers as well. Since the firm's growth is tied to a particular segment, changes in the size of the segment or in customer buying patterns may result in severe financial problems. Sales may also drop if new competitors appeal to the same market segment.

Texfi Industries, formed some 20 years ago to produce synthetic yarn, became the largest U.S. producer of polyester double-knits at the height of the double-knit fad. The end of the fad and the resulting sales declines almost bankrupted the company. It survived by exporting some goods to China and then moving away from its strategy of concentrated marketing and began producing and marketing women's fabrics as well as knits.[6]

Selecting a Strategy

Although most organizations adopt the strategy of differentiated marketing, there is no single best strategy. Any of the three alternatives may prove most effective in a particular situation. The basic determinants of a market matching strategy are (1) company resources, (2) product homogeneity, (3) stage in the product life cycle, and (4) competitors' strategies.

A concentrated marketing strategy may be a necessity for a firm with limited resources. Small firms, for example, may be forced to select small market targets because of limitations in financing, size of sales force, and promotional budgets.

On the other hand, an undifferentiated marketing strategy should be used for products perceived by consumers as relatively homogeneous. Marketers of grain sell their products on the basis of standardized grades rather than individual brand names. Some petroleum companies use a strategy of undifferentiated marketing in distributing their gasoline to the mass market.

The firm's strategy may also change as the product progresses through the various stages of the life cycle. During the early stages, an undifferentiated marketing strategy might be useful as the firm attempts to develop initial demand for the product. In the later stages, however, competitive pressures may result in modified products and marketing strategies aimed at smaller segments of the total market.

The strategies used by competitors also affect the choice of a market matching strategy. A firm may find it difficult to use an undifferentiated strategy if its competitors are actively cultivating smaller segments. In such instances, competition usually forces each firm to adopt a differentiated strategy.[7]

Tools Used in Marketing Planning

As more organizations discovered the benefits resulting from effective marketing planning, a number of planning tools were developed to assist in conducting this important function. The portfolio approach is commonly used by large, multiproduct firms. Two major portfolio concepts are the strategic business unit and the market share/market growth matrix. Both concepts can also assist marketers in small and medium-size organizations to develop marketing plans. In addition, the marketing audit is frequently used in evaluating marketing planning and marketing performance.

Strategic Business Units

Although smaller firms may offer only a few products and services to their customers, larger organizations frequently produce and market thousands of offerings to widely diverse markets. For example, Greyhound Corporation operates a bus company, Armour-Dial consumer products (makers of Dial soap), and a variety of business services ranging from mortgage insurance to restaurant management. Bell & Howell has a portfolio of business that includes the Charles E. Merrill publishing unit, DeVry technical schools, an audiovisual division, automated mail-handling equipment, and micrographics. Top management at major firms needs some method for determining the best way to evaluate these diverse businesses and to make decisions concerning promising product lines that warrant additional resources and those that should be pruned from the firm's product portfolio. Management at General Electric approached the problem in this way:

The GE system grew out of the company's problems in the late 1960s, when setbacks in several areas such as computers, jet engines, and international business proved costly overall. Revenues had steadily grown, but the growth was profitless.

To get profits growing along with revenues, GE decided it needed a new, company-wide approach. . . . Surveying the organization, management identified 43 units of various sizes, which it dubbed strategic business units. Each SBU . . . (had) a unique business mission within the company . . . (with) identifiable customers . . . and all its major business functions—manufacturing, engineering, finance, and marketing—within the control of the SBU manager.

SBUs superseded divisional organization. For example, three separate divisions—portable home products, food preparation products, and personal appliances—were merged into the Housewares Business Division.[8]

Strategic Business Units (SBUs)
Related product groupings of businesses within a multiproduct firm with specific managers, resources, objectives, and competitors; structured for optimal planning purposes.

Strategic business units (SBUs) are divisions composed of key businesses within multiproduct companies, with specific managers, resources, objectives, and competitors. SBUs may encompass a division, a product line, or a single product. SBUs can be evaluated as existing firms because they possess the following characteristics: (1) distinct missions, (2) their own manager, (3) identifiable customer segments, (4) their own competitors, and (5) the ability to be planned independently of other units of the firm.[9]

The consequence of this organizational arrangement is that each SBU can be evaluated according to its profit and growth potential. Such evaluations caused Greyhound Corporation to sell its Armour Food meat processing and packing subsidiary, a car rental company, a yarn business, and a British insurance company. The SBU concept resulted in Bell & Howell's decision to sell its consumer products business, which included its trademark cameras and movie projectors, and it also prompted General Electric to sell its line of small household appliances to Black & Decker.

During the 1970s, the SBU concept was quickly adopted by major firms including Union Carbide, Boise-Cascade, and International Paper. Although early experimenters like General Foods have since returned to a more traditional organizational structure, the SBU concept is utilized currently in about 20 percent of the largest manufacturing corporations in the United States.[10]

The Market Share/Market Growth Matrix

Market Share/Market Growth Matrix
Matrix developed by the Boston Consulting Group that enables a firm to classify its products and services in terms of the industry growth rate and its market share relative to competitive products.

To evaluate the strategic business units of the organization, some type of portfolio performance framework is needed. The most widely used framework was developed in the early 1970s by the Boston Consulting Group. The market share/market growth matrix is a four-quadrant matrix that plots market share—the percentage of a market controlled by a firm—against market growth potential. The market share plotted on the horizontal axis indicates the SBU's market share as compared with competitors in the industry. The market growth rate plotted on the vertical axis indicates the annual growth rate of that market. All of a firm's various businesses can be plotted in one of the four quadrants. As Figure 3.6 shows, the resulting quadrants are labeled cash cows, stars, dogs, and question marks, and each one requires a unique marketing strategy.

Cash cows represent a high market share and low market growth. Marketers want to maintain this status for as long as possible because these businesses are producing a strong cash flow. The funds can be used to finance the growth of other SBUs with high growth potential. As indicated in Figure 3.6, a product such as IBM's line of electronic typewriters serve as cash cows, generating surplus funds for investment in new computer technology.

Stars represent high market share and high market growth. These products or businesses are high growth market leaders. Although they generate

Figure 3.6
SBU Categories

Relative Market Share

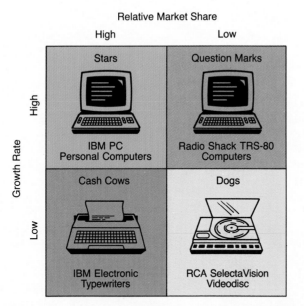

considerable income, even more funds are needed to finance the additional investments they require for further growth.

Dogs represent low market share and low market growth. Although dogs may generate some funds for the firm, their future prospects are poor, and marketers attempt to withdraw from these businesses or product lines as quickly as possible.

Question marks represent low market share and high market growth. These situations require that marketers make a basic go/no go decision. Due to the growth nature of the market, question marks typically require more cash than they are able to generate. Unless marketers can implement plans to convert these question marks to stars, the firm should pull out of these markets and pursue markets with greater potential.

Figure 3.7 shows how a large firm such as General Electric might begin the process of sorting out its various businesses and product lines according to profit and growth prospects. The three circles show the major categories: traditional "core" businesses (about one-third of total GE profits), the high-technology businesses (30 percent of profits and growing), and services (29 percent). Around these main groupings lie the remainder of the firm's businesses. Some are profitable, some lose money, and some, like microelectronics or Ladd Petroleum, have links to all three main businesses. These two businesses are likely to be permanent parts of GE, but the others must either be converted to stars in the very near future or be sold or closed.

Evaluating the Matrix Approach to Planning   The market share/market growth matrix emphasizes the importance of creating market offerings that position the firm to its best advantage. It also indicates that successful SBUs undergo a series of changes as they move through their life cycle. The successful product or business typically begins as a question mark, then becomes

Figure 3.7
Major Business Categories at General Electric

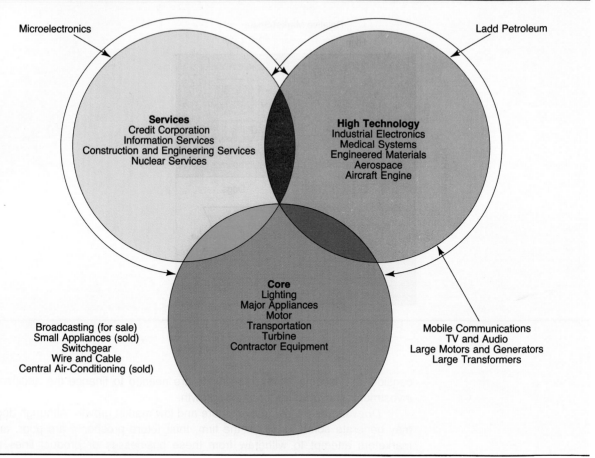

Microelectronics

Ladd Petroleum

Services
Credit Corporation
Information Services
Construction and Engineering Services
Nuclear Services

High Technology
Industrial Electronics
Medical Systems
Engineered Materials
Aerospace
Aircraft Engine

Core
Lighting
Major Appliances
Motor
Transportation
Turbine
Contractor Equipment

Broadcasting (for sale)
Small Appliances (sold)
Switchgear
Wire and Cable
Central Air-Conditioning (sold)

Mobile Communications
TV and Audio
Large Motors and Generators
Large Transformers

Source: Howard Banks, "General Electric—Going with the Winners," *Forbes* (March 26, 1984), p. 106

a star, and eventually develops into a cash cow, generating surplus funds to finance new stars. Ultimately it becomes a dog at the end of its life cycle and is eliminated from the firm's product offerings.

Critics of the matrix approach often point to the tendencies of some marketers to apply it in a largely mechanistic manner. In an attempt to develop a product line of stars, marketers may ignore the possible methods of converting products and services labeled as dogs. Or the firm with no stars may be forced to seek means of expanding market and sales opportunities of an existing product regardless of the label attached to it. Each organization must balance the advantages of the matrix approach against the potential shortcomings.

Marketing Audits

William S. Woodside, president of American Can Company, has been quoted as saying, "The roughest thing to get rid of is the Persian Messenger Syndrome, where the bearer of bad tidings is beheaded by the king. You should lean over backward to reward the guy who is first with the bad news. Most companies have all kinds of abilities to handle problems, if they only learn about them soon enough."[11]

If the marketing organization is to avoid the Persian Messenger Syndrome, it must institute periodic reviews of marketing plans and be willing to accept the objective results of the evaluations. For most organizations, this

Marketing Audit
Thorough, objective evaluation of an organization's marketing philosophy, goals, policies, tactics, practices, and results.

means using a marketing audit—a thorough, objective evaluation of an organization's marketing philosophy, goals, policies, tactics, practices, and results.[12]

A comprehensive marketing audit can provide a valuable—and sometimes disquieting—perspective on the performance of the firm's marketing plans. An excellent example of the need to assess performance is the pharmaceutical firm that was delighted with an 83 percent awareness rating for an advertising campaign but was shocked upon learning that this amounted to only a 28 percent intent-to-buy figure.[13]

A periodic review of marketing plans is invaluable both in identifying the tasks that the organization does well and in highlighting its failures. Periodic review, criticism, and self-analysis are crucial to the vitality of any organization. They are particularly critical to a function as diverse and dynamic as marketing.

Marketing audits are especially valuable in pointing out areas in which managerial perceptions differ sharply from reality. Methods of conducting audits are almost as diverse as the firms that use them. Some audits follow only informal procedures. Others involve elaborate checklists, questionnaires, profiles, tests, and related research instruments.

The marketing audit goes beyond the normal control system. The control process for marketing essentially asks: Are we doing things right? The marketing audit extends this question to: Are we also doing the right thing?

Marketing audits are applicable to all organizations—large or small, profitable or profitless, nonprofit or profit-oriented. Audits are particularly valuable when they are performed for the first time or when they are conducted after having been discontinued for several years. Not all organizations have implemented marketing audits, but the number of firms using them is expected to grow. According to one study, 28 percent of the firms surveyed had used a marketing audit.[14]

Sales Forecasting

Sales Forecast
Estimate of company sales for a specified future period.

A basic building block of marketing planning is the sales forecast—an estimate of the firm's sales or income for a specified future period. In addition to its use in marketing planning, the sales forecast plays a major role in production scheduling, financial planning, inventory planning and procurement, and the determination of personnel needs. An inaccurate forecast will result in incorrect decisions in each of these areas. The sales forecast is also an important tool for marketing control because it produces standards against which actual performance can be measured. Without such standards, no comparisons can be made. If no criterion of success exists, there is also no definition of failure.

Sales forecasts are either short run or long run. Short-run forecasts usually include a period of up to one year, whereas long-run forecasts typically cover a longer period. Both forecasts are developed in basically the same manner, but because more firms forecast sales for the coming year, short-run forecasting is discussed here.

Figure 3.8

Sales Forecasting Methods Used Regularly in 175 Firms

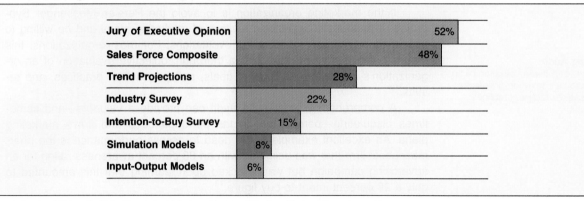

Source: Douglas J. Dalrymple, "Sales Forecasting Methods and Accuracy," *Business Horizons* (December 1975), p. 71.

Types of Forecasting Methods

Although forecasters utilize dozens of techniques to divine the future—ranging from complex computer simulations to crystal-ball gazing by professional futurists—two broad categories exist. *Quantitative* forecasting methods employ statistical techniques such as trend extensions based upon past data, computer simulation, and econometrics to produce numerical forecasts. *Qualitative* forecasting techniques are more subjective in nature. They include surveys of consumer attitudes and intentions, estimates by the field sales force, and predictions of key executives in the firm and in the industry. Since each method has advantages, most organizations utilize both in their attempts to predict future events.

A survey of forecasting techniques used by 175 firms revealed that qualitative measures such as sales force estimates and estimates by a jury of executives are most commonly used. The techniques used on a regular basis by the responding firms are shown in Figure 3.8.

Qualitative Forecasting Techniques

Qualitative techniques include (1) the jury of executive opinion, (2) estimates by the sales force, and (3) surveys of buyer intentions. The first two approaches rely upon experience and expectations. The jury of executive opinion method consists of combining and averaging the outlook of top executives from such areas as finance, production, marketing, and purchasing. It is particularly effective when top management is experienced and knowledgeable about situations that influence sales, open-minded concerning the future, and aware of the bases for their judgments.

The sales force composite is based upon the belief that organizational members closest to the marketplace—those with specialized product, customer, and competitor knowledge—are likely to have better insight concerning short-term future sales than any other group. It is typically a bottom-up approach since salespersons' estimates are usually combined at the district level, regional level, and national level to obtain an aggregate forecast of sales. Few firms rely solely upon the sales force composite, however. Since salespeople recognize the role of the sales forecast in determining expected performance in their territories, they are likely to estimate conservatively.

Jury of Executive Opinion
Qualitative sales forecasting method that combines and averages the outlook of executives from such functional areas as finance, production, marketing, and purchasing.

Sales Force Composite
Qualitative sales forecasting method in which sales estimates are based upon the combined estimates of the firm's sales force.

Moreover, their narrow perspectives on their limited geographic territories may prevent them from knowing about trends developing in other territories, forthcoming technological innovations, or major changes in company marketing strategies. Consequently, the sales force composite is often combined with other forecasting techniques in developing the final forecast.

Survey of Buyer Intentions
Qualitative sales forecasting method in which sample groups of present and potential consumers are surveyed concerning their purchase intentions.

A third method of forecasting, the survey of buyer intentions, uses mail questionnaires, telephone polls, or personal interviews to determine the intentions of a representative group of present and potential consumers. This technique is obviously limited to situations in which customers are willing to reveal their buying intentions. Moreover, customer expectations do not necessarily result in actual purchases.

Quantitative Forecasting Techniques

Quantitative techniques, which make use of past data, attempt to eliminate the guesswork of the qualitative forecasting methods. They include market tests, trend projections, and input-output models.

Market Test
Quantitative forecasting technique in which a new product, price, promotional campaign, or other marketing variable is introduced in a relatively small test-market location to assess consumer reactions under realistic market conditions.

Market tests are frequently used in assessing consumer response to new product offerings. The procedure typically involves establishing a small number of test markets to gauge consumer response to a new product under actual conditions. Market tests also permit the evaluation of different prices, different promotional strategies, and other marketing mix variations through comparisons in different test markets. The primary advantage of market tests is the realism it provides for the marketer. On the other hand, it is an expensive and time-consuming approach that communicates marketing plans to competitors before a product is introduced to the market. Test marketing is discussed in more detail in Chapter 9.

Trend Analysis
Quantitative sales forecasting method in which estimates of future sales are determined through statistical analyses of historical sales patterns.

Trend analysis involves forecasting future sales by analyzing the historical relationship between sales and time. It is based upon the assumption that the factors that collectively determined past sales will continue to exert similar influence in the future. If historical data is available, trend analysis can be performed quickly and inexpensively.

An example will make this clear. If sales were X last year and have been increasing at Y percent for the past several years, the sales forecast for next year would be calculated as follows:

$$\text{Sales Forecast} = X + XY.$$

In actual numbers, if last year's sales totaled 520,000 units and the average sales growth rate has been 5 percent, the sales forecast would be

$$\text{Sales Forecast} = 520,000 + (520,000 \times .05)$$
$$= 546,000.$$

The danger of trend analysis lies in its underlying assumption that the future is a continuation of the past. Any variations in the influencing determinants of sales will result in an incorrect forecast. In addition, historical data may not be readily available in some instances, most notably in the case of new products.

During periods of steady growth, the trend extension method of forecasting produces satisfactory results, but it implicitly assumes that the factors contributing to a certain level of output in the past will operate in the same manner in the future. When conditions change, the trend extension method often produces incorrect results. For this reason, forecasters increasingly use more sophisticated techniques and more complex mathematical models.

Input-Output Models
Quantitative forecasting techniques that show the impact on supplier industries of production changes in a given industry and that can be utilized in measuring the impact of changing demand in any industry throughout the economy.

Input-output models, which depict the interactions of various industries in producing goods, are being developed by the U.S. Department of Commerce and by private agencies. Since outputs (sales) of one industry are the inputs (purchases) of another, a change of outputs in one industry affects the inputs of other industries. Input-output models show the impact on supplier industries of increased production in a given industry and can be used to measure the impact of increased demand in any industry throughout the economy.

Steps in Sales Forecasting

Although sales forecasting methods vary, the most typical method begins with an environmental forecast of general economic conditions that the marketer uses to forecast industry sales and to develop a forecast of company and product sales. This approach is referred to as the *top-down method*.

Environmental Forecasting
Broad-based economic forecasting focusing upon the impact of external factors that affect a firm's markets.

Environmental Forecasting   These broad-based forecasts focus upon factors external to the firm that affect its markets. In environmental forecasting, projections are likely to be made of factors such as consumer spending/saving decisions, balance of trade surpluses and deficits, government expenditures, business investments, and inflation and unemployment levels. These projections can then be combined to develop an overall economic forecast. The most common measure of economic output is the nation's *gross national product* (GNP), the market value of all final products produced in a country in a given year. Trend extension is the most frequently used method of forecasting increases in the GNP.

Since many federal agencies and other organizations develop regular forecasts of the GNP, a firm may choose to use their estimates. These forecasts are regularly reported in such publications as *The Wall Street Journal* and *Business Week*.

Developing the Industry Sales Forecast   The general economic forecast is used with other relevant environmental factors in developing an industry sales forecast. Since industry sales are often related to the GNP or some other measure of the national economy, a forecast may begin by measuring the degree of this relationship and then applying the trend extension method to forecast industry sales. More sophisticated techniques, such as input-output analysis or multiple regression analysis, may also be used.

Forecasting Company and Product Sales   After the industry forecast has been completed, company and product forecasts are developed. They begin with a detailed analysis of previous years' performances. The firm's past and present market shares are reviewed, and product managers and regional and district sales managers are consulted about expected sales. Since an accelerated promotional budget or the introduction of new products may stimulate additional demand, the marketing plan for the coming year is also considered.

Product and company forecasts must evaluate many aspects, including sales of each product; future sales trends; sales by customer, territory, salesperson, and order size; financial arrangements; and other aspects. After a preliminary sales forecast has been developed, it is reviewed by the sales force and by district, regional, and national sales managers.

New Product Sales Forecasting Forecasting sales for new products is an especially hazardous undertaking because no historical data is available. Companies typically employ consumer panels to obtain reactions to the products and probable purchase behavior. Test market data may also be utilized.

Since few products are totally new, forecasters carefully analyze the sales of competing products that may be displaced by the new entry. A new type of fishing reel, for example, will compete in an established market with other reels. This substitute method provides the forecaster with an estimate of market size and potential demand.

Summary

Planning, the process of anticipating the future and determining the courses of action needed to achieve company objectives, is the basis for all strategy decisions. Strategic planning refers to strategy-oriented planning. Marketing planning is the implementation of planning activity as it relates to the achievement of marketing objectives.

The marketing planning process is based upon the overall organizational objectives. Opportunity analysis is a continual process of assessing environmental factors and comparing them with the objectives of the organization and its resources. Marketing objectives are based upon organizational objectives and result in the development of marketing plans. Market target analysis and the development of a marketing mix to satisfy chosen targets make up the marketing strategy of the organization.

The strategic business unit (SBU) concept, the market share/market growth matrix developed by the Boston Consulting Group, and the marketing audit are tools frequently used by marketing planners.

Effective strategic planning is regarded as a prerequisite to survival. It is an organization-wide responsibility involving chief executive officers, heads of operating units, and corporate strategic planning personnel. Strategic planning provides a basis for marketing planning, which is then translated into the development of marketing strategies.

There are three alternative strategies for matching the firm's offerings to specific market targets. Undifferentiated marketing refers to the strategy of firms that produce only one product or service and market it to all customers with a single marketing mix. By contrast, differentiated marketing occurs when a firm produces numerous products or services with different marketing mixes designed to satisfy smaller marketing segments. The third alternative is concentrated marketing, in which a firm concentrates all its marketing resources on a small segment of the total market.

Correct strategy decisions are dependent upon a number of situational variables. The basic determinants of a market matching strategy are (1) company resources, (2) degree of product homogeneity, (3) stage in the product life cycle, and (4) marketing strategies used by competitors.

Sales forecasting is an important component of both planning and controlling marketing programs. Forecasting techniques may be categorized as quantitative or qualitative. The most common approach to sales forecasting begins with an environmental forecast of the national economy. This forecast is used to develop an industry sales forecast, which in turn is used to develop company and product forecasts.

Solving the Stop-Action Case

Kent State University

To accomplish the objective of improving the image of Kent State University, a decision was made to feature prominent Kent State alumni in print media such as regional editions of *Time* and *Newsweek*, the *New York Times*, the *Cleveland Plain Dealer*, the *Canton Repository*, the *Pittsburgh Press*, and other regional publications. The ads, featuring major industry leaders such as Charles Pilliod of Goodyear, John Kapioltas of Sheraton Corporation, and Harry Bruce and Jim Martin of the Illinois Central Railroad, are reminiscent of American Express ads, with the KSU alumni card substituted for the credit card. The campaign, aimed at both prospective students and alumni, is a reminder of the benefits of the quality education offered at KSU.

Jan Zima, manager of communications services at Kent State University, summed up the marketing campaign as follows: "These ads are image pieces. We believe that Kent State is a fine university, and we are simply showing the great impact that Kent has had on the lives of people in this area."

But did the plan work? As William E. Shelton, KSU's vice-president for institutional advancement, points out, "The telling question, of course, is did the campaign have any impact. While this type of campaign does not

Photo sources: *Newsweek* cover courtesy of *Newsweek*. Copyright 1984 by Newsweek, Inc. All rights reserved. Suite success advertisement courtesy of Kent State University and DIVERSA, Inc., Kent, Ohio.

lend itself to specific quantifiable measures, we do think it was a positive effort. For example, our fall enrollment is the highest since 1976. This is significant in a state where demographics indicate a significant decline in the traditional pool of college students. We were the only university in northeast Ohio that experienced an increase in enrollment. The university set records in both the number of private gifts and total amount of contributions this year. Perhaps most importantly, however, is the apparent resurgence of pride within the university community and alumni. Our marketing effort was directed as much internally as externally."

Source: Zima quotation from "News from Kent" press release, June 5, 1984. Shelton quotation from personal correspondence, October 31, 1984.

Questions for Discussion

1. Distinguish between strategic planning and tactical planning.
2. Contrast marketing planning at different levels in the organization.
3. Identify the steps in the marketing planning process.
4. Explain the concept of the strategic window. Give an example.
5. Identify the two major components of a firm's marketing strategy.
6. Outline the basic features of undifferentiated marketing.
7. Contrast differentiated marketing with concentrated marketing.
8. Match the following strategies with the situations below. What strategy would be most appropriate in each of these situations?
   a. Undifferentiated marketing
   b. Differentiated marketing
   c. Concentrated marketing

_____ A product is entering the decline phase of the product life cycle.

_____ Management considers it essential to minimize production and inventory carrying costs.

_____ A new, small company is trying to gain a foothold in an industry.

_____ The major competitors are employing a differentiated marketing strategy.

_____ A firm lacks the financial resources of its major competitors.

_____ A firm is entering a large market made up of several homogeneous products such as grain.

_____ The market is composed of a series of homogeneous market segments, each having its own particular needs and wants.

9. Why is differentiated marketing the most costly marketing strategy?

10. Identify and discuss the major external and internal influences on marketing strategy.

11. Differentiate _cash cows, dogs, stars,_ and _question marks_ in the market share/market growth matrix.

12. Give two examples of products in each of the following quadrants of the market share/market growth matrix:
    a. Cash cows
    b. Dogs
    c. Stars
    d. Question marks
    Suggest marketing strategies for each product.

13. What are the potential dangers of rigid application of product portfolio models such as the market share/market growth matrix?

14. Explain the relationship between marketing planning and the marketing audit.

15. Compare and contrast each of the major types of forecasting methods.

16. Explain the steps involved in the forecasting process.

17. Discuss the advantages and shortcomings of basing sales forecasts exclusively on estimates developed by the firm's sales force.

18. Assume that growth in industry sales will remain constant for the coming year. Forecast company sales for the coming year based upon the following data:

    Year 1: $ 640,000
    Year 2: $ 700,000
    Year 3: $ 680,000
    Year 4: $ 760,000
    Year 5: $1,060,000

    What assumptions have you made in developing your forecast?

19. Suggest methods for forecasting sales for newly introduced products.

20. Which forecasting technique do you feel is most appropriate for each of the following:
    a. Prell shampoo
    b. New York Museum of Modern Art
    c. Office supplies retailer
    d. Fender guitars

Case: Piedmont Airlines

Of the smaller airlines that were around before deregulation, Piedmont Airlines has been the canniest. Most of its competitors jumped at the chance to drop small and medium-size cities from their routes. Piedmont—which calls Winston-Salem, North Carolina (pop. 140,000), home—disagreed. There was money to be made from Asheville (pop. 60,000), Jacksonville (pop. 26,000 plus 40,000 U.S. Marines at Camp Lejeune), and other North Carolina towns. Plenty of money, that is, *provided* passengers flew Piedmont to its Charlotte, North Carolina, hub and then took other Piedmont flights for longer hauls to such cities as Detroit, Miami, or New York.

The gamble, as President and Chief Executive William R. Howard, 61, points out, flew in the face of what wisdom there was in the immediate post-deregulation environment. "People thought routes that linked major cities were apples for the taking," says Howard, formerly Eastern's chief of labor relations. "But if we had started a service between Chicago and New York, nobody would have said, 'Thank God. We needed that!' Nobody would have given a damn."

So instead, Howard decided to find newly orphaned or neglected markets that would be grateful for the service and built a powerful Charlotte hub-and-spoke system. The strategy worked so well that in 1982 he repeated it, setting up a second hub in Dayton, Ohio, for flights to and from Flint, Michigan; Champaign-Urbana, Illinois; Fort Wayne, Indiana; and other cities. Last year Howard added a third hub—Baltimore-Washington International Airport.

By the end of 1983 Piedmont showed the biggest growth among the established airlines. Revenues climbed $229.5 million to $942.5 million. Profits were down 16 percent to $25.5 million, largely as a result of fare wars, but have since turned up again. Profitability will get a boost if Piedmont is successful in winning an American-style, two-tier wage agreement from its unions.

Howard—who collects vintage cars and modern motorcycles (he occasionally bikes to his office)—wants much more. On April 1, Piedmont began flights to Los Angeles from its Charlotte and Dayton hubs and is scheduled to fly to San Francisco in September. Given Howard's emphasis on happy customers, the inaugural flights to California presented a problem. The planes—long-range 727s being refurbished by Boeing—weren't ready. Piedmont had to use its shorter-range 727s, and the passengers had been promised nonstop trips. As it happened, the Dayton flight was blessed by favorable winds and made it. The Charlotte flight flew into head winds and the plane had to refuel in Oklahoma City. Howard had prepared letters of apology, which were passed out to the passengers, along with $50 in cash for those in first class and $20 for those in coach.

Even though the Los Angeles flights are making a profit, Howard's decision to fly to California bemuses some experts in the industry. Says a security analyst: "I'm not so sure it's not just vanity." Howard shrugs. Los Angeles and San Francisco topped the list of cities that his passengers wanted to go to but that Piedmont didn't serve, he says. He takes his cigar out of his mouth to allow the widest possible grin. The experts have been wrong before.

Questions

1. What type of marketing strategy is being employed by Piedmont Airlines? Explain why they selected this strategy.

2. What are the potential dangers of such a strategy? Suggest methods by which the firm's management can minimize these dangers.

Computer Applications

The sales forecast is a basic building block for marketing planning. A relatively simple quantitative forecasting technique that is frequently utilized for short-term forecasting during periods of steady growth is called *trend analysis*. This technique involves the extrapolation (or extension) of historical data into a specified future time period. The extrapolation is accomplished by fitting a trend equation to the past data on sales, market share, or earnings and using this trend equation to estimate a future time period. The equation for trend analysis is:

$$Y_c = a + bx$$

where

Y_c is the predicted amount of sales, market share, or earnings for the specified time period.

a is the estimated amount of sales, market share, or earnings at the time period when x is equal to 0.

b is the slope of the trend line. In other words, it is the average change in sales, market share, or earnings for each specified time period (year, month, etc.).

x is the time period used when the forecasts are made. An example might be one year, one month, or one quarter.

To use the trend analysis equation, the marketer must obtain estimates of a and b. These estimates are calculated from historical data using a technique called *least squares*. The following two equations are used for calculating a and b:

$$a = \frac{\Sigma Y}{n}$$

$$b = \frac{\Sigma xY}{\Sigma x^2}$$

The mathematical symbol Σ means "the sum of." The variable n refers to the total number of time periods.

Consider the following example. A small mail-order firm specializing in novelty items is seeking to forecast sales for 1987. The firm's president feels that trend extension is an appropriate forecasting technique because of the relatively stable growth in company sales and the short-term nature of the forecast. To calculate the needed data for the trend analysis equation, he has created the following table, beginning with a listing of annual sales for each year since the firm's establishment in 1978.

Year	n Time Period	Y Sales (Thousands of Dollars)	x	xY	x^2
1978	1	100	−4	−400	16
1979	2	112	−3	−336	9
1980	3	130	−2	−260	4
1981	4	160	−1	−160	1
1982	5	205	0	0	0
1983	6	210	1	210	1
1984	7	240	2	480	4
1985	8	280	3	840	9
1986	9	325	4	1300	16
		$1,762		1,674	60

Since the firm has been operating for an odd number of years, the mid-year of 1982 is coded 0. The years prior to 1982 are coded −1, −2, and so on. The years following 1982 are coded with a positive 1, 2, and so on. Should the data involve an even number of observations, the two mid-years are coded −1 and +1. The prior years are then coded in increments of −2 (−3, −5, −7, and so on); all subsequent years following the mid-years are coded in increments of +2 (+3, +5, +7, and so on). The analysis is completed by calculating ΣxY, Σx^2, and n. The first two values are determined by totaling the two columns labeled xY and x^2. Since the number of time periods included in this example is 9, the value of n is equal to 9. The calculated values for a and b are:

$$a = \frac{1,762}{9} = 195.8$$

$$b = \frac{1,674}{60} = 27.9.$$

Therefore, the trend line for this example is:

$$Y_c = a + bx$$

$$Y_c = 195.8 + 27.9x.$$

To forecast 1987 sales for the mail-order firm, it is necessary to count from the 1982 center value. Since the value for 1986 is 4, the value for 1987 would be 5. The forecast is then made by substituting the value of 5 for x in the formula.

1987 Annual Sales Forecast = 195.8 + 27.9(5)

= 335.3

= $335,300.

Directions: Use menu item 3 titled "Sales Forecasting" to solve each of the following problems.

Problem 1 The establishment of a "Birthday Surprise from Home" operation at Delta State University has proven to be a market success for its founder, junior marketing major Jennifer Glieson. A direct-mail brochure was prepared and mailed to the parents of each on-campus DSU student, offering to deliver personally a birthday cake, complete with a song and a personal message from the parents on the student's birthday for $20. During the first seven months of operation, Jennifer's part-time business has generated the following revenue:

September	$6,400
October	6,800
November	7,000
December	5,600
January	7,200
February	7,200
March	7,400

Forecast revenue for the month of April using the trend extension method.

Problem 2 Total annual sales for a video cassette rental chain are shown below. Forecast 1987 sales using the trend extension method.

1980	$ 1 million
1981	3 million
1982	6 million
1983	10 million
1984	11 million
1985	13 million
1986	14 million

Problem 3 During 1978, the first year of operation for Garden State University, enrollment totaled 1,200 students. The following year's enrollment grew to 2,100 students, and in 1980 the growth continued as 2,800 students attended the university. Enrollment for subsequent years was: 4,200 in 1981; 4,400 in 1982; 4,500 in 1983; 4,800 in 1984, 5,400 in 1985; and 6,000 in 1986. Use the forecasting model described above to estimate Garden State University enrollments for 1987 and 1988.

Problem 4 Ian Chandler was one of the first business-people in the United States to recognize the market potential of suntanning salons. The development of these solaria permitted users to obtain a rapid, natural tan in a very short time without the redness, burning, and drying out of the skin that all too frequently accompany the traditional approaches to tanning. Chandler opened his first Perfect Tan solarium in 1979 and has expanded over time as market acceptance grew. Annual sales revenues are as follows:

1979	$ 46,000
1980	78,000
1981	120,000
1982	132,000
1983	156,000
1984	190,000
1985	230,000
1986	278,000

Forecast Perfect Tan revenues for 1987 and 1988.

Problem 5 University Trivia, a newly designed board game aimed at taking advantage of the current trivia fad, was introduced eight months ago. Its sales have continued to grow each month, even though it carries a healthy price tag of $32. Moreover, there appears to be no seasonal variation in sales. Monthly unit sales of the product are as follows:

August	14,000 units
September	16,000 units
October	23,000 units
November	24,000 units
December	28,000 units
January	29,000 units
February	33,000 units
March	36,000 units

How many unit sales of University Trivia would you estimate for April? For May?

4

Marketing Research: Information for Decision Making

Key Terms

Learning Goals

1. To describe the development and current status of the marketing research function
2. To list the steps in the marketing research process
3. To differentiate the types and sources of primary and secondary data
4. To identify the methods of collecting survey data
5. To explain the various sampling techniques
6. To distinguish between marketing research and marketing information systems
7. To outline the current status of marketing information systems

Stop-Action Case

Mid-America Research

For years, the data collection mainstay of many marketing research firms was the door-to-door interview. To find out what average American homemakers thought about different products and services, researchers hired interviewers to knock on people's doors. Using this method, researchers targeted the exact cross section of consumers their clients wanted, based on neighborhood demographic patterns.

As times changed, the value of door-to-door research diminished. "Door-to-door, once the backbone of the industry, is dying fast," said William T. Field, vice-president and managing director of Mid-America Research (MAR). "It's too expensive, people aren't home anymore, women are working, our interviewers are nervous about going into homes, people hesitate to let strangers in."

The social forces that took women out of the home and into the work force also brought men into the supermarkets and other retail stores across the country. Men are now sharing their families' shopping chores—a trend marketing researchers could not investigate through daytime door-to-door interviewing.

Marketing researchers had to find a better method of tapping the opinions of typical male and female consumers who could no longer be found at home. One firm facing this challenge was Mid-America Research, a subsidiary of the advertising agency D'Arcy MacManus & Masius. To discover for clients the cereal box color that sells the most cereal, the TV commercial that gets the best response, the ingredient mix that tastes best in cocoa, MAR had to find a better way to gather the raw data that reflects consumer choice.

Assignment: Use the materials in Chapter 4 to recommend a course of action for Mid-America Research.

Photo Source: Courtesy of Mid-America Research.

Source: "Field Research: Alive and Well in the Malls," by Theodore J. Gage. Excerpts printed with permission from the May 23, 1983, issue of *Advertising Age*, pp. m-27, m-28. Copyright © 1983 by Crain Communications, Inc.

Chapter Overview _____

It has been said that the recipe for effective decisions is 90 percent information and 10 percent inspiration. All marketing management decisions depend
on the type, quantity, and quality of the information on which they are based.
A variety of sources exist for decision-oriented marketing data needs. Some
are well-planned investigations designed to elicit specific information. Other
valuable information may be obtained from sales-force reports, accounting
data, or published reports. Still other information may be obtained from controlled experiments or computer simulations.

A major source of information for marketing planning takes the form of
marketing research. The American Marketing Association defines marketing
research as the systematic gathering, recording, and analyzing of data about
problems relating to the marketing of goods and services.[1] The critical task of
the marketing manager is decision making. Managers must make effective
decisions that enable their firms to solve problems as they arise and must
anticipate and prevent future problems. Many times, though, managers are
forced to make decisions without sufficient information. Marketing research
aids the decision maker by presenting pertinent facts, analyzing them, and
suggesting possible action.

Chapter 4 deals with the marketing research function. Marketing research is closely linked with the other elements of the marketing planning
process. All marketing research should be done within the framework of the
organization's strategic plan. Research projects should be directed toward the
resolution of marketing decisions that conform to an overall corporate plan.
Alfred S. Boote, the marketing research director for the Singer Company, estimates that research costs 50 to 60 percent more for firms that lack a strategic
marketing plan because too much useless information is collected.[2]

Much of the material outlined in Chapters 3 and 5 on marketing planning
and forecasting and market segmentation is based on information collected as
a result of marketing research. Clearly, the marketing research function is the
primary source of the information needed to make effective marketing decisions.

A Perspective of the Marketing Research Function _____

Before looking at how marketing research is actually done, it is important to
get an overall perspective of the field. What activities are considered part of
the marketing research function? How did the field develop? Who is involved
in marketing research?

Marketing Research Activities

All marketing decision areas are candidates for marketing research investigations. As Figure 4.1 indicates, marketing research efforts are commonly centered around determining market potential, market share analysis, determination of market characteristics, sales analysis, and competitive product studies.

The Development of the Marketing Research Function

Marketing research is a relatively new field. More than a hundred years have
passed since N.W. Ayer conducted the first organized research project in
1879. A second important milestone in the development of marketing research

Figure 4.1
Selected Types of Marketing Research Conducted by Major Firms

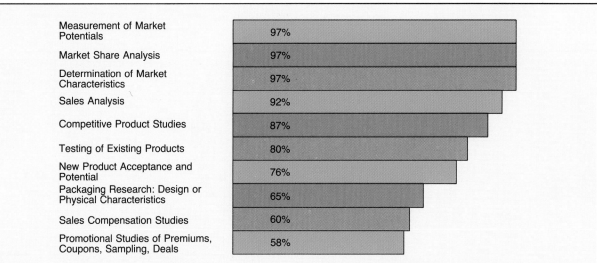

Measurement of Market Potentials	97%
Market Share Analysis	97%
Determination of Market Characteristics	97%
Sales Analysis	92%
Competitive Product Studies	87%
Testing of Existing Products	80%
New Product Acceptance and Potential	76%
Packaging Research: Design or Physical Characteristics	65%
Sales Compensation Studies	60%
Promotional Studies of Premiums, Coupons, Sampling, Deals	58%

Source: Dik Warren Twedt, ed., *1983 Survey of Marketing Research*
(Chicago: American Marketing Association, 1984) p. 41.

occurred in 1911 when Charles C. Parlin organized and became manager of the nation's first commercial research department at the Curtis Publishing Company.

Parlin actually got his start as a marketing researcher by counting soup cans in Philadelphia's garbage! Parlin was employed as a sales representative for advertising space in the *Saturday Evening Post*. He had failed to sell advertising space to the Campbell Soup Company because the firm believed that the magazine reached primarily working-class readers who made their own soup rather than spend 10 cents for a can of prepared soup. Campbell's was targeting its product at higher income people who could afford to pay for convenience. So Parlin began counting the soup cans contained in the garbage of different neighborhoods. To Campbell's surprise, Parlin's research revealed that more canned soup was sold to the working class than to the wealthy, who had servants to make soup for them. Campbell's soup quickly became a *Saturday Evening Post* client.[3]

Much of the early research represented little more than written testimonials received from purchasers of the firm's products. Research became more sophisticated during the 1930s as the development of statistical techniques led to refinements in sampling procedures and greater accuracy in research findings.[4] However, mistakes still occurred. The *Literary Digest* conducted a major national study of U.S. households selected at random from lists of telephone numbers and auto registration records and reported that Alf Landon—not Franklin D. Roosevelt—would be elected president. The fiasco resulted from a failure to realize that many voters (most of whom were apparently Democrats) did not have telephones or automobiles in 1936.

Marketing Research Participants

Total annual expenditures for marketing research are estimated at over $1 billion. Virtually all major consumer goods companies are actively researching

Figure 4.2
The Breakdown of Corporate Marketing Research Budgets

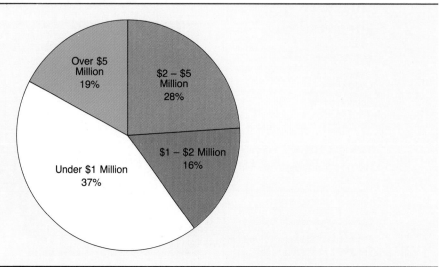

Source: "Corporate Research Budgets Rose 9% in '83: AMA Survey,"
Marketing News (May 25, 1984), p. 11.

their marketplace. But so are industrial goods manufacturers, service businesses, banks, and nonprofit organizations such as hospitals. The breakdown of marketing research budgets is shown in Figure 4.2.

The Marketing Research Process

How is marketing research actually conducted? The starting point, of course, is the need for information to make a marketing decision. This information need can relate to a specific marketing decision or an ongoing set of decisions. If an information need is perceived, the marketing research process can be used to produce the needed marketing knowledge.

The marketing research process can be divided into six specific steps: (1) defining the problem; (2) exploratory research; (3) formulating a hypothesis; (4) research design; (5) collecting data; and (6) interpretation and presentation. Figure 4.3 diagrams the marketing research process from the information need to the research-based decision.

Problem Definition

Someone once remarked that well-defined problems are half solved. Problems are barriers that prevent the accomplishment of organizational goals. A clearly defined problem permits the researcher to focus the research process on securing the necessary data to solve the problem. Sometimes it is easy to pinpoint problems. Top executives at Republic Airlines once stood in airport lines in order to spot passenger complaints. The two most common gripes were inadequate flight information and cold in-flight coffee.[5] Once these problems were identified, they were corrected without further research.

Figure 4.3
The Marketing Research Process

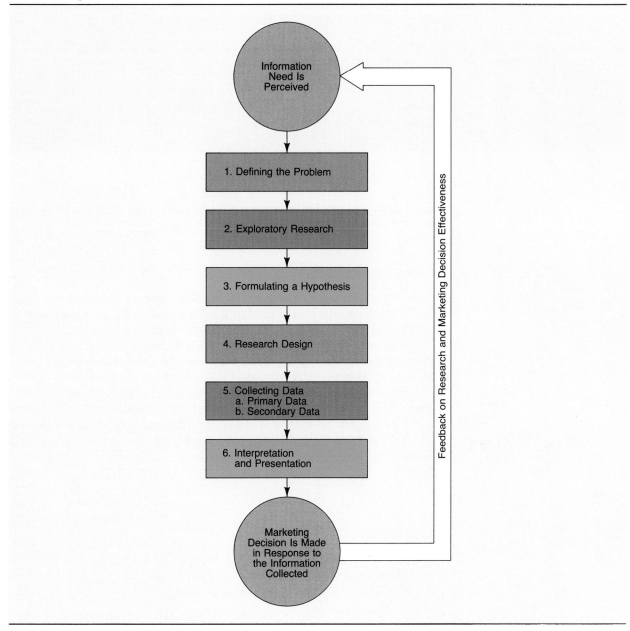

Exploratory Research

Exploratory Research
Discussing a marketing problem with informed sources within a firm, as well as with wholesalers, retailers, customers, and others outside the firm, and examining secondary sources of information.

Searching for the cause of a problem allows the researcher to learn about the problem area and to focus on specific areas for study in seeking solutions. This search, often called **exploratory research**, consists of discussing the problem with informed sources within the firm and with wholesalers, retailers, customers, and others outside the firm and examining secondary sources of information. Marketing researchers often refer to internal data collection as the *situation analysis* and to exploratory interviews with informed persons outside the firm as the *informal investigation*. Exploratory research also involves eval-

Table 4.1

Income Statement for the Venture Company for the
Year Ended December 31, 198X

Sales		$57,830,000
Cost of Goods Sold		32,910,000
Gross Margin		$24,920,000
Expenses:		
Selling Expenses	$7,530,000	
Other Expenses	3,010,000	
		10,540,000
Profit before Taxes		$14,380,000
Income Taxes		7,190,000
Profit after Taxes		$ 7,190,000

uating company records, such as sales and profit analyses of the company's
and its competitors' products.

Using Internal Data

An organization's sales records contain valuable sources of information. Analysis of these records should provide a basis for obtaining an overall view of
company efficiency and a clue to the problem under investigation.

The basis for analysis of internal data is traditional accounting data provided by the accounting department and usually summarized on the firm's
financial statements. Table 4.1 shows a simplified income statement.

Basic financial statements are often too broad to be very useful in marketing analysis. Where nondetailed accounts are used, their main contribution
is that they assist the analyst in raising more specific questions. The income
statement in Table 4.1 shows that the company earned a profit for the period
involved and that selling expenses represent approximately 13 percent of
sales.

$$\text{Cost/Sales Ratio} = \frac{\$7,530,000}{\$57,830,000} = 13\%.$$

Comparison of the 13-percent selling expense to sales ratio with previous
years may hint at possible problems, but it will not specifically reveal the cause
of the variation. To discover the cause, a more detailed breakdown is necessary.

Sales Analysis Table 4.2 shows a typical breakdown of sales by territories.

This kind of breakdown becomes part of an overall sales analysis. The purpose of the sales analysis—the in-depth evaluation of a firm's sales—is to
obtain meaningful information from the accounting data.

Easily prepared from company invoices stored on computer tapes, the
sales analysis can be quite revealing for the marketing executive. As Table
4.2 shows, the sales force in District 4 has a much higher cost/sales ratio than
the sales force in other districts.

To evaluate the performance of the salespersons in the five selected
districts, the marketing executive must have a standard of comparison. District

Sales Analysis
In-depth evaluation of a firm's sales.

Table 4.2

Sales and Expense Analysis of Selected Districts

District	Average Salary	Average Expenses	Average Sales Costs	Average Sales	Cost/ Sales Ratio
1	$33,600	$10,400	$44,000	$654,000	6.7%
2	31,900	12,800	44,700	534,000	8.4
3	37,200	13,100	50,300	790,000	6.4
4	35,200	12,300	48,000	380,000	12.6
5	34,200	11,700	35,900	580,000	7.9

Sales Quota
Level of expected sales against which actual results are compared.

4, for example, may be a large territory with relatively few industrial centers. Consequently, the costs involved in obtaining sales will be higher than for other districts.

The standard by which actual and expected sales are compared typically results from a detailed sales forecast by territories, products, customers, and salespersons. Once the sales quota—the level of expected sales by which actual results are compared—has been established, it is a simple process to compare the actual results with the expected performance. Table 4.3 compares actual sales with the quota established for salespersons in District 4.

Even though Shapiro had the smallest amount of sales for the period, her performance was better than expected. However, the district sales manager should investigate Chandler's performance since it represented only 81 percent of quota.

Iceberg Principle
Theory suggesting that collected data in summary form often hides (obscures) important evaluative information.

The performance of the salespersons in District 4 provides a good illustration of the iceberg principle, which suggests that important evaluative information is often hidden by aggregate data. The tip of the iceberg represents only one-tenth of its total size. The remaining nine-tenths lies hidden beneath the surface of the water. Summaries of data are useful, but the marketing researcher must be careful that they do not actually conceal more than they reveal. If the sales breakdown by salesperson for the district had not been available, Chandler's poor sales might have been partially concealed by the good sales performances of the others.

Other possible breakdowns for sales analysis include customer type, product, method of sale (mail, telephone, or personal contact), type of order (cash or credit), and size of order. Sales analysis is one of the least expensive and most important sources of marketing information.

Table 4.3

Sales Breakdown of Selected Sales Representatives in District 4

Salesperson	Quota	Actual	Performance to Quota
Holtzman	$336,000	$382,000	114%
Thompson	428,000	453,000	106
Shapiro	318,000	325,000	102
Chandler	446,000	360,000	81
Total	$1,528,000	$1,520,000	

Table 4.4

Allocation of Marketing Costs

Marketing Costs	By Customer		By District		
	Large	Small	A	B	C
Advertising	$140,000	$300,000	$200,000	$100,000	$140,000
Selling	520,000	620,000	380,000	380,000	380,000
Physical Distribution	330,000	260,000	280,000	140,000	170,000
Credit	4,000	26,000	16,000	6,000	8,000
Total	$994,000	$1,206,000	$876,000	$626,000	$698,000

Marketing Cost Analysis
Evaluation of such items as selling costs, billing, and advertising to determine the profitability of particular customers, territories, or product lines.

Marketing Cost Analysis   A second source of internal information is marketing cost analysis—the evaluation of such items as selling costs, billing, warehousing, advertising, and delivery expenses in order to determine the profitability of particular customers, territories, or product lines.

Marketing cost analysis requires a new way of classifying accounting data. *Functional accounts* must be established to replace the traditional natural accounts used in financial statements. These traditional accounts, such as salary, must be reallocated to the purpose for which the expenditure was made. A portion of the original salary account, for example, will be allocated to selling, inventory control, storage, billing, advertising, and other marketing costs. In the same manner, an account such as supply expenses will be allocated to the functions that utilize supplies.

The costs allocated to the functional accounts will equal those in the natural accounts. But instead of showing only total profitability, they can show the profitability of, say, particular territories, products, customers, salespersons, and order sizes. The most common reallocations are to products, customers, and territories or districts. Table 4.4 shows how they can be made.

The marketing decision maker can then evaluate the profitability of particular customers and districts on the basis of the sales produced and the costs incurred in producing them.

Table 4.5 indicates that District B is the most profitable region and District A is unprofitable. Attention can now be given to plans for increasing sales or reducing expenses in this problem district to make market coverage of the area a profitable undertaking.

Table 4.5

Income Statement for Districts A, B, and C

	District			
	A	B	C	Total
Sales	$2,600,000	$2,000,000	$1,910,000	$6,510,000
Cost of Sales	1,750,000	1,350,000	1,200,000	4,300,000
Gross Margin	850,000	650,000	710,000	2,210,000
Marketing Expenses	876,000	626,000	698,000	2,100,000
Contribution of Each Territory	$ (26,000)	$ 24,000	$ 12,000	$ 10,000

Formulating Hypotheses

Hypothesis
Tentative explanation about some specific event. A hypothesis is a statement about the relationship between variables and includes clear implications for testing this relationship.

After the problem has been defined and an exploratory investigation conducted, the marketer should be able to formulate a hypothesis, a tentative explanation about some specific event. A hypothesis is a statement about the relationship between variables and carries clear implications for testing this relationship.

A marketer of industrial products might formulate the following hypothesis: *Failure to provide 72-hour delivery service will reduce our sales by 20 percent*. Such a statement may prove correct or incorrect. The formulation of this hypothesis does, however, provide a basis for investigation and an eventual determination of its accuracy. Also, it allows the researcher to move to the next step: development of the research design.

Lever Brothers' Pepsodent toothpaste had been on the market since 1944, but by the mid-1960s surveys were indicating that young consumers were dissatisfied with current offerings in two areas: tooth whitening and breath freshening. Lever Brothers began work on its hypothesis that a combination toothpaste and mouthwash could become a successful market entry. The end result of the firm's hypothesis testing was Close-Up toothpaste.[6]

Research Design

Research Design
Series of advanced decisions that, when taken together, comprise a master plan or a model for conducting marketing research.

The research design represents a comprehensive plan for testing the hypothesis formulated about the problem. Research design refers to a series of decisions that, taken together, comprise a master plan or model for the conduct of the investigation. Heublein, a marketer of alcoholic products, is concerned about environmental factors that might impact its markets so it has set up an environmental monitoring system that scans published data to pick up environmental trends and the like.[7]

Sometimes published data is not enough, so the research design must call for a direct test of a hypothesis. Producers at Paramount Pictures were fearful that the planned death of Mr. Spock in *Star Trek II—The Wrath of Khan* would turn "Trekkies" against the movie, so a sample research design was formulated. The movie with Mr. Spock dying was shown to participants at a science-fiction meeting in Kansas City. The audience loved the movie, and Paramount Pictures decided to leave Mr. Spock dead.[8]

Data Collection

Primary Data
Information or statistics being collected for the first time during a marketing research study.

Secondary Data
Previously published data.

A major step in the research design is determining what data is needed to test the hypothesis. Data is classified as primary or secondary. Primary data refers to data that is collected for the first time during a marketing research study. The Kansas City screening of *Star Trek II—The Wrath of Khan* is an example of primary research. Secondary data is previously published matter. It serves as an extremely important source of information for marketing researchers such as those at Heublein.

Collecting Secondary Data

Not only is secondary data important to the marketing researcher, it is also very abundant. The overwhelming quantity of secondary data available at little or no cost challenges the researcher to select only pertinent secondary data.

Secondary data consists of two types: internal and external. Internal secondary data includes records of sales, product performances, sales force activities, and marketing costs. External data is obtained from a variety of sources. Governments—local, state, and federal—provide a wide variety of secondary data. Private sources also supply secondary data for the marketing decision maker.

Both external and internal data can be obtained from computerized data bases. A data base refers to any collection of data that is retrievable through a computer. A considerable amount of published information is available in this way. Some firms create their own data bases that include sales and marketing cost records.

There are three basic types of on-line data bases:

1. Reference data bases refer to information on a specific topic. Many libraries are equipped with such facilities.
2. Full data bases produce the complete article being sought.
3. Source data bases provide detailed information listings. A listing of export trade opportunities is an example.[9]

The growth in popularity of data bases has led to an expansion of such services. The offerings of some on-line data base services are outlined in Table 4.6.

Government Data   The federal government is the nation's most important source of marketing data, and the most frequently used government statistics are census data. Although the U.S. government spent more than $1 billion conducting the last Census of Population, census information is available for use at no charge at local libraries, or it can be purchased on computer tapes for instantaneous access at a nominal charge. In addition to the Census of Population, the Bureau of the Census also conducts a Census of Housing (which is combined with the Census of Population), a Census of Business, a Census of Manufacturers, a Census of Agriculture, a Census of Minerals, and a Census of Governments.

The census is so detailed for large cities that breakdowns of population characteristics are available by city block. Local retailers and shopping-center developers can easily gather specific information about customers in the immediate neighborhood without spending the time or money to conduct a comprehensive survey.

So much information is produced by the federal government that marketing researchers often purchase summaries such as the *Monthly Catalog of the United States Government Publications*, the *Statistical Abstract of the United States*, the *Survey of Current Business*, and the *County and City Data Book*. Published annually, the *Statistical Abstract* contains a wealth of current data. The *Survey of Current Business*, updated monthly, focuses on a variety of industrial data. The *County and City Data Book*, typically published every three years, provides a variety of data for each county and each city over 25,000 residents.

State and city governments serve as other important sources of information on employment, production, and sales activities. In addition, university bureaus of business and economic research often collect and disseminate such information.

Data Base
Any collection of data that is retrievable through a computer.

Table 4.6

Some Data on On-Line Data Base Services

On-Line Service[a]	What It Offers	Basic Fee	Prime-Time Hourly Fees	Off-Hour Hourly Fees
Bibliographic Retrieval Services (BRS) 1200 Rte. 7 Latham, N.Y. 12110 800 833-4707 800 553-5566 from N.Y.	More than 80 data bases, principally bibliographic references covering physical and social sciences, business, education, special emphasis on medicine, including access to MEDLARS	$50 start-up (or contract for minimum annual use)	$15 to $105 plus 4¢ to $1 per citation plus $3 to $26/hr. for telecommunications	
	BRS After Dark (includes about 35 BRS data bases)	$75 start-up		$6 to $21 (2 hour/ month minimum)
CompuServe 5000 Arlington Centre Blvd. P.O. Box 20212 Columbus, Ohio 43220 800 848-8199	National and international news wires, investment data, *Grolier's Encyclopedia*, airline guide, home banking, interactive games, computer conferencing, bulletin board, software exchange	$40 start-up (includes five free hours)	$12.50 (300 baud); $15 (1,200 baud); *Surcharges on some services and transactions; local access from about 150 cities*	$6 (300 baud); $12.50 (1,200 baud)
Data Resources, Inc. (DRI) 29 Hartwell Ave. Lexington, Mass. 02173 800 257-5114	More than 100 key economic and financial data bases; includes international and industry-sector data, demographic and stock market data, forecasting and simulation models	$500 to $7,000/year (can get fee waived by paying higher hourly fees)	$28 *Additional charges for accessing results of economic forecasts and other industry statistics*	$18
DIALOG Information Retrieval Service 3460 Hillview Ave. Palo Alto, Cal. 94304 800 227-1927 800 982-5838 in Cal.	More than 200 science, technology, general news and business data bases; principally bibliographic references with abstracts; some full texts; nationwide electronic Yellow Pages with ten million phone listings	$50 user's manual; 100 free hours in first month	$25 to $100 plus $6 to $8/hour for telecommunications	
	KNOWLEDGE INDEX, the DIALOG off-hour service, includes 23 data bases covering agriculture, electronics, engineering, medicine, news, business and legal information	$35 start-up (includes two free hours and $50 manual)		$24

Note: Hourly fees may depend in part on the speed of the modem you use. Speeds are expressed in terms of baud rates—a 1,200-baud modem receives data four times as quickly as a 300-baud modem.
[a]The out-of-state, toll-free numbers shown are for ordering the service, not for accessing it.

Source: Reprinted with permission from "Let a Data Base Get You the Facts," *CHANGING TIMES* Magazine (October 1984), p. 48. Copyright Kiplinger Washington Editors, Inc.

(continued)

Table 4.6

Some Data on On-Line Data Base Services (continued)

On-Line Service[a]	What It Offers	Basic Fee	Prime-Time Hourly Fees	Off-Hour Hourly Fees
Dow Jones News/Retrieval P.O. Box 300 Princeton, N.J. 08540 800 257-5114	Full-text news from *The Wall Street Journal* and other Dow Jones sources, emphasis on business and financial information and stock data; also provides sports scores, *Grolier's Encyclopedia*, weather reports, movie reviews, airline guide, electronic mail, shopping services	$75 start-up (free with Dow Jones software)	$36 to $72 *Fees are double for 1,200 baud*	$9 to $54
LEXIS Mead Data Central 9393 Springboro Pike P.O. Box 933 Dayton, Ohio 45401 513 865-6800	Archives of federal and state law; regulations; codes; libraries of tax and other specialty law; English and French law	$110/month	$20 plus $9 to $18/search $8/hour for telecommunications	$20 plus $4.50 to $9/search
MEDLARS National Library of Medicine 8600 Rockville Pike Bethesda, Md. 20209 301 496-6193	Biomedical data bases containing references to worldwide literature (three-day training program required of all users)	None	$22 average	$15 average *$15/month minimum, royalty charges for some files*
NewsNet 945 Haverford Rd. Bryn Mawr, Pa. 19010 800 345-1301	More than 200 full-text data bases, including UPI news wires, industry newsletters, *Howard Ruff's Financial Success Report*, government publications, press releases of interest to business; coverage includes investment, taxation, computer products	None	$24 to $120 (300 baud) *Fees are double for 1,200 baud*	25% off
NEXIS Mead Data Central (same address as LEXIS)	Full-text articles from more than 120 newspapers, magazines, professional and trade journals, and wire services; NAARS—a data base of annual reports and proxy statements of most major companies	$50/month *Also available to LEXIS and NEXIS subscribers: data bases with financial data on major companies, patent law; clipping service for $18/month*	Same hourly fees as LEXIS	
The Source 1616 Anderson Rd. McLean, Va. 22102 800 336-3366	General business and sports news with keyword index, investment data (including on-line stock trading and real-time quotations), electronic mail, games, shopping, travel reservations	$50 start-up (includes lifetime subscription to *SourceWorld* newsletter)	$20.75 (300 baud); $25.75 (1,200 baud); ($10/month minimum)	$7.75 (300 baud); $10.75 (1,200 baud) *Local access from about 500 cities*

Private Data Many private organizations provide information for the marketing executive. For data on activities in a particular industry, trade associations are excellent sources. Advertising agencies continually collect information on the audience reached by various media. A wide range of valuable data is found in the annual "Survey of Buying Power" published by *Sales and Marketing Management* magazine.

Several national firms also offer information to businesses on a subscription basis. The largest of these, A.C. Nielsen Company, collects data every two months on product sales, retail prices, display space, inventories, and promotional activities of competing brands of food and drug products. Its data sample consists of about 1,600 supermarkets, 750 drugstores, and 150 mass merchandisers.

Secondary Data: Strengths and Weaknesses

The use of secondary data offers two important advantages: (1) the assembly of secondary data is almost always less expensive than the collection of primary data; and (2) less time is involved in locating and using secondary data. Figure 4.4 shows the estimated time involved in completing a research study requiring primary data. Although the time involved in a marketing research study will vary considerably depending on such factors as the research subject and the scope of the study, an additional time and cost investment is required when primary data is needed.

Figure 4.4
Time Requirements for a Primary Data Research Project

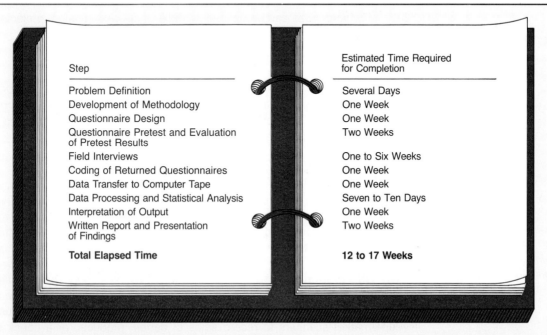

Step	Estimated Time Required for Completion
Problem Definition	Several Days
Development of Methodology	One Week
Questionnaire Design	One Week
Questionnaire Pretest and Evaluation of Pretest Results	Two Weeks
Field Interviews	One to Six Weeks
Coding of Returned Questionnaires	One Week
Data Transfer to Computer Tape	One Week
Data Processing and Statistical Analysis	Seven to Ten Days
Interpretation of Output	One Week
Written Report and Presentation of Findings	Two Weeks
Total Elapsed Time	**12 to 17 Weeks**

Source: Estimates by Alfred S. Boote, Corporate Director of Market Research, The Singer Company. Quoted in "Everyone Benefits from Closer Planning, Research Ties," *Marketing News* (January 9, 1981), p. 30. Used by permission of the American Marketing Association.

The researcher, however, must be aware of two potential limitations of secondary data: the data may be obsolete, or its classifications may not be usable in the proposed research study. Published information can quickly become obsolete. A marketing researcher analyzing the population of the Orlando, Florida, metropolitan market in early 1986 discovers that most of the 1980 census data is obsolete due to the influx of residents to the area. Also, data may have been collected previously on the basis of county or city boundaries, but the marketing manager may require data broken down by city blocks or census tracts. In such cases, the marketing researcher may not be able to rearrange the secondary data in usable form and may have to begin collecting primary data.

Collecting Primary Data

The collection of primary data requires that two questions be answered: (1) Who is going to collect the data? and (2) How is the data going to be collected?

The Assignment of Data Collection Responsibilities   Although most large companies have their own marketing research departments, many smaller ones depend on independent marketing research firms to conduct their research studies. Even large firms typically rely on outside agencies to provide interviewers, and they often farm out some research studies to independent agencies as well. The decision of whether to conduct a study through an outside organization or internally is usually based on cost. Another consideration is the reliability and accuracy of the information collected by the agency.

Research is likely to be contracted to outside groups when the following requirements are met:

1.   Problem areas can be defined in terms of specific research projects.
2.   There is a need for specialized know-how or equipment.
3.   Intellectual detachment is a requirement.[10]

An outside group is often able to provide technical assistance and expertise not available within the firm. Also, the use of outside groups helps ensure that the researcher is not conducting the study only to validate the wisdom of a favorite theory or package design.

Primary Data Collection Alternatives

The marketing researcher has three alternatives in the collection of primary data: observation, survey, or controlled experiment. No single method is best in all circumstances, and any of these methods may prove the most efficient in a particular situation.

The Observation Method   Observational studies are conducted by actually viewing the overt actions of the person being studied. They may take the form of a traffic count at a potential location for a fast-food franchise, the use of supermarket scanners to record sales of certain products, or a check of license plates at a shopping center to determine where shoppers live.

A.C. Nielsen's audimeter records the times television sets are turned on and which channels are viewed. This information shows the audience size, which is the primary determinant of television advertising rates.

High technology has increasingly evolved in the field of marketing research. Firms such as BehaviorScan use supermarket scanners to track the purchasing patterns of consumers in eight cities throughout the country. BehaviorScan uses scanners to record the purchases of some 2,500 households. Consumer purchases are then related to product advertisements seen on local cable television channels. Advertisers can quickly determine how their products sell under different marketing plans.[11]

The Survey Method   Some information cannot be obtained through observation. The researcher must ask questions to obtain information on attitudes, motives, and opinions. The most widely used approach to collecting primary data is the survey method. Three kinds of surveys exist: telephone, mail, and personal interviews.

Telephone Interviews   This survey method is inexpensive and fast for obtaining small quantities of relatively impersonal information. Since many firms have leased WATS services (telephone company services that allow businesses to make unlimited long-distance calls for a fixed rate per state or region), the cost of telephone interviewing has been reduced.

Telephone interviews account for an estimated 55 to 60 percent of all primary marketing research. A national survey revealed that one woman in five had been interviewed by telephone in 1980 compared with one in seven only two years earlier. The percentage of men who had participated in telephone interviews had grown from one in ten in 1978 to one in seven in 1980.[12]

Telephone interviews are, however, limited to simple, clearly worded questions. They cannot show respondents a picture of the item under discussion. Also, it is extremely difficult to obtain information on personal characteristics of respondents, and the survey may be prejudiced by the omission of households without phones or with unlisted numbers.

One survey reported that alphabetical listings in telephone directories excluded one-third of blacks with telephones and one-fourth of large-city dwellers. They underrepresented service workers and separated and divorced persons. In addition, the population mobility creates problems in choosing names from telephone directories. As a result, a number of telephone interviewers have resorted to using digits selected at random and matched to telephone prefixes in the geographic area to be sampled. This technique is designed to correct the problem of sampling households having unlisted numbers.[13]

Mail Surveys   This approach allows the marketing researcher to conduct national studies at a reasonable cost. Whereas personal interviews with a national sample may be prohibitive in cost, the researcher can contact each potential respondent for the price of a postage stamp. Costs can be misleading, however. For example, returned questionnaires may average only 40 to 50 percent depending on the length of the questionnaire and respondent interest. Also, as seen in Figure 4.5, some mail surveys include money to gain the reader's attention, which further increases costs. Unless additional information is obtained from nonrespondents, the results of mail interviews are likely to be biased, since there may be important differences in the characteristics of respondents and nonrespondents. For this reason, follow-up questionnaires are sometimes mailed to respondents, or telephone interviews are used to gather additional information.

Figure 4.5
Using a Monetary System in a Mail-Based Survey

Ted Thomas Research

P.O. Box 7740, Philadelphia, PA 19101

Dear Doctor:

I am writing to you in the hope that you may have attended The American College of Physicians Convention in Atlanta recently. If you did, your cooperation in completing this short questionnaire will aid technical exhibiting companies in making next year's meeting even more meaningful and enjoyable to you.

The attached questionnaire is designed to measure the impact of... and your interest in...activities that took place during the convention. And since the basis of your responses is your memory, please don't refer to any materials that you may still have in your possession. Your "top-of-the-mind" recall is important to us. No need to identify yourself.

Your help on this project is most certainly appreciated. Please use the post-paid envelope included to speed your reply back to me.

Thanks again.

Sincerely,

Robert D. Ritchie
Vice President

P.S. Please accept this new dollar bill as a small token of our appreciation for your help.

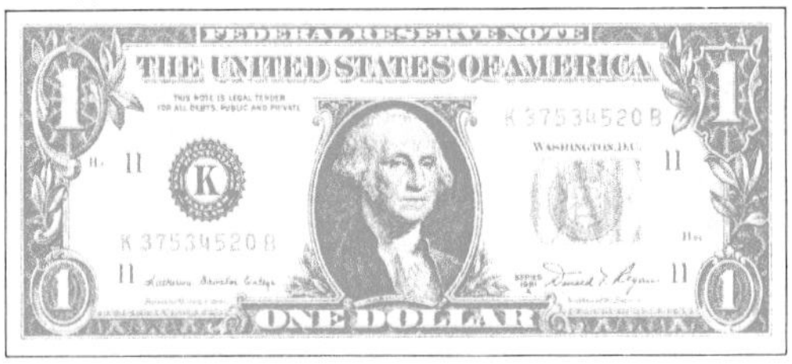

Source: Reprinted with permission of Ted Thomas Associates, Inc.

In 1980, the U.S. Bureau of the Census conducted the largest mail survey in history when it mailed census questionnaires to 80 million households. A number of questions were raised, including the difficulties of developing an accurate population count utilizing mail questionnaires. Another sensitive subject concerned confidentiality of answers. The 85 percent response rate was a pleasant surprise to Census Bureau officials and to researchers throughout the world who rely upon mail surveys to obtain research data.[14]

Personal Interviews This survey method is typically the best means of obtaining detailed information, since the interviewer has the opportunity to establish rapport with each respondent and can explain confusing or vague questions. Although mail questionnaires are carefully worded and often pretested to eliminate potential misunderstandings, misunderstandings can occur anyway. When an employee of the U.S. Department of Agriculture accidentally ran into and killed a cow with his truck, a department official sent the farmer an apology and a form to be filled out. The form included a space for "disposition of the dead cow." The farmer responded, "kind and gentle."[15]

Personal interviews are slow and the most expensive method of collecting data. However, their flexibility coupled with the detailed information that can be collected often offset these limitations. Recently marketing research firms have rented locations in shopping centers where they have greater ac-

Return to the Stop-Action Case

Mid-America Research

With the awareness that home interviews may never again be an effective tool for marketing researchers, executives at Mid-America Research located their field operations in four shopping malls in Chicago and Atlanta. These locations give the company's field interviewers ready access to traditional homemakers and men as well as nontraditional working mothers and single women. According to MAR executive William T. Field, consumers interviewed in shopping malls represent a cross section of the American buying public.

At its location at the Randhurst Mall in Mount Prospect, Illinois, a Chicago suburb, Mid-America Research has a staff of 25 day interviewers and 25 night interviewers who stop shoppers and ask questions about different products and services. Although the interview setting is different from earlier days of marketing research, the basic approach to field research remains the same.

"You have to love people, you have to enjoy interviewing, you have to learn not to take rejection personally," said MAR field interviewer Cathy Tomanek. "No matter how sophisticated the research gets or how big the organization gets, it's still a matter of getting consumers' personal opinions and convincing them their opinions are important."

Source: "Field Research: Alive and Well in the Malls," by Theodore J. Gage. Excerpts reprinted with permission from the May 23, 1983 issue of *Advertising Age*, p. m-27, m-28. Copyright © 1983 by Crain Communications, Inc.

cess to potential buyers of the products in which they are interested. Interviews conducted in shopping centers are typically referred to as mall intercepts. Downtown retail districts and airports are other on-site locations for marketing research.

Focus Group Interview
Information-gathering procedure in marketing research that typically brings eight to twelve individuals together in one location to discuss a given subject.

Focus group interviews have been widely used in recent years as a means of gathering research information. In a focus group interview, eight to twelve individuals are brought together in one location to discuss a subject of interest. Although the moderator typically explains the purpose of the meeting and suggests an opening discussion topic, he or she is interested in stimulating interaction among group members to develop the discussion of numerous points. Focus group sessions, which are often one or two hours long, are usually taped so the moderator can devote full attention to the discussion. The ideas for both Revlon's Charlie fragrance and Virginia Slims cigarettes originated in focus group interviews.

Experiment
Scientific investigation in which a researcher controls or manipulates a test group (or groups) and compares those results with the results of a group (or groups) that did not receive the controls or manipulations.

The Experimental Method   The final and least-used method of collecting marketing information is that of controlled experiments. An experiment is a scientific investigation in which a researcher controls or manipulates a test group or groups and compares the results with that of a control group that did not receive the controls or manipulations. Although such experiments can be conducted in the field or in a laboratory setting, most have been conducted in the field. To date, the most common use of this method by marketers has been in test marketing, a topic that is discussed later in the text.

As Chapter 3 pointed out, marketers often attempt to reduce their risks by *test marketing*, or introducing the product or marketing strategy into an area, then observing its degree of success. Marketers usually pick test areas that are reflective of what they envision as the market for their product. Seattle was used as a test market for Pepsi Free because Pepsi outsells Coca-Cola in the Emerald City, and Seattle and Milwaukee share the lead for the highest per-capita consumption of diet soft drinks.[16]

The major problem with controlled experiments is controlling all variables in a real-life situation. The laboratory scientist can rigidly control temperature and humidity. But how can the marketing manager determine the effect of, say, reducing the retail price through refundable coupons when the competition simultaneously issues such coupons? Experimentation will become more common as firms develop sophisticated competitive models for computer analysis. Simulation of market activities promises to be one of the great new developments in marketing.

Sampling Techniques[17]

Sampling is one of the most important aspects of marketing research because it involves the selection of respondents upon which conclusions will be based. The total group that the researcher wants to study is called the population (or universe). For a political campaign, the population would be all eligible voters. For a new cosmetic line, it might be all women in a certain age bracket.

Information is rarely gathered from the total population during a survey. If all sources are contacted, the results are known as a census. Unless the total population is small, the costs will be so great that only the federal government will be able to afford them (and it uses this method only once every ten years). Instead, researchers select a representative group called a sample. Samples can be classified as either probability samples or nonprobability samples.

A probability sample is a sample in which every member of the population has an equal chance of being selected. Examples of probability samples include a simple random sample, a stratified sample, and a cluster sample.

The basic type of probability sample is the simple random sample, where every item in the relevant universe has an equal opportunity of being selected. The military draft lottery of more than a decade ago is an example. Each day of the year—and those males born on that day—had an equal opportunity of being selected, thus establishing a conscription list. A stratified sample is a probability sample constructed so that randomly selected subsamples of different groups are represented in the total sample. It differs from quota sampling (discussed in the section that follows) because the subsamples are drawn randomly. Stratified samples are an efficient sample methodology in uses like opinion polls, where various groups hold divergent viewpoints. A cluster sample is a situation where areas or clusters are selected, then all or a sample within each become respondents. This probability sample is very cost-efficient and may be the best option where the population cannot be listed or enumerated. A good example would be a market researcher who identified various U.S. cities and then randomly selected supermarkets within those cities to study.

By contrast, a nonprobability sample is arbitrary, and standard statistical tests cannot be applied. Examples of nonprobability samples are the convenience sample and the quota sample. A convenience sample is a nonprobability sample based on the selection of readily available respondents. Broadcasting's "on-the-street" interviews are a good example. Marketing researchers sometimes use it in exploratory research, but not in definitive stud-

Population (or Universe)
Total group that the researcher wants to study.

Census
Collection of data from all possible sources in a population or universe.

Probability Sample
Sample in which every member of the population has an equal chance of being selected.

Simple Random Sample
Basic type of probability sample in which every item in the relevant universe has an equal opportunity of being selected.

Stratified Sample
Probability sample that is constructed so that randomly selected subsamples of different groups are represented in the total sample.

Cluster Sample
Sampling technique in which geographic areas or clusters are selected, then all or a sample within them become respondents.

Nonprobability Sample
Arbitrary sample in which most standard statistical tests cannot be applied to the collected data.

Convenience Sample
Nonprobability sample based on the selection of readily available respondents.

Quota Sample
Nonprobability sample that is divided
so that different segments or groups
are represented in the total sample.

ies. A quota sample is a nonprobability sample that is divided so that different segments or groups are represented in the total sample. An example would be a survey of auto import owners that included 33 Nissan owners, 31 Toyota owners, 7 BMW owners, and so on.

Interpretation and Presentation

A number of marketing research books contain information on how to cope with the many problems involved in surveying the public. Among these problems are designing the questionnaires; selecting, training, and controlling the field interviewers; editing, coding, tabulating, and interpreting the data; presenting the results; and following up on the survey.

It is imperative that marketing researchers and research users cooperate at every stage in the research design. Too many studies go unused because marketing management believes the results are too restricted due to lengthy discussions of research limitations or unfamiliar terminology.

Occasional misunderstandings between marketing researchers and the manager-user may lead to friction between the parties and failure to utilize the research findings effectively. Figure 4.6 lists several complaints that each party may express about the other. These complaints reflect a lack of understanding of the needs and capabilities of both parties. Such complaints can often be settled by involving both managers and researchers in specifying needed information, developing research designs, and evaluating the research findings. The research report should include recommendations, and whenever

Figure 4.6

Common Complaints between Managers and Marketing Researchers

Management Complaints about Marketing Researchers	Marketing Researcher Complaints about Management
Research is not problem-oriented. It tends to provide a plethora of facts, not actionable results or direction.	Management doesn't include research in discussions of basic fundamental problems. Management tends to ask only for specific information about parts of problems.
Researchers are too involved with techniques. They tend to do research for research's sake, and they appear to be reluctant to get involved in management "problems."	Management pays no more than lip service to research and doesn't really understand or appreciate its value. Research isn't given enough corporate status.
Research is slow, vague, and of questionable validity. It depends too much on clinical evidence.	Management has a propensity to jump the gun — not allowing enough time for research. Management draws preliminary conclusions based on early or incomplete results.
Researchers can't communicate; they don't understand, and they don't talk the language of management. In many cases, researchers are inexperienced and not well rounded.	Management relies more on intuition and judgment than on research. Research is used as a crutch, not a tool. Management tends to "typecast" the marketing researcher.

Source: Reprinted by permission from "Communication Gap Hinders Proper Use of Market Research," *Marketing Insights*
(February 7, 1968), p. 7. Copyright 1968 by Crain Communications, Inc.

possible, an oral report should explain, expand upon, or clarify the written summary. These efforts also increase the likelihood of management's utilizing the research findings.

Marketing Information Systems

Many marketing managers discover that their information problems result from an overabundance—not a paucity—of marketing data. Their sophisticated computer facilities may provide them with daily printouts about sales in 30 market areas, about 100 different products, and about 6,400 customers. Managers sometimes solve the problem of too much information of the wrong kind in the wrong form by sliding the printouts to the edge of the desk, where they quietly fall into the wastebasket. Data and information are not synonymous terms. Data refers to statistics, opinions, facts, or predictions categorized on some basis for storage and retrieval. Information is data relevant to the marketing manager in making decisions.

Obtaining relevant information appears simple enough. One can establish a systematic approach to information management by installing a planned marketing information system (MIS) The ideal marketing information system should be a designed set of procedures and methods for generating an orderly flow of pertinent information for use in making decisions, providing management with the current and future states of the market, and indicating market responses to company and competitor actions.[18] The marketing information system is a subset of the firm's overall management information system (also often called an MIS) that deals specifically with marketing information.

A properly constructed MIS can serve as the nerve center for the company, providing instantaneous information suitable for each level of management. It can monitor the marketplace continuously so that management can adjust actions as conditions change.

The role of marketing information in a firm's marketing system can be illustrated with the analogy of how an automatic heating system works. Once the objective of a particular temperature setting (say 68 degrees Fahrenheit) has been established, information about the actual temperature is collected and compared with the objective, and a decision based on this comparison is made. If the temperature drops below the established figure, the decision is to activate the furnace until the temperature reaches the established level. If the temperature is too high, the decision is to turn off the furnace.

Deviation from the firm's goals of profitability, improved return on investment, or greater market share may necessitate changes in price structures, promotional expenditures, package design, or other marketing alternatives. The firm's MIS should be capable of revealing such deviations and of suggesting changes that will result in attaining the established goals. Creating an effective MIS, however, is more easily said than done. Several firms' attempts have succeeded only in further complicating their data-retrieval systems.

Data
Statistics, opinions, facts, or predictions categorized on some basis for storage and retrieval.

Information
Data relevant to the marketing manager in making decisions.

Marketing Information System (MIS)
Set of procedures and methods designed to generate an orderly flow of pertinent information for use in making decisions, providing management with the current and future states of the market, and indicating market responses to company and competitor actions.

Marketing Research and the Marketing Information System

Many marketing executives think their organizations are too small to make use of a marketing information system. Others contend that their marketing research departments provide adequate research data for decision making. Such contentions often result from a misconception of the services and func-

Figure 4.7

Information Components of the Firm's Marketing Information System

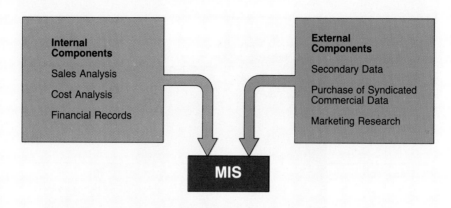

By focusing daily on the marketplace, the MIS provides a continuous systematic and comprehensive study of areas that indicate deviations from established goals. The up-to-the-minute information allows problems to be corrected before they adversely affect operations.

tions performed by the marketing research department. Marketing research has already been described as typically focusing on a specific problem or project; its investigations have a definite beginning, middle, and end.

Marketing information systems, on the other hand, are much wider in scope, involving the continual collection and analysis of marketing information. Figure 4.7 indicates the various information inputs—including marketing research studies—that serve as components of a firm's MIS.

Robert J. Williams, creator of the first marketing information system, explained the difference:

The difference between marketing research and marketing intelligence is like the difference between a flash bulb and a candle. Let's say you are dancing in the dark. Every 90 seconds you're allowed to set off a flash bulb. You can use those brief intervals of intense light to chart a course, but remember everybody is moving, too. Hopefully, they'll accommodate themselves roughly to your predictions. You may get bumped and you may stumble every so often, but you can dance along.

On the other hand, you can light a candle. It doesn't yield as much light, but it's a steady light. You are continually aware of the movements of other bodies. You can adjust your own course to the courses of the others. The intelligence system is a kind of light. It's no great flash on the immediate state of things, but it provides continuous light as situations shift and change.[19]

By focusing daily on the marketplace, the MIS provides a continuous systematic and comprehensive study of areas that indicate deviations from established goals. The up-to-the-minute information allows problems to be corrected before they adversely affect operations.

Current Status of Marketing Information Systems

Marketing information systems have progressed a long way from the days when they were responsible primarily for clerical activities (and usually at an increased cost over the old method). Today managers have available special computer programs, remote access consoles, better data banks, direct communication with the computer, and assignment of authority to the computer for

Figure 4.8
Current and Future Allocation of MIS Resources

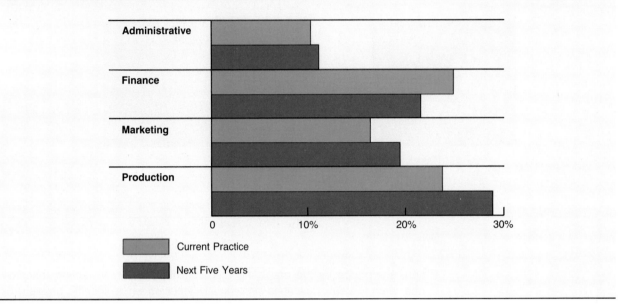

Current Practice

Next Five Years

Source: C. Richard Roberts and Louis E. Boone, "MIS Development in American Industry: The Apex,"
Journal of Business Strategy (Spring 1983). Reprinted by permission of the authors.

review and referral. In some instances, the computer simulates market conditions and makes decisions based on the results of the model. But how does the marketer's information system relate to similar systems for decision makers in other functional areas?

As noted earlier, marketing information systems are major components of the firm's overall management information system—the information base for decision making in all functional areas. A recent survey of the 500 largest firms in the United States focused on the allocation of overall management information resources to each of the functional areas. A total of 202 companies responded by indicating the approximate percentage of their total information system resources—including hardware, software, facilities, and personnel—allocated to four organizational functions: administrative, finance, marketing, and production. Figure 4.8 shows their responses and their predictions of relative allocations for the next five years.

Although production and finance currently receive most of the management information system's resources, additional resources are expected to be devoted to marketing during the next five years.

Successful Marketing Information Systems

Although only a few large companies currently have sophisticated computer-based marketing information systems, considerable attention is focused on their contributions. By the end of the decade, most medium-size companies will have established their own marketing information systems. General Mills is a good example of a firm with a successful MIS in operation.

The General Mills computer supplies each zone, regional, and district manager with a daily teletype report on (1) the previous day's orders by brand and (2) current projections of monthly sales compared with the monthly total projected the week before. Each of the 1,700 products is analyzed in terms of current profitability and projected annual profitability as compared with target projections made at the beginning of the year. Problem products that require management attention are also listed in the daily report. A similar report looks for problem areas in each region and breaks down each problem by cause.[20]

Developing an MIS

Construction of a marketing information system requires the full support of top management. Management not only must be truly enthusiastic about the potential of the system, but also must believe that it is top management's place to oversee its development. Too often technical staff are left to build the system without that important management contribution. The next step involves a review and appraisal of the entire marketing organization and the policies that direct it. The marketing managers' responsibilities must be clearly defined. If the system is to measure their performances against company plans, then each person's area of accountability must be specified.

Once the organization is readied for development of the system, its level of sophistication must be determined. Before this can be done, the company's needs and costs of meeting those needs must be carefully considered. The ability of managers to develop and effectively use a sophisticated system must also be considered. Managers must be able to state their specific information needs. A questionnaire, such as the one illustrated in Table 4.7, can be used to pinpoint specific information requirements and devise a reporting system that notes exceptions.

As marketing research becomes increasingly scientific and is combined by a growing number of organizations into fully functional information systems, decision makers benefit by making informed decisions about problems and opportunities. Sophisticated computer simulations make it possible to consider alternative courses of action by posing a number of "what if" situations. Computer-based marketing information systems will clearly play a major role in future marketing research activities.

Table 4.7
Sample Questionnaire for Determining Marketing Information Needs

1. What types of decisions are you regularly called upon to make?	6. What information would you like to receive daily? weekly? monthly? yearly?
2. What types of information do you need to make the decision?	7. What magazines and trade journals would you like to receive regularly?
3. What types of information do you regularly get?	8. What types of data analysis programs would you like to receive?
4. What types of special studies do you periodically request?	
5. What types of information would you like to get but are not currently receiving?	9. What are four improvements you would like to see made in the present marketing information system?

Source: Philip Kotler, "A Design for the Firm's Marketing Nerve Center," *Business Horizons* (Fall 1966), p. 70.
Copyright © 1966 by the Foundation for the School of Business at Indiana University. Reprinted by permission.

Summary

Information is vital for marketing planning and decision making. No firm can operate without detailed information on its market. Information may take several forms: one-time marketing research studies, secondary data, internal data, and the output of a marketing information system.

Marketing research, an important source of information, deals with studies that collect and analyze data relevant to marketing decisions. It involves the specific delineation of problems, research design, collection of secondary and primary data, interpretation of research findings, and presentation of results for management action.

Marketing research started when Charles C. Parlin, an advertising space sales representative for the *Saturday Evening Post*, counted empty soup cans in Philadelphia's trash in an effort to convince the Campbell Soup Company to advertise in the magazine. Today, the most common marketing research activities are determining market potential, market share analysis, determination of market characteristics, sales analysis, and competitive product studies. Annual expenditures for marketing research now exceed $1 billion, and most large companies have internal market research departments. However, outside suppliers still remain vital to the research function. Some of these outside research suppliers perform the complete research task, while others specialize in limited areas or provide other data services.

The marketing research process can be divided into six specific steps: (1) defining the problem; (2) exploratory research; (3) formulating hypotheses; (4) research design; (5) collecting data; and (6) interpretation and presentation. A clearly defined problem allows the researcher to obtain the relevant decision-oriented information. Exploratory research refers to information gained both outside and inside the firm. Hypotheses—tentative explanations of some specific event—allow the researcher to set out a specific research design, the series of decisions that, taken together, comprise a master plan or model for the conduct of the investigation. The data collection phase of the marketing research process can involve either or both primary data (original data) and secondary data (previously published data). Primary data can be collected by the firm's own researchers or by independent marketing research companies. Three alternative methods of primary data collection can be used: observation, survey, or experimental. After the data is collected, it is important that researchers interpret and present it in a way that is meaningful to management.

An increasing number of firms have installed planned marketing information systems. Properly designed, the MIS will generate an orderly flow of decision-oriented information as the marketing executive needs it. The number of firms with planned marketing information systems will grow in the years ahead as more managers recognize their contribution in dealing with the information explosion.

Photo Source: Courtesy of Mid-America Research.

Solving the Stop-Action Case

Mid-America Research

On a typical day, MAR interviewers stop dozens of potential subjects to find those who are willing to cooperate in a marketing research study. Willing participants are taken to MAR's mall offices where they fill out detailed questionnaires on such varied products as toothpaste, coffee, and breakfast cereal. Participants may be confronted with questions concerning 50 different attributes of hair spray—Is it too sticky? Is the container too large or too small? Does it have an appealing odor?—or they may be given a coffee taste test involving a series of different samples as well as water and crackers to clear their palates between sips.

To a great extent, the success of this research is linked to the competence of the interviewers, most of whom are women. Although they must follow instructions to the letter, interviewers must also be able to convince reluctant consumers to participate and to reassure those who appear to be ill-at-ease. Interviewing skills are continually honed in interview training sessions.

So successful is this mall-based research that companies vie with one another to capture mall leases. "No one infringes on another company's territory," said MAR executive William Field. "Randhurst is our mall, and no other company can come in and do research here. If the client of another research firm wants interviews (here), they contract with us or their research company subcontracts."

Mid-America Research also conducts focus group interviews at its various mall locations. Each focus group participant is recruited according to the specific needs of MAR's corporate clients. Groups made up of working men and women meet during evening hours, while those made up of nonworking women are arranged during the day. Although working women and men are also considered major purchasing forces, their inclusion in focus groups lags behind that of nonworking women.

Source: "Field Research: Alive and Well in the Malls," by Theodore J. Gage. Excerpts reprinted with permission from the May 23, 1983, issue of *Advertising Age*, p. m-27, m-28. Copyright © 1983 by Crain Communications, Inc.

Questions for Discussion

1. It seems that political predictions often miss their mark. Consider the prediction error made by the *Literary Digest* in the Alf Landon–Franklin D. Roosevelt presidential campaign of 1936; the Truman–Dewey presidential race in 1948; and Reagan's landslide victory over Carter in 1980. What implications do these results have for marketing researchers?

2. Outline the development and current status of the marketing research function.

3. Outline the major types of market, product, and sales research.

4. List and explain the various steps in the marketing research process.

5. You have been asked to determine the effect on Gillette of Schick's introduction of a revolutionary new blade that is guaranteed to give a hundred nick-free shaves. Outline your approach to the study.

6. Distinguish between primary and secondary data.

7. What advantages does the use of secondary data offer the marketing researcher? What potential limitations exist in using such data?

8. Compare and contrast sales analysis and market cost analysis.

9.   Look up the most recent "Survey of Buying Power" in *Sales and Marketing Management* magazine. What marketing implications can be drawn about the data describing your community or one nearby?

10.   Collect from secondary sources the following information:
      a.   Retail sales in Springfield, Ohio, for last year
      b.   Number of persons over sixty-five in Medford, Oregon
      c.   Earnings per share for Ford last year
      d.   Bituminous coal production in the United States in a recent year
      e.   Consumer price index for last August
      f.   Number of households earning more than $25,000 in Miami, Florida

11.   Distinguish among surveys, experiments, and observational methods of data collection.

12.   Explain the differences between probability and nonprobability samples and identify the various types of each.

13.   Identify and give an example of each of the three methods of gathering survey data. Under what circumstances should each be used?

14.   What are the major problems in using telephone interviews?

15.   Under what circumstances would probability sampling techniques be used?

16.   Suggest several instances in which a cluster sample rather than a simple random sample might be used in gathering primary data.

17.   Under what circumstances should a firm use an outside marketing research firm to conduct research studies?

18.   Frank Antonelli, marketing vice-president of the Digital Time Company, refuses to involve himself with the activities of his marketing research staff. He explains that he has hired competent professionals for the research department, and he does not plan to meddle in their operation. Critically evaluate Antonelli's position.

19.   Distinguish between marketing research and marketing information systems.

20.   What is the current status of marketing information systems?

Case: Hill Top Research

It's generally considered less than polite to raise an arm just so someone else can take a whiff, but it's perfectly acceptable in the name of science.

"No, there's no modesty involved," said Ransom F. Wall, who took part in an armpit test to check the effectiveness of a new deodorant soap.

Like the other male subjects, Wall shucked his shirt, lifted an elbow and offered his armpit to the nose of a product tester at Hill Top Research, an independent firm in suburban Miamiville, Ohio.

"You know you're on a test and, after all, we're all supposed to be adults," Wall said.

Female subjects donned a bib for the test.

Maryellen Mailey considers Wall lucky. She was rejected for the test because she didn't smell bad enough.

"I was really disappointed. I'd been looking forward to it," said Mailey, who has, for three decades, lathered, sweated, sniffed, and chewed for administrators of previous tests at Hill Top.

Source: Reprinted from "This Job Is the Pits, But Some Body Has To Do It," Bellevue (Wash.), *Journal-American* (April 4, 1984), p. C 6. Used by permission of the Associated Press.

This Is How They Test Underarm Deodorant at
Hill Top Research in Miamiville, Ohio.

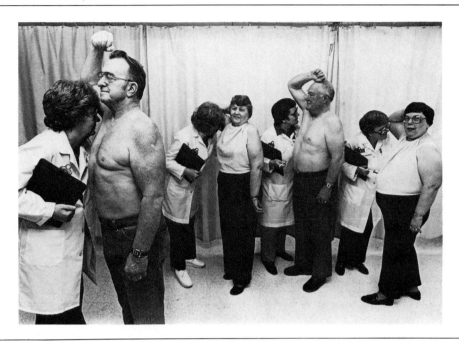

Photo Source: AP/Wide World Photos, Inc.

"Yeah," said her husband, Bruce, who was accepted for the test. "That's because she'd already planned how she was going to spend her bonus."

Hill Top tests American-made products ranging from deodorants to mouthwash to toilet paper to cosmetics and drugs.

The subjects are not told the names of the products.

"I feel we're helping science," said Bea Weiderhold. "I think it's a great thing. You feel like you're doing your bit for someone else."

Questions

1. How could this type of product research be used by Hill Top's clients?

2. This test is concerned with which steps in the marketing research process?

3. What other information might Hill Top's client want to know about the new deodorant soap? Discuss.

Computer Applications

Sales analysis is defined in this chapter as the in-depth evaluation of a firm's sales. This information is obtained from the organization's sales reports, customer purchase orders, invoices, and other accounting data. The sales analysis concept is explained in detail on pages 96–97. The following problems deal with sales analysis.

Directions: Use menu item 4 titled "Sales Analysis" to solve each of the following problems.

Problem 1 A Fresno, California-based corporation organizes its sales force into three sales regions: A, B, and C. The average salaries in these regions are $35,000; $40,000; and $45,000, respectively. Region A sales personnel average $700,000 in sales; Region B sales representatives, $640,000; and Region C personnel, $945,000. Selling expenses average $10,000 in all regions. Calculate the cost/sales ratios for the three regions.

Problem 2 The sales force for Emmons Associated Industries, of Greenville, South Carolina, is divided into four sales zones. Average sales for representatives in the various zones are as follows: A—$410,000; B—$394,000; C—$427,000; and D—$433,000. The average sales compensation in the four zones are: A—$26,000; B—$29,000; C—$31,000; and D—$30,500. Average selling costs are relatively low, with zone D being the most expensive at $6,340. Other average selling costs figures are: A—$6,100; B—$5,950; and C—$5,825. Determine the cost/sales ratios for each of Emmons' four sales zones.

Problem 3 Cynthia Dobler, a marketing consultant, has been hired to analyze the sales of a Bozeman, Montana firm. Management is particularly concerned with Division 4's average selling expense of $26,400. The Bozeman firm operates five divisions with the following average sales salaries:

Division 1 $28,100
Division 2   32,050
Division 3   26,750
Division 4   29,000
Division 5   30,125

Average selling expenses for personnel in the divisions are:

Division 1 $ 6,760
Division 2   6,950
Division 3   8,925
Division 4   26,400
Division 5   13,500

The average sales per representative in these divisions are:

Division 1 $384,000
Division 2   446,000
Division 3   492,000
Division 4   576,000
Division 5   482,000

What should Dobler tell management about the firm's cost/sales ratios?

Problem 4 The St. Louis Division of a Springfield, Missouri, firm employs five sales representatives. All were assigned annual sales quotas of $425,000. The division's manager, Duane Washington, is now preparing an analysis of how his people did in 1986. The actual sales results were as follows:

1. Zimmerman $416,000
2. Stack   458,000
3. Furberbush   381,000
4. Bonnell   411,000
5. Matson   444,000

a. Calculate the performance to quota ratio for each of the sales representatives in the St. Louis Division.
b. What is the overall performance to quota ratio for the St. Louis Division?

Problem 5 The Upper New England Division of a Lawrence, Massachusetts company has a seven-person sales force to cover Vermont, New Hampshire, and Maine. For 1986, the following quotas were assigned according to the sales potential of the territory:

Territory 1 $364,000
Territory 2   385,000
Territory 3   475,000
Territory 4   428,000
Territory 5   390,000
Territory 6   410,000
Territory 7   435,000

At the close of business on December 31, 1986, the following annual sales volumes were reported:

Territory 1 $390,000
Territory 2   385,000
Territory 3   435,000
Territory 4   410,000
Territory 5   445,000
Territory 6   415,000
Territory 7   428,000

a. Calculate the performance to quota ratios for each of the seven territories.
b. What is the overall performance to quota ratio for the Upper New England Division?

PART THREE

Market Segmentation and Buyer Behavior

5 Market Segmentation

Key Terms

market
consumer goods
industrial goods
market segmentation
geographic segmentation
Consolidated Metropolitan
  Statistical Area (CMSA)
Primary Metropolitan
  Statistical Area (PMSA)
Metropolitan Statistical Area
  (MSA)
demographic segmentation
family life cycle
Engel's laws
life-style
psychographic
  segmentation
AIO statements
benefit segmentation
product segmentation
end-use application
  segmentation
market target
  decision analysis

Learning Goals

1. To explain what is meant by a market
2. To outline the role of market segmentation in the development of a marketing strategy
3. To discuss the four bases for segmenting consumer markets
4. To describe the three bases for segmenting industrial markets
5. To explain how market target decision analysis can be used in segmenting markets

Stop-Action Case

The Ford Thunderbird

Photo Source: Courtesy of Ford Division, Ford Motor Company.

There was a time in the not-too-distant past when owning a Ford Thunderbird was the dream of millions of American drivers. The sporty two- and four-seater T-Birds of the 1950s were so valuable that many were passed on lovingly from buyer to buyer. These classic T-Birds became collectors' items and increased in value as time went on.

The allure of the Thunderbird faded during the 1970s when the Ford Motor Company changed the car's basic design. Instead of a sleek, European-style sports car, Ford executives believed the country was ready for a new T-Bird image: boxy, less luxurious, and significantly larger. Disappointing sales proved them wrong. T-Bird devotees abandoned the new model in droves, many turning instead to racy Japanese and European imports. Jack Fales, Jr., president of Advertising Design Associates of Enfield, Connecticut, expressed the feelings of many former Thunderbird owners: "I had three T-Birds—the '65, the '67 and the '69—then they changed the styling, and I didn't like it at all anymore. It looked bigger, less European, and they cheapened the insides."

These design changes coincided with a marketing shift. While the earlier T-Birds were marketed as personal luxury cars, the T-Birds of the early 1970s were aimed at the mass market. When Ford marketers decided to return to the personal, luxury-car approach in 1975, upper-income consumers were not receptive. They had already been turned off by the T-Bird design.

Realizing its design error, Ford introduced a totally redesigned Thunderbird in 1983. Touted by Ford as the "best Thunderbird ever built, with quality, fit, and finish equal to the claim," the new car received glowing critical acclaim: "To say that this car is the best new Thunderbird in years is a dramatic understatement," said *Road & Track*. "The new Coupe is a most serious effort at returning to the concept of a 'personal car,' an enthusiast's performance GT," said *Autoweek*. "We trust the public will know a good thing when it sees one," said *Car and Driver*.

But Ford marketing executives knew that glowing reviews like these were no guarantee of sales success—especially since many potential buyers thought of the new Thunderbird in terms of its ill-fated predecessor. To change the car's image, Ford developed a plan to target the new T-Bird to young, upwardly mobile professionals and executives. With its new, sophisticated look and $10,000-plus price tag, the car seemed a natural for these up-scale consumers. Finding these executives and professionals and convincing them to consider the new Thunderbird were the challenges Ford marketers faced.

Assignment: Use the materials in Chapter 5 to recommend a way for Ford to find and attract up-scale consumers to the new Thunderbird.

Sources: Meg Cox, "Ford Pushing Thunderbird with VIP Plan," *The Wall Street Journal* (October 17, 1981), p. 33; and Ford Motor Company's promotional brochure, *1983 Thunderbird, Pure Form, Pure Function*.

Chapter Overview

Before a marketing mix strategy can be implemented, the marketer must first identify, evaluate, and select a market target. The starting point is to understand what is meant by a market.

A market is people and institutions, but they alone do not make a market. A real estate salesperson would be unimpressed by news that 50 percent of a marketing class raised their hands in response to the question: Who wants to buy a condominium in Fort Lauderdale? More pertinent would be the answer to this question: How many of them have $20,000 for the downpayment and can qualify for the mortgage loan? A market requires not only people or institutions and the willingness to buy, but also purchasing power and authority to buy.

Market
Group of people who possess purchasing power and the authority and willingness to purchase.

A successful salesperson quickly learns how to pinpoint which individual in an organization or household has the authority to make particular purchasing decisions. Without this knowledge, too much time can be spent convincing the wror g person that the product or service should be bought.

Types of Markets

Products are often classified as either consumer goods or industrial goods. Consumer goods are products purchased by the ultimate consumer for personal use. Industrial goods are products purchased for use either directly or indirectly in the production of other goods or services for resale. A similar dichotomy can also be used for services. Most products purchased by individual consumers—books, records, and clothes, for example—are consumer goods. Rubber and raw cotton, however, are generally purchased by manufacturers and are therefore classified as industrial goods. Rubber is used in many products by a producer such as Goodyear Tire & Rubber Company; a manufacturer such as Burlington Industries converts raw cotton into cloth.

Consumer Goods
Products purchased by the ultimate consumer for personal use.

Industrial Goods
Products purchased for use either directly or indirectly in the production of other goods for resale.

Sometimes the same product is destined for different uses. The spark plugs purchased for the family car constitute a consumer good, but spark plugs purchased by American Motors for use on its American Eagle four-wheel-drive line is an industrial good, since it becomes part of another good destined for resale. (Some marketers use the term commercial goods to refer to industrial goods not directly used in producing other goods.) The key to proper classification of goods is to determine the purchaser and the reasons for the purchase.

The Role of Market Segmentation

The world is too large and filled with too many diverse people and firms for any single marketing mix to satisfy everyone. Unless the product or service is an item such as an unbranded, descriptive-label detergent aimed at the mass market, an attempt to satisfy everyone may doom the marketer to failure. Even a seemingly functional product like toothpaste is aimed at specific market segments. Crest focused on tooth-decay prevention; Stripe was developed for children; Close-Up hints at enhanced sex appeal; and Aim promises both protection and a taste children like.

The auto manufacturer who decides to produce and market a single model to satisfy everyone will encounter seemingly endless decisions about such variables as the number of doors, type of transmission, color, styling, and engine size. In its attempt to satisfy everyone, the firm may be forced to

Market Segmentation
Process of dividing the total market into several relatively homogeneous groups with similar product or service interests, based upon such factors as demographic or psychographic characteristics, geographic locations, or perceived product benefits.

compromise in each of these areas and, as a result, may discover that it does not satisfy anyone very well. Other firms that appeal to particular segments—the youth market, the high-fuel-economy market, the larger-family market, and so on—may capture most of the total market by satisfying the specific needs of these smaller market segments. This process of dividing the total market into several relatively homogeneous groups is called market segmentation Marketing mixes are then adjusted to meet the needs of specified market segments. Market segmentation can be used by both profit-oriented and nonprofit organizations.

Segmenting Consumer Markets

Market segmentation results from a determination of factors that distinguish a certain group of consumers from the overall market. These characteristics—such as age, sex, geographic location, income and expenditure patterns, and population size and mobility, among others—are vital factors in the success of the overall marketing strategy. Toy manufacturers such as Ideal, Hasbro, Mattel, and Kenner study not only birthrate trends, but also shifts in income and expenditure patterns. Colleges and universities are affected by such factors as the number of high-school graduates, changing attitudes toward the value of college educations, and increasing enrollment of older adults. Figure 5.1 identifies four commonly used bases for segmenting consumer markets.

Geographic segmentation, the dividing of an overall market into homogeneous groups on the basis of population location, has been used for hundreds of years. The second basis for segmenting markets is *demographic segmentation*—dividing an overall market into homogeneous groups based

Figure 5.1
Segmentation Bases for Consumer Markets

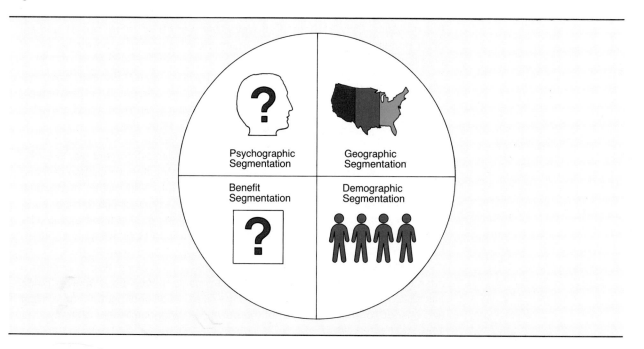

Psychographic Segmentation

Geographic Segmentation

Benefit Segmentation

Demographic Segmentation

upon characteristics such as age, sex, and income level. Demographic segmentation is the most commonly used method of subdividing total markets.

The third and fourth bases represent relatively recent developments in market segmentation. *Psychographic segmentation* utilizes behavioral profiles developed from analyses of the activities, opinions, interests, and life-styles of consumers in identifying market segments. The final basis, *benefit segmentation*, focuses on benefits the consumer expects to derive from a product or service. These segmentation bases can be important to marketing strategies provided they are significantly related to differences in buying behavior.

Geographic Segmentation

Geographic Segmentation
Dividing a population into homogeneous groups on the basis of location.

A logical starting point in market segmentation is the examination of population characteristics. It is not surprising, therefore, that one of the earliest bases for segmentation was geographic segmentation

Although the 1986 U.S. population is about 249 million, it is not distributed evenly. Instead, it is concentrated in states with major metropolitan areas.

States not only vary in population density, but also in pronounced population shifts. Recent data reveal that the populations of Alaska, Nevada, Utah, Texas, Florida, Wyoming, Oklahoma, and Arizona each grew by at least 9 percent between 1980 and 1983, while the populations of the District of Columbia, Michigan, Ohio, Iowa, and Indiana actually declined.[1] Census data also indicate three major population shifts: (1) to the Sunbelt states of the Southeast and Southwest; (2) from interior states to seacoast states; and (3) to the West.

Population shifts are expected to continue. Overall, the U.S. population is expected to grow 18.1 percent from the 1980 census to the year 2000. Three states are expected to lead this growth: Nevada, with a 140.1 percent increase; Wyoming, with a 112.9 percent increase; and Arizona, with a 105.4 percent increase.[2]

Population shifts among states become even more apparent with this fact: 40 percent of the U.S. population were not born in the states where they now reside. In 1900, the figure was 20 percent. The states varied widely on this measure. Only 21 percent of Nevadans were born there, but 81 percent of all Pennsylvanians are natives. Again, the data confirms the movement of people to the South and West.

Population shifts have also occurred within states. Farmers have migrated steadily to urban areas since 1800, and the percentage of farm dwellers has dropped below 4 percent. The 50 largest metropolitan areas are listed in Table 5.1 account for one-half of the total U.S. population.

The United States traditionally has been a mobile society. Less than 17 percent of all Americans move each year, down from 20 percent two decades ago. This slowdown is attributed to three factors: a higher percentage of home ownership, increased housing prices, and higher interest rates on mortgages. The number of in-county moves accounts for virtually all of this decline. Intercity moves have consistently remained at a higher rate.[3] If this trend continues, it will have a decided impact on marketers' use of geographic segmentation.

The move from urban to suburban areas after World War II created a need to redefine the urban marketplace. Primarily middle-class families made this shift. The move radically changed the cities' traditional patterns of retailing and has led to a disintegration of the downtown shopping areas of many U.S.

The 50 Largest Metropolitan Areas

		1982 Population				1982 Population
1.	New York	17,589,000	26.	Portland, Ore.	1,332,000
2.	Los Angeles	11,930,000	27.	New Orleans	1,300,000
3.	Chicago	7,974,000	28.	Columbus, Ohio	1,267,000
4.	Philadelphia	5,713,000	29.	Buffalo	1,218,000
5.	San Francisco	5,515,000	30.	Norfolk	1,201,000
6.	Detroit	4,630,000	31.	Indianapolis	1,182,000
7.	Boston	3,988,000	32.	Sacramento	1,165,000
8.	Houston	3,458,000	33.	San Antonio	1,135,000
9.	Washington	3,339,000	34.	Providence	1,089,000
10.	Dallas	3,143,000	35.	Hartford	1,021,000
11.	Cleveland	2,808,000	36.	Charlotte	1,003,000
12.	Miami	2,790,000	37.	Rochester, N.Y.	979,000
13.	Pittsburgh	2,403,000	38.	Salt Lake City	970,000
14.	St. Louis	2,377,000	39.	Louisville	955,000
15.	Atlanta	2,243,000	40.	Dayton	937,000
16.	Baltimore	2,218,000	41.	Memphis	924,000
17.	Minneapolis	2,194,000	42.	Oklahoma City	922,000
18.	Seattle	2,178,000	43.	Birmingham	890,000
19.	San Diego	1,962,000	44.	Greensboro, N.C.	869,000
20.	Tampa	1,721,000	45.	Nashville	865,000
21.	Denver	1,721,000	46.	Albany, N.Y.	833,000
22.	Cincinnati	1,672,000	47.	Honolulu	782,000
23.	Phoenix	1,609,000	48.	Richmond, Va.	778,000
24.	Milwaukee	1,572,000	49.	Orlando	762,000
25.	Kansas City	1,454,000	50.	Jacksonville	756,000

Source: Reprinted from *U.S. News & World Report*
(May 14, 1984), p. 16. Copyright 1984 U.S. News & World Report, Inc.

cities. It has rendered traditional city boundaries almost meaningless for marketing purposes. In an effort to correct this situation, the government now classifies urban data using three categories:

Consolidated Metropolitan Statistical Area (CMSA)
Major population concentration, including the 25 or so urban giants like New York, Chicago, and Los Angeles.

- A Consolidated Metropolitan Statistical Area (CMSA) includes the 25 or so urban giants like New York, Chicago, and Los Angeles. It must include two or more Primary Metropolitan Statistical Areas.

Primary Metropolitan Statistical Area (PMSA)
Major urban area within a CMSA; Long Island's Nassau and Suffolk counties are PMSAs within the larger New York CMSA.

- A Primary Metropolitan Statistical Area (PMSA) is a major urban area within a CMSA—an urbanized county or counties with social and economic ties to nearby areas. PMSAs are identified within areas of one million plus populations. Long Island's Nassau and Suffolk counties would be part of the New York CMSA. Aurora–Elgin would be part of the Chicago CMSA. And Oxnard–Ventura would be part of the Los Angeles CMSA.

Metropolitan Statistical Area (MSA)
Large, free-standing urban area such as Sheboygan, Wisconsin, and Syracuse, New York for which detailed marketing-related data is collected by the U.S. Census Bureau.

- A Metropolitan Statistical Area (MSA) is a freestanding urban area with an urban center population of 50,000 and a total MSA population of 100,000 or more. MSAs exhibit social and economic homogeneity. They are usually bordered by nonurbanized counties. Moorhead, Minnesota; Peoria, Illinois; and Sheboygan, Wisconsin are examples.[4]

Figure 5.2
The Location of PMSAs and MSAs within the Chicago CMSA

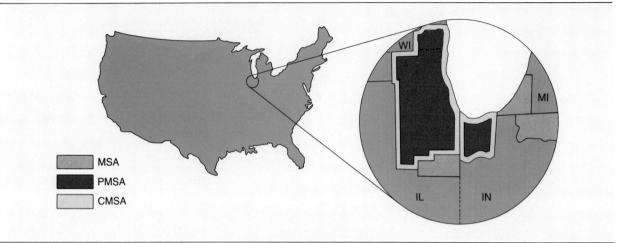

Source: "Definitions of Consolidated Metropolitan Statistical Areas, Primary Metropolitan Statistical Areas,
and Metropolitan Statistical Areas by Office of Management and Budget," (June 30, 1983), Bureau of the Census,
United States Department of Commerce, U.S. Government Printing Office, Washington, D.C.

Figure 5.2 illustrates areas designated as PMSAs, and MSAs in the Chicago CMSA.

Using Geographic Segmentation

There are many instances where markets for products and services may be segmented on a geographic basis. Regional variations in consumer tastes often exist. Per-capita consumption of Mexican food, for example, is higher in the Southwest than in New England. Basements, a mainstay in many homes in the North, are relatively rare in the South and Southwest.

Residence location within a geographic area is an important geographic variable. Urban dwellers may have less need for automobiles than their suburban and rural counterparts, and suburban dwellers spend proportionally more on lawn and garden care than people in rural or urban areas. Both rural and suburban dwellers may spend more of their household income on gasoline and automobile needs than urban households.

Climate is another important factor. Snowblowers, snowmobiles, and sleds are important products in the northern sections of the United States. Residents of the Sunbelt states may spend proportionally less of their total income on heating and heating equipment and more on air conditioning. Climate also affects patterns of clothing purchases.

Geographic segmentation is useful only when differences in preference and purchase patterns for a product emerge along regional lines. Moreover, geographic subdivisions of the overall market tend to be rather large and often too heterogeneous for effective segmentation without careful consideration of additional factors. In such cases, several segmentation variables may need to be utilized.

Demographic Segmentation _____

Demographic Segmentation
Dividing a population into homogeneous groups based upon characteristics such as age, sex, and income level.

The most common approach to market segmentation is demographic segmentation—dividing consumer groups according to demographic variables. These variables—age, sex, income, occupation, education, household size, and stage in the family life cycle, among others—are typically used to identify market segments and to develop appropriate marketing mixes. Demographic variables are often used in market segmentation for three reasons:

1. They are easy to identify and measure.
2. They are associated with the sale of many products and services.
3. They are typically referred to in describing the audiences of advertising media so media buyers and others can easily pinpoint the desired market target.[5]

Vast quantities of data are available to assist the marketing planner in segmenting potential markets on a demographic basis. Sex is an obvious variable for segmenting many markets, because many products are sex specific. Research by American Express revealed that women viewed credit cards as a male-specific product. Only 16 percent of all American Express Cards were held by women. So American Express targeted its marketing efforts at this largely untapped market segment. Three years later, 21 percent of its cards were held by women. One out of every three new cardholders is female.[6]

Age, household size, family life cycle stage, and income and expenditure patterns are important factors in determining purchase patterns. The distinct differences based upon demographic factors justify their frequent use as a basis for segmentation.

Age—Important Demographic Segmentation Variable

The bulk of the U.S. population growth during the 1980s will be concentrated in two age groups—young to middle-age adults between 30 and 45 and persons 65 years and older. Both markets represent potentially profitable market targets.

The young to middle-age adult segment includes family households with demands for such goods as homes, furniture, recreation, clothes, toys, and food. The median age of the U.S. population is now 31.6 years.[7] This age group is expected to account for two-thirds of the population growth during the 1980s. The anticipated configuration of the U.S. population in the year 2000 is shown in Figure 5.3.

Not long ago, there was no such thing as a senior adult market because few people reached old age. At present, however, nearly 27 million people, 11.6 percent of the population, are 65 or older.[8] It is encouraging to this year's retiree to learn that at age 65 his or her average life expectancy is more than an additional 16 years. Senior adults represent an important market segment in today's economy.

Each age group represents different consumption patterns, and each serves as the market target for several firms. For instance, Gerber traditionally has been extremely successful in aiming at the infants' and children's market. Table 5.2 lists some of the types of merchandise most often purchased by the various age groups.

Figure 5.3
The Age Distribution of U.S. Population in 2000

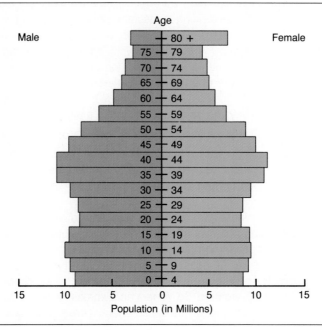

Source: U.S. Department of Commerce, Bureau of the Census, *Current Population Reports,*
Series P–25, No. 922 (Washington, D.C.: U.S. Government Printing Office, 1982), p. 11.

Table 5.2
Buying Patterns for Different Age Groups

Age	Name of Age Group	Merchandise
0–5	Young Children	Baby food, toys, nursery furniture, children's wear
6–19	School Children (Including Teenagers)	Clothing, sports equipment, records, school supplies, food, cosmetics, used cars
20–34	Young Adult	Cars, furniture, houses, clothing, recreational equipment, purchases for younger age segments
35–49	Younger Middle-Aged	Larger homes, better cars, second cars, new furniture, recreational equipment
50–64	Older Middle-Aged	Recreational items, purchases for young marrieds and infants
65 and Over	Senior Adults	Medical services, travel, drugs, purchases for younger age groups

Segmentation by Family Life Cycle Stage

Family Life Cycle
Process of family formation and dissolution that includes five major stages: (1) young single, (2) young married without children, (3) other young, (4) middle-age, and (5) older.

The family life cycle is the process of family formation and dissolution. Using this concept, the marketing planner combines the family characteristics of age, marital status, and number and ages of children to develop a marketing strategy.

Patrick E. Murphy and William A. Staples have proposed a five-stage family life cycle with several subcategories. The stages of the family life cycle are shown in Table 5.3.

Table 5.3
Family Life Cycle Stages

			Percent of U.S. Population
1.	Young Single *(under 35)*		8.2
2.	Young Married without Children *(under 35)*		2.9
3.	Other Young *(under 35)*		19.1
	a.	Young Divorced without Children	
	b.	Young Married with Children	
	c.	Young Divorced with Children	
4.	Middle-Aged *(35–64)*		45.4
	a.	Middle-Aged Married without Children	
	b.	Middle-Aged Divorced without Children	
	c.	Middle-Aged Married with Children	
	d.	Middle-Aged Divorced with Children	
	e.	Middle-Aged Married without Dependent Children	
	f.	Middle-Aged Divorced without Dependent Children	
5.	Older *(65 and older)*		7.2
	a.	Older Married	
	b.	Older Unmarried (Divorced, Widowed)	
6.	Other		17.2
	All Adults and Children Not Accounted for by Family Life Cycle Stages		

Source: Adapted with permission from Patrick E. Murphy and William A. Staples, "A Modernized Family Life Cycle," *Journal of Consumer Research* (June 1979), p. 16.

[a]Percentage of total expenditures.
[b]Includes transportation, health care, entertainment, personal care, reading education, tobacco, miscellaneous, cash contributions, and personal insurance and pensions.
Source: *News*, U.S. Department of Labor, Bureau of Labor Statistics, Washington, D.C. (December 19, 1984), Table 2.

The behavioral characteristics and buying patterns of persons in each life cycle stage often vary considerably. Young singles have relatively few financial burdens; tend to be early purchasers of new fashion items; are recreation oriented; and make purchases of basic kitchen equipment, cars, and vacations. By contrast, young marrieds with young children tend to be heavy purchasers of baby products, homes, television sets, toys, and washers and dryers. Their liquid assets tend to be relatively low, and they are more likely to watch television than young singles or young marrieds without children. The empty-nest households in the middle-age and older categories with no dependent children are more likely to have more disposable income; more time for recreation, self-education, and travel; and more than one member in the labor force than their full-nest counterparts with younger children. Similar differences in behavioral and buying patterns are evident in the other stages of the family life cycle.[9]

Analysis of life cycle stages often gives better results than reliance on single variables such as age. The buying patterns of a 25-year-old bachelor are very different from those of a father of the same age. The family of five headed by parents in their forties is a more likely prospect for the World Book Encyclopedia than the childless, 40-year-old divorced person.

Marketing planners can use published data such as census reports and divide their markets into more homogeneous segments than would be possible if they were analyzing single variables. Such data is available for each classification of the family life cycle.

The Changing Household

Slightly more than half of the households in the United States today contain only one or two persons. This development is in marked contrast to households that averaged 5.8 persons when the first census was taken in 1790.

The U.S. Department of Commerce cites several reasons for the trend toward smaller households: lower fertility rates; the tendency of young people to postpone marriage; the increasing tendency among younger couples to limit the number of children; the ease and frequency of divorce; and the ability and desire of many young single adults and the elderly to live alone.

More than 19 million people live alone today—about 23 percent of all households. The single-person household has emerged as an important market segment with a special title: *SSWD* (single, separated, widowed, and divorced). SSWDs buy one-third of all passenger cars.[10] They are also customers for single-serving food products, such as Campbell's Soup for One and Green Giant's single-serving casseroles.

The average household size today is 2.7 persons. While married-couple households continue to dominate, they will probably account for only 33 percent of all 1995 households compared to 61 percent in 1980. The number of unmarried individuals living together grew three-and-one-half times between 1970 and 1982. As a result, the Census Bureau has designated another category—*POSLSQ*—for unmarried people of the opposite sex living in the same quarters.

Market Segmentation Based on Income and Expenditure Patterns

Markets were defined earlier as people with purchasing power. A common method of segmenting the consumer market is on the basis of income. Fashionable specialty shops stocking designer clothing make most of their sales to high-income shoppers. Other retailers aim their appeals at middle-income groups. Still others focus almost exclusively on low-income shoppers.

The estimated number of households in various income groups in 1990 is shown in Figure 5.4. This information is further classified by age of the head of household, illustrating that two segmentation variables can be used jointly.

Household expenditures can be divided into two categories: (1) basic purchases of essential household needs, and (2) other purchases made at the discretion of household members after necessities have been purchased. Total discretionary purchasing power is estimated to have tripled since 1950.

Engel's Laws

Engel's Laws
Statements on spending behavior, comprised of three generalizations: As family income increases, (1) a smaller percentage of income goes for food; (2) the percentage spent on household operations, housing, and clothing remains constant; and (3) the percentage spent on other items increases.

How do expenditure patterns vary with increased income? More than a hundred years ago, Ernst Engel, a German statistician, published what became known as Engel's laws—three general statements based on his studies of the impact of household income changes on consumer spending behavior. According to Engel, as family income increases:

1. A smaller percentage of expenditures goes for food;
2. The percentage spent on housing and household operations and clothing remains constant; and
3. The percentage spent on other items (such as recreation and education) increases.

what is your Target ?

Figure 5.4
Households Classified by Age and Income: Estimates for 1990

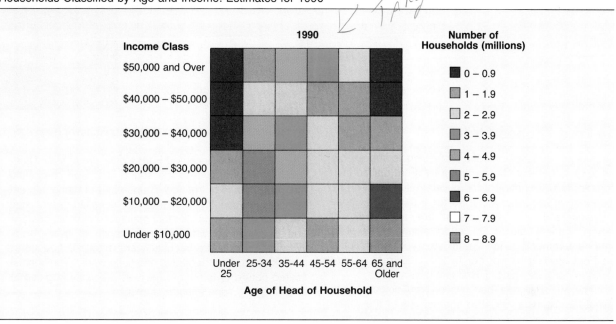

Source: Reprinted from "The Bourgeois Bulge," *Forbes* (April 30, 1984), p. 64.

Are Engel's laws still valid? Table 5.4 supplies the answers. A steady decline in the percentage of total income spent on food, beverages, and tobacco occurs from low to high incomes. Although high-income families spend a greater absolute amount on food purchases, their purchases represent a smaller percentage of their total expenditures than is true of low-income families. The second law is partly correct, since percentage expenditures for housing and household operations remain relatively unchanged in all but the very lowest income group. The percentage spent on clothing, however, increases with in-

Table 5.4
Family Expenditures by Income Groups

Category	Family Income				
	$5,000 to $9,999	$10,000 to $14,999	$15,000 to $19,999	$20,000 to $29,999	$30,000 and over
Food and Beverages	14%[a]	13%	13%	12%	11%
Housing and Related Items	50	45	43	43	44
Apparel and Services	3	3	3	3	4
Other Goods and Accessories[b]	33	38	41	42	42

[a]Percentage of total expenditures
[b]Includes transportation, health care, entertainment, personal care, reading, education, tobacco, miscellaneous, cash contributions, and personal insurance and pensions.
Source: *News*, U.S. Department of Labor, Bureau of Labor Statistics, Washington, D.C. (December 19, 1984), Table 2.

Return to the Stop-Action Case

The Ford Thunderbird

To entice performance-oriented professionals and executives to give the new Thunderbird a try, Ford mailed invitations to 406,270 potential car buyers, offering them the opportunity to test drive a T-Bird for a day. Ford chose the candidates for its "VIP Program" from national lists of business leaders, based on certain salary and professional requirements. Each candidate received a letter from Ford, inviting him or her to come down to a Ford showroom for a day-long, T-Bird test drive.

The VIP Program had two primary objectives: to eliminate consumers' negative impressions of the Thunderbird and to introduce them to the new, aerodynamic Thunderbird. "Our intent was not to sell cars," said Ford spokesperson Geri Opera. "Rather, we wanted to develop an awareness among people who would never even consider buying a Ford."

Those who accepted Ford's offer drove their Thunderbirds around town to the sound of a tape comparing the performance of the new Thunderbird to that of a great symphony orchestra. "For a car to be called great," said the voice on the tape, "it must maintain a delicate balance and demonstrate virtuoso performance in every area. When all aspects are beautifully orchestrated, it becomes a work of art. Thunderbird is one such work." The sophisticated nature of this message was precisely targeted to an intelligent, upper-income audience.

Source: Telephone conversation with Geri Opera, assistant manager of public affairs, Ford Division, Ford Motor Company, July 22, 1984.

creased income. Households that earn less than $10,000 annually spend a smaller percentage of their income on clothing than those who earn more than $10,000. The third law is also true with the exception of medical and personal care, which appear to decline with increased income.

Engel's laws provide the marketing manager with useful generalizations about the types of consumer demand that evolve with increased income. They can also be useful for the marketer evaluating a foreign country as a potential market target.

Psychographic Segmentation _____

Although geographic and demographic segmentation traditionally have been the primary bases for dividing consumer and industrial markets into homogeneous segments to serve as market targets, marketers have long recognized the need for fuller, more lifelike portraits of consumers in developing marketing programs. Even though traditionally used variables such as age, sex, family life cycle, income, and population size and location are important in segmentation, life-styles of potential customers may prove equally important.

Life-style
The way people decide to live their lives, including family, job, social activities, and consumer decisions.

Life-style refers to the consumer's mode of living; it is how an individual lives. Consumers' life-styles are regarded as a composite of their individual psychological makeups—their needs, motives, perceptions, and attitudes. A life-style also bears the mark of many other influences such as reference groups, culture, social class, and family members. A frequently used classification system for life-style variables is shown in Table 5.5.

Table 5.5

AIO Statement Dimensions

Activities	Interests	Opinions	Demographics
Work	Family	Themselves	Age
Hobbies	Home	Social Issues	Education
Social Events	Job	Politics	Income
Vacation	Community	Business	Occupation
Entertainment	Recreation	Economics	Family Size
Club Membership	Fashion	Education	Dwelling
Community	Food	Products	Geography
Shopping	Media	Future	City Size
Sports	Advertisements	Culture	Stage in Life Cycle

Source: Joseph T. Plummer, "The Concept and Application of Life Style Dimensions," *Journal of Marketing* (January 1974), p. 34. Used by permission of the American Marketing Association.

Using Psychographic Segmentation

Psychographic Segmentation
Dividing a population into homogeneous groups on the basis of behavioral and life-style profiles developed by analyzing consumer activities, opinions, and interests.

AIO Statements
Collection of statements contained in a psychographic study to reflect activities, interests, and opinions of the respondents.

In recent years, a new technique has been developed that promises to elicit more meaningful bases for segmentation. Although definitions vary among researchers, psychographic segmentation generally means the psychological profiles of different consumers developed from asking consumers to agree or disagree with AIO statements, which are several hundred statements dealing with activities, interests, and opinions. Some of these dimensions are listed in Table 5.5.

Hundreds of psychographic studies have been conducted on products and services ranging from beer to air travel. A national study of household food buying identified four distinct segments based on psychographic research. Of the 1,800 adults interviewed, 98 percent could be categorized into one of the following groups:

- *Hedonists*, who represent 20 percent of the population, want the good life—foods that taste good, are convenient, and inexpensive. They aren't worried about sugar, fat, cholesterol, salt, calories, additives, or preservatives. They are most likely young, male, and without children. Hedonists are above average consumers of soft drinks, beer, margarine, presweetened cereal, candy, and gum.

- *Don't Wants*, another 20 percent of the population, are the exact opposite of the Hedonists. They avoid all the "no-no" ingredients in some processed foods. They will sacrifice taste and convenience and will pay more to obtain foods without sugar, artificial ingredients, cholesterol, and fat. They are concerned about calories and nutrition. In effect, their avoidance behavior is more health oriented than diet conscious. This segment is older: more than half are over age 50. They tend to be better educated, live in large urban areas, and don't have children living at home. The Don't Wants are major consumers of decaffeinated coffee, fruit juices, wine, unsalted butter, corn oil margarine, nutritionally fortified cereal, yogurt, and sugar-free foods and beverages.

- *The Weight Conscious*, who comprise about one-third of the population, are primarily concerned about calories and fat. They like convenience foods but try to avoid cholesterol, sugar, and salt. They're not particularly nutrition or taste conscious and don't avoid foods simply because they have artificial ingredients or preservatives. Members of this segment tend to have higher incomes, and many are women employed full time. Given their concern for calories, the Weight Conscious are above-average consumers of iced tea, diet soft drinks, diet margarine, and sugar-free candy and gum.

■   *The Moderates*, the final 25 percent of the population, are average in everything. They balance the trade-offs they make in food selection and don't exhibit strong concerns about the avoidance factors. They closely profile the population in demographics, and their consumption levels are average for the foods and beverages listed in the study.[11]

The marketing implications of psychographic segmentation are considerable. Some of these are suggested in a study of heavy users of eye makeup and shortening, excerpted in Table 5.6. Psychographic profiles produce a much richer description of a potential market target and should assist promotional decisions in attempting to match the company's image and its product offerings with the type of consumer using the product.

Psychographic segmentation often serves as a component of an overall marketing strategy in which markets are also segmented on the basis of demographic/geographic variables such as age, city size, education, family life cycle stage, and geographic location. These more traditional bases provide the marketer with accessibility to consumer segments through orthodox communications channels like newspapers, radio and television advertising, and other promotional outlets. Psychographic studies may then be implemented to develop lifelike, three-dimensional profiles of the life-styles of the firm's market target. When combined with demographic/geographic characteristics, psychographics emerge as an important tool in understanding the behavior of present and potential market targets.

Benefit Segmentation

A fourth approach to market segmentation focuses on such attributes as product usage rates and the benefits derived from the product. These factors may reveal important bases for pinpointing prospective market targets. One analysis of 34 segmentation studies indicated that benefit analysis provided the best predictor of brand use, level of consumption, and product type selected in 51 percent of the cases.[12] Many marketers now consider benefit segmentation the most useful approach to classifying markets.

Benefit Segmentation
Dividing a population into homogeneous groups on the basis of benefits consumers expect to derive from a product or service.

Usage Rates

Marketing managers may divide potential segments into two categories: users and nonusers. Consider the case of greeting cards. Between 92 and 95 percent of the 7 billion cards sold in the United States each year are purchased by women. While men are essentially nonusers of this product, they will buy a card for a specific occasion. Men will also buy bigger and more expensive cards than women.[13]

Users may be categorized as heavy, moderate, and light. In some product categories, such as air travel, car rentals, dog food, and hair coloring, less than 20 percent of the population accounts for more than 80 percent of the

Table 5.6

Profile of Heavy Users of Eye Makeup and Shortening

Heavy User of Eye Makeup		Heavy User of Shortening
Young, Well-Educated, Lives in Metropolitan Areas	**Demographic Characteristics**	Middle-Aged, Medium to Large Family, Lives Outside Metropolitan Areas
Also a Heavy User of Liquid Face Makeup, Lipstick, Hair Spray, Perfume	**Product Use**	Also a Heavy User of Flour, Sugar, Canned Lunch Meat, Cooked Pudding, Catsup
Fashion Magazines, "The Tonight Show," Adventure Programs	**Media Preferences**	*Reader's Digest*, Daytime TV Serials, Family-Situation TV Comedies
	Activities, Interests, and Opinions (AIO Statements)	
"An important part of my life and activities is dressing smartly." "I want to look a little different from others." "I like what I see when I look in the mirror." "I take good care of my skin." "I would like to spend a year in London or Paris." "I like ballet." "I like to serve unusual dinners."	*Agrees More than Average with*	"I love to bake and frequently do." "I save recipes from newspapers and magazines." "I love to eat." "I enjoy most forms of housework." "Usually I have regular days for washing, cleaning, etc., around the house." "I am uncomfortable when my house is not completely clean." "I try to arrange my home for my children's convenience." "Our family is a close-knit group." "Clothes should be dried in the fresh air and out-of-doors." "I would rather spend a quiet evening at home than go out to a party."
"I enjoy most forms of housework." "I furnish my home for comfort, not for style." "If it was good enough for my mother, it's good enough for me."	*Disagrees More than Average with*	"My idea of housekeeping is once over lightly." "Classical music is more interesting than popular music." "I like ballet." "I'd like to spend a year in London or Paris."

Source: "Personality and Consumer Behavior" by Wells & Beard, in *Consumer Behavior: Theoretical Sources,* Ward/Robertson Eds., © 1973, pp. 195–196. Adapted by permission of Prentice-Hall, Inc., Englewood Cliffs, N.J.

total purchases. Even for such widely used products as coffee and soft drinks, half of all U.S. households account for almost 90 percent of the total usage.[14]

An early study of usage patterns by Dik Warren Twedt divided users into two categories: light and heavy. Twedt's analysis of consumer-panel data revealed that 29 percent of the sample households could be characterized as heavy users of lemon-lime soft drinks. This group represented 91 percent of sales in the product category.[15] It is not surprising that usage rates are important segmentation variables for Coca-Cola, Pepsi-Cola, and 7-Up.

Heavy users often can be identified through analysis of internal records. Retail stores and financial institutions have records of charge-card purchases and other transactions. Warranty records may also be used.[16]

Product Benefits

Market segments may also be identified by the benefits the buyer expects to derive from a product or brand. In a pioneering investigation, Daniel Yankelovich revealed that much of the watch industry operated with little understanding of the benefits watch buyers expect in their purchases. At the time of the study, most watch companies were marketing relatively expensive models through jewelry stores and using prestige appeals. However, Yankelovich's research revealed that about one-third of the market reported they purchased the lowest-priced watch and another 46 percent focused on durability and overall product quality. The U.S. Time Company decided to focus its product benefits on those two categories and to market its Timex watches in drugstores, variety stores, and discount houses. Within a few years of adopting the new segmentation approach, U.S. Time Company became the largest watch company in the world.[17]

Benefit segmentation has also been employed successfully in a number of other consumer markets. One study, for example, revealed seven market segments based on the perceived benefits of drinking liquor. "Mood modification" was the objective of a consumer group that sought to escape stress, boredom, and so forth, while another segment sought "social lubrication," believing that liquor improved social interaction.[18]

Segmenting Industrial Markets

While the bulk of market segmentation research has concentrated on consumer markets, the concept also applies to the industrial sector. The overall process is similar. For example, many of IBM's competitors have decided to compete against the computer giant by specializing in specific market segments. Qantel services small hotels and football and athletic teams. Control Data concentrates on the engineering and scientific markets. NCR markets many of its computers to banks and retailers.[19]

Three industrial market segmentation approaches—geographic segmentation, product segmentation, and segmentation by end-use application—are shown in Figure 5.5.

Geographic Segmentation

Geographic segmentation is useful in industries where the bulk of the customers is concentrated in specific geographical locations. This approach can be used effectively in the automobile industry, concentrated in the Detroit area, or the tire industry, centered in Akron. It might also be used where markets are limited to just a few locations. The oil-field equipment market, for example, is largely concentrated in cities like Houston, Dallas, and Tulsa.

Product Segmentation

Product Segmentation
Dividing an industrial market into homogeneous groups on the basis of product specifications identified by industrial buyers.

Product segmentation can be used in the industrial marketplace. Industrial users tend to have much more precise product specifications than ultimate consumers do. Thus, industrial products often fit narrower market segments than consumer products. Designing an industrial good or service to meet specific buyer requirements is a form of market segmentation.

Figure 5.5
Segmentation Bases for Industrial Markets

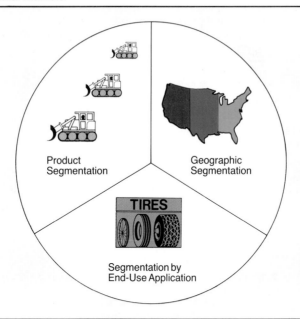

Segmentation by End-Use Applications

**End-Use Application
Segmentation**
Dividing an industrial market into
homogeneous groups on the basis
of precisely how different industrial
purchasers will use the product.

A third segmentation base is end-use application segmentation, or precisely
how the industrial purchaser will use the product. For example, a manufacturer
of printing equipment may serve markets ranging from a local utility to a bicycle manufacturer to the U.S. Department of Defense. Each end-use of the
equipment may dictate unique specifications of performance, design, and
price. Regardless of how it is done, market segmentation is as vital to industrial marketing as it is to consumer marketing.

Market Target Decision Analysis

Market Target Decision Analysis
Evaluation of potential market
segments by dividing the overall
market into homogeneous groups.
Cross classifications may be based
on variables such as type of market,
geographic location, frequency of
use, or demographic characteristics.

Identifying specific market targets is an important aspect of overall marketing
strategy. Clearly delineated market targets allow management to effectively
employ their marketing strategies. D'Lites, a franchised chain of diet-oriented
restaurants, is targeted at active 30 to 40-year-old executives earning over
$25,000 a year, who play racquetball and other sports. Atlanta was picked as
the original location for D'Lites because its population contained many people
that fit the profile of the market target customer.[20] Market target decision analysis played a major role in the start of D'Lites.

Market target decision analysis is a useful tool in the market segmentation process. Targets are chosen by segmenting the total market on the
basis of any given characteristic. The following example illustrates the application of market target decision analysis.[21]

Figure 5.6
Market Target for Typewriters

	East	Midwest	West
Consumer Market			
Industrial Market			

Photo Source: Courtesy of International Business Machines Corporation.

Applying Market Target Decision Analysis

Consider the decisions of a small firm that analyzes the market potential for a proposed line of typewriters. Because of limited financial resources, the company must operate on a regional basis. The grid in Figure 5.6 illustrates the firm's first two decisions: choosing a geographic area and marketing the typewriters to the ultimate consumer. The typewriter company could have also chosen the industrial market, but a separate marketing strategy would have

Figure 5.7
Market Target for Typewriters Sold to Consumers in the Eastern United States

	Income			
	Less than $10,000	$10,000 – $19,999	$20,000 – $29,999	Over $30,000
Young Single				
Young without Children				
Young with Children				
Middle-Aged with Children				
Middle-Aged without Children				
Older				
Other				

Photo Source: Courtesy of International Business Machines Corporation.

been required since each of the markets in Figure 5.6 represent unique and distinguishing characteristics.

The next step involves the decision to market the typewriters to high-income households in the young and middle-age stages of the family life cycle, which in turn requires evaluating the market for typewriters as gifts for school-age children. These decisions are shown in Figure 5.7 on page 140. Data can be gathered about the size of the market target in the eastern United States and the firm's predicted market share.

The cross classifications in Figure 5.7 can be further subdivided to gather more specific data about the characteristics of the proposed market target. The potential bases for segmenting markets are virtually limitless, and although divisions are sometimes made intuitively, they are usually supported by concrete data.

The preceding illustration used geographic and demographic segmentation bases, but benefit and psychographic segmentation can also be used in market target decision analysis. Similarly, geographic, product, and end-use application segmentation bases can be used in targeting industrial market segments.

Summary

A market consists of people or organizations with the necessary purchasing power and willingness to buy. The authority to buy must also exist. Markets can be classified by the type of products they handle. Consumer goods are products purchased by the ultimate consumer for personal use. Industrial goods are products purchased for use either directly or indirectly in the production of other goods and services for resale. Products are typically targeted at specific market segments. The process of dividing the total market into several homogeneous groups is called market segmentation.

Consumer markets can be divided on the bases of geographic, demographic, psychographic, or benefit segmentation. Geographic segmentation is the process of dividing the overall market into homogeneous groups on the basis of population location. It is one of the oldest forms of segmentation. The continual shifts in the U.S. population means that considerable effort must go into identifying the various geographic segments. The most commonly used form of segmentation is demographic segmentation, which classifies the overall market into homogeneous groups based upon characteristics such as age, sex, and income levels. Psychographic segmentation is a relatively new approach. It uses behavioral profiles developed from analyses of the activities, opinions, interests, and life-styles of consumers to identify market segments. The fourth approach, benefit segmentation, may be the most useful. It segments markets on the basis of the perceived benefits consumers expect to derive from a product or service.

Benefit segmentation is also useful in industrial markets. There are three bases for industrial market segmentation: geographic segmentation, product segmentation, and segmentation by end-use applications. Geographic segmentation is commonly used in concentrated industries. A second industrial market segmentation base is by product. Industrial markets are characterized by precise product specifications, making this approach feasible. Segmentation by end-use applications is the final base. This approach is predicated upon how the industrial purchaser will use the good or service.

Market target decision analysis is a useful tool in the market segmentation process. It involves developing a grid that outlines the various market segments by their distinguishing characteristics. All bases for segmentation can be employed in market target decision analysis, which can be used for both consumer and industrial markets.

Solving the Stop-Action Case

Photo Source: Courtesy of Ford Division, Ford Motor Company.

The Ford Thunderbird

Between mid-July 1983, when the VIP Program first began, and November 1983, when it ended, some 14,000 high-income consumers took a day-long, Thunderbird test drive. To quantify their responses, Ford asked each driver to fill out a detailed, product-evaluation questionnaire rating the Thunderbird in relation to what they had expected before they drove the car and in comparison to other cars of the same type in which they had driven. The questionnaire also asked the drivers to indicate their level of satisfaction with specific Thunderbird features and their inclination to buy a T-Bird some time in the future.

One out of ten drivers who answered the questionnaire said that they planned to buy a T-Bird, while 84 percent said that they planned to recommend the car to a friend. Many said that the only reason they set foot in a Ford dealership was the special VIP offer. A typical response was given by Richard Laughlin, director of financial reporting for Kentucky Fried Chicken in Louisville, Kentucky, who had not driven an American car in years. "We were looking to replace our older Toyota with a Honda Accord. But the T-Bird is a very, very, nice car. The luxury and comfort of the interior was great, and it had both performance and options. I'm real tempted."

Part of Ford's marketing plan was to have the T-Bird driven around town. "We wanted to have the car seen driving up to the right theaters, restaurants, and country clubs, driven by influential people," said Thomas Wagner, a Ford marketing executive. In many cases this worked, but in others it did not. Richard Laughlin used the test drive to take his 12-year-old son to a soccer practice, while another man drove his T-bird to a memorial service.

Despite Ford's planning, the program sometimes appealed to the wrong people. Richard Laughlin's 12-

year-old son, for example, became a more devoted fan than his father. "He and his friends must have spent five hours on Saturday sitting in the T-Bird, playing with the radio and the automatic seat adjustments," said the elder Laughlin. Although Nancy Stakoe, owner of a Detroit dry-cleaning business, liked the car, she felt it was the wrong car for her family. "I've got four kids of driving age," said Stakoe, "and they might get carried away driving this really cool car."

Ironically, despite Ford's efforts to market the T-Bird to up-scale consumers, some drivers considered the car a letdown from what they were used to. Jay Johnson, program director for an Indianapolis radio station, was embarrassed driving the car around town. "The T-Bird is obviously a less prestigious car than my Mercedes," said Johnson. "When people saw me drive that, they asked, 'Did you lose your job?'"

Despite the drawbacks of the VIP plan and despite its intent to increase awareness, not sales, the plan was an important factor in the T-Bird sales boom. Annual sales were 366 percent higher in December 1983 than they were in December 1981. T-Bird car sales outpaced those of any other Ford model. While sales for all Fords increased by 28 percent between July 1983 and July 1984, Thunderbird sales skyrocketed by 51 percent.

Source: Meg Cox, "Ford Pushing Thunderbird with VIP Plan," *The Wall Street Journal* (October 17, 1983), pp. 33, 49.

Questions for Discussion

1.   The typical BMW buyer is a business executive or professional who is college educated and earns an $80,000 annual household income. The BMW buyer is also a trend-setter who is socially and culturally active. Discuss the segmentation bases used in this description.

2.   Explain why each of the four components of a market is needed for a market to exist.

3.   Pizzas are consumer goods; iron ore is an industrial good. What about trucks—are they consumer goods or industrial goods? Defend your answer.

4.   Identify and briefly explain the bases for segmenting consumer markets.

5.   Match the following bases for market segmentation with the items below:
     a.   Geographic segmentation
     b.   Demographic segmentation
     c.   Psychographic segmentation
     d.   Benefit segmentation
     _____ A government-financed study divided U.S. households into five categories of eating patterns: meat eaters; healthy eaters; conscientious eaters; "in a dither" eaters; and on-the-go eaters.
     _____ Bamberger's decision to emphasize suburban department stores. (Its only downtown outlet is the original store in Newark, New Jersey.)
     _____ "7-Up, clear, crisp with no caffeine."
     _____ Spiegel Inc. targets its catalogs at 25 to 54-year-old working women with household incomes of $34,000.

6.   Analyze the future growth prospects of the geographic area in which you live.

7.   Identify the major population shifts that have occurred in recent years. How do you account for these shifts?

8.   Distinguish among CMSAs, PMSAs, and MSAs.

9.   Why is demographic segmentation the most commonly used approach to market segmentation?

10. The NFL strike in 1982 caused a major problem for marketers who targeted their products at affluent younger males, since commercials during National Football League games are a primary method of reaching this group. Substitute broadcasts of Canadian Football League and small college games reached only about half of the NFL audience. Research also indicated that baseball games tend to draw older, less affluent males. If you were such an advertiser, how would you have dealt with the NFL strike?

11. Explain why the household growth rate is substantially higher than the increase in population.

12. A study by the U.S. Census Bureau dealt with the ancestral background of Americans. Nearly 29 percent of all Americans claim some German ancestry, over 24 percent of our population is partially Irish, and over 22 percent have some English roots. How could a marketer use this demographic information?

13. How can life-styles be used in market segmentation?

14. Explain the use of product usage rates as a segmentation variable.

15. What market segmentation base would you recommend for the following?
     a.   Professional soccer team
     b.   Porsche sports car
     c.   Columbia Records
     d.   Scope mouthwash

16.   Identify and briefly explain the bases for segmenting industrial markets.

17.   What is meant by market target decision analysis?

18.   Show how market target decision analysis can help select market segments that the firm should attempt to reach.

19.   Illustrate how the four consumer-oriented segmentation bases can be used in market target decision analysis.

20.   Illustrate how the three industrial market segmentation bases can be used in market target decision analysis.

Case: The Seattle Symphony Orchestra

The Seattle Symphony Orchestra uses psychographic research developed by Gilmore Research for a local broadcaster to segment Seattle Symphony audiences. Gilmore concluded that Seattle had six life-style and value groups, each of about equal size. The exact number of groups varies from city to city; for example, Dallas has five, and Kansas City, seven.

Seattle's six groups are characterized as follows:

- Group 1:   [ ] The city's "old guard"
               [ ] Wealthy (over 20 percent earn in excess of $50,000 annually)
               [ ] Civic leaders, achievers

- Group 2:   [ ] Young professionals 35–44
               [ ] Trend-setters
               [ ] Both spouses have high-income jobs

- Group 3:   [ ] Primarily housewives
               [ ] Home-centered
               [ ] Family-oriented
               [ ] Traditional
               [ ] Conservative

- Group 4:   [ ] Primarily male
               [ ] Financially secure blue-collar workers
               [ ] Heavy buyers of recreational equipment (the Winnebago crowd)
               [ ] Not generally inclined toward the arts and community activities

- Group 5:   [ ] Lower income people (half made less than $20,000)
               [ ] Pessimistic
               [ ] Heavy buyers of fast food
               [ ] Heavy TV watchers
               [ ] Eighty percent are 25–44
               [ ] These people have difficulty finding jobs

- Group 6:   [ ] Fixed incomes
               [ ] Retired people and the military
               [ ] Home-centered
               [ ] Half are unmarried
               [ ] Little involvement in community affairs
               [ ] Followers, not leaders

Source: Melinda Bargreen, "Arts Market: Tuning Into Lifestyles to Target Audiences," *The Seattle Times* (November 13, 1983), pp. G-1, G-8.

Concentrations of the various groups have been classified by zip codes. Heavy populations of Groups 1, 2, and 3 who have attended an arts event have also been targeted by zip code. The Seattle Symphony then concentrates its direct mail efforts in these particular zip codes. The symphony also tells potential corporate sponsors of the demographics of its audience.

The Seattle Symphony now fills 85 percent of its seats, or approximately the national average. Its $300,000 marketing and public relations budget produces $1.9 million in ticket sales.

Questions

1. What is your assessment of the Seattle Symphony's use of psychographic segmentation? Discuss.

2. What other types of segmentation might be useful to the Seattle Symphony? Explain.

3. Do you think other arts groups would be able to use psychographic segmentation in their promotional efforts? Discuss.

Computer Applications

In one of the earliest reported studies of how consumer expenditure patterns change when household income increases, German statistician Ernst Engel proposed three general conclusions:

1.   A smaller percentage of the household budget will be allocated to food purchases;

2.   The percentage of the household budget spent on housing, household operations, and clothing will remain constant; and

3.   The percentage spent on other items (such as education and recreation) and the percentage devoted to savings/investments will increase.

These generalizations became known as Engel's laws.

Directions: Use menu item 5 titled "Engel's Laws" to solve each of the following problems.

Problem 1 The Smythe family, of Middlebury, Connecticut, uses a budget to monitor and control household expenditures. The family has just prepared this year's budget to reflect the salary increases that both spouses expect at the beginning of the year. The general categories of expenditures and savings and the amounts allocated to each category are shown below.

Is the Smythe's budget for this year consistent with Engel's laws? With which, if any, of the laws is the Smythe budget in conflict?

Budget Category	Last Year's Expenditures	This Year's Budgeted Amount
Food	$18,000	$19,500
Clothing and Housing	24,000	29,250
Other	18,000	16,250
Total	$60,000	$65,000

Problem 2 Sandra Sergetti is a single, 26-year-old marketing research analyst at a major consumer goods company in Cincinnati, Ohio. Last year Sandra saved $3,200 and spent the remainder as follows: food, $6,400; housing and clothing, $12,800; and miscellaneous (including entertainment and vacations), $9,600. But a recent promotion and salary increase has prompted Sergetti to reevaluate her personal budget. She has decided to use a payroll deduction program to increase her savings to $4,200, go on a diet and cut her food expenditures to $5,600, increase her housing and clothing outlays slightly to $14,000, and spend the rest of next year's $35,000 salary on miscellaneous items (including a short winter vacation). Does Sergetti's budget conflict with Engel's laws? If so, how?

Problem 3 Ed and Cindy Stoddard, of Thousand Oaks, California, have never used a formal household budget. But the couple does engage in an annual ritual of sitting in front of their fireplace every New Year's Eve, evaluating the past year and making some general plans for the coming year. The discussion this past December 31 went something like this:

Cindy: Well, this year was certainly good to us, with each of us getting a $5,000 raise effective tomorrow.

Ed: Yes, I agree. So maybe it is about time we moved on that house with the For Sale sign that we drive past every day.

Cindy: Ed, you read my mind every time! I don't care if it does increase our spending on housing from $15,000 to $19,500 next year. We could make it up somewhere else in our spending plans.

Ed: Well, we still have to eat, but we could eat fewer steaks and cut back on our percentage spent on food. My quick tally of the checkbook shows we spent $8,000 on food items this year. We could try to hold our food spending to, say, $9,000 next year.

Cindy: And I would be willing to spend our vacation at the beach rather than flying to Europe like we planned. According to my mental calculator, that means we would have $3,500 left from our $32,000 take-home pay next year for miscellaneous—including the vacation. That's $500 less than the $4,000 we allocated for miscellaneous spending this past year out of our combined $27,000 in take-home pay.

Ed: Cindy, next New Year's Eve we've just got to start talking about a savings and investment plan. . . .

Do the Stoddards' financial plans conflict with Engel's laws? If so, how?

Problem 4 Fred Addison is a relief pitcher with the New York Mets. Addison, who is 23 and single, has just completed best year of his baseball career, posting a 9–7 win/loss record with 16 saves. His agent has just negotiated a new contract for next year that will boost Addison to $250,000 from the $180,000 he earned last year. The agent, an attorney and a CPA, has also developed a personal budget for Addison that reflects his raise and the fact that the young pitcher will marry soon. Since the couple plans to start a family right away, the bride-to-be has decided to give up her teaching position in suburban Westchester County. Determine whether the agent's proposed budget coincides with Engel's laws. (Hint: Taxes and the agent's fees should be included in the "Other" category.)

Budget Category	Last Year's Expenditures	This Year's Budgeted Amount
Clothing	$ 9,000	$ 25,000
Food	9,000	11,000
Entertainment	18,000	18,000
Travel	5,000	15,000
Housing	27,000	27,000
Professional Fees	18,000	25,000
Taxes	54,000	75,000
Savings and Investments	40,000	54,000
Total	$180,000	$250,000

Problem 5 Cedric and Heather Brannigan, of Boca Raton, Florida, have recently consulted a financial planner to assist them in developing a household budget and in making investments. In the process, the planner made several suggestions about the Brannigans' personal expenditures. The planner, noting that the couple's combined income would increase next year by 12 percent, suggested that the Brannigans purchase the beachfront condominium they had been considering. The planner pointed out that, while their monthly housing costs would rise 50 percent above their current rent, most of the increase would be tax deductible as an interest expense. However, Heather was interested in using the additional income to purchase stocks and bonds rather than to serve as a down-payment on the condo. Last year's expenditures and next year's budget proposals are shown below.

Budget Category	Expenditures	Planner's Proposed Budget for Next Year	Heather's Proposed Budget for Next Year
Food	$ 14,000	$ 15,000	$ 15,000
Beverages	1,000	2,000	2,000
Clothing	20,000	22,000	22,000
Housing	17,000	25,000	17,000
Entertainment	10,000	11,000	11,000
Investments	5,000	5,000	17,000
Other	33,000	32,000	28,000
Total	$100,000	$112,000	$112,000

a.   Does the planner's suggestion conflict with Engel's laws?

b.   How consistent is Heather's proposed budget with Engel's laws?

6 Consumer Behavior

Learning Goals

1. To explain the classification of behavioral influences in consumer decisions
2. To identify the interpersonal determinants of consumer behavior
3. To identify the personal determinants of consumer behavior
4. To outline the steps in the consumer decision process
5. To differentiate among routinized response behavior, limited problem solving, and extensive problem solving

Photo Source: Yamaha International Corporation, Specialty Products Division.

Stop-Action Case

The Yamaha PortaTone PC-1000

A person's general attitude toward a product category is often a determining factor in whether or not he or she will become a purchaser. Chapter 6 defines *attitudes* as a person's enduring favorable or unfavorable evaluations, emotional feelings, or pro and con action tendencies toward an object or idea. Playing a keyboard instrument is an example in which negative attitudes have an adverse effect on sales. While many people would like to play such an instrument, nonmusicians shy away from it because they believe it is too difficult to learn.

Many consumers avoid buying traditional pianos because of their size and price. Understandably, nonmusicians are unwilling to invest thousands of dollars in an instrument they are unsure they will like. Parents are even less likely to invest this amount of money in their children, who change their minds and musical preferences almost as readily as their clothes. So when Yamaha decided to introduce a new keyboard instrument, they faced a sizable challenge.

Assignment: Use the materials in Chapter 6 to suggest a way in which Yamaha could change consumer attitudes toward purchasing a keyboard instrument.

Source: Information provided by Yamaha International Corporation, Specialty Products Division, 1985.

Chapter Overview _____

Consumer Behavior
Acts of individuals in obtaining and
using goods or services, including
the decision processes that precede
and determine these acts.

Consumer behavior consists of the acts of individuals in obtaining and using
goods and services, including the decision processes that precede and determine these acts.[1] This definition includes both the ultimate consumer and the
purchaser of industrial products. A major difference in the purchasing behavior
of industrial consumers and ultimate consumers is that additional influences
from within the organization may be exerted on the industrial purchasing
agent.

   This chapter assesses interpersonal and personal influences on consumer behavior. Chapter 7 deals with industrial and organizational buyer behavior.

Classifying Behavioral Influences: Personal and Interpersonal

Since the study of consumer behavior involves attempts to understand human
behavior in purchase/nonpurchase situations, it is not surprising to learn that
consumer researchers borrow extensively from other areas such as psychology and sociology. The work of Kurt Lewin, for example, provides an excellent
classification of influences on buying behavior. Lewin's work is also used in
motivation theory, which is part of the management discipline, because it is a
general model of behavior. Lewin's proposition was:

$$B = f(P,E),$$

where behavior (B) is a function (f) of the interactions of personal influences
(P) and the pressures exerted upon them by outside forces in the environment (E).[2]

   This statement is usually rewritten for consumer behavior as follows:

$$B = f(I,P),$$

where consumer behavior (B) is a function (f) of the interaction of interpersonal determinants (I), like reference groups and culture, and personal determinants (P), like attitudes, on the consumer. Understanding consumer behavior requires an understanding of both the individual's psychological makeup
and the influences of others. A general model of the interpersonal and personal determinants of consumer behavior is shown in Figure 6.1.

The Consumer Decision Process

Consumer behavior may be viewed as a decision process, and the act of
purchasing is merely one point in the process. To understand consumer behavior, the events that precede and follow the purchase must be examined.
The steps in the consumer decision process are problem recognition, search,
evaluation of alternatives, purchase decision, purchase act, and postpurchase
evaluation. The decision process is utilized by the consumer in solving problems and in taking advantage of opportunities that arise. Such decisions permit consumers to correct differences between their actual and desired states.
Feedback from each decision serves as additional experience to rely upon in
subsequent decisions.

   This process is demonstrated by the young couple whose only television
set has been declared irreparable by the service representative. The need to
purchase a new set is clearly recognized since it is a primary form of recrea-

Figure 6.1
Personal and Interpersonal Determinants of Consumer Behavior

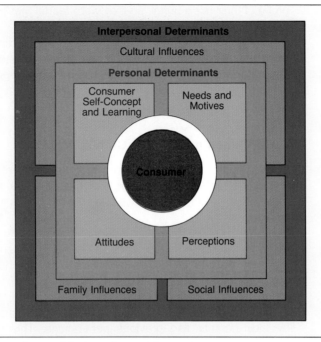

Source: C. Glenn Walters and Gordon W. Paul, *Consumer Behavior: An Integrated Framework*
(Homewood, Ill.: Richard D. Irwin, 1970), p. 14. © by Richard D. Irwin, Inc. Reprinted by permission.

tion for their young children. The couple questions their friends and acquaintances who have bought televisions recently. They pore over consumer-oriented reports on new models. After all the necessary information is collected,
the couple evaluates the various models on the basis of what is important to
them—reliability and price. They decide to buy a new set the next weekend.
The actual purchase is completed at a local discount store the next Saturday.
The new set is hooked up, and the young family sits back to evaluate their
purchase.

This process is common to consumer purchase decisions. It is introduced here to provide an advance perspective of the field of consumer behavior. An expanded discussion of the consumer decision process concludes this
chapter after the reader has an overview of the various factors that impact
consumer behavior.

Interpersonal Determinants of Consumer Behavior

People are social animals. They often buy products and services that will enable them to project a favorable image to others. These influences may result
from three categories of interpersonal determinants of consumer behavior: cultural influences, social influences, and family influences.

Cultural Influences

Culture is the broadest environmental determinant of consumer behavior.
Sometimes it is a very elusive concept for marketers to handle. General Mills
knew that few Japanese homes had ovens, so it designed a Betty Crocker

cake mix that could be made in the widely used electric rice cookers. The product failed because of a cultural factor. Japanese homemakers are very proud of their rice's purity, so they were fearful that a cake flavor would be left in their cookers.[3]

Culture
Complex of values, ideas, attitudes, and other meaningful symbols created by people to shape human behavior and the artifacts of that behavior as they are transmitted from one generation to the next.

Culture can be defined as "the complex of values, ideas, attitudes, and other meaningful symbols created by people to shape human behavior and the artifacts of that behavior, transmitted from one generation to the next."[4] It is the completely learned and handed-down way of life that gives each society its own peculiar flavor or values.

Core Values in the U.S. Culture

While cultural values do change over time, there are always some basic core values that are slow to change. For example, the work ethic and the accumulation of wealth have always played a big part in the development of American society.

Many people thought the generation that grew up in the 1960s had permanently altered American core values. This generation was the product of the baby boom that followed World War II and the Korean conflict. It was raised with the conservative values of the 1950s. Free time was spent watching television shows like "Ozzie and Harriet" and "Father Knows Best." As they matured, this generation seemed to rebel against most of the values held by their parents and previous generations. This was the generation that shocked traditional cultural values with its long hair, antiwar protests, marijuana, and Woodstock festival. Despite the turmoil of the 1960s, most American core values survived. What are the flower children of the 1960s doing now? They have passed on to early middle age, crossing that dreaded barrier, age 30. They have adopted many of the values held by their parents, including worrying about the younger generation. Most baby boomers are now too concerned with mortgages and receding hair lines to protest anything besides high taxes. Even Rolling Stone Mick Jagger observed: "I can't go on pretending to be 18 much longer."[5]

There are trends and shifts in cultural values, yet traditionally these changes have been gradual, not revolutionary like those of the 1960s generation. Because rapid technological shifts may alter this pace in the future, marketers must constantly assess cultural norms.[6] One of the most recent cultural trends is the search for more interpersonal relationships rather than the self-centered orientation that characterized recent American value structures. In short, many people are motivated by a desire for increased friendship.[7] This trend has been noted by marketers who now feature more family and friendship groups in their scenarios for commercials. Michelob's restaurant scenes are a good example.

Cultural Influences: An International Perspective

Cultural differences are particularly important for international marketers. This topic is more fully explored in Chapter 19, but it is important to point out that cultural differences do result in different attitudes, mores, and folkways. All have an impact on marketing strategy. Consider the case of the candy company that introduced a new chocolate bar with peanuts in Japan. The candy bar failed because Japanese folklore suggests that eating chocolate with peanuts leads to nosebleed.[8]

Marketing strategies that have proven successful in one country often cannot be applied directly in international markets because of cultural differences. For example, an inept translation of Schweppes Tonic Water caused the product to be advertised as "bathroom water" in Italy.[9] Similarly, the Chinese had difficulty selling "Fang Fang" lipstick, "White Elephant" batteries, and "Pansy" men's underwear in the United States.[10]

U.S.-based international marketers face competition from firms in Germany, France, the Soviet Union, Japan, and several other countries, as well as from firms in the host nation. Therefore, they must become familiar with all aspects of the local population, including its cultural heritage. This can be accomplished by treating each country as additional market segments that must be thoroughly analyzed before developing a marketing mix.

Subcultures

Subcultures
Subgroups of a culture with their own distinguishing mode of behavior.

Cultures are not homogeneous entities with universal values. Within each culture are numerous subcultures —subgroups with their own distinguishing modes of behavior. Any culture as heterogeneous as that of the United States is composed of significant subcultures based on factors such as race, nationality, age, rural-urban location, religion, and geographic distribution.

Inhabitants of the Southwest display a life-style that emphasizes casual dress, outdoor entertaining, and water recreation. Mormons refrain from buying tobacco and liquor. Blacks may exhibit interest in products and symbols of their African heritage. Orthodox Jews purchase kosher or other traditional foods.

The two largest ethnic subcultures in the United States are blacks and Hispanics. Together they account for over 41 million of the U.S. population, or a little over 18 percent of the total.[11] However, many sources say that the census data undercounts both of these subcultures. Not only are these two ethnic subcultures large, but they also make up a disproportionate part of many important U.S. markets.

Black Consumption Patterns Blacks represent the largest racial/ethnic subculture in the United States, some 26.5 million strong. They account for about 11.7 percent of the U.S. population and $140 billion in purchasing power.[12] There are several striking differences between the black and white populations. According to the U.S. Department of Commerce, about 34 percent of blacks are below the poverty level compared to 11 percent of whites. Also, the black population is very young. The median age for blacks is six years younger than for whites.[13]

While marketers recognize that no group of 26.5 million people can be considered a homogeneous market segment for all products, a number of marketing studies have compared consumption patterns of blacks and whites. The major findings are

- Blacks are very loyal to national brands.

- Blacks save a higher percentage of their income than do whites.

- Blacks spend less on food, housing, medical, and automobile transportation than equivalent whites. They spend more for clothing and nonautomobile transportation. Blacks and whites spend about the same on recreation, leisure, home furnishings, and equipment.

- Blacks tend to buy larger domestic automobiles rather than foreign-made vehicles.

- Blacks buy more milk, soft drinks, and liquor than whites but less tea and coffee.[14]

The most distinguishing feature of black consumers is their brand loyalty. Blacks have been slow to shift to generic and private brands. In fact, it is estimated that blacks may account for 30 to 40 percent of the sales of many national brands. The Wellington Group, a New Jersey-based market research and business development company, found the following to be among the brand favorites of blacks: Listerine, Tide, Pine-Sol, Clorox, S.O.S., Reynolds Wrap, Minute Maid, Maxwell House, Gold Medal, Crisco, Skippy, Kraft mayonnaise, Vaseline Intensive Care, Campbell's baked beans, and Scott towels.[15]

Marketers—whether in majority- or minority-owned firms—must choose their strategies carefully when attempting to reach the growing black market. The product or service must be positioned correctly and the appropriate promotional media selected. S.C. Johnson, of Racine, Wisconsin, for instance, was successful in promoting Edge shaving gel to black males. Since the hair follicles of many black men have bumps that lead to nicks, Edge's introductory advertising campaign stressed the theme "Beat the bumps." Edge was a product that met the needs of the black marketplace.[16]

Hispanic Consumption Patterns   Hispanics are the nation's second largest subculture. The U.S. Spanish-speaking population is increasing by more than one-half million a year and is becoming a very important market segment. This is particularly true in metropolitan Miami, whose Cuban population of 690,000 is exceeded only by Havana's; Greater Los Angeles, whose 2.1 million Hispanic population is second only to Mexico City's; and New York, whose Puerto Rican population of 1.4 million is greater than San Juan's.

In total, 6.4 percent of the U.S. population, or 14.6 million people, reported they were of Spanish-speaking origin. In the following five states, the Hispanic population represented more than 10 percent of the total population: New Mexico (36.6 percent), Texas (21 percent), California (19.2 percent), Arizona (16.2 percent), and Colorado (11.7 percent).[17] Overall, the U.S. Spanish-speaking population amounts to a market with $60 billion of purchasing power.[18]

Hispanics are probably a more heterogeneous subculture than blacks due to their variety of national backgrounds. Mexico is identified as the birthplace of 59.4 percent of the U.S. Hispanic population. Other places of origin are Puerto Rico, 15.1 percent; Central or South America, 7.4 percent; Cuba, 5.9 percent; and other locales, 12.2 percent.[19]

Hispanic consumption of certain products is disproportionate to that of the white majority. Some specific examples are

- Hispanics purchase 1.5 times as much beer as other population segments.

- Los Angeles Hispanics buy 5 times as much juice, 3.5 times as many baby-food products, 3 times as many cans of spaghetti, 1.8 times as many soft drinks, and 1.5 times as many bottles of shampoo as the rest of the population.

These figures reflect the facts that Hispanics typically have larger families and they dine out less than other population segments.[20] But, like blacks, the most noticeable characteristic of Hispanic consumption patterns is brand loyalty.[21] The Hispanic subculture, therefore, is of particular importance to marketers of national brands.

Social Influences

The second interpersonal determinant of consumer behavior is the social influences that impact purchase behavior. Children's earliest awareness is their membership in a very important group, the family. From this group they seek total satisfaction of their physiological and social needs. As they grow older, they join other groups—neighborhood play groups, school groups, Girl Scouts, Little League, and groups of friends, among others—from which they acquire both status and roles.

Status
Relative position of any individual member in a group.

Status is the relative position of any individual member in the group; roles are what the other members of the group expect of the individual who is in any particular position within the group. Some groups (like the Boy Scouts) are formal, and others (like friendship groups) are informal. Groups of either sort supply each member with both status and roles; in doing so, they influence the member's activities.

Roles
Behavior that members of a group expect of individuals who hold a specific position within the group.

The Asch Phenomenon

Although most persons view themselves as individuals, groups are often highly influential in purchase decisions. In situations where individuals feel that a particular group or groups are important, they tend to adhere in varying degrees to the general expectations of that group.

The surprising impact that groups and group norms can exhibit on individual behavior has been called the Asch phenomenon, which was first documented in the following study conducted by psychologist S. E. Asch:

Asch Phenomenon
Occurrence first documented by psychologist S. E. Asch, which illustrates the effect of the reference group on individual decision making.

Eight subjects are brought into a room and asked to determine which of a set of three unequal lines is closest to the length of a fourth line shown some distance from the other three. The subjects are to announce their judgments publicly. Seven of the subjects are working for the experimenter and they announce incorrect matches. The order of announcement is arranged such that the naive subject responds last. In a control situation, 37 naive subjects performed the task 18 times each without any information about others' choices. Two of the 37 subjects made a total of 3 mistakes. However, when another group of 50 naive subjects responded after hearing the unanimous but incorrect judgment of the other group members, 37 made a total of 194 errors, all of which were in agreement with the mistake made by the group.[22]

This widely replicated study illustrates the impact of groups upon individual choice making. Marketing applications range from the choice of automobile models and residential locations to the decision to purchase at least one item at a home party.

Reference Groups

Groups whose value structures and standards influence a person's behavior are called reference groups. Consumers usually try to keep their purchase behavior in line with what they perceive to be the values of their reference group.

Reference Groups
Groups with which an individual identifies to the point where the groups dictate a standard of behavior for the individual.

The extent of reference group influence varies widely. For the influence to be great, two factors must be present:

1.   The item must be one that can be seen and identified by others.
2.   The item must also be conspicuous; it must stand out, be unusual, and be a brand or product that not everyone owns.

The status of the individual within the reference group produces three subcategories: a *membership group*, where the person actually belongs to, say, a country club; an *aspirational group*, in which a person desires to associate with a group; and a *disassociative group*, with which the individual does not want to be identified with by others.

Although a reference group can be a membership group, it is not essential that the individual be a member for the group to serve as a point of reference. This concept helps explain the use of athletes in advertisements.

Social Classes

Although people prefer to think of the United States as the land of equality, a well-structured class system does exist. Research conducted a number of years ago by W. Lloyd Warner identified a six-class system within the social structure of both small and large cities. An updated description of the members of each class and an estimate of its population percentage are shown in Table 6.1.

Class rankings are determined by occupation, source of income (not amount), education, family background, and dwelling area. Income is not a primary determinant; a pipefitter paid at union scale earns more than many college professors, but his or her purchase behavior may be quite different. Thus the adage "A rich man is a poor man with money" is incorrect from a marketing viewpoint.

Richard Coleman illustrates the behavior of three families, all earning less than $35,000 a year but all in decidedly different social classes. The upper-middle-class family in this bracket—a young lawyer or college professor and family—is likely to spend its money buying a home in a prestigious neighborhood, buying expensive furniture from high-quality stores, and joining social clubs.

At the same time, the lower-middle-class family—headed by a grocery store owner or a sales representative—will probably purchase a good house in a less expensive neighborhood. It buys more furniture from less expensive stores and typically has a savings account at the local bank.

The lower-class family—headed by a truck driver or welder—spends less money on the house but buys one of the first new cars sold each year and owns one of the largest color television sets in town. It stocks its kitchen with appliances—symbols of security.[23]

The role of social class in determining consumer behavior continues to be a source of debate in the field of marketing. Some have argued against using social class as a market segmentation variable. Others disagree as to whether income or social class is the best base for market segmentation. The findings tend to be mixed. One recent study revealed that social class was the superior segmentation variable for food and non-soft-drink/non-alcoholic-beverage markets. Social class also influenced shopping behavior and evening television watching. Income was the superior segmentation variable for major appliances, soft drinks, mixes, and alcoholic beverages. For other categories, like clothing, a combination of the two variables was the best approach.[24]

Opinion Leaders

Opinion Leaders
Individuals in a group who serve as information sources for other group members.

Each group usually contains a few members who can be considered **opinion leaders**, or trend-setters. These individuals are likely to purchase new products before others do and to serve as information sources for others in the group.[25]

Table 6.1

Social Class in America

Status Group	Membership Prototypes, Consumption Themes	Population Share
Upper-Upper	Socially prominent families, usually inherited wealth, often third or fourth generation. "Prep school" backgrounds the rule, ideally followed by Ivy League, Seven Sisters collegiate experience. Expenditures understated: emphasis on travel, arts patronage, civic leadership, exclusive clubs, "proper upbringing" for children, "classic" clothes.	0.3%
Lower-Upper	*Nouveau riche* business founders; celebrities in entertainment, sports, government; first-generation executive and professional elite. Consumption tends to be conspicuous—large houses, expensive cars, luxurious vacations, lavish parties. Incomes range from four times the national mean on up: many of America's richest rank here.	1.2%
Upper-Middle	Corporate management, owners of medium-size businesses, moderately successful professionals. College backgrounds, degrees from "standard" or "superior" schools is the norm. Family income ordinarily double or triple national average, once middle-age is reached. Spending in individualized "good taste" is goal. This is America's "quality market" along with classes above.	12.5%
Lower-Middle	Mostly white-collar workers in sales, technical, administrative support jobs, small-business ownership; some socially ambitious blue-collar families. Education usually more years than average for people in their age group; incomes run 20–30 percent above the mean ideally (but not necessarily). Being "respectable," "doing the right thing," following media lead in consumption are characteristic.	32.0%
Working Class *(Formerly Upper-Lower)*	Blue-collar workers dominant—from construction, assembly lines, service occupations (i.e., police, bartenders, deliverymen), transportation. Incomes range from somewhat below average up to twice the national mean, depending on union affiliation, how many family members are working. "Keeping up with the times" in cars, appliances, and recreation is consumption hope. Family, neighborhood, workmates are center of social life; a parochial worldview.	38.0%
Lower Class *(Formerly Lower-Lower)*	Unskilled, semi-skilled but sometimes jobless; habitually unemployed "on welfare." Unassimilated ethnics, "poor whites" with limited education ("hillbillies"), and disadvantaged blacks. "Too many children" and illegitimacy frequent. Apathy, fatalism, and impulsive consumption are more characteristic than "trying to get up and out."	16.0%

Source: This updating of the Warner view results from research by Richard P. Coleman and associates in Kansas City (since the 1950s) and in Boston (during the 1970s); it has been abstracted from *Social Status in the City* by Richard P. Coleman and Bernice Neugarten (San Francisco: Jossey-Bass, 1971) and *Social Standing in America* by Richard Coleman and Lee Rainwater (New York: Basic Books, 1978).

Generalized opinion leaders are rare; instead, individuals tend to be opinion leaders for specific products and services. Their distinguishing characteristics are considerable knowledge and interest in a particular product or service. Their interest in the product motivates them to seek out information from mass media, manufacturers, and other supply sources, and, in turn, they transmit this information to their non-opinion-leader associates through interpersonal communications. Opinion leaders are found within all segments of the population.

Direct, Two-Step, and Multistep Communication Flows

Information about products, retail outlets, and ideas flow through a number of channels. In some cases, the flows are from radio, television, and other mass media to opinion leaders, and then from opinion leaders to the masses of the population. Elihu Katz and Paul Lazarsfeld referred to this channel as the two-step process of communication.[26] In other instances, the information flow is

Figure 6.2
Alternative Channels for Communication Flows

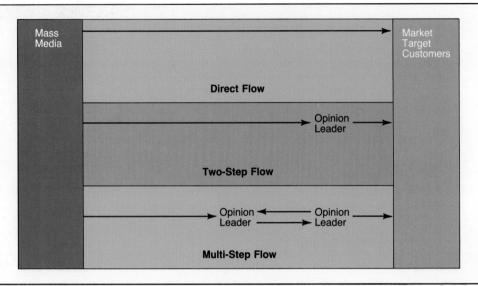

direct. Continuing access to communications channels allows much information to be transmitted directly to individuals who represent the organization's market target with no intermediaries. Another channel for information flows is a multistep flow. In this case, the flows are from mass media to opinion leaders then on to other opinion leaders before being disseminated to the general public. Figure 6.2 illustrates the three types of communication flows.

Applying the Opinion Leadership Concept

Opinion leaders play a crucial role in interpersonal communication. The fact that they distribute information and advice to others indicates their potential importance to marketing strategy. Opinion leaders, for instance, can be particularly useful in the launch of new products.

Ford Motor Company utilized the opinion leadership concept when it developed a special *VIP Program* to introduce its aerodynamically restyled Thunderbird. Over 400,000 performance-oriented professionals and executives, who traditionally had been inclined to buy imports, were offered a new Thunderbird to drive for a day. Follow-up surveys indicated that 84 percent of the recipients planned to recommend the car to others and one in ten test-drivers actually became Thunderbird owners.

Family Influence

One's family is also an interpersonal determinant of consumer behavior. The influence of household members is often significant in the purchase decision process. Because of the close, continuing interactions among family members, the family often represents the strongest source of group influence on the individual. Most people are members of at least two families during their lifetimes—the family into which they are born and the one they eventually form as they marry and have children.

The establishment of a new household results in new marketing opportunities. A new household means a new house or apartment and accompanying furniture. The need for refrigerators, vacuum cleaners, and a watercolor painting for the living room is dependent not on the number of persons comprising the household but on the number of households.

Less than 60 percent of all U.S. households now include a married couple. The tremendous growth of single and other nonfamily households has caused the average household size to fall to 2.7 persons.[27] In fact, it is estimated that 25 percent of all households will be single-person households by 1990.[28] This suggests a tremendous future opportunity for many marketers.

Another market is established for parents who are left alone when children move away from home. These parents may find themselves with a four-bedroom residence and a half acre of lawn to maintain. Lacking maintenance assistance from their children and no longer needing the large house, they become customers for townhouses, condominiums, and high-rise apartments in larger cities. Some become residents of St. Petersburg, Sun City, or other centers for retired persons. Others become market targets for medical insurance, travel, and hearing aids. Designing houses specifically for senior citizens is one effort to reach that market.

Household Roles

Historically, the wife made the majority of the family purchases, and the husband worked at a paying job most of the day. Even though the preferences of the children or the husband may have influenced her decisions, the wife usually was responsible for food buying and most of the clothing purchases.

Two forces have changed the female's role as sole purchasing agent for most household items. First, a shorter work week provides each wage-earning household member with more time for shopping. Second, there are a large number of women in the work force. In 1950, only one-fourth of married women were employed outside the home; now, over 50 percent are working wives. Studies of family decision making have shown that working wives tend to exert more influence in decision making than nonworking wives. Households with two wage earners also exhibit a large number of joint decisions and an increase in night and weekend shopping.

These changing roles of household members have led many marketers to adjust their marketing programs. For example, *The Wall Street Journal* recently noted: "In the world of TV commercials, dads now instruct their kids about Crest toothpaste, cook Aunt Jemima waffles for breakfast, cruise supermarket aisles for Kraft cheese, and change diapers with Johnson & Johnson baby powder. Teenagers cook Uncle Ben's rice for dinner, and the whole family pitches in to prepare Minute Rice."[29]

Although an infinite variety of roles can be played in household decision making, four role categories are often used: (1) autonomic—an equal number of decisions is made by each partner; (2) male dominant; (3) female dominant; and (4) syncratic—most decisions are jointly made by male and female.[30] Figure 6.3 shows the roles played by household members in the purchase of a number of products.

Figure 6.3
Role Categories in Household Decisions

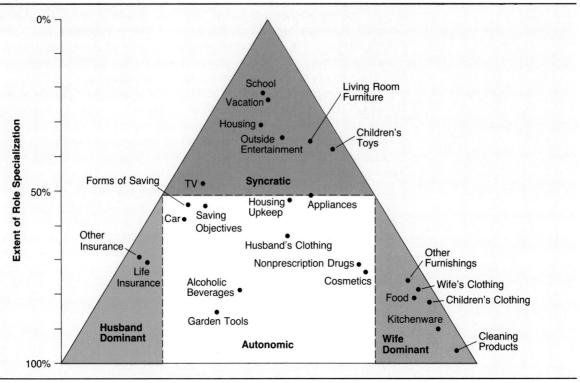

Source: Harry L. Davis and Benny P. Rigaux, "Perception of Marital Roles in Decision Processes,"
Journal of Consumer Research (June 1974), p. 57. Reprinted by permission from the
Journal of Consumer Research published by the Journal of Consumer Research, Inc.

Children's Roles in Household Purchasing

The role of children in purchasing evolves as they grow older. Children's early influence is generally centered around toys to be recommended to Santa Claus and the choice of cereal brands. Younger children are also important to marketers of fast-food restaurants.

In general, as children gain maturity, they increasingly influence their clothing purchases. One study revealed that teenage boys in the 13 to 15-year age group spend an average of $19.45 a week, while teenage girls spend $20.70. Between the ages of 16 and 19, the average weekly expenditure of boys is $43.30, while girls spend $45.30. Thirteen to fifteen-year-old teenage boys spend most of their money on food, movies, entertainment, and clothing. Girls in the same age group buy clothing, food and snacks, tickets for movies and entertainment, and jewelry. Sixteen to nineteen-year-old boys spend most of their money on dating, entertainment, automobiles and gasoline, clothing, and food and snacks, while girls in the same age group buy clothing, cosmetics, automobiles and gasoline, movie and entertainment tickets, and food and snacks.[31]

Teenagers—The Family's New Purchasing Agent

The growing number of married and divorced mothers who work has a decided impact on household purchasing patterns. Recent research shows that both teenage boys and girls play an important role in their family's grocery purchases. According to a recent survey of 1,002 teenagers conducted by the Beta Research Corporation, 64 percent shopped for food at one time or another, and 36 percent shopped at least once a week. Six out of ten of these teens helped write the family shopping list. Forty-two percent selected what their families purchased, 18 percent chose both the product and the specific brand, while another 24 percent selected just the brand.

Only slightly more girls than boys did the shopping. The incidence of teenage shopping is nearly equal for various income levels, family makeups, and market sizes. Overall, teens spend about 15 percent of the family's total food budget, averaging $24 per shopping trip.

Little advertising has been targeted at these important buyers. Research suggests that radio and magazines, not the traditional newspaper shopping sections, may be the best way to reach this audience. These young shoppers are not only a sizable part of the current market for many products, they are also the future market. Brand loyalties built now may last for decades. For example, a Yankelovich survey showed that 29 percent of adult women still drink the same coffee they did as teenagers. The growing role of teenage shoppers is certainly an important new development in the study of consumer behavior.[32]

Personal Determinants of Consumer Behavior

Consumer behavior is a function of both interpersonal and personal influences. The personal determinants of consumer behavior, as shown in Figure 6.1, include the individual's needs and motives, perceptions, attitudes, and self-concept. The interaction of these factors with interpersonal influences cause the individual to act.

Needs and Motives

Need
Lack of something useful; a discrepancy between a desired state and the actual state.

Motives
Inner states that direct people toward the goal of satisfying a felt need.

The starting point in the purchase decision process is the recognition of a felt need. A need is simply the lack of something useful. It is an imbalance between the consumer's actual and desired state. The consumer is typically confronted with numerous unsatisfied needs, but a need must be sufficiently aroused before it can serve as a motive to buy something.

Motives are inner states that direct people toward the goal of satisfying a felt need. The individual is moved to take action to reduce a state of tension and to return to a condition of equilibrium.

Hierarchy of Needs

Although psychologists disagree on specific classifications, a useful theory of the hierarchy of needs has been developed by A. H. Maslow. Maslow's hierarchy is shown in Figure 6.4. His list is based on two important assumptions:

1. People are wanting animals whose needs depend on what they already possess. A satisfied need is not a motivator; only those needs that have not been satisfied can influence behavior.

2. People's needs are arranged in a hierarchy of importance. After one need has been at least partially satisfied, another emerges and demands satisfaction.[33]

Figure 6.4
Hierarchy of Needs

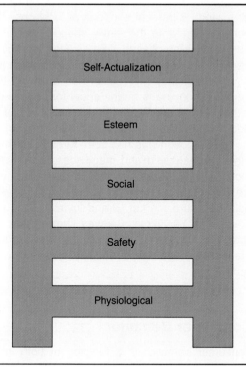

Self-Actualization

Esteem

Social

Safety

Physiological

Source: A. H. Maslow, "A Theory of Human Motivation," *Psychological Review* (July 1943), pp. 370–396.

Physiological Needs   The primary needs for food, shelter, and clothing that are present in all humans and must be satisfied before the individual can consider higher-order needs are physiological needs. After the physiological needs are at least partially satisfied, other needs enter the picture.

Safety Needs   The second-level safety needs include security, protection from physical harm, and avoidance of the unexpected. Gratification of these needs may take the form of a savings account, life insurance, the purchase of radial tires, or membership in a local health club. American Express advertisements also target this need.[34]

Social Needs   Satisfaction of physiological and safety needs leads to the third level—the desire to be accepted by members of the family and other individuals and groups—the social needs. The individual may be motivated to join various groups, to conform to their standards of dress and behavior, and to become interested in obtaining status as means of fulfilling these needs.

Esteem Needs   The higher-order needs are more prevalent in developed countries where a sufficiently high per-capita income has allowed most consumers to satisfy the basic needs and to concentrate on the desire for status, esteem, and self-actualization. These needs, which are near the top of the ladder, are more difficult to satisfy. At the esteem level is the need to feel a sense of accomplishment, achievement, and respect from others. The competitive need to excel—to better the performance of others—is almost a universal human trait.

The esteem need is closely related to social needs. At this level, however, the individual desires not just acceptance but also recognition and respect. The person has a desire to stand out from the crowd in some way.

Self-Actualization Needs   The top rung of the ladder of human needs is self-actualization, the need for fulfillment, for realizing one's own potential, for using one's talents and capabilities totally. Maslow defines self-actualization this way: "The healthy man is primarily motivated by his needs to develop and actualize his fullest potentialities and capabilities. What man can be, he must be."[35]

Maslow points out that a satisfied need is no longer a motivator. Once the physiological needs are satiated, the individual moves on to the higher-order needs. Consumers are periodically motivated by the need to relieve thirst or hunger, but their interests are most often directed toward satisfaction of safety, social, and other needs in the hierarchy.

Perception

Several years ago, a U.S. pharmaceutical firm developed Analoze, a cherry-flavored combination pain killer and stomach sweetener that could be taken without water. The product failed because consumers associated the ritual of taking pills and a glass of water with pain relief.[36] Analoze was not perceived as an effective remedy because it violated their experience with other pain killers.

Individual behavior resulting from motivation is affected by how stimuli are perceived. Perception is the meaning that each person attributes to incoming stimuli received through the five senses—sight, hearing, touch, taste, and smell. The Lean Cuisine ad in Figure 6.5 demonstrates advertising that appeals to multiple senses.

Perception
Manner in which an individual interprets a stimulus; the often highly subjective meaning that one attributes to an incoming stimulus or message.

Psychologists once assumed that perception was an objective phenomenon, that the individual perceived only what was there to be perceived. Only recently have researchers come to recognize that what people perceive is as much a result of what they want to perceive as of what is actually there. This does not mean that dogs may be viewed as pigeons or shopping centers as churches. A retail store stocked with well-known brand names and staffed with helpful, knowledgeable sales personnel is perceived differently from a largely self-service discount store.

The perception of an object or event is the result of the interaction of two types of factors:

1.   *Stimulus factors:* characteristics of the physical object, such as size, color, weight, or shape; and

2.   *Individual factors:* characteristics of the individual, including not only sensory processes but also experiences with similar items and basic motivations and expectations.

Perceptual Screens

The individual is continually bombarded with many stimuli, but most are ignored. To have time to function, people must respond selectively. The determination of which stimuli they do respond to is the problem of all marketers. How can the consumer's attention be gained so he or she will read the adver-

Figure 6.5
Stouffer's Uses More Than One Sense Mode to Create
a Favorable Perception of Its Lean Cuisine Frozen Foods

tisement, listen to the sales representative, or react to the point-of-purchase display? Figure 6.6 shows how PepsiCo attempts to capture the consumer's attention.

Even though studies have shown that the average consumer is exposed to more than 500 advertisements daily, most of these ads never break through people's perceptual screens—the perceptual filters through which messages must pass. Sometimes breakthroughs are accomplished in the printed media through large ads. Doubling the size of an ad increases its attention value by about 50 percent. Using color in newspaper ads, in contrast to the usual black and white ads, is another effective way of breaking through the reader's perceptual screen. Other contrast methods include using a large amount of white space around a printed area or using white type on a black background.

In general, the marketer seeks to make the message stand out, to make it sufficiently different from other messages that it gains the attention of the prospective customer. Menley & James Laboratories followed the practice of running hay-fever radio commercials for their Contac capsules only on days when the pollen count was above certain minimum levels. Each commercial was preceded by a live announcement of the local pollen count.

The psychological concept of closure also accomplishes the objective of making a message stand out. *Closure* refers to the tendency of people to

Perceptual Screens
Perceptual filters through which messages must pass.

Figure 6.6

PepsiCo's Tipper Display: Attracting Attention in Supermarkets

Source: Reproduced with permission of PepsiCo, Inc., owner of registered trademarks
Pepsi, Diet Pepsi, Pepsi Light, Mountain Dew, and Pepsi Free.

produce a complete picture. Advertisements that allow consumers to do this are successful in breaking through perceptual screens. Salem cigarettes once asked people to complete the advertising theme "You can take Salem out of the country, but. . . ." Kellogg at one time used outdoor advertising with the last "g" omitted at the billboard's edge.[37] During another Kellogg campaign promoting the use of fruit with cereal, they emphasized the point by replacing the "lls" in Kellogg with bananas; for another campaign featuring a 25-cent coupon offer, Kellogg emphasized the promotion by replacing the "o" in their brand name with a quarter, as Figure 6.7 illustrates.

With such selective perception at work, it is easy to see the importance of the marketer's efforts to obtain a "consumer franchise" in the form of brand loyalty to a product. Satisfied customers are less likely to seek information about competing products. Even when it is forced on them, they are not as likely as others to allow it to pass through their perceptual filters. They simply tune out information that is not in accord with their existing beliefs and expectations.

Subliminal Perception

Is it possible to communicate with persons without them being aware of the communication? In 1957, the words *eat popcorn* and *drink Coca-Cola* were flashed on the screen of a New Jersey movie theater every five seconds at 1/300th of a second. Researchers reported that these messages, although too

Figure 6.7
Examples of Closure

Subliminal Perception
Receipt of information at a subconscious level.

short to be recognizable at the conscious level, resulted in a 58 percent increase in popcorn sales and an 18 percent increase in Coca-Cola sales. After these findings were published, advertising agencies and consumer protection groups became intensely interested in **subliminal perception**—the receipt of incoming information at a subconscious level.

Subliminal advertising is aimed at the subconscious level of awareness to avoid viewers' perceptual screens. The goal of the original research was to induce consumer purchasing while keeping consumers unaware of the source of their motivation to buy. Further attempts to duplicate the test findings, however, have invariably been unsuccessful.

Although subliminal advertising has been universally condemned (and declared illegal in California and Canada), it is exceedingly unlikely that it can induce purchasing except in those instances where the person is already inclined to buy. The reasons for this are:

1. Strong stimulus factors are required to even gain attention.

2. Only a very short message can be transmitted.

3. Individuals vary greatly in their thresholds of consciousness.[38] Messages transmitted at the threshold of consciousness for one person will not be perceived at all by some people and will be all too apparent to others. The subliminally exposed message "Drink Coca-Cola" may go unseen by some viewers, while others may read it as "Drink Pepsi-Cola," "Drink Cocoa," or even "Drive Slowly."

Despite early fears, research has shown that subliminal messages cannot force the receiver to purchase goods that he or she would not consciously want.

Attitudes

Attitudes
One's enduring favorable or unfavorable evaluations, emotional feelings, or pro or con action tendencies.

Perception of incoming stimuli is greatly affected by attitudes. In fact, the decision to purchase a product is based on currently held attitudes about the product, the store, or the salesperson. **Attitudes** are a person's enduring favorable or unfavorable evaluations, emotional feelings, or pro or con action tendencies in regard to some object or idea. They are formed over a period of time through individual experiences and group contacts and are highly resistant to change.

Because favorable attitudes are likely to be conducive to brand preferences, marketers are interested in determining consumer attitudes toward their products. Numerous attitude scaling devices have been developed for this purpose.[39]

Attitude Components

There are three related components of an attitude: cognitive, affective, and behavioral. The cognitive component refers to the individual's information and knowledge about an object or concept. The affective component deals with feelings or emotional reactions. The behavioral component involves tendencies to act or to behave in a certain manner. In considering the decision to shop at a warehouse-type food store, the individual would obtain information from advertising, trial visits, and input from family, friends, and associates (cognitive). The consumer would also receive input from others about their acceptance of shopping at this type of store, as well as information about the type of people who shop there (affective). The shopper may ultimately decide to make some purchases of canned goods, cereal, and bakery products there but continue to rely on a regular supermarket for major food purchases (behavioral).

All three components exist in a relatively stable and balanced relationship to one another and combine to form an overall attitude about an object or idea. Figure 6.8 illustrates the three attitude components.

Figure 6.8
Attitude Components

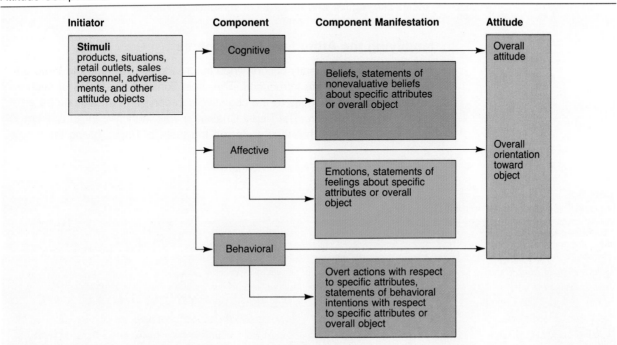

Source: Adapted from M. J. Rosenberg and C. I. Hovland, *Attitude Organization and Change*
(New Haven, Conn.: Yale University Press, 1960), p. 3. Reprinted by permission.

Changing Consumer Attitudes

Given that a favorable consumer attitude is a prerequisite to marketing success, how can a firm lead prospective buyers to adopt this kind of attitude toward its products? The marketer has two choices: to attempt to change consumer attitudes making them consonant with the product, or to first determine consumer attitudes then change the product to match them. If consumers view the product unfavorably, the firm may choose to redesign it to better conform with their desires. It may make styling changes, vary ingredients, change package size, or switch retail stores.

The other course of action—changing consumer attitudes—is much more difficult. A famous study of coffee drinkers revealed surprisingly negative attitudes toward those who serve instant coffee. The two imaginary shopping lists in Figure 6.9 were shown to a sample of 100 homemakers. Half were shown List 1 and half List 2. Each respondent was then asked to describe the hypothetical shopper who purchased the groceries. The only difference in the lists was the instant versus the regular coffee.

The woman who bought instant coffee was described as lazy by 48 percent of the women evaluating List 1, but only 24 percent of those evaluating List 2 described the woman who bought regular coffee as lazy. Forty-eight percent described the instant coffee purchaser as failing to plan household purchases and schedules well; only 12 percent described the purchaser of regular coffee this way.

But consumer attitudes often change with time. The shopping list study was repeated 20 years later, and the new study revealed that much of the stigma attached to buying instant coffee had disappeared. Instead of describing the instant coffee purchaser as lazy and a poor planner, most respondents thought she was a working woman.[40] Nonetheless, General Foods took no chances when it introduced its new freeze-dried Maxim as a coffee that "tastes like regular and has the convenience of instant."

Modifying the Attitudinal Components

Attitude change frequently occurs when inconsistencies among the three attitudinal components are introduced. The most common examples of such inconsistencies are changes to the cognitive component of an attitude as a result of new information. The Pepsi Challenge was launched in an attempt to convince consumers that they preferred the taste of Pepsi, giving them new

Figure 6.9
Shopping Lists Used in the Instant Coffee Study

Shopping List 1	Shopping List 2
1½ lbs. of hamburger	1½ lbs. of hamburger
2 loaves of Wonder Bread	2 loaves of Wonder Bread
Bunch of carrots	Bunch of carrots
1 can Rumford's Baking Powder	1 can Rumford's Baking Powder
Nescafé Instant Coffee	*1 lb. Maxwell House coffee (drip grind)*
2 cans Del Monte peaches	2 cans Del Monte peaches
5 lbs. potatoes	5 lbs. potatoes

Source: Mason Haire, "Projective Techniques in Marketing Research," *Journal of Marketing* (April 1950), pp. 649–656. Reprinted from the *Journal of Marketing* published by the American Marketing Association.

Return to the Stop-Action Case

The Yamaha PortaTone PC-1000

Yamaha has developed a unique portable keyboard instrument, the PortaTone PC-1000, to entice nonmusicians to consider purchasing a Yamaha product. The PC-1000 is a modern-day player piano programmed to provide a fully orchestrated musical performance including melody, obbligato, bass and chords, rhythm accompaniment, and drum fill-ins, as well as 12 orchestra voices including the clarinet, guitar, and violin.

The PC-1000's performance is programmed by special Yamaha Playcards that are placed into a slot on the instrument. The slot "reads" the playing instructions from a magnetic strip at the bottom of the Playcard song sheet. As the notes are read, the keyboard plays, rendering the entire performance without the player touching the keyboard. Beginners who want to play along can do so by following lights above the keys that show them which notes to play.

information that might lead to increased sales. A recent Life Savers advertising campaign built around the theme that a Life Saver contains only ten calories was designed to correct misconceptions in the minds of many consumers about the candy's high caloric content.

The affective component may be altered by relating the use of the new product or service to desirable consequences for the user. The growth of health clubs can be attributed to their success in promoting the benefits of being trim and physically fit.

The third alternative in attempting to change attitudes is to focus upon the behavioral component by inducing the person to engage in behavior that contradicts currently held attitudes. Attitude-discrepant behavior may occur if the consumer is given a free sample of a product. Trying the product may lead to an attitude change.

Learning

Learning
Changes in behavior, immediate or expected, that occur as a result of experience.

Drive
Strong stimulus that impels action.

Cue
Any object existing in the environment that determines the nature of the response to a drive.

Marketing is as concerned with the process by which consumer decisions change over time as with describing those decisions at any one point. Thus the study of how learning takes place is important. Learning refers to changes in behavior, immediate or expected, as a result of experience.

The learning process includes several components. The first component, drive, is any strong stimulus that impels action. Examples of drives are fear, pride, desire for money, thirst, pain avoidance, and rivalry.

The cue, the second component of the learning process, is any object existing in the environment that determines the nature of the response to a drive. Examples of cues are a newspaper advertisement for a new French restaurant, an in-store display, and an Exxon sign on an interstate highway. For the hungry person, the shopper seeking a particular item, or the motorist needing gasoline, these cues may result in a specific response to satisfy a drive.

Response
Individual's reaction to cues and drive.

A **response** is the individual's reactions to the cues and drive. Responses might include such reactions as purchasing a package of Gillette Trac II blades, dining at Burger King, or deciding to enroll at a particular college or university.

Reinforcement
Reduction in drive that results from an appropriate response.

Reinforcement is the reduction in drive that results from a proper response. The more rewarding the response, the stronger the bond becomes between the drive and the purchase of that particular product. Should the purchase of Trac II blades result in closer shaves through repeated use, the likelihood of their purchase in the future is increased.

Applying Learning Theory to Marketing Decisions[41]

Learning theory has some important implications for marketing strategists. A desired outcome like repeat purchase behavior has to be developed gradually. *Shaping* is the process of applying a series of rewards and reinforcements so that more complex behavior can evolve over time. Both promotional strategy and the product itself play a role in the shaping process.

Figure 6.10 shows the application of learning theory and shaping procedures to a typical marketing scenario. Assume that marketers are attempting to motivate consumers to become regular buyers of a certain product. An initial product trial is induced by a free sample package that includes a substantial discount coupon on a subsequent purchase. This illustrates the use of a cue as a shaping procedure. The purchase response is reinforced by satisfactory product performance and a coupon for the next purchase.

Figure 6.10
Application of Learning Theory and Shaping Procedure to Marketing

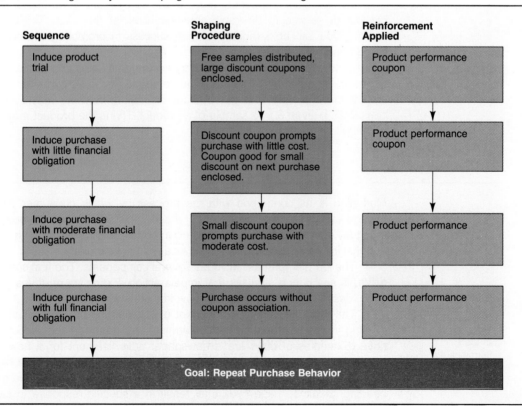

Source: Adapted from Michael L. Rothschild and William C. Gaidis, "Behavioral Learning Theory:
Its Relevance to Marketing and Promotions," *Journal of Marketing* (Spring 1981), p. 72.

The second stage is to entice the consumer to buy the product with little financial risk. The large discount coupon enclosed in the free sample prompts such an action. The package that is purchased has a smaller discount coupon enclosed. Again, the reinforcement is satisfactory product performance and the second coupon.

The third step would be to motivate the person to buy the item again at a moderate cost. The discount coupon accomplishes this objective, but this time there is no additional coupon in the package. The only reinforcement is satisfactory product performance.

The final test comes when the consumer is asked to buy the product at its true price without a discount coupon. Satisfaction with product performance is the only continuing reinforcement. Thus repeat purchase behavior has been literally shaped by effective application of learning theory within a marketing strategy context.

The introduction of Kellogg's Nutri-Grain brand sugarless whole grain cereal illustrates the use of learning theory. Coupons worth 40 cents off— about a third of the product's cost—were distributed to elicit trial purchases by consumers. Inside boxes of the new cereal were additional cents-off coupons of lesser value.[42] Figure 6.11 indicates Kellogg's attempt to shape future purchase behavior.

Figure 6.11
Kellogg's Nutri-Grain Campaign Illustrates the Use of Learning Theory

Figure 6.12
Self-Concept Theory Components

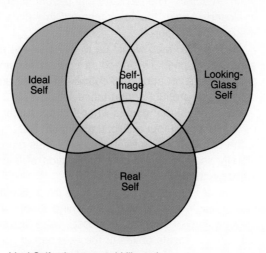

Ideal Self—the way you'd like to be
Self-Image—the way you see yourself
Real Self—you as you are
Looking-Glass Self—the way you think others see you

Source: John Douglas, George A. Field, and Lawrence X. Tarpey, *Human Behavior in Marketing*
(Columbus, Ohio: Charles E. Merrill Publishing Co., 1967), p. 65. Reprinted by permission.

Self-Concept Theory

Self-Concept
Mental conception of one's self,
comprised of four components: real
self, self-image, looking-glass self,
and ideal self.

The consumer's self-concept plays an important role in consumer behavior. Individuals are physical and mental entities possessing multifaceted pictures of themselves. One young man, for example, may view himself as intellectual, self-assured, moderately talented, and a rising young business executive. People's actions, including their purchase decisions, are related to their mental conception of self—their self-concept. The response to direct questions like "Why do you buy Senchal?" is likely to reflect this desired self-image.

The concept of self is the result of the interaction of many of the influences—both personal and interpersonal—affecting buyer behavior. Individual needs, motives, perception, attitudes, and learning lie at the core of an individual's conception of self, in addition to the environmental factors of family, social, and cultural influences.

As Figure 6.12 indicates, the self has four components: real self, self-image, looking-glass self, and ideal self. The real self is an objective view of the total person. The self-image, the way individuals view themselves, may distort the objective view. The looking-glass self, the way individuals think others see them, may also be quite different from self-image, since people often choose to project a different image to others. The ideal self serves as a personal set of objectives, since it is the image to which the individual aspires.

In purchasing goods and services, people are likely to choose products that move them closer to their ideal self-image. Those who see themselves as scholars are more likely than others to join literary book clubs. The young woman who views herself as a budding tennis star may become engrossed in evaluating the merits of graphite versus steel rackets and may view any cheaply made imports with disdain. The college graduate on the way up the organizational ladder at a bank may hide a love for bowling and instead take up golf, having determined that golf is the sport for bankers.

Figure 6.13

Steps in the Consumer Decision Process

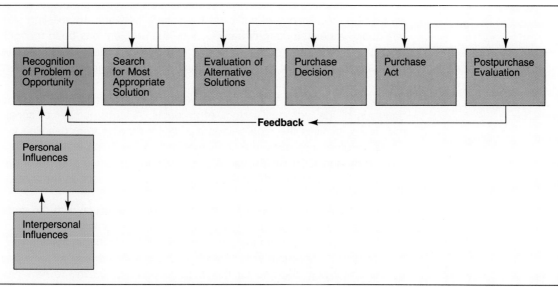

Sources: C. Glenn Walters and Gordon W. Paul, *Consumer Behavior: An Integrated Framework* Homewood,
Ill.: Richard D. Irwin, Inc., 1970), p. 18, and James F. Engel, Roger D. Blackwell, Paul W. Miniard, *Consumer
Behavior,* fifth edition (Hinsdale, Ill: The Dryden Press, 1986), pp. 29–35.

The Consumer Decision Process

Consumer behavior research traditionally has focused on such specific areas as attitudes, personality, and the influence of reference groups on the individual. To see these fragments in their proper perspective, a model of the entire process is required. This model, shown in Figure 6.13, makes possible the integration of the various components of consumer behavior and assists in understanding the complex relationships among them. It also provides a means of integrating new research findings in the search for a more complete explanation of why consumers behave as they do. The total model approach can be used in major buying situations, such as a first-time purchase of a new product or the purchase of a high-priced, long-lived article. By contrast, it can also be applied to cases of routine purchases handled by the individual in a largely habitual manner, such as the purchase of a newspaper or a particular brand of chewing gum.

Both personal and interpersonal influences act on the individual to create a recognition that a problem exists. This recognition triggers the consumer decision process. The steps of this process are outlined in the following sections.

Problem Recognition

The first stage in the decision process occurs when the consumer becomes aware of a discrepancy of sufficient magnitude between the existing state of affairs and a desired state of affairs. Once the problem has been recognized, it must be defined so that the consumer may seek out methods for its solution. As a consequence of problem recognition, the individual is motivated to achieve the desired state.

Perhaps the most common cause of problem recognition is a routine depletion of the individual's stock of products. A large number of consumer purchases involves the replenishment of items ranging from gasoline to groceries. In other instances, the consumer may possess an inadequate assortment of products. The individual whose hobby is gardening may make regular purchases of different fertilizers, seeds, or gardening tools as the size of the garden grows.

A third cause of problem recognition is dissatisfaction with the consumer's present brand or product type. This situation is common in the purchase of a new automobile, new furniture, or a new fall wardrobe. In many instances, the consumer's boredom with current products and a desire for novelty may be the underlying rationale for the decision process leading to new product purchases.

Another important factor in problem recognition is changed financial status. The infusion of added financial resources from such sources as a salary increase, a second job, or an inheritance may permit the consumer to make purchases that previously had been postponed.

Search

The second step in the decision process is search, the gathering of information related to the attainment of a desired state of affairs. This stage permits the identification of alternative means of problem solution.

Search may be internal or external. Internal search is a mental review of stored information relevant to the problem situation. This includes both actual experiences and observations plus memories of personal communications and exposures to persuasive marketing efforts.

External search is the gathering of information from outside sources by the consumer who is involved in the search process. Outside information sources may include family members, friends and associates, store displays, sales representatives, brochures, and such product-testing publications as *Consumer Reports*.

In many instances, problems are solved by the consumer through internal search. The individual merely relies upon stored information in making a purchase decision. Achieving favorable results using Du Pont's Rain Dance car polish may sufficiently motivate a consumer to repurchase this brand rather than to consider possible alternatives. Since external search involves both time and effort, the consumer will rely upon it only when adequate information is unavailable in memory.

Alternative brands for consideration and possible purchase are identified during the search process. The number of brands that a consumer actually considers in making a purchase decision is known as the evoked set. In some instances, the consumer is aware of the brands worthy of further consideration; in other situations, the external search process involves the acquisition of information necessary to permit the consumer to identify those brands that

Evoked Set
In consumer decision making, the number of brands that a consumer actually considers before making a purchase decision.

comprise the evoked set. Not all brands are included in the evoked set. Sometimes the consumer is unaware of certain brands, others are rejected as too costly, while still others have been tried previously and considered unsatisfactory. Unfavorable word-of-mouth communication or negative reactions to advertising or other marketing efforts may also result in the elimination of some brands from the evoked set. While the number of brands in the evoked set will vary by product categories, research indicates that the number is likely to be as few as four or five brands.[43]

Evaluation of Alternatives

The third step in the consumer decision process involves the evaluation of alternatives identified during the search process. Actually, it is difficult to completely separate the second and third steps since some evaluation takes place simultaneously with the search process as consumers accept, discount, distort, or reject incoming information as they receive it.

Since the outcome of the evaluation stage is the choice of a brand or product in the evoked set (or, possibly, the search for additional alternatives should all alternatives identified during the search process prove unsatisfactory), the consumer must develop a set of evaluative criteria for use in making the selection. Evaluative criteria may be defined as those features the consumer considers in making a choice among alternatives. These criteria can either be objective (government tests of miles per gallon or comparison of retail prices) or subjective (favorable image of Calvin Klein sportswear). Commonly used evaluative criteria include price, reputation of the brand, perceived quality, packaging, size, performance, durability, and color. Evaluative criteria for detergents include suds level and smell as indicators of cleaning power. Most research studies indicate that consumers utilize six or fewer criteria in the evaluation process.[44]

The Purchase Decision and the Purchase Act

The end result of the search and alternative evaluation stages of the decision process is the actual purchase decision and the act of making the purchase. The consumer has evaluated each of the alternatives in the evoked set, utilizing his or her personal set of evaluative criteria, and has narrowed the alternatives to one.

Another decision facing the consumer is the purchase location. Consumers tend to make store choice decisions by considering such factors as location, price, assortment, store personnel, store image, physical design, and services. In addition, store selection is influenced by the product category. Some consumers choose the convenience of in-home shopping via telephone or mail order rather than complete the transaction in a retail store.[45]

Postpurchase Evaluation

The purchase act results in satisfaction to the buyer and removal of the discrepancy between the existing state and the desired state or dissatisfaction with the purchase. It is also common for consumers to experience some postpurchase anxieties. Leon Festinger refers to the postpurchase doubt as **cognitive dissonance** [46]

Dissonance is a psychologically unpleasant state that occurs when an imbalance exists among a person's *cognitions* (knowledge, beliefs, and atti-

Evaluative Criteria
In consumer decision making, the features considered in a consumer's choice of alternatives.

Cognitive Dissonance
Postpurchase anxiety that results when an imbalance exists among an individual's cognitions (knowledge, beliefs, and attitudes).

tudes). For example, consumers may experience dissonance after choosing a particular automobile over several alternative models when several of the rejected models have some desired features not available with the chosen model.

Dissonance is likely to increase (1) as the dollar value of the purchase increases, (2) when the rejected alternatives have desirable features not present in the chosen alternative, and (3) when the decision is a major one. The consumer may attempt to reduce dissonance in a variety of ways. He or she may seek out advertisements and other information supporting the chosen alternative or seek reassurance from acquaintances who are satisfied purchasers of the product. The individual may also avoid information favoring the unchosen alternative. The Toyota purchaser is likely to read Toyota advertisements and to avoid Nissan and Volkswagen ads. The cigarette smoker may ignore the magazine articles reporting links between smoking and cancer.

Marketers can assist in reducing cognitive dissonance by providing informational support for the chosen alternative. Automobile dealers recognize "buyer's remorse" and often follow up purchases with a warm letter from the president of the dealership, who offers personal handling of any customer problems and includes a description of the product's quality and the availability of convenient, top-quality service.

A final method of dealing with cognitive dissonance is for the consumer to change opinions, thereby restoring the cognitive balance. In this instance, the consumer may ultimately decide that one of the rejected alternatives would have been the best choice and may decide to purchase it in the future.[47]

Should the purchase prove unsatisfactory, the consumer's purchase strategy must be revised to allow need satisfaction to be obtained. Whether satisfactory or not, feedback on the results of the decision process will serve as experience to be called upon in similar buying situations in the future.

Classifying Consumer Problem-Solving Processes

The consumer decision process varies on the basis of the problem-solving effort that is required. There are three categories of problem-solving behavior: routinized response behavior, limited problem solving, and extended problem solving.[48] The classification of a particular purchase according to this framework clearly impacts the consumer decision process.

Routinized Response Behavior   Many purchases are made on the basis of a preferred brand or selection from a limited group of acceptable brands. This type of rapid consumer problem solving is referred to as routinized response behavior. The evaluative criteria are set and the available options identified. External search is limited in cases of routinized response behavior. The routine purchase of regular brands of beer, cigarettes, or soft drinks are examples.

Limited Problem Solving   Consider the situation where the consumer has set evaluative criteria but encounters a new, unknown brand. The introduction of a new fragrance line is an example of a limited problem-solving situation. The consumer knows the evaluative criteria but has not assessed the new brand on the basis of these criteria. A medium amount of time and external search is involved in such situations. Limited problem solving is affected by the multitude of evaluative criteria and brands, the extent of external search, and the process by which preferences are determined.

Extended Problem Solving   Analoze, a product described earlier was not clearly classified by consumers. Extended problem solving results from such situations where the brand is difficult to categorize or evaluate. The first step is to compare the item with similar ones, such as Analoze was compared to other pain killers. The consumer needs to understand the item before evaluating alternatives. In the case of Analoze, the evaluation was negative. Most extended problem-solving efforts are lengthy and involve considerable external search.

Regardless of the type of problem solving, the steps in the basic model of the consumer decision process remain valid. The problem-solving categories described here relate only to the time and effort that is devoted to each step in the process.

Summary

Consumer behavior refers to the way people select, obtain, and use goods and services. Both interpersonal and personal factors determine patterns of consumer behavior.

There are three interpersonal determinants of consumer behavior: cultural influences, social influences, and family influences. Culture, the broadest of these three influences, refers to behavioral values that are created and inherited by a society. The work ethic and the accumulation of wealth were the original determinants of American culture. Cultural norms can change over time, although traditionally the pace of change is slow. However, it may occur at a faster pace in the future. An example of a recent shift in values is the desire for expanded friendship rather than self-centered activities.

Cultural influences are particularly significant in international marketing, but they are also crucial factors in domestic marketing. Increased attention is being devoted to the consumption behavior patterns of U.S. subcultures. The two largest American subcultures are blacks and Hispanics, both of which are growing market segments.

Social influences concern the nonfamily group influences on consumer behavior. The role that groups play in individual decision making was demonstrated by research conducted by S. E. Asch. If a group's values or standards impact individual behavior, it is said to be a reference group for that person. The importance of reference groups on specific product and brand decisions varies.

Social class ranking is another factor that influences consumer behavior. The existence of a U.S. class system was demonstrated by W. Lloyd Warner years ago. Opinion leaders, or trend-setters, are another important social influence on consumer behavior. The reaction of these people to new products is highly influential in the future success of the good or service. Marketers must make special efforts to appeal to these flagships of consumer behavior.

Family influences are the third interpersonal determinant of consumer behavior. Family purchasing patterns vary. In some cases, the female is dominant; in others, the male. Some purchase decisions are made jointly while others are made separately, but the number of such decisions is roughly equal between male and female. The traditional role for the female was the family's purchasing agent. This situation is now in flux, and more teenagers are doing the shopping for the household.

The personal determinants of consumer behavior are needs and motives, perceptions, attitudes, and self-concept. Learning theory also plays a role in consumer behavior processes.

A need is the lack of something useful, while motives are the inner states that direct individuals to satisfy such needs. A. H. Maslow proposed a hierarchy of needs that started with basic physiological needs and proceeded to progressively higher levels of needs—safety, social, esteem, and self-actualization. Perception is the meaning that people assign to incoming stimuli received through the five senses. Because most of these stimuli are screened or filtered out, the marketer's task is to break through these screens to effectively present the sales message. Attitudes are a person's evaluations and feelings toward an object or idea. There are three components of attitudes: cognitive (what the person knows), affective (what the person feels about something), and behavioral (how the person tends to act). Learning refers to changes in behavior, immediate or expected, as a result of experience. The learning theory concept can be useful in building consumer loyalty for a particular brand. The self-concept refers to an individual's conception of self. Self-concept theory has important implications for marketing strategy, such as in the case of targeting advertising messages.

The consumer decision process consists of six stages: problem recognition, search, evaluation of alternatives, purchase decision, purchase act, and postpurchase evaluation. The process varies on the basis of the problem-solving effort that is required. Routinized response behavior, limited problem solving, and extended problem solving are the three categories of problem-solving behavior.

Solving the
Stop-Action Case

The Yamaha PortaTone PC-1000

The Yamaha PortaTone PC-1000 encourages beginners to overcome their musical fears by enabling them to play at their own pace. A beginner who selects the Free Tempo mode can press the melody keys, according to the directions given by the illuminated melody lamp, at whatever pace he or she feels comfortable. The programmed accompaniment follows along and even stops if a wrong key is pressed. Beginners can learn to play chords in a similar way. Chord lamps light up over groups of three or four keys to produce the desired musical effect. The Playcard system also enables beginners to practice the same musical phrase or phrases over and over again until they are mastered.

The PC-1000 gives more advanced players the flexibility to use only parts of the programmed musical instruction. By cancelling the melody or chords on the magnetic strip, players can choose their own musical interpretations yet still have a musical accompaniment in the form of obbligato, bass, rhythm, and drum fill-ins.

Photo Source: Yamaha International Corporation, Specialty Products Division.

Nonmusicians who want to master popular tunes are attracted to the Yamaha PortaTone PC-1000 because of its large selection of Playcards that feature the music of Paul McCartney and other popular artists. The instrument is especially attractive to teenagers, who are targeted by Yamaha as one of their primary markets, because of its portability and price. The PC-1000 weighs only 12.8 pounds and can be easily carried in one hand. With a suggested retail price of $749, it is more affordable than a traditional piano. Yamaha's successful product resulted from the firm's ability to change consumer attitudes toward keyboard instruments.

Source: Information provided by Yamaha International Corporation, Specialty Products Division, 1985.

Questions for Discussion

1. Relate the model of consumer behavior developed in this chapter to the formula proposed by psychologist Kurt Lewin for classifying behavioral influences.

2. How does culture impact buying patterns?

3. Discuss the cultural values or norms that have had the greatest impact on your purchase behavior.

4. For which of the following products is reference-group influence likely to be strong?
   a. Rolex watch
   b. Skis
   c. Shaving lather
   d. 10-speed bicycle
   e. Portable radio
   f. Cigarettes
   g. Electric blanket
   h. Contact lenses

5. Identify the opinion leaders in a group to which you belong. Why are these people the group's opinion leaders?

6. List two products for which the following family members might be most influential:
   a. Mother
   b. 6-year-old child
   c. Father
   d. Teenage son
   e. Teenage daughter
   f. 2-year-old child

7. Relate social class to consumer behavior.

8. Which two social classes contain the largest membership? The smallest?

9. How do needs and motives influence consumer behavior?

10. Identify and briefly explain each of the levels in Maslow's hierarchy of needs.

11. Based on Maslow's hierarchy, which needs are being referred to in the following advertising slogans:
    a. "No caffeine. Never had it. Never will." (7-Up)
    b. "Where a man belongs." (Camel cigarettes)
    c. "The most beautiful summer evenings start with Red." (Johnnie Walker Red Label Scotch)
    d. "Don't leave home without it." (American Express Card)

12. Poll your friends about subliminal perception. How many believe that marketers can control consumers at a subconscious level? Report the results of this survey to your marketing class.

13. How can learning theory be applied to marketing strategy?

14. Cite examples of shaping procedures being used in marketing applications.

15. Outline your own ideal self, looking-glass self, self-image, and real self.

16. Relate each of the following to the appropriate component of the self-concept:
    a. "Three more semesters until I finish the degree, get a good job, and move into my own apartment."
    b. "I'm outgoing and a fun person. My friends see me as a terrific mixer and extremely witty."
    c. "It's true that I'm outgoing and fun to be with, but I'm also much too hesitant when meeting people, especially older people."
    d. "Debby is a C student, has average athletic abilities, and is quite involved in the ecology movement."

17. Select a recent shopping experience. Then analyze your attitudes relating to your consumer behavior in this instance. Be sure your assessment considers all three components of an attitude.

18. Relate a recent purchase you made to the consumer decision process outlined in this chapter.

19. Under what circumstances is cognitive dissonance most likely to occur? What steps may be taken to reduce it?

20. Differentiate among routinized response behavior, limited problem solving, and extended problem solving.

Case: American Saw & Manufacturing Company

It only took "Hack-man" 7 blades and 26 minutes and 6 seconds to saw the compact car completely in half. Why did he do it? Hack-man was a promotional event sponsored by American Saw & Manufacturing Company to highlight its Lenox hacksaw blades.

The Hack-man event was staged on a Saturday afternoon so employees from both shifts and their families could watch it. The company sponsored an employee contest to guess how long it would take Hack-man to do his work. The event was covered by local television stations and newspapers. Hack-man posters and caps were developed to promote Lenox blades. Smaller bulletins were available to dealers as mailing pieces and point-of-sale handouts.

Hack-man was helpful in building pride in the products employees make. It was also designed to promote Lenox blades to their distribution channels, specifically the electrical, plumbing, and construction wholesale trades. To do this, American Saw had to deal with the perceptions of that marketplace. One American Saw executive put it this way: "There really isn't much excitement about a hacksaw blade. You have to try to build some." Hack-man was able to dramatically demonstrate the qualities of Lenox blades.

Since the car-cutting event, Hack-man has worked in many trade show booths attended by plumbing, electrical, and building contractors who recognize him immediately as "the guy who cut the car in half." Hack-man's continued promotional contribution through demonstration sawing improved sales by a significant amount, and Lenox's share of the market has grown appreciably.

Source: Courtesy of American Saw & Mfg. Co.

American Saw liked the Hack-man promotion so much that in the fall of 1984 it had Hack-man cut a 30-foot-long Fruehauf tanker in half. The winner of a contest to guess Hack-man's tanker-sawing time won 10 troy ounces of gold.

Sources: Information provided by American Saw & Manufacturing Company, updated May 11, 1984. The quote is from *The Wall Street Journal* (December 31, 1981), p. 31. Information courtesy of American Saw & Manufacturing Company.

Questions

1. What aspect of consumer behavior was Hack-man dealing with in this demonstration? Discuss.

2. Can you think of other ways that Hack-man could improve the consumer's attitude toward Lenox blades?

3. What other products could benefit from dramatic demonstrations like Hack-man? Why?

Computer Applications

Two important concepts discussed in connection with the consumer decision process are *evoked set* and *evaluative criteria*. An evoked set is defined in Chapter 6 as the number of brands a consumer actually considers in his or her search behavior. Evaluative criteria are those features the consumer considers in selecting a specific purchase option. Both concepts are described in detail on pages 174–175.

Consumers develop various methods for making purchase choices from alternative products or brands. For major purchases and cases where considerable risk is present, potential buyers may score or rank the brands that comprise their evoked set on the basis of various evaluative criteria. Then the question becomes how to best make the actual purchase decision. Approaches to this problem include (1) the overall scoring method, (2) the weighted scoring method, and (3) the minimum score method.[1]

Overall Scoring Method. This approach to ranking alternative purchase possibilities uses the highest total score to select a brand from among the evoked set. All of the evaluative criteria are considered of equal importance, and the brand with the highest overall score is chosen.

Weighted Scoring Method. The second approach involves assigning different weights to the various evaluative criteria in accordance with the consumer's perception of their relative importance. Once the variables are assigned their weighted scores, they are totaled and the brand with the highest score is selected.

Minimum Score Method. This approach sets a floor for one or more of the evaluative criteria below which a brand will not be selected. For example, should the consumer decide that a brand must receive a ranking of 4 or more on the "service availability," a brand ranked 3 for this criterion would be rejected even though it might receive the highest overall score. The minimum score method is frequently used in conjunction with either the overall scoring method or the weighted scoring method.

It should be noted that these methods are representative of quantitative approaches to a typically qualitatively-oriented subject. Not all consumers behave in such a fashion. Moreover, those who do may differ significantly in their scoring evaluations. The problems that follow refer to a specific consumer's perceptions of a purchasing situation in which the individual has already determined the evaluative criteria and the evoked set.

---

[1] A similar approach is discussed in David L. Kurtz, H. Robert Dodge, and Jay E. Klompmaker, *Professional Selling*, 4th ed. (Plano, Texas: Business Publications, Inc., 1985).

Directions: Use menu item 6 titled "Evaluation of Alternatives" to solve each of the following problems.

Problem 1 An Oakland, Michigan, consumer is considering four brands of washing machines (the evoked set). The consumer has decided to evaluate the brands on the bases of price, quality, warranty, and service availability (the evaluative criteria). The consumer has also decided to give each model a score of 1 (poor) to 5 (best) on each of the evaluative criteria. These scores are shown below.

Evoked Set	Evaluative Criteria: Decision Factors			
	(A)	(B)	(C)	(D) Service
Alternatives	Price	Quality	Warranty	Availability
1. Washmaster	4	3	4	4
2. Magic Washer	4	4	4	4
3. Wonder Machine	2	5	5	5
4. The Marvel	5	5	4	2

a.   Which model would the consumer select using the overall scoring method?

b.   Suppose the consumer considers price 50 percent more important than any of the other evaluative criteria. Which model would be selected?

c.   Suppose the consumer, using the overall scoring method, also decides that he or she will not accept

any model that scored lower than 3 on any variable. Which model would be selected?

d.   Would your response to Question c change if the consumer used the weighted scoring method?

Problem 2 Alice Jarvis, of Bristol, Pennsylvania, is attempting to select a new car based on the following criteria: price, trade-in allowance, styling, riding comfort, and fuel economy. Jarvis had earlier narrowed her decision to four models: Elegance, Standard, Speedo, and Majestic. She then decided to rate each model on each of the specified evaluative criteria. Jarvis used a 3 to represent "excellent," 2 for "good," and 1 for "fair." Her rankings are shown below.

Evoked Set	Evaluative Criteria: Decision Factors				
	(A)	(B) Trade-in	(C)	(D) Riding	(E) Fuel
Alternatives	Price	Allowance	Styling	Comfort	Economy
1. Elegance	2	2	3	3	2
2. Standard	2	2	2	2	3
3. Speedo	3	3	3	3	1
4. Majestic	3	3	1	1	3

a.   Which model would the consumer select using the overall scoring method?

b.   Suppose that the consumer considers that fuel economy, price, and trade-in allowance are each 50 percent more important than the other two evaluative criteria. Which model would she select?

c.   Suppose that Jarvis, using the overall scoring method, also decides she will not accept any model

that is rated lower than good on fuel economy, price, and trade-in allowance. Which model would she prefer?

d.   Would Jarvis's decision in Question c change if she decides to use the weighted scoring method?

Problem 3 Like Alice Jarvis in Problem 2, Hal Eckleburger is also contemplating the purchase of a new car. In fact, he and Jarvis conferred before assigning the ratings for the Elegance, Standard, Speedo, and Majestic. However, Eckleburger also considers another auto model, the Olympic, to be a viable option. His rankings are shown below.

Evoked Set	Evaluative Criteria: Decision Factors				
Alternatives	(A) Price	(B) Trade-in Allowance	(C) Styling	(D) Riding Comfort	(E) Fuel Economy
1. Elegance	2	2	3	3	2
2. Standard	2	2	2	2	3
3. Speedo	3	3	3	3	1
4. Majestic	3	3	1	1	3
5. Olympic	3	2	2	2	2

a. Which model would the consumer select using the overall scoring method?

b. Suppose Eckleburger considers riding comfort and fuel economy 100 percent more important than styling and price, and trade-in allowance 200 percent more important than styling. Which model would he select?

c. Suppose that Eckleburger, using the overall scoring method, also decides that he will not accept a car that is rated lower than good on any variable. Which model would he select?

d. Would Eckleburger's decision in Question c change if he had used the weighted scoring method?

Problem 4 Ed Jacoby, of Montclair, New Jersey, is considering the purchase of a new refrigerator. His evoked set consists of five brands: Chillmaster, Super Fridge, Excellence, Keep Fresher, and Best Fridge. Jacoby's evaluative criteria are price, energy efficiency, appearance, ice-making feature, and reversible doors. He decides to use a seven-point rating scale in making his assessment. Scores range from 1 (unacceptable or the absence of the feature) to 7 (perfect). Jacoby's scores are shown below.

Evoked Set	Evaluative Criteria: Decision Factors				
Alternatives	(A) Price	(B) Energy Efficiency	(C) Appearance	(D) Ice-Making Feature	(E) Reversible Doors
1. Chillmaster	4	5	5	7	1
2. Super Fridge	7	5	7	7	1
3. Excellence	2	2	7	7	7
4. Keep Fresher	3	4	2	7	7
5. Best Fridge	7	7	4	1	7

a. Which model would the consumer select using the overall scoring method?

b. Suppose Jacoby considers price and energy efficiency to be 100 percent more important than the other criteria. Which model would he select if he assigns this weight to price and energy efficiency?

c. Suppose Jacoby, using the overall scoring method, decides that an ice maker and reversible doors are absolutely essential. What model would he select?

d. Would Jacoby's decision in Question c change if he used a weighted scoring method?

Problem 5 Walter Sweneger, director of purchasing for Dakota Industries, of Fargo, North Dakota, is a very orderly decision maker. When he was asked to purchase a snow blower, Sweneger developed a 100-point scoring system to evaluate different models on the bases of price, ease of use, power, warranty, and ease of maintenance. The maximum score is 100. Sweneger's evoked set consists of five brands: Snow Tosser, White Energy, Super Blower, The Remover, and Expert Blower. His scores are shown below.

Evoked Set	Evaluative Criteria: Decision Factors				
Alternatives	(A) Price	(B) Ease of Use	(C) Power	(D) Warranty	(E) Ease of Maintenance
1. Snow Tosser	70	75	65	60	70
2. White Energy	95	45	75	99	100
3. Super Blower	45	85	85	100	100
4. The Remover	75	75	80	45	60
5. Expert Blower	99	50	55	70	60

a. Which method would Sweneger select using the overall scoring method?

b. Suppose Sweneger considers price and power to be 100 percent more important than the other criteria. Which model would he select if he assigns this weight to price and power?

c. Suppose that Sweneger, using the overall scoring method, decides that he will not accept any snow blower that scores less than 50 on any evaluative criterion. Which brand would he select?

d. Would Sweneger's decision in Question c change if he used the weighted scoring method described in Question b?

7 Organizational Buying Behavior

Key Terms

organizational market
industrial (producer) market
trade industries
value added by
  manufacturing
Standard Industrial
  Classification (SIC)
derived demand
joint demand
straight rebuy
modified rebuy
new task buying
buying center
reciprocity
bids
specifications

Learning Goals

1. To list the components of the organizational market
2. To describe the nature and importance of the organizational market
3. To identify the major characteristics of industrial markets and industrial market demand
4. To describe organizational purchasing behavior
5. To classify organizational purchasing situations
6. To explain the buying center concept
7. To compare government markets with other organizational markets

Stop-Action Case

NutraSweet® Brand Sweetener

It all started innocently enough back in 1966. James Schlatter, a chemist working for G. D. Searle, a Skokie, Illinois-based pharmaceutical company, was testing a possible compound for the treatment of ulcers when he happened to touch his fingers to his mouth. The sweet taste surprised Schlatter since neither of the compound's component amino acids—aspartic acid and phenylalanine—tasted sweet on its own. This fortuitous event marked the discovery of aspartame, a substance that is 200 times sweeter than sugar but without sugar's calories, six times sweeter than cyclamate but without cyclamate's link to cancer, and one-and-one-half times sweeter than saccharin but without saccharin's link to cancer and bitter aftertaste.

Searle secured the patent to use aspartame as a sweetener and then began the long, arduous process of gaining Food and Drug Administration (FDA) approval. In July 1981, Searle received its first important FDA go-ahead when the agency approved aspartame's use as a food additive in such dry mixes as presweetened cereal, flavored instant coffee and tea mixes, and chewing gum. Two years later, the FDA approved aspartame's use in carbonated soft drinks.

This approval opened up the enormous diet soft-drink market to Searle—a market that accounts for nearly one out of every four carbonated soft-drink sales in the United States. Between 1970 and 1983, diet soft drinks were sweetened exclusively with saccharin. Saccharin's sole U.S. manufacturer, the Sherwin Williams Chemical Company, saw its sales rise by about 40 percent in a decade as more and more Americans became diet conscious. With annual sales of all products containing saccharin totaling some $3 billion, Searle saw a golden opportunity to step into the market with NutraSweet, the brand name of its aspartame product.

NutraSweet had one major drawback—its price. Whereas the cost of saccharin was about $4 a pound, the cost of the same amount of NutraSweet was approximately $100. With time running out on its exclusive patent, which is due to expire in 1992, G. D. Searle had to find a way to convince soft-drink producers to switch to NutraSweet. "It's a taste versus cost trade-off," said Bonnie Cook, a beverage analyst at the Robinson Humphrey Company. "Aspartame has a superior taste. But there is a significant price differential. . . . The question is whether consumers can be convinced it's worth paying a premium price for."

Assignment: Use the materials in Chapter 7 to recommend a way for G. D. Searle to convince soft-drink producers to begin using NutraSweet.

Source: Leslie Wayne, "Searle's Push into Sweetness," *New York Times* (October 24, 1982), Section 2, p. F4.

Chapter Overview _____

Organizational Market
Market that includes four major
components: producer firms, trade
industries, governments, and
institutions.

Over 15 million businesses and individuals are involved in the organizational market. The consumer market has been defined as individuals who purchase goods and services for personal use. The organizational market can be divided into four major categories: (1) the industrial (producer) market, (2) trade industries (wholesalers and retailers), (3) governments, and (4) institutions.

Organizational marketers face decisions similar to those of their consumer-oriented market counterparts.[1] But important differences exist both in the characteristics of market targets and in the development of appropriate marketing mixes. Professor James D. Hlavecek recognized the differences between the consumer market and the industrial segment of the organizational market when he noted: "Overall, the strategic and tactical emphasis and elements in the industrial and consumer marketing mixes are as different as silicon chips and potato chips."[2]

The first two chapters of Part Three dealt with market segmentation and personal and interpersonal influences on buyer behavior. In Chapter 7, attention is shifted to buying behavior in the organizational market. This chapter concludes the section on market segmentation and buyer behavior. The next part of the textbook discusses the product element of the marketing mix, including a comprehensive classification system for industrial products.

Components of the Organizational Market

The industrial market is a major component of the organizational market. The industrial (producer) market consists of individuals and firms that acquire goods and services to be used, directly or indirectly, to produce other goods and services. An American Airlines purchase of the new fuel-efficient Boeing 757 plane, a wheat purchase by General Mills for its cereals, and the purchase of light bulbs and cleaning materials for an Owens-Illinois manufacturing facility all represent industrial purchases by producers. Some products aid in producing another product or service (the new plane); others are physically used up in the production of a product (the wheat); and still others are routinely used in the day-to-day operations of the firm (the maintenance items). Producers include manufacturing firms; the farmers and other resource industries: construction contractors; and providers of such services as transportation, public utilities, finance, insurance, and real estate.

Industrial (Producer) Market
Component of the organizational
market consisting of individuals and
firms that acquire goods and
services to be used, directly or
indirectly, to produce other goods
and services.

The second component of the organizational market consists of trade industries, which are organizations such as retailers and wholesalers who purchase for resale to others. In most instances, such resale products as clothing, appliances, sports equipment, and automobile parts are finished goods that are marketed to customers in the selling firm's market area. In other instances, some processing or repackaging may take place. For example, retail meat markets may make bulk purchases of sides of beef and convert them into individual cuts for their customers. Lumber dealers and carpet retailers may purchase in bulk, then provide quantities and sizes to meet customers' specifications. In addition to resale products, trade industries also buy cash registers, computers, display equipment, and other products required to operate their business. These products (as well as maintenance items and the purchase of such specialized services as marketing research studies, accounting services, and consulting) all represent organizational purchases. Detailed discussions of the trade industries are presented in later chapters: wholesaling in Chapter 11 and retailing in Chapter 12.

Trade Industries
Component of the organizational
market comprised of retailers or
wholesalers who purchase goods for
resale to others.

Governments at the federal, state, and local levels represent the third category of organizational purchasers. This important component of the organizational market purchases a wide variety of products, ranging from highways to F–16 fighter aircraft. The primary motivation of government purchasing is to provide some form of public benefit, such as national defense or public welfare.

Institutions, such as hospitals, universities, and museums and other nonprofit groups comprise the fourth component of the organizational market. The purchasing behavior of the institutional sector is similar to that of the other components of the organizational market. A thorough discussion of the institutional market is presented in Chapter 20..

Size of the Organizational Market

Value Added by Manufacturing
Difference between the price charged for a manufactured good and the cost of the raw materials and other inputs.

The producer component of the organizational market accounts for about half the value of all the manufactured goods in the United States. The value added by manufacturing—the difference between the price charged by manufacturers and the cost of their inputs—totals about $838 billion.[3]

The size and scope of the organizational market are shown in Table 7.1. The producer, trade industry, and government components employ more than 110 million workers in more than 15 million organizations. Producers account for approximately 85 percent of the total number of organizations and two-thirds of total employment. However, there are differences among the three

Table 7.1
The Organizational Market: Size and Scope

Category	Number of Organizations	Number of Employees	Employees per Organization
Industrial Producers			
Agriculture, Forestry, Fisheries	3,486,000	3,571,000	1
Mining	181,000	1,028,000	6
Construction	1,412,000	5,756,000	4
Manufacturing	569,000	20,286,000	36
Transportation, Public Utilities	570,000	6,552,000	11
Finance, Insurance, Real Estate	2,179,000	6,270,000	3
Services	4,777,000	30,090,000	6
Total	13,174,000	73,553,000	6
Trade Industries			
Wholesaling Establishments	383,000	4,120,000	11
Retailers	1,855,000	16,638,000	9
Total	2,238,000	20,758,000	9
Governments			
Federal Government	1	2,862,000	
State Governments	50	3,747,000	
Local Governments	82,290	9,324,000	
Total	82,341	15,933,000	194
Overall Totals	15,494,341	110,244,000	

Source: *Statistical Abstract of the United States* (Washington, D.C.: U.S. Government Printing Office, 1984), pp. 272, 303, 421, 533, 798.

components. As expected, employees per unit in the government sector are significantly larger than in the producer and trade industry segments. Also, there are more than three times as many retail establishments as manufacturers. However, the average manufacturing firm employs 36 people, compared with 9 employees in the average retail establishment.

Characteristics of the Industrial Market

The industrial market can be distinguished from the consumer market on the bases of three distinctive characteristics: (1) geographic market concentration, (2) a relatively small number of buyers, and (3) a unique classification system called SIC codes.

Geographic Market Concentration

The market for industrial goods in the United States is more concentrated geographically than the consumer market. Figure 7.1 shows the concentration in eastern states like New Jersey, New York, and Pennsylvania; Sunbelt states like California, North Carolina, and Texas; and the Great Lakes states of Illinois, Indiana, Michigan, and Ohio. These ten states, in which about 50 percent of the U.S. population resides, account for 57 percent of the $1.9 billion in annual manufacturing shipments.[4]

Limited Number of Buyers

In addition to geographic concentration, the industrial market is made up of a limited number of buyers. Industrial purchasers at four companies represent two-thirds of the entire U.S. automobile tire output. The total U.S. aluminum

Figure 7.1
Geographic Concentration of Manufacturing Facilities in the United States

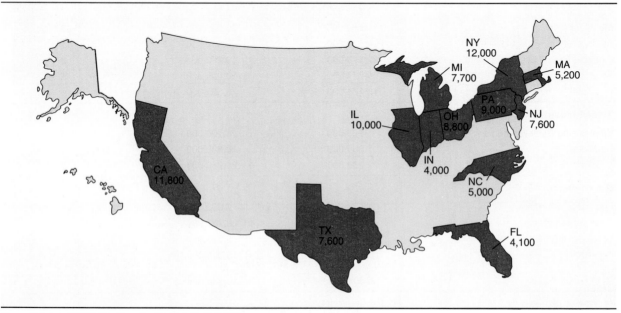

sheet plate and foil industry includes a total of only 55 manufacturing facilities. Even in industries made up of a larger number of producers, a relatively small percentage of the total industry accounts for a large percentage of the total industrial market. While factories employing 20 or more workers represent only one-third of the total U.S. manufacturing industry, they account for 95 percent of the total industry output.

The concentration of the industrial market—both in terms of the number of buyers and geographic concentration—greatly influences the marketing strategies used in serving it. Some companies have set up a national accounts sales organization that deals solely with buyers at company headquarters. A separate field sales organization is then used to service buyers at regional production facilities. Wholesalers are used less frequently in the industrial field than in the marketing of consumer goods, and the marketing channel for industrial goods is typically much shorter than for consumer goods. In addition, advertising plays a much smaller role in the industrial market. It is used primarily as an aid to personal selling and to enhance the reputation of the industrial marketer and its products and services.

Standard Industrial Classification (SIC) Codes

Marketers are aided in their efforts to reach the geographically concentrated and limited number of industrial buyers by a wealth of statistical information. The federal government is the largest single source of information. Every five years it conducts a Census of Manufacturers as well as a Census of Retailing and Wholesaling, which provide detailed information on industrial establishments, output, and employment. Specific industry studies are summarized in the annual *U.S. Industrial Outlook,* a government publication providing statistical data and discussing industry trends.

Trade associations and business publications provide additional information on the industrial market. Private firms such as Dun & Bradstreet publish detailed reports on individual firms. These data serve as useful starting points for analyzing industrial markets.

Standard Industrial Classification (SIC)
Numerical system developed by the U.S. government that subdivides the industrial marketplace into detailed market segments.

The federal government's Standard Industrial Classification (SIC) system greatly simplifies the process of focusing on an industrial market target. This numerical system subdivides the industrial marketplace into more detailed market segments. The SIC codes are divided into the following broad industry divisions, into which all types of organizations can be classified:

- 01–09   Agriculture, Forestry, Fishing
- 10–14   Mining
- 15–17   Contract Construction
- 20–39   Manufacturing
- 40–49   Transportation and Other Public Utilities
- 50–51   Wholesale Trade
- 52–59   Retail Trade
- 60–67   Finance, Insurance, and Real Estate
- 70–89   Services
- 91–97   Government—Federal, State, Local, and International
- 99   Others

Each major category within these classifications is assigned its own two-digit number; three- and four-digit numbers subdivide the industry into smaller

Figure 7.2
The Standard Industrial Classification System

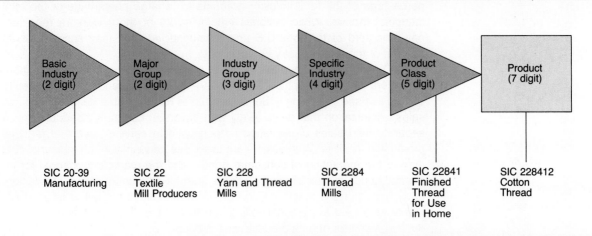

segments. For example, a major group such as the printing, publishing and allied industries is assigned SIC 27. A specific three-digit industry group such as books is SIC 273. The next category, specific industries, would use the fourth digit. Book printing, for example, is SIC 2732.[5]

In the Census of Manufacturers, the Census Bureau also assembles industrial data at two additional levels: five-digit *product classes* and seven-digit *product* or *commodity categories*. Figure 7.2 illustrates the classification system and the detail in which data is available.

Since most published data on industrial markets utilize the SIC system, the SIC codes are invaluable tools in analyzing the industrial marketplace. The detailed information for each market segment provides the marketer with a comprehensive description of the activities of potential customers on both a geographic and a specific industry basis.

Characteristics of Industrial Market Demand

Considerable differences exist in the marketing of consumer and industrial products. Gillette's Paper Mate division had long been a successful provider of medium-priced ballpoint pens to consumer markets. But this market is becoming increasingly divided into low- and premium-priced segments. So Paper Mate decided to come out with new offerings at both ends of the price spectrum.

The firm also decided to enter the office supplies field—an industrial market. It established a special commercial sales force to promote its pens to industrial buyers. Paper Mate also acquired Liquid Paper, an established name in the office supplies field. Liquid Paper's industrial marketing strengths are seen as complementing the consumer marketing in which Paper Mate has specialized.[6] The Gillette division clearly recognized that the industrial marketplace was different from the consumer markets in which they had traditionally competed. The unique characteristics of industrial settings require that marketing strategies be tailored to the special requirements of this marketplace.

Return to the Stop-Action Case

NutraSweet® Brand Sweetener

To compensate for the extra expense of using Nutra-Sweet in their sugar-free products, some manufacturers simply raised the prices of their products. When producers of sugar-free powdered soft drinks switched to NutraSweet several years ago, prices of their products increased on an average of 22 percent. But, in spite of the added cost, sales of these products increased 44 percent in 1983. Many analysts attributed this sales gain to NutraSweet.

But Searle had a more difficult time selling Nutra-Sweet to Coca-Cola and PepsiCo: neither firm wanted to raise the price of its diet soft drinks. To keep costs down, both firms initially used a blend of NutraSweet and saccharin. But research conducted by Searle revealed that 7 out of 10 diet-soda drinkers did not like the blend's taste. Even worse, the blend was turning these consumers against NutraSweet.

Consequently, Searle decided against the blend compromise. It insisted that Coke and Pepsi use aspartame 100 percent or risk having their supplies cut off—a demand Searle now makes for all products using aspartame.

Searle offered a promotion to the soft-drink industry that reduced the price per pound by roughly 20 percent.

In 1984, both Coca-Cola and PepsiCo began using NutraSweet exclusively. Although the cost of producing the soft drinks increased, product sales also increased. In 1984, diet soft drinks expanded its market share 30 percent.

Since November 1984, all major soft-drink companies have switched 100 percent to using NutraSweet: PepsiCo was the first, followed by Coca-Cola and then other soft-drink firms. Because of the increased demand for NutraSweet, Searle also reduced the price per pound of the sweetener.

The use of NutraSweet in diet soft drinks has expanded the potential of the soft-drink market. According to Brian G. Dyson, president of Coca-Cola USA, the addition of NutraSweet to Diet Coke improved the soda's taste enough to attract male consumers who are "less likely to make taste sacrifices for dieting." Dyson added, "NutraSweet will allow a taste never before achievable in (diet) soft drinks and will boost the industry's growth." This increased consumer demand helped offset the additional cost of NutraSweet to producers of diet soft drinks.

Sources: "Sweet-Talking the Public," *Newsweek* (January 28, 1985), p. 57; "How Sweet It Is," *Time* (August 28, 1983) p. 44; and "Sweet Profits May Flow from Aspartame," *Business Week* (September 5, 1983), p. 42.

What are the primary characteristics of industrial market demand? Most lists would include the following: derived demand, joint demand, inventory adjustments, and demand variability.[7]

Derived Demand

Derived Demand
Linkage between desires to make industrial purchases and the desires of customers for the firm's output.

The term derived demand refers to the linkage between desires to make industrial purchases and the desires of customers for the firm's output. For example, the demand for cash registers (an industrial good) is partially derived from demand at the retail level (consumer products). Increased retail sales may ultimately result in greater demand for cash registers.

On the other hand, the "downsizing" of automobile engines by auto manufacturers in an attempt to develop smaller, fuel-efficient cars adversely affects spark plug manufacturers such as Champion. Since the four-cylinder engines use fewer plugs than bigger cars, Champion's total sales may decline drastically unless total auto sales increase dramatically or unless Champion can increase its share of the total market.

Joint Demand

The demand for some industrial products is related to the demand for other industrial goods to be used jointly with the first item, a concept known as joint demand. Coke and iron ore are required to make pig iron. If the coke supply is reduced, there will be an immediate effect on the demand for iron ore.

Inventory Adjustments

Changes in inventory policy can have an impact on industrial demand. Assume that a two-month supply of raw materials is considered the optimal inventory in a particular industry. Now suppose economic conditions or other factors dictate that this level be increased to a 90-day supply. The raw materials supplier would then be bombarded with a tremendous increase in new orders. Thus, inventory adjustments can be a major determinant of industrial demand.

Demand Variability

Derived demand in the industrial market is linked to immense variability in industrial demand. Assume the demand for industrial product A is derived from the demand for consumer product B—an item whose sales volume has been growing at an annual rate of 10 percent. Now suppose that the demand for product B slowed to a 5 percent annual increase. Management might decide to delay further purchases of product A, using existing inventory until market conditions were clarified. Therefore, even modest shifts in the demand for product B greatly affect product A's demand. This disproportionate impact that changes in consumer demand have upon industrial market demand is called the *accelerator principle*.

Basic Categories of Organizational Products _____

There are two general categories of organizational products: capital items and expense items. *Capital items* are long-lived business assets that must be depreciated over time. *Depreciation* is the accounting concept of charging a portion of a capital item as a deduction against the company's annual revenue for purposes of determining its net income. Examples of capital items include major installations like new plants and office buildings as well as equipment.

Expense items, by contrast, are products and services that are used within a short period of time. For the most part, they are charged against income in the year of purchase. Examples of expense items include the supplies that are used in operating the business, ranging from paper clips to machine lubricants.

Chapter 8 presents a comprehensive classification of industrial products. The initial breakdown of capital and expense items is useful because buying behavior varies significantly depending upon how a purchase is treated from an accounting viewpoint. Expense items may be bought routinely and with minimal delay, while capital items involve major fund commitments and are thus subject to considerable review by the purchaser's personnel. Differences in organizational purchasing behavior are discussed next.

Organizational Buying Behavior _____

Organizational buying behavior tends to be more complex than the consumer decision process described in Chapter 6. There are several reasons for this increased complexity:

1. Many persons may exert influence in organizational purchases, and considerable time may be spent in obtaining the input and approval of various organizational members.

2. Organizational buying may be handled by committees, with greater time requirements for majority or unanimous approval.

3. Many organizations attempt to utilize several sources of supply as a type of "insurance" against shortages.

4. Organizational buyers are influenced by both rational (cost, quality, delivery reliability) and emotional (status, fear, recognition) needs.

Most organizations have attempted to systematize their purchases by employing a professional buyer—the purchasing manager or buyers or buying committee in the case of retailers and wholesalers. These technically qualified professional buyers are responsible for handling much of the organization's purchases and for securing needed products at the best possible price. Unlike the ultimate consumer who makes periodic purchase decisions, a firm's purchasing department devotes all its time and effort to determining needs, locating and evaluating alternative sources of supply, and making purchase decisions.

The Complexity of Organizational Purchases

Where major purchases are involved, negotiations may take several weeks or even months, and the buying decision may rest with a number of persons in the organization. The choice of a supplier for industrial drill presses, for example, may be made jointly by the purchasing agent and the company's production, engineering, and maintenance departments. Each of these principals may have a different point of view to be taken into account in making a purchase decision. As a result, representatives of the selling firm must be well versed in the technical aspects of the product or service and capable of interacting socially and professionally with managers of the various departments involved in the purchase decision. In the transportation equipment industry, for instance, it takes an average of 4.9 face-to-face presentations to make a sale. Figure 7.3 shows the average number of sales calls required to complete a sale in a variety of industries.

An Illustration of a Typical Organizational Purchase

The manufacturer of a reinforced fiberglass utility lighting pole faced a complicated decision process that involved the members of several departments and months of negotiations before a sale could be made. The new pole had several advantages over the traditional steel, wood, or aluminum pole: it was light weight, had nonelectrical conducting and noncorrosive properties, never needed painting, and met all strength requirements. Its major disadvantage, other than purchaser unfamiliarity, was its high initial purchase price compared to the metal alternatives. The decision process began with the manager of the

Figure 7.3

Average Number of Sales Calls by Industry

Industry	Average Number of Calls to Close a Sale
Food and Kindred Products	2.6
Furniture and Fixtures	3.8
Paper and Allied Products	4.7
Petroleum/Refining and Related Industries	4.0
Primary Metal Industries	3.9
Transportation Equipment	4.9
Transportation by Air	4.1
Business Services	5.6
Automotive Repair, Services, and Garages	5.0

Source: "Industrial Sales Call Tops $137, But New 'Cost to Close' Hits $589," *Marketing News* (May 1, 1981),
p. 1. Used by permission of the American Marketing Association.

utility company. Next, the utility's purchasing department manager was contacted who, in turn, contacted the engineering head. After a list of alternative suppliers and materials was prepared by purchasing and approved by engineering, the purchasing manager then discussed the organization's needs with salespeople representing three suppliers. The salespeople met with the heads of the stores department and the marketing department and with the engineering department manager. After a series of meetings with the salespeople and numerous discussions among the utility's various department heads, a decision was made to submit the new fiberglass pole to a test conducted by the engineering department. The results of the test were reported to the various department heads. Bids were then requested from Suppliers A, B, and C. These bids were reviewed by the department heads, who ultimately decided to select the new fiberglass pole offered by Supplier B. This complex decision process is diagrammed in Figure 7.4.[8]

Classifying Organizational Buying Situations

Organizational buying behavior is affected by situational variables. Organizational purchase decisions vary in terms of the degree of effort and involvement by different levels within the organization. There are three generally recognized organizational buying situations: straight rebuy, modified rebuy, and new task buying.[9]

Straight Rebuy

Straight Rebuy
Recurring purchase decision where an item that has performed satisfactorily is purchased again by a customer.

A straight rebuy is a recurring purchase decision where an item that has performed satisfactorily is purchased again by a customer. This organizational buying situation occurs when a purchaser is pleased with the good or service and the terms of sale are acceptable. The buyer sees little reason to assess other options, so the purchaser follows a routine buying format.

Low-cost products like paper clips and number 2 pencils for an office are typical examples. If the purchaser is pleased with the products and their prices and terms, future purchases will probably be treated as a straight rebuy from the current vendor. Even expensive items specially designed for a customer's needs can be treated as a straight rebuy in some cases. For example, the

Figure 7.4
The Decision to Purchase a New Type of Utility Pole

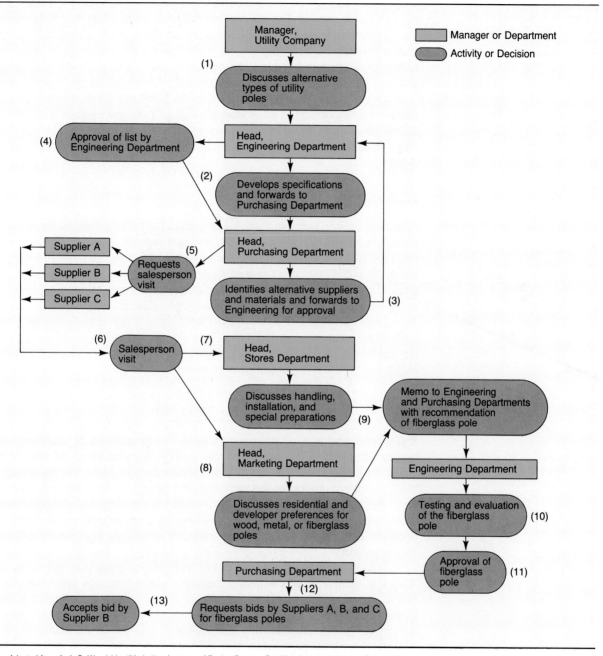

Source: Adapted from Arch G. Woodside, "Marketing Anatomy of Buying Process Can Help Improve Industrial Strategy,"
Marketing News (May 1, 1981), sec. 2, p. 11. Used by permission of the American Marketing Association.

Department of Defense is committed to buying about 7000 M–1 Abrams tanks. This is an expensive product specifically designed to replace the M–60 as the main U.S. battle tank.

Marketers facing straight rebuy situations should concentrate on maintaining a good relationship with the buyer by providing adequate service and delivery. Competitors are faced with the difficult task of presenting a unique sales proposal that will break this chain of repurchases.

Modified Rebuy

A modified rebuy is a situation where purchasers are willing to reevaluate their available options. The appropriate decision makers feel that it may be to their advantage to look at alternative product offerings, using established purchasing guidelines. This might occur if a marketer allows a straight rebuy situation to deteriorate because of poor service or delivery. Perceived quality and cost differences can also create a modified rebuy situation.

Organizational marketers want to move purchasers into a straight rebuy position by responding to all of their product and service needs. Competitors, on the other hand, try to move buyers into a modified rebuy situation by correctly assessing the factors that would make buyers reconsider their decisions.

New Task Buying

New task buying refers to first-time or unique purchase situations that require considerable effort on the part of the decision makers. After such a need has been identified, evaluative criteria can be established and an extensive search launched. Alternative product and service offerings and vendors are considered. For example, when a firm enters a new field, it has to seek suppliers of component parts that have not previously been purchased.

Organizational marketers should work closely with the purchaser in the case of new task buying situations. This will allow them to study the factors the purchaser considers important and to design their marketing proposal to match the needs of the organizational buyer.

The Buying Center Concept _____

The buying center is a vital concept to the understanding of organizational buying behavior.[10] The buying center simply refers to everyone who is involved in some fashion in an organizational buying action. For example, a buying center can include the architect who designs a new research laboratory, the scientist who will use the facility, the purchasing manager who screens contractor proposals, the chief executive officer who makes the final decision, and the vice-president for research who signs the formal contracts for the project.

Buying centers are not part of the firm's formal organizational structure. They are informal groups whose composition varies from one purchase situation to another. Buying centers typically include anywhere from 4 to 20 participants.[11] Buying centers tend to evolve as the purchasing process moves through its various stages. They also vary from one firm to the next.

Buying center participants play different roles in the purchasing process. These roles are generally recognized as users, gatekeepers, influencers, deciders, and buyers. Each of these is defined in Table 7.2.

The critical task for the organizational marketer is to be able to determine the specific role and the relative buying influence of each buying center participant. Sales presentations and information can then be tailored to the appropriate role that the individual plays at each step in the purchase process. Organizational marketers have also found that while their initial, and in many cases most extensive, contacts are all with the purchasing department, the buying center participants having the greatest influence often are not in the purchasing department.

Table 7.2
Buying Center Roles

Role	Description
Users	As the role name implies, these are the personnel who will be using the product in question. Users may have anywhere from inconsequential to an extremely important influence on the purchase decision. In some cases, the users initiate the purchase action by requesting the product. They may even develop the product specifications.
Gatekeepers	Gatekeepers control information to be reviewed by other members of the buying center. The control of information may be in terms of disseminating printed information or advertisements or through controlling which salesperson will speak to which individuals in the buying center. To illustrate, the purchasing agent might perform this screening role by opening the gate to the buying center for some sales personnel and closing it to others.
Influencers	These individuals affect the purchasing decision by supplying information for the evaluation of alternatives or by setting buying specifications. Typically, technical personnel such as engineers, quality control personnel, and research and development personnel are significant influences to the purchase decision. Sometimes individuals outside of the buying organization can assume this role (e.g., an engineering consultant or an architect who writes very tight building specifications).
Deciders	Deciders are the individuals who actually make the buying decision, whether or not they have the formal authority to do so. The identity of the decider is the most difficult role to determine: buyers may have formal authority to buy, but the president of the firm may actually make the decision. A decider could be a design engineer who develops a set of specifications that only one vendor can meet.
Buyers	The buyer has *formal* authority for selecting a supplier and implementing all procedures connected with securing the product. The power of the buyer is often usurped by more powerful members of the organization. Often the buyer's role is assumed by the purchasing agent, who executes the clerical functions associated with a purchase order.

Source: Adapted from Frederick E. Webster, Jr. and Yoram Wind, *Organizational Buying Behavior* (Englewood Cliffs, N.J.: Prentice-Hall, 1972), pp. 77–80. This adaptation is reprinted from Michael D. Hutt and Thomas W. Speh, *Industrial Marketing Management*, second edition (Hinsdale, Ill.: The Dryden Press, 1985), p. 103. Used by permission of Prentice-Hall, Inc. and CBS College Publishing.

Reciprocity

Reciprocity
Highly controversial practice of extending purchasing preference to suppliers who are also customers.

A highly controversial practice in a number of organizational buying situations is reciprocity, the extension of purchasing preference to suppliers who are also customers. For example, an office-equipment manufacturer may favor a particular supplier of component parts if the supplier has recently made a major purchase of the manufacturer's products. Reciprocal arrangements were traditionally used in industries with homogeneous products with similar prices, such as the chemical, paint, petroleum, rubber, and steel industries.

Two other forms of reciprocity have been used. *Reverse reciprocity* is the practice of extending supply privileges to firms who provide needed supplies. In times of shortages, reverse reciprocity occasionally emerges as firms attempt to obtain raw materials and parts to continue operations. A more recent reciprocity spinoff is the *voluntary price rollback,* where purchasers request vendors to agree to temporary price cuts or freezes. While no threats are made, it is difficult for a supplier to refuse a request from a major purchaser. This sometimes forces the vendor to ask for concessions from its own work force and/or employees.[12]

The various forms of reciprocity suggest the close links that exist between the various elements of the organizational marketplace. Although some reciprocal agreements still exist, both the Justice Department and the Federal Trade Commission view them as attempts to reduce competition. Federal intervention is common in cases where agreements are used systematically.[13]

Government Markets

Government is a sizable portion of many organizational markets in 1986. The federal government is a primary market of industrial producer Colt Industries, as the ad in Figure 7.5 illustrates. There are many similarities between other organizational markets and government markets. Both seek to purchase many similar goods and services. However, there are differences in the way items are produced, primarily due to the numerous regulations that impact government markets.

Bids
Written sales proposals from vendors.

Specifications
Written description of a product or a service needed by a firm. Prospective bidders use this description first to determine whether they can manufacture the product or deliver the service and then to prepare a bid.

Selling to Government Markets

Most government purchases, by law, must be made on the basis of bids, or written sales proposals, from vendors. As a result, government buyers develop specifications—specific descriptions of needed items—for prospective bidders.

The General Services Administration, through its Office of Federal Supply and Services, buys many commercial items for use by other agencies;

Figure 7.5
Colt Industries Serves a Variety of Organizational Markets, Including The United States Air Force

Source: Courtesy of Colt Industries, Inc.

however, a large number of other federal agencies also maintain procurement functions. Most states have offices comparable to the GSA.[14]

Prospective government suppliers can learn of opportunities for sales by contacting the various government agencies. Most contracts are advertised by each agency, and information on bidding procedures can be obtained directly from the agency. Directories explaining procedures involved in selling to the federal government are available from the Government Printing Office, and most states provide similar information.

Problems and Opportunities   The GSA was once unable to find three bidders for some $50,000 in purchases of facial tissue, filing cabinets, garbage cans, and table napkins. Despite its immense size, the government market is often viewed as unprofitable by many suppliers. A survey conducted by *Sales & Marketing Management* reported that industrial marketers registered a variety of complaints about government purchasing procedures. These included excessive paperwork, bureaucracy, needless regulations, emphasis on low bid prices, decision-making delays, frequent shifts in procurement personnel, and excessive policy changes.[15]

On the other hand, marketers generally credit the government with being a relatively stable market. Once an item is purchased by the government, the probability of additional sales is good. Other marketers cite such advantages as the instant credibility established by sales to the federal government, timely payment, excise tax and sales tax exemptions, acceptance of new ideas, and reduced competition.

One survey reported that 68 percent of its organizational respondents did not maintain a separate government sales manager or sales force. But many firms report success with specialized government marketing efforts. J. I. Case, Goodyear, Eastman Kodak, and Sony are examples.

Recent Developments for Government Markets

Four recent actions have impacted the federal government market. Similar developments have influenced some state and local governments.[16] The federal developments are:

1. The Office of Management and Budget requires that government agencies use a single set of procurement regulations, the so-called Federal Acquisition Regulation (FAR). The intent is to reduce the red tape and excessive regulation that currently characterizes the federal government market. By combining government procurement regulations in one plain-English document, the FAR has made it easier for private contractors to know exactly what the government wants. By giving government contracting officers greater discretion in carrying out federal procurement policy, the FAR has also made the system more flexible in dealing with the variations in private contractors.[17]

2. In an attempt to reduce spending, the Pentagon, the GSA, and other government buyers are turning to more off-the-shelf goods rather than issuing special-order contracts.

3. Life-cycle costing—the cost of using a product over its lifetime, not just the initial bid price—is now accepted by the GSA. In fact, life-cycle costing procurement of typewriters is estimated to have saved the government $9 million over a three-year period.[18]

4. A variety of reforms are being implemented in the GSA. Most of these involve streamlining its organization, increasing procurement efficiency, and improving its counseling of would-be suppliers.

Summary

The organizational market is divided into four segments: the industrial (producer) market; trade industries, including wholesalers and retailers; governments; and institutions. The industrial market consists of individuals and firms that acquire goods and services to be used, directly or indirectly, to produce other goods and services. Trade industries are organizations such as retailers and wholesalers who purchase for resale to others. The primary motivation of government purchasing at the federal, state, and local levels is to provide some form of public benefit. The purchasing behavior of institutions, such as hospitals, universities, and other nonprofit groups, is similar to that of the other components of the organizational market.

Geographic concentration in the industrial market is verified by the fact that ten states—California, Illinois, Indiana, Michigan, New Jersey, New York, North Carolina, Ohio, Pennsylvania, and Texas—account for about 57 percent of manufacturing shipments in the United States. The limited number of buyers in the marketplace is illustrated by the fact that while only one-third of all U.S. plants employ over 20 people, these larger facilities account for 95 percent of total industrial output. SIC codes (Standard Industrial Classification codes) are the government's system of subdividing the industrial marketplace into more detailed product/service industries or market segments.

Industrial market demand is characterized by derived demand, joint demand, inventory adjustments, and demand variability. All of these factors influence the nature and extent of industrial market demand.

The systematic nature of organizational buying is reflected by the use of purchasing managers who direct such efforts. Major organizational purchases may require an elaborate and lengthy decision-making process that involves many people. Purchase decisions typically depend on price, service, certainty of supply, and product efficiency.

Organizational buying situations differ. A straight rebuy is a recurring purchase decision where an item that has performed satisfactorily is purchased again by a customer. A modified rebuy is a situation where purchasers are willing to reevaluate their available options. New task buying refers to first-time or unique purchase situations that require considerable effort on the part of the decision makers.

The buyer center concept refers to everyone who is involved in some fashion in an organizational buying action. There are five buying center roles: users, gatekeepers, influencers, deciders, and buyers.

The chapter ends with a discussion of government markets. This is a sizable organizational market that exhibits both similarities and differences with other components of organizational buying.

Solving the Stop-Action Case

NutraSweet® Brand Sweetener

In recognizing the important role the consumer would play in the success of NutraSweet, Searle developed a marketing strategy to promote its industrial product to a consumer audience. The theme of its initial ad campaign was "Introducing NutraSweet. You can't buy it, but you're gonna love it."

In 1983, Searle launched a major advertising campaign—the nation's first consumer-oriented marketing plan for a food ingredient. According to Robert Shapiro, president of Searle's NutraSweet division, "It isn't easy to convince the public that a sugar-free sweetener can be good-tasting and safe. This is the only way to break the credibility barrier."

Searle's advertising message focused on telling consumers what NutraSweet isn't. Ads informed consumers that NutraSweet isn't artificial (it is made from natural proteins), it isn't suspected of causing any serious health problems, and it doesn't have an unpleasant aftertaste.

Hoping to expand consumer awareness of a newcomer, Searle treated the ingredient as if it were a product by giving it a catchy name and logo.

But Searle's marketing strategy was broader-based than simply gaining consumer acceptance. By preselling NutraSweet to the public, the company wanted to make the ingredient irresistible to product manufacturers. "We have to create consumer loyalty to NutraSweet in order to give our customers an instant 'reason why' to support

their product claims," said Timothy Healy, vice-president of marketing for the NutraSweet Group. Otherwise the company would have problems convincing product makers to agree to a key part of Searle's plan to gain widespread name recognition—by attaching the NutraSweet logo on the front of their packages, as they all do.

Searle's marketing strategies have paid off. Sales of NutraSweet exploded from $13 million in 1981 to about $600 million in 1984. And they are expected to climb higher. The market for NutraSweet may be expanded to new product categories, including orange juice, yogurt, and ice cream, pending FDA approval.

As Americans continue to be more and more diet conscious, the future of NutraSweet seems secure. A potential threat, however, is that Searle's exclusive patent on aspartame expires in 1992. The company's successful marketing plan may simply have led the way for a host of imitators.

Source: "Sweet-Talking the Public," *Newsweek* (January 28, 1985), p. 57.

Questions for Discussion

1. Identify a market opportunity that exists in some specific organizational market. Explain why you think this situation represents a good opportunity.

2. Name the four components of the organizational market and give two examples of each component.

3. Give two examples of products or services that are most likely to be purchased by each component of the organizational market.

4. Comment on the following statement: "There is really no need to separate the study of organizational buying behavior and consumer buying behavior."

5.   What are the three characteristics of the industrial market? Show how each of the features affects the marketing strategy used by firms serving the market.

6.   Describe the geographic concentration in the industrial market.

7.   Discuss the number and location of industrial buying prospects.

8.   How are SIC codes used by organizational marketers?

9.   Contrast organizational buying behavior and consumer purchasing behavior.

10.   Discuss the issue of reciprocity.

11.   Identify the major characteristics of industrial market demand.

12.   Give two examples of how derived demand, joint demand, inventory adjustments, and the accelerator principle have affected industrial market demand.

13.   How do inventory adjustments impact industrial market sales?

14.   Discuss the demand variability that exists in industrial markets.

15.   Identify and give two examples of each of the types of organizational buying situations.

16.   Describe the roles involved in the buying center concept and identify which person in an organization would most likely play each role.

17.   In what ways is the government market similar to other organizational markets? How do they differ?

18.   How does the extensive use of bids in government purchasing affect the marketing strategies employed in this market?

19.   Why do some firms ignore while other firms pursue sales opportunities in the government marketplace?

20.   Identify the recent developments affecting the government market. Which marketing mix components are most affected by each of these developments?

Case: J. M. Smucker Company

"With a name like Smucker's, it has to be good!" This amusing slogan, coupled with a sound marketing program for its jellies and preserves has made the J. M. Smucker Company a successful, well-known firm to its customers. Yet the firm has been equally successful in the industrial market. Smucker's produces filling bases that are used by other manufacturers in such products as yogurt and bakery items. The tasks involved in marketing strawberry preserves to ultimate consumers is significantly different from the tasks of marketing a related strawberry filling to a manufacturer of yogurt.

Smucker's: A Consumer Goods Marketer   In marketing its jellies and preserves to the consumer market, the J. M. Smucker Company engages in the classic marketing tasks of identifying market targets and developing an appropriate marketing mix. Each new product to be sold in retail food outlets is carefully developed, tested, and targeted for specifically chosen consumer segments. A company sales force calls on larger accounts, while independent intermediaries also make calls on retail and wholesale channel members. Promotional programs are designed to stimulate consumer demand and to provide incentives for retailers to handle Smucker's products. Pricing decisions

Source: Michael D. Hutt and Thomas W. Speh, *Industrial Marketing Management*, second edition, (Hinsdale, Ill.: The Dryden Press, 1985), pp. 10–11. Copyright © 1985 CBS College Publishing. Reprinted by permission of CBS College Publishing.

reflect cost, prices of competitors, and consumer demand. All areas of marketing strategy are included in the Smucker's plan.

Smucker's: An Industrial Marketer   A radically different marketing program is used in the industrial segment. The market consists of manufacturers who might use Smucker products in the goods they produce. Smucker's products will lose their identity in the manufacturing process as they are blended into forms such as cakes, cookies, or yogurt.

Once a potential industrial customer is identified, a Smucker's sales representative will call on the account. In some instances, the initial contact is with top management. More typically, the early contacts are with the individual in charge of research and development. Early discussions typically center on specifications for the texture and composition of the required goods.

These specifications are provided to the research and development division at Smucker's and samples are developed. The samples are then supplied to the potential customer who may request further modifications. It is not uncommon for a period of months to pass and a series of modifications to occur before a mixture is finally approved. Next, attention turns to price, and the salesperson's contact point shifts to the purchasing department. Since large quantities are involved (truckloads or drums rather than jars), a few cents per pound can be significant to both parties. Quality and service are also major criteria in the decision.

Once a contract has been signed, the product will be shipped directly from the Smucker's warehouse to the manufacturer's plant. The salesperson will follow up frequently with the purchasing agent and the plant manager. The ultimate sales for Smucker's will depend upon both the manufacturer's satisfaction with Smucker's products and on the performance of the manufacturer's product in the marketplace.

Questions
1.   What similarities and differences exist between Smucker's consumer and organizational marketing efforts? Discuss.

2.   Why is J. M. Smucker Company considered an effective organizational marketer?

3.   Identify other firms that successfully market both consumer and organizational products. What can be learned from these examples?

Computer Applications

Because many organizational purchasers make buying decisions on the basis of competitive bids from alternative suppliers, determination of the most appropriate bid is an important assignment for industrial marketers. One method of quantifying this task is to use the concept of *expected net profit (ENP)*. The formula for calculating ENP is as follows:

$$\text{Expected Net Profit} = P(\text{Bid} - \text{Costs})$$

where

P = the probability of the buyer accepting the bid
Bid   = the bid price of the product or project
Costs = the estimated total costs of the product or project

Consider the following example. A firm is contemplating submission of a bid for a job that is estimated to cost $23,000. One executive has proposed a bid of $60,000; another, $50,000. Although it is impossible to determine the buyer's reactions to either of these bids, the firm's marketing director estimates a 40 percent chance of the buyer accepting Bid 1 ($60,000) and a 60 percent chance that Bid 2 ($50,000) will be accepted. The two alternative bids can be evaluated as follows:

Bid 1
ENP = 0.40($60,000 − $23,000)

    = 0.40($37,000)

    = $14,800.

Bid 2
ENP = 0.60($50,000 − $23,000)

    = 0.60($27,000)

    = $16,200.

The expected net profit formula indicates that Bid 2 would be best since its expected net profit is $1,400 higher than the ENP of Bid 1.

The most difficult task in applying the ENP concept is estimating the probability that a certain bid will be accepted. However, this is not a valid reason for failing to quantify an estimate. Experience can provide the foundation for such estimates. The calculation of ENP is particularly useful in permitting organizational marketers to compare alternative competitive strategies. It is especially useful in industries where marketers are involved in preparing and submitting hundreds of bids as a regular component of their marketing programs.

Directions: Use menu item 7 titled "Competitive Bidding" to solve each of the following problems.

Problem 1 Jacob Weissman, director of marketing at Empire Corporation, based in Schenectady, New York, is considering offering a large industrial product to a local buyer at one of two possible prices. The first price, which Weissman refers to as Alternative A, is $25,000. Alternative B is a price of $30,000. Weissman's total costs involved in producing the item amount to $15,000. Weissman believes that the likelihood of the customer accepting the $25,000 bid is 70 percent. However, he feels that only a 40 percent chance exists that the buyer will accept the bid at the higher price. Use the ENP formula to recommend a course of action for Empire Corporation. What should Weissman do in this case?

Problem 2 Camden Industries, of Camden, New Jersey, has developed a new industrial scrubber. Its marketing executives are actively working on a large sale to the leading firm in their market target, a firm whose purchase decisions are frequently imitated by other firms in the industry. One of Camden's executives has proposed a price of $75,000 per unit, while another has suggested $85,000. Total costs of the scrubber average $50,000 per unit. Camden's marketing research department has assigned a 58 percent probability of the buyer accepting the lower price and a 42 percent probability of purchase at the higher price. Use the ENP formula to recommend a bid price for the scrubber.

Problem 3 A California-based defense contractor has developed a new generation of fighter aircraft. The firm's marketing executives are in the process of completing the proposal and are discussing the price tag they should attach to each plane. Should the U.S. Department of Defense elect to purchase the fighter, the order would amount to 400 aircraft. Total costs in developing and producing the fighters are $8 billion. Management is considering two prices for the fighter: $25 million and $28 million. The executive board thinks the probability of the Pentagon accepting the first price is 55 percent, while the probability of it accepting the higher price is expected to be 45 percent. Use the ENP formula to determine which of the two prices the defense contractor should select.

Problem 4 Alladin Industries, of Fort Wayne, Indiana, has been supplying Cleveland Manufacturing with a certain rivet for years. Cleveland Manufacturing treats these purchases from Alladin as what is referred to in this chapter as a straight rebuy. Alladin's price of $350 per thousand rivets has remained unchanged for the past three years. But the cost of producing the rivet has recently risen from $275 to $300 per thousand. Alladin would like to pass the $25 cost increase along to Cleveland Manufacturing in the form of a price increase. However, its marketing director expects that a 20 percent chance exists that Cleveland Manufacturing would locate a different supplier. At $350 per thousand, the director is completely confident that the Cleveland firm will continue to be an Alladin Industries customer. What should Alladin's management do in this case?

Problem 5 James Staggers is a sales representative for The Copy Connection, an office equipment distributor in Provo, Utah. Staggers is currently attempting to sell a small, low-volume copier to a local contractor. He believes that his best approach is to prepare a single proposal at a reasonable price. The firm's copier is available in two models: Model A, which costs The Copy Connection $1,200; and the slightly faster Model B, which costs The Copy Connection $1,300. Staggers's manager has given him authority to negotiate any price above $1,400 for Model A and $1,500 for Model B. Staggers has assigned an estimated probability of closing the sale to each of several alternative prices. The alternatives are shown in the accompanying table.

What model and price should Staggers propose to the contractor?

Alternative Prices	Probability of Sale
$1,500 for Model A	30%
$1,500 for Model B	35
$1,750 for Model A	15
$1,750 for Model B	25
$1,850 for Model A	5
$1,850 for Model B	15

PART FOUR

Product/Service Strategy

8 Introduction to Product/Service Strategy

Key Terms

product
warranty
product life cycle
adoption process
consumer innovators
diffusion process
convenience goods
shopping goods
specialty goods
installations
accessory equipment
industrial distributor
component parts
   and materials
raw materials
supplies
MRO items
goods-services continuum
services

Learning Goals

1. To explain the concept of the product life cycle
2. To identify the determinants of the speed of the adoption process
3. To explain the methods for accelerating the speed of adoption
4. To identify the classifications for consumer goods and to briefly describe each category
5. To identify the types of industrial goods
6. To explain the key distinguishing features of services

ARM & HAMMER Baking Soda

By 1970 ARM & HAMMER baking soda, a product marketed by the ARM & HAMMER division of Church & Dwight Company, was a staple on grocers' shelves. It was developed in 1846 by John Dwight, who set up a processing and packaging plant in his kitchen. By 1970, the company was selling 2.3 million cases of baking soda a year.

Despite its strong sales, Church and Dwight's management were convinced that they could extend the product life cycle of their baking soda and reach an enormous untapped sales potential. Senior executives, including Robert A. Davies, III, then vice-president of marketing of the ARM & HAMMER division, saw the product as a sleeper with unlimited potential consumer use. Consumers were already using this colorless, odorless, salty white powder with the chemical name of sodium bicarbonate as a refrigerator cleanser, a bath-water treatment, a skin-rash treatment, a deodorizer, a plaque remover, and a leavening agent. But Davies was determined to expand the product's applications even further. Years later, Davies, who would become Church & Dwight's president and chief executive officer, said: "I regard (baking soda) as a mine where we've only tapped the first vein. There are a lot more veins; I don't know how many, but a lot more." Davies' efforts were aimed at nothing less than extending the product life cycle of ARM & HAMMER baking soda.

Assignment: Use the materials in Chapter 8 to recommend a way for Church & Dwight's ARM & HAMMER division to extend its baking soda's product life cycle.

Photo Source: Reprinted with the permission of the ARM & HAMMER Division of Church & Dwight Co., Inc. ARM & HAMMER is a registered trademark of Church & Dwight Co., Inc.

Source: Jack J. Honomichl, "The Ongoing Saga of 'Mother Baking Soda'," *Advertising Age* (September 20, 1982), p. m-22.

Chapter Overview _____

The first three parts of the book dealt with preliminary marketing considerations such as marketing research and consumer behavior. Now the attention shifts to the firm's marketing mix.

The chapters in Part Four analyze the decisions and problems involved with the first element of the marketing mix—the product or products offered to the firm's market target. Planning efforts begin with the choice of products to offer the market target. The other variables of the marketing mix—pricing structures, distribution channels, and promotional plans—must be based on product planning.

A narrow definition of the word *product* focuses on the physical or functional characteristics of a good or service. For example, a video cassette recorder is a rectangular container of metal and plastic with wires connecting it to a television set, accompanied by a series of special tapes for recording and viewing. But the purchaser has a much broader view of the recorder. Some buyers may want to use the recorder to see soap operas they missed because of work; others may be interested in the warranty and service facilities of the manufacturer; and many others may want it to rent or purchase recently released movies for home viewing.

Marketing decision makers must have this broader conception of product in mind and realize that people are buying *want satisfaction.* For example, most consumers know little about the gasoline they buy. In fact, many view it not as a product at all, but rather as a premium they must pay for the privilege of driving their car.

The consumer's conception of a product may be altered by such features as packaging, labeling, or even the retail outlet at which the product is purchased. An image of high quality has been created for Maytag appliances by virtue of the advertising campaign featuring the Maytag repairer as the loneliest person in town. Maytag's standard of high product quality is responsible for its strong consumer franchise.

Some products have few or no physical attributes. A haircut and blow-dry by the local hairdresser only produces well-groomed hair. A tax counselor only produces advice. Therefore, a broader view of products must include services. Consequently, a product is a bundle of physical, service, and symbolic attributes designed to produce consumer want satisfaction. Figure 8.1 reflects this broader definition by identifying the various components of the total product.

An important feature of many products is the product warranty—the guarantee to the buyer that the manufacturer will replace the product or refund its purchase price if it proves defective during a specified period of time. Warranties increase consumer purchase confidence and often represent an important means by which demand is stimulated. Figure 8.2 is an example of a warranty that protects consumers against product defects. Zippo guarantees that its lighters will be repaired or replaced free of charge, regardless of age or condition. This kind of warranty enhances the image of the firm and its products.

The Magnuson-Moss Warranty Act (1975) gives the Federal Trade Commission the power to develop regulations affecting warranty practices for any product costing more than $15 that is covered by a written warranty. While the act does not require firms to give warranties, it is designed to assist the consumer in comparison shopping. Warranties must be easy to read and understand, and firms offering them must also establish mechanisms for processing consumer complaints.[1]

Product
Bundle of physical, service, and symbolic attributes designed to produce consumer want satisfaction.

Warranty
Guarantee to the buyer that the manufacturer will replace a product or refund its purchase price if the product proves to be defective during a specified period of time.

Figure 8.1
The Total Product Concept

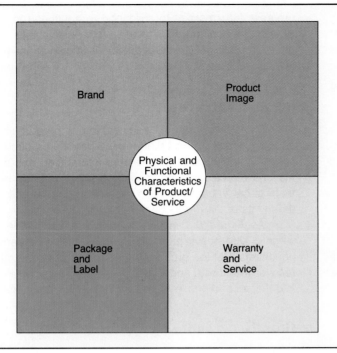

Figure 8.2
The Zippo Warranty

The Product Life Cycle

Product Life Cycle
Four stages through which a successful product passes— introduction, growth, maturity, and decline.

Products, like individuals, pass through a series of stages. Whereas humans progress from infancy to childhood to adulthood to retirement to death, successful products progress through four basic stages: introduction, growth, maturity, and decline. This progression is known as the product life cycle, which is depicted in Figure 8.3.

Introduction

The firm's objective in the early stages of the product life cycle is to stimulate demand for the new market entry. Since the product is not known to the public, promotional campaigns stress information about its features. They also may be directed toward marketing intermediaries in the channel to induce them to carry the product. In this phase, the public becomes acquainted with the merits of the product and begins to accept it.

As Figure 8.3 indicates, losses are common during the introductory stage due to heavy promotion and extensive research and development expenditures. But the groundwork is being laid for future profits. Firms expect to recover their costs and to begin earning profits when the new product moves into the second phase of its life cycle—the growth stage.

Growth

Sales volumes rise rapidly during the growth stage as new customers make initial purchases and early buyers repurchase the product. Word-of-mouth and mass advertising induce hesitant buyers to make trial purchases. Five million personal computers (defined as computers selling for less than $10,000 and bought for home use) were purchased in 1983, more than 41 times the number purchased in 1980. These machines, now in the growth stage, are currently being used in about 14 percent of all U.S. homes.[2]

As the firm begins to realize substantial profits from its investment during the growth stage, the product attracts competitors. Success breeds imitation,

Figure 8.3
Stages in the Product Life Cycle

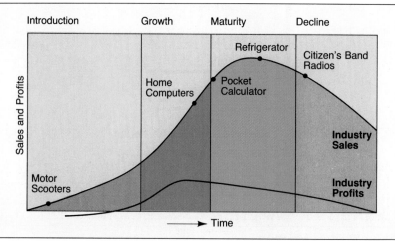

and other firms inevitably rush into the market with competitive products. In fact, the majority of firms in a particular market enter during the growth stage.

Maturity

Industry sales continue to grow during the early part of the maturity stage, but eventually they reach a plateau as the backlog of potential customers is exhausted. By this time, a large number of competitors have entered the market, and profits decline as competition intensifies.

In the maturity stage, differences among competing products diminish as competitors discover the product and promotional characteristics most desired by the market. Heavy promotional outlays emphasize subtle differences among competing products, and brand competition intensifies.

For the first time in the product life cycle, available products exceed industry demand. Companies attempting to increase their sales and market share must do so at the expense of competitors. As competition intensifies, the competitors tend to cut prices in an attempt to attract new buyers. Even though a price reduction may be the easiest method of inducing additional purchases, it is also one of the simplest moves for competitors to duplicate. Reduced prices result in decreased revenues for all firms in the industry unless the price cuts produce enough increased purchases to offset the loss in revenue on each item sold.[3]

Decline

In the final stage of the product's life, innovations or shifting consumer preferences bring about an absolute decline in industry sales. The safety razor and electric shaver replaced the straight razor years ago. More recently, universal life insurance policies are now replacing whole life insurance policies because of a shift in consumer preferences. As Figure 8.4 indicates, the decline stage of an old product doubles as the growth stage for a new market entry.

Figure 8.4
Overlap of Life Cycles for Products A and B

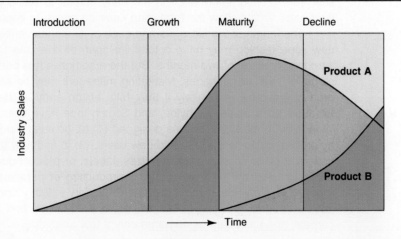

Figure 8.5
Fad Cycles

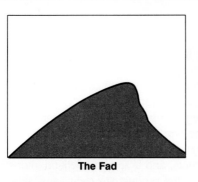
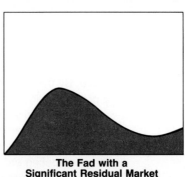

The Fad   **The Fad with a
                                       Significant Residual Market**

Source: Reprinted from Chester R. Wasson, *Dynamic Competitive Strategy and Product Life Cycles*, 3rd ed. (Austin, Texas: Austin Press, 1978), p. 13.

Industry profits decline and in some cases actually become negative as sales fall and firms cut prices in a bid for the dwindling market. Manufacturers gradually begin to leave the industry in search of more profitable products.

The traditional product life cycle needs to be distinguished from fad cycles. Fashions and fads have a profound influence on marketing strategy. *Fashions* are currently popular products that tend to follow recurring life cycles.[4] Women's apparel fashions provide the best examples. The mini skirt was reintroduced in 1982 after being out of fashion for over a decade.

By contrast, *fads* are fashions with abbreviated life cycles. Consider popular music for teenagers. Disco gave way to punk and new wave, which were replaced by new music, a take-off on rock-and-roll.[5] Most fads experience short-lived popularity and then quickly fade. However, there are some fads that maintain a residual market among certain market segments. Both of these fad cycles are shown in Figure 8.5.

Utilizing the Product Life Cycle Concept

The product life cycle concept provides important insights about developments at the various stages of the product's life. Knowledge that profits assume a predictable pattern through the stages and that promotional emphasis must shift from product information in the early stages to brand promotion in the later ones should allow the marketing decision maker to improve planning.

The length of the life cycle and each of its stages varies considerably. A new shoe fashion may have a total life span of one calendar year, with an introductory stage of two months. But the automobile has been in the maturity stage for over two decades. Marketing managers may be able to extend the product life cycle indefinitely if they take action early in the maturity stage. Products such as Jell-O, nylon, and Scotch tape have been given extended lives through marketing moves designed (1) to increase the frequency of use by present customers, (2) to add new users, (3) to find new uses for the products, and (4) to change package sizes, labels, or product quality.[6] Nylon was originally used by the military in the production of parachutes, thread, and rope. Next, it revolutionized the women's hosiery industry and has since been used in producing stretch socks, sweaters, panty hose, body stockings, tires, carpets, and ball bearings, to name only a few products.

Figure 8.6
Hypothetical Life Cycle for Denim Fabric

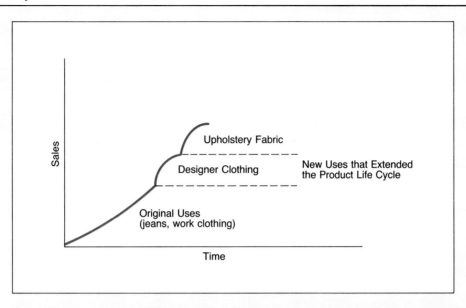

Denim is another product whose life was extended through the development of new uses, as Figure 8.6 indicates. Denim was pioneered in the 1850s by Levi Strauss and Company in the form of durable jeans and work shirts. Later, work jackets were added, but for more than 100 years the products had been aimed at a market consisting of children, teenagers, and blue-collar adults.

The fashion changes of the 1970s and 1980s converted the Levi name into a status symbol as the denim fabric—and the Levi label—began to appear on premium-priced clothing. Dress suits were made from denim. Other markets for denim included automobile seat covers, backpacks, and hats.

The changes in both organizational and environmental conditions and the adjustments in marketing efforts at each stage in the product life cycle are summarized in Table 8.1.

Consumer Adoption Process

Adoption Process
Series of stages in the consumer decision process regarding a new product, including awareness, interest, evaluation, trial, and rejection or adoption.

Consumers also make decisions about the new product offering. In the adoption process, potential consumers go through a series of stages from learning of the new product to trying it and deciding to purchase it regularly or to reject it. These stages in the consumer adoption process can be classified as:

1. *Awareness*. Individuals first learn of the new product but lack information about it.

2. *Interest*. They begin to seek information about it.

3. *Evaluation*. They consider whether or not the product is beneficial.

4. *Trial*. They make a trial purchase to determine its usefulness.

5. *Adoption/Rejection*. If the trial purchase is satisfactory, they decide to make regular use of the product.[7]

Table 8.1

Organizational and Environmental Conditions with Appropriate
Marketing Efforts for Various Product Life Cycle Stages

		Organizational Conditions	Environmental Conditions	Marketing Efforts
Introduction		High Costs Inefficient Production Levels Cash Demands	Few or No Competitors Limited Product Awareness and Knowledge Limited Demand	Stimulate Demand Establish High Price Offer Limited Product Variety Increase Distribution
Growth		Smoothing Production Lowering Costs Operation Efficiencies Product Improvement Work	Expanding Markets Expanded Distribution Competition Strengthens Prices Soften a Bit	Cultivate Selective Demand Product Improvement Strengthen Distribution Price Flexibility
Maturity:	**Early Maturity**	Efficient Scale of Operation Product Modification Work Decreasing Profits	Slowing Growth Strong Competition Expanded Market Heightened Competition	Emphasize Market Segmentation Improve Service and Warranty Reduce Prices
	Late Maturity	Low Profits Standardized Production	Faltering Demand Fierce Competition Shrinking Number of Competitors Established Distribution Patterns	Ultimate in Market Segmentation Competitive Pricing Retain Distribution
Decline			Permanently Declining Demand Reduction of Competitors Limited Product Offerings Price Stabilization	Increase Primary Demand Profit Opportunity Pricing Prune and Strengthen Distribution

Source: Adapted from Burton H. Marcus and Edward M. Tauber, *Marketing Analysis and Decision Making*
(Boston: Little, Brown, 1979), pp. 115–16. Copyright © 1979 by Burton H. Marcus and
Edward M. Tauber. Reprinted by permission of Little, Brown and Company.

The marketing manager needs to understand the adoption process so
that he or she can move potential consumers to the adoption stage. Once the
manager is aware of a large number of consumers at the interest stage, steps
can be taken to stimulate sales. For example, Gillette introduced Aapri Apricot
Facial Scrub by mailing 15 million samples to households in the United States
and Canada. Total sampling costs for the new skin product designed to compete with Noxzema, Pond's, and Oil of Olay were $4.1 million.[8] Sampling is a
technique that reduces the risk of evaluation and trial, moving the consumer
quickly to the adoption stage.

Return to the Stop-Action Case

ARM & HAMMER Baking Soda

Starting in 1970, Church & Dwight took a number of steps to extend ARM & HAMMER baking soda's product life cycle and to capitalize on the brand's respected name and logo. These moves fell into four categories:

1. An ongoing effort was made via public relations and package copy to maintain the volume from established uses of baking soda.

2. New, high-volume uses were aggressively promoted via advertising and reinforced by public relations and package copy. Baking soda was marketed as a deodorizer for refrigerators and freezers, cat litter, kitchen drains, and septic tanks. It was also promoted as a swimming pool water ph stabilizer and alkalinity reserve and as a plaque remover.

3. Flanker products, which aimed the basic baking soda product at specific consumer groups, were developed. These specially packaged products included a line of scented rug and room deodorizers and a cat litter deodorizer.

4. New products were developed to ride on the coattails of the ARM & HAMMER trademark. These included a heavy-duty laundry detergent, an oven cleaner, and a liquid laundry detergent.

Adopter Categories

Consumer Innovators
First purchasers of new products and services.

Some people purchase a new product almost as soon as it is placed on the market. Others wait for additional information and rely on the experiences of the first purchasers before making trial purchases. **Consumer innovators**— *first purchasers*—are likely to be present in each product area. Some families were first in the community to buy color television sets. Some doctors are first to prescribe new drugs, and some farmers plant new hybrid seeds much earlier than their neighbors. Some people are quick to adopt new fashions, and some drivers made early use of automobile diagnostic centers.

A number of investigations analyzing the adoption of new products has resulted in the identification of five categories of purchasers based on relative time of adoption. These categories, shown in Figure 8.7, are innovators, early adopters, early majority, late majority, and laggards.

Diffusion Process
Acceptance of new products and services by the members of a community or social system.

The **diffusion process** is the acceptance of new products and services by the members of a community or social system. Figure 8.7 shows this process as following a normal distribution. A few people adopt at first; then the number of adopters increases rapidly as the value of the innovation is apparent. The rate finally diminishes as fewer potential consumers remain in the nonadopter category.

Since the categories are based on a normal distribution, standard deviations are used to partition them. Innovators are the first 2.5 percent to adopt the new product; laggards are the last 16 percent to do so. Excluded from Figure 8.7 are the nonadopters—those who never adopt the innovation.

Figure 8.7
Categories of Adopters on the Basis of Relative Time of Adoption

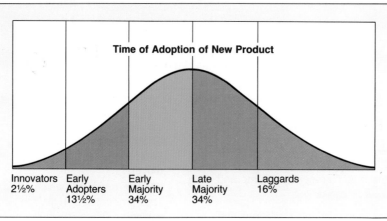

Identifying the First Adopters

Locating first buyers of new products represents a challenge for the marketing manager. If first buyers can be reached early in the product's development or introduction, they can serve as a test market, evaluating the products and making suggestions for modifications. Since early purchasers are often opinion leaders from whom others seek advice, their attitudes toward new products are quickly communicated to others. Acceptance or rejection of the innovation by these purchasers can help forecast the expected success of the new product.

Unfortunately, first adopters of one new product are not necessarily first adopters of other products or services. A large number of research studies has, however, established some general characteristics of most first adopters.

First adopters tend to be younger, have a higher social status, be better educated, and enjoy a higher income than others. They are more mobile than later adopters and change both their jobs and home addresses more often. They are also more likely to rely on impersonal information sources than are later adopters, who depend more on promotional information from the company and word-of-mouth communication.[9]

Rate of Adoption Determinants

Frisbees progressed from the product introduction stage to the market maturity stage in a period of six months. But it took the U.S. Department of Agriculture 13 years to convince corn farmers to use hybrid seed corn—an innovation capable of doubling corn yields. The adoption rate is influenced by five characteristics of the innovation:

1. *Relative advantage*—the degree to which the innovation appears superior to previous ideas. The greater the relative advantage—manifested in terms of lower price, physical improvements, or ease of use—the faster the adoption rate.

2. *Compatibility*—the degree to which the innovation is consistent with the values and experiences of potential adopters. The failure of Analoze, the

waterless pain remedy discussed earlier, resulted largely from consumers' unwillingness to accept a product whose directions for use conflicted drastically with consumer custom.

3. *Complexity*—the relative difficulty of understanding the innovation. The more difficult the new product is to understand or to use, the longer it will take to be generally accepted in most cases.

4. *Divisibility*—the degree to which the innovation can be used on a limited basis. First adopters face two types of risk, financial losses and ridicule by others, if the new product proves unsatisfactory. The option of sampling the innovation on a limited basis allows these risks to be reduced and generally accelerates the rate of adoption.

5. *Communicability*—the degree to which the results of using the product are observable or communicable to others. If the superiority of the innovation can be displayed in a tangible form, the adoption rate will be increased.[10]

These five characteristics can be implemented to some extent by the marketing manager to accelerate the rate of adoption. Product complexity must be overcome by informative promotional messages. Products should be designed to emphasize their relative advantages and, whenever possible, should be divisible for sample purchases. If divisibility is physically impossible, in-home demonstrations or trial placements in the home can be used. Positive attempts must also be made to ensure compatibility of the innovation with the adopters' value systems.

These actions are based on extensive research studies of innovators in agriculture, medicine, and consumer goods. They should pay off in increased sales by accelerating the rate of adoption in each of the adopter categories.

Consumer Goods and Industrial Goods: A Definition

How a firm markets a product depends largely on the product itself. For example, Chanel stresses subtle promotions in prestige media such as *The New Yorker* and *Vogue* magazines and markets its perfumes through department stores and specialty shops. Hershey markets its candy products through candy wholesalers to thousands of supermarkets, variety stores, discount houses, and vending machine companies. A firm manufacturing and marketing forklifts may use sales representatives to call on industrial buyers and ship its product either directly from the factory or from regional warehouses.

Product strategy differs for consumer goods and industrial goods. As defined earlier, *consumer goods* are products destined for use by the ultimate consumer, and *industrial goods* are products used directly or indirectly in producing other goods for resale. These two major categories can be further subdivided.

Consumer Goods: Characteristics

Although a number of classification systems have been suggested, the system most often used is based on consumer buying habits. The three categories of consumer goods are convenience goods, shopping goods, and specialty goods.[11]

Convenience Goods
Products that consumers want to
purchase frequently, immediately,
and with a minimum of effort.

Convenience Goods   The products that the consumer wants to purchase frequently, immediately, and with a minimum of effort are called convenience goods. Milk, bread, butter, eggs, and beer (the staples of most 24-hour convenience food stores) are all convenience goods. So are newspapers, chewing gum, magazines, M&M's, and the items found in most vending machines.

Convenience goods are usually sold by brand name and are low priced. Many of them—such as bread, milk, and gasoline—are staple items, and the consumer's supply must be constantly replenished. In most cases, the buyer has already decided to purchase a particular brand of gasoline or candy or to buy at a particular store and spends little time deliberating about the purchase decision. Products purchased on the spur of the moment and out of habit when the supply is low are referred to as *impulse goods*.

The consumer rarely visits competing stores or compares price and quality in purchasing convenience goods. The possible gains from such comparisons are outweighed by the costs of acquiring the additional information. This does not mean, however, that the consumer is destined to remain permanently loyal to one brand of beer, candy, or cigarettes. People continually receive new information from radio and television advertisements, billboards, and word-of-mouth communication. Since the price of most convenience goods is low, trial purchases of competing brands or products are made with little financial risk, and often new habits are developed.

Since the consumer is unwilling to spend much effort in purchasing convenience goods, the manufacturer must strive to make them as convenient as possible. Candy, cigarettes, and newspapers are sold in almost every supermarket, variety store, service station, and restaurant. Where retail outlets are physically separated from a large number of consumers, the manufacturer constructs small "stores" in the form of vending machines and places them in spots that are convenient for customers (such as office buildings and factories).

Retailers usually carry several competing brands of convenience products and are unlikely to promote any particular one. The promotional burden, therefore, falls on the *manufacturer*, who must advertise extensively to develop consumer acceptance of the product. The Coca-Cola promotional program consists of radio and television commercials, magazine ads, billboards, and point-of-purchase displays in stores. These efforts to motivate the consumer to choose Coke over competing brands are a good example of a manufacturer's promotion designed to stimulate consumer demand.

Shopping Goods
Products purchased only after the
consumer has made comparisons of
competing goods in competing
stores on bases such as price,
quality, style, and color.

Shopping Goods   In contrast to convenience goods, shopping goods are purchased only after the consumer has made comparisons of competing goods in competing stores on bases such as price, quality, style, and color. The purchaser of shopping goods lacks complete information prior to the shopping trip and gathers information during it.

A woman intent on adding a new dress to her wardrobe may visit many stores, try on a number of dresses, and spend days making the final choice. She may follow a regular route from store to store in surveying competing offerings and ultimately will select the dress that most appeals to her. New stores carrying assortments of shopping goods must ensure that they are located near other shopping goods stores so that they will be included in shopping expeditions.

Shopping goods are typically more expensive than convenience goods and are most often purchased by women. In addition to women's apparel, shopping goods include such items as appliances, furniture, jewelry, and shoes.

Some shopping goods are considered *homogeneous;* that is, the consumer views them as essentially the same. Others are considered *heterogeneous*—essentially different. Price is an important factor in the purchase of homogeneous shopping goods, while quality and styling are relatively more important in the purchase of heterogeneous goods.[12]

Important features of shopping goods are physical attributes, price, styling, and place of purchase. The store's name and reputation has a considerable influence on consumer buying behavior. The brand is often of lesser importance, in spite of the large amounts of money manufacturers often spend promoting their brands.

Since buyers of shopping goods expend some effort in making their purchases, manufacturers of shopping goods utilize fewer retail stores than for convenience goods. Retailers and manufacturers work closely in promoting shopping goods, and retail purchases are often made directly from the manufacturer or its representative rather than the wholesaler. Fashion merchandise buyers for department stores and specialty shops make regular buying trips to regional and national markets in New York, Dallas, and Los Angeles. Buyers for furniture retailers often go directly to the factories of furniture manufacturers or attend furniture trade shows.

Specialty Goods   The specialty goods purchaser is well aware of what he or she wants and is willing to make a special effort to obtain it. The nearest Cartier dealer may be 50 miles away, for example, but the watch purchaser willing to spend several thousand dollars will go there to buy this prestigious watch.

Specialty Goods
Products with unique characteristics that cause the buyer to prize them and to make a special effort to obtain them.

Specialty goods possess some unique characteristics that cause the buyer to prize that particular brand. For these products, the buyer has complete information prior to the shopping trip and is unwilling to accept substitutes.

Specialty goods are typically high priced and are frequently branded. Since consumers are willing to exert considerable effort to obtain them, fewer retail outlets are required. Mercury outboard motors and Porsche sports cars may be handled by only one or two retailers for each 100,000 people.

Applying the Consumer Goods Classification System

The three-way classification system allows the marketing manager to gain additional information for use in developing a marketing strategy. Once a new food product has been classified as a convenience good, insights are gained about marketing needs in branding, promotion, pricing, and distribution methods. Table 8.2 summarizes the impact of the consumer goods classification system on the development of an effective marketing mix.

But the classification system also poses problems. The major problem is that it suggests only three categories into which all products must fit. Some products fit neatly into one of the categories, but others fall into the grey areas between categories.

For example, how should a new automobile be classified? It is expensive, sold by brand, and handled by a few exclusive dealers in each city. But before classifying it as a specialty good, other characteristics must be considered. Most new-car buyers shop extensively among competing models and

Table 8.2

Marketing Impact of the Consumer Goods Classification System

Factor	Convenience Goods	Shopping Goods	Specialty Goods
Consumer Factors			
Planning Time Involved in Purchase	Very Little	Considerable	Extensive
Purchase Frequency	Frequent	Less Frequent	Infrequent
Importance of Convenient Location	Critical Importance	Important	Unimportant
Comparison of Price and Quality	Very Little	Considerable	Very Little
Marketing Mix Factors			
Price	Low	Relatively High	High
Advertising	By Manufacturer	Both	Both
Channel Length	Long	Relatively Short	Very Short
Number of Retail Outlets	Many	Few	Very Small Number; Often One per Market Area
Store Image	Unimportant	Very Important	Important

auto dealers before deciding on the best deal. A more effective way to utilize the classification is to consider it a continuum representing degrees of effort expended by the consumer, as Figure 8.8 illustrates.[13] If this is done, the new-car purchase can be located between the categories of shopping and specialty goods but nearer the specialty goods end of the continuum.

A second problem with the classification system is that consumers differ in their buying patterns. One person will make an unplanned purchase of a new Honda Prelude, while others will shop extensively before purchasing a car. But one buyer's impulse purchase does not make the Prelude a convenience good. Goods are classified by the purchase patterns of the majority of buyers.

Classification of Industrial Goods

Industrial goods can be subdivided into five categories: installations, accessory equipment, component parts and materials, raw materials, and industrial supplies. Industrial buyers are professional consumers; their job is to make effective purchase decisions. The purchase decision process involved in buying supplies of flour for General Mills, for example, is much the same as that used in buying the same commodity for Pillsbury. Thus the classification system for industrial goods must be based on product uses rather than on consumer buying patterns.

Figure 8.8

Product Classification Continuum

Convenience Good   Shopping Good   Specialty Good

Installations

Specialty goods of the industrial market are called installations. Included in this classification are such major capital items as new factories and heavy machinery, new planes for United Airlines, or locomotives for the Burlington Northern.

Since installations are relatively long-lived and involve large sums of money, their purchase represents a major decision for an organization. Negotiations often extend over a period of several months and involve the participation of numerous decision makers. In many cases, the selling company must provide technical expertise. When custom-made equipment is involved, representatives of the selling firm work closely with the buyer's engineers and production personnel to design the most feasible product for the buying firm.

Price is almost never the deciding factor in the purchase of installations. The purchasing firm is interested in the product's efficiency and performance over its useful life. The firm also wants a minimum of breakdowns. "Down time" is expensive because employees are nonproductive (but are still paid) while the machine is being repaired.

Since most of the factories of firms purchasing installations are geographically concentrated, the selling firm places its promotional emphasis on well-trained salespeople who often have a technical background. Most installations are marketed directly on a manufacturer-to-user basis. Even though a sale may be a one-time transaction, contracts often call for regular product servicing. In the case of extremely expensive installations, such as computer and electronic equipment, some firms lease the installations rather than sell them outright and assign personnel directly to the lessee to operate or to maintain the equipment.

Accessory Equipment

Fewer decision makers are usually involved in purchasing accessory equipment—capital items that are usually less expensive and shorter-lived than installations. Although quality and service still remain important criteria in purchasing accessory equipment, the firm is likely to be much more price conscious. Accessory equipment includes such products as desk calculators, hand tools, portable drills, small lathes, and typewriters. Although these goods are considered capital items and are depreciated over several years, their useful life is generally much shorter than that of an installation.

Because of the need for continuous representation and the more widespread geographic dispersion of accessory equipment purchasers, a wholesaler—often called an industrial distributor—contacts potential customers in each geographic area. Technical assistance is usually not necessary, and the manufacturer of accessory equipment often can effectively utilize wholesalers in marketing the firm's products. Manufacturers also use advertising more than installation producers do.

Component Parts and Materials

Whereas installations and accessory equipment are used in producing the final product, component parts and materials are the finished industrial goods that actually become part of the final product. Champion spark plugs make a new Chevrolet complete; batteries are often added to Mattel toys; tires are included with a Dodge pickup truck. Some fabricated materials, such as flour, undergo further processing before producing a finished product.

Purchasers of component parts and materials need a regular, continuous supply of uniform quality goods. These goods are generally purchased on contract for a period of one year or more. Direct sale is common, and satisfied customers often become permanent buyers. Wholesalers sometimes are used for fill-in purchases and in handling sales to smaller purchasers.

Raw Materials

Raw Materials
Industrial goods such as farm products (wheat, cotton, soybeans) and natural products (coal, lumber, iron ore) used in producing final products.

Farm products—such as cattle, cotton, eggs, milk, pigs, and soybeans—and *natural products*—such as coal, copper, iron ore, and lumber—constitute **raw materials**. They are similar to component parts and materials in that they are used in producing the final product.

Since most raw materials are graded, the purchaser is assured of standardized products with uniform quality. As with component parts and materials, direct sale of raw materials is common, and sales are typically made on a contractual basis. Wholesalers are increasingly involved in the purchase of raw materials from foreign suppliers.

Price is seldom a deciding factor in the purchase of raw materials, since it is often quoted at a central market and is virtually identical among competing sellers. Purchasers buy raw materials from the firms they consider most able to deliver in the quantity and the quality required.

Supplies

Supplies
Regular expense items necessary in the daily operation of the firm but not part of the final product.

MRO Items
Supplies for an industrial firm, categorized as maintenance items, repair items, or operating supplies.

If installations represent the "specialty goods" of the industrial market, then operating supplies are the "convenience goods." **Supplies** are regular expense items necessary in the daily operation of the firm, but not part of the final product.

Supplies are sometimes called **MRO items** because they can be divided into three categories: 1) *maintenance items*, such as brooms, floor-cleaning compounds, and light bulbs; 2) *repair items*, such as nuts and bolts used in repairing equipment; and 3) *operating supplies*, such as heating fuel, lubricating oil, and office stationery.

The regular purchase of operating supplies is a routine aspect of the purchasing agent's job. Wholesalers are very often used in the sale of supplies due to the items' low unit prices, small sales, and large number of potential buyers. Since supplies are relatively standardized, price competition is frequently heavy. However, the purchasing agent spends little time in making purchase decisions. He or she frequently places telephone or mail orders or makes regular purchases from the sales representative of the local office supply wholesaler.

Services

Both industrial buyers and ultimate consumers are frequent purchasers of services as well as goods.[14] Services—ranging from necessities such as electric power and medical care to luxuries such as foreign travel, backpacking guides, ski resorts, and tennis schools—now account for about half of the average consumer's total expenditures. While *product* was defined earlier in the chapter to include both tangible and intangible items, differences do exist between tangible products and intangible services. In addition, services account for two-thirds of the private (nongovernment) labor force; they are therefore important enough to require careful analysis.

Figure 8.9
After the Sale Service: A Critical Component in Burroughs' Definition of Product

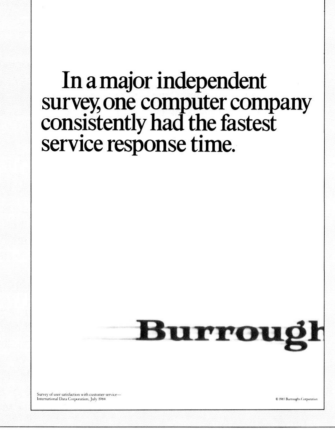

Source: Courtesy of Burroughs Corporation.

Defining Services

Services are difficult to define. Consider the rapidly expanding area of computer software. Is software a product or a service? Among taxing authorities the definitions vary considerably. The federal government asks whether anything tangible has been sold. The state of Washington considers custom-designed software a service and packaged programs a product.[15]

Some marketers provide a combination of goods and services to their customers. An optometrist may give eye examinations (a service) and sell contact lenses and eyeglasses (goods). As suggested in Figure 8.9, some services are an integral part of the marketing of physical goods. For example, a Burroughs sales representative may emphasize the firm's service capabilities. These illustrations suggest that some method of alleviating definitional problems in the marketing of services is needed.

One useful method is the utilization of a product spectrum, which shows that most products have both goods and services components. Figure 8.10 presents a **goods-services continuum**—a method for visualizing the differences and similarities of goods and services.[16] A tire is a pure good, although the service of balancing may be sold along with it or included in the total price. Hair styling is a pure service. In the middle ranges of the continuum are products with both goods and services components. The satisfaction that results

Goods-Services Continuum
Method for visualizing the differences and similarities of goods and services.

Figure 8.10
The Goods-Services Continuum

Services
Intangible tasks that satisfy
consumer and industrial user needs
when efficiently developed and
distributed to chosen market
segments.

from dining in an exclusive restaurant is derived not only from the food and drink, but also from the services rendered by the establishment's personnel. Services, then, can be defined as intangible tasks that satisfy consumer and industrial user needs when efficiently developed and distributed to chosen market segments.

Classifying Consumer and Industrial Services

Literally thousands of services are offered to consumers and industrial users. In some instances, they are provided by specialized machinery with almost no personal assistance, such as an automated car wash. In other cases, they are provided by skilled professionals with little reliance on specialized equipment, such as accountants and management consultants. Figure 8.11 provides a means of classifying services based on the degree of reliance on equipment in providing the service and the degree of skill possessed by the people who provide the service.[17]

Features of Services

Services have four key features with major marketing implications:

1.   Services are intangible.
2.   They are perishable.
3.   Their standardization is difficult.
4.   Buyers are often involved in their development and distribution.

Intangibility   Services do not have tangible features that appeal to consumers' sense of sight, hearing, smell, taste, or touch. They are therefore difficult to demonstrate at trade fairs, to display in retail stores, and to illustrate in magazine advertisements. They are nearly impossible to sample, and they cannot make use of many other forms of sales promotion. Consequently, imaginative personal selling is usually essential in marketing services.

Furthermore, buyers are often unable to judge the quality of a service prior to purchase. Because of this, the reputation of the service's vendor is often a key factor in a buyer's decision.

Perishability   The utility of most services is short-lived, therefore, they cannot be produced ahead of time and stored for periods of peak demand. Vacant

Figure 8.11
Types of Service Businesses

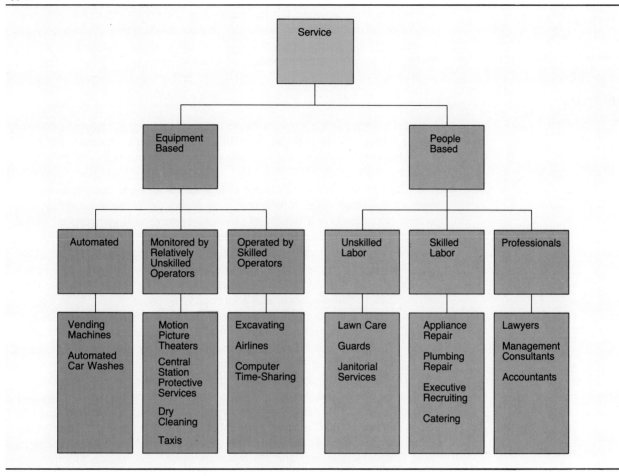

seats on an airplane, idle dance instructors, and empty motel rooms represent economic losses that can never be recovered. Sometimes, however, idle facilities during slack periods must be tolerated so the firm will have sufficient capacity for peak periods. Electric and gas utilities, resort hotels, telephone companies, and airlines all face the problem of perishability.

Difficulty of Standardization   It is often impossible to standardize offerings among sellers of the same service or even to assure consistency in the services provided by one seller. No two paint jobs from the same house painter are identical. Although standardization is often desirable, it occurs only in the case of equipment-based firms such as those offering automated banking services or automated car washes. Creative marketing is needed to adapt nonstandardized services to the unique needs of individual customers.

Involvement of Buyers   Buyers often play major roles in the marketing and production of services. The house painter's customer may provide samples of the desired colors for the house and the trim and may offer suggestions at several stages during the painting process. Different firms often want unique blends of insurance coverage, and the final policy may be developed after several meetings between the purchaser and the insurance agent. Although purchaser specifications also play a role in the creation of major products such as installations, the interaction of buyer and seller at both the production and distribution stages is a common feature of services.

Summary

A critical variable in the firm's marketing mix is the product it plans to offer its market target. The best price, most efficient distribution channel, and most effective promotional program cannot gain continuing purchases of an inferior product.

Consumers view products not only in physical terms but more often in terms of expected want satisfaction. The broad marketing conception of a product encompasses a bundle of physical, service, and symbolic attributes designed to produce this want satisfaction.

All successful products pass through the four stages of the product life cycle: introduction, growth, maturity, and decline. Consumers also go through a series of stages in adopting new product offerings: initial awareness, interest, evaluation, trial purchase, and adoption or rejection.

Although first adopters of new products vary among product classes, several common characteristics have been isolated. First adopters are often younger, better educated, and more mobile, and they have higher incomes and higher social status than later adopters.

The rate of adoption for new products depends on five characteristics: (1) relative advantage, the degree of superiority of the innovation over the previous product; (2) compatibility, the degree to which the new product or idea is consistent with the value system of potential purchasers; (3) complexity of the new product; (4) divisibility, the degree to which trial purchases on a small scale are possible; and (5) communicability, the degree to which the superiority of the innovation can be transmitted to other potential buyers.

Products are classified as either consumer or industrial goods. Consumer goods are used by the ultimate consumer and are not intended for resale or further use in producing other products. Industrial goods are used either directly or indirectly in producing other products for resale.

Differences in consumer buying habits can be used to further classify consumer goods into three categories: convenience goods, shopping goods, and specialty goods. Industrial goods are classified on the basis of product uses. The five categories in the industrial goods classification are installations, accessory equipment, component parts and materials, raw materials, and industrial supplies.

About half of all personal consumption expenditures go to the purchase of services—intangible tasks that satisfy consumer and industrial user needs when efficiently developed and distributed to chosen market segments. The marketing of services has many similarities to the marketing of goods, but there are also significant differences. The key features of services are their intangibility and perishability, the difficulty of standardizing them, and the involvement of buyers in their development and distribution.

Once the firm's products have been classified, the marketing manager is provided with a number of insights in making decisions about distribution channels, price, and promotion—the three other variables of the marketing mix.

Solving the Stop-Action Case

ARM & HAMMER Baking Soda

Photo Source: Reprinted with the permission of the ARM & HAMMER Division of Church & Dwight Co., Inc. ARM & HAMMER is a registered trademark of Church & Dwight Co., Inc.

When the ARM & HAMMER division of Church & Dwight started its promotional campaign in the early 1970s, it focused on using baking soda as a refrigerator air freshener. Ads test marketing this approach on the West Coast proved so successful that the ARM & HAMMER division quickly expanded the campaign nationwide. Within 13 months, the company's market research showed a jump from 1 percent to 57 percent in the number of households using baking soda as a refrigerator deodorant. This astounding success translated into a 72 percent sales volume increase between 1971 and 1974.

The ARM & HAMMER division then began advertising other related uses for baking soda. Its use as a freezer deodorizer was introduced through an extensive advertising campaign that more than doubled the number of households that used baking soda for this purpose. To deal with the problem of consumers putting a box of baking soda in the refrigerator or freezer and forgetting about it, the ARM & HAMMER division launched another advertising campaign promoting baking soda as a sink-drain deodorizer. The idea behind this campaign was to encourage consumers to pour their baking soda down the drain, thus forcing them to regularly replenish their supply. By June 1977, 67 percent of all households claimed to have used baking soda as a drain deodorizer, up from 43 percent in November 1975.

The ARM & HAMMER name was further enhanced by the introduction of a nonpolluting laundry detergent, a product that met with immediate success. "We had a $25 million business almost overnight," said Burton B. Staniar, a Church & Dwight group business manager. This success gave Church & Dwight confidence that it could sell almost any product that used the ARM & HAMMER name. "The ARM & HAMMER name has such phenomenal strength, such good equity, it was hard to do anything wrong," said Staniar.

Church & Dwight's success at finding new products and creating new uses for old products was in large measure the result of an extensive marketing research program conducted by Behavioral Analysis Inc., a research organization headed by Richard Reiser. "We've done just about every kind of study there is," said Reiser. "This continuity is important because we've been able to build a comprehensive body of knowledge which probably wouldn't result from a bunch of unrelated ad hoc studies."

By 1981, baking soda's annual sales had grown to 5 million cases a year, up from 2.3 million in 1970. Consumer use has also changed considerably due to Church & Dwight's promotional campaigns. A little more than half of current volume is generated by uses which didn't exist in 1970, while remaining volume is generated by uses which existed in 1970 and have continued viable. For example, baking soda's use as a leavening agent in baking was the same in 1981 as in 1970. Approximately 200,000 cases a year were still used for baking despite the explosion of other uses—a trend that points to the value of Church & Dwight's promotional campaign. According to *Advertising Age,* "The introduction of new uses for baking soda did not take from the established uses of 1970; indeed it expanded the tonnage they represented, if not the relative importance."

In recent years, the ARM & HAMMER division has focused its marketing efforts on the use of baking soda as a dentifrice and plaque remover and as a personal care application in the bath. Church & Dwight's success in extending the product life cycle of its baking soda products is best measured in dollars and cents. With 1983 net sales topping $152 million—nearly ten times the level recorded in 1969—there is little reason to doubt that "mother baking soda," as it is known to company employees, will be around for many years to come.

Sources: Jack J. Honomichl, "The Ongoing Saga of 'Mother Baking Soda'," *Advertising Age* (September 20, 1982), p. M-3; and Church & Dwight Co., *1983 Annual Report.*

Questions for Discussion

1. Differentiate between the definition of product used in Chapter 8 and the narrower, traditional definition.

2. Justify the inclusion of services in the definition of product.

3. Select a specific product in each stage of the product life cycle (other than those shown in Figure 8.3). Explain how the marketing strategies vary by life cycle stage for each product.

4. Suggest several means by which the life cycle of a product, such as Scotch tape, can be extended.

5. Identify and briefly explain the stages in the consumer adoption process.

6. Describe each of the determinants of the rate of adoption.

7. Choose a newly introduced product with which you are familiar and make some positive suggestions to accelerate its adoption rate.

8. Suggest some practical uses for currently known facts about the consumer innovator.

9. Home burglar alarm systems using microwaves are a fast-growing product in the home-security market. Such systems operate by filling rooms with microwave beams that set off alarms when an intruder intercepts one of them. What suggestions can you make to accelerate the rate of adoption for this product?

10. Why is the basis used for categorizing industrial goods different from that used for categorizing consumer goods?

11. Of what possible value is a classification scheme that allows an automobile tire to be both a consumer and an industrial good?

12. What determines whether a product is a consumer good or an industrial good?

13. Compare a typical marketing mix for convenience goods with a mix for specialty goods.

14. Give two illustrations from your own experience of each of the following kinds of goods: convenience goods, shopping goods, and specialty goods. Justify your classifications.

15. Explain how a suit can be a convenience good for one person, a shopping good for a second, and a specialty good for a third. Does this fact destroy the validity of the consumer goods classification? Support your answer.

16. Classify the following consumer goods:
    a. Furniture   e. Porsche 944
    b. Puma running shoes   f. Binaca breath freshener
    c. Felt-tip pen   g. Sports Illustrated magazine
    d. Swimsuit   h. Original oil painting

17. Outline the typical marketing mix for a shopping good.

18. Classify the following products into the appropriate industrial goods category. Briefly explain your choice for each product.
    a. Calculators   e. Paper towels
    b. Land   f. Nylon
    c. Light bulbs   g. Airplanes
    d. Wool   h. Tires

19. How will the marketing mix for installations differ from the mix for raw materials? Support your answer with specific illustrations.

20. Identify and explain the key features of services.

Case: American Honda Motor Company

"It's sexy," purrs rock star Grace Jones on television screens around the country. The Honda motor scooter that Jones and fellow rocker Adam Ant are pitching may or may not be sexy, but it is indisputably different from scooters of the past. Rakishly designed with a wedge-shaped nose, the $1,300 Elite model sports such engineering features as an electric starter instead of the old kick pedal, an automatic transmission, a water-cooled engine, and a digital speedometer.

American Honda Motor Company is spending $6 million and archrival Yamaha Motor Corp. USA $1 million in marketing drives to persuade Americans to ride such sleek new machines—and to develop a mass market in the U.S. where others have failed.

White-Collar Crowd   Scooters are popular abroad, but they have never caught on with U.S. consumers, who until recently had bought only 50,000 of them since World War II. Italy's Piaggio, maker of the Vespa, the dominant brand in the past, withdrew from the U.S. market last year rather than meet pollution control standards for its few exports to the U.S.

Honda and Yamaha are following distinctly different marketing strategies. Honda is targeting so-called early adopters—trendy and affluent 16- to 25-year-olds—on the theory that their elders will follow them into scooters as they did into designer jeans. Honda's TV ads aim for this market, with a racier version on MTV. A smaller print campaign will appear in *People, Us, Teen, National Lampoon,* and *Rolling Stone.* To grab the student market, Honda is offering a small, 85-lb. bike with a 49cc engine that retails for $400. "Honda is putting all its eggs in the youth basket," says Dennis J. Stefani, manager of product planning at Yamaha USA.

Yamaha, on the other hand, is going straight for the over-30, white-collar crowd. Understated advertising calls its Riva line "transportation for people who are already there." The print-only campaign is running in *Time, Newsweek, Sports Illustrated,* and *People.* To counter the cheaper Hondas, Yamaha just cut the price on its smallest scooter, the Riva 50, from $659 to $559.

Quieter and Simpler   Motorcycle makers badly need a new U.S. product because aging baby boomers are buying fewer machines, and Honda and Yamaha think scooters may be the answer. So far the market looks promising. Honda, which has built a 70% market share since introducing its first models with little fanfare last year, sold some 35,000 scooters so far this year. Manufacturers expect to sell 50,000 units in 1984, but the number may go much higher. They aim for 250,000 scooters in a few years, despite some skepticism that the scooter will prove to be a fad, like mopeds in the 1970s. If they are right, other makers—including Japan's Suzuki Motor Co. and Piaggio—may start shipping to the U.S.

Manufacturers believe that Americans will be won over by the new scooters because they are quieter and simpler to operate than motorcycles or the old-style European scooters, and most are more powerful than mopeds. Part of the marketing plan is to disassociate scooters from motorcycles. Yamaha's research shows that potential scooter owners are older, wealthier, and better educated than motorcyclists. And many are female. Women own only 8% of the motorcycles on the road, but they are buying nearly half of the new scooters at some dealerships.

Photo Source: Courtesy of American Honda Motor Co. Inc.

"The new scooters are extremely good looking, and they are practical, short-haul transportation," says Don J. Brown, an industry consultant and president of Hancock-Brown Corp. in Costa Mesa, Calif. "We think the scooter is here to stay." A broad dealer network, which Vespa never achieved, should help. Although some motorcycle dealers at first shunned scooters as playthings, some 1,000 of Honda's 1,700 dealers are signed up to carry scooters, while one-third of Yamaha's 1,500 dealers are selling them.

Source: "Motor Scooters Finally Make a Dent in the U.S. Market," reprinted from the July 16, 1984 issue of *Business Week* by special permission, pp. 31, 35, © 1984 by McGraw-Hill, Inc.

Questions

1. How would you place the Honda Motor Scooter in the product life cycle? Explain your decision.

2. Relate this case to the chapter's discussion of the determinants of the rate of adoption.

Computer Applications

The creation of new product and service offerings for industrial purchasers, organizational buyers, or ultimate consumers is an expensive and risk-filled undertaking. Since marketers usually face a number of alternatives from which to choose a product or service to offer their selected market targets, they need a method to use in evaluating the most appropriate use of the firm's limited financial and human resources. A commonly used technique for its investment is *return on investment (ROI)*. This quantitative tool is particularly useful in evaluating proposals for alternative courses of action.

ROI is equal to the rate of profit (net profit divided by sales) multiplied by the firm's turnover rate (sales divided by the required investment). The formula for calculating ROI is as follows:

$$ROI = \frac{Net\ Profit}{Sales} \times \frac{Sales}{Investment}.$$

Consider the example of a proposed new product for which the firm's marketers estimate that a $200,000 investment will be required. The company expects to achieve $500,000 in sales, with a projected net profit of $40,000. The proposed product's ROI is calculated as follows:

$$ROI = \frac{\$40,000}{\$500,000} \times \frac{\$500,000}{\$200,000}$$

$$= .08 \times 2.5$$

$$= 20\ percent.$$

Whether or not the 20 percent return on investment is acceptable depends on similar ROI calculations for alternative uses of company funds. In addition, the marketing decision makers are likely to consider carefully such variables as the fit of the proposed product or service with existing product lines and with long-range marketing plans.

In comparing ROIs of different proposals, it is important to recognize several factors that can affect ROI calculations. In situations where different depreciation schedules are being used, profits—and therefore ROI—will vary. External conditions can also affect ROI. Favorable economic conditions may be associated with high rates of return, while lower rates may be more common during economic downturns. A third factor affecting ROI is the time period over which product development expenditures are made. The ROI of a product that requires considerable developmental work may be adversely affected.[1]

---

[1] These factors are suggested in J. Fred Weston and Eugene F. Brigham, *Essentials of Managerial Finance* (Hinsdale, Ill.: The Dryden Press, 1985), pp. 156–157.

Directions: Use menu item 8 titled "Return on Investment" to solve each of the following problems.

Problem 1 The management of Southern Michigan Industries, of Jackson, Michigan, is considering the development of a new type of industrial shears. The estimated cost to develop the new product is $4 million. The firm expects to sell $20 million of the shears, producing a profit of $2 million. What is the ROI for the new industrial product?

Problem 2 Atlanta-based Affiliated Dental Clinics markets franchises to young dentists just starting their practices. The company projects that a franchisee will earn $30,000 in the first year of operation based upon $180,000 in professional fees. Total first-year expenses of $150,000 include franchise fees, dental equipment, personnel, rent, utilities, and other set-up costs. In addition, the $150,000 includes interest charges on a special financial arrangement Affiliated Dental Clinics has developed for new dentists with limited current funds but high future-revenue expectations. What is the typical first year's ROI for a dentist who establishes an Affiliated Dental Clinic?

Problem 3 Light Manufacturing, Inc., of Sacramento, California, has marketed an industrial drill for years. Currently sales are $5 million annually, but last year Light Manufacturing earned only $150,000 on the drill because of the rapidly rising cost of component parts. A recent proposal from the production department suggests that shifting to less expensive components would increase profits to $300,000 while maintaining sales at $5 million. However, this would require several plant layout changes costing $1.25 million. What is the ROI of the proposed switch to less expensive parts?

Problem 4 A Jonesboro, Arkansas, inventor has developed a new fad item that is so secret that she refuses to divulge any details about it until she completes a licensing proposal for a major novelty manufacturer in Memphis. One part of the proposal is a return-on-investment calculation. The inventor estimates that the manufacturer would have to spend a total of $15 million in production and promotional outlays to successfully launch the fad item. Sales are estimated to total $60 million. After subtracting such expenses as shipping, retail price discounts necessary to motivate retailers to carry the item in inventory, and licensing fees, the firm should earn profits of $10 million. What ROI should the inventor include on her proposal to the novelty manufacturer?

Problem 5 SKI Industries, of La Crosse, Wisconsin, has developed a new type of ski. Special placement tests at ski instruction schools throughout the United States proved highly successful. In fact, ski instructors preferred the new skis by a three-to-one margin over their current skis. The firm's top management estimates that they would be able to generate $10 million in revenue from the sale of the skis at wholesale prices. However, development expenses for the prototype skis are estimated at $4 million. Management believes that the new line would add $1 million to the firm's annual profits. Calculate the ROI for the proposed new line of skis.

9 Elements of Product/Service Strategy

Key Terms

product mix
product line
cannibalizing
line extension
product positioning
product managers
venture team
concept testing
test marketing
brand
brand name
trademark
generic name
brand recognition
brand preference
brand insistence
brand extension
family brand
individual brands
manufacturers'
    (national) brands
private brands
generic products
label
Universal Product Code
product liability

Learning Goals

1. To identify the major product mix decisions that must be made by marketers
2. To explain why most firms develop a line of related products rather than a single product
3. To identify alternative new product strategies and the determinants of the success of each
4. To identify and explain the various organizational arrangements for new product development
5. To list the stages in the product development process
6. To explain the role of brands, brand names, and trademarks
7. To describe the major functions of the package
8. To explain the functions of the Consumer Product Safety Commission and the concept of product liability

Predetermining Product Success

Somewhere in the back of every marketing manager's mind is the fact that two out of every three products on store shelves eventually fail. This thought almost certainly occurred to marketers at G.D. Searle & Co. when Equal, Searle's tabletop, nonsaccharin sugar substitute, was ready to be marketed. Searle executives knew they were dealing with a new kind of product that was sure to attract a great deal of attention.

Working with Glendenning, a consulting firm, Searle developed a promotional strategy and creative advertising for Equal. To determine how to position Equal—as a "no saccharin" product or as a "tastes like sugar" product—Searle conducted focus group interviews and learned that "taste" was the more effective positioning.

According to Marcel C. Durot, Searle's vice-president and general manager of consumer products, the marketing success of Equal depended on three major marketing decisions: (1) determining how the mix of all the marketing elements fit together, (2) determining the price/volume relationship of the product, and (3) determining the media weight level that was appropriate to attain the awareness, trial, and repeat goals. Marketers also faced the problem of predicting market response. If Searle's projections were too low, they would lose a significant amount of business when potential customers walked out of stores empty-handed. If projections were too high, they would face costly, unsold inventory.

The Pillsbury Company faced an equally important decision when it was ready to market a new refrigerated dough product called "Pipin Hot Loaf." Marketing executives were unsure whether all three versions of the product—white, rye, and wheat—would gain national acceptance.

With millions of dollars invested in product development, both Searle and Pillsbury had to find a way to measure public acceptance of their products well before they were marketed on a national level. Larry Gibson, director of corporate marketing research at General Mills, emphasized the point when he admitted, "Most new products we start working on turn out to be bad ideas."

Assignment: Use the materials in Chapter 9 to recommend a course of action for Searle and Pillsbury.

Source: "To Test or Not to Test Seldom the Question," *Advertising Age* (February 20, 1984), p. M-10.

Photo Source: Courtesy of NutraSweet® Group, G.D. Searle & Co.

Chapter Overview

Chapter 8 considered several basic product concepts. This chapter expands the discussion of products and services by examining the product mix and new product planning. A starting point is to consider the concept of a product mix.

Product Mix
Assortment of product lines and individual offerings available from a marketer.

A product mix is the assortment of product lines and individual offerings available from a marketer. Its two primary components are product line, a series of related products, and individual offerings that make up a product line.

Product Line
Various related goods offered by a firm.

Product mixes are typically measured by width of assortment and depth of assortment. *Width* of assortment refers to the number of product lines that the firm offers, while *depth* of assortment refers to the number of different product offerings in a particular product line.[1] Philip Morris Incorporated offers an assortment of consumer product lines—cigarettes, beer, and soft drinks. These product lines would be considered the width of the Philip Morris product mix. The depth is determined by the number of individual offerings within each product line. For example, their soft-drink line consists of 7-Up, Diet 7-Up, Like Cola and Sugar Free Like Cola; their cigarette line is headed by Marlboro; and their beer line by Miller and Miller Lite. The width and depth of the Philip Morris product mix is depicted in Figure 9.1.

The Existing Product Mix

The starting point in any product planning effort for an established firm is to assess its current product mix. What product lines does it now offer? How deep are the offerings within each of the product lines? The marketer wants to look for gaps in the assortment that can be filled by new products or modified versions of existing products.

Cannibalization

Cannibalizing
Product that takes sales from another offering in a product line.

The firm wants to avoid a costly new product introduction that will adversely affect sales of one of its existing products. A product that takes sales from another offering in a product line is said to be cannibalizing the line. Such was the case in 1964 when Maxim instant coffee was introduced. Marketers

Figure 9.1
The Philip Morris Product Mix

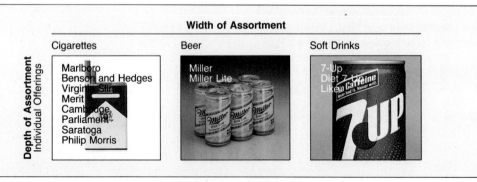

Sources: Reprinted by permission of Philip Morris Incorporated, Miller Brewing Company, and The Seven-Up Company.

at General Foods hoped that the popularity of the Maxwell House name would help Maxim. It did, but it also took millions of sales dollars from the established offering.[2] While the introduction of a new product will inevitably take some sales from related products already being marketed, marketing research should ensure that the new offering will guarantee sufficient additional sales to warrant the investment involved in its development and market introduction.

Line Extension

An important rationale for assessing the current product mix is to determine whether line extension is feasible. A line extension refers to the development of individual offerings that appeal to different market segments but are closely related to the existing product line. If cannibalization can be minimized, line extension provides a relatively cheap way of increasing sales revenues at minimal risk. Hershey's Krackel candy bar was outsold about four to one by Nestlé's Crunch, but Hershey's addition of a larger bar—the Big Block—allowed it to nearly double the sales of Krackel.[3] This situation illustrates the line extension of an existing Hershey product.

After the assessment of the existing product mix has been made and the appropriate line extensions considered, marketing decision makers must turn their attention to product line planning and the development of new products.

Line Extension
New product that is closely related to other products in the firm's existing product line.

The Importance of Product Lines

Firms that market only one product are rare today. Most offer their customers a product line—a series of related products. Polaroid Corporation, for example, began operations with a single product, a polarized screen for sunglasses and other products. Then, in 1948, it introduced the world's first instant camera. For the next 30 years, these products proved to be sufficient for annual sales and profit growth. By 1983, however, instant cameras accounted for only about 60 percent of Polaroid's sales. The company had added hundreds of products in both industrial and consumer markets, ranging from nearly 40 different types of instant films for various industrial, medical, and other technical operations to batteries, sonar devices, and computer image recorders.[4] Several factors account for the inclination of firms such as Polaroid to develop a complete line rather than concentrate on a single product.

Desire to Grow

A company places definite limitations on its growth potential when it concentrates on a single product. In a single 12-month period, Lever Brothers introduced 21 new products in its search for market growth and increased profits. A study by Booz, Allen & Hamilton management consultants revealed that information-processing firms expect new products to contribute approximately 43 percent of corporate profits in 1986. Manufacturers of consumer durables expect new products to bring in about 36 percent of company profits by the same year. New products are being introduced at an ever-increasing rate to meet these product growth targets. While each of the surveyed firms introduced an average of five new products between 1976 and 1982, these corporations planned to double that number through 1986.[5]

Firms often introduce new products to offset seasonal variations in the sales of their current products. Since the majority of soup purchases are made during the winter months, Campbell Soup Company has made attempts to tap the warm-weather soup market. A line of fruit soups to be served chilled was test marketed, but results showed that U.S. consumers were not yet ready for fruit soups. The firm continued to search for warm-weather soups, however, and in the early 1980s, it added gazpacho and other varieties to be served chilled.

Optimal Use of Company Resources

By spreading the costs of company operations over a series of products, it may be possible to reduce the average production and marketing costs of all products. Texize Chemicals Company started with a single household cleaner and learned painful lessons about marketing costs when a firm has only one major product. Management rapidly added the products K2r and Fantastik to the line. The company's sales representatives can now call on marketing intermediaries with a series of products at little more than the cost of a single product. In addition, Texize's advertising produces benefits for all products in the line. Similarly, production facilities can be used economically in producing related products. For example, Chrysler has designed a convertible, van, and sports car from the K car design.[6] Finally, the expertise of all the firm's personnel can be utilized more economically for a line of products than for a single product.

Increasing Company Importance in the Market

The company with a line of products is often more important to both consumers and marketing intermediaries than is the firm with only one product. Shoppers who purchase a tent often buy related items, such as tent heaters, sleeping bags and air mattresses, camping stoves, and special cookware. Recognizing this tendency, the Coleman Company now includes in its product line dozens of items associated with camping. The firm would be little known if its only product were lanterns. Similarly, new cameras from Eastman Kodak help the firm sell more film—a product that carries a 60 percent profit margin.[7]

Consumers and marketing intermediaries often expect a firm that manufacturers and markets small appliances to also offer related products under its brand name. The Maytag Company offers not only washing machines but also dryers, since many consumers prefer matching appliances. Gillette markets not only razors and blades but also a full range of grooming aids, including Right Guard deodorants/antiperspirants, Foamy Shave Cream, Aapri Facial Scrub and Moisturing Creme, and the Silkience line of hair care products (shampoo, conditioner, and hair spray).

Exploiting the Product Life Cycle

As its output enters the maturity and decline stages of the product life cycle, the firm must add new products if it is to prosper. The regular addition of new products to the firm's line helps ensure that it will not become a victim of product obsolescence. The development of the compact laser disc player in the early 1980s was accompanied by a steady reduction in retail price. The impact of this innovation was to shift audio cassette tapes from the late growth stage to the maturity stage, as all major record producers began to offer the compact disc option to record buyers.

New Product Planning

The product development effort requires considerable advance planning. New products are the lifeblood of any business firm, and a steady flow of new entries must be available if the firm is to survive. Some new products may involve major technological breakthroughs. For example, Procter & Gamble has filed patent applications for a male baldness cure, a margarine that cuts cholesterol in the blood, and a plaque-eliminating dental product.[8] Other new products are simple product-line extensions. In other words, a new product is simply a product new to either the company or the customer. A recent survey revealed that only about 10 percent of new product introductions were truly new products.

The Product Idea Mortality Curve

New product development is risky and expensive. Approximately two-thirds of all new products fail after they are on store shelves.[9] As the product mortality curve shown in Figure 9.2 reveals, dozens of new-product ideas are required to produce even one successful product. As ideas are evaluated and tested, most are discarded in the firm's pursuit of products that will enjoy sufficient marketplace success to justify the required investment.

Product Development Strategies

The firm's strategy for new product development should vary in accordance with the existing product mix and the extent to which current market offerings match overall marketing objectives. The current market position of the firm's products and services will also affect the product development strategy used by the firm's marketers. Figure 9.3 identifies the four alternative strategies facing the marketing manager: product improvement, market development, product development, and product diversification.

Product Positioning
Consumer's perception of a product's attributes, use, quality, and advantages and disadvantages.

A *product improvement strategy* refers to a modification in existing products. Product positioning often plays a major role in such strategy. **Product positioning** refers to the consumer's perception of a product's attributes, use,

Figure 9.2
The Product Idea Mortality Curve

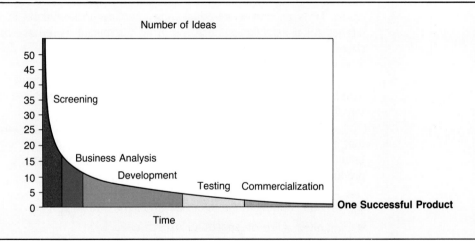

Figure 9.3

Forms of Product Development

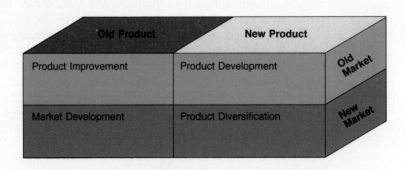

Sources: Charles E. Meisch, "Marketers, Engineers Should Work Together in 'New Product' Development Departments," *Marketing News* (November 13, 1981), p. 10. Earlier discussion of these strategies is credited to H. Igor Ansoff, "Strategies for Diversification," *Harvard Business Review* (September–October 1957), pp. 113–124. See Philip Kotler, *Principles of Marketing*, 2nd ed. (Englewood Cliffs, N.J.: Prentice-Hall, Inc., 1983), pp. 34, 52.

quality, and advantages and disadvantages in relation to competing brands. Marketing research methodology allows marketers to analyze consumer preferences and to construct product positioning maps that plot a product in relationship to competitive offerings.[10]

Product positioning has permitted manufacturers to make their products more appealing to even the smallest consumer segments. For example, auto buyers can select from more than 69,000 possible versions of a new Ford Thunderbird. This strategy is in sharp contrast to that of Japanese manufacturers who target only the largest consumer segments and limit the range of model choice because of vast shipping distances. The Honda Accord, for example, comes in only 32 versions.[11]

A *market development strategy* concentrates on finding new markets for existing products. Market segmentation, discussed in Chapter 5, is a useful tool in such an effort. The ARM & HAMMER division's penetration of new markets with an established product is illustrative of this strategy.

Product development strategy, as it is defined here, refers to the introduction of new products into identifiable or established markets. Sometimes the new product is the firm's first entry in a particular marketplace. In other cases, firms choose to introduce new products into markets in which they already have established positions in an attempt to increase overall market share. These new offerings are called *flanker brands*. Butcher's Blend dry dog food is Ralston Purina's flanker to their Dog Chow line.[12]

Product diversification strategy refers to the development of new products for new markets. In some cases, the new market targets are complementary to existing markets; in others, they are not.

In every new product decision, the firm's marketers should make certain that the new entry is consistent with the firm's overall strategic orientation. A beverage firm, for example, uses four strategic requirements for a new product:

■   It must appeal to the under-21 age segment.

■   It must utilize off-season or excess capacity.

- It must successfully penetrate a new product category for the firm.
- Alternatively, it could become a cash cow that funds other new products.[13]

New product planning is a complex area. The critical nature of product planning decisions requires an effective organizational structure.

The Organizational Structure for New Product Development _____

An effective organizational structure is required to stimulate and coordinate new product development. Most firms assign new product development to one or more of the following alternatives: new product committees, new product departments, product managers, or venture teams.

New Product Committees

The most common organizational arrangement for new product development is the new product development committee. It is typically composed of representatives of top management in such areas as marketing, finance, manufacturing, engineering, research, and accounting. Committee members are less concerned with the conception and development of new product ideas than with reviewing and approving new product plans. Publishing houses, for instance, often have editorial review committees that must approve new project ideas before an editor can work with an author in developing a new book.

Since the members of new product committees are key executives in the functional areas, their support for any new product plan is likely to result in an approval for further development. However, new product committees tend to be slow in making decisions and conservative in their views, and sometimes they compromise so members can get back to their regular company responsibilities.

New Product Departments

Many companies establish a separate, formally organized new product department. The organization of a department overcomes the limitations of the new product committee system and makes new product development a permanent, full-time activity. The department is responsible for all phases of the product's development within the firm, including screening decisions, development of product specifications, and coordinating product testing. The head of the department has substantial authority and typically reports to the president or the top marketing officer.

Product Managers

Product Managers
Individuals in a manufacturing firm assigned a product or product line and given complete responsibility for determining objectives and establishing marketing strategies.

Product managers, also called brand managers, are individuals assigned one product or product line and given responsibility for determining its objectives and marketing strategies. Procter & Gamble assigned the first product manager in 1927 when it made one person responsible for Camay soap.[14] The product manager concept is now widely accepted by marketers. Johnson & Johnson, Richardson-Vicks, and General Mills are examples of firms employing product managers.

Product managers set prices, develop advertising and sales promotion programs, and work with sales representatives in the field. Although product managers have no line authority over the field sales force, the objective of increasing sales for the brand is the same, and managers attempt to help salespeople accomplish their task. In multiproduct companies, product managers are key people in the marketing department. They provide individual attention to each product, while the firm as a whole has a single sales force, marketing research department, and advertising department that all product managers can utilize.

In addition to having primary responsibility for marketing a particular product or product line, the product manager is often responsible for new product development, the creation of new product ideas, and recommendations for improving existing products. These suggestions become the basis for proposals submitted to top management.

The product manager system is open to one of the same criticisms as the new product committee: New product development may get secondary treatment because of the manager's time commitments for existing products. Although a number of extremely successful new products have resulted from ideas submitted by product managers, it cannot be assumed that the skills required for marketing an existing product line are the same as those required for successfully developing new products.[15]

Venture Teams

Venture Team
Organizational strategy for identifying and developing areas for new products by combining the management resources of technological innovation, capital, management, and marketing expertise.

The venture team concept is an organizational strategy for developing new product areas by combining the management resources of technological innovations, capital, management, and marketing expertise. Like new product committees, venture teams are composed of specialists from different areas of the organization: engineering representatives for expertise in product design and the development of prototypes; marketing staff members for development of product concept tests, test marketing, sales forecasts, pricing, and promotion; and financial accounting representatives for detailed cost analyses and decisions concerning the concept's probable return on investment.

Unlike committees, venture teams do not disband after every meeting. Team members are assigned a project as a major responsibility, and teams possess the necessary authority to both plan and implement a course of action. To stimulate product innovation, the venture team is typically linked directly with top management, but it functions as a separate entity apart from the organization. Some sources also differentiate venture teams from task forces. A new product task force is an interdisciplinary group on temporary assignment that works through functional departments. Their basic task is to coordinate and integrate the work of the functional departments on a specific project. By contrast, venture teams work independently and are not tied to functional departments.[16]

The venture team must meet such criteria as prospective return on investment, uniqueness of the product, existence of a well-defined need, degree of the product's compatibility with existing technology, and strength of patent protection. Although the venture team is considered temporary, the actual life span of these groups is flexible, often extending over a number of years. When the commercial potential of a new product has been demonstrated, the product may be assigned to an existing division, become a division within the company, or serve as the nucleus of a new company.

Stages in the New Product Development Process

After the firm has organized for new product development, it can establish procedures for evaluating new product ideas. The new product development process involves six stages: (1) idea generation, (2) screening, (3) business analysis, (4) development, (5) testing, and (6) commercialization. At each stage, management faces the decision to abandon the project, continue to the next stage, or seek additional information before proceeding further.

Idea Generation

New product development begins with ideas that emanate from many sources: the sales force, customers who write letters asking, "Why don't you . . .," marketing employees, research and development specialists, competitive products, retailers, and inventors outside the company. It is important for the firm to develop a system for stimulating new ideas and for rewarding persons who develop them.

Screening

This critical stage involves separating ideas with potential from those incapable of meeting company objectives. Some organizations use checklists to determine whether product ideas should be eliminated or subjected to further consideration. These checklists typically include such factors as product uniqueness, availability of raw materials, and compatibility of the proposed product with current product offerings, existing facilities, and capabilities. In other instances, the screening stage consists of open discussions of new product ideas among representatives of different functional areas in the organization. Screening is an important stage in the developmental process because any product ideas that proceed beyond this stage will cost the firm time and money.[17] Table 9.1 presents some basic criteria for the screening process.

Table 9.1

Basic Criteria for Preliminary Screening

The item should be in a field of activity in which the corporation is engaged.

If the idea involves a companion product to others already being manufactured, it should be made from materials to which the corporation is accustomed.

The item should be capable of being produced on the type and kind of equipment that the corporation normally operates.

The item should be easily handled by the corporation's existing sales force through the established distribution pattern.

The potential market for the product should be at least $_____.

The market over the next five years should be expected to grow at a faster rate than the GNP.

Return on investment, after taxes, must reach a minimum level of ____ percent.

Source: Reprinted from William S. Sachs and George Benson, *Product Planning and Management* (Tulsa, Okla.: PennWell Books, 1981), p. 231.

Business Analysis

Product ideas surviving the initial screening are subjected to a thorough business analysis. The analysis involves an assessment of the potential market, its growth rate, and the likely competitive strengths of the new product. Decisions must be made about the compatibility of the proposed product with such company resources as financial support for necessary promotion, production capabilities, and distribution facilities.

Concept testing, or the consideration of the product idea prior to its actual development, is an important aspect of the business analysis stage. **Concept testing** is a marketing research project that attempts to measure consumer attitudes and perceptions relevant to the new product idea. Focus groups and in-store polling can be effective methods for assessing a new product concept.

Concept Testing
Measuring consumer attitudes and perceptions of a product idea prior to its actual development.

Development

Product ideas with profit potential are converted into a physical product. The conversion process is the joint responsibility of the development engineering department, which turns the original concept into a product, and the marketing department, which provides feedback on consumer reactions to product designs, packages, colors, and other physical features. Numerous changes may be necessary before the original mock-up is converted into the final product.

The series of tests, revisions, and refinements should result ultimately in the introduction of a product with great likelihood of success. Some firms obtain the reactions of their own employees to proposed new product offerings. Employees at Levi Strauss test new styles by wearing them and reporting on the various features. Thom McAn asks its workers to report regularly over an eight-week testing period on shoe wear and fit.

Occasionally, attempts to be the first with a new product result in the product's premature introduction. The Kellogg Company and several other cereal makers experienced this problem several years ago when they all failed in their attempts to introduce freeze-dried fruit cereal. In the rush to be first on the market with the new offering, they did not perfect the product. The small, hard pellets of real fruit took too long to reconstitute in the bowl, and millions of bowls of cereal went into garbage cans.[18]

Testing

To determine consumer reactions to a product under normal conditions, many firms test market their new product offerings. Up to this point, consumer information has been obtained by submitting free products to consumers, who then give their reactions. Other information may come from shoppers asked to evaluate competitive products. Test marketing is the first stage at which the product or service must perform in a real-life environment.

Test marketing is the process of selecting a specific city or television-coverage area considered reasonably typical of the total market and introducing the product or service with a complete marketing campaign in this area. A carefully designed and controlled test allows management to estimate sales for a full-scale introduction. Figure 9.4 indicates U.S. test-market cities frequently used by marketers.

Test Marketing
Process of selecting a specific city or television-coverage area considered reasonably typical of a new total market and introducing the product with a marketing campaign in this area.

Figure 9.4

Recommended Test Markets

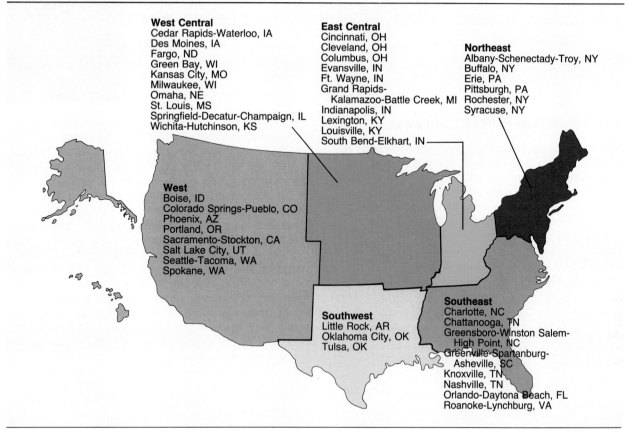

West Central
Cedar Rapids-Waterloo, IA
Des Moines, IA
Fargo, ND
Green Bay, WI
Kansas City, MO
Milwaukee, WI
Omaha, NE
St. Louis, MS
Springfield-Decatur-Champaign, IL
Wichita-Hutchinson, KS

East Central
Cincinnati, OH
Cleveland, OH
Columbus, OH
Evansville, IN
Ft. Wayne, IN
Grand Rapids-
    Kalamazoo-Battle Creek, MI
Indianapolis, IN
Lexington, KY
Louisville, KY
South Bend-Elkhart, IN

Northeast
Albany-Schenectady-Troy, NY
Buffalo, NY
Erie, PA
Pittsburgh, PA
Rochester, NY
Syracuse, NY

West
Boise, ID
Colorado Springs-Pueblo, CO
Phoenix, AZ
Portland, OR
Sacramento-Stockton, CA
Salt Lake City, UT
Seattle-Tacoma, WA
Spokane, WA

Southwest
Little Rock, AR
Oklahoma City, OK
Tulsa, OK

Southeast
Charlotte, NC
Chattanooga, TN
Greensboro-Winston Salem-
    High Point, NC
Greenville-Spartanburg-
    Asheville, SC
Knoxville, TN
Nashville, TN
Orlando-Daytona Beach, FL
Roanoke-Lynchburg, VA

Source: Dancer Fitzgerald Sample, Inc.

Some firms omit test marketing and move directly from product development to full-scale production. They cite four problems with test marketing:

1. Test marketing is expensive. As one marketing executive at Ralston Purina pointed out:

    It's very difficult to run a little [test market] for six months or a year in three or four markets across the United States and then project what your sales volume is going to be two or three years in the future, mainly because you're testing in such small localities, generally to keep your costs down.[19]

2. Competitors who learn about the test market often disrupt the findings by reducing the price of their products in the test area, distributing cents-off coupons, installing attractive in-store displays, or giving additional discounts to retailers to induce them to display more of their products. In a court settlement, Hartz Mountain once agreed not to engage in advertising designed to disrupt the test of a new pet product by a subsidiary of A. H. Robins.

3. Long-lived durable goods, such as dishwashers, hair dryers, and compact laser disc players, are seldom test marketed due to the major finan-

Return to the Stop-Action Case

Predetermining Product Success

Why must marketers know if a product will succeed before it is marketed nationally? The primary reason is money. New product failure can translate into multimillion-dollar losses during a national product launch. Although test marketing will eliminate most of these losses if the decision is made to discontinue an unsuccessful product, it adds a substantial cost of its own. According to Gian Fulgoni, president of Information Resources, Inc., new product testing in 2 percent of the U.S. market can cost a company $3.1 million. The costs break down in the following way:

Item	Approximate Cost
Product Costs	
R & D	$ 800,000
Pilot Production	750,000
Advertising	
Production	150,000
Spot Purchases	600,000
Promotion	
Consumer and Trade	200,000
Marketing Research	
Sales Audits	200,000
Controlled Distribution	200,000
Consumer Research	200,000
Total Cost	$3,100,000

Despite the skyrocketing costs, studies have shown that the success of new-product testing has improved little over the years. Fulgoni explains the reason for this failure.

"Historically, too many marketers have introduced new products using the Mother Robin approach—i.e., once it looks ready, push it out of the nest and hope you don't hear a crash. Too seldom is test marketing designed to increase the odds of success. Too often it is designed for a simple go/no go decision.

"Increasing the odds of success, in turn, means trying alternative strategies. It means measuring the payout of marketing supports. It means manipulating and fine-tuning the business proposition while in test market. Yet, by and large, marketers haven't done so. In fact, (a recent) *Wall Street Journal* article (said) that one-third of all companies do not formally measure the performance of new products."

With the cost of test marketing so high, continued Fulgoni, its "job . . . must become not a go/no go decision, but rather an optimization of financial results for a product which simply must go."

The only way for test marketers to meet these new demands is through the development of new, more sophisticated technologies.

Source: Gian Fulgoni, "Test Marketing in the '80s," speech presented to the Proprietary Association, New York City, December 8, 1983.

cial investment required for the development, the need to develop a network of dealers to distribute the products, and the parts and servicing required. A company such as Whirlpool invests from $1 million to $33 million in the development of a new refrigerator. To develop each silicon chip that performs a single function in an Apple microcomputer costs approximately $1 million and takes from one to fifteen months. Producing a prototype for a test market is simply too expensive, so the go/no go decision for the new durable product is typically made without the benefit of test-market results.[20]

4.   Test marketing a new product or service communicates company plans to competitors prior to its introduction. The Kellogg Company discovered

a new product with sales potential by learning of the test marketing of a new fruit-filled tart designed to be heated in the toaster and served for breakfast. Kellogg rushed a similar product into full-scale production and became the first national marketer of the product Pop Tarts. Other test-marketed products beaten into the national market by competitors include Helene Curtis' Arm in Arm deodorant (preempted by Church & Dwight's ARM & HAMMER deodorant); General Foods' Maxim (Nestlé's Taster's Choice); Hills Brothers High Yield Coffee (Procter & Gamble's Folger's Flakes); and Hunt–Wesson's Prima Salsa tomato sauce (Chesebrough–Ponds' Ragu Extra Thick & Zesty).[21]

The decision to skip the test-marketing stage should be based on the conclusion that the new product or service has an extremely high likelihood of success. The cost of developing a new detergent, for example, from idea generation to national marketing has been estimated at $25 million! Even if a company experiences losses on a product or service that fails at the test-marketing stage, the firm saves itself from incurring even greater losses and embarrassment in the total market. Otherwise, the product or service may join the ranks of such monumental failures as Du Pont's Corfam synthetic leather with losses of more than $100 million or Polaroid's ill-fated Polavision instant movie system, whose development and production costs were estimated at between $200 million and $500 million.[22]

Commercialization

The few product ideas that survive all the steps in the development process are ready for full-scale marketing. Marketing programs must be established, outlays for necessary production facilities must be made, and the sales force, marketing intermediaries, and potential customers must be acquainted with the new product. A systematic approach to new product development is essential.

Systematic planning of all phases of new product development and introduction can be accomplished through the use of such scheduling methods as the Program Evaluation and Review Technique (PERT) and the Critical Path Method (CPM). These techniques, developed originally by the U.S. Navy in connection with construction of the Polaris missile and submarine, map out the sequence in which each step must be taken and show the time allotments for each activity. Detailed PERT and CPM flowcharts coordinate all activities involved in the development and introduction of new products.

Product Deletion Decisions

Although many firms devote a great deal of time and resources to the development of new products, the thought of eliminating old ones is painful for many executives. Often, sentimental attachments to marginal products with declining sales prevent objective decisions to drop them.

To avoid waste, product lines must be pruned, and old, marginal products must eventually be eliminated. Marketers typically face this decision during the late maturity and early decline stages of the product life cycle. Periodic reviews of weak products should be conducted to eliminate them or to justify retaining them.

In some instances, a firm will continue to carry an unprofitable product to provide a complete line of goods for its customers. Even though most grocery stores lose money on bulky, low unit-value items such as salt, they continue to carry them to meet shopper demand.

Shortages of raw materials have prompted some companies to discontinue the production and marketing of previously profitable items. Due to such a shortage, Alcoa discontinued its Alcoa aluminum foil.

In other cases, profitable products are dropped because they fail to fit into the firm's existing product line. The introduction of automatic washing machines necessitated the development of low-sudsing detergents. Monsanto produced the world's first detergent of this sort, All, in the 1950s. All was an instant success, and Monsanto was swamped with orders from supermarkets throughout the nation. The Monsanto sales force was primarily involved in marketing industrial chemicals to large-scale buyers, and the company would have needed a completely new sales force to handle the product. Nine months after the introduction of All, Procter & Gamble introduced the world's second low-sudsing detergent, Dash. Because the Procter & Gamble sales force handled hundreds of products, the company could spread the cost of contacting dealers over all its products. Monsanto had only All. Rather than attempt to compete, Monsanto sold All in 1958 to Lever Brothers, a Procter & Gamble competitor that had a marketing organization capable of handling the product.

Product Identification

Manufacturers identify their products with brand names, symbols, and distinctive packaging; so do certain large retailers, such as JCPenney and Sears. Almost every product that is distinguishable from another contains a means of identification for the buyer. Sunkist Growers literally brands its oranges with the name Sunkist. The purchasing agent for a construction firm can turn over a sheet of aluminum and find the name and symbol for Alcoa. Choosing the means of identifying the firm's output represents a major decision for the marketing manager.

Brands, Brand Names, and Trademarks

Brand
A name, term, sign, symbol, design, or some combination used to identify the products of one firm and to differentiate them from competitive offerings.

Brand Name
Part of the brand consisting of words or letters that comprise a name used to identify and distinguish the firm's offerings from those of competitors.

Trademark
Brand that has been given legally protected status. Protection is granted solely to the brand's owner.

A brand is a name, term, sign, symbol, design, or some combination used to identify the products of one firm and to differentiate them from competitive offerings. A brand name is that part of the brand consisting of words or letters that comprise a name used to identify and distinguish the firm's offerings from those of competitors.[23] It is, therefore, that part of the brand which can be vocalized. A trademark is a brand that has been given legal protection; the protection is granted solely to the brand's owner. The term *trademark* includes not only the pictorial design, but also the brand name. More than 500,000 trademarks are currently registered in the United States.[24]

For the consumer, the process of branding allows repeat purchases of the same product, since the product is identified with the name of the firm producing it. The purchaser thus can associate the satisfaction derived from a hot dog, for example, with the brand name Corn King Franks. For the marketing manager, the brand serves as the cornerstone of the product's image. Once consumers have been made aware of a particular brand, its appearance becomes additional advertising for the firm. Shell Oil's symbol of a seashell is instant advertising to motorists who view it while driving.

Well-known brands also allow the firm to escape some of the rigors of price competition. Although any chemist will confirm that all brands of aspirin contain the same amount of the chemical acetylsalicylic acid, Bayer has developed so strong a reputation that it can successfully market its aspirin at a higher price than competitive products. Well-known gasoline brands typically sell at slightly higher prices than independent brands because many purchasers feel that they are buying higher-quality gasoline.

What Constitutes a Good Brand Name?   Effective brand names are easy to pronounce, recognize, and remember. Short names like Busch, Gleem, Klear, and Off! meet these requirements. Multinational marketing firms face a particularly acute problem in selecting brand names; an excellent brand name in one country may prove disastrous in another. When Standard Oil decided to reduce its number of gasoline brands from three (Esso, Enco, and Humble) to one, company officials ruled out Enco, because in Japanese the word means stalled car. The ultimate choice was Exxon—a unique, distinctive name. Exxon was picked from some 10,000 possible names generated by a computer. It was checked for potential translation problems in 56 languages and 113 dialects. The firm also conducted a worldwide legal search to be sure no one else had the rights to the new name.[25]

Every language has *o* and *k* sounds, and *okay* has become an international word. Every language also has a short *a* so that Coca-Cola and Texaco are effective brands in any country. An advertising campaign for E-Z washing machines failed in the United Kingdom, however, because the British pronounce *z* as zed.

For 21 years, Nissan Motor Corporation marketers struggled with an easily mispronounced brand name for its Datsun cars and trucks. Datsun encountered difficulty in the United States and other English-speaking nations where some people pronounce the *a* like the *a* in hat, while others pronounce it like the *o* in got. Finally, Nissan marketers decided to change the name of all its automobile products to Nissan. Total costs of the change in the more than 135 countries serviced by Nissan were estimated as high as $150 million.[26]

The brand name should give the buyer the right connotation. The Tru-Test name used on the True Value Hardware line of paints produces the desired image. Accutron suggests the quality of the high-priced and accurate timepiece sold by Bulova.

The brand name must also be legally protectable. The Lanham Act (1946) states that registered trademarks must not contain words in general use, such as automobile or suntan lotion. These generic words actually describe a particular type of product and thus cannot be granted exclusively to any company.

Generic Name
Brand name that has become a generally descriptive term for a product.

When a unique product becomes generally known by its original brand name, the brand name may be ruled as a descriptive generic name; if this occurs, the original owner loses exclusive claim to it. For example, in 1983 the U.S. Supreme Court ruled that the trademark for Parker Brothers' Monopoly was invalid because it had become a general term for such games. The case involved Parker Brothers, who first produced Monopoly in 1935, and a San Francisco State University economics professor who developed a game called Anti-Monopoly.[27] The generic names *nylon, aspirin, escalator, kerosene,* and *zipper* were at one time brand names. Other generic names that were once brand names include *cola, yo-yo, linoleum,* and *shredded wheat.*

There is a difference between brand names that are legally generic and those that are generic in the eyes of many consumers. Jell-O is a brand name owned exclusively by General Foods, but to most consumers Jell-O is the descriptive name for gelatin desserts. Legal brand names like Jell-O are often used by consumers as descriptive names. Many English and Australian consumers use the brand name Hoover as a verb for vacuuming. Similarly, Xerox is such a well-known brand name that it is frequently, but incorrectly, used as a verb. To protect its valuable trademark, Xerox Corporation has placed advertisements in *Writer's Digest*, a trade magazine for writers. The advertising copy in Figure 9.5 explains that Xerox is a brand name and registered trademark and should not be used as a verb.

To prevent their brand names from being ruled descriptive and available for general use, most owners take steps to inform the public of their exclusive ownership of the name. Coca-Cola uses the ® symbol for registration immediately after the names *Coca-Cola* and *Coke* and sends letters to newspapers, novelists, and others who use Coke with a lower-case letter informing them that the name is owned by Coca-Cola.[28] These companies face the dilemma of attempting to retain exclusive rights to a brand name when it is generic to a large part of the market.

Since any dictionary name may eventually be ruled generic, some companies create new words for their brand names. Names such as Tylenol, Keds, Rinso, and Kodak have been created by their owners.

Measuring Brand Loyalty   Brands vary widely in consumer familiarity and acceptance. While a boating enthusiast may insist on a Johnson outboard motor, one study revealed that 40 percent of U.S. homemakers could not identify the brands of furniture in their own homes. Brand loyalty can be measured in three stages: brand recognition, brand preference, and brand insistence.

Figure 9.5
Xerox Corporation Advertisement Designed to Protect the Firm's Brand Name

Brand recognition is a company's first objective for its newly introduced products—to make them familiar to the consuming public. Often this is achieved through offers of free samples or discount coupons for purchases. Several new brands of toothpaste have been introduced on college campuses in free sample kits called Campus Pacs. Once consumers have used a product, it moves from the unknown to the known category, and the probability of its being repurchased is increased provided the consumer was satisfied with the trial sample.

Brand preference is the second stage of brand loyalty. In this stage, consumers, relying on previous experience with the product, will choose it over its competitors if it is available. A college student who prefers Stroh's beer will usually switch to another brand if it is not available at the tavern where he or she is to meet friends after an evening class. Companies with products at the brand preference stage are in a favorable position for competing in their industry.

Brand insistence, the ultimate stage in brand loyalty, is that situation in which consumers will accept no alternatives and will search extensively for the product. A product at this stage has achieved a monopoly position with that particular group of consumers. Although brand insistence is the goal of many firms, it is seldom achieved. Only the most exclusive specialty goods attain this position with a large segment of the total market.

The Importance of Brand Loyalty   A study of 12 patented drugs illustrates the importance of brand acceptance. The sample included well-known drugs like Librium and Darvon. The research indicated that patent expiration had minimal effect on the drugs' market shares or price levels. This resiliency was credited to the brand loyalty for the pioneer product in the field.[29] Another measure of the importance of brand loyalty is found in the Brand Utility Yardstick used by J. Walter Thompson advertising agency. These ratings measure the percentage of buyers who remain brand loyal even if a 50-percent cost savings was available from generic products. Beer consumers were very loyal, with 48 percent refusing to switch brands. Sinus-remedy buyers were also brand loyal with a 44 percent rating. By contrast, only 13 percent of the aluminum-foil buyers would not switch to the generic product.[30]

Some brands are so popular that they are carried over to unrelated products because of their marketing advantages. The decision to use a popular brand name for a new product entry in an unrelated product category is known as brand extension. It should not be confused with line extension, which refers to new sizes, styles, or related products. Brand extension, by contrast, refers only to carrying over the brand name.

Examples of brand extension are abundant in contemporary marketing. Fisher-Price, well known for its toys, is now marketing preschool playwear.[31] Similarly, General Foods has extended its Jell-O brand to Jell-O Pudding Pops, Jell-O Slice Creme, and Jell-O Gelatin Pops. Although most people associate the Mrs. Paul's brand with fish sticks, it has been extended to frozen fried chicken.[32]

Family Brands and Individual Brands   Brands can be classified as family brands or individual brands. A family brand is a single brand name used for several related products. General Electric has a complete line of kitchen appliances under the GE name. Johnson & Johnson offers a line of baby powder, lotions, disposable diapers, plastic pants, and baby shampoo under one name.

On the other hand, a manufacturer may choose to utilize individual brands, items known by their own brand names rather than by the names of the companies producing them or by an umbrella name covering similar items. Lever Brothers, for example, markets Aim, Close-Up, and Pepsodent toothpastes; All and Wisk laundry detergents; Imperial margarine; Caress, Dove, Lifebuoy, and Lux bath soaps; and Shield deodorant soap. Beatrice Foods markets Bonkers cat food; Milk Duds and Good and Plenty candy; and Arrowhead and Great Bear bottled waters. Individual brands are more expensive to market because a new promotional campaign must be developed to introduce each new product to its market target. But they are an extremely effective aid to implementing a market segmentation strategy.

When family brands are used, a promotional outlay benefits all the products in the line. For example, a new addition to the Heinz line gains immediate recognition because the family brand is well known. Use of family brands also makes it easier to introduce the product to the customer and to the retailer. Since grocery stores stock an average of some 10,256 items, they are reluctant to add new products unless they are convinced of potential demand. A marketer of a new brand of turtle soup would have to promise the grocery-store buyer huge advertising outlays for promotion and evidence of consumer buying intent before getting the product into the stores. With its dominant share of the U.S. soup market, the Campbell Soup Company could merely add turtle soup to its existing line and secure store placements more easily than could another company with individual brand names.

Family brands should be used only when the products are of similar quality, or the firm will risk harming its product image. Using the Mercedes-Benz name on a new, less-expensive auto might severely tarnish the image of the other models in the Mercedes-Benz product line.

Individual brand names should be used for dissimilar products. Campbell Soup Company once marketed a line of dry soups under the brand name Red Kettle. Large marketers of grocery products, such as Procter & Gamble, General Foods, and Lever Brothers, employ individual brands to appeal to unique market segments. These brands also enable the firm to stimulate competition within the organization and to increase total company sales. Consumers who do not want Tide can choose Cheer, Dash, or Oxydol—all Procter & Gamble products—rather than purchase a competitor's brand.

Manufacturers' Brands or Private Brands?

Most of the brands mentioned in this chapter have been brands offered by manufacturers, commonly termed manufacturers' (national) brands. But many large wholesalers and retailers also place their own brands on the products they market. The brands offered by wholesalers and retailers are usually called private brands. Sears, the nation's largest retailer, sells its own brands—Kenmore, Craftsman, DieHard and Harmony House. Safeway shelves are filled with such company brands as Bel Air, Canterbury, Cragmont, Party Pride, Manor House, and Scotch Buy. In total, these private brands represent 28 percent of the total retail sales in all U.S. Safeway stores. The growth of private brands and generic products has greatly expanded the number of alternatives available to consumers. There are now about 28,000 nationally advertised brands in the United States.[33]

The growth of private brands is largely attributed to the fact that they allow retailers and wholesalers to maintain control over the product's image, quality, and price. Private brands are usually sold at lower prices than the national brands offered by manufacturers.

Generic Products   Food and household staples characterized by plain labels, little or no advertising, and no brand names are called generic products. These "no-name" products were first sold in Europe, where their prices were as much as 30 percent below brand-name products. They now capture about 40 percent of total volume in European supermarkets.

Generics account for between 5 and 15 percent of selected food and nonfood sales and are found in over 60 percent of all U.S. supermarkets throughout the country. The most popular generic products in U.S. supermarkets include canned green beans and corn, jams, jellies and preserves, peanut butter, tea bags, plastic household bags, light- and heavy-duty detergents, paper towels, and toilet tissue.[34]

Battle of the Brands   Competition between manufacturers' brands and the private brands offered by wholesalers and large retailers has been called "the battle of the brands." Although the battle appears to be intensifying, the marketing impact varies widely among industries. One survey showed that private brands represented 40 percent of the market in replacement tires but only 20 percent of gasoline sales.[35]

The growth of private brands has paralleled the growth of chain stores in the United States, most of which has occurred since the 1930s. Chains that market their own brands become customers of the manufacturer, which places the chains' private brand names on the products it produces.

Such leading manufacturers as Westinghouse, Armstrong Rubber, and Heinz are obtaining larger and larger percentages of their total income by selling private-label goods. Private-label sales to Sears and other major customers account for about 45 percent of Whirlpool's sales.

Polaroid is now manufacturing private-label instant cameras for Sears. Although some manufacturers refuse to produce private-brand goods, most regard such production as reaching another segment of the total market.

Great inroads have been made into the dominance of manufacturers' national brands. Private brands and generics have proven that they can compete with national brands and have often succeeded in producing price reductions by national brand marketers to make them more competitive.

Packaging

Questions about packaging must also be addressed in a firm's product strategy. When Kimberly-Clark was designing one version of Kleenex, it asked several consumers to keep diaries listing their tissue usage. The study resulted in a new Kleenex package containing 60 tissues, the average number of times the product is used when someone has a cold.[36]

Packaging represents a vital component of the total product concept. Its importance can be inferred from the size of the packaging industry. Approximately $60 billion is spent annually on packaging in the United States, and the industry is comparable in size with the automobile and meat-packing industries.

The package has several objectives. These can be classified under three general goals:

1.   To protect against damage, spoilage, and pilferage;

2.   To assist in marketing the product; and

3.   To be cost effective.

Protection against Damage, Spoilage, and Pilferage

The original packaging objective was to offer physical protection. The typical product is handled several times between manufacture and consumer purchase, and its package must protect the contents against damage. Furthermore, perishable products must be protected against spoilage in transit, storage, or awaiting consumer selection.

Another important role provided by many packages for the retailer is the prevention of pilferage. At the retail level, pilferage is estimated to cost retailers between $8 million and $9 million each day. Many products are packaged with oversize cardboard backing too large to fit into a shoplifter's pocket or purse. Large plastic packages are used in a similar manner on such products as eight-track and cassette tapes.

Assistance in Marketing the Product

The package designers of the 1980s frequently use marketing research in testing alternative designs. Increasingly scientific approaches are utilized in designing a package that is attractive, safe, and esthetically appealing. Kellogg, for instance, tested Nutri-Grain's package as well as the product itself.[37]

In a grocery store containing as many as 15,000 different items, a product must capture the shopper's attention. Walter Margulies, chairman of Lippincott & Margulies advertising, summarizes the importance of first impressions in the retail store: "Consumers are more intelligent, but they don't read as much. They relate to pictures." Margulies also cites another factor: One of every six shoppers who needs eyeglasses does not wear them while shopping. Consequently, many marketers offering product lines are adopting similar package designs to create more visual impact in the store. Packaging Stouffer's frozen foods in orange boxes and the adoption of common package designs by such product lines as Weight Watchers foods and Planters nuts represent attempts to dominate larger sections of retail stores.[38]

Packages can also offer the consumer convenience. Pump dispenser cans facilitate the use of products ranging from mustard to insect repellent. Pop-top cans provide added convenience for soft drinks, beer, and other food products. The six-pack carton, first introduced by Coca-Cola in the 1930s, can be carried with minimal effort by the food shopper.

A growing number of firms provide increased consumer utility with packages designed for reuse. Peanut butter jars and jelly jars have long been used as drinking glasses. Bubble bath can be purchased in plastic bottles shaped like animals and suitable for bathtub play. Packaging is a major component in Avon's overall marketing strategy. The firm's decorative reusable bottles have even become collectibles.

Cost-Effective Packaging

Although packaging must perform a number of functions for the producer, marketer, and consumer, it must accomplish them at a reasonable cost. Packaging currently represents the single largest item in the cost of producing a can of beer. It also accounts for 55 percent of the total cost of the single-serving packets of sugar found in restaurants.[39]

An excellent illustration of how packaging can be cost effective is provided by the Swedish firm Tetro-Pak that pioneered aseptic packaging for products like milk and juice. Aseptic packaging wraps a laminated paper around a sterilized product and seals it off. The big advantage of this packaging technology is that products can be kept unrefrigerated for months. Aseptically packed milk, for instance, will keep its nutritional qualities and flavor for six months. With 60 percent of a supermarket's energy bill going for refrigeration, aseptic packaging is certainly cost effective. The paper packaging is also cheaper than the cans and bottles used for unrefrigerated fruit juices. Handling costs can also be reduced in many cases.[40]

The Metric Revolution in Packaging and Product Development

Marketers in the United States are increasingly adopting the metric system in their packaging and product development decisions. Metrics is a standard of weights and measures used throughout most of the world. Most soft drinks now come in half-liter bottles as a substitute for pints and quarts. Many canned and packaged foods list metric equivalents to ounces and pounds on their labels.

The metric revolution has clearly affected the development of new products and their packaging. One survey found that 34 percent of all new products were designed in metrics, while 16 percent of the firms studied reported losing some sales because they did not offer a metric product.[41]

U.S. marketers must make the switch to metrics if they are to continue to compete in the world marketplace. Such firms as Caterpillar Tractor, John Deere, International Harvester, and IBM have been using metrics for years in their foreign trade. The switch to metrics should increase export sales of small U.S. firms that cannot afford to produce two sets of products for different markets.

Labeling

Label
Descriptive part of a product's package, listing brand name or symbol, name and address of the manufacturer or distributor, ingredients, size or quantity of the product, and/or recommended uses, directions, or serving suggestions.

Although in the past the label was often a separate item applied to the package, most of today's plastic packages contain it as an integral part of the package. Labels perform both promotional and informational functions. A label in most instances contains the brand name or symbol, the name and address of the manufacturer or distributor, the product composition and size, and recommended uses for the product.

Consumer confusion and dissatisfaction over such incomprehensible sizes as giant economy size, king size, and family size led to passage of the Fair Packaging and Labeling Act (1966). The act requires a label to offer adequate information concerning the package contents and a package design that facilitates value comparisons among competitive products.

Food and Drug Administration regulations require that the nutritional contents be listed on the label of any food product to which a nutrient has been added or for which a nutritional claim has been made. Figure 9.6 shows a label listing the nutritional ingredients.

Voluntary packaging and labeling standards have also been developed in a number of industries. As a result, the number of toothpaste sizes was reduced from 57 to 5 and the number of dry detergent sizes from 24 to 6. In other industries, such as drug, food, fur, and clothing, federal legislation has been enacted to force companies to provide information and to prevent branding that misleads the consumer. Marketing managers in such industries must be fully acquainted with these laws and must design packages and labels that are in compliance.

Figure 9.6
Product Label with the Zebra-Stripe Universal Product Code

Universal Product Code (UPC)   The Universal Product Code (UPC) designation is another very important part of a label or package. Figure 9.6 shows the zebra-stripe UPC on the Green Giant Chopped Spinach label. In other cases, the code lines are printed right into the package, such as on a can of Tab.

The Universal Product Code, introduced in 1974 as an attempt to cut expenses in the supermarket industry, are codes read by optical scanners that print the item and its price on the cash register receipt. Some 95 percent of all packaged grocery items contain the UPC lines.

While the cost of UPC scanners is high—about $125,000 for a four-lane supermarket—they do permit considerable cost savings. The advantages include:

Universal Product Code
Special codes on packages read by optical scanners.

1. Labor savings, because products are no longer individually priced;

2. Faster customer check-out times;

3. Better inventory control since the scanners can be tied to inventory records;

4. Fewer errors in entering purchases at the check-out counter.

The Universal Product Code is a major asset to marketing research in the industries involved with it. But despite its advantages, UPC still faces several obstacles. Many consumers still do not understand the purpose and advantages of the UPC scanners. In some localities, regulations specifically require individually priced items, thus negating the labor-savings advantage of UPC scanners. Overall, it is obvious that the Universal Product Code is going to play an even greater role in product management in the coming decade.[42]

Product Safety _____

If the product is to fulfill its mission of satisfying consumer needs, it must, above all, be safe. Manufacturers must design their products to protect the consumers who use them. Packaging plays an important role in product safety. Aspirin bottle tops have been made child-proof (and virtually parent-proof) by St. Joseph's and Bayer since 1968. This safety feature is estimated to have reduced by two-thirds the number of children under five years of age who have swallowed accidental doses of aspirin.

Prominently placed safety warnings on the labels of such potentially hazardous products as cleaning fluids and drain cleaners inform users of the dangers of these products and urge them to store the products out of the reach of children. Changes in product design have reduced the dangers involved in the use of such products as lawn mowers, hedge trimmers, and toys.

The Consumer Product Safety Commission

Federal and state legislation have long played a major role in promoting product safety. Many of the piecemeal federal laws passed over a period of 50 years were unified by the Consumer Product Safety Act (1972), which created a powerful regulatory agency—the Consumer Product Safety Commission (CPSC). The new agency has assumed jurisdiction over every consumer product except food, automobiles, and a few other products already regulated by other agencies.

The CPSC has the authority to ban products without a court hearing, order the recall or redesign of products, and inspect production facilities. It can charge managers of accused companies with criminal offenses. It has a national, toll-free "hotline" (800-638-CPSC) that receives about 120,000 inquiries each year. Research on consumer accidents resulted in the list of common dangers shown in Table 9.2.

The Concept of Product Liability

Product Liability
Concept that manufacturers and marketers are responsible for injuries and damages caused by their products.

Product liability refers to the concept that manufacturers and marketers are responsible for injuries and damages caused by their products. There has been a tremendous increase in product liability suits in recent years. Although many of these claims are settled out of court, others are decided by juries who have sometimes awarded multimillion-dollar settlements.

Not only have marketers stepped up efforts to ensure product safety, but product liability insurance has become an essential ingredient in any new or existing product strategy. Premiums for this insurance have risen at an alarming rate, and, in some cases, coverage is almost impossible to obtain. A Detroit producer of components for pleasure boats discovered that its liability insurance premiums had increased from $2,500 to $160,000 in a two-year period even though the insurance company had never paid a claim on the firm's behalf.

Efforts are underway in several states to exempt companies from liability for injuries or property loss resulting from misuse of the products or from customer negligence. Such an exemption would have protected the retailer who paid damages to two men hurt by a lawn mower they lifted off the ground to trim a hedge.

CPSC activities and the increased number of liability claims have prompted companies to improve their safety standards voluntarily. For many companies, safety has become a vital ingredient of the broad definition of product.

Table 9.2
Some of the Most Dangerous Consumer Products

Rank	Item	National Estimates of Injuries Requiring Emergency Room Treatment
1.	Stairs or Steps	789,032
2.	Bicycles or Accessories	571,196
3.	Floors or Flooring Materials	489,077
4.	Baseballs	477,790
5.	Basketballs	461,678
6.	Footballs	424,884
7.	Knives	364,741
8.	Chairs, Sofas, Sofabeds, Stools	292,229
9.	Tables	254,823
10.	Doors	244,840
11.	Nails, Screws, Carpet Tacks, and Thumbtacks	229,566
12.	Ceilings and Walls	187,829
13.	Playground Equipment	180,827
14.	Glass Doors, Windows, and Panels	154,627
15.	Drinking Glasses	134,579
16.	Skating	131,829
17.	House Structures, Repair or Construction	123,886
18.	Glass Bottles or Jars	121,349
19.	Fences or Fence Posts	107,758
20.	Bathtubs, Showers, and Enclosures	102,686

Source: U.S. Consumer Product Safety Commission, "Product Summary Report and NEISS Estimates of National Injury Incidents: 1983."

Summary

A product mix is the assortment of product lines and individual offerings available from a marketer. The two primary components are product line, a series of related products, and individual offerings, or single products. Product mixes are assessed in terms of width and depth of assortment. Width of assortment refers to the variety of product lines offered, while depth refers to the number of individual offerings. Firms usually produce several related products rather than a single product to achieve the objectives of growth, optimal use of company resources, and increased company importance in the market.

Many new product ideas are required to produce one commercially successful product. The success of a new product depends on a host of factors and can result from four alternative product development strategies: product improvement, market development, product development, and product diversification.

New product organizational responsibility in most large firms is assigned to new product committees, new product departments, product managers, or venture teams. New product ideas evolve through six stages before their market introduction: (1) idea generation, (2) screening, (3) business analysis, (4) development, (5) testing, and (6) commercialization.

While new products are added to the line, old products may be dropped. The typical causes for product eliminations are unprofitable sales and failure to fit into the existing product line.

Product identification may take the form of brand names, symbols, distinctive packaging, labeling, and the Universal Product Code. Effective brand names should be easy to pronounce, recognize, and remember; they should give the right connotation to the buyer; and they should be legally protectable. Brand loyalty can be measured in three stages: brand recognition, brand preference, and brand insistence. Marketing managers must decide whether to use a single family brand for their product line or an individual brand for each product. Retailers have to decide the relative mix of manufacturers' and private brands as well as generic products that they will carry.

Modern packaging is designed to (1) protect against damage, spoilage, and pilferage; (2) assist in marketing the product; and (3) be cost effective. The metric revolution is also having a significant impact on U.S. packaging. Labels identify the product, producer, content, size, and uses of a packaged product. Most products also contain a Universal Product Code designation so that optical check-out scanners can be used.

Product safety has become an increasingly important component of the total product concept. This emphasis on making products safe for the consumer has occurred through voluntary attempts by product designers to reduce hazards, through various pieces of legislation, and through the establishment of the Consumer Product Safety Commission. The concept of product liability, or the legal responsibility of a producer or marketer for injuries or damages caused by a defective product, is also becoming increasingly important.

Predetermining Product Success

Both G.D. Searle and Pillsbury saw no other choice but to test market their products before introducing them on a national level. To gain as much information as possible from this market research at the lowest possible cost, both companies turned to BehaviorScan®, a system developed by Information Resources, Inc.

BehaviorScan® monitors the buying habits of select groups of "average" Americans to determine what they buy at what price and how advertising influences their purchases. What sets BehaviorScan® apart from other test-marketing systems is its reliance on such high-technology items as supermarket scanners, cable television hookups, and computers.

The BehaviorScan® system works in the following way. Approximately 2,500 residents are chosen in one or more of the company's eight test cities, which include Marion, Indiana; Pittsfield, Massachusetts; Midland, Texas; Eau Claire, Wisconsin; Visalia, California; Rome, Georgia; Grand Junction, Colorado; and Williamsport, Pennsylvania. These test-marketing participants are given

Photo Source: Courtesy of Information Resources Inc.

Sources: "To Test or Not to Test Seldom the Question," *Advertising Age* (February 20, 1984), p. M-10; and Fern Schumer, "The New Magicians of Marketing Research," *FORTUNE* (July 25, 1983), pp. 72–73.

special I.D. cards that they present to store cashiers when they check out their purchases. Every purchase they make is recorded and analyzed right at the check-out counter by Universal Product Code scanners—devices that emit laser beams that read the set of bars printed on most packaged goods. BehaviorScan® equips each of the 10 to 15 supermarkets and drugstores in the community with these scanners, at a cost of up to $2 million, as a way of ensuring that every purchase will be tracked.

"It's an expensive route for us to go," said Gian Fulgoni, president of the BehaviorScan® parent company, Information Resources, Inc. "But people aren't loyal to just one store and we have to capture all their purchases." The scanners feed information about product purchases into the BehaviorScan® central computer in Chicago.

Many products are advertised on cable television. Cable gives marketers the flexibility to advertise a new product to a small, select segment of the population and then to track the public's reaction to the ad and product. "The system allows the manufacturer to measure the purchases of products under different marketing plans," said Fulgoni. "It's important because a company can increase the chances of having a successful product once the right marketing plan is known. It's more than a new product being tested," Fulgoni continued. "It's the advertising, the promotion, and the price that we can measure as well."

One of the most valuable functions of BehaviorScan® is to tell advertisers which television programs their buyers tune to, thus enabling them to aim their messages at specific target audiences. For example, when BehaviorScan® marketers monitored evening TV viewing in test cities on February 11, 1983, they found that 46 percent of Heinz Ketchup buyers watched the fifth installment of the TV movie "Winds of War," while only 18 per-

cent tuned into the "Dukes of Hazzard" and 15 percent to the "Powers of Matthew Star." "Imagine the millions of dollars to be saved through the efficiency of advertising to the right audience," said Information Resources president Fulgoni.

When G.D. Searle was ready to introduce Equal, it test marketed the product at BehaviorScan® sites in Pittsfield, Massachusetts, and Marion, Indiana. Results of the testing gave Searle the marketing information it needed to determine how the marketing mix elements fit together, to determine the price/volume relationship (two prices were tested), and to determine the most effective media weight level (two media weight levels were tested).

From the testing, Searle learned that the elements of the marketing mix for Equal worked together effectively, that the lower of the two tested prices produced a more profitable volume, and that the higher media plan of the two plans tested was less effective. Test results also enabled Searle marketers to gauge the size of the potential market for Equal at over $50 million in annual sales.

After an 18-month trial of its Pipin Hot Loaf, Pillsbury also made some important marketing decisions. For example, test market results convinced Pillsbury not to offer a rye version of its new product prior to the national launch.

Information Resources chairman of the board John Malec believes that these test-marketing research advances mark the beginning of a new revolution. "Some day," he mused, "we could identify the different demographic segments and when the commercial breaks come on, we send the high-income group a high-income type of ad and the low-income group a low-income type of ad. It would be a direct mail approach for broadcast and perhaps the most valuable marketing tool ever devised."

Questions for Discussion

1. What is meant by a product mix? How is the concept used in making effective marketing decisions?

2. Outline the product mix of a firm that operates in your geographic area. What can you learn from this analysis? Discuss.

3. Why do most business firms market a line of related products rather than a single product?

4. Explain the product idea mortality curve.

5. Outline the alternative organizational structures for new product development.

6. Why has the product manager concept become so popular among multiproduct firms?

7. Identify the steps in the new-product development process.

8. A firm's new-product idea suggestion program has produced a design for a portable car washer that can be attached to a garden hose. Outline a program for deciding whether the product should be marketed by the firm.

9. What is the chief purpose of test marketing? What potential problems are involved in it?

10. General Foods gave up on Lean Strips, a textured vegetable protein strip designed as a bacon substitute, after eight years of test marketing. Lean Strips sold well when bacon prices were high but poorly when they were low. General Foods hoped to offer a protein analog product line that also included Crispy Strips, a snack and salad dressing item. Consumers liked the taste of Crispy Strips, but it was too expensive for repeat purchases, and the product was abandoned before Lean Strips' demise. General Foods decided to concentrate on new product categories instead of individual items like Lean Strips. What can be learned from General Foods' experience with Lean Strips?

11. List the characteristics of an effective brand name. Illustrate each characteristic with an appropriate brand name.

12. Give an example of each of the following:
    a. Brand   e. Individual brand
    b. Brand name   f. National brand
    c. Trademark   g. Private brand
    d. Family brand

13. What are the chief advantages of using family brands? Under what circumstances should individual brands be used?

14. The Lanham Act grants exclusive usage of specified trademarks to their owners. Such marks assist consumers by allowing them to distinguish between a preferred product and those of competitors. Yet many trademarks are quite similar in sound, color, or appearance. In instances of possible trademark infringement, a legal decision must be made. The following examples are actual trademark cases in which decisions have been reached. In which of these instances would you have ruled that trademark infringement has occurred? Defend your ruling.

    a. *Jockey* men's underwear and hosiery vs. *Jockey* shoe polish
    b. *Mustang* automobiles vs. *Mustang* mobile homes
    c. *All* detergent vs. *All Out* rust remover
    d. Miller *Lite* beer vs. Budweiser *Light*
    e. *Space Saver* clothes drying racks vs. *Space Server* belt and tie hangers
    f. *Pepsi* soft drinks vs. *Pepsup* barbecue sauce
    g. *Triox* insecticides vs. *Tri-X* fertilizer
    h. *Dial* soap vs. *Di-All* insecticide (with clock dial on label)
    i   *English Leather* toiletries vs. *London Leather* toiletries
    j. *Pepsodent* dentrifice vs. *Pearlident* dentifrice*

15. Identify and briefly explain each of the three stages of brand loyalty.

16. Why do so few brands reach the brand insistence stage? Discuss.

17. Campbell Soup Company's Belgian candy company, Godiva Chocolates, introduced a designer line called "Bill Blass Chocolates." The premium chocolates sold for $14 per pound. Relate this action to the material discussed in Chapter 9.

18. Exxene, a $1 million manufacturer of antifog coatings for goggles, was sued for trademark infringement by Exxon Corp. The oil company giant claimed that it had nearly exclusive rights to the letters *EXX* regardless of what followed it.

*Source: Adapted from Richard H. Buskirk, *Principles of Marketing* (Hinsdale, Ill.: The Dryden Press, 1975), pp. 268–271. Used by permission of the author.

Four-and-a-half years later, a jury awarded Exxene $250,000 in damages instead. Exxon filed an appeal. Relate this case to the textbook discussion of trademarks.

19. Identify the product development strategy being employed in each of the following examples. Defend your answers.

   a. AT&T's decision to enter a new market by developing a new line of personal computers

   b. Procter & Gamble's development of a new pump dispenser package as an alternative to the familiar Crest tube package of toothpaste.

   c. Columbia Record Club offer of membership in its new Columbia Video Club to its current members

   d. Marketing of Johnson & Johnson baby oil as a suntan lotion.

20. Explain the chief functions of the Consumer Product Safety Commission. What steps can it take to protect consumers from defective and hazardous products?

Case: Beatrice Companies, Inc.

Beatrice Companies, Inc. started as a creamery in Beatrice, Nebraska, in 1894. The founder was an unemployed butter and egg seller. Today, Beatrice is the largest food and consumer products firm in the United States. Its 9,000 products produce an annual sales volume of $13.5 billion.

Beatrice is huge, but, until recently, it was relatively unknown. The firm acquired 400 companies over the years; each is run separately, often by its previous owner. Beatrice's $2.8 billion acquisition of Esmark in 1984 was its biggest purchase. Beatrice brands include Meadow Gold ice cream, Tropicana citrus juice, Avis, La Choy, International Playtex, Wesson Oil, Peter Pan Peanut Butter, and Butterball Turkey.

Television viewers of the 1984 Summer Olympics were introduced to a changed strategy at Beatrice. The firm's commercials showed its various brands along with the line "Beatrice, you've known us all along." A similar advertising campaign was run in national magazines. Beatrice's objective was to build corporate name familiarity so that it could be used for future product offerings.

Source: James Litke, "Beatrice: Building an Identity," *The Seattle Times/The Seattle Post Intelligencer* (August 26, 1984), p. C-4 (AP story); Milton Maskowitz, "After Operating in Obscurity, Beatrice Wants to Be Known," *Journal–American* (August 26, 1984), p. F-1 (syndicated column).

Questions

1. If you were part of Beatrice's top management, would you have advocated adoption of this advertising campaign? Why or why not?

2. Relate Beatrice's new strategy to the discussion of brands that appears in this chapter.

3. Identify other firms that face situations similar to that of Beatrice Companies, Inc. Should they adopt a similar product strategy? Why or why not?

Computer Applications

In Chapter 6, three approaches to making choices from available alternatives were described. The first approach, the *overall scoring method,* involves scoring or ranking each of the evaluative criteria (or decision factors) used in choosing among available alternatives. The alternative with the highest total score is selected. The second approach, the *weighted scoring method,* involves assigning different weights to the various decision factors in accordance with the decision maker's perception of their relative importance. The weighted scores are then totaled and the alternative with the highest score is selected. The final approach, the *minimum score method,* establishes a minimum score for one or more of the decision factors. Any alternative with a score below this specified minimum is rejected, regardless of its overall score. The minimum score method can be used in conjunction with either the overall scoring method or the weighted scoring method.

These approaches are described in detail on page 182. While these approaches were used earlier in making consumer purchase decisions, they can also be used to quantify the alternatives in product strategy decisions ranging from the selection of a package design to choosing a brand name.

Directions: Use menu item 6 titled "Evaluation of Alternatives" to solve each of the following problems.

Problem 1 Standard Enterprises, of Flint, Michigan, is considering one of three package designs for its electronic components. The firm identified three major factors to consider in this decision: safety, promotional appeal, and ease of storage. Standard's management has scored each of the package designs on a scale of 1 (poor) to 5 (excellent) for each of the three decision factors. These scores are shown below.

Evoked Set Alternatives	Evaluative Criteria: Decision Factors		
	(A) Safety	(B) Promotional Appeal	(C) Ease of Storage
Package Design #1	4	2	2
Package Design #2	2	5	2
Package Design #3	5	1	4

a. Which package design would the company select using the overall scoring method?

b. Suppose that management considers safety 100 percent more important than any other decision factor. Which package design would be selected?

c. Suppose that management, using the overall scoring method, also decides that it will not accept any package design that scored less than 2 on any factor. Which package design would be selected?

d. Would your response to Question c change if management used the weighted scoring method?

Problem 2 Oklahoma City Industries is trying to pick one of three line extensions to its line of batteries. The alternatives are named Sparky, Big Lite, and Light Forever. Management is evaluating these options on the basis of compatibility with the existing line, production lead time, and potential profitability. The product development group at Oklahoma City Industries has rated each alternative on a system of 3 (excellent), 2 (good), and 1 (fair). These ratings are shown below.

Evoked Set Alternatives	Evaluative Criteria: Decision Factors		
	(A) Compatibility	(B) Lead Time	(C) Profitability
1. Sparky	1	2	3
2. Big Lite	1	3	2
3. Light Forever	2	3	2

a. Which line extension should Oklahoma Industries select using the overall scoring method?

b. Suppose that management considers potential profitability 200 percent more important than any other evaluative factor. Which line extension would be selected?

c. Suppose that management, using the overall scoring method, will not accept any line extension rated less than good on any factor. Which line extension would be selected?

Problem 3 Terry O'Connell, marketing vice-president at an Elmira, New York, toy company, must select a brand name for use on a new toy line targeted at preschool children. The five finalists, coded A, B, C, D, and E to maintain their secrecy, have all been cleared by the firm's legal department. O'Connell's marketing research department has concluded that the marketing impact of the brand names varies among the various parties involved in the toy-buying decision: parents, grandparents, and the children themselves. Each brand name has been evaluated for each group on a five-point scale ranging from excellent (5) to unacceptable (1). The rankings are shown below.

	Evaluative Criteria: Decision Factors		
Evoked Set **Alternatives**	**(A)** **Impact with** **Grandparents**	**(B)** **Impact with** **Parents**	**(C)** **Impact with** **Children**
1. Brand A	4	4	3
2. Brand B	4	2	5
3. Brand C	2	5	2
4. Brand D	3	3	4
5. Brand E	5	5	2

a. Which brand name would be selected using the overall scoring method?

b. Suppose that O'Connell considers the brand name's marketing impact with children to be 200 percent more important than its impact on parents and grandparents. Which brand name should he select?

c. Suppose that O'Connell, using the overall scoring method, decides that he will not accept a brand name rated less than 3 by any of the parties who might be involved in a purchase decision. Which brand name should he select?

d. Would O'Connell's decision in Question c change if he used the weighted scoring method?

Problem 4 Miguel Fernandez, marketing director of a Bakersfield, California, garden tool manufacturer, is in the process of choosing one of five new retail display racks. Fernandez is considering four major factors: promotional appeal, maximum display inventory, cost, and convenient size. He has scored each of the display designs on a scale ranging from 1 (poor) to 5 (excellent) for each of the decision factors. Fernandez's ratings are shown below.

	Evaluative Criteria: Decision Factors			
Evoked Set **Alternatives**	**(A)** **Promotional** **Appeal**	**(B)** **Maximum** **Inventory**	**(C)** **Cost**	**(D)** **Convenient** **Size**
Display Rack #1	5	3	3	4
Display Rack #2	4	4	1	5
Display Rack #3	3	5	5	2
Display Rack #4	3	3	5	3
Display Rack #5	5	5	1	5

a. Which display will Fernandez select if he uses the overall scoring method?

b. Suppose that Fernandez considers convenient size to be the least important of the four decision factors. Promotional appeal and maximum inventory are considered to be 100 percent more important than convenient size, and cost is considered 400 percent more important than convenient size. Which display rack should Fernandez select if he applies these weights to the various decision factors?

c. Suppose that Fernandez, using the overall scoring method, also decides that he will not accept any display rack with less than a 3 rating on any decision factor. Which display should he select?

d. Would your response to Question c change if Fernandez decides to use the weighted scoring method in making his decision?

Problem 5 Maureen D'Angelo, director of marketing at Bennett Industries, of Scranton, Pennsylvania, wants to add a line extension to her firm's offering of toothbrushes. Various toothbrush configurations are under consideration. These alternatives are labeled Option 1, Option 2, Option 3, Option 4, and Option 5. Five factors will be used to evaluate each of the five options: profitability, produc-tion lead time, compatibility with the existing product line, adaptability to the standard Bennett Industries' in-store display, and the retailer's margin. D'Angelo has rated each of the possible line extensions by each variable. Her scoring system ranges from 1 (poor) to 5 (excellent). The specific scores are shown below.

Evoked Set	Evaluative Criteria: Decision Factors				
Alternatives	(A) Profitability	(B) Production Lead Time	(C) Compatibility	(D) Adaptability	(E) Retail Margin
Option #1	2	4	3	2	2
Option #2	5	5	5	2	3
Option #3	3	3	3	3	3
Option #4	3	3	4	3	3
Option #5	5	2	2	5	5

a.   Which line extension option should D'Angelo select using the overall scoring method?

b.   Suppose that D'Angelo decides to assign a weight of 400 percent more to the retail margin than to pro-duction lead time due to the importance of accep-tance of the new toothbrush line by retailers. In ad-dition, she decides to weight adaptability 300 percent more important than production lead time, to weight profitability 200 percent more important than production lead time, and to weight compati-bility with the existing product line 100 percent more important than production lead time. Which line ex-tension option should she select?

c.   Suppose that D'Angelo, using the overall scoring method, decides to reject any option rated less than 3 on any factor. Which line extension option would she select?

d.   Would your response to Question c change if D'An-gelo decided to use the weighted scoring method in making her selection from among the available al-ternatives?

PART FIVE

Distribution Strategy

10 Introduction to Channel Strategy

Key Terms

distribution channels
marketing intermediary
wholesaling
retailers
reverse channel
channel captain
intensive distribution
selective distribution
exclusive distribution
exclusive dealing agreement
closed sales territories
tying agreement
vertical marketing systems
   (VMS)
franchise

Learning Goals

1. To explain the role of distribution channels in marketing strategy
2. To describe the various types of distribution channels
3. To explain the concept of channel leadership
4. To outline the major channel strategy decisions
5. To identify and discuss the various types of vertical marketing systems
6. To discuss conflict and cooperation in the distribution channel

Porsche

The American love affair with the automobile is perhaps best epitomized in the Porsche, as evidenced by new-Porsche sales which doubled between 1980 and 1983. To the 22,000 Americans who spend between $25,000 and $50,000 for a new Porsche each year, the 911, 928, and 944 represent the ultimate in styling, performance, and image. This sales success was achieved by Volkswagen of America, which imported, marketed, and serviced Porsches with a 330-dealer network that also handled Audis—and occasionally Volkswagens.

But Porsche president Peter Schutz expressed concerns about the U.S. distribution arrangement for his firm's cars. He was disturbed by reports of inventory shortages at many dealerships. To avoid losing a sale, these dealers were forced to purchase cars, at a premium, from other Porsche dealers and then pass along these additional costs to their customers. Schutz also felt that dealers carrying both Volkswagens and Porsches presented a confused image to the car-buying public. High inventory costs, difficulty in obtaining Porsches matching precise customer specifications, occasional service complaints, and inconsistent resale values were other problems. Schutz also felt that it was simply a matter of time before one of the Japanese auto companies began marketing a high-performance sports car in the United States, and he wanted to be certain that the strongest possible distribution system was in place for Porsche before the anticipated Japanese competition materialized.

Porsche executive John A. Cooke summed up Schutz's concern: "It's essential that we establish the right solutions—not just do the traditional thing—if we are to serve our customers at a level they expect, commensurate with the product."

Assignment: Use the materials in Chapter 10 to recommend a course of action for Porsche.

Source: Cook quotation from Matt DeLorenzo, "Porsche Casts a Pall on Franchise System," *Automotive News* (February 20, 1984), p. 57.

Chapter Overview

Part Four considered the first marketing mix variable: product development and strategy. Part Five discusses the activities, decisions, and marketing intermediaries involved in moving products and services to consumers and industrial users. Basic channel strategy is the beginning focus for a discussion of the distribution function and its role in the marketing mix.

Chapter 10 analyzes such basic issues as the role and types of distribution channels, channel strategy decisions, and conflict and cooperation in the channel of distribution. Chapters 11 and 12 deal with wholesaling and retailing—the marketing institutions in the distribution channel. Although not considered part of the distribution channel, physical distribution is a vital facilitating agency that assists regular channel members. It is discussed separately in Chapter 13. The starting point of Part Five is an examination of what marketers call distribution channels.

Americans, who drink enough coffee to equal an annual per-capita consumption of 12 pounds of coffee beans (representing 20 percent of all coffee grown in the world), look primarily to the Latin American countries for their supplies. Boeing aircraft, which is assembled in Washington State, is marketed to numerous overseas and domestic airlines. The Honda Accord bought by someone in Dallas was probably made in Columbus, Ohio. In each case, methods must be devised to bridge the gap between producer and consumer.

Distribution channels are used to provide consumers with a convenient means of obtaining the products and services they desire. Distribution channels refer to the various marketing institutions and the interrelationships responsible for the physical and title flow of goods and services from producer to consumer or industrial user. Marketing intermediaries, or middlemen, are the marketing institutions in the distribution channel. A marketing intermediary is a business firm operating between the producer and the consumer or industrial purchaser. The term therefore includes both wholesalers and retailers.

Wholesaling is the activities of persons or firms who sell to retailers, other wholesalers, and industrial users but do not sell in significant amounts to ultimate consumers. The terms *jobber* and *distributor* are considered synonymous with wholesaler in this book.

Confusion can result from the practices of some firms that operate both wholesaling and retailing operations. Sporting goods stores, for example, often maintain a wholesaling operation in marketing a line of goods to high schools and colleges as well as operating retail stores. For the purposes of this text, it is simpler to conceive of these operations as separate entities.

A second source of confusion is the misleading practice of some retailers who claim to be wholesalers. Such stores may actually sell at wholesale prices and can validly claim to do so. However, stores that sell products purchased by individuals for their own use and not for resale are by definition retailers, not wholesalers.

Distribution Channels
Marketing institutions and their interrelationships responsible for the physical and title flow of goods and services from producer to consumer or industrial user.

Marketing Intermediary
Business firm, either wholesale or retail, that operates between the producer of goods and the consumer or industrial user; sometimes called a middleman.

Wholesaling
Activities of those who sell to retailers, other wholesalers, and industrial users, but not in significant amounts to ultimate consumers.

Retailers
Firms that sell products or services to the ultimate consumer and not for resale.

The Role of Distribution Channels in Marketing Strategy

Distribution channels play a key role in marketing strategy because they provide the means by which goods and services are conveyed from producers to consumers and users. Marketing intermediaries exist at both the wholesale and retail levels. As specialists in the performance of marketing functions—rather than producing or manufacturing functions—they perform these activities more efficiently than producers or consumers. The importance of distribution channels and marketing intermediaries can be explained in terms of the utility they create and the functions they perform.

The Creation of Utility

Distribution channels create three types of utility for consumers. *Time utility* is created when distribution channels make products and services available for sale when the consumer wants to purchase them. *Place utility* is created when goods and services are available at a convenient location. *Ownership* (or *possession*) *utility* is created when title to the goods passes from the producer or intermediary to the purchaser. Possession utility can also result from transactions in which the title does not pass to the purchaser, such as in the case of a rental car.

Swimwear, as illustrated in Figure 10.1, provides a good example of how the distribution channel creates time utility. Designing the 1986 Jantzen swimwear line began in January 1985 with preliminary designs, interviews with fab-

Figure 10.1
Distribution Channels Provide Time Utility for Jantzen Swimwear

ric suppliers concerning fabric and color innovations, and informal sessions where Jantzen marketers and designers thrashed out ideas prior to developing the final prototypes. This process continued until May 1985 when the specific prototype garments were selected for the 1986 line.

From May until late August, fabrics were ordered and small quantities of the swimsuits were produced as samples for Jantzen sales representatives. Because of the long lead time involved in receiving fabric, orders for fabric to be used in producing the 1986 line were also placed during this period. Full-scale production on some basic 1986 styles began in July.

A sales convention featuring the 1986 swimwear line was held in late August, and the sales representatives began seeking retail orders in mid-September. Delivery dates on swimwear vary from late November until late May. Early deliveries are made to retail outlets in Florida, Hawaii, and other warm-weather, winter vacation locations. The bulk of all swimwear deliveries occurs during January, February, and March. Late deliveries typically take place in northern cities, and the selling season declines sharply after the Fourth of July.

The provision of place utility is illustrated by flight insurance vending machines in airport terminals or a stock of *TV Guides* near a supermarket checkout counter. Similarly, the offices of a real estate broker, escrow company, or lending institution are often used to create ownership utility. Legal title and possession of a new home is often transferred to a buyer in these settings.

Types of Distribution Channels

Literally hundreds of marketing channels exist today, and it is obvious that there is no such thing as one best distribution channel. The best channel for Mary Kay Cosmetics is direct from manufacturer to consumer through a sales force of 200,000 beauty consultants. The best channel for frozen french fries may be from food processor to agent marketing intermediary to merchant wholesaler to supermarket to consumer. Instead of searching for the best channel for all products, the marketing manager must analyze alternative channels in light of consumer needs to determine the most appropriate channel (or channels) for the firm's products and services.[1]

Even when the proper channels have been chosen and established, the marketing manager's channel decisions have not ceased. Channels, like so many marketing variables, change, and today's ideal channel may prove disastrous in a few years.

Until the 1960s, the typical channel for beer was from brewery to local distributor (wholesaler) to local pubs, where most beer was consumed. Today, two-thirds of beer purchases are made "off premises" in supermarkets, convenience stores, and the like. So the channels for modern brewers must reflect these changes in consumer buying patterns.

Alternative Distribution Channels

Figure 10.2 depicts the major channels available for marketers of consumer and industrial products and services. In general, industrial products channels tend to be shorter than consumer goods channels due to geographic concentrations of industrial buyers and a relatively limited number of purchasers. In addition, retail sales are characteristic only of consumer goods purchases; therefore, the retailer is not found in industrial channels. Service channels also

Figure 10.2

Channel Alternatives in the Marketing of Consumer and
Industrial Products and Services

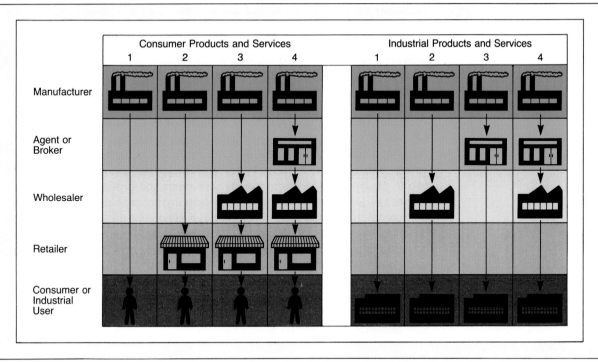

tend to be short. This is due to the intangibility of services and the need to maintain personal relationships in the channel.

Producer to Consumer or Industrial User   The simplest, most direct distribution channel is not necessarily the most popular, as evidenced by the relatively small percentage of dollar volume of sales that moves along this route. Less than 5 percent of all consumer goods move from producer to consumer. For a company like Avon, the direct producer to consumer channel is very effective. Mail-order houses are other examples of firms whose products move directly from manufacturer to consumer.

Direct channels are much more important to the industrial goods market. Most major installations, accessory equipment, and even component parts and raw materials are marketed through direct contacts between seller and buyer.

Producer to Wholesaler to Retailer to Consumer   The traditional channel for consumer goods proceeds from producer to wholesaler to retailer to user. It is the method used by small retailers and by literally thousands of small producers that make limited lines of products. Small companies with limited financial resources utilize wholesalers as immediate sources of funds and as a means to reach the hundreds of retailers who will stock their products. Small retailers rely on wholesalers as buying specialists who ensure a balanced inventory of goods produced in various regions of the world.

The wholesaler's sales force is responsible for reaching the market with the producer's output. Many manufacturers also use specialized sales representatives, called missionary salespersons, to contact their retailer accounts.

These representatives serve as sources of marketing information, but they do not actually sell the product.

Producer to Wholesaler to Industrial User   Similar characteristics in the industrial market often lead to the utilization of marketing intermediaries between the producer and industrial purchaser. The term *industrial distributor* is commonly utilized in the industrial market to refer to those wholesalers who take title to the goods they handle. Office equipment is a good example of this channel.

Producer to Agent to Wholesaler to Retailer to Consumer   Where products are produced by a large number of small companies, a unique intermediary—the agent—performs the basic function of bringing buyer and seller together. The agent is, in fact, a wholesaling intermediary who does not take title to the goods. The agent merely represents the producer or the regular wholesaler (who does take title to the goods) in seeking a market for the manufacturer's output or in locating a source of supply for the buyer. Chapter 11 describes two types of wholesaling intermediaries—merchant wholesalers, who take title to the goods they handle, and agent wholesaling intermediaries, who do not take title to the goods.

Agents are used in such industries as canning and frozen food packing. In these industries, many producers supply a large number of geographically scattered wholesalers. The agent wholesaling intermediary performs the service of bringing buyers and sellers together.

Producer to Agent to Wholesaler to Industrial User   Similar conditions often exist in the industrial market, where small producers attempt to market their offerings to large wholesalers. The agent wholesaling intermediary, often called a *manufacturers' representative*, serves as an independent sales force in contacting the wholesaler buyers.

Producer to Agent to Industrial User   Where the unit sale is small, merchant wholesalers must be used to cover the market economically. By maintaining regional inventories, they achieve transportation economies by stockpiling goods and making the final small shipment over a short distance. Where the unit sale is large and transportation accounts for a small percentage of the total product cost, the producer to agent to industrial user channel is usually employed. The agent wholesaling intermediaries become, in effect, the company's industrial sales force.

Service Provider to Consumer or Industrial User   Distribution of services to both consumers and industrial users is usually simpler and more direct than for industrial and consumer goods. In part, this is due to the intangibility of services. The marketer of services is often less concerned with storage, transportation, and inventory control; shorter channels are typically used.

Another consideration is the need for continuing personal relationships between performers and users of many services. Consumers will remain clients of the same insurance agent, bank, or travel agent as long as they are reasonably satisfied. Likewise, public accounting firms and attorneys are retained on a relatively permanent basis by industrial buyers.

Service Provider to Agent to Consumer or Industrial User   When marketing intermediaries are used by service firms, they are usually agents or brokers. Common examples include insurance agents, securities brokers, travel agents, and entertainment agents. For instance, travel and hotel packages are sometimes created by intermediaries and then marketed at the retail level by travel agents to both vacationers and firms wanting to offer employee incentive awards.

A Special Note on Channel Strategy for Consumer Services   A dominant patronage motive for many consumer services, such as banks, motels, and auto rental agencies, is convenient location. It is absolutely essential that careful consideration be given to retail site selection. Banks in particular have been sensitive to locating branches in suburban shopping centers and malls to meet the needs of customers in those areas. The wide acceptance of retail banking has led to the installation of automated electronic tellers that enable customers to withdraw funds and to make deposits when a bank's offices are closed.

Multiple Distribution Channels

The use of more than one channel for similar products is increasingly commonplace. In some instances, multiple channels (or dual distribution) are utilized when the same product is marketed both to the ultimate consumer and to industrial users. Dial soap, for example, is distributed to grocery wholesalers, who deliver it to food stores, which market it to consumers. But a second distribution channel also exists: large retail chains and motels purchase the soap directly from the manufacturer.

In other cases, the same product is marketed through a variety of types of retail outlets. A basic product such as a paint brush is carried in inventory by the traditional hardware store; it is also handled by such nontraditional retail outlets as auto accessory stores, building-supply outlets, department stores, discount houses, mail-order houses, supermarkets, and variety stores. Each retail store may utilize different distribution channels.

Figure 10.3 illustrates one of the numerous channels used in marketing Firestone automobile tires. They are distributed to General Motors and Ford, where they serve as component parts for new cars; to Firestone-owned retail outlets; to tire wholesalers, who sell them to retail gas stations; and to franchised Firestone outlets. Each channel enables the manufacturer to serve a different market.

Reverse Channels

Reverse Channel
Path goods follow from consumer to manufacturer, in an effort to recycle used products or by-products.

While the traditional concept of marketing channels involves the movement of products and services from producer to consumer or industrial user, there is continued interest in reverse channels. Reverse channels refer to the backward movement of goods from the user level to the producer, or recycling, level.

Reverse channels will increase in importance as raw materials become more expensive and as additional laws are passed to control litter and the disposal of packaging materials such as soft-drink and beer bottles. The reverse channel concept is illustrated in Figure 10.4, where consumers are paid for returning empty cans and bottles to a redemption center. Reverse channels are also dependent upon adequate technology for both recycling and recovery.

In some instances, the reverse channel consists of traditional marketing intermediaries. In the soft-drink industry, retailers and local bottlers perform these functions. In other cases, manufacturers take the initiative by establish-

Figure 10.3
The Firestone-Owned Retail Outlet Channel: One of Many Channels for
Firestone Automobile Tires

Source: Courtesy of The Firestone Tire & Rubber Company.

ing redemption centers. For the last three years, the Reynolds Metals Company has recycled more cans than it has sold. Since it began its nationwide consumer recycling business in 1968, Reynolds has recycled more than 2 billion pounds of consumer-generated aluminum—an amount equivalent to nearly 50 billion beverage cans—and paid recyclers more than $500 million. A Reynolds executive summarized the importance of this reverse channel as follows: "Aluminum recycling has become increasingly important to Reynolds because it saves energy and conserves natural resources, while providing us with a vital domestic source of raw materials. . . . Each time aluminum is recycled we save 95 percent of the energy required to produce the metal from ore."[2] Other reverse channel participants may include community groups that organize "clean-up" days and develop systems for recycling paper products and specialized organizations developed for waste disposal and recycling.

Reverse Channels for Product Recalls and Repairs   Reverse channels are also used for product recalls and repairs. Ownership of some products (like tires) is registered so that proper notification can be sent in case of recalls. For example, in the case of automobile recalls, owners are advised to have the problem corrected at their dealership. Similarly, reverse channels have been used for repairs to some products. The warranty for a small appliance might specify that if repairs are needed in the first 90 days, the item should be returned to the dealer. After that period, the product should be returned to the factory. Such reverse channels are a vital element of product recalls and repair procedures.

Figure 10.4

The Can Redeemer by Envipco Pays Consumers Five Cents for
Each Empty Can. Lasers Sort Brands by Their UPC Code

Source: Courtesy of Environmental Products Corporation.

Channel Leadership

Channel Captain
Dominant and controlling member of
a marketing channel.

The dominant and controlling member of the channel is called the channel
captain.[3] Historically, the channel leadership role was performed by the producer or wholesaler, since retailers tend to be both small and localized. However, retailers are increasingly taking on the role of channel captain as large
chains assume traditional wholesaling functions and even dictate product design specifications to the manufacturer.

Producers as Channel Captains   Since producers and service providers
typically create new product and service offerings and enjoy the benefits of
large-scale operations, they fill the role of channel captain in many marketing
channels. Examples of such manufacturers include Armstrong Cork, General
Electric, Magnavox, Sealy Mattress, and Western Auto Stores.

Retailers as Channel Captains   Retailers are often powerful enough to
serve as channel captains in many industries. Larger chain operations may
bypass independent wholesalers and utilize manufacturers as suppliers in producing the retailers' private brands at quality levels specified by the chains.
Major retailers, such as Kmart, Sears, JCPenney, and Montgomery Ward,
serve as leaders in many of the marketing channels with which they are associated.

Wholesalers as Channel Captains   Although the relative influence of wholesalers has declined since 1900, they continue to serve as vital members of
many marketing channels. IGA, Inc. is a good example. With over 3,200

stores in 48 states and with a total sales volume equaling $8.3 billion in 1983, IGA is the largest voluntary food group in the world. These stores are serviced by 62 distribution centers owned by 27 wholesalers.

Channel Strategy Decisions

Marketers face several channel strategy decisions. The selection of a specific distribution channel is the most basic of these decisions, but the level of distribution intensity must also be determined. Channel decision makers must also address the issue of vertical marketing systems.

Selection of a Distribution Channel

What makes a franchised retail dealer network best for the Ford Motor Company? Why do operating supplies often go through both agents and merchant wholesalers before being purchased by the industrial firm? Why do some firms employ multiple channels for the same product? The firm must answer many such questions in choosing distribution channels. The choice is based on an analysis of market, product, producer, and competitive factors. Each factor is important, and the factors are often interrelated. But the overriding consideration is where, when, and how consumers choose to buy the product or service. Consumer orientation is as important to channel decisions as it is in other areas of marketing strategy.

Market Factors   A major determinant of channel structure is whether the product is intended for the consumer or the industrial market. Industrial purchasers usually prefer to deal directly with the manufacturer (except for supplies or small accessory items), but most consumers make their purchases from retail stores. Often products for both industrial users and consumers are sold through more than one channel.

The needs and geographic location of the firm's market affect channel choice. Direct sales are possible where the firm's potential market is concentrated. A small number of potential buyers also increases the feasibility of direct channels. Consumer goods are purchased by households everywhere. Since these households are numerous and geographically dispersed and since they purchase a small volume at a given time, marketing intermediaries must be employed to market products to them.

Jostens has successfully captured 40 percent of the market for high school class rings and yearbooks by using a direct, in-school sales force numbering more than 1,000. These highly educated and motivated sales representatives average $50,000 per year in commissions. Changes in the market have prompted Jostens to place more emphasis on its retail jewelry program in recent years. Through this program, many sales representatives work more closely with local retailers to distribute class rings to complement in-school distribution.

Order size will also affect the channel decision. Producers are likely to use shorter, more direct channels in cases where retail customers or industrial buyers place relatively small numbers of large orders. Retailers often employ buying offices to negotiate directly with manufacturers for large-scale purchases. Wholesalers may be used to contact smaller retailers.

Shifts in consumer buying patterns also influence channel decisions. The desire for credit, the growth of self-service, the increased use of mail-order houses, and the greater willingness to purchase from door-to-door salespeople all affect a firm's marketing channel.

Product Factors Product factors also play a role in determining optimal distribution channels. Perishable products, such as fresh produce and fashion products with short life cycles, typically move through relatively short channels directly to the retailer or the ultimate consumer. For example, Nabisco Brands Inc. distributes its cookies and crackers from the bakery to retail shelves. Chips Ahoy!, Fig Newtons, Oreos, Ritz crackers, and other Nabisco brands are delivered to retail customers, as Figure 10.5 shows, by a fleet of 1,800 company-owned trucks and a 3,000-member sales force. As another example, each year Hines & Smart Corporation ships some 5 million pounds of live lobsters in specially designed styrofoam containers directly to restaurants and hotels throughout North America.

Complex products, such as custom-made installations or computer equipment, are typically sold by the producer to the buyer. As a general rule, the more standardized the product, the longer the channel. Standardized goods usually are marketed by wholesalers. Products that require regular service or specialized repair service usually are not distributed through channels employing independent wholesalers. Automobiles are marketed through a franchised network of retail dealers whose employees receive training on how to properly service the cars.

Another generalization about distribution channels is that the lower the unit value of the product, the longer the channel. Convenience goods and industrial supplies with typically low unit prices are frequently marketed through relatively long channels. Installations and more expensive industrial and consumer goods employ shorter, more direct channels.

Producer Factors Companies with adequate financial, managerial, and marketing resources are less compelled to utilize intermediaries in marketing their products. A financially strong manufacturer can hire its own sales force, warehouse its own products, and grant credit to retailers or consumers. A

Figure 10.5
Nabisco Brands, Inc.'s Fleet of 1,800 Trucks Is an Important
Part of the Firm's Distribution System

Source: Courtesy of Nabisco Brands, Inc.

Table 10.1

Factors Affecting Distribution Channel Selection

	Characteristics of Short Channels	**Characteristics of Long Channels**
Market Factors	Industrial user	Consumers
	Geographically concentrated	Geographically diverse
	Technical knowledge and regular servicing is required	Technical knowledge and regular servicing is not required
	Large orders	Small orders
Product Factors	Perishable	Durable
	Complex	Standardized
	Expensive	Inexpensive
Producer Factors	Manufacturer has adequate resources to perform channel functions	Manufacturer lacks adequate resources to perform channel functions
	Broad product line	Limited product line
	Channel control is important	Channel control is not important
Competitive Factors	Manufacturer feels that independent marketing intermediaries are inadequately promoting products	Manufacturer feels that independent marketing intermediaries are adequately promoting products

weaker firm must rely on marketing intermediaries for these services (although some large retail chains purchase all of the manufacturer's output, thereby bypassing the independent wholesaler). Production-oriented firms may be forced to utilize the marketing expertise of marketing intermediaries to replace the lack of finances and management in their organization.

A firm with a broad product line is usually able to market its products directly to retailers or industrial users since its sales force can offer a variety of products. Larger total sales permit the selling costs to be spread over a number of products and make direct sales feasible. The single-product firm often discovers that direct selling is an unaffordable luxury.

The manufacturer's need for control over the product also influences channel selection. If aggressive promotion is desired at the retail level, the producer chooses the shortest available channel. For new products, the producer may be forced to implement an introductory advertising campaign before independent wholesalers will handle the items.

Competitive Factors   Some firms are forced to develop unique distribution channels because of inadequate promotion of their products by independent marketing intermediaries. Avon's famous shift to house-to-house selling was prompted by intense competition in retail stores with similar lines of cosmetics.

Table 10.1 summarizes the factors affecting the selection of a distribution channel and examines the effect of each factor upon the overall length of the channel.

Determining Distribution Intensity

Adequate market coverage for some products could mean one dealer for 50,000 people. American Home Products defines adequate coverage for Anacin and Dristan headache and cold remedies as almost every supermarket, discount store, drugstore, and variety store, plus many vending machines. The degree of distribution intensity can be viewed as a continuum with three general categories: intensive distribution, selective distribution, and exclusive distribution.

Intensive Distribution
Market coverage strategy in which a manufacturer of a convenience good attempts to saturate the market with the product.

Intensive Distribution   Producers of convenience goods practice intensive distribution when they provide saturation coverage of the market, enabling the purchaser to buy the product with a minimum of effort. Examples of goods distributed in this way include soft drinks, candy, gum, cigarettes, and pens.

For example, Bic pens, lighters, and shavers can be purchased in more than 200,000 retail outlets in the United States. Consumers can find Bic products in food, drug, and mass merchandise/variety outlets and in convenience stores, service stations, and office supply dealers. Bic's distribution channel involves direct sales to such huge chains as Kmart, Walgreen, and Kroger as well as sales to wholesalers with a wide spectrum of retail-store clients. According to Bic spokesperson Leah Colihan, "Because Bic is a manufacturer of mass market, consumable goods, we strive to have distribution in as many retail outlets as possible."[4]

The American Time Company also uses an intensive distribution strategy for its Timex watches. Consumers can buy a Timex in many jewelry stores, the traditional retail outlet for watches. In addition, they can find Timex watches in department stores, discount stores, drugstores, hardware stores, and variety stores.

Mass coverage and low unit prices make the use of wholesalers almost mandatory for such distribution. An important exception to this generalization is Avon Products, which sells directly to the consumer through a nationwide network of neighborhood sales personnel. These representatives purchase directly from the manufacturer and service a limited area of about 100 households with cosmetics, toiletries, jewelry, and toys.

Selective Distribution
Market coverage strategy in which a firm chooses only a limited number of retailers to handle its product line.

Selective Distribution   Selective distribution involves the selection of a small number of retailers in a market area to handle the firm's product line. By limiting the number of retailers, the firm can reduce its total marketing costs while establishing better working relationships within the channel. Cooperative advertising, in which the manufacturer pays a percentage of the retailer's advertising expenditures and the retailer prominently displays the firm's products, can be utilized for mutual benefit, and marginal retailers can be avoided. Where product service is important, the manufacturer usually provides dealer training and assistance. Price cutting is less likely, since fewer dealers are handling the firm's line. For example, Massachusetts-based Epicure Products, Inc. requires its dealers to be technically proficient in marketing and servicing the firm's high-fidelity speakers. Dealers are also required to maintain listening rooms for the convenience of customers.[5]

Exclusive Distribution
Market coverage strategy in which a firm grants exclusive rights to a wholesaler or retailer to sell in a particular geographic area.

Exclusive Distribution   When producers grant exclusive rights to a wholesaler or retailer to sell in a geographic region, they are practicing exclusive distribution—an extreme form of selective distribution. The best example of exclusive distribution is within the automobile industry.[6]

Some market coverage may be sacrificed through a policy of exclusive distribution, but this loss is offset by the development and maintenance of an image of quality and prestige for the products and the reduced marketing costs associated with a small number of accounts. Producers and retailers cooperate closely in decisions concerning advertising and promotion, inventory to be carried by the retailers, and prices.

Return to the Stop-Action Case

Porsche

After serious deliberations concerning the perceived shortcomings of the U.S. Porsche distribution system and the threat of significant new Japanese competition, Porsche president Peter Schutz drafted a proposal for sweeping changes in the current channel. His proposal, if implemented, would sever Porsche's ties with Volkswagen of America and would replace the present dealership network with a three-tiered distribution system:

1.   A central distribution network in Reno, Nevada
2.   Forty company-owned Porsche Centers located throughout the United States
3.   Conversion of the current franchised dealerships into franchised Porsche agencies

The new agency arrangement would mean that the franchised agencies would no longer follow the traditional industry practice of purchasing cars from the auto maker for resale. Instead, the proposed plan called for them to order new cars directly from the nearest Porsche Center as sales were made. The plan also shifted such functions as new-car preparation and delivery from the dealers to the Porsche Centers.

Schutz's proposal produced immediate negative reactions from the franchised Porsche dealers. Some referred to the February 14, 1984, proposal as a "Valentine's Day Massacre" when they learned that the proposed plan would reduce their commissions from the current 16 to 18 percent under the Volkswagen of America arrangement to 8 percent. In addition, they would face new competition from the 40 Porsche Centers, which would market cars directly to the public as well as supplying them to the franchised Porsche agents.

Robert McElwaine, president of the American International Automobile Dealers Association (AIADA), summarized the Porsche dealers' reactions to the proposed changes:

Porsche's proposal would put the dealers in the position of competing with factory-owned stores under circumstances where the dealer would not be able to carry any inventory nor have any clear idea of his market potential. These dealers have made huge investments in their dealerships under the premise that they would be able to buy and sell Porsche autos.

Clearly, Porsche president Schutz's proposed new U.S. distribution network faced intense opposition by its channel members. He would have to decide whether the merits of his proposed plan were sufficient to offset the risk of wrenching apart, perhaps permanently, his American distribution system.

Sources: McElwaine quotation from "Dealer Groups Assail Changes by Porsche," *Automotive News* (February 20, 1984), p. 54; and "Porsche, Volkswagen Sued by Distributor on Shift in U.S. Sales," *The Wall Street Journal* (March 7, 1984), p. 4.

The Legal Problems of Exclusive Distribution   The use of exclusive distribution presents a number of potential legal problems in three areas—exclusive dealing agreements, closed sales territories, and tying agreements. While none of these practices is illegal per se, all may be ruled illegal if they reduce competition or tend to create a monopoly situation.

Exclusive Dealing Agreement
Understanding between a manufacturer and a marketing intermediary that prohibits the intermediary from handling the product lines of the manufacturer's competitors.

Exclusive Dealing Agreements   An exclusive dealing agreement prohibits a marketing intermediary (either a wholesaler or, more typically, a retailer) from handling competing products. Producers of high-priced shopping goods, specialty goods, and accessory equipment often require such agreements as assurance by the marketing intermediary of total concentration on the firm's product line. These contracts are considered violations of the Clayton Act if the producer's or the dealer's sales volume represents a substantial percentage of total sales in the market or sales area. The courts have ruled that sellers who are initially entering the market can use exclusive dealing agreements as a means of strengthening their competitive position. But the same agreements are considered violations of the Clayton Act when used by firms with sizable market shares, since competitors may be barred from the market because of the agreements.

Closed Sales Territories
Restricted geographic selling regions specified by a manufacturer for its distributors.

Closed Sales Territories   Producers with closed sales territories restrict the geographic territories for each of their distributors. Although the distributors may be granted exclusive territories, they are prohibited from opening new facilities or marketing such products outside their assigned territories. The legality of closed sales territories depends on whether the restrictions decrease competition. If competition is lessened, closed sales territories are considered to be in violation of the Federal Trade Commission Act and of provisions of the Sherman Act and the Clayton Act.

The legality of closed sales territories is also determined by whether they are horizontal or vertical. Horizontal territorial restrictions involve agreements by retailers or wholesalers to avoid competition among products from the same producer. Such agreements have consistently been declared illegal. However, the U.S. Supreme Court has ruled that vertical territorial restrictions—those between the producer and the wholesaler or retailer—may be legal. While the ruling was not entirely clear-cut, such agreements are likely to be legal in cases where the manufacturer occupies a relatively small part of the market. In such cases, the restrictions may actually increase competition among competing brands. The wholesaler or retailer faces no competition from other dealers carrying the manufacturer's brand and can therefore concentrate on effectively competing with other brands.[7]

Tying Agreement
Understanding between a marketing intermediary and a manufacturer that requires the intermediary to carry the manufacturer's full product line in exchange for an exclusive dealership.

Tying Agreements   The third legal question of exclusive dealing involves the use of a tying agreement, an agreement that requires a dealer who wishes to become the exclusive dealer for a producer's products to also carry other products by the producer. In the clothing industry, for example, such an agreement may require the dealer to carry a line of less popular clothing in addition to the fast-moving items.

Tying agreements violate the Sherman Act and the Clayton Act when they lessen competition or create monopoly situations by keeping competitors out of major markets. For this reason, the International Salt Company was prohibited from selling salt as a tying product with the lease of its patented salt-dispensing machines for snow and ice removal. The Supreme Court ruled that such an agreement unreasonably eliminated competition among sellers of salt.

Vertical Marketing Systems _____

Vertical Marketing Systems (VMS)
Professionally managed and centrally programmed marketing channel networks structured to achieve operating economy and maximum impact.

The traditional marketing channel has been described as a "highly fragmented network in which vertically aligned firms bargain with each other at arm's length, terminate relationships with impunity, and otherwise behave autonomously."[8] This potentially inefficient system of distributing goods is gradually being replaced by vertical marketing systems (VMS)—"professionally managed and centrally programmed networks preengineered to achieve operating economies and maximum impact."[9] VMS produce economies of scale through their size and by eliminating duplicated services. As Table 10.2 indicates, three types prevail—corporate, administered, and contractual.

Table 10.2

Vertical Marketing Systems

Type of System	Description	Examples
Corporate	Channel owned and operated by a single organization	Hartmarx, Firestone, Sherwin-Williams
Administered	Channel dominated by one powerful member who acts as a channel captain	Magnavox, General Electric, Kraftco, Corning Glass
Contractual	Channel coordinated through contractual agreements among channel members	*Wholesaler Sponsored Voluntary Chain:* IGA, Western Auto Stores, Associated Druggists, Sentry Hardware *Retail Cooperative:* Associated Grocers *Franchise Systems:* H & R Block, 7-Eleven Stores, Century 21 Real Estate, AAMCO Transmission, Coca-Cola Bottlers

Corporate System

Where there is single ownership of each stage of the marketing channel, a corporate vertical marketing system exists. IBM has opened its own retail outlets. Holiday Inn owns a furniture manufacturer and a carpet mill. Hartmarx (formerly Hart, Schaffner & Marx) markets its Hart, Schaffner & Marx, Pierre Cardin, Austin Reed, and other brands through its company-owned network of 259 stores as well as through independent retailers throughout the United States.

Administered System

Channel coordination is achieved through the exercise of power by a dominant channel member in an administered vertical marketing system. Magnavox obtains aggressive promotional support from its retailers because of the strong reputation of its brand. Although the retailers are independently owned and operated, they cooperate with the manufacturer because of the effective working relationships built up over the years.

Contractual System

The most significant form of vertical marketing systems is the contractual vertical marketing system, which accounts for nearly 40 percent of all retail sales. Instead of the common ownership of channel components that characterized the corporate VMS or the relative power of a component of an administered system, the contractual VMS is characterized by formal agreements among channel members. In practice, there are three types of agreements: the wholesaler-sponsored voluntary chain, the retail cooperative, and the franchise.

Wholesaler-Sponsored Chain   The wholesaler-sponsored voluntary chain represents an attempt by the independent wholesaler to preserve a market for the firm's products by strengthening the firm's retailer customers. To enable the independent retailers to compete with the chains, the wholesaler enters into a formal agreement with a group of retailers in which the retailers agree to use a common name, have standardized facilities, and purchase the wholesaler's products. Often the wholesaler develops a line of private brands to be stocked by the members of the voluntary chain.

A common store name and similar inventory allows the retailers to achieve cost savings on advertising, since a single newspaper ad promotes all the retailers in the trading area. McKesson & Robbins Drug Company has established a large voluntary chain in the retail drug industry.

Retail Cooperatives   A second type of contractual VMS is the retail cooperative, which is established by a group of retailers who set up a wholesaling operation to better compete with the chains. The retailers purchase shares of stock in the wholesaling operation and agree to buy a minimum percentage of their inventory from the firm. The members may also choose to use a common store name and to develop their own private brands to carry out cooperative advertising. Retail cooperatives have been extremely successful in the grocery industry, accounting for one-fifth of all retail grocery sales.

Franchise
Contractual arrangement in which a wholesaler or retail dealer agrees to meet the operating requirements of a manufacturer.

Franchising   A third type of contractual VMS is the franchise—a contractual arrangement in which dealers (franchisees) agree to meet the operating requirements of a manufacturer or other franchisor. The dealers typically receive a variety of marketing, management, technical, and financial services in exchange for a specified fee.

Although franchising has attracted considerable interest during the past two decades, the concept actually began over a century earlier when the Singer Company established franchised sewing machine outlets after the Civil War. Early impetus for the franchising concept came after 1900 in the automobile industry. Increasing automobile travel created demands for nationwide distribution of gasoline, oil, and tires, for which franchising was also used.[10] The soft-drink industry is another example of a franchise: a contractual arrangement exists between the syrup manufacturer and the wholesale bottler.

The franchising format that has created the most excitement in retailing during the past 20 years has been the retailer franchise system sponsored by the service firm. McDonald's is an excellent example of such a franchise operation. The company brings together suppliers and an 8,000-unit chain of hamburger outlets. It provides a proven system of retail operation (the operations manual for each outlet weighs several pounds) and lower prices through its purchasing power on meat, buns, napkins, and necessary supplies. In return, the franchisee pays a fee of about $350,000 for the use of the McDonald's name and a percentage of gross sales. Other familiar examples are Hertz, Century 21 and Red Carpet real estate agencies, Tantrific tanning salons, Pizza Hut, Howard Johnson's, and Weight Watchers.

McDonald's is a familiar example of a franchise that has adapted its market offerings to match changing consumer demands. The early McDonald's outlets offered a severely restricted menu and little or no seating. Their current counterparts provide an expanded menu, including breakfast fare, and ample seating capacity to accommodate from 100 to 300 diners. These efforts are aimed at obtaining even more of the $107 billion spent annually in U.S. eating and drinking establishments.[11] Figure 10.6 lists the five largest U.S. fast-food restaurants and their 1983 sales volumes. Currently, the average American eats out 3.5 times in seven days and spends one of three food dollars on meals away from home.[12]

Fast-food franchising has already proven itself in the international market. McDonald's hamburgers are consumed in Tokyo, London, and Paris. Ken-

Figure 10.6
The Five Largest Fast-Food Restaurants

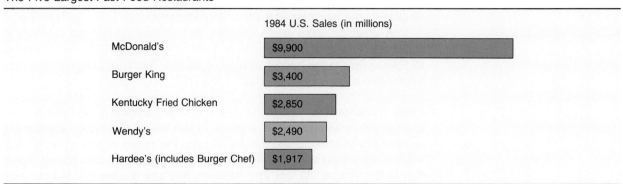

1984 U.S. Sales (in millions)

McDonald's — $9,900
Burger King — $3,400
Kentucky Fried Chicken — $2,850
Wendy's — $2,490
Hardee's (includes Burger Chef) — $1,917

Source: "Restaurant Franchising in the Economy," *Restaurant Business* (March 20, 1984), p. 170.

tucky Fried Chicken has opened more than 1,500 restaurants outside the United States in locations as diverse as Tokyo, Cologne, and London. In some countries, adjustments to U.S. marketing plans have been made to accommodate local needs. Although their menu is rigidly standardized in the United States, McDonald's executives approved the addition of wine to the menu in French outlets. Also, Kentucky Fried Chicken substituted french fries for mashed potatoes to satisfy its Japanese customers.[13]

The median investment for a franchise varies tremendously from one business area to another. For example, the investment required for a company-owned restaurant franchise recently averaged $285,000. Similarly, automotive products and services franchises required a $75,000 investment, and tax preparation services franchises averaged $8,000.[14]

Since 1971, the Federal Trade Commission has been engaged in a concentrated attempt to minimize potential abuses of the franchise system. The FTC has a rule called *Disclosure Requirements and Prohibitions Concerning Franchising and Business Opportunities*, designed to protect would-be investors by requiring disclosure of factual information concerning franchisor claims, guarantees, franchising experience, occurrence of any bankruptcy, and evidence of the moral character of the key personnel in the franchise. Also specified are services to be provided by each party and the specific terms of the franchising agreement, including all costs involved.

Whether corporate, administered, or contractual, vertical marketing systems are already a dominant factor in the consumer goods sector of the U.S. economy. An estimated 64 percent of the available market is currently in the hands of retail components of VMS.

Overcoming Conflict in the Distribution Channel

Distribution channels must be organized and regarded as a systematic cooperative effort if operating efficiencies are to be achieved. Yet channel members often perform as separate, independent, and even competitive forces. Too often, marketing institutions within the channel believe it extends only one step forward or backward. They think in terms of suppliers and customers rather than of vital links in the total channel.[15]

Channel conflict can evolve from a number of sources:

A manufacturer may wish to promote a product in one manner . . . while his retailers oppose this. Another manufacturer may wish to get information from his retailers on a certain aspect relating to his product, but his retailers may refuse to provide this information. A producer may want to distribute his product extensively, but his retailers may demand exclusives. A supplier may force a product onto its retailers, who dare not oppose, but who retaliate in other ways, such as using it as a loss leader. Large manufacturers may try to dictate the resale price of their merchandise; this may be less or more than the price at which the retailers wish to sell it. Occasionally a local market may be more competitive for a retailer than is true nationally. The manufacturer may not recognize the difference in competition and refuse to help this channel member. There is also conflict because of the desire of both manufacturers and retailers to eliminate the wholesaler.[16]

Types of Conflict

Two types of conflict—horizontal or vertical—may occur. Horizontal conflict may occur between channel members at the same level, such as two or more wholesalers or two or more retailers, or between marketing intermediaries of the same type, such as two competing discount stores or several retail florists. More often, however, horizontal conflict occurs between different types of marketing intermediaries who handle similar products. The retail druggist competes with variety stores, discount houses, department stores, convenience stores, and mail-order houses, all of which may be supplied by the producer with identically branded products. Consumer desires for convenient, one-stop shopping have led to multiple channels and the use of numerous outlets for many products.

Vertical conflict occurs between channel members at different levels—between wholesalers and retailers or between producers and wholesalers or retailers. Vertical conflict occurs frequently and is often the more severe form of conflict in the channel. Conflict may occur between producers and retailers when retailers develop private brands to compete with the producers' brands, or when producers establish their own retail stores or create a mail-order operation which competes with retailers. Conflict between producers and wholesalers may occur when the producer attempts to bypass the wholesaler and make direct sales to retailers or industrial users. In other instances, wholesalers may promote competitive products.

A third type of vertical conflict may occur between wholesalers and retailers. Retailers may believe that wholesalers fail to offer credit or to allow returns on the same basis as they provide for other types of retail outlets. Wholesalers may complain that retailers are making sales to institutions that previously dealt directly with the wholesaler. A wholesaler in the sporting goods field, for example, may argue that sales by retail sporting goods outlets directly to local school systems are unfairly competing with its own sales force.[17]

Cooperation in the Distribution Channel

The basic antidote to channel conflict is effective cooperation among channel members. However, channels usually have more harmonious relationships than conflicting ones; if they did not, the channels would have ceased to exist long ago. Cooperation is best achieved by considering all channel members as part of the same organization. Achieving cooperation is the prime responsibility of the dominant member of the channel, the channel captain, who must provide the leadership necessary to ensure efficient functioning of the channel.

Summary

Distribution channels refer to the various marketing institutions and the interrelationships responsible for the physical and title flow of goods and services from producer to consumer or industrial user. Wholesaling and retailing intermediaries are the marketing institutions in the distribution channel.

Distribution channels bridge the gap between producer and consumer. By making products and services available when and where the consumer wants to buy and by arranging for transfer of title, marketing channels create time, place, and ownership utility.

A host of alternative distribution channels are available for makers of consumer products, industrial products, and services. They range from contacting the consumer or industrial user directly to using a variety of marketing intermediaries. Multiple channels are also increasingly commonplace today. A unique distribution system is the reverse channel used in recycling, product recalls, and in some service situations.

Channel leadership is primarily a matter of relative power within the channel. The channel leader is called the channel captain.

Basic channel strategy decisions involve channel selection, the level of distribution intensity, and the use of vertical marketing systems. The selection of a distribution channel is based on market, product, producer, and competitive factors. The decision on distribution intensity involves choosing from among intensive distribution, selective distribution, or exclusive distribution. The issue of vertical marketing systems also has to be explored by the marketing manager. Three major types of vertical marketing systems exist: corporate, administered, and contractual, which includes wholesaler-sponsored chains, retail cooperatives, and franchises.

Channel conflict is a problem in distribution channels. There are two types of conflict: horizontal, between the channel members at the same level; and vertical, between channel members at different levels. Marketers should work toward cooperation among all channel members as the remedy for channel conflict.

Solving the Stop-Action Case

Porsche

Given the intense negative reactions by franchised U.S. Porsche dealers to his proposed new distribution network, Porsche president Schutz's response was straightforward. He rejected the proposal to overhaul Porsche's franchise distribution system and made immediate moves designed to end the potential channel conflict. As John Cook, president of Porsche Cars North America, put it, "We need an enthusiastic organization."

However, Schutz did decide to end his 15-year relationship with Volkswagen of America when Volkswagen's contract expired in 1984. "We feel that for our limited number of vehicles we don't see a role for a middleman between importer and dealer," Schutz explained.

The result of severing the ties with Volkswagen of America is that Porsche has a direct linkage with its franchised U.S. dealers. Certain components of the original proposal are being implemented, such as the installation of a computer link at each dealership to provide Porsche owners with computerized service records and new

customers with a means of locating specially equipped models.

Schutz is confident that potential channel conflict resulting from the original proposal has been minimized. As he pointed out, "We demonstrated that we are sensitive to dealer feelings and that we are flexible."

Source: Schutz and Cook quotations from Matt DeLorenzo, "Porsche Changes Its Mind," *Automotive News* (March 19, 1984), p. 1.

Questions for Discussion

1. Chipwich, an ice cream and chocolate-chip cookie snack, is marketed via vendor carts as well as supermarkets. Relate Chipwich's distribution strategy to the material presented in Chapter 10.

2. Explain the role of distribution channels in marketing strategy.

3. Explain how distribution channels create utility.

4. Outline the various types of distribution channels.

5. Which marketing channel is the traditional channel? Give some reasons for its frequent use.

6. What types of products are most likely to be distributed through direct channels?

7. Outline the distribution channels used by a local firm. Why were these particular channels selected by the company?

8. Under what circumstances is the retailer likely to assume a channel leadership role?

9. Explain and illustrate the major factors affecting distribution channel selection.

10. Why would manufacturers choose more than one channel for their products?

11. One generalization of channel selection mentioned in the chapter was that low-unit-value products require long channels. How can you explain the success of a firm (such as Avon) that has a direct channel for its relatively low-unit-value products?

12. Outline situations in which reverse channels might be used.

13. Which degree of distribution intensity is appropriate for each of the following:
    a. *Time* magazine   e. KitchenAid food processors
    b. Volvo automobiles   f. Yamaha motorcycles
    c. Dove soap   g. Fostoria crystal
    d. Homelite chain saws

14. Why would a manufacturer deliberately choose to limit market coverage through a policy of exclusive coverage?

15. Outline the legal problems of exclusive distribution.

16. Explain and illustrate each type of vertical marketing system.

17. Interview a franchisee in the local area. What are the dealer requirements of this particular franchise?

18. What advantages does franchising offer the small retailer? Discuss.

19. Differentiate between vertical and horizontal channel conflict.

20. In what ways could the use of multiple channels produce channel conflict?

Case: Accountants Microsystems Inc.

Rapidly growing Accountants Microsystems Inc., of Bellevue, Washington, markets software packages to accountants. Unlike many other software companies, Accountants Microsystems decided to stay in its specialized market rather than move into less sophisticated or mass-appeal software programs.

But the four-year-old firm realized it faced a potential problem. The cost of marketing software was going up rapidly, while software prices were declining. Accountants Microsystems realized that it needed an efficient distribution channel, so it turned to certified agents—independent businesspeople who pay no fees to join the organization. Certified agents are not franchisees, employees, or dealers. Accountants Microsystems trains the certified agents, pays their advertising expenses, and finances their accounts receivable. Certified agents do not face competition from distributors or original equipment manufacturers since Accountants Microsystems distributes exclusively through its certified agent channel.

Source: Carol Smith Monkman, "AMI Succeeds with Textbook Strategy," *Journal–American* (June 5, 1984), p. D-1.

Questions
1. Identify the alternative distribution channels available to Accountants Microsystems. Do you think they made the right choice? Why or why not?

2. Explain how the firm avoided any future channel conflicts.

3. What other products and services could use the certified agent distribution channel? Discuss.

Computer Applications

Decison tree analysis, a quantitative technique used in identifying alternative courses of action, assigning probability estimates for the profits or sales associated with each alternative, and indicating the course of action with the highest profit or sales, was first introduced in Chapter 2. Although the technique was used in Chapter 2 to assess the impact of environmental variables on marketing decisions, it can also be applied to channel strategy decisions. The technique is summarized on page 58.

Directions: Use menu item 2 titled "Decision Tree Analysis" to solve each of the following problems.

Problem 1 A Topeka, Kansas, firm with $10 million in annual sales is considering bypassing its independent wholesaling intermediaries and setting up its own retail outlets. Should the new distribution arrangement prove successful, the firm's management estimates that next year's sales would increase to $15 million. Management also feels that sales will decline to $8 million if the new distribution system is unsuccessful. The odds of success are calculated to be 60 percent. Should the firm elect to continue its current distribution channel, sales volume is expected to remain at $10 million. Should the Topeka firm set up its own retail outlets?

Problem 2 A producer of industrial supplies in Joliet, Illinois, is seriously considering the replacement of its current network of industrial distributors with its own sales force. The firm's director of marketing believes that the establishment of a quality sales force could increase next year's sales to $30 million—$5 million more than the $25 million in sales expected under the current distribution system. In addition, he feels that this sales increase can be achieved with no increase in selling costs. But the marketing director also believes that the conversion to a new distribution channel could cause next year's sales to decline to $10 million unless the firm is successful in attracting, training, and motivating high-quality sales representatives. Since management is confident of its ability to create an effective selling organization, it assigns a 70 percent probability of success. Use the decision tree analysis to suggest a course of action for the firm.

Problem 3 A consumer goods company headquartered in Hyattsville, Maryland, believes that it can increase its current $50 million annual sales volume to as much as $65 million if it replaces its current selective distribution arrangement with a strategy of intensive distribution. While the firm's vice-president of marketing believes that the probability of such a sales increase is only 30 percent, she is also convinced that no possibility exists for sales to fall below $50 million if the firm moves to intensive distribution. If the firm elects to continue its selective distribution, sales are expected to rise to $55 million. Recommend a course of action for the firm based upon the decision tree analysis model.

Problem 4 A Gunnison, Colorado-based firm is in the process of choosing one of two possible wholesalers to distribute its Christmas novelty items. A marketing research consultant retained by the firm has prepared both a best-case and worst-case forecast for each wholesaler. The researcher estimates a probability of 50/50 for the occurrence of his "best" and "worst" cases. The potential sales volumes for the two wholesalers are as follows:

Forecast	First Wholesaler	Second Wholesaler
Best Case	$3 million	$5 million
Worst Case	$2 million	$1 million

Which wholesaler should the firm select?

Problem 5 A West German firm has chosen Davenport, Iowa, for its U.S. offices and production facility. The firm's top management is currently evaluating which type of vertical marketing system (VMS) to implement in the United States. Although the firm has eliminated the corporate VMS from consideration due to the costs involved, its marketers have concluded that it is possible to establish a contractual VMS or an administered VMS. In response to a request to develop sales forecasts for the firm's products in the United States, an American consulting firm has produced two estimates: an optimistic forecast labeled Barnburner and a most-likely forecast labeled Expected. The probabilities of the occurrence of these alternative forecasts are 30 percent and 70 percent, respectively. The potential sales payoffs for each option are shown below:

Forecast	Administered VMS	Contractual VMS
Barnburner	$50 million	$40 million
Expected	$16 million	$22 million

Which of the two VMS options should the West German firm select?

11 Wholesaling

Learning Goals

1. To identify the functions performed by marketing institutions
2. To explain how marketing intermediaries improve channel efficiency
3. To distinguish between merchant wholesalers and agents and brokers
4. To identify the major types of merchant wholesalers and where each type might be used
5. To describe the major types of agents and brokers

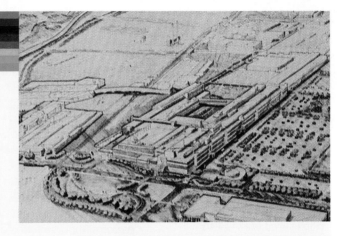

Stop-Action Case

Buick City

For the past 80 years Buick purchasers have been supplied with automobiles from the firm's Flint, Michigan, auto-assembly plant. But over the years, the facility had become increasingly inefficient, especially when compared with its Japanese counterparts who could build the same number of cars with half the employees, half the investment, and an assembly plant roughly half the size. The bad news finally arrived in Flint in the form of a General Motors Corporation announcement of a 1986 plant closing.

But Lloyd E. Reuss, Buick's general manager, was determined to find a way to save the Flint facility and the jobs of its 8,000 employees. He and a team of Buick's senior executives submitted a series of proposals to the parent GM headquarters for new auto-assembly operations. After turning down 26 diffferent ideas, GM finally accepted a proposal to assemble GM's new full-sized, front-wheel drive autos scheduled for introduction in 1986.

The plan that Reuss submitted to headquarters involved a total revamping of the traditional approach to auto assembly. No longer would Buick components be shipped from other facilities in distant cities. The new concept, which became known as Buick City, called for building cars from scratch, with every operation located under one roof. As Reuss explained the restructuring, "Our plan is to return to the original 1930s concept of what was then also called Buick City—a total integrated plant with steel entering one door and a car coming out the other."

Buick's strategy/design team identified four key success factors that would enable the firm to compete with the Japanese. Herbert Stone, the plant's general manager, enumerated these factors: "Number one, we had to build a quality automobile—world-class quality. Two, we had to be cost effective. We couldn't afford many of the old practices—like 20 or 30 repair crews to fix mistakes that never should have been made in the first place. Three, from a systems standpoint, we just had to have new . . . ways of manufacturing and assembling cars. And four, we had to have all our people squarely behind any program we came up with. All employees, all suppliers, everyone had to support our goals."

A key element in the plan was to reduce inventory costs. Not only did the parent GM organization have an estimated $9 billion tied up in inventory, with about half of these goods in storage or transit, its delivery system was often erratic. Storage, handling, and transportation costs added $3 billion a year to GM's cost of doing business.

The totally integrated Buick City approach and the need to reduce inventory costs forced Reuss and his management team to rethink the firm's current distribution channel. As a major industrial producer, Buick used a direct channel for some of its inventory needs and relied upon specialized wholesalers for others. If the new Buick City concept was to succeed, Reuss would have to create an entirely new working relationship with Buick's industrial suppliers and marketing intermediaries—a relationship that left the status quo behind.

Assignment: Use the materials in Chapter 11 to recommend a course of action for Buick City executives.

Sources: Stone quotation from *The Buick City Strategy* (New York: Conference Board, November 1, 1984). The Buick facility is described in Arthur M. Spinella, "Buick City: Hawk Bares Talons," *Ward's Auto World* (June 1983).

Chapter Overview _____

Wholesaler
Wholesaling intermediary who takes title to the goods handled; also called jobber or distributor.

Wholesaling Intermediary
Broad term that describes not only wholesalers but also agents and brokers who perform important wholesaling activities without taking title to the goods.

Chapter 10 introduced the concept of channel strategy and the role of wholesalers and retailers. This chapter expands the discussion by dealing exclusively with wholesaling; the next chapter concentrates on retailing. Part Five ends with a discussion of physical distribution in Chapter 13.

Wholesaling involves the activities of persons or firms who sell to retailers and other wholesalers or to industrial users, but not in significant amounts to ultimate consumers. The term wholesaler is applied only to wholesaling intermediaries who take title to the products they handle. Wholesaling intermediaries is a broader term that describes not only marketing intermediaries who assume title to the goods they handle, but also agents and brokers who perform important wholesaling activities without taking title to the goods. Under this definition, then, a wholesaler is a merchant intermediary.

Wholesaling activity also exists in the marketing of some services. For example, wholesaling intermediaries operate in the travel industry. They are largely responsible for the GIT (Group Inclusive Tour) market where "land packages" (hotels and meals) are offered to retail travel agents who combine them with air travel for their customers as a complete prepaid vacation.

The most recent Census of Wholesale Trade lists nearly 383,000 wholesaling establishments with a total sales volume of $1.26 trillion. Wholesaling intermediaries are concentrated in the Middle Atlantic and East North Central states. The New York City metropolitan area alone accounts for 11 percent of all wholesale trade.

Functions of Wholesaling Intermediaries _____

The route that goods follow on the way to the consumer or industrial user is actually a chain of marketing institutions. Goods that "bypass" the marketing intermediaries in the chain and move directly from manufacturer to consumer constitute only 3 percent of the total in the consumer goods market. Some consumers complain that marketing intermediaries are an unnecessary cost in the distribution system. Many discount retailers claim lower prices as a result of direct purchases from manufacturers. Chain stores often assume wholesaling functions and bypass the independent wholesalers.

Are these complaints and claims valid? Are wholesaling intermediaries the "dinosaurs" of the late 1980s? Answers to these questions can be discerned by considering the functions and costs of these marketing intermediaries.

Services Provided by Wholesaling Intermediaries

A marketing institution can continue to exist only as long as it performs a service that fulfills a need. Its demise may be slow but inevitable once other channel members discover they can survive without it. Table 11.1 examines a number of possible services provided by wholesaling intermediaries. It is important to note that numerous types of wholesaling intermediaries exist and that not all of them provide every service listed in Table 11.1. Producer-suppliers and their customers, who rely on wholesaling intermediaries for distribution, select those intermediaries providing the desired combination of services.

The listing of possible services provided by wholesaling intermediaries clearly indicates the provision of marketing utility—time, place, and possession

Table 11.1

Possible Wholesaling Services for Customers and Producer-Suppliers

Service	Service Provided for	
	Customers	Producer-Suppliers
Buying Anticipates customer demands and possesses knowledge of alternative sources of supply; acts as purchasing agent for their customers.	X	
Selling Provides a sales force to call upon customers, thereby providing a low-cost method of servicing smaller retailers and industrial users.		X
Storing Provides a warehousing function at lower cost than most individual producers or retailers could provide. Reduces the risk and cost of maintaining inventory for producers and provides customers with prompt delivery service.	X	X
Transporting Customers receive prompt delivery in response to their demands, reducing their inventory investments. Wholesalers also break-bulk by purchasing in economical carload or truckload lots, then reselling in smaller quantities to their customers, thereby reducing overall transportation costs.	X	X
Providing Market Information Serves as important marketing research input for producers through regular contacts with retail and industrial buyers. Provides customers with information about new products, technical information about product lines, reports on activities of competitors, industry trends, and advisory information concerning pricing changes, legal changes, etc.	X	X
Financing Aids customers by granting credit that might not be available were the customers to purchase directly from manufacturers. Provides financing assistance to producers by purchasing goods in advance of sale and through prompt payment of bills.	X	X
Risk-Taking Assists producers by evaluating credit risks of numerous distant retail customers and small industrial users. Extension of credit to these customers is another form of risk-taking. In addition, the wholesaler responsible for transportation and stocking goods in inventory assumes risk of possible spoilage, theft, or obsolescence.	X	X

or ownership—by these intermediaries. The services also reflect the provision of the basic marketing functions of buying, selling, storing, transporting, risk-taking, financing, and supplying market information.

The critical marketing functions—transportation and convenient product storage; reduced costs of buying and selling through reduced contacts; marketing information; and financing—form the basis of evaluating the efficiency of any marketing intermediary. The risk-taking function is present in each of the services provided by the wholesaling intermediary.

Transportation and Product Storage Wholesalers transport and store products at locations convenient to customers. Manufacturers ship products from their warehouse to numerous wholesalers, who then ship smaller quantities to retail outlets in locations convenient to purchasers. A large number of wholesalers assume the inventory function (and cost) for the manufacturer.

They benefit through the convenience afforded by local inventories. The manufacturer benefits through reduced cash needs, since its products are sold directly to the retailer or wholesaler.

Costs are reduced at the wholesale level through the making of large purchases from the manufacturer. The wholesaler receives quantity discounts from the manufacturer and incurs lower transportation costs because economical carload or truckload shipments are made to the wholesaler's warehouses. At the warehouse, the wholesaler divides the goods into smaller quantities and ships them to the retailer over a shorter distance (but at a higher rate) than would be the case if the manufacturer filled the retailer's order directly from a central warehouse.

Reduced Contacts Often Lower Costs   As the computer application for Chapter 1 demonstrates, when a marketing intermediary represents numerous producers, the costs involved in buying and selling often decrease. The transaction economies are shown by the example in Figure 11.1. In this illustration, five manufacturers are marketing their outputs to four different retail outlets. A total of 20 transactions result if no intermediary is utilized. By adding a wholesaling intermediary, the number of transactions is reduced to nine.

A Source of Information   Because of their central position between the manufacturer and retailers or industrial buyers, wholesalers serve as important information links. Wholesalers provide their retail customers with useful infor-

Figure 11.1
Achieving Transaction Economy with Wholesaling Intermediaries

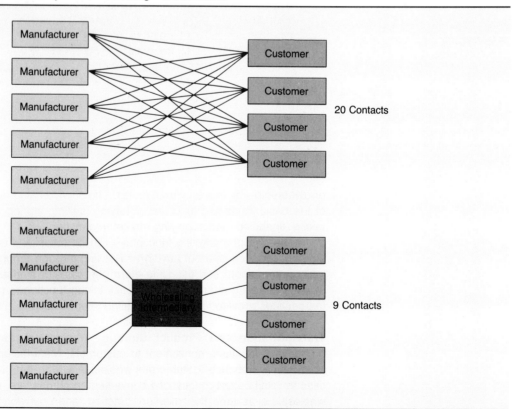

mation about new products. In addition, they supply manufacturers with information about the market acceptance of their product offerings.

Source of Financing   Wholesalers also serve a financing function. They often provide retailers with goods on credit, allowing the retailers to minimize their cash investment in inventory and pay for most of the goods as they are sold. This allows them to benefit from the principle of leverage, whereby a minimum amount spent on goods in inventory inflates the return on invested funds.

Wholesalers of industrial goods provide similar services for the purchasers of their goods. In the steel industry, intermediaries (referred to as metal service centers) currently market one-fourth of all steel shipped by U.S. mills. One such center, the Earle M. Jorgensen Company in Los Angeles, stocks 18,000 items for sale to many of the 50,000 major metal users who buy in large quantities directly from the steel mills but who turn to service centers for quick delivery of special orders. While an order from the mills may take several weeks for delivery, a service center can usually deliver locally within 24 hours. To attract business from key customers, such as AMF, which makes bicycles locally, Jorgensen carries inventory for them without demanding a contract. The cost and the risk of maintaining the stock are assumed by the service center in order for it to provide overnight delivery service for its customers.[1]

Marketing Channel Functions: Who Should Perform Them?

While wholesaling intermediaries often perform a variety of valuable functions for their manufacturer, retailer, and other wholesaler clients, these functions could be performed by other channel members. Manufacturers may choose to bypass independent wholesaling intermediaries by establishing networks of regional warehouses, maintaining large sales forces to provide market coverage, serving as sources of information for their retail customers, and assuming the financing function. In some instances, they may decide to push the responsibility for some of these functions through the channel on to the retailer or the ultimate purchaser. Large retailers who choose to perform their own wholesaling operations face the same choices.

A fundamental marketing principle applies to marketing channel decisions:

Marketing functions must be performed by some member of the channel. They can be shifted, but they cannot be eliminated.

Large retailers who bypass the wholesaler and deal directly with the manufacturer will either assume the functions previously performed by wholesaling intermediaries, or these functions will be performed by the manufacturer. Similarly, a manufacturer who deals directly with the ultimate consumer or with industrial buyers will assume the functions of storage, delivery, and marketing information previously performed by marketing intermediaries. Intermediaries can be eliminated from the channel, but the channel functions must be performed by someone.

The potential gain for the manufacturer or retailer is summarized in Table 11.2. The table shows the potential savings if channel members perform the wholesale functions as effectively as the independent wholesaling intermediary. Such savings, indicated in the net profit column, could be used to

Table 11.2

Median Net Profits and Turnover Rates of Selected Wholesalers

Kind of Business	Profits as a Percentage of Net Sales[a]	Annual Turnover Rate[b]
Automotive Parts and Supplies	3.7%	4.2
Beer, Wine, and Distilled Beverages	2.5	14.3
Clothing and Furnishings	3.6	7.8
Confectionery	1.4	13.0
Dairy Products	1.4	43.1
Drugs, Proprietaries, and Sundries	1.9	7.6
Electrical Appliances, Television and Radio Sets	2.9	7.4
Farm Machinery and Equipment	1.7	2.8
Furniture and Home Furnishings	3.7	8.6
Groceries, General Line	1.5	6.2
Hardware	3.8	5.9
Meats and Meat Products	0.9	39.6
Petroleum and Petroleum Products	1.5	32.0
Tires and Tubes	2.2	6.7
Tobacco and Tobacco Products	0.9	17.5

[a]Return on net sales.
[b]Net sales to inventory.
Source: "The Ratios," *Dun's Business Monthly* (February 1983), pp. 116–117.

reduce retail prices, to increase the profits of the manufacturer or retailer, or both.

The most revealing information in Table 11.2 is the low profit rates earned by most wholesalers. Four types of wholesalers (meats and meat products, tobacco and tobacco products, confectionery, and dairy products) earned less than 1.5 percent net profit as a percentage of net sales, while the group with the highest profits as a percentage of sales (hardware) earned 3.8 percent.

Table 11.2 also indicates a positive relationship between annual turnover rate (as measured by total sales divided by the average inventory) and net profits as a percentage of net sales. Wholesaling intermediaries such as those in dairy and meat products enjoyed relatively high turnover rates. These rates permitted the firms to generate sufficient financial returns with lower net profits (on a percentage of net sales basis) than many of the other intermediaries with lower turnover rates.

Types of Wholesaling intermediaries

Various types of wholesaling intermediaries are present in different marketing channels. Some provide a wide range of services or handle a broad line of products, while others specialize in a single service, product, or industry. Figure 11.2 classifies wholesaling intermediaries by two characteristics: *ownership* (whether the wholesaling intermediary is independent, manufacturer-owned, or retailer-owned) and *title flows* (whether title passes from the manufacturer to the wholesaling intermediary). There are three basic types of ownership: (1) independent wholesaling intermediaries, (2) manufacturer-owned sales offices and branches, and (3) retailer-owned cooperatives and buying

Figure 11.2

Major Types of Wholesaling Intermediaries

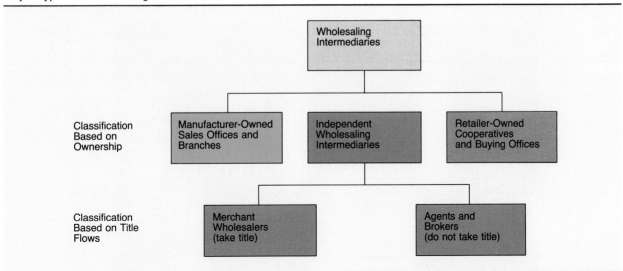

offices. The two types of independent wholesaling intermediaries are merchant wholesalers who do take title to goods and agents and brokers who do not.

Manufacturer-Owned Facilities

For several reasons, an increasing volume of products is being marketed directly by manufacturers through company-owned facilities. Some products are perishable; some require complex installation or servicing; others need aggressive promotion; still others are high-unit-value goods that the manufacturer can sell profitably to the ultimate purchaser. Among those who have shifted from the use of independent wholesaling intermediaries to the use of company-owned channels are manufacturers of apparel, construction materials, lumber, paint, paper, and piece goods.[2] More than half of all industrial goods are sold directly to users by manufacturers, and slightly less than one-third of all products are marketed through manufacturer-owned channels.[3]

Sales Branches and Offices The basic distinction between a company's sales branches and sales offices is that a sales branch carries inventory and processes orders to customers from available stock. Branches duplicate the storage function of independent wholesalers and serve as offices for sales representatives in the territory. They are prevalent in the marketing of chemicals, commercial machinery and equipment, motor vehicles, and petroleum products. Operating expenses for the 26,892 sales branches in the United States average 8.9 percent of sales. General Electric has sales branches in every major city in the United States. Its subsidiary, General Electric Supply Corporation, provides regular contacts and overnight delivery to GE retailers and industrial purchasers.

Since warehouses represent a substantial investment in real estate, small manufacturers and even large firms developing new sales territories may choose to use a public warehouse—an independently owned storage facility. For a rental fee, manufacturers can store their goods in any of the

Sales Branch
Establishment maintained by a manufacturer that serves as a warehouse for a particular sales territory, thereby duplicating the services of independent wholesalers. Sales branches carry inventory and process orders to customers from available stock.

Public Warehouse
Independently owned storage facility that stores and ships products for a rental fee.

Figure 11.3
Chicago's Merchandise Mart Center

Source: Courtesy of Merchandise Mart of Chicago.

more than 10,000 public warehouses in the United States for shipment by the warehouses to customers in the area. Warehouse owners will package goods into small quantities to fill orders and will even handle billing for manufacturers. Public warehouses can also provide a financial service for manufacturers by issuing warehouse receipts for inventory. Manufacturers can use these receipts as collateral for bank loans.

A sales office, by contrast, does not carry inventory but serves as a regional office for the firm's sales personnel. Sales offices in close proximity to the firm's customers help reduce selling costs and improve customer service. The listing of a firm in the local telephone directory often results in new sales for the local representative. Many buyers prefer to telephone the office of a supplier rather than take the time to write to distant suppliers. Since the nation's 13,629 sales offices do not perform a storage function, their operating expenses are relatively low, averaging 3.1 percent of total sales.

Other Outlets for Manufacturers' Products In addition to using a sales force and regionally distributed sales branches, manufacturers often market their products through trade fairs and merchandise marts. A trade fair (or a trade exhibition) is a periodic show where manufacturers in a particular industry display their wares for visiting retail and wholesale buyers. The New York City toy fair and the furniture show in High Point, North Carolina, are annual events for manufacturers and purchasers of toys and furniture. The cost of making a face-to-face contact with a prospective customer at a trade fair is only 41 percent of the cost of a personal sales call. In addition, such exhibitions represent effective methods of generating additional sales. One study of

Sales Office
Manufacturer's establishment that serves as a regional office for salespeople but does not carry inventory.

Trade Fair
Periodic shows where manufacturers in a particular industry display wares for visiting retail and wholesale buyers.

Figure 11.4
Types of Wholesale Trade Operations as a Percentage of Total Wholesale Sales

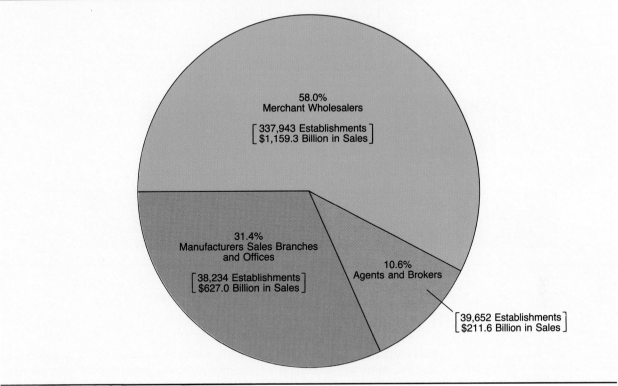

Source: U.S. Department of Commerce, Bureau of the Census, *1982 Census of Business, Wholesale Trade* (Washington, D.C.: U.S. Government Printing Office, 1984).

attendees at the National Computer Conference revealed that within the 11 months following the conference, four out of five attendees had purchased at least one product on display and that the average purchase had been $254,100.[4]

A merchandise mart provides space for permanent exhibits where manufacturers rent showrooms for their product offerings. The largest is The Merchandise Mart in Chicago, shown in Figure 11.3. This facility is two blocks long, a block wide, and 24 floors high. The entire Mart Center complex includes 7 million square feet, consisting of The Merchandise Mart, The Apparel Center, and Expocenter/Chicago, hosts 33 industry markets each year, and accounts for more than 1.4 million buying visits by retailers, designers, architects, and industrial purchasers. Industries represented at The Mart Center include residential furnishings, office furnishings, floor coverings, giftware, apparel, and business products. The Mart Center enables exhibitors in these industries to display their latest products in a central location. Over one million items are on permanent exhibit.[5]

Merchandise Mart
Permanent exhibition facility where manufacturers rent showrooms to display products for visiting retail and wholesale buyers, designers, and architects.

Independent Wholesaling Intermediaries

As Figure 11.4 indicates, independent wholesaling intermediaries account for 90 percent of the wholesale establishments and approximately two-thirds of the wholesale sales in the United States. They can be divided into two categories—merchant wholesalers and agents and brokers.

Figure 11.5
Classification of Independent Wholesaling Intermediaries

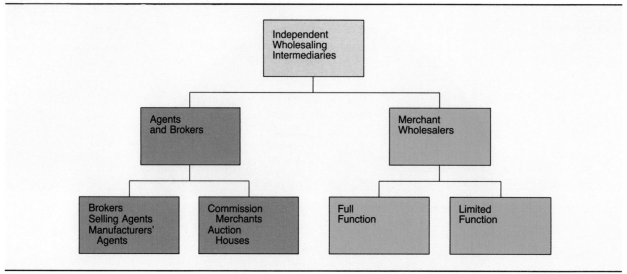

Merchant Wholesaler
Wholesaling intermediary who takes title to the goods handled.

Merchant Wholesalers   The merchant wholesaler takes title to the goods handled. Merchant wholesalers account for slightly more than 58 percent of all sales at the wholesale level, with 1985 sales of about $1 trillion.[6] They can be further classified as full-function or limited-function wholesalers, as indicated in Figure 11.5.

Full-Function Merchant Wholesalers   A complete assortment of services for retailers and industrial purchasers is provided by full-function merchant wholesalers. These wholesalers store merchandise in convenient locations, thereby allowing their customers to make purchases on short notice and to minimize their inventory requirements. They also usually maintain sales forces to call regularly on retailers, make deliveries, and extend credit to qualified buyers. In the industrial goods market, full-function merchant wholesalers (often called industrial distributors) usually market machinery, inexpensive accessory equipment, and supplies.

Full-function merchant wholesalers prevail in industries where retailers are small and carry large numbers of relatively inexpensive items, none of which is stocked in depth. The drug, grocery, and hardware industries have traditionally been serviced by full-function merchant wholesalers.

A unique type of service wholesaler emerged after World War II as grocery retailers began to stock high-profit-margin nonfood items. Because food store managers knew little about such products as health and beauty items, housewares, paperback books, records, and toys, the rack jobber provided the necessary expertise. This wholesaler supplies the racks, stocks the merchandise, prices the goods, and makes regular visits to refill the shelves. In essence, rack jobbers rent space from retailers on a commission basis. They have expanded into discount, drug, hardware, and variety stores.

Rack Jobber
Full-function merchant wholesaler who markets specialized lines of merchandise to retail stores and provides the services of merchandising and arrangement, pricing, maintenance, and stocking of display racks.

Return to the Stop-Action Case

Buick City

Members of Buick's strategy/design team decided to take a first-hand look at the Japanese auto-assembly system by touring the facilities at Toyota City outside Tokyo. There they analyzed a system called *kan-ban*, a just-in-time inventory system made possible by close cooperative efforts between Toyota and its wholesaler-suppliers. This approach transformed Toyota's operations into a hand-to-mouth system. It also allowed them to dramatically reduce their inventory costs and to improve the quality of their components and finished products.

Instead of maintaining inventory capable of filling the firm's needs for several weeks, Toyota relied completely on its wholesaler-suppliers, since inventory on hand at any one time might last no longer than several hours. In fact, their description of an ideal inventory system involved a supply truck arriving at the plant just as the last item in inventory was being used. Major savings resulted from dramatically reduced inventory and warehousing costs and from shifting the responsibility for missed deliveries and defects in components from the manufacturer to the supplier. Suppliers who miss deliveries or who fail to maintain specified quality levels quickly become *former* suppliers.

Buick executives decided to make the just-in-time inventory system a central element of the Buick City design. But for the system to work, they needed to convince such major suppliers as Jones & Laughlin to relocate their facilities near the Buick City complex. "Ideally, we would envision delivering parts directly to the assembly line with little or no inventory float at all, thereby keeping costs down and helping us to improve our competitive position," said GM president James McDonald. As Buick City officials looked to the immediate future, they realized that they had to decide how to implement the just-in-time inventory system. They had to determine how best to ensure timely delivery of the supplies they needed.

Source: McDonald quotation in Andrew Sharkey, *Just-in-Time's Time Has Come*, report to the Steel Service Center Institute, 1984, p. 2. See also Ripley Watson, Jr., "GM Revamping Its 'Buick City' Operations," *Journal of Commerce* (July 21, 1983).

Since full-function merchant wholesalers perform a large number of services, their operating expenses average nearly 13 percent, and sometimes as high as 20 percent, of sales. Attempts to reduce the costs of dealing with these wholesalers have led to the development of a number of limited-function intermediaries.

Limited-Function Merchant Wholesalers   Four types of limited-function merchant wholesalers are cash-and-carry wholesalers, truck wholesalers, drop shippers, and mail-order wholesalers. The cash-and-carry wholesaler performs most wholesaling functions with the exception of financing and delivery. These wholesalers first appeared on the marketing scene in the grocery industry during the depression era of the 1930s. In an attempt to reduce costs, retailers began driving to wholesalers' warehouses, paying cash for their purchases, and making their own deliveries. By eliminating the delivery and financing functions, cash-and-carry wholesalers were able to reduce their operating costs to approximately 9 percent of sales.

Although feasible for small stores, this kind of wholesaling is generally unworkable for large-scale grocery stores. Chain store managers are unwilling to perform the delivery function, and cash-and-carry these days is typically

Cash-and-Carry Wholesaler
Limited-function merchant wholesaler who performs most wholesaling functions except financing and delivery.

one department of a regular full-service wholesaler. The cash-and-carry wholesaler has proven successful, however, in the United Kingdom, where 600 such operations produce over $1 billion a year in sales.

Truck Wholesaler
Limited-function merchant wholesaler who markets perishable food items. Also known as a truck jobber.

The truck wholesaler, or truck jobber, markets perishable food items such as bread, tobacco, potato chips, candy, and dairy products. Truck wholesalers make regular deliveries to retail stores and perform the sales and collection functions. They also aggressively promote their product lines. The high costs of operating delivery trucks and the low dollar volume per sale mean relatively high operating costs of 15 percent.

Drop Shipper
Limited-function merchant wholesaler who receives orders from customers and forwards them to producers who ship directly to the customers.

A drop shipper receives orders from customers and forwards them to producers, who ship directly to the customers. Although drop shippers take title to the goods, they never physically handle or even see them. Since they perform no storage or handling function, their operating costs are a relatively low 4 to 5 percent of sales.

Drop shippers operate in fields where products are bulky and customers make their purchases in carload lots. Transportation and handling costs represent a substantial percentage of the total cost of such products as coal and lumber. Drop shippers do not maintain an inventory of these products, thereby eliminating the expenses of loading and unloading carload shipments. Their major service is the development of a complete assortment of customers. Since various types and grades of coal and lumber are produced by different companies, drop shippers can assemble a complete line to fill any customer's order.

Mail-Order Wholesaler
Limited-function merchant wholesaler who utilizes catalogs instead of a sales force to contact customers in an attempt to reduce operating expense.

The mail-order wholesaler is a limited-function merchant wholesaler who relies on catalogs rather than a sales force to contact retail, industrial, and institutional customers. Purchases are then made by mail or telephone by relatively small customers in outlying areas. Mail-order operations are found in the hardware, cosmetics, jewelry, sporting goods, and specialty foods lines, as well as in general merchandise.

Table 11.3 compares the various types of merchant wholesalers in terms of services provided. Full-function merchant wholesalers and truck wholesalers are relatively high-cost intermediaries due to the number of services they

Table 11.3
Services Provided by Merchant Wholesalers

Services	Full-Function Wholesalers	Limited-Function Wholesalers			
		Cash-and-Carry Wholesalers	Truck Wholesalers	Drop Shippers	Mail-Order Wholesalers
Anticipates Customer Needs	Yes	Yes	Yes	No	Yes
Carries Inventory	Yes	Yes	Yes	No	Yes
Delivers	Yes	No	Yes	No	No
Provides Market Information	Yes	Rarely	Yes	Yes	No
Provides Credit	Yes	No	No	Yes	Sometimes
Assumes Ownership Risk by Taking Title	Yes	Yes	Yes	Yes	Yes

perform, while cash-and-carry wholesalers, drop shippers, and mail-order wholesalers provide fewer services and have relatively lower operating costs.

Agents and Brokers   A second group of independent wholesaling intermediaries—the agents and brokers—may or may not take possession of the goods, but they never take title. They normally perform fewer services than the merchant wholesalers and are typically involved in bringing together buyers and sellers. Agent wholesaling intermediaries can be classified into five categories—commission merchants, auction houses, brokers, selling agents, and manufacturers' agents.

The commission merchant who predominates in the marketing of agricultural products, takes possession when the producer ships goods such as grain, produce, and livestock to a central market for sale. Commission merchants act as the producer's agents and receive an agreed-upon fee when the sale is made. Since customers inspect the products and since prices fluctuate, commission merchants receive considerable latitude in making decisions. The owner of the goods may specify a minimum price, but the commission merchant will sell them on a "best price" basis. The merchant's fee is deducted from the price and remitted to the original owner.

Auction houses bring buyers and sellers together in one location and allow potential buyers to inspect the merchandise before purchasing it. Auction houses' commissions are often based on the sale price of the goods. Sotheby Parke Bernet of New York, London, and Los Angeles is a well-known auction house specializing in works of art. Other auction houses handle used cars, livestock, tobacco, fur, fruit, and other commodities.

Brokers bring buyers and sellers together. Brokers operate in industries characterized by a large number of small suppliers and purchasers—real estate, frozen foods, and used machinery, for example. They represent either the buyer or the seller in a given transaction, but not both. Brokers receive a fee from the client when the transaction is completed. Since the only service they perform is negotiating for exchange of title, their operating expense ratio can be as low as 2 percent.

Because brokers operate on a one-time basis for sellers or buyers, they cannot serve as an effective marketing channel for manufacturers seeking regular, continuing service. A manufacturer who seeks to develop a more permanent channel utilizing agent wholesaling intermediaries must evaluate the use of the selling agent or the manufacturers' agent.

Selling agents have often been referred to as independent marketing departments, since they can be responsible for the total marketing program of a firm's product line. Typically, a selling agent has full authority over pricing decisions and promotional outlays and often provides financial assistance for the manufacturer. The manufacturer can concentrate on production and rely on the expertise of the selling agent for all marketing activities. Selling agents are common in the coal, lumber, and textile industries. In the coal industry, for example, A. T. Mossey Company, of Richmond, Virginia, and Primary Coal, Inc., of New York, are selling agents. For small, poorly financed, production-oriented manufacturers, they may prove the ideal marketing channel.

While manufacturers may utilize only one selling agent, they typically use a number of manufacturers' agents, who often refer to themselves as manufacturers' reps. These independent salespeople work for a number of manufacturers of related but noncompeting products and receive commissions based on a specified percentage of sales. Although some commissions are as

Agents and Brokers
Independent wholesaling intermediaries who may or may not take possession of goods but who never take title to goods.

Commission Merchant
Agent wholesaling intermediary who takes possession of goods when they are shipped to a central market for sale, acts as the producer's agent, and collects an agreed-upon fee at the time of sale.

Auction Houses
Establishments that bring buyers and sellers together in one location for the purpose of permitting buyers to examine merchandise before purchasing it.

Brokers
Agent wholesaling intermediaries who do not take title or possession to goods and whose primary function is to bring buyers and sellers together.

Selling Agent
Agent wholesaling intermediary responsible for the total marketing program of a firm's product line.

Manufacturers' Agent
Agent wholesaling intermediary who represents a number of manufacturers of related but noncompeting products and receives a commission based on a specified percentage of sales.

high as 23 percent of sales, they usually average between 7 and 13 percent.[7] Unlike selling agents, who may be given exclusive world rights to market a manufacturer's product, manufacturers' agents operate in a specified territory.

Manufacturers' agents reduce their total selling costs by spreading the cost per sales call over a number of different products. An agent in the plumbing supplies industry, for example, may represent a dozen manufacturers.

Manufacturers develop their marketing channels through the use of manufacturers' agents for several reasons. First, when they are developing new sales territories, the costs of adding salespeople to "pioneer" the territory may be prohibitive. Agents, who are paid on a commission basis, can perform the sales function in these territories at a much lower cost.

Second, firms with unrelated lines may need to employ more than one channel. One line of products may be marketed through the company's sales force. Another may be marketed through independent manufacturers' agents. This is particularly common where the unrelated product line is a recent addition and the firm's sales force has had no experience with it.

Finally, small firms with no existing sales force may turn to manufacturers' agents to gain access to their market. A newly organized firm producing pencil sharpeners may use office equipment and supplies agents to reach retailers and industrial purchasers.

The importance of selling agents has declined since 1940 because manufacturers desire to better control their marketing programs. In contrast, the volume of sales by manufacturers' agents has more than doubled and now comprises 37 percent of all sales by agent wholesaling intermediaries. The nation's 20,000 agents account for more than $48 billion in sales. Table 11.4 provides a comparison of the major types of agents and brokers on the basis of services performed by each.

Retailer-Owned Facilities

Retailers also assume numerous wholesaling functions in an attempt to reduce costs or to provide special service. Independent retailers occasionally band together to form buying groups to achieve cost savings through quantity purchases. Other groups of retailers establish retailer-owned wholesale facilities as a result of the formation of a cooperative chain. Larger-size chain re-

Table 11.4

Services Provided by Agents and Brokers

Services	Commission Merchants	Auction Houses	Brokers	Manufacturers' Agents	Selling Agents
Anticipates Customer Needs	Yes	Some	Some	Yes	Yes
Carries Inventory	Yes	Yes	No	No	No
Delivers	Yes	No	No	Some	No
Provides Market Information	Yes	Yes	Yes	Yes	Yes
Provides Credit	Some	No	No	No	Some
Assumes Ownership Risk by Taking Title	No	No	No	No	No

Figure 11.6

Operating Expenses as Percentages of Sales by Wholesaling Intermediaries

Merchant Wholesalers	12.7%
Manufacturers' Sales Branches	8.9%
Manufacturers' Agents	6.6%
Commission Merchants	4.8%
Brokers	3.2%
Manufacturers' Sales Offices	3.1%
Auction Houses	3.0%

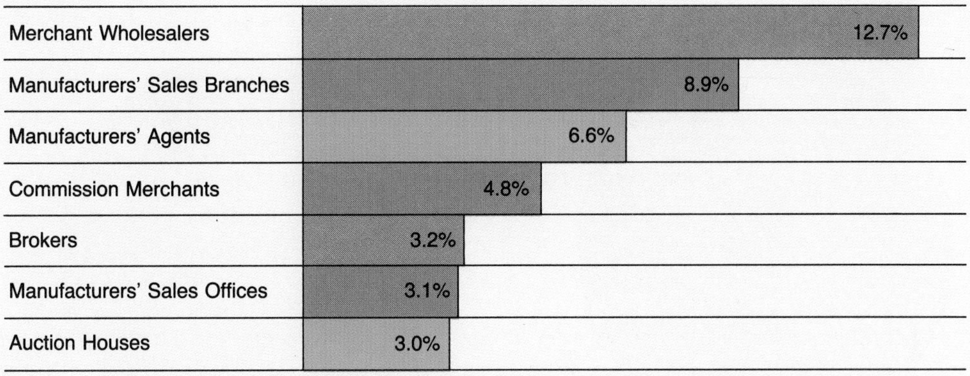

Source: U.S. Department of Commerce, Bureau of the Census, *1977 Census of Business, Wholesale Trade—Geographic Area Series 52-19* (Washington, D.C.: U.S. Government Printing Office, 1980).

tailers often establish centralized buying offices to negotiate large-scale purchases directly with manufacturers for the members of the chain. For a discussion of these facilities, see Chapter 10.

Costs of the Wholesaling Intermediary

Costs of the various wholesaling intermediaries are calculated as a percentage of total sales. Figure 11.6 lists the costs for each major category. The chief conclusion to be drawn from the table is that expense variations result from differences in the number of services provided by each intermediary. Cost ratios are highest for merchant wholesalers and manufacturers' sales branches because both provide such services as maintenance of inventories, market coverage by a sales force, and transportation. Auction houses perform only one service: bringing buyers and sellers together. As a consequence, they have the lowest expense ratios. Of course, these ratios are averages and will vary among firms within each category, depending on the actual services provided.

Independent Wholesaling Intermediaries— A Durable Marketing Institution

Many marketing observers of the 1920s felt that the end had come for independent wholesaling intermediaries as chain stores grew in importance and attempted to bypass them. Over the ten-year period from 1929 to 1939, the independent wholesalers' sales volume did indeed drop, but it has increased since then. Figure 11.7 shows how the relative shares of total wholesale trade have changed since 1929.

While the period from 1929 to the present has seen the decline in importance of agents and brokers and the increase in importance of company-owned channels, it is also true that independent wholesaling intermediaries are far from obsolete. In fact, they are responsible for over two-thirds of all wholesale trade. Their continued importance is evidence of their ability to ad-

Figure 11.7

Changes in Market Shares of the Wholesaling Intermediaries 1929–1982

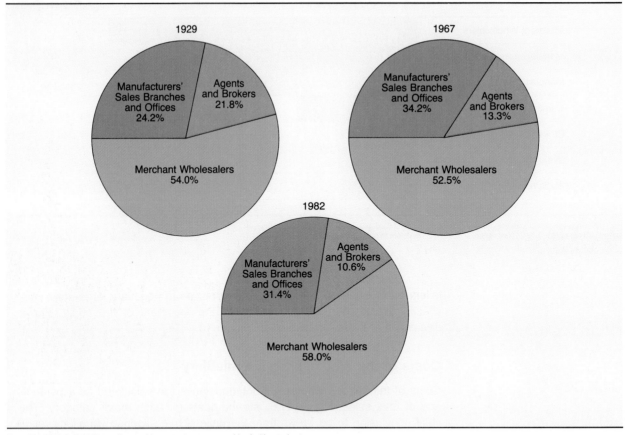

Note: Petroleum bulk station and assembler percentages are combined with merchant
wholesaler data for 1929 and 1967 for comparison with 1982 data.
Source: 1929 and 1967 data from James R. Moore and Kendall A. Adams, "Functional Wholesaler Sales Trends
and Analysis," in *Combined Proceedings* (Chicago: American Marketing Association, 1976), p. 402. 1982 data
from U.S. Department of Commerce, Bureau of the Census. *1982 Census of Business, Wholesale Trade*
(Washington, D.C.: U.S. Government Printing Office, 1984).

just to changing conditions and changing needs. Their market size proves
their ability to continue to fill a need in many marketing channels.

Summary

Wholesaling involves the activities of persons or firms who sell to retailers and
other wholesalers or to industrial users, but not in significant amounts to ultimate consumers. Wholesaling intermediaries is a broader term that describes
not only intermediaries who assume title to the goods they handle, but also to
agents and brokers who perform important wholesaling activities without taking title to the goods. The three types of wholesaling intermediaries are manufacturer-owned facilities, merchant wholesalers, and agents and brokers.
Merchant wholesalers take title to the goods they handle. Agents and brokers
may take possession of the goods but do not take title. Merchant wholesalers
include full-function wholesalers, rack jobbers, cash-and-carry wholesalers,
truck wholesalers, drop shippers, and mail-order wholesalers. Commission
merchants, auction houses, brokers, selling agents, and manufacturers'

agents are classified as agent wholesaling intermediaries because they do not take title to goods.

The operating expenses of wholesaling intermediaries vary considerably, depending on the services provided and the costs involved. The services include storage facilities in conveniently located warehouses, market coverage by a sales force, financing for retailers and manufacturers, market information for retailers and manufacturers, transportation, and, specifically for retailers, management services, retail sales training, and merchandising assistance and advice.

Although the percentage of wholesale trade by manufacturer-owned facilities has increased since 1929, independent wholesaling intermediaries continue to account for 90 percent of all wholesale establishments and over two-thirds of total wholesale trade. They accomplish this by continuing to provide desired services to manufacturers, retailers, and industrial buyers.

Solving the Stop-Action Case

Buick City

To implement its just-in-time inventory system and to ensure that quality specifications were met, Buick executives decided to use a direct channel for its exterior surface steel and to work with a wholesaling intermediary to fill its needs for steel components. Jones & Laughlin, a major U.S. steel manufacturer, was chosen to fill the first need, and Kasle Steel served as Buick's wholesaler-supplier for steel components. Jones & Laughlin was actually involved in both channels, since it served as Kasle's supplier for steel. Once the steel arrived at Kasle's facilities, it received minor pre-production processing such as cutting-to-length, slitting, and burning to meet specific Buick purchase requirements.

To accommodate Buick City's needs, Kasle Steel built a $7.5 million facility in an industrial park adjacent to the Buick plant. This proximity enables Kasle to deliver some 60,000 tons of steel each year directly to the assembly line at the moment it is needed. The firm's contract with Buick requires assembly-line delivery every four hours.

This plan, although innovative and rewarding, also creates enormous challenges for both Kasle and Buick. Without a safety net of back-up inventory, Kasle must deliver defect-free steel to keep the assembly line moving. Herbert D. Stone, Buick City's general manager, summarizes the new approach:

We're building Buick City without a safety net. This is a strategic move to force discipline into a

manufacturing system that used to operate with convenient—but expensive—fallbacks. One of our safety nets, for example, was a warehouse full of parts. Buick City has only hours of materials on hand. There is no allowance for warehousing. In the past, we had inspectors on the dock sampling incoming parts and sorting out defects. Working without a safety net you don't inspect parts. You rely on the supplier to ship only perfect products.

While risky, this system promises enormous benefits for the General Motors subsidiary. It will reduce raw material inventory levels from $250 million to less than $125 million. In the end, the new Buick City approach to auto assembly will save Buick about $400 a car. The result is the ability of the firm to price its products more competitively.

As Buick City's wholesaler-supplier, Kasle Steel faces the substantial risk of losing its major account if it proves unable to meet its product commitments. But it stands to gain, since what its executives learn at Buick City can be applied readily for other customers. And being in on the ground floor of the Buick City operation gives Kasle an edge over wholesaling competitors. As Kasle owner–president Leonard Kasle points out, "Whenever you can find some unique way to service a customer by tailoring your process to suit his needs, you create a niche for yourself from which you cannot be dislodged."

Sources: Stone quotation from *The Buick City Strategy* (New York: Conference Board, November 1, 1984). Kasle quotation from Michael A. Verespej, "Gambling on Service," *Industry Week* (May 14, 1984), pp. 28–29.

Questions for Discussion

1. In outlying areas of Central America, Quaker Oats products are distributed by wholesaling intermediaries on three to five different levels. The first intermediary buys the products in lots of several cases and then breaks bulk by selling to other wholesalers in smaller quantities. They, in turn, resell in smaller quantities to other intermediaries. The Quaker Oats products continue to be resold until finally a peddler on a mule travels into the jungles with a couple of cans and several other manufacturers' products to resell to small retailers called *pulperios*. Discuss the contributions made by this unique wholesaling system.

2. Distinguish between a wholesaler and a retailer.

3. In what ways do wholesaling intermediaries assist manufacturers? How do they assist retailers?

4. Explain how wholesaling intermediaries can assist retailers in increasing their return on investment.

5. Distinguish between sales offices and sales branches. Under what conditions might each type be used?

6. Explain the strength of wholesale volume through manufacturers' sales offices and branches even though the percentage of total wholesale sales through brokers and selling agents has been declining.

7. What role does the public warehouse play in marketing channels?

8. Distinguish merchant wholesalers from agents and brokers.

9. Which major type of wholesaling intermediary represents the most frequently used marketing channel? Which major type is least often used?

10. Comment on the following statements: Drop shippers are good candidates for elimination. All they do is process orders. They don't even handle the goods.

11. Why is the operating expense ratio of the merchant wholesaler higher than that of the typical agent or broker?

12. List the following wholesaling intermediaries in ascending order on the basis of operating expense percentage: full-function merchant wholesaler, cash-and-carry wholesaler, broker, manufacturers' sales branch, truck wholesaler.

13. Why does the truck wholesaler have a relatively high operating expense ratio?

14. Match each of the following industries with the most appropriate wholesaling intermediary:

    _____ Grocery   a.   Drop shipper

    _____ Potato chips   b.   Truck wholesaler

    _____ Coal   c.   Auction house

_____ Grain   d.   Manufacturers' agent

_____ Antiques   e.   Full-function merchant wholesaler

                       f.   Commission merchant

15.   In what ways are commission merchants and brokers different?

16.   The term *broker* also appears in the real estate and securities fields. Are these brokers identical to the agent wholesaling intermediaries described in this chapter?

17.   Distinguish between a manufacturers' agent and a selling agent.

18.   Why do commission merchants, unlike most other agents and brokers, take possession of the products they market?

19.   Under what conditions would a manufacturer utilize manufacturers' agents for a marketing channel?

20.   What type of firm is likely to utilize selling agents?

Case: Brady Marketing

When Macy's California in San Francisco sold 800 sets of General Housewares Corp.'s Magnalite Professional Cookware in two weeks—turning over the $239 item at almost three times the normal rate—the major credit went neither to the retailer, Macy's, nor to the manufacturer, GHC. The person most responsible for the successful sale was Frank Brady, the manufacturer's representative who created the merchandising concept. Brady repackaged each set of pots and pans in wine storage cases to coincide with the National Wine Convention in San Francisco. Then he sweetened the offering by including a free cookbook and an invitation to cooking demonstrations (on Magnalite Professional Cookware) at Mirassou Vineyards in San Jose.

Brady represents a small but growing number of manufacturers' agents in the housewares industry who have dramatically expanded the role of the traditional rep. It used to be "a salesman opened up a catalog of wares and took orders, item by item," says Gary Riley, president of the Cookware Division of GHC in Terre Haute, Ind. Brady, he notes, is a marketer, sensitive to the needs of consumers and retailers alike.

In the housewares industry, few manufacturers have the advertising dollars to "pull" consumers into stores with national ad campaigns or the direct salespeople in the field to train and motivate retailers to sell their products. Manufacturers are forced to rely on the retailer to move products off the shelf. The results are mixed.

While most specialty stores cater to customers and are familiar with the products they carry, the large department stores are frequently staffed by people with little knowledge or interest in specific products. "That's where we fit in," says 37-year-old Brady, who brings to the manufacturer the complete services of a marketing department in the field.

Last year Brady Marketing reported total net sales of around $20 million. . . . Seven commissioned salespeople and more than 100 part-time demonstrators are organized to create personal merchandising programs, train retail salespeople, and develop advertising and special events. "If we help a person make money," theorizes Brady, "the more money we're going to make." Brady Marketing mixes and matches promotions to create a differ-

Source: Adapted from Sara Delano, "Pushing Products through the Pipeline," Reprinted with permission, INC. magazine, February 1984, pp. 119, 121, 124, 127. Copyright © 1984 by INC. Publishing Company, 38 Commercial Wharf, Boston, MA 02110.

Photo courtesy of The Brady Marketing Company, Inc.

ent program for each retailer. "You don't need to reinvent the wheel every time, but the details must change to fit the personality of the retail store and the local consumer. For example, because Macy's customers in northern California tended to be more familiar with the Krup's food slicer than The Broadway's southern California shoppers, Brady Marketing suggested that the company offer a free salami with each purchase, rather than focusing on demonstrations.

Brady Marketing spends at least eight hours prior to actual demonstrations explaining products and sales approaches to demonstrators. Unlike many retailers and manufacturers that hire demonstrators practically off the street, Brady Marketing screens all prospects by telephone before interviewing them. Of those interviewed, about 50 percent are accepted. "We're not interested in someone with heavy demo experience," says Brady. The company values communication skills, patience, and creativity.

In 1981, Frank Brady decided to expand his business by leasing a 2,000-square-foot warehouse. "It was a way to protect our customer base of small retail accounts," he says. Because specialty-store owners don't have the confidence to purchase the amount of inventory they should, the warehouse allows the specialty stores—which represent about 30 percent of Brady's business—to order in small quantities and receive overnight shipment on orders.

Seeing yet another opportunity, Brady also formed a new division, Culinary Parts Unlimited. CPU provides retailers with replacement parts for appliances—including glass carafes, filter paper, and pasta disks—items that retailers prefer not to stock. Demonstrators and retail salespeople simply hand customers brochures that list CPU's toll-free telephone number. Instead of calling a manufacturer's service center and waiting six weeks for delivery, a customer can expect shipment from CPU within 48 hours.

Since 1980, Brady has purposely winnowed down the number of manufacturers he represents from 20 to 12 in order to allow him to provide the marketing and merchandising it takes to push products through stores successfully. Although he intends to keep that number at the current level or lower, he does plan to diversify. "We're looking for other high-quality products that require an explanation," says Brady. That could be exercise equipment, hi-tech furniture, or ski clothing. "We're not selling cookware," he emphasizes, "we're selling quality and fashion." As a reflection of his own aggressiveness, however, he defines more narrowly future manufacturers he intends to represent: "We're interested in companies that aren't satisfied with 10 percent or 15 percent growth a year . . . companies that have the financial resources, the desire, and the sense of urgency to move at a faster clip."

Questions

1. What type of wholesaling intermediary is Brady Marketing? Explain your reasoning for classifying Brady Marketing as you did.

2. Identify the various wholesaling functions performed by Brady Marketing.

3. Why do you think Brady Marketing has been so successful? Discuss.

Computer Applications

Inventory turnover, the number of times the dollar value of the firm's average inventory is sold annually, is an important ratio in evaluating the performance of wholesaling intermediaries and their retailer customers. Since trade associations publish average inventory turnover rates for different types of firms, products, and geographic areas, a comparison of the firm's turnover with those of similar organizations provides tangible evidence of the firm's performance. In addition, comparing current turnover rates with turnover in prior years enables marketers to evaluate changes in performance over time.

Inventory turnover rates are also likely to be reflected in the markups of a marketing intermediary. In most instances, wholesaling intermediaries with relatively low turnover rates charge higher average markups than those with higher turnover rates. (Exceptions occur in instances where a wholesaler performs few services in comparison with another wholesaler who might have a similar annual turnover rate but performs a large number of services for its customers.)

To calculate the rate of inventory turnover for a wholesaling intermediary, the firm's average inventory for the year must be known. Average inventory can be determined by adding beginning and ending inventories and dividing by 2. Inventory turnover is then calculated by one of the following formulas, depending on whether the firm's inventory is recorded at *retail* (the price at which the products will be sold to the wholesaler's customers) or *cost* (the prices paid for the products in inventory):

$$\text{Inventory Turnover Rate (at retail)} = \frac{\text{Sales}}{\text{Average Inventory}}.$$

$$\text{Inventory Turnover Rate (at cost)} = \frac{\text{Cost of Goods Sold}}{\text{Average Inventory}}.$$

The following example illustrates the two methods of determining annual inventory turnover rates. Wholesaler A, with $100,000 in sales and an average inventory of $20,000 (at retail), has an annual turnover rate of 5. Wholesaler B, with a cost of goods sold of $120,000 and an average inventory of $30,000 (at cost), has an annual turnover rate of 4.

Wholesaler A:

$$\text{Inventory Turnover Rate (at retail)} = \frac{\text{Sales}}{\text{Average Inventory}}$$

$$= \frac{\$100,000}{\$20,000} = 5.$$

Wholesaler B:

$$\text{Inventory Turnover Rate (at cost)} = \frac{\text{Cost of Goods Sold}}{\text{Average Inventory}}$$

$$= \frac{\$120,000}{\$30,000} = 4.$$

In instances where average inventory is recorded at cost and only the selling price of the inventory is known, the markup percentage must be subtracted from the selling price to calculate the inventory turnover rate on a cost basis. For example, consider the operations of a small wholesaler who carries an average inventory at a cost of $750,000, generates annual sales of $3,850,000, and operates on a 15 percent markup percentage on the selling price. To calculate the firm's inventory turnover rate, the $3,850,000 total sales must be reduced by the 15 percent markup for a total of $3,272,500. The second formula can then be used to determine the firm's turnover rate.

$$\text{Inventory Turnover Rate (at cost)} = \frac{\text{Cost of Goods Sold}}{\text{Average Inventory}}$$

$$= \frac{\$3,272,500}{\$750,000}$$

$$= 4.4.$$

Directions: Use menu item 9 titled "Inventory Turnover" to solve each of the following problems.

Problem 1 The Book Source is a book jobber (wholesaler) in Bangor, Maine. The firm carries an average inventory at a cost of $1 million. Its annual sales are approximately $8 million. The Book Source operates on a 20 percent markup percentage on selling price. What is the annual turnover rate for The Book Source?

Problem 2 A Mankato, Minnesota, wholesaling intermediary carries an average inventory recorded at cost of $7 million. Its total cost of goods sold is $35 million. What is the firm's inventory turnover rate?

Problem 3 Phoenix Mart is a merchandise mart in Phoenix, Arizona. Merchandise is displayed for retailers who can order for shipment directly from the factories of the firms that exhibit their product lines there. But since many of the manufacturers' factories are located in distant cities, Phoenix Mart requires its tenants to carry modest inventories. Total inventories at Phoenix Mart average $1,750,000 (at retail). The mart's management estimates that about $10.5 million in merchandise (at retail) is sold out of these inventories each year. What is the annual inventory turnover rate for the inventories carried at Phoenix Mart?

Problem 4 A Wayne, Nebraska, wholesaler began 1986 with an inventory of $3 million at retail. During the year, the wholesaler decided to increase its overall inventory position to better serve its customers. The firm ended 1986 with a $4 million inventory (at retail). Sales in 1986 were $28 million. What was the wholesaler's inventory turnover rate for the year?

Problem 5 A wholesaler in Covington, Kentucky, had a $10 million cost-based inventory on January 1, 1986, but was able to reduce it to $9 million by the end of the year. The firm had a 24 percent markup percentage on selling price. Its 1986 sales volume was $50 million. Calculate the 1986 inventory turnover rate for the Covington wholesaler.

Retailing

Key Terms

retailing
wheel of retailing
planned shopping center
retail image
atmospherics
limited-line store
general merchandise retailer
department store
mass merchandiser
discount house
off-price retailer
outlet malls
hypermarkets
chain stores
scrambled merchandising
teleshopping

Learning Goals

1. To explain the evolution of retailing
2. To outline the various elements of retailing strategy
3. To identify and explain each of the five bases for categorizing retailers
4. To describe the concept of scrambled merchandising
5. To explain the role of teleshopping in retailing

Kmart

Kmart was suffering from an image problem. The chain's more than 2,000 stores had a reputation for selling low-quality, private-brand merchandise at rock-bottom prices. To attract low-income and lower-middle-income customers over the years, Kmart had taken a no-frills approach to many of its products. During the 1970s, for example, it instructed its shirt manufacturers to reduce costs by using lighter-weight fabrics, eliminating pockets and flaps, and reducing the amount of thread used in each shirt. As a result of this marketing decision, Kmart stocked only one kind of men's dress shirt—the Challenger, priced at $8.97. The store's most expensive dresses also sold for such bargain-basement prices as $13 and $17. Kmart's nonapparel lines reflected the same low-price/low-quality image. Customers looking for shower curtains would find only one line selling for $1.97. If they wanted a better quality product, they had to go to another store.

Although Kmart customers wanted low prices, it soon became apparent that they also wanted quality. By the mid-1970s, the stores' own marketing research showed that quality played an increasingly important role in consumers' buying decisions. While customers regularly returned to Kmart to buy low-price staples such as shampoo, increasingly they shopped elsewhere for fashion items and other major purchases.

Assignment: Use the materials in Chapter 12 to recommend a course of action for Kmart.

Photo Source: Courtesy of Kmart.

Source: "Kmart, Looking Brighter," *Chain Store Age, General Merchandise Edition*, (September 1983), p. 37.

Chapter Overview

Retailing is the third distribution component considered in Part Five. Chapter 10 introduced basic concepts in channel strategy, and Chapter 11 discussed wholesaling intermediaries. This chapter explores retailing, which often links the consumer with the rest of the distribution channel. The final chapter of this section deals with physical distribution.

The nation's two million retail outlets serve as contact points between channel members and the ultimate consumer. In a very real sense, retailers are the distribution channel for most consumers, since the typical shopper has little contact with manufacturers and virtually none with wholesaling intermediaries. Retailers represent the consumer as a purchasing agent to the rest of the distribution channel. The services provided by retailers—location, store hours, quality of salespeople, store layout, selection, and returns policy, among others—are often more important than the physical product in developing consumer images of the products and services offered. Both large and small retailers perform the major channel activities: creating time, place, and possession utility.

Retailers are both customers and marketers in the channel. They market products and services to ultimate consumers, and they also are the customers of wholesalers and manufacturers. Because of this critical location in the channel, retailers often perform an important feedback role. They obtain information from customers and transmit it to manufacturers and other channel members.

Retailing
All activities involved in the sale of products and services to the ultimate consumer.

Retailing may be defined as all of the activities involved in the sale of products and services to the ultimate consumer. Although the bulk of all retail sales occurs in retail stores, the definition of retailing also includes several forms of nonstore retailing. Nonstore retailing involves such activities as telephone and mail-order sales, vending machine sales, and direct house-to-house solicitations.

The Evolution of Retailing

Early retailing can be traced to the establishment of trading posts, such as the Hudson Bay Company, and to pack peddlers who carried their wares to outlying settlements. The first important retail institution in the United States was the general store, a general merchandise store stocked to meet the needs of a small community or rural area. Here, customers could buy clothing, groceries, feed, seed, farm equipment, drugs, spectacles, and candy.

The basic needs that caused the general store to develop also doomed it to a limited existence. Since storekeepers attempted to satisfy the needs of customers for all types of goods, they carried a small assortment of each good. As communities grew, new stores opened, and they concentrated on specific product lines, such as drugs, dry goods, groceries, and hardware. The general stores could not compete, and their owners either converted them into more specialized, limited-line stores or closed them. Today, general stores still do exist in some rural areas. Only a few hundred stores are still operating, mostly in rural areas of the South and West.

Wheel of Retailing
Hypothesis stating that new types of retailers gain a competitive foothold by offering lower prices through reduction or elimination of services. Once established, they add more services, their prices gradually rise, and they are vulnerable to the emergence of a new low-price retailer with minimum services.

The Wheel of Retailing

Marketing professor Malcolm P. McNair attempted to explain the patterns of change in retailing through what has been termed the wheel of retailing. According to this hypothesis, new types of retailers gain a competitive foothold by offering lower prices to their customers through the reduction or elimination of services. Once they are established, however, they add more services, and their prices gradually rise. They then become vulnerable to a new low-price retailer who enters with minimum services—and the wheel turns.

Most of the major developments in retailing appear to fit the wheel pattern. Early department stores, chain stores, supermarkets, discount stores, hypermarkets, and catalog retailers all emphasized limited service and low prices. For most of these retailers, price levels gradually increased as services were added.

There have been some exceptions, however. Suburban shopping centers, convenience food stores, and vending machines were not built around low-price appeals. However, the wheel pattern has been present often enough in the past that it should serve as a general indicator of future developments in retailing.[1]

Retailing Strategies

While much of the discussion of marketing decisions so far in the text has centered upon manufacturers, the same concepts apply to retail marketers. The decision framework for retailers, like manufacturers and wholesalers, centers upon the two fundamental steps of (1) analyzing, evaluating, and ultimately selecting a *market target*, and (2) developing a *marketing mix* designed to profitably satisfy the chosen market target. The retailer must determine his or her market target. Then a product or service offering must be developed to appeal to that consumer group. Prices must be set and location and distribution decisions made. Finally, a promotional strategy has to be developed. The components of retailing strategy are presented in Figure 12.1.

The Market Target

Like other marketers, retailers must start by selecting the market target to which they wish to appeal. Marketing research is often used in this aspect of retail decision making. West Coast-based Mervyn's, part of the Dayton Hudson Group, defines its market target as a woman in her mid-twenties with one or more children. She works in a white-collar position, and her average family income is $25,000.[2]

Market segmentation is a valuable tool for retailers. Pittsburgh's Kaufmann's department store offers lunch-hour seminars, late hours, and career-planning workshops. All of these efforts are directed at attracting working women.[3] Statistics indicate working women spend considerably more for clothing than do either men or nonworking women, so demographic segmentation helped Kaufmann's determine its prime market target.

Sometimes a retailer finds it necessary to shift its strategy. Jos. A. Banks Clothiers, Inc., a retail outlet and mail-order firm owned by Quaker Oats, traditionally concentrated on a 45-year-old customer base. Management decided to shift its orientation to affluent 20 to 30-year-olds to take advantage of its popular new line of preppy clothing.[4] These examples suggest that market target selection is as vital an aspect of retailers' marketing strategy as it is for any other marketer.

Figure 12.1
Components of Retail Strategy

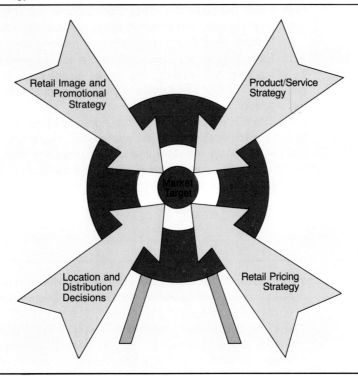

Product/Service Strategy

Retailers must also determine their offerings with respect to:

- General product/service categories
- Specific lines
- Specific products
- Inventory depth
- Width of assortment

The starting point is to assess the general product/service categories the firm currently offers or plans to offer in the future. A variety of factors can influence product and/or service offerings. For example, the discount price policies of warehouse supermarkets force these retailers to restrict their product offerings to about 1,500 items—a sharp contrast to the 15,000 found in traditional supermarkets.[5]

Montgomery Ward provides an interesting study of the evolution of a product strategy.[6] Ward's was traditionally a mass merchandiser patterned after the Sears model. When Mobil bought the retailer, management decided to move it into discounting with the Jefferson-Ward chain. Later Ward's decided to reverse that strategy.

Ward's product line is a significant aspect of their current strategy. Management has cut weak-selling items from Ward's product mix wherever possible. The new Ward's products are grouped in specialty departments like a department store. Brand names like Michelin, Black & Decker, Izod, RCA, and Monroe shock absorbers have been added to boost Ward's image to customers. Product strategy will clearly play a role in the future success of Montgomery Ward.

Retail Pricing Strategy

Pricing is another critical element of the retailing mix. The essential pricing decisions concern relative price levels. Does the store want to carry higher-priced merchandise like the steer desk offered by Neiman-Marcus, as illustrated in Figure 12.2, or lower-priced items like those handled by a discounter like Target? Other pricing decisions concern markups, markdowns, loss leaders, odd pricing, and promotional pricing. The retailer is the channel member with direct responsibility for the prices paid by consumers. Prices play a major role in buyer perceptions of the retail market.

Location and Distribution Decisions

Real estate professionals often point out that location may be the determining factor in the success or failure of a retail business. The location must be appropriate for the type and price of merchandise carried by the store. Stuckey's was originally set up in roadside locations to sell food and knickknacks, but

Figure 12.2

Spectacular His-and-Her Gift Set in the Neiman-Marcus Christmas Catalog: In 1984, for Him, a Desk in the Likeness of a Steer; for Her, a Desk Shaped Like a Horse. The Price? $65,000 Each.

Photo Source: Courtesy of Neiman-Marcus Company.

the proliferation of fast-food outlets have hurt the Pet Inc. operation. Stuckey's product line may also be out of place for its location. One food franchiser critically observed, "There just isn't much of a market anymore for high-quality rubber snakes."[7]

Planned Shopping Centers   The pronounced shift of retail trade away from the traditional downtown retailing districts and toward suburban shopping centers has been building since 1950. A planned shopping center is a group of retail stores planned, coordinated, and marketed as a unit to shoppers in their geographic trade area. These centers followed population shifts to the suburbs and concentrated on avoiding many of the problems associated with shopping in the downtown business district. They provide a convenient location for shoppers, as well as free parking facilities based upon the number and types of stores in the center. Shopping is facilitated by uniform hours of operation and by evening and weekend shopping hours. There are now about 23,000 shopping centers.[8]

Types of Shopping Centers   There are three types of planned shopping centers. The smallest and most common is the neighborhood shopping center, which is most often composed of a supermarket and a group of smaller stores such as a drugstore, a laundry and dry cleaner, a small appliance store, and perhaps a beauty shop and barber shop. These centers provide convenient shopping for perhaps 5,000 to 15,000 shoppers who live within a few minutes' commuting time of the center. They typically contain five to fifteen stores, and the product mix is usually confined to convenience goods and some shopping goods.

Community shopping centers serve 20,000 to 100,000 persons in a trade area extending a few miles. These centers are likely to contain 15 to 50 retail stores and a branch of a local department store or a large variety store as the primary tenant. In addition to the stores found in a neighborhood center, the community center is likely to have additional stores featuring shopping goods, some professional offices, and a branch of a bank or a savings and loan association.

The largest planned shopping center is the regional shopping center, a giant shopping district of at least 400,000 square feet of shopping space usually built around one or more major department stores and as many as 200 smaller stores. To be successful, regional centers must be located in areas where at least 250,000 people reside within 30 minutes' driving time of the center. The regional centers provide the widest product mixes and the greatest depth of each line.

Woodfield Mall, located in Schaumburg, Illinois, is one of the world's largest enclosed malls. Its 230 stores occupy three stories and overlook an ice-skating rink. An average of 50,000 shoppers are attracted each day, and total annual sales are estimated at $400 million. Four movie theaters, a hotel, and numerous high-rise office buildings nearby attract other people. The mall structure and its 10,800-car parking area are situated on a site almost as large as Vatican City. Like other huge regional malls, Woodfield serves as a substitute downtown for the Illinois community.[9]

Planned shopping centers account for almost 50 percent of all retail sales in the United States. Their growth has slowed in recent years, however, because the most lucrative locations are occupied and the market for such centers appears to have been saturated in many regions. The expansion and renovation of existing centers now account for approximately 50 percent of all construction activity.

Return to the Stop-Action Case

Kmart

Kmart ignored its marketing research until customer shopping patterns began to be translated into reduced profits. The net-profit-to-sales ratio declined steadily from a peak of 3 percent in 1976. Annual merchandise turnover rates plunged from eight in the mid-1970s to less than four in 1980. And 1980 profits fell 37.2 percent from the previous year. It was apparent that the retailing philosophy that had built Kmart into one of the nation's premier retailers had to be changed.

"We had to spread shoppers out and get them to buy in areas they haven't been buying before," explained Kmart president Samuel Leftwich. "We had to attract higher-income shoppers who, for example, would come in and go to our sporting goods or camera department but never think of buying apparel from us."

Source: "Kmart: Trying Harder, Looking Brighter," *Chain Store Age, General Merchandise Edition* (September 1983), p. 37.

Other Distribution Decisions   Retailers are also faced with a variety of other distribution decisions, many of which ensure that adequate quantities of stock are available when consumers want to buy. Montgomery Ward uses a 1,000-item "Never Out" program to guarantee that local stores have adequate stock and to pinpoint possible distribution channel breakdowns.[10]

Retail Image and Promotional Strategy

Retail Image
The consumer's perception of a store and the shopping experience it provides.

Atmospherics
Combination of physical store characteristics and amenities provided by the retailer that results in developing a retail image and attracting customers.

Retail image refers to the consumer's perception of a store and the shopping experience it provides. Promotional strategy is a key element in determining the consumer's image of the store. Another important element is atmospherics, the physical characteristics of a store and the amenities provided by the retailer that combine to develop the retail image and attract customers.

Consider the case of Byerly's, a Minnesota-based luxury supermarket chain that sells items as exotic as buffalo meat at $5 per pound and truffles at $45 per 7/8-ounce jar. Other luxury food retailers include Dierberg's in St. Louis, Lofino's in Dayton, Ohio, and Barlow's in Cedar Rapids, Iowa. These stores maintain their quality retail image by offering extensive services like in-store home economists and a product offering up to three times larger than a conventional supermarket. Stores like Byerly's typically do little advertising but instead concentrate on their retail image.[11]

In other situations, promotional strategies can be a major determinant of retail image. Price Chopper, a discount supermarket chain in Vermont, Massachusetts, and New York, used television ads to emphasize its stores' contributions to the community and, as a result, changed their image.[12]

Regardless of how it is accomplished, the objective of retail promotional strategy should be to position the consumer's perception of the store so that it is in line with other elements of the retailing mix. Retail image should also match the market target that is selected.

Figure 12.3
Bases for Categorizing Retailers

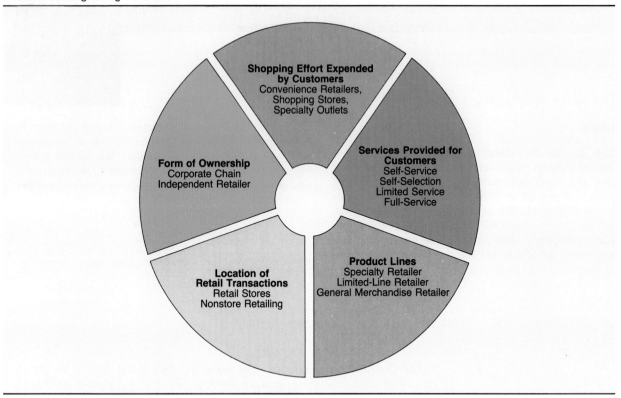

Types of Retailers

The nation's two million retailers come in a variety of forms. Since new types of retail operations continue to evolve in response to changing demands of their markets, no universal classification has been devised. The following bases can be used in categorizing them:

1.   Shopping effort expended by customers
2.   Services provided to customers
3.   Product lines
4.   Location of retail transactions
5.   Form of ownership

Any retailing operation can be classified according to each of the five bases. A 7-Eleven food store may be classified as a convenience store (category 1); self-service (category 2); relatively broad product lines (category 3); store-type retailer (category 4) and a member of a corporate chain (category 5). Figure 12.3 illustrates each basis utilized in classifying retail operations.

Classification by Shopping Effort

In Chapter 8, consumer goods were classified as convenience goods, shopping goods, and specialty goods, based on consumer purchase patterns in securing a particular product or service. This three-way classification system can be extended to retailers by considering the reasons consumers shop at a particular retail outlet. The result is a classification scheme in which retail stores are categorized as convenience, shopping, or specialty retailers.[13] This determination has a significant influence on the marketing strategies selected by a retailer. Convenience retailers focus on convenient locations, long store hours, rapid check-out service, and adequate parking facilities. Local food stores, gasoline retailers, and some barber shops may be included in this category.

Shopping stores typically include furniture stores, appliance retailers, clothing outlets, and sporting goods stores. Consumers will compare prices, assortments, and quality levels of competing outlets before making a purchase decision. Managers of shopping stores attempt to differentiate their outlets through advertising, window displays and in-store layouts, knowledgeable salespeople, and appropriate merchandise assortments.

Specialty retailers provide a combination of product lines, service, or reputation that results in consumers' willingness to expend considerable effort to shop there. Neiman-Marcus, Lord & Taylor, Tiffany & Co., and Saks Fifth Avenue have developed a sufficient degree of preference among many shoppers to be categorized as specialty retailers.

Classification by Services Provided

Some retailers seek to develop a differential advantage by developing a unique combination of service offerings for the customers who comprise their market target. It is possible to distinguish various retailer types by focusing on the services they offer. Figure 12.4 indicates the spectrum of retailer services from virtually no services (self-service) to a full range of customer services (full-service retailers).

Since the self-service and self-selection retailers provide few services to their customers, retailer location and price are important factors. These retailers tend to specialize in staple convenience goods that are purchased frequently by customers and require little product service or advice from retail personnel.

The full-service retail establishments focus on fashion-oriented shopping goods and specialty items and offer a wide variety of services for their clien-

Figure 12.4
Classification of Retailers on the Basis of Service Provided

	Self-Service	Self-Selection	Limited-Service	Full-Service
Characteristics	Very few services Price appeal Staple goods Convenience goods	Restricted services Price appeal Staple goods Convenience goods	Limited variety of services Less price appeal Shopping goods	Wide variety of services Fashion merchandise Specialty merchandise
Examples	Warehouse retailing Supermarkets Mail-order Automatic vending	Discount retailing Variety stores Mail-order retailing	Door-to-door Telephone sales Variety stores	Specialty stores Department stores

Source: Adapted from Larry D. Redinbaugh, *Retailing Management: A Planning Approach* (New York: McGraw-Hill, 1976), p. 12. Copyright 1976 McGraw-Hill Book Company. Used with the permission of McGraw-Hill Book Company.

tele. As a result, their prices tend to be higher than those of self-service retailers due to the higher operating costs associated with the services.

Classification by Product Lines

Retail strategies can also be based on the product lines that are carried. Grouping retailers by product lines produces three major categories: specialty stores, limited-line retailers, and general merchandise retailers.

Specialty Stores

A specialty store typically handles only part of a single line of products. However, this part is stocked in considerable depth for the store's customers. Specialty stores include meat markets, men's and women's shoe stores, bakeries, furriers, and millinery shops. Although some are operated by chains, most are run as independent, small-scale operations. They are perhaps the greatest stronghold of independent retailers who develop expertise in providing a very narrow line of products for their local market.

Specialty stores should not be confused with specialty goods. Specialty stores typically carry convenience and shopping goods. The label *specialty* comes from the practice of handling a specific, narrow line of merchandise.

Limited-Line Retailers

Limited-Line Store
A retail establishment that offers a large assortment of one-product lines or a few related product lines.

A large assortment of one line of products or a few related lines of goods are offered in the limited-line store. Its development paralleled the growth of towns when the population grew sufficiently to support them. These operations include such retailers as appliance stores, furniture stores, grocery stores, hardware stores, and sporting goods stores. Examples of limited-line stores are Toys R Us (toys); Levitz (furniture); Radio Shack and Playback (home electronics); Handy Dan and Handy Man (home repair products); Brain Factory (electronic calculators); and Lerner Shops (clothing). These retailers cater to the needs of people who want to select from a complete line in purchasing a particular product. Most retailers are in the limited-line category.

The Supermarket   A supermarket is a large-scale, departmentalized retail store offering a variety of food products, such as meats, produce, dairy products, canned goods, and frozen foods, in addition to various nonfood items. It operates on a self-service basis and emphasizes low prices and adequate parking facilities. Supermarkets offer low prices through a policy of self-service. Before the 1920s, however, food purchases were made at full-service grocery stores. Store personnel filled orders (often from customers' shopping lists), delivered goods, and often granted credit to their customers. Supermarkets exchanged these services for lower prices and quickly revolutionized food shopping in the United States and much of the world.[14]

Supermarket customers typically shop once or twice a week and make fill-in purchases between each major shopping trip. The 29,550 U.S. supermarkets represent only 19 percent of the nation's food stores. Yet they account for 71 percent of all food sales. The largest supermarket chains in the United States are Safeway, Kroger, American Stores, Winn-Dixie, and A & P.

With profit margins averaging only about 1 percent of sales after taxes, supermarkets compete through careful planning of retail displays to sell a large amount of merchandise each week and thereby retain a low investment in inventory. Product location within the store is studied carefully to expose the consumer to as much merchandise as possible and thereby increase impulse purchases.

Supermarkets carry nonfood products, such as magazines, records, small kitchen utensils, toiletries, and toys, for two reasons: Consumers have displayed a willingness to buy such items in supermarkets, and supermarket managers like the profit margin on these items, which is higher than that of food products. Nonfood sales account for 23.8 percent of all supermarket sales.

General Merchandise Retailers

General merchandise retailers may be distinguished from limited-line and specialty retailers by the large number of product lines they carry. The general store described earlier in this chapter is a primitive form of a general merchandise retailer—a retail establishment carrying a wide variety of product lines, all of which are stocked in some depth. Included in this category of retailers are variety stores, department stores, and such mass merchandisers as catalog retailers, discount stores, and off-price retailers.

Variety Stores   Retail firms that offer an extensive range and assortment of low-priced merchandise are called variety stores. The nation's 17,000 variety stores account for only about 1 percent of all retail sales.[15] Variety stores are not as popular as they once were. Many have evolved into or been replaced by other retailing categories such as discount stores.

Department Stores   The department store is actually a series of limited-line and specialty stores under one roof. By definition, it is a large retail firm handling a variety of merchandise that includes men's and boys' wear, women's wear and accessories, household linens and dry goods, home furnishings, and furniture. It serves the consumer as a one-stop shopping center for almost all personal and household items. Department stores account for about 10 percent of all retail sales.[16]

These retailers are organized around departments for the purpose of providing service, promotion, and control. A general merchandising manager is responsible for the store's product planning. Reporting to the general manager are the department managers. These managers typically run the departments almost as independent businesses; they are given considerable latitude in merchandising and layout decisions. Acceptance of the retailing axiom that well-bought goods are already half sold is indicated by the department manager's title of buyer.

The department store has been the symbol of retailing since the construction of the nation's first department store in 1863, the A.T. Stewart store in New York City. Almost every urban area in the United States has one or more department stores associated with its downtown and major shopping areas. Macy's Herald Square store in New York City is the world's largest department store; it contains more than two million square feet of space and produces gross sales of over $360 million each year. There are about 500,000 items available in 300 selling departments.

Department stores are known for offering their customers a wide variety of services, such as charge accounts, delivery, gift wrapping, and liberal return privileges. In addition, some 50 percent of their employees and 40 percent of their floor space are devoted to nonselling activities. As a result, they have relatively high operating costs, averaging from 45 to 60 percent of sales.

Department stores have faced intensified competition in the past 30 years. Their relatively high operating costs made them vulnerable to such new retailing innovations as discount stores, catalog merchandisers, and hyper-markets. In addition, department stores were usually located in downtown business districts and experienced the problems associated with limited parking, traffic congestion, and urban migration to the suburbs.

However, department stores have displayed a willingness to adapt to changing consumer desires. They have added bargain basements and expanded parking facilities in attempts to compete with discount operations and suburban retailers. They have also followed the movement of the population to the suburbs by opening major branches in outlying shopping centers. They have attempted to revitalize downtown retailing in many cities by modernizing their stores, expanding store hours, attracting the tourist and convention trade, and focusing on the residents of the central cities.

Mass Merchandisers   Mass merchandising has made major inroads on department stores' sales during the past two decades by emphasizing lower prices for well-known brand name products, high turnover of goods, and reduced services. The mass merchandiser often stocks a wider line of products than department stores but usually does not offer the depth of assortment in each line. Discount houses, off-price retailers, hypermarkets, and catalog retailers are all mass merchandisers.

Discount Houses   The birth of the modern discount house came at the end of World War II, when a New York-based company called Masters discovered that a large number of customers were willing to shop at a store that charged lower than usual prices and did not offer such traditional services as credit, sales assistance by clerks, and delivery. Soon, retailers throughout the country were following the Masters formula, either changing over from their traditional operation or opening new stores dedicated to discounting. At first, discount stores sold mostly appliances, but they have expanded into selling furniture, soft goods, drugs, and even food.

Discount operations had existed before World War II, but the early discounters usually sold goods from manufacturers' catalogs; they kept no stock on display and often limited potential customers. The more recent discounters operate large stores, advertise heavily, emphasize low prices for well-known brands, and are open to the public. Elimination of many of the "free" services provided by traditional retailers allows these operations to keep their markup 10 to 25 percent below those of their competitors. Consumers had become accustomed to self-service by shopping at supermarkets, and they responded in great numbers to this retailing innovation. Conventional retailers such as Kresge joined the discounting practice by opening its own Kmart stores.

As discount houses move into new product areas, there has been a noticeable increase in the number of services offered. Floors in the stores are often carpeted, credit is usually available, and many discounters are even dropping discount from their name. Although they still offer fewer services than other retailers, discounters' operating costs are increasing as they begin to resemble traditional department stores.

Kmart shoppers can choose from such designer labels as Calvin Klein, Sasson, Jordache, and Sergio Valente. Other brands with images of quality

Mass Merchandiser
Store that stocks a wider line of goods than that offered by a department store but usually does not offer the same depth of assortment.

Discount House
Store that charges lower-than-normal prices but may not offer many typical retail services such as credit, sales assistance, and home delivery.

and style now found at the discount giant include Seiko watches, Puma running shoes, Izod shirts, and Minolta and Pentax cameras.

Off-Price Retailer
Retailer who sells designer labels or well-known brand name clothing at less than typical retail prices.

Off-Price Retailing   The latest version of the discount house is the off-price retailer. These retail merchants buy only designer labels or well-known brand name clothing at regular wholesale prices or less and then pass these cost savings along to the consumer. Their inventory frequently changes as they take advantage of special price offers from manufacturers anxious to sell excess merchandise. Off-price retailers such as Loehmann's, Marshalls, T. J. Maxx, and Hit or Miss tend to keep their prices below traditional retailers by making purchases of fashion merchandise at less-than-normal wholesale prices and by offering fewer services. The result is dramatic consumer acceptance, making off-price retailing a major retailing growth trend.[17] While many off-price retailers are located in downtown areas or free-standing buildings, a growing trend is for them to concentrate in outlet malls, shopping centers consisting entirely of off-price merchandisers.

Outlet Malls
Shopping centers consisting entirely of off-price retailers.

Hypermarkets
Giant mass merchandisers of soft goods and groceries who operate on a low-price, self-service basis.

Hypermarkets—Shopping Centers in a Single Store   A relatively recent retailing development has been the introduction of hypermarkets—giant mass merchandisers who operate on a low-price, self-service basis and carry lines of soft goods and groceries. Hypermarkets are sometimes called superstores, although this latter term has also been used to describe a variety of large retail operations.[18] The hypermarket concept began in France and has since spread to Canada and the United States. Meijer's Thrifty Acres in suburban Detroit has 220,000 square feet of selling space (11 to 15 times that of the average supermarket) and more than 40 check-out counters. It sells food, hardware, soft goods, building materials, auto supplies, appliances, and prescription drugs, and it has a restaurant, a beauty salon, a barber shop, a branch bank, and a bakery. While the format may differ, more than a thousand superstores are currently in operation.

Catalog Retailers—Catalog, Showroom, and Warehouse   One of the major growth areas in retailing during the past decade has been that of catalog retailing. Catalog retailers mail catalogs to their customers and operate from a showroom displaying samples of each product handled by them. Orders are filled from a backroom warehouse. Price is an important factor for catalog store customers, and low prices are made possible by few services, storage of most of the inventory in the warehouse, reduced shoplifting losses, and the handling of products that are unlikely to become obsolete, such as luggage, small appliances, gift items, sporting equipment, toys, and jewelry. Some major catalog retailers include Best Products, Service Merchandise, Consumer Distributor, H. J. Wilson, Zales, and Gordon Jewelry Corporation. Mail-order catalog retailing is discussed later in the chapter.

Classification by Location of Retail Transactions

Some retailers choose to implement their marketing strategies outside the store environment. Although the overwhelming majority of retail transactions occur in retail stores, nonstore retailing is important for many products. Nonstore retailing includes direct selling, direct response retailing, and automatic merchandising machines. These kinds of sales account for nearly 10 percent of all retail sales.

Direct Selling

One of the oldest marketing channels was built around direct contact between the seller and the customer. Direct selling provides maximum convenience for the consumer and allows the manufacturer to control the firm's marketing channels. It is a minor part of the retailing picture and accounts for less than 1 percent of all retail sales.[19]

Direct selling is used by a number of merchandisers, including manufacturers of bakery products, dairy products, and newspapers. Amway distributors market a variety of consumer products directly to their customers, who are often friends and acquaintances. Firms emphasizing product demonstrations also tend to use the direct-selling channel. Among them are companies that sell vacuum cleaners (Electrolux), household items (Fuller Brush Company), encyclopedias (The World Book Encyclopedia), and insurance. Some firms, such as Stanley Home Products, use a variation called party selling, where a customer hosts a party to which neighbors and friends are invited. During the party, an independent salesperson makes a presentation of the products. The salesperson receives a commission based on the amount of products sold. The largest direct-selling retailers are Amway Corporation, Avon Products, Electrolux Corporation, Encyclopaedia Britannica, Home Interiors & Gifts, Jafra Cosmetics, Mary Kay Cosmetics, Princess House, Scott Fetzer (The Kirby Company, World Book), Shaklee Corporation, and Tupperware® Home Parties.

Direct-Response Retailing

The customers of direct-response retailers can order merchandise by mail, by telephone, or by visiting the mail-order desk of a retail store. Goods are then shipped to the customer's home or to the local retail store. Table 12.1 identifies a number of socioeconomic, external, and competitive factors that have contributed to the growing consumer acceptance of catalog retailing.

Many department stores and specialty stores issue catalogs to seek telephone and mail-order sales and to promote in-store purchases of items featured in the catalogs. Among typical department stores, telephone and mail-generated orders account for 15 percent of total volume during the Christmas season.[20]

Mail-order selling began in 1872, when Montgomery Ward issued its first catalog to rural Midwestern families. That catalog contained only a few items,

Table 12.1

Factors Contributing to the Success of Mail-Order Catalogs

Socioeconomic Factors	External Factors	Competitive Factors
More women joining the work force	Rising costs of gasoline	Inconvenient store hours
Population growing older	Availability of WATS (800) lines	Unsatisfactory service in stores
Rising discretionary income	Expanded use of credit cards	Difficulty of parking, especially near downtown stores
More single households	Low-cost data processing	"If you can't beat 'em join 'em" approach of traditional retailers
Growth of the "me generation"	Availability of mailing lists	

Source: John A. Quelch and Hirotaka Takeuchi, "Nonstore Marketing: Fast Track or Slow?" *Harvard Business Review* (July–August 1981), p. 77. Reprinted by permission of the *Harvard Business Review*. Copyright © 1981 by the President and Fellows of Harvard College; all rights reserved.

mostly clothing and farm supplies. Sears soon followed Ward's lead, and mail-order retailing became an important source of goods in isolated settlements.

In recent years mail-order sales have skyrocketed. It is estimated that 8 to 10 billion mail-order catalogs are distributed each year, 300 million of which are distributed by Sears alone.[21]

Mail-order houses offer a wide range of products, from novelty items (Spencer Gifts) to hunting and camping equipment (L.L. Bean) to an eighteenth-century Chinese screen priced at $60,000 (Horchow). Many mail-order catalog organizations also generate retail sales by having consumers buy from retail outlets of their catalog stores.

Direct-response retailing can also involve television commercials. Customers are typically given 24-hour telephone order service including toll-free numbers.

Automatic Merchandising

Automatic merchandising machines are a convenient way to purchase a vast array of convenience goods ranging from Pepsi-Cola to Marlboros to Michigan lottery tickets. The average American spends $1.35 a week in one or more of the approximately 6 million vending machines currently in operation. Coffee and soft-drink purchases represent nearly half of the $14.4 billion of products sold annually through vending machines.

The world's first vending machines dispensed holy water for a five-drachma coin in Egyptian temples around 215 B.C. However, the period of most rapid growth came after World War II when coffee and soft-drink vending machines were introduced in the nation's offices and factories.

A new generation of vending machines incorporating microprocessor technology is now being developed. These electronic devices are utilized in producing beverages such as coffee and soft drinks inside the machine, monitoring how much of each item is sold, and for collecting deposited money. This permits vending machine companies to integrate the sales data from the machines with financial and inventory control.

Where does the vending machine dollar go? According to the National Automatic Merchandising Association, 44 cents of each dollar goes for the product, 54.2 cents for operating expenses, and 2.8 cents for profit. Typically, the owner of the building receives more money from a machine for just allowing it on the premises than the owner of the machine does for installing, stocking, and servicing it.

Although automatic merchandising is important in the retailing of some products, it represents less than 1 percent of all retail sales. Future growth of the vending industry will depend upon the availability of a widely circulating one-dollar coin, because many of the prices of products which could be sold through vending machines are now in the range of from $1.50 to $4.50. This includes such items as complete food entrees, photographic film, flashlight batteries, and paperback books.[22]

Classification by Form of Ownership

A final method of categorizing retailers is by ownership. The two major types are corporate chain stores and independent retailers. In addition, independent retailers may join a wholesaler-sponsored voluntary chain, band together to form a retail cooperative, or enter into a franchise arrangement through contractual agreements with a manufacturer, wholesaler, or service organization. Each type has its own unique advantages and strategies.

Chain Stores

Chain stores are groups of retail stores that are centrally owned and managed and handle the same lines of products. The concept of chain stores is certainly not new. The Mitsui chain operated in Japan in the 1600s.

One major advantage that chain operations have over independent retailers is economies of scale. Volume purchases through a central buying office allows such chains as Safeway and Kroger to pay lower prices than independents. Since chains may have thousands of retail stores, they can use layout specialists, sales training, and accounting systems to increase efficiency. Advertising can also be used effectively. A single advertisement for Radio Shack in a national magazine benefits every Radio Shack store in the United States.

About 31 percent of all retail stores are part of some chain, and their dollar volume of sales amounts to more than one-third of all retail sales. Chains currently dominate four fields. They account for 92 percent of all department-store sales, almost 80 percent of all variety store sales, 49 percent of all food-store sales, and 50 percent of all retail shoe store sales. Table 12.2 lists the ten largest retailers in the United States.

For years, Sears has ranked as the nation's largest retailer. In fact, more than 24 million people now carry a Sears credit card. Appropriately, the firm's headquarters are located in the tallest building in the world, the 110-story Sears Tower in Chicago.

Many of the larger chains have expanded their operations to the rest of the world. Safeway operates supermarkets in Australia, Germany, and the United Kingdom. JCPenney, operating under the name Sarma, has retail operations in Belgium. Japanese shoppers, as shown in Figure 12.5, can frequent more than 2,000 7-Eleven stores.[23]

Table 12.2
The Ten Largest U.S. Retailers

Rank	Company	Sales (Thousands of Dollars)	Net Income as Percentage of Sales
1	Sears Roebuck (Chicago)	$30,019,800	2.9%
2	Safeway Stores (Oakland, Calif.)	17,632,821	0.9
3	Kmart (Troy, Mich.)	16,772,166	1.6
4	Kroger (Cincinnati)	11,901,892	1.2
5	JCPenney (New York)	11,413,806	3.4
6	Lucky Stores (Dublin, Calif.)	7,972,973	1.2
7	Household International (Prospect Heights, Ill.)	7,767,500	1.6
8	Federated Department Stores (Cincinnati)	7,698,944	3.0
9	American Stores (Salt Lake City)	7,507,772	1.2
10	Winn-Dixie Stores (Jacksonville, Fla.)	6,764,472	1.5

Figure 12.5
7-Eleven Stores Are Common in Japan

Source: Courtesy of The Southland Corporation.

Independent Retailers

Even though most retailers are small, independent operators, the larger-size chains dominate a number of fields. The U.S. retailing structure can be characterized as having a large number of small stores, many medium-size stores, and a small number of large stores. Even though only 7 percent of all stores have annual sales of $1 million or more, Figure 12.6 reveals that they account for almost two-thirds of all retail sales in the United States. On the other hand, almost half of all stores in the United States have sales of less than $100,000 each year.

Independents have attempted to compete with chains in a number of ways. Some were unable to do so efficiently and went out of business. Others have joined retail cooperatives, wholesaler-sponsored voluntary chains, or franchise operations. Still others have remained in business by exploiting their advantages of flexibility in operation and knowledge of local market conditions. The independents continue to represent a major part of U.S. retailing.[24]

Scrambled Merchandising

Scrambled Merchandising
Practice of some retailers who carry dissimilar product lines in an attempt to generate added sales volume.

It is becoming increasingly difficult to classify retailers because the traditional delineations no longer exist in many cases. Anyone who has attempted to fill a physician's prescription recently has been exposed to the concept of scrambled merchandising, the retail practice of carrying dissimilar lines in an at-

Figure 12.6

Comparison of Retail Trade by Number of Establishments and Sales Volume

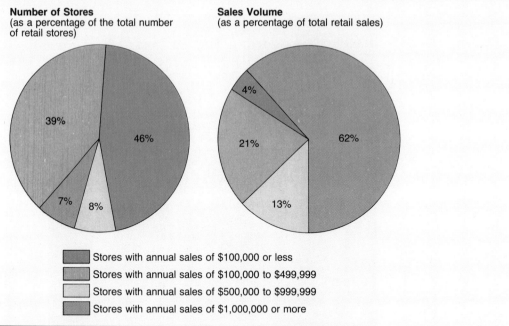

Number of Stores
(as a percentage of the total number
of retail stores)

Sales Volume
(as a percentage of total retail sales)

Stores with annual sales of $100,000 or less
Stores with annual sales of $100,000 to $499,999
Stores with annual sales of $500,000 to $999,999
Stores with annual sales of $1,000,000 or more

Source: U.S. Department of Commerce, Bureau of the Census, *1977 Census of Retail Trade, Establishment Size*
(Washington, D.C.: U.S. Government Printing Office, 1981), pp. 1–8.

tempt to generate added sales volume. The drugstore carries not only pre-scription and proprietary drugs, but also garden supplies, gift items, groceries, hardware, housewares, magazines, records, and even small appliances. The modern service station is one of the biggest practitioners of scrambled mer-chandising. Sailboats, wood-burning stoves, and dry cleaning are now avail-able at gas stations in Seattle. Bank card machines appear in Los Angeles service stations. Video games, snacks, and milk are often sold by these re-tailers. Scrambled merchandising may have come full circle at a McDonald's restaurant in Florida. It now sells gasoline.[25]

Many supermarkets rent video cassette movies, fill prescriptions, and stock such nonfood items as portable televisions, cameras, stereo equipment, citizen's band radios, and clothing such as jeans and T-shirts. A host of ser-vices from catering to cosmetology are also available at many supermarkets, as shown in Figure 12.7. Customers often can use bank credit cards for pay-ment. The best-selling product in dollar volume in drugstores is Polaroid Po-lacolor II film for instant movies. Other photographic materials—Kodak Koda-color C 110, disc, and PR 10 instant print films—also rank among the top ten drugstore sellers.[26] Shoppers at 25 Montgomery Ward stores in Los Angeles, San Diego, and Sacramento can obtain legal advice from Jacoby & Meyers legal clinics located in the store. These clinics, which lease space from Mont-gomery Ward, charge $25 for an initial consultation.[27]

Scrambled merchandising was born out of retailers' willingness to add dissimilar merchandise lines to satisfy consumer demand for one-stop shop-ping. Consider Sears' purchase of Coldwell Banker, a real estate firm, and Dean Witter Reynolds Inc., a stockbrokerage firm. Sears already has an insurance company, Allstate, operating within its stores. Scrambled merchan-

Figure 12.7
In Many Supermarkets Today, You Can Buy Much More than Food

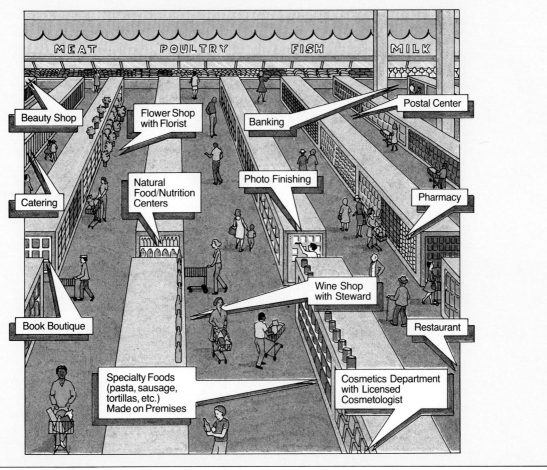

Source: Illustration by Bob Laird. *USA Today*, November 17, 1983. Reprinted by permission.

dising complicates manufacturers' channel decisions: in most cases, their attempts to maintain or increase market share will mean they must develop multiple channels to reach the diverse variety of retailers handling their products.

Teleshopping

Future retail purchases may be made through the use of interactive cable television systems such as Warner Amex's QUBE system. Best-selling author and television personality Richard Simmons appeared in a live, one-hour special titled "QUBE Presents Richard Simmons," as shown in Figure 12.8. During the interactive special, QUBE subscribers in Cincinnati were able to "touch in" on their hand-held QUBE console to order a copy of Richard Simmons's best-selling book *Never Say Diet*.

About 20 million households now have cable televisions, and the number is expected to grow significantly.[28] The growth of cable television has made teleshopping—retailing conducted through interactive cable television—practical in some areas. Consumers with these interactive cable capabilities are

Teleshopping
Innovative method of retailing conducted through interactive cable television.

Figure 12.8
Richard Simmons on QUBE

Source: Reprinted by permission of Warner Amex Cable Communications.

able to buy products and services displayed on their television screens, by merely pushing a button, as shown in Figure 12.9.

Teleshopping obviously offers an exciting new dimension for retailing, but it is not without its drawbacks. One survey found that only 10 percent of the 2,163 respondents expressed positive attitudes about teleshopping. Reasons for the low acceptance varied, but they included a desire to personally inspect the product, preference for going out to shop, and the fear of being tempted to purchase unneeded items.[29] Teleshopping via an interactive cable system is likely to be most effective for products where sight, feel, smell, and personal service are not important in the purchase decision.[30]

Summary

Retailing may be defined as all of the activities involved in the sale of products and services to the ultimate consumer. The evolution of retail institutions has generally been in accordance with the wheel of retailing, which holds that new types of retailers gain a competitive foothold by offering lower prices to their customers through the reduction or elimination of services. Once they are established, however, they add more services and increase their prices. They then become vulnerable to the next low-price retailer.

Retailers must develop a marketing mix similar to other marketers. A market target must be identified, then a product/service strategy has to be developed. Retail price strategies start with a determination of relative price levels before proceeding to issues like markdowns, odd pricing, and promotional strategy. Location is a primary aspect of a retailer's distribution function. Retail image refers to the consumer's perception of a store and the shopping experience it provides. Atmosphere, amenities, and promotional strategy play important roles in establishing a store's image.

Figure 12.9
An Example of Electronic, On-Line Ordering

Source: Courtesy of Viewdata Corporation of America, Inc.

Retailing has been affected by the development of planned shopping centers. Planned shopping centers are a group of retail stores planned, coordinated, and marketed as a unit to shoppers in their geographic area. Shopping centers can be classified as neighborhood, community, and regional centers.

Retailers are vital members of the distribution channel for consumer products. They play a major role in creating time, place, and possession utility. Retailers can be categorized on five bases: (1) shopping effort expended by customers; (2) services provided to customers; (3) product lines; (4) location of retail transactions; and (5) form of ownership. However, the trend toward scrambled merchandising sometimes makes it difficult to classify retailers. Scrambled merchandising refers to the practice of carrying dissimilar lines in an attempt to generate additional sales volume.

Retailers, like consumer goods, may be divided into convenience, shopping, and specialty categories based upon the efforts shoppers are willing to expend in purchasing products. A second method of classification categorizes retailers on a spectrum ranging from self-service to full-service. The third method divides retailers into three categories: limited-line stores, which compete by carrying a large assortment of one or two lines of products; specialty stores, which carry a very large assortment of only part of a single line of products; and general merchandise retailers, including department stores, variety stores, and mass merchandisers such as discount houses, off-price retailers, hypermarkets, and catalog retailers, all of which handle a wide variety of products.

A fourth classification method distinguishes between retail stores and nonstore retailing. While more than 90 percent of total retail sales in the United States takes place in retail stores, such nonstore retailing as direct selling, direct-response retailing, and automatic merchandising machines are important in marketing many types of products and services.

The fifth method of classification categorizes retailers by form of ownership. The major types include corporate chain stores, independent retailers, and independents who have banded together to form retail cooperatives or to join wholesaler-sponsored voluntary chains or franchises.

Chains are groups of retail stores that are centrally owned and managed and that handle the same lines of products. Chain stores dominate retailing in four fields: department stores, variety stores, food stores, and shoe stores. They account for more than one-third of all retail sales.

Chapter 12 concludes with a discussion of teleshopping, which is conducted through interactive cable television. Attention shifts to physical distribution in Chapter 13.

Solving the Stop-Action Case

Kmart

Kmart executives decided to adopt a totally new retailing strategy. The shift began in early 1980 when Bernard Fauber was appointed Kmart chairman. Since then, the store has undergone some dramatic shifts to attract middle-income and upper-middle-income customers and encourage lower-income customers to make larger purchases. Name brands that sold at relatively high prices were added to Kmart's traditional stock of low-price merchandise; stores were redecorated and modernized; risk-taking was encouraged. According to Fauber, "the shroud of restrictions" under which the buyers thought they were operating was removed. This has meant "less control-type supervision and more encouragement to try to experiment."

It also meant improved quality. Fauber urged his staff to "get away from these price categories that we mentally typed ourselves into. If you can't produce a tire gauge that will give you an accurate reading for 99 cents, get a $3 one. The consumer will buy it. In some instances we have just taken the quality out of the product."

Improved quality changes are most visible in Kmart's apparel lines. The chain's polyester, private-brand image has given way to 100 percent natural fibers or blended fabrics, many of which feature such brand names as Wrangler, Gitano, and Chic. Now, 25 percent of all Kmart's apparel is national-brand merchandise. New, stylish clothing is inspired by rock star Michael Jackson, the movie *Flashdance*, and the British safari look. "We were known for basic items, but now you find style and fashion treatments like the broader shoulders, the new squared-off shapes, and the elongated torso," said Kmart fashion consultant Joan Ragona. In addition,

Photo Source: Courtesy of Kmart.

customers can now depend on finding the current year's merchandise on store shelves. Kmart has abandoned its policy of buying only odd lots and closeouts of brands.

As a result, Kmart customers will no longer find the $8.97 Challenger men's dress shirt. In its place are three new labels ranging in price from $8.97 to $12.97. More expensive dresses costing as much as $55 have also been added, and suits for the working woman have become a store staple. All of these items use better fabrics and more thread than merchandise sold at Kmart during the 1970s.

Departments are being redecorated to highlight the new merchandise. Clothing departments that once had pipe racks and tile floors have been replaced by color-coordinated departments that feature modern fixtures, carpeting, and attractive displays. By the end of 1983, Kmart's new image was illustrated by consumer electronic departments in 800 stores, houseware shops with up-scale merchandise in 100 stores, newly revamped Homecare Centers in 45 stores, and "Names for Less" clothing departments in some 700 stores. Kmart's new strategy is clear: highlight well-known brand names and downplay store brands.

Kmart is also diversifying its merchandise mix according to the needs of specific markets. Kmart president Samuel Leftwich explains the strategy: "The Kmart customer is the customer who lives around the store. You have a high-end Kmart location and a low-end location. We'll tailor the assortment. For example, we wouldn't put

a home center in an area that was predominantly renters. In some stores, we'll have 20 percent 'Names for Less' and in other stores we might go up to 70 percent. You can put a very well-known brand name in one store and the customer will say, 'What the heck is this?'"

Kmart's new image has already started paying off. The chain's 1983 clothing sales increased by 11 percent to more than $4 billion and now account for 20 percent of the chain's profits. Overall sales increased by 10.9 percent in 1983, and net earnings rose by 88 percent to $492.3 million.

Chairman Fauber points out: "Nobody today says 'it can't be done,' or 'we have always done it some other way.' Now we say, 'Let's try it. Let's get out there and have a look at it and not waste a lot of time arguing about it around a table or trying to figure out why it won't work. Let's put it together and see if it will work.'"

Sources: "Kmart: Trying Harder, Looking Brighter," *Chain Store Age, General Merchandise Edition* (September 1983), p. 37; and Steve Weiner, "Kmart Upgrades Clothing Lines to Draw More Customers and Change Firm's Image," *The Wall Street Journal* (April 3, 1984), p. 35.

Questions for Discussion

1. Discuss the evolution of retailing.

2. List several examples of the wheel of retailing in operation. List examples that do not conform to this hypothesis. What generalizations can be drawn from this exercise?

3. Discuss the major elements of retailing strategy.

4. Location is considered a critical aspect of distribution strategy. Discuss.

5. Identify and describe the different types of shopping centers.

6. Outline the five bases for categorizing retailers.

7. Differentiate among convenience, shopping, and specialty retailers.

8. How are limited-line and specialty stores able to compete with general merchandise retailers such as department stores and discount houses?

9. A Louis Harris poll showed that supermarket shoppers rated rapid checkout as the most important criteria in choosing a supermarket. Variety of products was second, and price was third.[31] What does this study suggest for today's food marketers?

10. Identify the major types of general merchandise retailers.

11. Give reasons for the success of discount retailing in the United States.

12. Explain the concepts of off-price retailing and outlet malls.

13. Why are hypermarkets such an important part of today's retailing scene?

14. Identify and briefly explain each of the types of nonstore retailing operations.

15. Differentiate between direct selling and direct-response retailing.

16. Discuss the future of automatic merchandising.

17. Why has the practice of scrambled merchandising become so common in retailing?

18.   Computers are one of the fastest-growing aspects of retailing. Computer outlets include Radio Shack, Computerland, Compu Shop, Micro Age, and Computer Store. Relate this growth to the concepts discussed in Chapter 12.

19.   IBM has opened stores to serve small businesses and professionals like attorneys, physicians, dentists, and CPAs. How would you classify these stores?

20.   What is your assessment of the future of teleshopping via interactive cable television?

Case: Revco

It is not surprising that Revco drugstores have one of the highest profitability rates and earnings growth in the industry. The Ohio-based firm leaves little to chance when it comes to merchandising. Consider the shampoo shelf: Head & Shoulders is the nation's leading brand of shampoo, so Revco positions the standard-size package of the Procter & Gamble product on the left side of the shelf. To its right, they place the Revco label, which is similar to that of the national brand. In fact, the Revco product even says, "If You Like Head & Shoulders, Try Ours." Finally, the family-size package of Head & Shoulders is placed to the right of the Revco label.

Why does Revco spend so much effort lining up its shampoo? The retailer gets higher profit margins from its own private labels and larger sizes of national brands. And since most people are right-handed, they are more likely to reach for one of Revco's alternatives to Head & Shoulders' standard-size package.

The shampoo department is just one example of Revco's thoroughness and expertise. The firm analyzes all products by inches of shelf space and develops elaborate plans for each store. Revco places the pharmacy at the front rather than the back of the store to reduce personnel since an additional cash register will not be needed. Similarly, Revco does not have a salesperson for cosmetics. Instead, it displays cosmetics by brand name rather than product type. Revco management concluded that most women buy cosmetics by brand name and were more likely to make additional purchases if the entire product line of a particular label was displayed together.

Revco uses what it calls "everyday discount prices" rather than weekly specials. This policy eliminates periodic pricing decisions at the store level. The company does offer a 10 percent discount for senior adults on Revco label products and prescriptions, its two highest margin items. Revco works hard to build its older clientele; it knows that seniors are three times more likely to fill prescriptions than the store's younger customers.

Source: Eamonn Fingleton, "Knocking Off Head and Shoulders," *Forbes* (June 7, 1982), pp. 162, 164. Reprinted by permission.

Questions

1.   Would Revco's strategies be useful to retailers other than drugstores? Discuss.

2.   Describe how you think Revco decided on the strategies it employs. Discuss.

Computer Applications

A major pricing issue facing retailers and other channel intermediaries is *markups*, the amount added to a product's or service's cost to determine the selling price. The amount of the markup is typically the result of two factors:

a. the *services* performed by the retailer (other things equal, the greater the number of services provided for customers, the larger the required markup to cover their cost); and

b. the inventory turnover rate (other things equal, the greater the turnover rate, the smaller the markup required to cover the retailer's costs and to generate a profit).

Markups are important factors in the retailer's image among its present and potential customers. In addition, they affect the ability of the retailer to attract shoppers. Excessive markups may result in the loss of customers; inadequate markups may not generate sufficient funds to cover the cost of operations and return a profit.

Markups are typically stated as either a percentage of the selling price or the product's or service's cost. Two alternative formulas are used to calculate markups:

$$\text{Markup Percentage on Selling Price} = \frac{\text{Amount Added to Cost (the markup)}}{\text{Selling Price}}.$$

$$\text{Markup Percentage on Cost} = \frac{\text{Amount Added to Cost (the markup)}}{\text{Cost}}.$$

Consider the example of a product with an invoice cost of $.60 and a selling price of $1.00. The total markup (selling price less cost) is $.40. The two markup percentages are calculated as follows:

$$\text{Markup Percentage on Selling Price} = \frac{\$.40}{\$1.00} = 40\%.$$

$$\text{Markup Percentage on Cost} = \frac{\$.40}{\$.60} = 66.7\%.$$

To determine the selling price when only the cost and markup percentage on selling price are known, the following formula is used:

$$\text{Price} = \frac{\text{Cost in Dollars}}{100\% - \text{Markup Percentage on Selling Price}}.$$

In the example cited above, the correct selling price of $1.00 could be determined as follows:

$$\text{Price} = \frac{\$.60}{100\% - 40\%} = \frac{\$.60}{60\%} = \$1.00.$$

Similarly, the markup percentage can be converted from one basis (selling price or cost) to the other by using the following formulas:

$$\text{Markup Percentage on Selling Price} = \frac{\text{Markup Percentage on Cost}}{100\% + \text{Markup Percentage on Cost}}.$$

$$\text{Markup Percentage on Cost} = \frac{\text{Markup Percentage on Selling Price}}{100\% - \text{Markup Percentage on Selling Price}}.$$

Again, using the data from the previous example, the following conversions can be made:

$$\text{Markup Percentage on Selling Price} = \frac{66.7\%}{100\% + 66.7\%} = \frac{66.7\%}{166.7\%} = 40\%.$$

$$\text{Markup Percentage on Cost} = \frac{40\%}{100\% - 40\%} = \frac{40\%}{60\%} = 66.7\%.$$

Markups are based partially upon the marketer's judgment about the amounts consumers will be willing to pay for a given product or service. But when buyers refuse to pay the price or when improved products or fashion changes render current merchandise less salable, the marketer must give serious consideration to reducing the price of the product in the form of a *markdown*. The markdown percentage—the discount statistic that is typically advertised for the "sale" item—can be computed as follows:

$$\text{Markdown Percentage} = \frac{\text{Dollar Amount of Markdown}}{\text{"Sale" (New) Price}}.$$

Suppose no one has been willing to pay $1.00 for the item discussed above. The marketer has decided to reduce the selling price to $.79. Advertisements for the special "sale" item might emphasize that the product has been marked down 27 percent.

$$\text{Markdown Percentage} = \frac{\$.21}{\$.79} = 26.6\%.$$

Markdowns are sometimes used for evaluative purposes. For example, store managers or buyers in a large department store may be evaluated partially on the basis of the average markdown percentage on the product lines for which they are responsible.

Directions: Use menu item 10 titled "Markups" to solve Problems 1 through 5.
Use menu item 11 titled "Markdowns" to solve Problems 6 through 8.

Problem 1 A Bloomsburg, Pennsylvania, florist sells a special gift arrangement for $25. The florist's costs are $12.50. What are the florist's markup percentage on selling price and markup percentage on cost?

Problem 2 The Fish Market, an Anchorage, Alaska, seafood restaurant, sells a house wine for $9 a carafe. The wine actually costs the restaurant $3 per carafe. What are the restaurant's markup percentages on selling price and on cost?

Problem 3 A Rockford, Illinois, shoe store always adds a 40 percent markup (based on selling price) for its shoes. A shipment of men's shoes just arrived carrying an invoice cost of $45 per pair. What should the retail selling price be for each pair of the new shoes?

Problem 4 At a recent meeting of the management committee of Strowski and Daughter, a Youngstown, Ohio-area retailer, one of the buyers reported that a new line of dresses carried a markup percentage on cost of 66.67 percent. The firm's president asked the young buyer to determine the markup percentage on the selling price for the line. How should the buyer respond?

Problem 5 Suppose that the Idaho State University bookstore uses a markup percentage on selling price of 50 percent for its line of ISU T-shirts. What would the markup percentage on cost be for the T-shirts?

Problem 6 An economic downturn in the local area has adversely affected sales of a store's line of $150 dresses. The manager decides to mark these dresses down to $125. What markdown percentage should be featured in advertising for the sale items?

Problem 7 A Fresno, California, retailer pays $144 per dozen for a particular brand of men's shirts. The store attempted to sell these shirts at $30, but sales have been disappointing. In an attempt to stimulate additional sales, the store manager decides to mark the shirts down to $25. Determine the store's markdown percentage on the shirts.

Problem 8 An Altoona, Pennsylvania, bookstore has been selling a collection of local recipes for $9.95. The store buys the book from a local gourmet club for $4.00. No returns are allowed. The recipe collection has sold well, and only 17 copies remain. Management recently decided to make space for new inventory by putting the recipe books on the store's discount table at $5.95 each. Determine the bookstore's markdown percentage on the recipe book.

Key Terms

Learning Goals

1. To explain the role of physical distribution in an effective marketing strategy
2. To identify and compare the major components of a physical distribution system
3. To outline the suboptimization problem in physical distribution
4. To explain the impact of transportation deregulation on physical distribution activities
5. To compare the major transportation alternatives on the basis of such factors as energy efficiency, speed, dependability, cost, frequency of shipments, availability in different locations, and flexibility in handling products

Federal Express

In 1965 Frederick W. Smith, then a student at Yale University, wrote a paper for an economics course proposing a new kind of air-freight service. Smith envisioned an air-freight system totally independent of existing commercial passenger carriers and the uncertainties of their shifting schedules. He foresaw a small company, equipped with its own fleet of jets, that could efficiently and dependably move high-priority parcels to and from a large number of locations overnight. Unimpressed by the idea because of the regulatory climate that characterized the airline industry at the time and because of the probable hostility from commercial airlines, Smith's professor gave his report a "C." What happened next is American business history.

Seven years later, Smith put his idea into action and founded Federal Express, a company that has grown from ground zero to a $1.2 billion empire. During its introductory period, Federal Express's basic service was the delivery before noon the next day of small packages weighing less than 70 pounds. Due to such factors as an ingenious routing system that relayed packages to their destinations via a central sorting hub in Memphis; the deregulation of the airline industry that resulted in the tendency of commercial carriers to eliminate small, unprofitable cities from their routes; and the astounding success of the ad campaign it initiated in 1977—"When it absolutely, positively has to be there overnight"—Federal Express saw its overnight package count grow from 3,000 pieces in 1973 to 60,000 pieces in 1980.

While Federal Express had established itself as the leader in the small-package delivery service during this period, it could not rest on its laurels. It faced increasingly stiff competition from companies like Airborne Freight, Emery Air Freight, and the U.S. Postal Service. To maintain its competitive edge, Federal had to improve its existing service and perhaps offer a new range of services. Company executives knew that they could not maintain their hold on the market by clinging to the status quo.

Assignment: Use the materials in Chapter 13 to recommend a course of action for Federal Express.

Photo Source: This photograph is used pursuant to a license agreement with Federal Express Corporation.

Chapter Overview

Chapters 10, 11, and 12 concentrated on distribution channel strategy and the marketing activities of wholesaling and retailing. This chapter focuses specifically on the physical flow of goods. Improving customer service through more efficient physical distribution remains an important aspect of any organization's marketing strategy. This efficiency improvement can mean substantial cost savings.

Physical distribution involves a broad range of activities concerned with efficient movement of finished products from the end of the production line to the consumer. Physical distribution activities include such important decision areas as customer service, inventory control, materials handling, protective packaging, order processing, transportation, warehouse site selection, and warehousing. The term *logistics* is used interchangeably with physical distribution in this chapter.

Physical Distribution
Broad range of activities concerned with efficient movement of finished products from the end of the production line to the consumer. Includes customer service, transportation, inventory control, materials handling, order processing, and warehousing.

Importance of Physical Distribution

Increased attention has been focused in recent years on physical distribution activities. A major reason for this attention is that these activities represent a major portion of total marketing costs. Almost half of all marketing costs result from physical distribution functions.

Management's traditional focal point for cost cutting has been production. Historically, these attempts began with the industrial revolution of the 1700s and 1800s when businesses emphasized efficient production, stressing their ability to decrease production costs and improve the output levels of factories and production workers. But managers have begun to recognize that production efficiency has reached a point at which it is difficult to achieve further cost savings. More and more managers are turning to physical distribution activities as a possible area for cost savings.

In a recent year, U.S. industry spent about $300 billion on transportation, $180 billion on warehousing, $130 billion for inventory carrying costs, and $40 billion to administer and manage physical distribution. Total physical distribution costs amounted to $650 billion, approximately 21 percent of the nation's gross national product.[1]

The second—and equally important—reason for the increased attention on physical distribution activities is the role they play in providing customer service. By storing products in convenient locations for shipment to wholesale and retail customers, firms create time utility. Place utility is created primarily by transportation. These major contributions indicate the importance of the physical distribution component of marketing.

Customer satisfaction depends heavily on reliable movement of products to ensure availability. Eastman Kodak committed a major marketing error in the late 1970s when it launched a multimillion-dollar advertising campaign for its new instant camera before adequate quantities had been delivered to retail outlets. Many would-be purchasers visited the stores and, when they discovered that the new camera was not available, bought a Polaroid camera instead.

By providing consumers with time and place utility, physical distribution contributes to implementing the marketing concept. Robert Woodruff, former president of The Coca-Cola Company, emphasized the role of physical distribution in his firm's success when he stated that his organization's policy is to "put Coke within an arm's length of desire."

The Physical Distribution System

The study of physical distribution is one of the classic examples of the systems approach to business problems. The basic notion of a system is that it is a set of interrelated parts. The word is derived from the Greek word *systema*, which refers to an organized relationship among components. The firm's components include such interrelated areas as production, finance, and marketing. Each component must function properly if the system is to be effective and if organizational objectives are to be achieved.

A system may be defined as an organized group of parts or components linked together according to a plan to achieve specific objectives. The physical distribution system contains the following elements:

System
Organized group of parts or components linked together according to a plan to achieve specific objectives.

1. *Customer service:* What level of customer service should be provided?
2. *Transportation:* How will the products be shipped?
3. *Inventory control:* How much inventory should be maintained at each location?
4. *Materials handling:* How are efficient methods developed to handle products in the factory, warehouse, and transport terminals?
5. *Order processing:* How should the orders be handled?
6. *Warehousing:* Where will the products be located? How many warehouses should be utilized?

The above components are interrelated, and decisions made in one area affect the relative efficiency of other areas. Attempts to reduce transportation costs by utilizing low-cost, relatively slow water transportation may increase inventory costs because the firm may be required to maintain larger inventory levels to compensate for longer delivery times. The physical distribution manager must balance each component so that no single aspect is stressed to the detriment of the overall functioning of the distribution system.

The Problem of Suboptimization

The objective of an organization's physical distribution system may be stated as follows: to produce a specified level of customer service while minimizing the costs involved in physically moving and storing the product from its production point to the point where it is ultimately purchased. Marketers must first agree on the necessary level of customer service, then seek to minimize the total costs of moving the product to the consumer or industrial user. All physical distribution elements must be considered as a whole, rather than individually, when attempting to meet customer service levels at minimum cost. But sometimes this does not happen.

Suboptimization
Condition in which individual objectives are accomplished at the expense of broader organizational objectives.

Suboptimization is a condition in which the manager of each physical distribution function attempts to minimize costs, but, due to the impact of one physical distribution task on the others, the results are less than optimal. One writer explains suboptimization using the analogy of a football team made up of numerous talented individuals who seldom win games. Team members hold league records in a variety of skills: pass completions, average yards gained per rush, blocked kicks, and average gains on punt returns. Unfortunately, however, the overall ability of the team to accomplish the organizational goal—scoring more points than the opponents—is rarely achieved.[2]

Why does suboptimization occur frequently in physical distribution? The answer lies in the fact that each separate logistics activity is often judged by its ability to achieve certain management objectives, some of which are at cross-purposes with other objectives. Sometimes, departments in other functional areas take actions that cause the physical distribution area to operate at less than full efficiency.

Effective management of the physical distribution function requires some cost trade-offs. Some functional areas of the firm will experience cost increases while others will have cost decreases, resulting in the minimization of total physical distribution costs. Of course, the reduction of any physical distribution cost assumes that the level of customer service will not be sacrificed.[3]

Customer Service Standards

Customer Service Standards
Quality of service that a firm's customers will receive.

Customer service standards are the quality of service that the firm's customers will receive. For example, a customer service standard for one firm might be that 60 percent of all orders will be shipped within 48 hours after they are received, 90 percent in 72 hours, and all within 96 hours.

Setting the standards for customer service is an important marketing decision. Inadequate customer service may mean dissatisfied customers and the loss of future sales. The physical distribution department must delineate the costs involved in providing proposed standards. A conflict may arise when sales representatives make unreasonable delivery promises to their customers to obtain sales. In many cases, however, the need for additional inventory or the use of premium-cost transportation causes such a cost increase that the order proves unprofitable.

In an attempt to increase its share of the market, a major manufacturer of highly perishable food items set a 98 percent service level; that is, 98 percent of all orders were to be shipped the same day they were received. To meet this extremely high level of service, the firm leased warehouse space in 170 different cities and kept large stocks in each location. The large inventories, however, often meant the shipment of dated merchandise. Customers interpreted this practice as evidence of a low-quality product—or poor "service."[4]

Table 13.1 indicates specific objectives that might be developed for each factor involved in customer service. It also illustrates the importance of coordinating order processing, transportation, inventory control, and the other components of the physical distribution system in achieving these service standards.

American Airlines Has Strict Customer Service Standards

The next time you are at an American Airlines counter, someone with a stop watch and clipboard may well be hanging around. This person is there to see how long it takes you to get your ticket: the company standard says 85 percent of the passengers should not have to stand in line more than five minutes. When you land, you may find another American Airlines employee checking to see how long it takes to get the bags off the plane.

American Airlines employees are held to dozens of standards—and are checked constantly. Reservation phones must be answered within 20 seconds; 80 percent of the flights must take off within five minutes of departure time; 79 percent of the flights must arrive within 15 minutes of the published schedule; and 95 percent of the time a gate agent must be available to open

Table 13.1

Customer Service Standards

Service Factor	Objectives
Order-Cycle Time	To develop a physical distribution system capable of effecting delivery of the product within 8 days from the initiation of a customer order: • transmission of order—1 day • order processing (order entry, credit verification, picking and packing)—3 days • delivery—4 days
Dependability of Delivery	To ensure that 95% of all deliveries will be made within the 8-day standard and that under no circumstances will deliveries be made earlier than 6 days nor later than 9 days from the initiation of an order
Inventory Levels	To maintain inventories of finished goods at levels that will permit: • 97% of all incoming orders for class A items to be filled • 85% of all incoming orders for class B items to be filled • 70% of all incoming orders for class C items to be filled
Accuracy in Order Filling	To be capable of filling customer orders with 99% accuracy
Damage in Transit	To ensure that damage to merchandise in transit does not exceed 1%
Communication	To maintain a communication system that permits salespersons to transmit orders on a daily basis and that is capable of accurately responding to customer inquiries on order status within 4 hours

Source: From *Strategic Marketing* by David T. Kollat, Roger D. Blackwell and James F. Robeson, p. 316. Copyright ©
1972 by Holt, Rinehart and Winston. Reprinted by permission of CBS College Publishing.

the airplane cabin door on arrival. Cabins must have the proper supply of magazines. Performance summaries drawn up every month tell management how the airline is doing and where the problems lie. An outbreak of dirty ashtrays may be traced to a particular cleanup crew. The manager responsible for the crew will hear about it. His or her pay and promotion depend on meeting standards. If he or she fails to meet them three months running without extenuating circumstances, he or she may be looking for a job.[5]

Elements of the Physical Distribution System

The establishment of acceptable levels of customer service provides the physical distribution department a standard with which actual operations can be compared. The physical distribution system should be designed to achieve this standard by minimizing the total costs of the following components: (1) transportation, (2) warehouses and their locations, (3) inventory control, (4) order processing, and (5) materials handling. Relative costs for each component are illustrated in Figure 13.1.

Transportation

Transportation costs are the largest expense item in physical distribution. At Boise-Cascade Corporation, transportation costs are equal to 10 percent of sales, or $340 million. John B. Fery, chairman of the firm, declared:

Effective transportation makes us more competitive. Better customer service is just one of the reasons for this. Another reason is that by holding down overall freight costs, we keep our products competitively priced. Furthermore,

Figure 13.1
Where the Physical Distribution Dollar Goes

because goods in transit represent the greater share of our total inventories, close transportation control plays a big part in achieving asset management.[6]

The transportation system in the United States has historically been a regulated industry, much the same as the telephone and electricity industries. The railroads were first regulated under the Interstate Commerce Act of 1887. This act established the Interstate Commerce Commission (ICC), the first regulatory body in the United States. The ICC regulates railroads, slurry pipelines, motor carriers, and inland water carriers. The Federal Maritime Commission regulates U.S. ocean carriers.

Rate Determination

There are two basic freight rates: class and commodity. The class rate is the standard rate that is found for every commodity moving between any two destinations. Of the two rates, the class rate is the higher. The commodity rate is sometimes called a special rate, since it is given by carriers to shippers as a reward for either regular use or large-quantity shipments. It is used extensively by railroads and inland water carriers.

A third type of rate commonly used in the railroad industry today is the negotiated, or contract, rate. This type of rate was legalized by the Staggers Rail Act of 1980. It allows the shipper and railroad to negotiate a rate for a particular service. The terms of the rate, service, and so forth are then finalized in a contract between the two parties. As of 1984, over 12,000 such contracts have been established and filed with the ICC.[7]

Transportation Deregulation

The United States transportation industry has experienced federal deregulation, which began in 1977 with the removal of regulations for cargo air carriers not engaged in passenger transportation. The following year, the Airline Deregulation Act of 1978 was passed, granting considerable freedom to the airlines in establishing fares and in choosing new routes. With the passage of this act, the Civil Aeronautics Board began to be phased out; it was abolished in 1985.

In 1980, the Motor Carrier Act and the Staggers Rail Act significantly deregulated the trucking and railroad industries. These laws provided transportation carriers with the ability to negotiate rates and services, eliminating much of the bureaucracy that had traditionally hampered the establishment of new and innovative rates and services. Transporters are now able to base rates on a shipper's unique needs.

The new transportation environment has increased the importance of physical distribution managers, because their areas of responsibility are even more complex than in a highly regulated situation. It is now possible to simultaneously increase service levels and decrease transportation costs. General Foods recently negotiated a service-oriented contract with the Santa Fe Railroad in which highway trailers would be placed on rail cars and transported from Houston to Chicago. In obtaining the contract to ship 6 million pounds of General Foods' products each year, the railroad guaranteed the availability of sufficient truck capacity. As a bonus, it will receive an additional $75 per trailer used for each month in which 90 percent of its trailers make the trip in 96 hours or less.[8]

Classes of Carriers

Freight carriers are classified as common, contract, and private. *Common carriers*, sometimes called the backbone of the transportation industry, are for-hire carriers that serve the general public. Their rates and services are regulated, and they cannot conduct their operations without permission of the appropriate regulatory authority. Common carriers exist for all the modes of transport.

Contract carriers are for-hire transporters who do not offer their services to the general public. Instead, they establish specific contracts with certain customers and operate exclusively for a particular industry (most commonly the motor-freight industry). These carriers are subject to much less regulation than are common carriers.

Private carriers are not-for-hire carriers. Their operators transport products only for a particular firm and cannot solicit other transportation business. Since the transportation they provide is solely for their own use, there is no rate or service regulation.

In 1978 the ICC began to permit private carriers to also operate as common or contract carriers. Many private carriers have taken advantage of this new rule to operate their trucks fully loaded at all times. For instance, Nabisco's fleet of private carriers hauling the firm's products to regional warehouses should be able to reduce total transportation costs by transporting the products of other shippers on the return trip to the factory. Instead of returning in an empty truck, the Nabisco driver acts as a common carrier or contract carrier and receives a transport fee from the outside shipper.[9]

Major Transportation Modes

The physical distribution manager has five major transportation alternatives: railroads, motor carriers, water carriers, pipelines, and air freight. Figure 13.2 indicates the percentage of total ton-miles shipped by each major mode. The term *ton-mile* refers to moving one ton of freight one mile. Thus a three-ton shipment moved eight miles equals twenty-four ton-miles.

Figure 13.2

Percentage of Total Intercity Ton-Miles by the
Various Transport Modes: 1940–1982

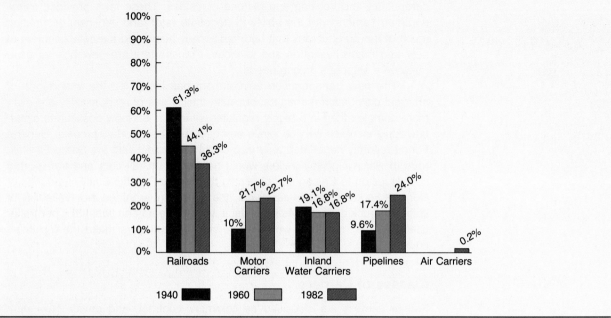

Sources: "Transportation in America," Transportation Policy Associates, Washington, D.C.; and *Yearbook of Railroad Facts* (Washington, D.C., Association of American Railroads, 1983), p. 32.

The water carriers' percentage has remained generally stable over the years, railroads have experienced a significant decrease, and pipelines and motor carriers have experienced substantial increases. Air carriers are dwarfed by the other transportation alternatives, accounting for less than 1 percent of all shipments.

Railroads: The Nation's Leading Transporter   The most frequently used method of transportation continues to be railroads by about a 1.5 to 1 margin over their nearest competitors. They represent the most efficient mode for the movement of bulk commodities over long distances.

Railroads move two-thirds of all U.S.-mined coal, and coal makes up more than 30 percent of total rail carloadings. Other major commodity groups represented in rail traffic are farm products, chemicals, minerals, and food products.

In recent years railroads have introduced many new services. One of the most familiar is piggyback—the movement of truck trailers and containers that ride as rail cargo, combining the long-haul, low-cost advantages of the railroad with the door-to-door flexibility of the truck. Piggyback is the fastest-growing segment of rail traffic, second only to coal in rank of carloadings.

Another development is the unit train, used extensively for the expeditious movement of coal, grain, and other high-volume shipments. The unit train is loaded entirely with a single commodity bound for a single destination; it returns to the starting point to reload and repeat the trip. The customer benefits from time and cost savings.

A similar concept is the run-through train, which bypasses intermediate terminals and avoids delays. The run-through train differs from the unit train in that it may carry a variety of commodities. The Chicago and North Western

Figure 13.3

The Union Pacific System's Run-Through Train
from Chicago to Los Angeles

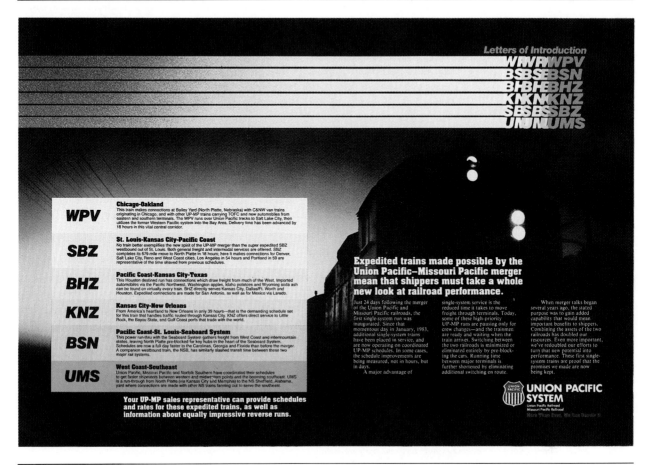

Source: Courtesy of the Union Pacific System.

Railroad and the Union Pacific system offer a run-through train from Chicago to Los Angeles. This train consistently covers the 2,050 miles in less than 48 hours, carrying daily more than 100 trailers and marine containers. Other run-throughs—between the Union Pacific system and Conrail at St. Elmo, Illinois, and with the Chessie System via Salem, Illinois—expedite boxcars and unit trains to their destinations, as exemplified in Figure 13.3.

The Changing Structure of the Railroad Industry   A major change in the structure of the railroad industry is the steady decline in the number of Class I railroads (those earning more than $50 million in annual gross revenues) primarily through consolidations and mergers. There were only 31 Class I railroads in 1983, and only 9 carriers controlled nearly 90 percent of Class I revenues, more than 92 percent of all revenue ton-miles and more than 89 percent of the nation's trackage. In the past, rail shippers had to resort to interlining—using more than one rail carrier when long distances between the shipment's origin and its destination were involved. As a result, it was easy for one railroad to simply blame other connecting railroads for service problems.

The increased number of rail mergers are typically "end-to-end," thereby providing shippers with single-carrier service from origin to destination.[10]

Motor Carriers: Flexible and Growing The trucking industry has shown dramatic growth over the past decades. Its prime advantage over the other transportation modes is its relatively fast, consistent service for both large and small shipments. Motor carriers concentrate on manufactured products, while railroads haul more bulk and raw material products. Motor carriers therefore receive greater revenue per ton shipped than do railroads. Motor carriers receive over 20 cents per ton-mile while railroads earn 3.2 cents per ton-mile.[11]

Less-than-truckload (LTL) shipments, those weighing less than 10,000 pounds, are consistently transported from coast to coast in less than six days. A typical example would be an 8,000-pound shipment of color televisions from San Diego to Charlotte, North Carolina. The shipment given to Consolidated Freightways on Friday at 4:00 p.m. is joined with others and by Saturday is in Tucumcari, New Mexico. By Sunday the shipment is in Oklahoma City, and on Monday it has arrived in Memphis. It is delivered to the receiver on Tuesday at 10:30 a.m.[12]

Water Carriers: Slow but Inexpensive There are basically two types of water carriers—the inland or barge lines and the ocean-going deepwater ships. Barge lines are efficient transporters of bulky, low-unit value commodities like grain, gravel, lumber, sand, and steel. A typical lower Mississippi River barge line, as Figure 13.4 illustrates, may be more than a quarter mile in length and 200 feet wide.

Figure 13.4
Barge Traffic: Low-Cost Transportation Mode

Source: Courtesy of Trailer Marine Transport Corporation.

Ocean-going ships operate on the Great Lakes, between United States port cities, and in international commerce. Water carrier costs average 0.6 cents per ton-mile.

Pipelines: Specialized Transporters   Even though the pipeline industry ranks second only to railroads in number of ton-miles transported, many people are barely aware of its existence. More than 213,000 miles of pipelines crisscross the United States. Pipelines serve as extremely efficient transporters of natural gas and oil products, as evidenced by the latter's average revenue per ton-mile of 1.2 cents.[13] Oil pipelines carry two types of commodities—crude (unprocessed) oil and refined products, such as gasoline and kerosene. There is also a slow but steady growth in the use of slurry pipelines. In this method of transport, a product such as coal is ground up into a powder, mixed with water, and transported in suspension through the pipeline.[14]

Although pipelines represent a low-maintenance, dependable method of transportation, they possess a number of characteristics that limit their use. Their availability in different locations is even more limited than water carriers, and their use is restricted to a relatively small number of products that can be transported in this manner. Finally, pipelines represent a relatively slow method of transportation. Liquids travel through pipelines at an average of only three or four miles per hour.

Air Freight: Fast but Expensive   The use of air carriers has been growing significantly. In 1961, U.S. domestic airlines flew about 1 billion ton-miles. By 1985 this figure had jumped to 5 billion ton-miles. However, air freight is still a relatively insignificant percentage of the total ton-miles shipped, amounting to one-fifth of 1 percent in 1985.[15]

Because of air freight's relatively high cost, it is used primarily for valuable or highly perishable products. Typical shipments consist of computers, furs, fresh flowers, high-fashion clothing, live lobsters, and watches. Air carriers often offset their higher transportation costs with reduced inventory holding costs and faster customer service.

One result of airline deregulation was the simplification of regulations concerning the creation of new airline companies. In the first three years following deregulation, new air carriers such as Midway, New York Air, People Express, Sun Pacific, Sun Air, Pacific Express, and Air Chicago began operations. All of these carriers are primarily passenger-oriented, although some freight service is available.[16] Figure 13.5 ranks the five transport modes on several bases.

Freight Forwarders: Transportation Intermediaries   Freight forwarders are considered transportation intermediaries because their function is to consolidate shipments to get lower rates for their customers. The transport rates on less-than-truckload (LTL) and less-than-carload (LCL) shipments are often twice as high on a per-unit basis as are the rates on truckload (TL) and carload (CL) shipments. Freight forwarders charge less than the higher rates but more than the lower rates. They make their profit by paying the carriers the lower rates. By consolidating shipments, freight forwarders offer their customers two advantages—lower costs on small shipments and faster delivery service than the LTL and LCL shippers.

Supplemental Carriers   The physical distribution manager can also utilize a number of auxiliary, or supplemental, carriers that specialize in transporting

Figure 13.5
Comparing the Transport Modes

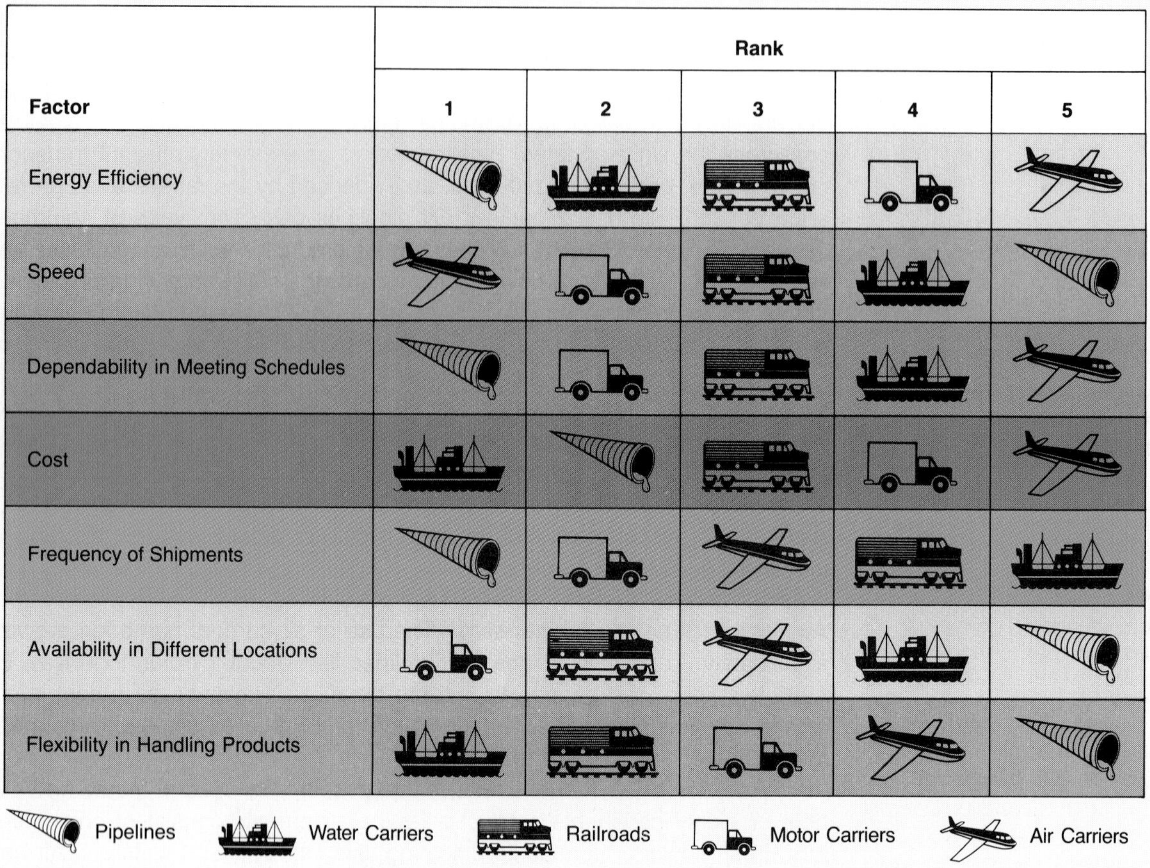

Factor	Rank				
	1	2	3	4	5
Energy Efficiency	Pipelines	Water Carriers	Railroads	Motor Carriers	Air Carriers
Speed	Air Carriers	Motor Carriers	Railroads	Water Carriers	Pipelines
Dependability in Meeting Schedules	Pipelines	Motor Carriers	Railroads	Water Carriers	Air Carriers
Cost	Water Carriers	Pipelines	Railroads	Motor Carriers	Air Carriers
Frequency of Shipments	Pipelines	Motor Carriers	Air Carriers	Railroads	Water Carriers
Availability in Different Locations	Motor Carriers	Railroads	Air Carriers	Water Carriers	Pipelines
Flexibility in Handling Products	Water Carriers	Railroads	Motor Carriers	Air Carriers	Pipelines

Pipelines   Water Carriers   Railroads   Motor Carriers   Air Carriers

Sources: The energy-efficiency rankings are reported in Eric Hirst, *Energy Intensiveness of Passenger and Freight Modes*, National Science Foundation, Oak Ridge National Laboratory, March 1972, p. 27. The other factors and rankings are based on a discussion in James L. Heskitt, Nicholas A. Glaskowsky, Jr., and Robert M. Ivie, *Business Logistics* (New York: Ronald Press, 1973), pp. 113–118. Used by permission.

small shipments. These carriers include bus freight services, United Parcel Service, and the U.S. Postal Service.

Intermodal Coordination   The various transport modes often combine their services to give shippers the service and cost advantages of each mode. Piggyback, discussed earlier and illustrated in Figure 13.6, is the most widely accepted form of coordination. The combination of truck and rail services generally gives shippers faster service and lower rates than either mode does individually, since each method is used where it is most efficient. Shipper acceptance of piggybacking has been tremendous. In 1955 fewer than 200,000 piggyback rail cars were shipped. By 1983 more than 2.3 million cars were involved. Piggyback shipments are expected to account for 40 percent of all rail-car loadings by 1995.[17] The ICC exempted piggyback service from government regulation, a move that is expected to increase competition and improve growth prospects for this concept.[18]

Another form of intermodal coordination is birdyback. Here, motor carriers deliver and pick up the shipment, and air carriers take it over the long

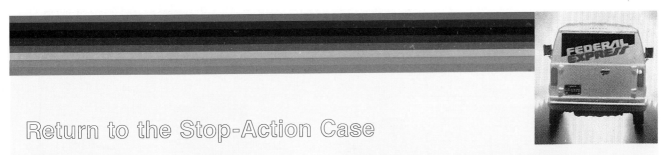

Return to the Stop-Action Case

Federal Express

From Federal Express's earliest years, company executives understood the importance of attracting customers and differentiating the company from other small-package delivery services. This marketing commitment began in 1974 when, although the company was losing $1 million a month, it spent $150,000 on television advertising in six key markets. The advertising campaign presented the following message:

America, you've got a new airline. The first major airline in over 30 years. There's no first class, no meals, no movies. In fact, no passengers. Just packages. Small important shipments that have to get where they're going overnight. And up to now have had to fly at the mercy of the passenger airlines. Not anymore. Federal Express. A whole new airline for packages only.

This advertising strategy boosted Federal's package volume from 3,000 to 10,000 pieces a night.

The next advertising campaign began in 1975 with ads that focused on Federal's competition—Emery Air Freight, then the leader in the small-package industry. Ads compared Federal's next-day delivery rate to Emery's, which showed that Federal's on-time delivery rate was way ahead of Emery's. Again, the campaign substantially boosted Federal's business. The campaign continued

with ads that said "Take Away Our Planes and We'd Be Just Like Everybody." This slogan positioned Federal against all other small-package delivery services.

Although by 1977 Federal Express had turned the financial corner and was beginning to earn a profit, company executives were concerned that they had not reached a large segment of the public. Federal Express decided to change its focus: Instead of explaining the system and its superiority, Federal concentrated on customers and their problems with the theme "When It Absolutely, Positively Has To Be There Overnight." The success of this campaign caused Federal Express's package volume to soar to 39,000 pieces a night.

Later commercials emphasized convenience, price, and service reliability and introduced the Courier Pak. The 1982 campaign, which featured a fast-talking man, increased Federal's visibility and success even more.

In 1983, Federal Express shifted its advertising emphasis from speed and reliability to specific superiorities of its service. Using the tag line—"Why Fool Around with Anyone Else?"—the ads communicated this message: "Express transactions are so important that when they go wrong, someone pays a big price. Therefore, it doesn't make sense to take a chance on anyone else."

Source: "Advertising Success at Federal Express," *Federal Express Report* (March 1984).

---

distance. Fishyback is a form of intermodal coordination between motor carriers and water carriers.

The Multimodal Transportation Company Another form of intermodal coordination is performed by multimodal transportation companies. Piggyback is generally performed by two separate companies: a railroad and a trucking company. A multimodal firm provides intermodal service in which all the modes of transportation are owned and operated by one company. The advantage to the shipper is that the one carrier service has responsibility from origin to destination. There can be no argument about which carrier caused the shipment to be late or who was responsible for a loss or damage.

The Denver and Rio Grande Western Railroad is an example of the above trend. In 1983 it received nationwide trucking service authorization from the ICC. In the same year, United States Lines, a large ocean carrier, received ICC approval to establish a nationwide trucking company serving as a feeder to the shipping company. In addition, Consolidated Freightways, one of the

Figure 13.6
Intermodal Coordination: An Important Aspect of Physical Distribution

Source: Courtesy of Chicago and North Western Transportation Company.

largest trucking companies in the United States, has been expanding into the air-freight forwarding business. Raymond F. O'Brien, chairman of CF, noted: "CF has no intention of becoming a railroad, but we do plan to offer various types of intermodal service as well as virtually any other kind of service a customer might want."[19]

Warehouses and Their Locations

Storage Warehouse
Traditional warehouse where products are stored prior to shipment.

Distribution Warehouse
Facility designed to assemble and then redistribute products to facilitate rapid movement of products to purchasers.

Two types of warehouses exist: storage and distribution. A storage warehouse stores products for moderate to long periods of time in an attempt to balance supply and demand for producers and purchasers. They are used most often by firms whose products are seasonal in supply or demand.

The distribution warehouse assembles and redistributes products, keeping them on the move as much as possible. Many distribution warehouses or centers actually store the goods physically for less than one day.

In an attempt to reduce transportation costs, manufacturers have developed central distribution centers. A manufacturer located in Philadelphia with customers in the Illinois, Wisconsin, and Indiana area could send each customer a direct shipment. But if each customer places small orders, the transportation charges for the individual shipments will be relatively high. A feasible solution is to send a large, consolidated shipment to a break-bulk center, a central distribution center that breaks down large shipments into several smaller ones and delivers them to individual customers in the area. For the manager in Philadelphia, the feasible break-bulk center might be located in Chicago.

Inversely, the make-bulk center consolidates several small shipments into one large shipment and delivers it to its destination. For example, a giant retailer like Safeway Stores may operate several satellite production facilities in a given area. Each plant can send shipments to a storage warehouse in Dallas. This, however, could result in a large number of small, expensive shipments. If a make-bulk center is created in San Francisco, and each supplier sends its shipments there, all deliveries bound for Dallas could be consolidated into one economical shipment.

The top five distribution center cities in the United States, as measured by the total number of break-bulk distribution centers, are Chicago, Los Angeles–Long Beach, the New York City area, Dallas–Fort Worth, and Atlanta.

Automated Warehouses

Warehouses lend themselves well to automation, with the computer the heart of the operation. Outstanding examples of automation at work are the six JCPenney Catalog Distribution Centers located throughout the country. In Penney's Manchester, Connecticut, center, which is shown in Figure 13.7—a facility larger than 35 football fields—a complex system of computers moves over 25,000 pieces of merchandise on and off more than 196,000 shelves

Figure 13.7
JCPenney Catalog Distribution Center in Manchester, Connecticut

each hour. The computers are involved in every phase of the distribution operation, including merchandise receipt, inventory tracking, order processing, packing and invoice preparation, and shipping.

Although automated warehouses may cost as much as $10 million, they can provide major savings to high-volume distributors such as grocery chains. They can "read" computerized store orders, choose the correct number of cases, and move them in the desired sequence to loading docks. These warehouses reduce labor costs, worker injuries, pilferage, fires, and breakage; they also assist in inventory control.

Location Factors

A major decision facing each company deals with the number and location of its storage facilities. The two general factors involved are (1) warehousing and materials handling costs and (2) delivery costs from the warehouse to the customer. The first costs are subject to economies of scale; therefore, on a per-unit basis, they decrease as volume increases. Delivery costs, on the other hand, increase as the distance from the warehouse location to the customer increases.

The specific location of the firm's warehouses presents a complicated problem. Factors that must be considered include (1) local, county, and state taxes; (2) local, county, and state laws and regulations; (3) availability of a trained labor force; (4) police and fire protection; (5) access to the various transport modes; (6) community attitude toward the proposed warehouses; and (7) the cost and availability of public utilities, such as electricity and natural gas.

Inventory Control Systems _____

Inventory control is a major component in the physical distribution system. Current estimates of inventory holding costs are about 25 percent per year. This means that $1,000 of inventory held for a single year costs the company $250. Inventory costs include such expenses as storage facilities, insurance, taxes, handling costs, opportunity costs for funds invested in inventory, and depreciation and possible obsolescence of the goods in inventory.[20]

EOQ (Economic Order Quantity) Model
Technique devised to determine the optimal order quantity of each product; the optimal point is determined by balancing the costs of holding inventory and the costs involved in placing orders.

Inventory control analysts have developed a number of techniques to help the physical distribution manager effectively control inventory. The most basic is the EOQ (economic order quantity) model. This technique emphasizes a cost trade-off between two fundamental costs involved with inventory: inventory holding costs that increase with the addition of more inventory, and order costs that decrease as the quantity ordered increases. As Figure 13.8 indicates, these two cost items are traded off to determine the optimal order quantity of each product.

The EOQ point in Figure 13.8 is the point at which total cost is minimized. By placing an order for this amount as needed, firms can minimize their inventory costs.

The Just-In-Time System

Just-in-Time (JIT) Inventory System
Inventory control system designed to minimize inventory at production facilities.

As the Buick City Stop-Action Case in Chapter 11 illustrates, a new approach to inventory control borrowed from the Japanese is rapidly gaining acceptance in the United States. This approach, known as the just-in-time (JIT) inventory system, involves minimizing inventory at each production facility. Manu-

Figure 13.8
The EOQ Model

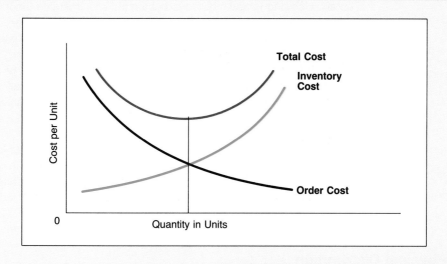

facturers prefer this system because it greatly reduces their levels of inventory carrying costs. Often, parts arrive the same day they are used in the production process. Just-in-time inventory control requires precise delivery schedules that place great emphasis on the purchaser's traffic department working with carriers to ensure timely delivery. The seller must also have efficient personnel to ensure that products arrive when they are scheduled. Because Dana Corporation, a major supplier to the car and truck industries, wants to assure its customers with timely delivery schedules, it is relocating production plants to be in close proximity to its major customers.[21]

Order Processing

Like customer service standards, order processing is a quasi-logistics function. The physical distribution manager is concerned with order processing because it directly affects the firm's ability to meet its customer service standards. If a firm's order processing system is inefficient, the company may have to compensate by using costly, premium transportation or increasing the number of field warehouses in all major markets.

Materials Handling Systems

Materials Handling
All activities involved in moving products within a manufacturer's production facilities, warehouses, and transportation company terminals.

Unitizing
Combination of as many packages as possible into one load, preferably on a pallet in order to produce faster product movement and reduce damage and pilferage.

All the activities associated in moving products within the manufacturer's plants, warehouses, and transportation company terminals comprise the materials handling component of physical distribution. These activities must be thoroughly coordinated for both intracompany and intercompany activities. The efficiency of plants and warehouses is dependent on an effective system.[22]

Two important innovations have been developed in the area of materials handling. One is known as unitizing—combining as many packages as possible into one load, preferably on a pallet (a platform, generally made of wood, on which products are transported). Unitizing can be accomplished by using steel bands to hold the unit in place or by shrink packaging. Shrink packages are constructed by placing a sheet of plastic over the unit and then heating it. As the plastic cools, it shrinks and holds the individual packages together securely. Unitizing is advantageous because it requires little labor per package, promotes fast movement, and minimizes damage and pilferage.

Containerization
Combination of several unitized loads of products into a single load to facilitate intertransport changes in transportation modes.

The second innovation is containerization, the combination of several unitized loads. It is typically a big box eight feet wide, eight feet high and ten, twenty, thirty, or forty feet long. Such containers allow ease of intertransport mode changes. A container of oil rig parts, for example, can be loaded in Tulsa and trucked to Kansas City, where it can be placed on a high-speed, run-through train to New York City. There it can be placed on a ship and sent to Saudi Arabia.

Containerization also markedly reduces the time involved in loading and unloading ships. Container ships can often be unloaded in less than 24 hours—a task that otherwise can take up to two weeks. In-transit damage is also reduced, because individual packages are not handled en route to the purchaser.

International Physical Distribution

The United States has experienced rapid growth in international trade since World War II. In 1983, U.S. merchandise exports totaled approximately $201 billion, and total imports amounted to $270 billion. Only ten years earlier, U.S. exports and imports totaled $71.6 billion and $74 billion, respectively. The growth of international commerce has placed new responsibilities on physical distribution departments.

A major problem facing international marketers is the flood of paperwork involved in exporting products. More than a hundred different international trade documents representing more than a thousand separate forms must be completed for each international shipment. The result is that an average export shipment requires approximately 36 employee hours for documentation and 27 employee hours for importing a shipment. Paperwork alone equals 7 percent of the total value of U.S. international trade. Many physical distribution departments are not large enough to employ international specialists, and they subcontract the work to *foreign freight forwarders,* wholesaling intermediaries who specialize in physical distribution outside the United States.

The major impetus to exporting has been the advent of containerization and container ships. One shipping company currently has container ships that can make a round trip between New York, Bremerhaven, and Rotterdam in fourteen days. Only four days are needed for crossing the Atlantic and another six for three port calls. This speed allows U.S. exporters to provide competitive delivery schedules to European markets.

Summary

Physical distribution involves a broad range of activities concerned with the efficient movement of finished products from the end of the production line to the consumer. Physical distribution, as a system, consists of six elements: (1) customer service, (2) transportation, (3) inventory control, (4) materials handling, (5) order processing, and (6) warehousing. These elements are interrelated and must be balanced for a smoothly functioning distribution system and to avoid suboptimization. The physical distribution department is one of the classic examples of the systems approach to business problems.

The goal of a physical distribution department is to produce a specified level of customer service while minimizing the costs involved in physically moving and storing the product from its production to the point where it is ultimately purchased.

The physical distribution manager has five transportation alternatives: railroads, motor carriers, water carriers, pipelines, and air freight. Intermodal transport systems are also available and are increasingly being used. Deregulation has had a profound effect on transportation in recent years. Many transporters are now free to develop unique solutions to shippers' needs.

Other important aspects of physical distribution involve warehouses and their locations; inventory control systems, including the popular just-in-time system; order processing; and materials handling systems. Chapter 13 concludes with a discussion of international physical distribution.

Solving the Stop-Action Case

Federal Express

Starting in 1979, Federal Express began expanding the range of its services and improving existing services. The Courier Pak overnight envelope was introduced to transport documents, reports, and other lightweight items overnight. In 1981, Federal took advantage of a new, free-enterprise approach adopted by the U.S. Postal Service, which made it possible for private companies to carry letter mail. The result: Federal's Overnight Letter, a service that accounted for 5,000 pieces of mail a night when first introduced and that skyrocketed to more than 75,000 pieces nightly over the next three years.

Federal made one of its most important service changes in 1982 when it bettered its own promised delivery time. Overnight packages would now be delivered by 10:30 a.m. instead of noon. Known as "Operation Earlybird," this earlier delivery time not only enabled consumers to get their priority mail by mid-morning, it also helped prepare Federal for the introduction in 1984 of electronic image transmission.

Federal has also followed a steady plan of geographic expansion. In 1983 new Metropolitan Areas were added to its service region. These additions enabled Federal to serve 85 percent of the population, moving it closer to its goal of reaching 95 percent of the population within the next few years. Growth has also included the acceptance of increasingly heavier packages. By July 1, 1984, Federal was accepting packages weighing up to 150

Photo Source: This photograph is used pursuant to a license agreement with Federal Express Corporation.

pounds, more than twice the accepted weight during the company's early years.

As a result of these service improvements, Federal Express handled over 300,000 packages a night at the close of 1983. With over a half million accounts and the ability to reach more than 179 million people in 40,000 communities with direct overnight service, Federal was still the market leader in the $3 billion express mail industry.

To cement its lead throughout the 1980s, Federal introduced ZapMail in 1984, a revolutionary electronic mail system that enables Federal to transmit and deliver, door to door within two hours, facsimile copies of documents that were delivered overnight in trucks and planes. With more than 42 percent of its revenue and 60 percent of its unit volume coming from reports, letters, blueprints, and other documents that could be sent electronically, Federal sees an enormous potential in this new service.

Federal is also undertaking a new international delivery service that promises delivery within 48 hours. On the back burner are other services that will enable Federal to maintain its competitive position. The company has its eye on the sky for the next market target. It is exploring such possibilities as putting its own fleet of satellites into space and providing financing, insurance, and technical assistance for other commercial users of space.

Throughout these changes, Federal has always maintained its focus on its primary market—businesses and individuals who must transport small packages overnight. Thomas R. Oliver, a Federal Express senior vice-president, commented: "Corporate America is littered with the burned-out hulks of companies that started out doing one thing and then tried to do something else." Federal's mission, he said, is to be a "fast and reliable carrier," regardless of whether the carrying is by plane, satellite, or van.

Source: David Stipp, "Helloooooo Electronics, Federal Says," *The Wall Street Journal* (April 28, 1982), p. 29.

Questions for Discussion

1. Why was physical distribution one of the last areas in most companies to be carefully studied and improved?

2. Outline the basic reasons for the increased attention to physical distribution management.

3. The text comments: "The study of physical distribution is one of the classic examples of the systems approach to business problems." Explain the statement.

4. What is the basic objective of physical distribution?

5. Explain the role of customer service standards in the physical distribution system.

6. Outline the evolution and the results of transportation deregulation.

7. Suggest the most appropriate method of transportation for each of the following products and defend your choices:

   a. Iron ore
   b. Dash detergent
   c. Heavy earth-moving equipment
   d. Crude oil
   e. Orchids
   f. Lumber

8. Discuss the new services offered by railroads.

9. Discuss the basic strengths and weaknesses of each mode of transportation.

10. Outline the current status in terms of ton-miles of the various transportation modes.

11. Which mode of transportation do you believe will experience the greatest ton-mile percentage during the 1980s? Why?

12. Under what circumstances are freight forwarders used?

13. Identify the major forms of intermodal coordination and give an example of a product likely to use each type.

14. Explain the role of multimodal transportation companies in physical distribution.

15. Differentiate between a storage warehouse and a distribution warehouse.

16. What factors should be considered in locating a new warehouse?

17. Explain the just-in-time system of inventory control.

18. Comment on the following statement: The popularity of physical distribution management is a fad; ten years from now it will be considered a relatively unimportant function of the firm.

19. Discuss the basic cost factors involved in the EOQ model. Does the basic EOQ model consider all relevant costs? Explain.

20. Discuss the similarities of and differences between domestic and international physical distribution.

Case: The Chinese Cabbage Problem

Peking—Here in this Chinese capital, winter time is cabbage time.

Trucks trundle through the streets dumping big loads of cabbage helter-skelter. The piles loom six feet high and higher. Workers are released from factories to stack and sort. Children play on it, leaping from mound to mound. Old men sleep in it, curled up among the leaves.

Cabbage dangles from the backs of bicycles and pedicabs. It spills over the tops of high-rise balconies and covers the roofs of courtyard-style houses. It flaps from the clotheslines of homes with yards and peeks out from beneath the beds of those without.

China may claim to be marching toward modernization, but the country still feeds its people as it has for millennia, directly from the land. Transportation is inadequate and storage is minimal, so when crops ripen, they are eaten. For two weeks in the summer, tomatoes appear in enormous abundance in the streets, are crushed under foot, and as suddenly as they proliferate, become scarce again. Melons, too, rot in the street in June and July and then vanish for another year.

But of all the harvests that fill the streets with a temporary abundance, cabbage is the most important. Unlike the summer crops, which follow each other in rapid succession, cabbage is almost all there will be the next three months. As soon as the weather grows chilly, the entire city buckles down to stash away enough of it to last until spring. . . .

But without a well-developed system of long-distance transport to bring variety and supply from warmer climates, keeping fruits and vegetables in city dwellers' diets remains a problem. The Chinese government estimates that rail transport can handle only 70 percent of the necessary cargo, and most is devoted to industrial use. Long-distance trucking is minimal, because of both the poor condition of the roads and the small number of available vehicles. . . .

Questions

1. What does this illustration suggest about the importance of physical distribution in a developing economy? Discuss.

2. What steps would you suggest the Chinese take to combat their annual cabbage problem? Explain your suggestions.

3. Can you cite any examples of where physical distribution failures have had a negative impact on the U.S. economy? Discuss.

Computer Applications

The physical distribution manager must balance two types of costs involved with inventory: (1) inventory holding costs that increase with the addition of more inventory and (2) order costs that decrease as the quantity ordered increases. The *economic order quantity (EOQ)* model is a particularly useful quantitative technique for determining the order size that most effectively balances these two different types of costs. It is described in more detail in this chapter on pages 366–367.

The following formula is used to determine the economic order quantity:

$$EOQ = \sqrt{\frac{2RS}{IC}}$$

where
EOQ = the economic order quantity (in units)
 R = the annual rate of usage
 S = the cost of placing an order
 I = the annual inventory carrying costs expressed as a percentage
 C = the cost per unit of the item. The "unit" may consist of a single item or a prepackaged box containing a dozen items, a gross, or even more.

In the above formula, R is an estimate based upon the demand forecast for the item. S is calculated from the firm's cost records. I is also an estimate based upon the costs of such items as handling, insurance, interest, storage, depreciation, and taxes. Since the costs of the item may vary over time, C is also likely to be an estimate. By inserting specific data into the formula, the EOQ can be determined. Consider, for example, the following data:

$$R = 6{,}000$$
$$S = \$8.50$$
$$I = 15 \text{ percent}$$
$$C = \$14.50$$
$$EOQ = \sqrt{\frac{(2)(6{,}000)(8.50)}{(14.50)(.15)}}$$
$$= 216.56.$$

Since the EOQ model involves a mathematical formula, the calculation often results in a fractional answer that must be rounded to the next whole number to determine the economic order quantity. Thus, the EOQ in the above example would be rounded to 217 units.

Even though the exact EOQ calculation has been determined to be 217 units, other factors may have to be considered. For instance, suppliers may place additional constraints on the ordering firm. In other cases, orders may be limited to even dozens or multiples of 100. In such instances, the economic order quantity must be adjusted to match these constraints.

Directions: Use menu item 12 titled "Economic Order Quantity (EOQ)" to solve the following problems.

Problem 1 An Albuquerque, New Mexico, retailer sells about 220 dozen of a certain brand of men's shirts each year. The wholesale cost is $145 per dozen. The retailer tries to keep the inventory as low as possible because of a 26 percent annual carrying cost. Each order costs the store $30 to place. Calculate the EOQ for the Albuquerque retailer.

Problem 2 Appliance City, of Roanoke, Virginia, sells 160 refrigerators annually. The store pays an average of $300 for these units, with each order costing $25 to place. The annual inventory carrying cost percentage is 10 percent. What is the appropriate EOQ for Appliance City?

Problem 3 A souvenir shop near Rapid City, South Dakota, pays 12 cents for each of the 30,000 postcards it sells annually. Inventory carrying costs are a modest 5 percent, and placing an order costs only $5. Calculate the EOQ for the South Dakota retailer.

Problem 4 A Pawtucket, Rhode Island, motorcycle shop has an order placement cost of $50 for its $75 helmets (wholesale cost). Its average annual inventory carrying cost is 15 percent. The shop sells 250 helmets each year.

a.   Determine the EOQ for the motorcycle helmets.

b.   Determine the most appropriate order size if the shop's supplier decides to require that all orders be placed in multiples of one dozen.

Problem 5 The owner of an El Paso, Texas, sporting goods retail store wants to calculate the EOQ for a certain line of tennis racquets. The racquets cost the store $20 and have an average inventory carrying cost of 25 percent. Each order costs $25. The El Paso store sells 600 of these racquets each year.

a.   Determine the economic order quantity for the tennis racquets.

b.   Suggest the most appropriate order size if the manufacturer insists that orders be placed in multiples of 10 racquets.

Promotional Strategy

Introduction to Promotion

Key Terms

promotion
marketing communications
AIDA concept
promotional mix
personal selling
advertising
sales promotion
public relations
publicity
pulling strategy
pushing strategy
percentage-of-sales method
fixed-sum-per-unit method
task-objective method

Learning Goals

1. To explain the relationship of promotional strategy to the process of communication
2. To explain the concept of the promotional mix and its relationship to the marketing mix
3. To identify the primary determinants of a promotional mix
4. To contrast the two major alternative promotional strategies
5. To list the objectives of promotion
6. To compare the primary methods of developing a promotional budget
7. To defend promotion against the public criticisms that are sometimes raised

Stop-Action Case

The Louisville Redbirds

A. Ray Smith owned a construction business in Tulsa until 1960 when he fell victim to baseball fever. Asked by city officials to help save Tulsa's minor league club, Smith and a number of other civic-minded citizens funded the team for one year. The next year Smith sold his construction company, bought the team outright, and made baseball his life.

The Redbirds, as Smith's team is now known, remained in Tulsa until 1977 when its stadium became unusable. From there, the team moved to New Orleans and then to Springfield, Illinois, for short, unhappy stays. "The powers that be looked on the minor leagues with contempt," said Smith. Equally limiting was the size of Springfield's baseball park, which accommodated only 4,800 fans.

When Louisville, Kentucky, offered his team the chance to play in its newly refurbished 32,000-seat stadium, Smith couldn't refuse. The 1970s had been bleak times for baseball fans in Louisville. Although baseball had been played there since the sport's earliest days, the city lost its Triple-A franchise in 1972 after it constructed a new 18,000-seat facility that accommodated the University of Louisville football team but that proved virtually unworkable as a baseball field.

Even though Smith's team was affiliated with the St. Louis Cardinals, a team whose regional location drew thousands of followers from the Louisville area, he realized that an effective marketing strategy had to be developed to attract fans to the stadium and induce them to become regular Redbirds followers. Because the city had gone nine years without a minor league team, promotional decisions had to be made to communicate information about the new team and to persuade fans to support it. "Used to be that people would go to the ballpark to watch the game," said Smith. "The crowd would be 80 percent men and boys. Now it's a whole family thing, and Disneyland is the model. People want entertainment, and they demand comfort and cleanliness. You don't give it to them and they'll stay home, no matter who's playing."

Assignment: Use the materials in Chapter 14 to recommend methods to be used by Louisville Redbirds' marketers to attract baseball fans.

Photo Source: Courtesy of Louisville Redbirds.

Source: Smith quotes from Frederick C. Klein, "Owner of Louisville Redbirds Finds Success in Baseball-as-Entertainment Philosophy," *The Wall Street Journal* (August 10, 1983), p. 27.

Chapter Overview

Thus far the text has examined two of the four broad variables of the marketing mix. Chapters 8 and 9 described the decisions and problems in choosing the right products and services for the firm's market target. Chapters 10 through 13 focused on distribution—the problems, activities, and marketing institutions involved in channeling selected products and services to the firm's market target. Part Six analyzes the third marketing mix variable—promotion. Chapter 14 introduces promotion and briefly describes the variables that comprise a firm's promotional mix—personal selling and nonpersonal selling—and the factors that determine the optimal mix. The objectives of promotion are identified, and the importance of developing promotional budgets and measuring the effectiveness of promotion are described. Finally, the importance of the business, economic, and social aspects of promotion are critically assessed. Chapter 15 discusses advertising, sales promotion, and the other nonpersonal selling elements of the promotional mix. Chapter 16 completes this section by focusing on personal selling.

Promotion
Function of informing, persuading, and influencing the consumer's purchase decision.

A good place to begin the discussion of promotion is by defining the term. Promotion is the function of informing, persuading, and influencing the consumer's purchase decision. Figure 14.1 depicts the relationship between the firm's promotional strategy and the other elements of the overall marketing strategy in accomplishing organizational objectives and producing utility for the consumer.

The marketing manager sets the goals and objectives of the firm's promotional strategy in accordance with overall organizational objectives and the goals of the marketing organization. Then, based on these goals, the various elements of the strategy—personal selling, advertising, sales promotion, publicity, and public relations—are formulated in a coordinated promotional plan. This becomes an integral part of the total marketing strategy for reaching selected consumer segments. Finally, the feedback mechanism, in such forms as marketing research and field reports, completes the system by identifying any deviations from the plan and by suggesting modifications for improvement.

Marketing Communications
Transmission from a sender to a receiver of messages dealing with buyer–seller relationships.

Promotional strategy is closely related to the process of communication. A standard definition of *communication* is the transmission of a message from a sender to a receiver. Marketing communications, then, are those messages that deal with buyer-seller relationships. Marketing communication is a

Figure 14.1
How Promotion Fits in the Total Marketing Mix

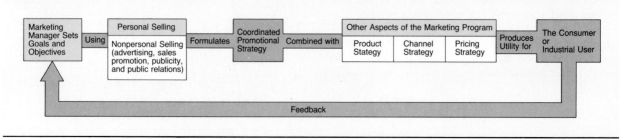

broader concept than promotional strategy since it includes word-of-mouth advertising and other forms of unsystematic communication. A planned promotional strategy, however, is certainly the most important part of marketing communications.

The Communications Process

Figure 14.2 shows a general communications process and its application to promotional strategy. The sender is the source of the communications system since he or she seeks to convey a message (a communication of information or advice or a request) to a receiver (the recipient of the communication). The message must accomplish three tasks to be effective:

1. It must gain the attention of the receiver.
2. It must be understood by both the receiver and the sender.
3. It must stimulate the needs of the receiver and suggest an appropriate method of satisfying these needs.[1]

AIDA Concept
Acronym for attention-interest-desire-action; the traditional explanation of the steps an individual must go through prior to making a purchase decision.

The three tasks are related to the **AIDA (attention-interest-desire-action) concept** proposed by E. K. Strong more than 50 years ago as an explanation of the steps an individual must go through before making a purchase decision. First, the potential consumer's attention must be gained. Once this is accomplished, the promotional message seeks to arouse interest in the product or service. If interest is aroused, the next stage is to stimulate consumer desire by convincing the would-be buyer of the product's ability to satisfy his or her needs. Finally, the sales presentation or advertisement attempts to produce action in the form of a purchase or a more favorable attitude that may lead to future purchases.

The message must be *encoded*, or translated into understandable terms, and transmitted through a communications medium. *Decoding* is the receiver's interpretation of the message. The receiver's response, known as *feedback*, completes the system. Throughout the process, *noise* can interfere with the transmission of the message and reduce its effectiveness.

The marketing manager is the sender in the system, as shown in Figure 14.2. The message is encoded in the form of sales presentations, advertisements, displays, or publicity releases. The *transfer mechanism* for delivering the message may be a salesperson, a public relations channel, or an advertising medium. The decoding step involves the consumer's interpretation of the sender's message. This is often the most troublesome aspect of marketing communications because consumers do not always interpret a promotional message in the same way as the sender. Since receivers are likely to decode messages based upon their own frames of reference or individual experiences, the sender must be careful to ensure that the message is encoded to match the target audience.

Feedback is the receiver's response to the message. It may take the form of attitude change, purchase, or nonpurchase. In some instances, firms may use promotion to create a favorable attitude toward their new products or services. Such attitude changes may result in future purchases. In other instances, the objective of the promotional communication may be to stimulate consumer purchases. Such purchases indicate positive responses to the firm, its product/service offerings, its distribution channels, its prices, and its pro-

Figure 14.2
Relating Promotion to the Communications Process

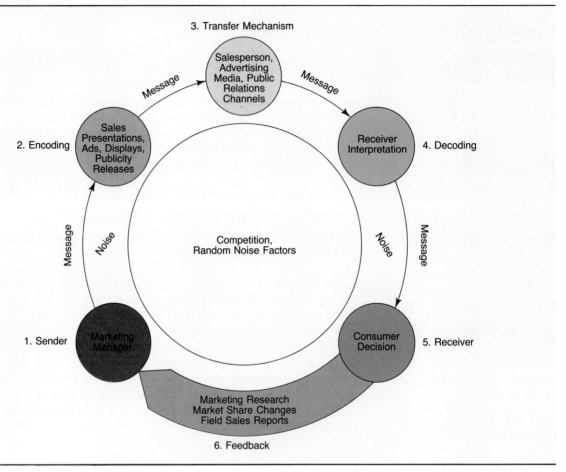

motion. Even nonpurchases may serve as feedback to the sender. They may result from ineffective communication in which the message was not believed or not remembered, or the message may fail to persuade the receiver that the firm's products or services are superior to its competitors. Feedback can be obtained from such techniques as marketing research studies and field sales reports.

Noise represents interference at some stage in the communications process. It may result from such factors as competitive promotional messages being transmitted over the same communications channel, misinterpretation of a sales presentation or advertising message, receipt of the promotional message by the wrong person, or random noise factors such as people conversing during a television commercial or leaving the room. When Sunlight liquid detergent was introduced with the promotional theme "containing real lemon juice," Sunlight marketers were shocked to discover that some consumers who received trial samples mistook the detergent for lemon juice. A few product misusers were even hospitalized.

Table 14.1 illustrates the steps in the communications process with several examples of promotional messages. Although the types of promotion may

Table 14.1

Examples of Marketing Communications

Type of Promotion	Sender	Encoding	Transfer Mechanism	Decoding by Receiver	Feedback
Personal Selling	Lanier Business Products	Sales presentation on new model word processor	Lanier sales representative	Office manager and employees in local firm discuss Lanier sales presentation and those of competing suppliers.	Order placed for the Lanier word processor
Two-Dollar-Off Coupon (Sales Promotion)	Domino's Pizza	Domino's marketing department and advertising agency	Coupon insert to Sunday newspaper	Newspaper reader sees coupon for pizza and saves it.	Pizza purchased by consumers using the coupon
Television Advertising	Walt Disney Enterprises	Advertisement for a new "G"-rated animated movie is developed by Disney's advertising agency.	Network television during programs with high percentage of viewers under 12 years old	Children see ad and ask their parents to take them; parents see ad and decide to take children.	Movie tickets purchased

Disney Graphic Source: © Walt Disney Productions

vary from a highly personalized sales presentation to such nonpersonal promotions as television advertising and two-dollar-off coupons, each form of promotion goes through each stage in the communications model.

The Promotional Mix

Promotional Mix
Blending of personal selling and nonpersonal selling (including advertising, sales promotion, and public relations) by marketers in an attempt to accomplish promotional objectives.

The promotional mix, like the marketing mix, involves the proper blending of numerous variables to satisfy the needs of the firm's market target and achieve organizational objectives. While the marketing mix is comprised of product, price, promotion, and distribution elements, the promotional mix is a subset of the overall marketing mix. With the promotional mix, the marketing manager attempts to achieve the optimal blending of various promotional elements to accomplish promotional objectives. The components of the promotional mix are personal selling and nonpersonal selling, including advertising, sales promotion, and public relations.

Personal selling and advertising are the most significant elements because they usually account for the bulk of a firm's promotional expenditures. However, all factors contribute to efficient marketing communications. A detailed discussion of each of these elements is presented in the chapters that follow. Here, only a brief definition is given to set the framework for the discussion of promotion.

Personal Selling

Personal Selling
Interpersonal influence process involving a seller's promotional presentation conducted on a person-to-person basis with the buyer.

Personal selling may be defined as a seller's promotional presentation conducted on a person-to-person basis with the buyer. It is a direct face-to-face form of promotion. Selling was the original form of promotion. Today it is estimated that 6 million people in the United States are employed in personal selling.

Nonpersonal Selling

Nonpersonal selling is divided into advertising, sales promotion, and public relations. Advertising is usually regarded as the most important of these forms.

Advertising
Paid, nonpersonal communication through various media by business firms, nonprofit organizations, and individuals who are in some way identified in the advertising message and who hope to inform or persuade members of a particular audience.

Advertising may be defined as paid, nonpersonal communications through various media by business firms, nonprofit organizations, and individuals who are in some way identified in the advertising message and who hope to inform or persuade members of a particular audience.[2] Advertising involves the mass media, such as newspapers, television, radio, magazines, and billboards. Businesses have come to realize the tremendous potential of this form of promotion, and, during recent decades, advertising has become increasingly important in marketing. Mass consumption makes advertising particularly appropriate for products that rely on sending the same promotional message to large audiences.

Sales Promotion
Marketing activities (other than personal selling, advertising, and publicity) that stimulate consumer purchasing and dealer effectiveness; includes displays, trade shows and expositions, demonstrations, and various nonrecurrent selling efforts.

Sales promotion includes marketing activities other than personal selling, advertising, and publicity that stimulate consumer purchasing and dealer effectiveness, such as displays, trade shows and expositions, product demonstrations, and various nonrecurrent selling efforts not used on a regular basis.[3] Sales promotion is usually practiced together with other forms of advertising to emphasize, assist, supplement, or otherwise support the objectives of the promotional program.

Public Relations
Firm's communications and relationships with its various publics.

Public relations is a firm's communications and relationships with its various publics. These publics include the organization's customers, suppliers, stockholders, employees, the government, the general public, and the society in which the organization operates. Public relations programs can be either formal or informal. The critical point is that every organization, whether or not it has a formally organized program, needs to be concerned about its public relations.

Publicity
Stimulation of demand by placing commercially significant news or obtaining favorable media presentation not paid for by an identified sponsor.

Publicity is an important part of an effective public relations effort. It can be defined as the nonpersonal stimulation of demand for a product, service, or organization by placing significant news about it in a published medium or by obtaining favorable presentation of it through radio, television, or the stage that is not paid for by an identified sponsor. Compared to personal selling, advertising, and even sales promotion, expenditures for public relations are usually low in most firms. Since they don't pay for it, companies have less control over the publication by the press of good or bad company news. For this reason, a consumer may find this type of news source more believable than if the news were disseminated directly by the company.

As Table 14.2 indicates, each type of promotion has both advantages and disadvantages. Even though personal selling has a relatively high cost per contact, there is less wasted effort than in nonpersonal forms of promotion such as advertising. Personal selling is often more flexible than the other forms because the salesperson can tailor the sales message to meet the unique needs—or objections—of each potential customer.

Table 14.2

Comparing Alternative Promotional Techniques

Type of Promotion	Personal or Nonpersonal	Cost	Advantages	Disadvantages
Advertising	Nonpersonal	Relatively inexpensive per contact	Appropriate in reaching mass audiences; allows expressiveness and control over message	Considerable waste; difficult to demonstrate product; difficult to close sales; difficult to measure results
Personal Selling	Personal	Expensive per contact	Permits flexible presentation and gains immediate response	Costs more than all other forms per contact; difficult to attract qualified salespeople
Sales Promotion	Nonpersonal	Can be costly	Gains attention and has immediate effect	Easy for others to imitate
Public Relations	Nonpersonal	Relatively inexpensive; publicity is free	Has high degree of believability	Not as easily controlled as other forms

Source: Adapted from David J. Rachman and Elaine Romano, *Modern Marketing*
(Hinsdale, Ill.: The Dryden Press, 1980), p. 450.

On the other hand, advertising is an effective means of reaching mass audiences with the marketer's message. Sales promotion techniques are effective in gaining attention, and public relations efforts such as publicity frequently have a high degree of believability compared to other promotional techniques. The task confronting the marketer is to determine the appropriate blend of each of these techniques in marketing the firm's products and services.

Developing an Optimal Promotional Mix

The blending of advertising, personal selling, sales promotion, and public relations to achieve marketing objectives is the promotional mix. Since quantitative measures to determine the effectiveness of each mix component in a given market segment are not available, the choice of a proper mix of promotional elements is one of the most difficult tasks facing the marketing manager. Factors affecting the promotional mix are: (1) nature of the market, (2) nature of the product, (3) stage in the product life cycle, (4) price, and (5) funds available for promotion.

Nature of the Market

The marketer's target audience has a major impact upon the type of promotion to be used. In cases where there is a limited number of buyers, personal selling may prove highly effective. However, markets characterized by a large number of potential customers scattered over a large geographic area may make the cost of contact by personal salespeople prohibitive. In such instances, advertising may be extensively used. The type of customer also affects the promotional mix. A market target made up of industrial purchasers or retail and wholesale buyers is more likely to be served by firms relying heavily upon personal selling than is a market target consisting of ultimate consumers.

Nature of the Product

A second important factor in determining an effective promotional mix is the product itself. Highly standardized products with minimal servicing requirements are less likely to depend upon personal selling than custom products that are technically complex and require servicing. Consumer goods are more likely to rely heavily upon advertising than are industrial goods.

Within each product category, promotional mixes vary. For example, installations typically involve heavy reliance upon personal selling compared to the marketing of operating supplies. By contrast, the marketing mix for convenience goods is likely to involve more emphasis on manufacturer advertising and less on personal selling. On the other hand, personal selling plays an important role in the marketing of shopping goods, and both personal selling and nonpersonal selling are important in the marketing of specialty goods. A personal selling emphasis is also likely to be more effective in the marketing of products involving trade-ins.

Stage in the Product Life Cycle

The promotional mix must be tailored to the stage in the product life cycle. In the introductory stage, heavy emphasis is placed on personal selling to inform the marketplace of the merits of the new product or service. Salespeople contact marketing intermediaries to secure interest and commitment to handle the new product. Trade shows and exhibitions are frequently used to inform and educate prospective dealers and ultimate consumers. Advertising at this stage is mostly informative, and sales promotional techniques, such as product samples and cents-off coupons, are designed to influence consumer attitudes and stimulate initial purchases.

As the product or service moves into the growth and maturity stages, advertising becomes relatively more important in persuading consumers to make purchases. Personal-selling efforts continue to be directed at marketing intermediaries in an attempt to expand distribution. As more competitors enter the marketplace, advertising stresses product differences to persuade consumers to purchase the firm's brand. Reminder advertisements begin to appear in the maturity and early decline stages.

Price

Price of the product or service is the fourth factor that affects the choice of a promotional mix. Advertising is the dominant promotional mix component for low-unit-value products due to the high costs per contact of personal selling. The cost of an industrial sales call, for example, is estimated at $205. As a result, it has become unprofitable to promote lower-value products and services through personal selling. Advertising, by contrast, permits a low promotional expenditure per sales unit because it reaches mass audiences. For low-value consumer products, such as chewing gum, soft drinks, and snack foods, advertising is the most feasible means of promotion.

Return to the Stop-Action Case

The Louisville Redbirds

Louisville Redbirds owner A. Ray Smith realized that minor league baseball teams are not the only ones worried about designing a promotional mix aimed at bringing in the fans. Ticket sales are also a chronic concern of major league clubs, as witnessed by their big-time, big-money promotional efforts. Smith decided to begin his plans by studying the promotional campaigns of the major league clubs. One recent major league success took place in Chicago.

With 35 promotional events spread out over 81 home games, the Chicago White Sox recently undertook the most ambitious promotional schedule in its history. Included was a $300,000 cash advertising budget that was boosted to $1.5 million by trade arrangements with radio and television stations. Corporate tie-ins were also a key promotional feature. In exchange for contributions that ranged from $6,000 to $100,000, as many as 20 corporate commercials featuring White Sox players were aired on the White Sox-owned cable TV station, and local radio carried an additional 25 radio spots. Team mascots, elaborate fireworks displays, and all-star jacket, beach towel, poster, and ring giveaway days also drew in the fans.

The California Angels placed its promotional dollars on such proven standbys as advertising, in-park promotions, mascots, and musical themes. The team also took extraordinary steps to strengthen ties with the Hispanic, black, and Asian communities through community relations committees and speakers bureaus.

In recent years, the Oakland A's spent about $1 million annually in advertising designed to convince fans that a few hours at the ballpark is more fun than theater, movies, or any other form of entertainment. The team's marketers also decided to upgrade their giveaways to include such items as Adidas workout kits. Marketing research targeted their audience promotions to the 25–34 age group—a group interested in upscale merchandise.

Many teams, including the New York Mets, wrap up their seasonal advertising campaigns by mid-July. As the Mets' advertising agency representative stated, "If the Mets aren't on a winning track by then, no amount of advertising will help. And if they are, they won't need much advertising."

Source: Quotation from "Baseball Urges Fans to Root for the Home Team," *Advertising Age* (April 2, 1984), p. 59.

Funds Available for Promotion

A real barrier to implementing any promotional strategy is the size of the promotional budget. A 30-second television commercial on recent Super Bowl telecasts cost the advertiser $500,000! Even though the message was received by millions of viewers and the cost per contact was relatively low, such an expenditure would exceed the entire promotional budget of thousands of firms. For many new, smaller firms, the cost of mass advertising is prohibitive, and they are forced to seek less expensive, less efficient methods. Neighborhood retailers may not be able to advertise in metropolitan newspapers or on local radio and television stations. They may choose to concentrate their promotional budgets on a well-trained group of retail salespeople and devote a smaller amount of advertising dollars on a Yellow Pages listing in the telephone directory, periodic advertisements in a neighborhood weekly newspaper, store window signs, and in-store displays.

Table 14.3 summarizes the factors influencing the determination of an appropriate promotional mix.

Table 14.3

Factors Influencing the Promotional Mix

Factor		Emphasis on	
		Personal Selling	Advertising
Nature of the Market	Number of Buyers	Limited Number	Large Number
	Geographic Concentration	Concentrated	Dispersed
	Type of Customer	Industrial Purchaser	Ultimate Consumer
Nature of the Product	Complexity	Custom-Made, Complex	Standardized
	Service Requirements	Considerable	Minimal
	Type of Good	Industrial	Consumer
	Use of Trade-Ins	Trade-Ins Common	Trade-In Uncommon
Stage in the Product Life Cycle		Introductory and Early Growth Stages	Latter Part of Growth Stages and Maturity and Early Decline Stages
Price		High Unit Value	Low Unit Value

Promotional Strategy—Pull or Push

Essentially, there are two promotional alternatives that may be employed: a pulling strategy and a pushing strategy. A pulling strategy is a promotional effort by the seller to stimulate final-user demand, which then exerts pressure on the distribution channel. When marketing intermediaries stock a large number of competing products and exhibit little interest in any one particular product, a pulling strategy may be necessary to motivate them to handle the product. In such instances, personal selling by the manufacturer is largely limited to contacting intermediaries, providing requested information about the product, and taking orders. The plan is to build consumer demand for the product by means of advertising so channel members must stock the product to meet that demand. Since most retailers want to stimulate repeat purchases by satisfied customers, the manufacturer's promotional efforts that result in shopper requests for the retailer to stock the item will usually succeed in getting that item on the retailer's shelves. Advertising and sales promotion are the most commonly used elements of promotion in a pulling strategy.

By contrast, a pushing strategy relies more heavily on personal selling. Here the objective is promoting the product to the members of the marketing channel rather than to the final user. This can be done through cooperative advertising allowances, trade discounts, personal selling efforts by the firm's sales force, and other dealer supports. Such a strategy is designed to produce marketing success for the firm's products by motivating representatives of wholesalers and/or retailers to spend a disproportionate amount of time and effort in promoting these products to customers.[4]

While these are presented as alternative strategies, it is unlikely that many companies depend entirely upon either strategy. In most cases, a combination of the two methods is employed.

Timing is another factor to consider in developing a promotional strategy. The relative importance of advertising and selling changes during the different phases of the purchase process. During the pretransactional period (prior to the actual sale), advertising is usually more important than personal selling. It is often argued that one of the primary advantages of a successful advertising program is that it assists the salesperson in approaching the prospect. Selling becomes more important than advertising during the transactional phase of the process. In most situations, personal selling is the actual mechanism of closing the sale. In the posttransactional stage, advertising regains primacy in the promotional effort. It affirms the customer's decision to buy a particular good or service and reminds the customer of the product's favorable qualities.

Objectives of Promotion

Determining the precise objectives of promotion has always been a perplexing problem for management. What specific tasks should promotion accomplish? The answer to this question seems to be as varied as the sources one consults. Generally, however, the following are considered objectives of promotion: (1) to provide information, (2) to increase demand, (3) to differentiate the product, (4) to accentuate the value of the product, and (5) to stabilize sales.

Providing Information

The traditional function of promotion was to inform the market about the availability of a particular product. Indeed, a large part of current promotional efforts is still directed at providing product information to potential customers. For example, the typical newspaper advertisement for a university or college extension course program emphasizes informative features, such as the availability, time, and place of different courses.

When Volvo recently introduced a new and more luxurious line of cars, the firm's management stressed the car's reputation for longevity and reliability. Figure 14.3 shows how Volvo marketers used industry statistics that measure the average life expectancies of different models to emphasize Volvo's strengths.

Stimulating Demand

The primary objective of most promotional efforts is to increase the demand for a specific brand of product or service. Successful promotion can shift demand, thereby resulting in increased sales.

Differentiating the Product

A frequent objective of the firm's promotional effort is *product differentiation*. Homogeneous demand means consumers regard the firm's output as virtually identical with the products of its competitors. In these cases, the individual firm has almost no control over such marketing variables as price. A differentiated demand schedule, by contrast, permits more flexibility in marketing strategy, such as price changes. For example, the high quality and distinctiveness of Cross pens are widely advertised, resulting in Cross's ability to ask and obtain a price 100 times that of some disposable pens.

Accentuating the Value of the Product

Promotion can point out more ownership utility to buyers, thereby accentuating the value of a product. The good or service might then be able to command a higher price in the marketplace. For example, status-oriented advertising may

Figure 14.3
Using Advertising to Inform

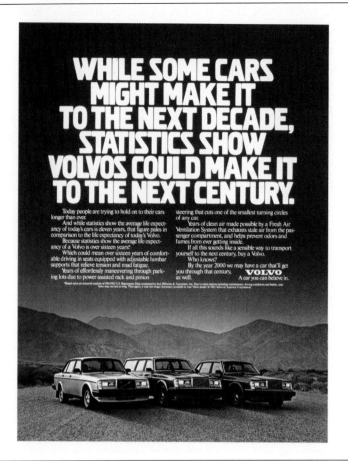

Source: Courtesy of Volvo of America Corporation.

allow some retail clothing stores to command higher prices than others. The demand curve—that schedule of amounts of a product or service a firm expects consumers to purchase at different prices—facing a prestige store may be less responsive to price differences than that of a competitor without a quality reputation.

When Weight Watchers introduced a new line of reformulated frozen foods, it sought to convince dieters that, besides being low in calories, its entrees were delectable. Figure 14.4 shows how a single promotion can stimulate demand, differentiate the product, and accentuate its value.

Stabilizing Sales

For the typical firm, sales are not uniform throughout the year. Sales fluctuations may be caused by cyclical, seasonal, or irregular demand. Stabilizing these variations is often an objective of the firm's promotional strategy.

Coffee sales follow a seasonal pattern: purchases and consumption increase during the colder winter months. Figure 14.5 illustrates the efforts of General Foods Corporation marketers to stimulate summer sales of its Sanka brand decaffeinated coffee.

Figure 14.4

Use of Promotion to Stimulate Demand, Differentiate a
Product, and Accentuate Its Value

Budgeting for Promotional Strategy

Promotional budgets may differ not only in amount but also in composition. Industrial firms generally invest a larger proportion of their budgets for personal selling than for advertising, while the reverse is usually true of most producers of consumer goods.

Evidence suggests that sales initially lag behind promotion for structural reasons (filling up the retail shelves, low initial production, and lack of buyer knowledge). This produces a threshold effect where there are few sales but a substantial initial investment in promotion. A second phase might produce returns (sales) proportional to a given promotional expenditure; this would be the most predictable range. Finally, the area of diminishing returns is reached when an increase in promotional spending does not produce a proportional increase in sales.

For example, an initial expenditure of $40,000 may result in the sale of 100,000 product units for a consumer goods manufacturer. An additional $10,000 expenditure may sell 30,000 more units, and another $10,000 may

Figure 14.5
Using Advertising to Stabilize Sales

Source: Advertisement courtesy of General Foods Corporation. SANKA is a
registered trademark of General Foods Corporation.

produce the sale of 35,000 more units. The cumulative effect of the expenditures and repeat sales has resulted in increasing returns to the promotional outlays. However, as the advertising budget moves from $60,000 to $70,000, the marginal productivity of the additional expenditure may fall to 28,000 units. At some later point, the return may actually become zero or negative as competition intensifies, markets become saturated, and less effective advertising media are employed.

To test the thesis that there is a saturation point for advertising, Anheuser-Busch once quadrupled its advertising budget in several markets. After three months, the company's distributors demanded an advertising cut. Many claimed that beer consumers came into their stores saying, "Give me anything *but* Bud."[5]

The ideal method of allocating a promotional budget would be to expand it until the cost of each additional increment equals the additional incremental revenue received. In other words, the most effective allocation procedure is to increase promotional expenditures until each dollar of promotional expense is matched by an additional dollar of profit. This procedure—called *marginal analysis*—results in the maximization of the input's productivity. The difficulty arises in identifying the optimal point, which requires a precise balancing of marginal expenses for promotion and the resulting marginal receipts.

Traditional methods of allocating a promotional budget are percentage of sales, fixed sum per unit, meeting the competition, and task-objective.

Percentage-of-Sales Method
Promotional budget allocation method in which the funds allocated for promotion during a time period are based upon a specified percentage of either past or forecasted sales.

The **percentage-of-sales method** is a very common way of allocating promotional budgets. The percentage can be based on either past (such as the previous year) or forecasted (estimated current year) sales. While the simplicity of this plan is appealing, it is not an effective way of achieving basic promotional objectives. Arbitrary percentage allocations, whether applied to historical or future sales figures, fail to provide the flexibility that is required. Furthermore, such reasoning is circular since the advertising allocation depends upon sales rather than vice versa, as it should be. Consider, for example, the implications of a decline in sales.

Fixed-Sum-Per-Unit Method
Promotional budget allocation method in which promotional expenditures are a predetermined dollar amount for each sales or production unit.

The **fixed-sum-per-unit method** differs from percentage of sales in only one respect: It applies a predetermined allocation to each sales or production unit. This can also be based on either historical or forecasted figures. Producers of high-value, consumer durable goods, such as automobiles, often use this budgeting method.

Another traditional approach is simply to match competitors' outlays—in other words, meet competition—on either an absolute or a relative basis. However, this kind of approach usually leads to a status quo situation with each company retaining its percentage of total sales. Meeting the competition's budget does not necessarily relate to the objectives of promotion and, therefore, seems inappropriate for most contemporary marketing programs.

Task-Objective Method
Promotional budget allocation method under which a firm defines its goals and then determines the amount of promotional spending needed to accomplish them.

The **task-objective method** of developing a promotional budget is based upon a sound evaluation of the firm's promotional objectives, and, as a result, is better attuned to modern marketing practices. It involves two sequential steps.

1. The organization must *define the realistic communication goals* the firm wants the promotional mix to accomplish—for example, a 25 percent increase in brand awareness or a 10 percent rise in consumers who realize that the product has certain specific differentiating features. The key is to quantitatively specify the objectives to be accomplished. They then become an integral part of the promotional plan.

2. The organization must *determine the amount (as well as type) of promotional activity required to accomplish each of the objectives* that has been set. These units combined become the firm's promotional budget.

A crucial assumption underlies the task-objective approach—that the productivity of each promotional dollar is measurable. That is why the objectives must be carefully chosen, quantified, and accomplished through promotional efforts. Generally, an objective like "We wish to achieve a 5 percent increase in sales" is a marketing objective, because a sale is a culmination of the effects of *all* elements of the marketing mix. Therefore, an appropriate promotional objective might be "To make 30 percent of the market target aware of the one-hour optical service concept."

While promotional budgeting is always difficult, recent research studies and more frequent use of computer-based models make it less of a problem than it has been in the past.

Measuring the Effectiveness of Promotion _____

It is widely recognized that part of a firm's promotional effort is ineffective. John Wanamaker, a successful nineteenth-century retailer, observed: "I know half the money I spend on advertising is wasted, but I can never find out which half."

Measuring the effectiveness of promotional expenditures has become an extremely important research issue, particularly among advertisers. Studies aimed at this measurement dilemma face several major obstacles, one of them being the difficulty of isolating the effect of the promotional variable.

Most marketers would prefer to use a *direct-sales-results test* to measure the effectiveness of promotion. This test ascertains for each dollar of promotional outlay the corresponding increase in revenue. The primary difficulty is controlling the other variables operating in the marketplace. A $1.5 million advertising campaign may be followed by an increase in sales of $20 million. However, this increase may be due more to a sudden price hike by the leading competitor than to the advertising expenditure. Therefore, advertisers are turning to establishing and assessing achievable, measurable objectives.

With the increasing sophistication of marketing analysts, analytical techniques, and computer-based marketing information systems, historical data on promotional expenditures and their effects are being subjected to even more scrutiny. More and more is being learned about measuring and evaluating the effects of promotional activity. Other assessment methods include sales inquiries, determination of change in attitudes toward the product, and improvement in public knowledge and awareness. One indicator of advertising effectiveness would be the elasticity or sensitivity of sales to promotion based on historical data concerning price, sales volume, and advertising expenditures.

It is difficult for the marketer to conduct research in a controlled environment such as other disciplines use for research. The difficulty in isolating the effects of promotion causes many marketers to abandon all attempts at measurement. Others, however, turn to indirect evaluation. These researchers concentrate on the factors that are quantifiable, such as recall (how much is remembered about specific products or advertisements) and readership (the size and composition of the audience). The basic problem is the difficulty in relating these variables to sales. Does extensive ad readership actually lead to increased sales? Another problem is the high cost of research in promotion. To correctly assess the effectiveness of promotional expenditures may require a significant investment.

The Value of Promotion _____

Promotion has often been the target of criticism. Common criticisms may include:

- "Promotion contributes nothing to society."
- "Most advertisements and sales presentations insult my intelligence."
- "Promotion 'forces' consumers to buy products they cannot afford and do not need."
- "Advertising and selling are economic wastes."
- "Salespersons and advertisers are usually unethical."

Consumers, public officials, and marketers agree that too many of these complaints are true.[6] Some salespersons do use unethical sales tactics. Some product advertising is directed at consumer groups that can least afford to purchase the particular item. Many television commercials do contribute to the growing problem of cultural pollution.

While promotion can certainly be criticized on many counts, it is important to remember that promotion plays a crucial role in modern society. This point is best explained by looking at the importance of promotion at the business, economic, and societal levels.

Business Importance

Promotional strategy has become increasingly important to business enterprises—both large and small. The long-term increase in outlays for promotion is well documented and certainly attests to management's faith in the ability of promotional efforts to produce additional sales. It is difficult to conceive of an enterprise that would not attempt to promote its product or service in some manner or another. Most modern institutions simply cannot survive in the long run without promotion. Business must communicate with the public.

Nonbusiness enterprises also have recognized the importance of promotional efforts. The United States government spends over $228 million a year on advertising and ranks twenty-eighth among all U.S. advertisers. The Canadian government is the leading advertiser in Canada, promoting many programs and concepts. Religious organizations have acknowledged the importance of promoting what they do. Even labor organizations have used promotional channels to make their viewpoints known to the public at large. The National Wildlife Federation advertisement shown in Figure 14.6 effectively points out the conservation efforts of this organization to protect the 3,000 bald eagles remaining in the United States.

Economic Importance

Promotion has assumed a degree of economic importance, if for no other reason than the employment of thousands of people. More importantly, however, effective promotion has allowed society to derive benefits not otherwise available. For example, the criticism that promotion costs too much isolates an individual expense item and fails to consider the possible effect of promotion on other categories of expenditures.

Promotional strategies that increase the number of units sold permit economies in the production process, thereby lowering the production costs assigned to each unit of output. Lower consumer prices then allow these products to become available to more people. Similarly, researchers have found that advertising subsidizes the informational content of newspapers and the broadcast media.[7] In short, promotion pays for many of the enjoyable entertainment and educational aspects of contemporary life as well as lowering product costs.

Social Importance

Criticisms such as "most promotional messages are tasteless" and "promotion contributes nothing to society" sometimes ignore the fact that no commonly accepted set of standards or priorities exists within our social framework. We live in a varied economy characterized by consumer segments with differing needs, wants, and aspirations. What is tasteless to one group may be quite informative to another. Promotional strategy is faced with an "averaging" problem that escapes many of its critics. The one generally accepted standard in a market society is freedom of choice for the consumer. Customer

Figure 14.6
Promotional Message for a Nonprofit Organization

Source: Courtesy of National Wildlife Federation.

buying decisions eventually determine what is acceptable practice in the marketplace.

Promotion has become an important factor in the campaigns to achieve socially oriented objectives, such as stopping smoking, family planning, physical fitness, and the elimination of drug abuse. Promotion performs an informative and educational task that makes it extremely important in the functioning of modern society. As with everything else in life, it is how one uses promotion, not the using itself, that is critical.

Summary

This chapter provides an introduction to promotion, the third variable in the marketing mix (product, distribution, promotional, and pricing strategies). Promotional strategy is closely related to the marketing communications system, which includes the elements of sender, message, encoding, transfer mechanism, decoding, receiver, feedback, and noise. The major components of promotional strategy are personal selling and nonpersonal selling (advertising, sales promotion, and public relations). These elements are discussed in Chapters 15 and 16.

Developing an effective promotional strategy is a complex matter. The elements of promotion are related to the type and value of the product being promoted, the nature of the market, the stage of the product life cycle, and the funds available for promotion, as well as to the timing of the promotional effort. Personal selling is used primarily for industrial goods, for higher-value items, and during the transactional phase of the purchase decision process. Advertising, by contrast, is used primarily for consumer goods, for lower-value items during the later stages of the product life cycle, and during the pretransactional and posttransactional phases.

A pushing strategy, which relies on personal selling, attempts to promote the product to the members of the marketing channel rather than to the final user. A pulling strategy concentrates on stimulating final-user demand, primarily in the mass media through advertising and sales promotion.

The five basic objectives of promotion are (1) to provide information, (2) to stimulate demand, (3) to differentiate the product, (4) to accentuate the value of the product, and (5) to stabilize sales.

Although it has become the target of much criticism, promotion plays an important role in the business, economic, and social activities of the nation.

Solving the Stop-Action Case

The Louisville Redbirds

A. Ray Smith was convinced that effective promotion is second only to winning as a technique for bringing in the fans. Working in conjunction with such local firms as Ford, PepsiCo, and Armour Meats, the Redbirds gave away thousands of T-shirts and helmets on special, jointly sponsored nights. On a weekly basis, they also make a special effort to attract certain groups of fans. Every Thursday is *Ladies Nite*, and every Sunday is *Senior Citizens Nite*. The club has also used such slogans as "Baseball—A Great Catch for Louisville" to promote ticket sales.

One of the most successful promotions run by the Redbirds is "Strikeitrich," in which fans are asked to guess attendance totals at several home games and for the entire season. Over 111,000 fans have entered the contest in an attempt to win the $21,000 grand prize. Contest publicity included newspaper and radio ads and bus-stop billboard displays.

"Of all the promotions we've had," said Smith, "that one was the epitome. It increased awareness of what we were trying to do; it created fan interest; and the final reward was the biggest prize ever." Smith added, "That had to be the largest, most impressive, best-managed promotion in any sport."

Photo Source: Courtesy of Louisville Redbirds.

(*continued*)

Smith's specialty, however, is "soft" promotion. Critical components of his marketing strategy involve a competitive team comprised of potential major league players and a ballpark atmosphere that encourages fans to return throughout the summer to watch the Redbirds play. Entertainment and gaiety are key elements in this plan. Between innings a Dixieland ensemble provides a musical break in the stands, and another combo entertains before-game picnickers. The concession stands, staffed by an army of teenagers dressed in red, white, and blue uniforms, offer such nontraditional snacks as nachos, fried chicken, pork tenderloin, and freshly squeezed orange juice. They also sell so many Redbirds caps that nearly every fan wears one to the game. T-shirts, pennants, and pencils all carrying the Redbirds insignia are also available.

The festive atmosphere often peaks around the seventh inning when the stadium scoreboard features a race among three electronic horses. Unofficial betting is popular, and winners as well as losers are encouraged to try their luck again at the next home game. Smith's own presence also encourages fan support. Dressed in a checkered sports jacket, the Redbirds' owner works the crowd, shaking hands with every fan he sees.

These efforts, combined with an excellent sports facility, low ticket and concession prices, and the team's winning performance, bring in about 1 million fans a season. No other minor league team comes close to that mark. In fact, in recent years the team's per-game attendance has exceeded that of such major league clubs as the Cleveland Indians, Minnesota Twins, Pittsburgh Pirates, and Seattle Mariners.

Although the Redbirds' promotional style is much more subdued than that of many other major and minor league teams, its effect is everywhere. Smith is so confident of his system that he is projecting 1.5 million fans a year within five years. "We might be minor league in New York, but in Louisville, on a summer night, we're the best thing going, and that includes TV."

Sources: First Smith quotation from George Rorrer and Stan Denny, *Redbirds: Thanks a Million* (Louisville, Kentucky: *The Courier–Journal and Louisville Times,* 1983), p. 11. Second Smith quotation from Frederick C. Klein, "Owner of Louisville Redbirds Finds Success in Baseball-as-Entertainment Philosophy," *The Wall Street Journal* (August 10, 1983), p. 27.

Questions for Discussion

1. Relate the steps in the communications process to promotional strategy.

2. Explain the concept of the promotional mix and its relationship to the marketing mix.

3. What mix of promotional variables would you use for each of the following?
    a. Delco auto batteries
    b. Lawnboy lawn mowers
    c. A management consulting service
    d. Industrial drilling equipment
    e. Women's sports outfits
    f. Customized business forms

4. "Perhaps the most critical promotional question facing the marketing manager concerns when to use each of the components of promotion." Comment on this statement, and relate your response to the goods classification, product value, marketing channels, price, and the timing of the promotional effort.

5. Identify the major determinants of a promotional mix and describe how they affect the selection of an appropriate blending of promotional techniques.

6. Relate the AIDA concept to the marketing communications process.

7. Explain the concept of noise and its causes.

8. Under what circumstances should a pushing strategy be used in promotion? When would a pulling strategy be effective?

9. What are the primary objectives of promotion?

10. Why is it difficult to measure the effectiveness of promotional efforts?

11. Identify and briefly explain the alternative methods for developing a promotional budget.

12. Develop a hypothetical promotional budget for the following firms. Ignore dollar amounts by using percentage allocations to the various promotional variables, such as 30 percent to personal selling, 60 percent to advertising, and 10 percent to public relations.
    a.   Avis Car Rentals
    b.   Days Inn
    c.   A manufacturer of industrial chemicals
    d.   Aetna Life Insurance Company

13. How should a firm attempt to measure the effectiveness of its promotional efforts?

14. Develop a plan for measuring the effectiveness of a current advertising campaign with which you are familiar.

15. Identify the major public criticisms sometimes directed toward promotion. Prepare a defense for each criticism.

16. Many professionals, such as attorneys, physicians, and dentists, are now allowed to promote their services through media advertising. What effect is this likely to have on the practices of professionals who advertise?

17. When paperback book sales suffered a downturn, several of the major publishers adopted new promotional strategies. Fawcett Books began using 30-cents-off coupons to promote its Coventry romance series. New American Library, on the other hand, established a returns policy that rewarded dealers with high sales. The new policy also contained penalties to discourage low volume by retail book outlets. Relate these promotional strategies to the material discussed in this chapter.

18. The Ridge Tool Company, of Elyria, Ohio, recently honored a promotional offer it had made in a 1931 issue of *Popular Science*. The ad had offered a wrench for $.20. Ridge Tool sent the wrench, which now sells for $4.20, and even returned the customer's $.20. How could an action of this type fit into Ridge Tool's overall promotional strategy?

19. The Justice Bedding Company, of Chepachet, Rhode Island, has developed a product it believes is better than an electric blanket. What type of promotional strategy would you devise for Justice Bedding's new electric mattress?

20. Develop a promotional strategy to expand the membership of a campus organization to which you belong or with which you are familiar.

Case: Reverend Moon and a Texan Named Hunt

Although word-of-mouth advertising is generally considered a positive addition to a formal promotional mix, such uncontrolled communications frequently prove detrimental. Entenmann's, a Warner-Lambert subsidiary and the world's largest baker of fresh cake products, was once rumored to be owned by the Reverend Sun Myung Moon's Unification Church. Paid advertising, press conferences, and formal letters of denial to the nation's news media were all used by the firm to combat this erroneous word-of-mouth communication.

Another widely reported consumer misperception involved Hunt–Wesson Foods, a Norton Simon subsidiary based in California. A false rumor spread across the country that the firm was owned by a rich Texan named Hunt. Hunt–Wesson marketers decided to battle the rumor with their own word-of-mouth communications. The following advertisement shows how Hunt–Wesson developed a special promotion designed to simulate word-of-mouth to dispel the misconception.

Source: Courtesy of Hunt-Wesson Foods, Inc.

Questions

1.   Explain how firms can make positive use of word-of-mouth communications. Relate your answer to the discussion of the opinion leader in Chapter 6.

2.   What steps would you recommend that firms take to minimize the likelihood of false information being spread by word-of-mouth?

Computer Applications

A number of traditional methods for allocating a promotional budget are described in this chapter. They include percentage of sales, fixed sum per unit, meeting the competition, and task-objective methods. These problems focus upon the various methods for promotional budgeting.

Directions: Use menu item 13 titled "Promotional Budget Allocations" to solve each of the following problems. To solve Problem 5, also use menu item 3 titled "Sales Forecasting" to calculate data needed to solve the problem.

Problem 1 Heathcliff Clothiers, of Largo, Maryland, has allocated $12,600 for its 1987 promotional budget. The allocation was calculated by basing the budget on the same percentage allocation used during 1986. During 1986, the store generated sales of $180,000 and spent a total of $10,800 on promotion. How much sales revenue does Heathcliff Clothiers expect to produce in 1987?

Problem 2 Barry Abruscato, marketing manager for Zale Fashions, is in the process of developing a promotional budget for 1987. Total expected sales for 1987 amount to $675,000. Abruscato has collected the following historical sales and promotional expenditures data for the firm:

Year	Annual Sales	Promotional Outlays
1982	$520,000	$33,800
1983	580,000	38,860
1984	620,000	37,200
1985	640,000	37,760
1986	652,000	32,600

Abruscato has also collected data on sales and promotional outlays of his three major competitors. Town & Country Fashions spent $37,560 on promotion and generated 1986 sales of approximately $820,000. The promotional budget at Miss Patti's was $75,400, and total sales amounted to $1.4 million. The Style Shop, Zale Fashions' largest competitor, generated $1.5 million in sales in 1986 and spent $80,000 on promotion.

a. What percentage of 1987 sales should Abruscato include in his 1987 promotional budget if he bases his budget on the percentage used for 1986 sales? How many dollars would be allocated to promotion?

b. Suppose Abruscato decides to use the average percentage allocated for promotion over the past five years. He determines this average by calculating total sales and total promotional outlays since 1982 and then divides total promotional outlays by total sales. What percentage would he include in his 1987 promotional budget using this method? How many dollars would he allocate to promotion?

c. Abruscato is also considering meeting competition by basing his promotional budget on the average promotional outlays of each of his three major competitors. What percentage would he use for promotion if he utilizes this approach? How many dollars would he allocate to promotion in 1987 if this approach is implemented?

Problem 3 Terry Simpson, manager of Reno Import Motors, has decided to use the fixed-sum-per-unit method to determine the appropriate promotional budget amount for 1987. He plans to base the precise sum upon the average for other automobile dealers in his market area. Available data reveal the following:

Dealer	Per-Car Promotional Expenditures
A	$ 37
B	48
C	65
D	85
E	110

Simpson forecasts 1987 sales to amount to 1,400 cars. How much should he allocate on a per-unit basis to promotion in 1987? What will his total promotional budget be in 1987?

Problem 4 Golden Bear Enterprises was founded six years ago in San Francisco. Its growth has been substantial, and the firm has expanded into several cities in northern California. Sales and annual promotional expenditures for the past six years are as follows:

Year	Annual Sales	Promotional Expenditures
1981	$1,400,000	$ 58,800
1982	2,300,000	92,000
1983	3,000,000	135,000
1984	3,700,000	185,000
1985	4,500,000	243,000
1986	5,700,000	302,000

The 1987 sales forecast is $6,500,000. The firm's four major competitors have the following annual sales and promotional outlays:

Competitor	Estimated Current Annual Sales	Estimated Promotional Budget
A	$3,800,000	$159,600
B	4,200,000	298,200
C	6,700,000	335,000
D	9,200,000	496,800

a. What percentage of 1987 sales should Golden Bear Enterprises include in its 1987 promotional budget if the budget is based on the percentage allocated for 1986 sales? How many dollars would be allocated to promotion?

b. Suppose the firm's marketers decide to use the average percentage allocated for promotion over the past six years. They determine this average by calculating total sales and total promotional outlays since 1981 and then divide total promotional outlays by total sales. What percentage would be included in the 1987 promotional budget? How many dollars would be allocated to promotion?

c. The firm's marketers are also considering simply meeting competition by basing their promotional budget on the average promotional outlays of each of the four major competitors. What percentage would be used for promotion if this approach is implemented?

Problem 5 Barbara Whitmore, marketing vice-president of Foster Designs, plans to allocate 6.5 percent of 1987 sales to promotion. To develop her budgets, she needs to forecast sales for 1987. Annual sales for previous years are shown below.

Year	Annual Sales
1978	$ 7,200,000
1979	8,100,000
1980	8,800,000
1981	9,500,000
1982	10,000,000
1983	10,600,000
1984	11,200,000
1985	11,800,000
1986	12,800,000

Estimate 1987 sales by using menu item 3 titled "Sales Forecasting." This sales forecasting technique is described on page 87. Once 1987 sales have been estimated, calculate the amount of funds Whitmore should allocate for promotion in 1987.

Advertising, Sales Promotion, and Public Relations

Key Terms

advertising
positioning
product advertising
institutional advertising
informative advertising
persuasive advertising
reminder advertising
advocacy advertising
advertising agency
comparative advertising
retail advertising
cooperative advertising
pretesting
posttesting
sales promotion
point-of-purchase
    advertising
specialty advertising
public relations
publicity

Learning Goals

1. To explain the current status and historical development of advertising
2. To identify the major types of advertising
3. To list and discuss the major advertising media
4. To explain how advertising effectiveness is determined
5. To outline the organization of the advertising function
6. To describe the process of creating an advertisement
7. To identify the principal methods of sales promotion
8. To explain the role of public relations and publicity in an organization's promotional strategy

Photo Source: Courtesy of New York Penta Hotel.

New York Penta Hotel

For years the New York Statler was the laughingstock of Manhattan's hotel industry. Despite its enviable location in the heart of New York's bustling garment district and across the street from Madison Square Garden, one of the nation's premier sports facilities, the Statler had earned a reputation as a second-class hotel. Those who knew the Statler best—travel agents and others in the hotel business—identified it as a hotel with frayed carpets, peeling wallpaper, a poor reservations system, and inadequate security. They also knew it as a hotel that had changed hands numerous times in its 65-year history, most recently to a European hotel chain named Penta.

The Statler's new executives faced two enormous challenges. First, they had to renovate the deteriorating hotel, a job that would cost at least $20 million. They also had to convince travelers and travel agents that the hotel *would* be upgraded. Since previous owners had made repeated promises about renovations that never materialized, the hotel and travel industries greeted Penta's new promises with a healthy skepticism. "We had a credibility problem," said Richard Graves, director of marketing for the newly named New York Penta Hotel. "We had to overcome the fact that people kept saying, 'we've heard that promise before'."

Assignment: Use the materials in Chapter 15 to suggest methods for improving the New York Penta's image as it improves its facilities.

Source: Graves quotation from telephone interview, May 1, 1984.

Chapter Overview

As Chapter 14 explained, promotion consists of both personal and nonpersonal elements. In this chapter the nonpersonal elements of promotion—advertising, sales promotion, and public relations—are examined. These elements play a critical role in the promotional mixes of thousands of organizations.

For most organizations, advertising represents the most important type of nonpersonal promotion. This chapter examines advertising objectives, the importance of planning for advertising, and the different types of advertisements and media choices. Both retail advertising and manufacturer (national) advertising are discussed and the alternative methods of assessing the effectiveness of an advertisement are examined. Sales promotion and public relations—including publicity—are also discussed.

Advertising

Advertising
Paid, nonpersonal communication through various media by business firms, nonprofit organizations, and individuals who are identified in the advertising message and who hope to inform or persuade members of a particular audience.

If you sought to be the next member of the U.S. Senate, you would need to communicate with every possible voter in your state. If you had developed new computer software and went into business to market it, your chances of success would be slim without informing and persuading students, businesspeople, and other potential customers of the usefulness of your offering. In these situations you would discover, as have countless others, the need to use advertising to communicate to buyers. In the previous chapter, advertising was defined as a paid, nonpersonal communication through various media by business firms, nonprofit organizations, and individuals who are in some way identified in the advertising message and who hope to inform or persuade members of a particular audience.

Today's widespread markets make advertising an important part of business. Since the end of World War II, advertising and related expenditures have risen faster than the gross national product and most other economic indicators. Furthermore, about 200,000 workers are employed in advertising.

Six corporations—Procter & Gamble, Sears, Beatrice Companies, General Motors, R. J. Reynolds, and Philip Morris—each spent more than $500 million on advertising in 1983. The total expenditure for advertising in the United States in 1983 was about $76 billion, or approximately $330 per capita.

Advertising expenditures vary among industries and companies. Cosmetics companies are often cited as an example of firms that spend a high percentage of their funds on advertising and promotion. Chicago management consultants Schonfeld & Associates, Inc., studied 5,000 firms and calculated their average advertising expenditures as a percentage of sales. Estimates for selected industries are given in Figure 15.1. Wide differences exist among industries, as shown in the figure. Advertising spending can range from one-fifth of 1 percent in an industry like petroleum refining to more than 21 percent of sales in the phonograph/audio cassette industry.

Historical Development

Some form of advertising probably existed since the development of the exchange process. Most early advertising was vocal; criers and hawkers sold various products, made public announcements, and chanted advertising slogans like this one:

One-a-penny, two-a-penny, hot-cross buns
One-a-penny, two for tuppence, hot-cross buns.

Figure 15.1

Estimates of Average Advertising as a Percentage of Sales in Ten Industries

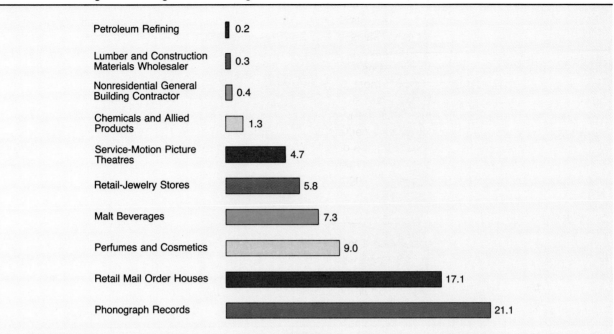

Source: Schonfeld & Associates, Inc., 2550 Crawford Ave., Evanston, IL., 60201, (312)869-5556

Criers were common in colonial America. The cry of "Rags! Any Rags? Any wool rags?" filled the streets of Philadelphia in the 1700s.

Signs were also used in early advertising. Most were symbolic in their identification of products or services. In Rome, a goat signified a dairy, a mule driving a mill signified a bakery, and a boy being whipped signified a school.

Later, the development of the printing press greatly expanded advertising's capabilities. A 1710 advertisement in the *Spectator* billed one dentifrice as "the Incomparable Powder for cleaning Teeth, which has given great satisfaction to most of the Nobility and Gentry in England." Colonial newspapers such as Benjamin Franklin's *Gazette* also featured advertising. In fact, many newspapers carried it on their front page. Most of these advertisements would be called classified ads today. A few national advertisers such as Lorillard, a producer of tobacco products, also began to use newspaper advertising at this time. As the example from William Henry Harrison's 1840 presidential campaign in Figure 15.2 illustrates, political advertising focusing upon image (including the visual symbol of the log cabin) have been a part of the nation's political scene for almost 150 years.

Volney Palmer organized the first advertising agency in the United States in 1841. George P. Rowell was another advertising pioneer. Originally, advertising agencies simply sold ad space. Services like advertising research, copywriting, and planning came later. In the early 1900s, Claude C. Hopkins used a large-scale consumer survey on home-baked beans before launching a campaign for Van Camp's Pork and Beans. Hopkins claimed that home-baked beans were difficult to digest and suggested that consumers try Van Camp's beans. He advocated the use of "reason-why copy" to show why people should buy the product.

Figure 15.2
Person Marketing: Political Advertising in 1840

Source: Courtesy of President Benjamin Harrison Home, Indianapolis, Indiana.

Some early advertising promoted products of questionable value, such as patent medicines. As a result, a reform movement in advertising developed during the early 1900s, and some newspapers began to screen their advertisements. *Saturday Evening Post* publisher Cyrus Curtis began rejecting certain types of advertising, such as medical copy that claimed cures and advertisements for alcoholic beverages. In 1911, the forerunner of the American Advertising Federation drew up a code of improved advertising.

One identifying feature of advertising in the twentieth century is its concern for researching the markets that it attempts to reach. Originally, advertising research dealt primarily with media selection and the product. Then, advertisers became increasingly concerned with determining the appropriate *demographics*—characteristics such as the age, sex, and income level of potential buyers. Understanding consumer behavior has now become an important aspect of advertising strategy. Behavioral influences in purchase decisions, often called *psychographics,* can be useful in describing potential markets for advertising appeals. As described in Chapter 5, these influences include such factors as life-style and personal attitudes. Increased information about consumer psychographics has led to improved advertising decisions.

The emergence of the marketing concept, with its emphasis on a companywide consumer orientation, expanded the role of advertising as marketing communications assumed greater importance in business. Today, the average American is exposed to 565 advertisements daily.[1] Advertising provides an efficient, inexpensive, and fast method of reaching the much-sought-after consumer. Its extensive use currently rivals that of personal selling. Advertising has become a key ingredient in the effective implementation of the marketing concept.

Advertising Objectives

Traditionally, advertising objectives were stated in terms of direct sales goals. A more realistic approach, however, is to view advertising as having communications objectives that seek to inform, persuade, and remind potential customers of the product. Advertising seeks to condition the consumer to have a favorable viewpoint toward the promotional message. The goal is to improve the likelihood that the customer will buy a particular product. In this sense, advertising illustrates the close relationship between marketing communications and promotional strategy.

Where personal selling is the primary component of a firm's marketing mix, advertising may be used in a support role to assist salespeople. Much of Avon's advertising is aimed at assisting the neighborhood salesperson by strengthening the image of Avon, its products, and its salespeople. The well-known advertisement for McGraw-Hill Publications, shown in Figure 15.3, illustrates the important role advertising can play in opening doors for the sales force.

Figure 15.3
Use of Advertising to Assist Personal Selling

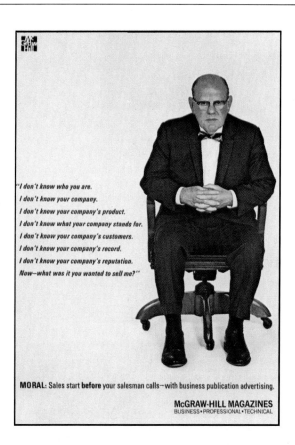

"I don't know who you are.
I don't know your company.
I don't know your company's product.
I don't know what your company stands for.
I don't know your company's customers.
I don't know your company's record.
I don't know your company's reputation.
Now—what was it you wanted to sell me?"

MORAL: Sales start **before** your salesman calls—with business publication advertising.

McGRAW-HILL MAGAZINES
BUSINESS • PROFESSIONAL • TECHNICAL

Advertising Planning

Advertising planning begins with the marketing objectives and strategies derived from the overall objectives of the organization. These marketing objectives and strategies are the basis for marketing communications objectives and strategies. Effective research is an essential input for both marketing and advertising planning. The results of the research allow management to make strategic decisions that are translated into tactical areas such as budgeting, copywriting, scheduling, and media selection. Posttests are used in measuring the effectiveness of advertising and serve as the basis for feedback concerning needs for possible adjustment. The elements of advertising planning are shown in Figure 15.4.

There is a real need to follow a sequential process in advertising decisions. Novice advertisers are often overly concerned with the technical aspects of advertisement construction and ignore the more basic steps, such as market analysis. The type of advertisement employed in a particular situation is related in large part to the planning phase of this process.

Figure 15.4
Elements of Advertising Planning

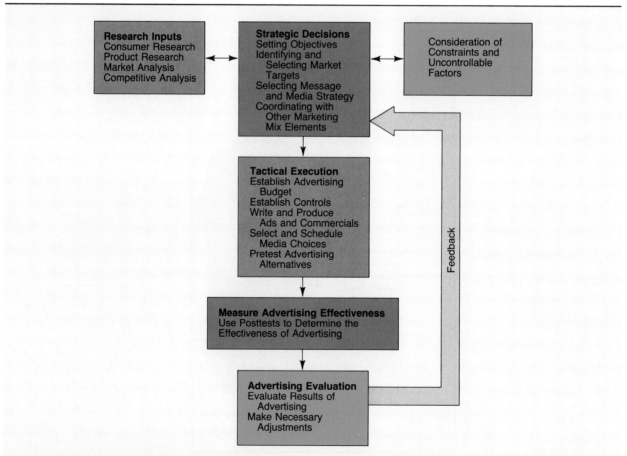

Source: Adapted from S. Watson Dunn and Arnold M. Barban, *Advertising: Its Role in Modern Marketing* (Hinsdale, Ill.: The Dryden Press, 1982), p. 202.

Positioning

Positioning
Developing a marketing strategy
aimed at a particular market
segment and designed to achieve a
desired position in the mind of the
prospective buyer.

One of the most widely discussed strategies in advertising is the concept of positioning, which involves the development of a marketing strategy aimed at a particular segment of the market and designed to achieve a desired position in the mind of the prospective buyer. While advertising experts continue to debate its effectiveness and origin, positioning has been used by hundreds of firms since its inception a little more than a decade ago. The strategy is applied primarily to products that are not leaders in their particular industries. These products are apparently more successful if their advertising concentrates on specific "positions" in the minds of consumers. As Professors David A. Aaker and J. Gary Shansby point out, a variety of positioning strategies are available to the advertiser. An object can be positioned by:

1.   Attributes *(Crest is a cavity fighter.)*
2.   Price/quality *(Sears is a value store.)*
3.   Competitor *("Avis is only number two in rent-a-cars, so why go with us? We try harder.")*
4.   Application *(Gatorade is for quick, healthful energy after exercise and other forms of physical exertion.)*
5.   Product user *(Miller is for the blue-collar, heavy beer drinker.)*
6.   Product class *(Carnation Instant Breakfast is a breakfast food.)*

A common positioning technique is to position some aspect of the firm's marketing mix against the leading brand. A classic example is 7-Up. With the image of being a mixer for older people's drinks, 7-Up was missing the primary market for soft drinks—children, teenagers, and young adults. So the firm developed its UnCola campaign to first identify the product as a soft drink and then to position it as an alternative to cola.

Success in positioning requires a careful, well-researched plan:

The selection of a positioning strategy involves identifying competitors, relevant attributes, competitor positions, and market segments. Research-based approaches can help in each of these steps by providing conceptualization even if the subjective judgments of managers are used to provide the actual input information to the position decision.[2]

Types of Advertisements

Product Advertising
Nonpersonal selling of a good or
service.

Institutional Advertising
Promoting a concept, an idea, a
philosophy, or the goodwill of an
industry, company, organization, or
person.

Informative Advertising
Promotions that seek to announce
the availability of and develop initial
demand for a product, service,
organization, person, idea, or cause.

There are essentially two types of advertisements—product and institutional. Product advertising deals with the nonpersonal selling of a particular good or service. It is the type that comes to the average person's mind when he or she thinks about advertisements. Institutional advertising, by contrast, is concerned with promoting a concept, an idea, a philosophy, or the goodwill of an industry, company, organization, person, or government agency. It is a broader term than *corporate advertising,* which is typically limited to nonproduct advertising sponsored by profit-seeking firms. Institutional advertising is often closely related to the public relations function of the enterprise.

As pointed out in the previous chapter, advertising can be subdivided into informative, persuasive, and reminder categories. Informative advertising seeks to develop initial demand for a product, service, organization, person, idea, or cause. It tends to characterize the promotion of any new market

Figure 15.5

Institutional Advertising: Informative, Persuasive, and Reminder Oriented

Source: Courtesy of AT&T, © AT&T 1985; American Association of Advertising Agencies;
and the Advertising Council (Keep America Beautiful, Inc.).

entry because the objective is often simply to announce its availability. Informative advertising is used in the introductory stage of the product life cycle.

Persuasive advertising seeks to develop demand for products, services, organizations, people, ideas, or causes. It is a competitive type of promotion used in the growth and early part of the maturity stages of the product life cycle.

Reminder advertising seeks to reinforce previous promotional activity by keeping the name of the product, service, organization, person, idea, or cause before the public. It is used in the latter part of the maturity stage as well as throughout the decline stage of the product life cycle. Figure 15.5 shows examples of informative, persuasive, and reminder ads used by institutional advertisers.

Persuasive Advertising
Competitive promotions that seek to develop demand for products, services, organizations, people, ideas, or causes.

Reminder Advertising
Promotions that seek to reinforce previous promotional activity by keeping the name of the product, service, organization, person, idea, or cause in front of the public.

Advocacy Advertising

One form of persuasive institutional advertising that has grown in use during the past decade is advocacy advertising. **Advocacy advertising**, sometimes referred to as *cause advertising,* can be defined as any kind of paid public communication or message, from an identified source and in a conventional medium of public advertising, which presents information or a point of view bearing on a publicly recognized controversial issue.[3] Such advertising is designed to influence public opinion, to affect current and pending legislation, and to gain a following.

Advocacy advertising has been utilized effectively by such nonprofit organizations as Mothers Against Drunk Driving (MADD), Planned Parenthood, the National Rifle Association, and "right to life" anti-abortion groups. (Uses of advocacy advertising are examined in Chapter 20.) In recent years, profit-seeking companies (particularly energy and resource firms) with a stake in

Advocacy Advertising
Paid public communication or message that presents information on a point of view bearing on a publicly recognized controversial issue.

some issue have turned to advocacy advertising. Among the firms that have used advocacy advertising in taking aggressive positions on particular issues and seeking to convince the public of their viewpoints are Mobil Oil and Bethlehem Steel.

Media Selection

One of the most important decisions in developing an advertising strategy is media selection. A mistake at this point can cost a company literally millions of dollars in ineffective advertising. The advertising media selected by the marketer must be capable of accomplishing the communications objectives of informing, persuading, and reminding potential customers of the product, service, person, or idea.

Research should identify the market target to determine its size and characteristics and then match the target with the audience and the effectiveness of the available media. The objective is to achieve adequate media coverage without advertising beyond the identifiable limits of the potential market. Finally, alternative costs should be compared to determine the best possible media purchase.

Figure 15.6 compares the various advertising media on the basis of their shares of overall advertising expenditures. Newspapers and television are the

Figure 15.6
Percentage of Total Advertising in the Various Media

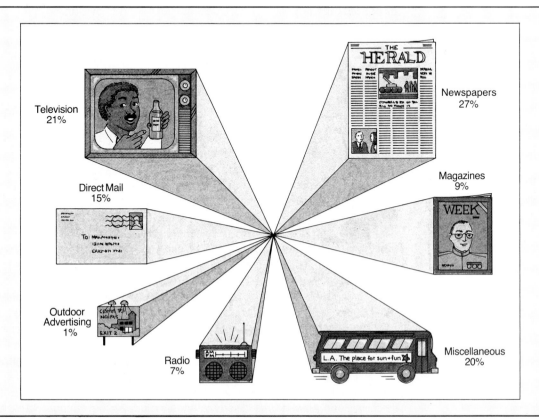

Source: *Statistical Abstract of the United States* (Washington, D.C.: Government Printing Office, 1984), p. 567.

leading advertising media, with radio and outdoor advertising ranking at the bottom. During the 35 years since 1950, newspapers, radio, and magazines have experienced declines in their market shares, while television has grown tremendously.

Newspapers

Newspaper advertising continues to dominate local markets. It accounts for 27 percent of total advertising revenues. Newspapers' primary advantages are flexibility (advertising can be varied from one locality to the next), community prestige (newspapers have a deep impact on the community), intensive coverage (in most locations 90 percent of the homes can be reached by a single newspaper), reader control of exposure to the advertising message (unlike electronic media, readers can refer back to newspapers), coordination with national advertising, and merchandising services (such as promotional and research support). The disadvantages are a short life span, hasty reading (the typical reader spends only 20 to 30 minutes reading the newspaper), and poor reproduction.[4]

Magazines

Magazines, which are divided into such diverse categories as consumer, farm, and business publications, account for about 9 percent of national advertising, of which 45 percent appears in weekly magazines. The primary advantages of magazine advertising are the selectivity of market targets, quality reproduction, long life, the prestige associated with some magazines, and the extra services offered by many publications. The primary disadvantage is that magazines lack the flexibility of newspapers, radio, and television.

Reader's Digest is the nation's leading magazine in terms of annual paid subscriptions, with 17.9 million. Other leading magazines include two that focus upon the growing numbers of subscribers who are over 50, several women's magazines, one magazine targeted at young adult males, a weekly guide for television viewers, and a news magazine.

Television

Although television ranks second to newspapers with a 21 percent share of overall advertising revenues, the relative attractiveness of the two media differ in local and national markets. A major component of total newspaper advertising revenues is the local markets. By contrast, television is the dominant medium for national advertising. Television advertising can be divided into four categories: network, national, local, and cable. Columbia Broadcasting System, National Broadcasting Company, and American Broadcasting Company are the three major national networks. Their programs usually account for a substantial portion of total television advertising expenditures. A national "spot" is nonnetwork broadcasting used by a general advertiser. Local advertising spots, used primarily by retailers, consist of locally developed and sponsored commercials. Cable television is a rapidly growing medium, currently serving more than 34 million people in 40.5 percent of all U.S. households. Total cable advertising revenues were $383 million in 1983, with Anheuser-Busch, Procter & Gamble, and General Foods as the largest advertisers. Television advertising offers the advantages of impact, mass coverage, repetition, flexibility, and prestige. Its disadvantages include relinquishing control of the

Return to the Stop-Action Case

New York Penta Hotel

One of the first objectives of New York Penta marketing executives was to determine the target audience for their advertising campaign. They had to know exactly whom they must convince that Penta had advanced from second-class status. According to marketing director Richard Graves, the answer was partially determined by the firm's relatively small advertising budget. In addition, hotel management recognized that the image of a hotel whose promises of improvement were regularly broken was limited to people in the hotel and travel industries. "We didn't have to tell our story to John Q. Public," said Graves. "The general public never knew about the promised renovations that never happened."

Because the hotel's image problems were limited to marketing intermediaries such as travel agencies and to persons responsible for large bookings, Penta marketers decided to concentrate its $500,000 advertising budget on ads in such trade publications as *Travel Weekly, Meetings & Conventions,* and *Women's Wear Daily.* The latter publication was included in the media package because of the hotel's proximity to New York's garment district, which attracts tens of thousands of traveling executives each year.

Source: Graves quotation from telephone interview, May 1, 1984.

promotional message to the telecaster (who can influence its impact), high costs, high mortality rates for commercials, some public distrust, and a lack of selectivity.

Radio

Advertisers using the medium of radio can also be classified as network, national, and local. Radio accounts for about 7 percent of total advertising revenue and 12 percent of local expenditures. Its advantages are immediacy (studies show most people regard radio as the best source for up-to-date news), low cost, flexibility, practical and low-cost audience selection, and mobility. Its disadvantages include fragmentation (Boise, Idaho, for example, has a population of 100,000 and 20 radio stations), the temporary nature of the message, and less research information than for television.

Direct Mail

Sales letters, postcards, leaflets, folders, broadsides (larger than folders), booklets, catalogs, and house organs (periodical publications issued by organizations) are all forms of direct-mail advertising. The advantages of direct mail are selectivity, intensive coverage, speed, format flexibility, complete information, and the personalization of each mailing piece. Disadvantages of direct mail are its high cost per reader, its dependence on the quality of the mailing list, and some people's annoyance with it. This situation led the Direct Mail/Marketing Association in 1971 to establish its Mail Preference Service. This consumer service sends name-removal forms to people who do not wish to receive direct-mail advertising. It also provides add-on forms for those who like to receive a lot of mail. Approximately 15 percent of total advertising is spent on direct mail.

Outdoor Advertising

Posters (commonly called billboards), painted bulletins or displays (such as those that appear on the walls of buildings), and electric spectaculars (large, illuminated, and sometimes animated signs and displays) make up outdoor advertising. This form of advertising has the advantages of communicating quick and simple ideas, repetition, and the ability to promote products that are available for sale nearby. Outdoor advertising is particularly effective in metropolitan and other high-traffic areas. Disadvantages of the medium are the brevity of its message and public concern over aesthetics. The Highway Beautification Act of 1965, for example, regulates outdoor advertising near interstate highways. This medium accounts for approximately 1 percent of all advertising. Figure 15.7 shows the classic billboard for Coppertone, which research studies indicate is the best remembered design ever displayed.[5]

Figure 15.8 compares the various advertising media on the basis of each medium's major strengths and weaknesses.

Organization of the Advertising Function

Although the ultimate responsibility for advertising decision making often rests with top marketing management, the organization of the advertising function varies among companies. A producer of a technical industrial product may be served by one person within the company, whose primary task is writing copy submitted to trade publications. A consumer goods company, on the other hand, may have a large department staffed with advertising specialists.

Figure 15.7
Effective Use of Outdoor Advertising by Suntan Lotion Marketer

Source: Courtesy of Coppertone.

Figure 15.8

Advantages and Disadvantages of the Various Advertising Media

Media	Advantages	Disadvantages
Newspapers 	Flexibility Community Prestige Intense Coverage Reader Control of Exposure Coordination with National Advertising Merchandising Service	Short Life Span Hasty Reading Poor Reproduction
Magazines 	Selectivity Quality Reproduction Long Life Prestige Associated with Some Magazines Extra Services	Lack of Flexibility
Television 	Great Impact Mass Coverage Repetition Flexibility Prestige	Temporary Nature of Message High Cost High Mortality Rate for Commercials Evidence of Public Lack of Selectivity
Radio 	Immediacy Low Cost Practical Audience Selection Mobility	Fragmentation Temporary Nature of Message Little Research Information
Outdoor Advertising 	Communication of Quick and Simple Ideas Repetition Ability to Promote Products Available for Sale Nearby	Brevity of the Message Public Concern over Esthetics
Direct Mail 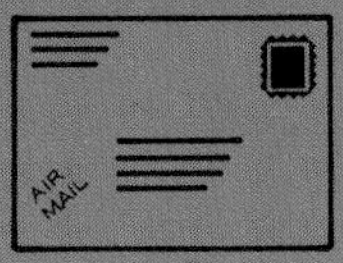	Selectivity Intense Coverage Speed Flexibility of Format Complete Information Personalization	High Cost per Person Dependency on Quality of Mailing List Consumer Resistance

Source: Based on S. Watson Dunn and Arnold M. Barban, *Advertising: Its Role in Modern Marketing*,
6th ed. (Hinsdale, Ill.: The Dryden Press, 1986).

The advertising function is usually organized as a staff department reporting to the vice-president (or director) of marketing. The director of advertising is an executive position heading the functional activity of advertising. The individual in this slot should be not only a skilled and experienced advertiser, but also an effective communicator within the organization. The success of a firm's promotional strategy depends upon the advertising director's willing-

Figure 15.9
Advertising Agency Organization Chart

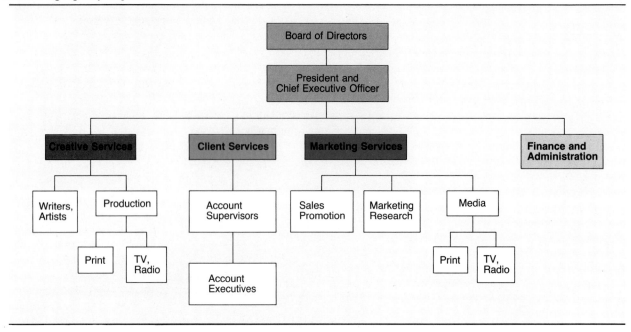

ness and ability to communicate both vertically and horizontally. The major tasks typically organized under advertising include advertising research, design, copywriting, media analysis, and, in some cases, sales promotion.

Advertising Agencies

Advertising Agency
Marketing specialist firm used to assist advertisers in planning and implementing advertising programs.

Many major advertisers make use of one of the more than 8,000 independent advertising agencies in the United States. The advertising agency is a marketing specialist firm that assists the advertiser in planning and preparing advertisements. There are several reasons why most large advertisers use an agency for at least a portion of their advertising. Agencies are typically staffed with highly qualified specialists who provide a degree of creativity and objectivity that is difficult to sustain in a corporate advertising department. In some cases, they also reduce the cost of advertising because the advertiser can avoid many of the fixed expenses associated with maintaining an internal advertising department. Finally, since agencies are typically compensated by the media used (typically in the form of a 15 percent discount based upon advertising expenditures), their services are available for the advertiser at little cost. However, effective use of an advertising agency requires a close relationship between the advertiser and the agency.

Figure 15.9 shows the organization chart for a large advertising agency. While the titles may vary among agencies, the major operational functions may be classified as creative services, account management, research, and promotional services. Young & Rubicam, Ted Bates Worldwide, J. Walter Thompson Company, and Ogilvy & Mather are the largest advertising agencies in the world. Each agency has worldwide billings of over $2 billion.

Creating an Advertisement

The final step in the advertising process—the development and preparation of an advertisement—should flow logically from the promotional theme selected. It should be a complementary part of the marketing mix, and its role in the total marketing strategy should be carefully determined. Major factors to consider when preparing an advertisement are its creativity, its continuity with past advertisements, and possibly its association with other company products.

What should an advertisement accomplish? Regardless of the exact appeal that is chosen, an advertisement should (1) gain attention and interest, (2) inform and/or persuade, and (3) eventually lead to buying action.

Gaining attention should be productive, that is, it should instill some recall of the product or service. Consider the case of the Gillette Company, which had a chimpanzee shave a man's face in a commercial. After tests in two cities, one Gillette spokesperson lamented, "Lots of people remembered the chimp, but hardly anyone remembered our product. There was fantastic interest in the monkey, but no payoff for Gillette."[6] The advertisement gained the audience's attention, but it failed to lead to buying action. An advertisement that fails to gain and hold the receiver's attention is ineffective.

An advertisement should also inform and/or persuade. For example, insurance advertisements are informative—they typically specify the features of the policy—and they are persuasive—they may use testimonials in attempting to persuade prospects.

Stimulating buying action is often difficult because an advertisement cannot actually close a sale. Nevertheless, if the ad gains attention and informs or persuades, it is probably well worthwhile. Too many advertisers fail to suggest how the receiver can purchase a product if he or she so desires. This is a shortcoming that should be eliminated.

Figure 15.10 illustrates the evolution of an advertisement from idea to finished product. Marketers of Colombian coffee elevated the image of a Colombian farmer and his burro to the status of a trademark. Incorporating this image in new advertising, a thought sketch is converted into a rough layout. The layout is further refined until the final version of the advertisement is ready to print.

Comparative Advertising

Comparative Advertising
Nonpersonal selling efforts that make direct promotional comparisons with leading competitive brands.

Comparative advertising is an advertising strategy in which the firm's advertising messages make direct promotional comparisons with leading competitive brands. The strategy is best employed by firms that do not lead the market. Most market leaders do not mention the names of competing products in their own advertisements. Rather than giving competitors a "free ride," they simply do not acknowledge that competitive products even exist. Procter & Gamble and General Foods, for example, traditionally have devoted little of their huge promotional budgets to comparative advertising. But many firms do use it extensively. An estimated 23 percent of all radio and television commercials make comparisons to competitive products. Here are some examples.

- Scope mouthwash prevents "medicine breath," but Listerine is never mentioned.

Figure 15.10
How to Build an Ad

Source: Courtesy of the National Federation of Coffee Growers of Colombia.

- Minute Maid lemonade is better than the "no-lemon lemonade," a reference to General Foods' Country Time brand.
- Suave antiperspirant will keep you just as dry as Ban Ultra Dry does and for a lot less.
- Nationwide, more Coca-Cola drinkers prefer the taste of Pepsi.

Marketers who contemplate using comparative advertising in their promotional strategies should take precautions to assure that they can substantiate their claims. Comparative advertising has the potential of producing lawsuits, so practitioners must be especially careful. Advertising experts disagree about the long-term effects of comparative advertising. The conclusion is likely to be that comparative advertising is a useful strategy in a limited number of circumstances.

Celebrity Testimonials: Advantages and Disadvantages

In attempting to improve the effectiveness of their advertising, a number of marketers utilize celebrities to present their advertising messages. Well-known examples include Michael Jackson and Lionel Ritchie for Pepsi Cola, model Cheryl Tiegs for Cover Girl makeup and Sears sportswear, James Garner and Mariette Hartley for Polaroid, former Dallas Cowboy Walt Garrison for Dodge and Skoal smokeless tobacco, and Bill Cosby for Jell-O pudding.

The primary advantage of using big-name personalities is that they may improve product recognition in a promotional environment filled with hundreds of competing 20- and 30-second commercials. (Advertisers use the term *clutter* to describe this situation.) For this technique to succeed, the celebrity must be a credible source of information for the item being sold. Cheryl Tiegs is an effective spokeswoman for Cover Girl, since her exuberant personality and beauty are compatible with the Cover Girl message of clean makeup aimed at young women. By contrast, sophisticated actress Ann Blyth is less effective in her advertisements for Hostess cupcakes. Celebrity advertisements are ineffective when there is no reasonable relationship between the celebrity and the advertised product or service.

Millions of Americans are currently very sports and celebrity oriented. Therefore, there is opportunity for firms to profitably sponsor athletes or sporting events. However, such promotion should clearly be an adjunct to existing promotional programs. There are several principles that corporate sponsors should consider before getting involved. First, they must be selective and specific. A market target should be pinpointed and a sport or celebrity carefully matched to that target and objective. Second, sports interest trends should be followed carefully. Too often firms get involved without assessing the strength of the trend. Third, they must be original and look for a special focus. Is it possible to come up with a unique concept? Fourth, firms should analyze the results in the short and long term. Sponsorship is a business decision that should pay off in profits.

Retail Advertising

Retail Advertising
Nonpersonal selling by stores that offer goods or services directly to the consuming public.

Retail advertising is all advertising by stores that sell goods or services directly to the consuming public. While accounting for a sizable portion of total annual advertising expenditures, retail advertising varies widely in its effectiveness. One study showed that consumers were often suspicious of retail price advertisements. Source, message, and shopping experience seemed to affect consumer attitudes toward these advertisements.[7]

The basic problem is that advertising is often treated as a secondary activity in retail stores. Advertising agencies are rarely used, except in the case of some retail giants. Instead, store managers are usually given the responsibility of advertising as an added task to be performed along with their normal functions. The basic step in correcting this deficiency is to give one individual both the responsibility and the authority for developing an effective retail advertising program.

Cooperative Advertising
Sharing of advertising costs between a retailer and the manufacturer of a good or service.

Cooperative Advertising   Sharing of advertising costs between the retailer and the manufacturer or wholesaler is called **cooperative advertising** For example, Ocean Pacific Sportswear may pay 50 percent of the cost of a retail store's newspaper advertisement that features its product lines. Cooperative advertising resulted from the media practice of offering lower rates to local advertisers than to national advertisers. Later, cooperative advertising was seen as a method of improving dealer relations. From the retailer's viewpoint, it permits a store to secure advertising that it would not otherwise have.

Assessing the Effectiveness of an Advertisement _____

Because advertising represents a major expenditure for many firms, it is imperative to determine whether a chosen campaign is accomplishing its promotional objectives. The determination of advertising effectiveness, however, is one of the most difficult undertakings in marketing. It consists of two primary elements—pretesting and posttesting.

Pretesting

Pretesting
Assessment of an advertisement before it is actually used.

Pretesting is the assessment of an advertisement's effectiveness before it is actually used. It includes a variety of evaluative methods. To test magazine advertisements, the Batten, Barton, Durstine & Osborn ad agency cuts ads out of advance copies of magazines, then "strips in" the ads it wants to test. Interviewers later check the impact of the advertisements on readers who receive free copies of the revised magazine.

Another ad agency, McCann-Erickson, uses a *sales conviction test* to evaluate magazine advertisements. Interviewers ask heavy users of a particular item to pick which of two alternative advertisements would convince them to purchase it.

Potential radio and television advertisements are often screened by consumers who sit in a studio and press two buttons—one for a positive reaction to the commercial, the other for a negative reaction. Sometimes, proposed ad copy is printed on a postcard that also offers a free product; the number of cards returned is viewed as an indication of the copy's effectiveness. *Blind product tests* are also often used. In these tests, people are asked to select unidentified products on the basis of available advertising copy. Mechanical means of assessing how people read advertising copy are yet another method. One mechanical test uses an eye camera to photograph how people read ads: its results help determine headline placement and advertising copy length.

Posttesting

Posttesting
Assessment of an advertisement's effectiveness after it has been used.

Posttesting is the assessment of advertising copy after it has been used. Pretesting is generally a more desirable testing method than posttesting because of its potential cost savings. However, posttesting can be helpful in planning future advertisements and in adjusting current advertising programs.

In one of the most popular posttests, the *Starch Readership Report*, interviewers ask people who have read selected magazines whether they have read various ads in them. A copy of the magazine is used as an interviewing aid, and each interviewer starts at a different point in the magazine. For larger ads, respondents are also asked about specifics, such as headlines and copy. Figure 15.11 shows an advertisement for Clairesse haircolor lotion with the actual Starch scores. All readership, or recognition, tests assume that future sales are related to advertising readership.

Unaided recall tests are another method of posttesting advertisements. Here, respondents are not given copies of the magazine but must recall the ads from memory. Interviewers for the Gallup and Robinson market-research

Figure 15.11
Magazine Advertisement with Starch Scores

The "Seen %" label indicates the percentage of readers interviewed who saw the illustration.

The "Ad-As-A-Whole" label indicates the percentage of readers interviewed who: "Noted" the ad in the issue, "Associated" it with a specific advertiser or product, and "Read Most" (more than 50%) of the written material in the ad. This label summarizes the total readership of the ad.

The "Signature %" label indicates the percentage of readers who saw the logo or signature.

The "Read %" and "Read Some %" labels indicate the percentage of readers interviewed who read the headline and some or all of the body copy.

Source: Courtesy of Starch INRA Hooper, Inc.

firms require people to prove they have read a magazine by recalling one or more of its feature articles. The people who remember particular articles are given cards with the names of products advertised in the issue. They then list the ads they remember and explain what they remember about them. Finally, the respondents are asked about their potential purchase of the product. A readership test concludes the Gallup and Robinson interview. Burke Research Corporation uses telephone interviews the day after a commercial appears on television to test brand recognition and the effectiveness of the advertisement.

Inquiry tests are another popular posttest. Advertisements sometimes offer a gift, generally a sample of the product, to people who respond to the advertisement. The number of inquiries relative to the cost of the advertisement is used as a measure of effectiveness. *Split runs* allow advertisers to test two or more ads at the same time. Under this method, a publication's production run is split in two: half the magazines use Advertisement A and half use Advertisement B. The relative pull of the alternatives is then determined by inquiries.

Regardless of the exact method used, marketers must realize that pretesting and posttesting are expensive, and they must, therefore, plan to use them as effectively as possible.

Sales Promotion Methods

Sales Promotion
Marketing activities (other than personal selling, advertising, and publicity) that stimulate consumer purchasing and dealer effectiveness.

The second type of nonpersonal selling is sales promotion. Sales promotion may be defined as those marketing activities, other than personal selling, advertising, and publicity, that stimulate consumer purchasing and dealer effectiveness. It includes such activities as displays, trade shows and exhibitions, demonstrations, and various nonrecurrent promotional efforts not in the ordinary routine.[8]

Sales promotional techniques may be used by all members of a marketing channel: manufacturers, wholesalers, and retailers. In addition, sales promotional activities are typically targeted at specific markets. For example, a manufacturer such as Texize Corporation might use trial sample mailings of a new spot remover to consumers and a sales contest for wholesalers and retailers who handle the new product. In both instances, the sales promotion techniques are designed to supplement and extend the other elements of the firm's promotional mix.

Firms that wish to use sales promotion can choose from various methods—point-of-purchase advertising; specialty advertising; trade shows; samples, coupons, and premiums; contests; and trading stamps. More than one of these options may be used in a single promotional strategy, but probably no promotional strategy has ever used all of the options in a single program. While they are not mutually exclusive, promotions are generally employed on a selective basis.

Point-of-Purchase Advertising

Point-of-Purchase Advertising
Displays and other promotions located near where a buying decision is actually made.

Point-of-purchase advertising refers to displays and other promotions located near where a buying decision is actually made. The in-store promotion of consumer goods is a common example. Such advertising may be useful in supplementing a theme developed in another area of promotional strategy. A life-size display of a celebrity used in television advertising is a very effective in-store display. Another example is the familiar L'eggs store displays, in which pantyhose packaged in plastic eggs completely altered marketing practices in this industry.

Specialty Advertising

Specialty Advertising
Sales promotion technique that involves the use of articles such as key rings, calendars, and ballpoint pens that bear the advertiser's name, address, and advertising message.

Specialty advertising is a sales promotion technique that utilizes useful articles carrying the advertiser's name, address, and advertising message to reach the target consumers. The origin of specialty advertising has been traced to the Middle Ages, when wooden pegs bearing the names of artisans were given to prospects to be driven into their walls and to serve as a convenient place upon which to hang armor.[9]

Examples of contemporary advertising specialties carrying the firm's name include ashtrays, balloons, calendars, coffee mugs, key rings, matchbooks, pens, personalized business gifts of modest value, pocket secretaries, shopping bags, memo pads, paperweights, glasses, yardsticks, and hundreds of other items.

Advertising specialties help reinforce previous or future advertising and sales messages. An A.C. Nielsen survey found that both the general public and businesses were more likely to purchase from firms using specialty advertising.[10]

Trade Shows

To influence channel members and resellers in the distribution channel, it has become a common practice for sellers to participate in *trade shows*. These shows are often organized by an industry's trade association and may be part of the association's annual meeting or convention. Vendors serving the industry are invited to the show to display and demonstrate their products for the association's membership. An example is the Hanover Fair, an industrial technology show held annually in Hanover, Germany. The 1985 Hanover Fair attracted over 650,000 visitors from 120 different countries to its 5 million square feet of display area. Shows are also used to reach the ultimate consumer. Home and recreation shows, for instance, allow businesses to display and demonstrate home care, recreation, and other consumer products to the entire community.

Samples, Coupons, and Premiums

The distribution of samples, coupons, and premiums is probably the best-known sales promotion technique. *Sampling* is the free distribution of a product in an attempt to obtain future sales. The distribution may be done on a door-to-door basis, by mail, via demonstrations, or by inclusion in packages containing other products. Sampling is especially useful in promoting new products.

Coupons offer a discount, usually some specified price reduction, on the next purchase of a product. They are redeemable at retail outlets that receive a handling fee from the manufacturer. Mail, magazine, newspaper, and package insertions are the standard methods of distributing coupons.

Premiums are items given free, or at a low cost, with the purchase of another product. They have proved effective in motivating consumers to try new products or different brands. Premiums should have some relationship with the purchased item. For example, the service department of an auto dealership might offer its customers ice scrapers. Premiums are also used to obtain direct mail purchases. The value of premium giveaways runs into billions of dollars each year.

Contests

Firms often sponsor contests to introduce new products and services and to attract additional customers. Contests, sweepstakes, and games offer substantial prizes in the form of cash or merchandise as an inducement to potential customers.

In recent years, a number of court rulings and legal restrictions have placed limitations on the use of contests. As a result, firms contemplating the use of this promotional technique should use the services of a specialist.

Trading Stamps

A sales promotion technique similar to premiums is *trading stamps*. Customers receive trading stamps with their purchases in various retail establishments. The stamps can be saved and exchanged for gifts, usually in special redemption centers operated by the trading-stamp company. The degree to which the consumer benefits by trading stamps depends on the relative value of the goods offered. Although the trading stamp industry was founded by Sperry & Hutcheson in 1896, the heighth of their popularity as a sales promotion tool occurred during the 1950s and 1960s. They have been distributed by such retailers as gasoline stations, grocer retailers, mail-order houses, and savings and loan associations. The extent of their usage seems to depend on factors including relative price levels, location of redemption centers, and legal restrictions.

Public Relations

Public Relations
A firm's communications and relationships with its various publics.

The previous chapter defined public relations as the firm's communications and relationships with its various publics, including customers, employees, stockholders, suppliers, the government, and the society in which it operates. Public relations efforts date back to 1889, when George Westinghouse hired two people to publicize the advantages of alternating current to counter the arguments for direct-current electricity.

Public relations still remains an efficient indirect communications channel for promoting products, although it typically has broader objectives than other aspects of promotional strategy. It is concerned with the prestige and image of all parts of the organization. Examples of nonmarketing-oriented public relations objectives are a company's attempt to gain favorable public opinion during a long strike and an open letter to Congress published in a newspaper during congressional debate on a bill affecting a particular industry. Although in some companies the public relations department is not an arm of the marketing division, the activities of the public relations department invariably have an impact on promotional strategy.

Public relations is now a $2-billion-a-year industry employing 123,000 people in both the nonprofit and profit-oriented sectors. There are approximately 1,200 public relations firms in the United States, ranging in size from Hill & Knowlton, with over 1,000 employees, to one-person operations. Only 49 of these agencies exceed $1 million in annual revenues.

Public relations is considered to be in a period of major growth as a result of increased environmental pressure for better communication between industry and the public. Many top executives are becoming involved. Lee Iacocca's efforts to publicize the justification for federal loan guarantees for Chrysler Corporation are an illustration. A survey of 185 chief executives concluded that 92 percent of them spend more time on public relations now than they did five years ago. Nearly 40 percent of the respondents reported that public relations accounted for 25 to 50 percent of their time.[11]

Publicity

Publicity
Stimulation of demand by placing significant news or obtaining favorable presentation not paid for by an identified sponsor.

The part of public relations that is most directly related to promoting a firm's products or services is publicity. Publicity can be defined as the nonpersonal stimulation of demand for a product, service, idea, person, or organization by placing significant news about it in a published medium or obtaining favorable presentation of it upon radio, television, or stage that is not paid for by an identified sponsor.[12] Since it is designed to familiarize the general public with the characteristics, services, and advantages of a product, service, idea, person, or organization, publicity is an information activity of public relations. While the costs associated with it are minimal in comparison to other forms of promotion, publicity is not entirely cost-free. Publicity-related expenses include the costs of employing marketing personnel assigned to create and submit publicity releases, printing and mailing costs, and other related expense items.

Some publicity is used to promote a company's image or viewpoint, but a significant amount provides information about products, particularly new ones. Because many consumers accept information in a news story more readily than they accept it in an advertisement, publicity releases are often sent to media editors for possible inclusion in news stories. In some cases, the information in a publicity release about a new product or service provides valuable assistance to a newspaper or magazine writer, and information of this sort eventually is published.

Publicity releases are sometimes used to fill voids in a publication and other times are used in regular features. In either case, publicity releases serve as a valuable supplement to advertising.

Today, public relations has to be considered as an integral part of promotional strategy even though its basic objectives extend far beyond just attempting to influence the purchase of a particular good. Public relations programs—and especially publicity—make a significant contribution to the achievement of promotional goals.

Summary

Advertising, sales promotion, public relations, and publicity—the nonpersonal selling elements of promotion—are not twentieth century phenomena. Advertising, for instance, can trace its origin to very early times. Today, these elements of promotion have gained professional status and serve as vital aspects of most organizations, both profit and nonprofit.

Advertising, a nonpersonal sales presentation usually directed to a large number of potential customers, seeks to achieve communications goals rather than direct sales objectives. It strives to inform, persuade, and remind potential customers of the product, service, person, idea, or organization being promoted.

Advertising planning begins with the objectives and strategies formulated for the entire organization. Research is frequently used to make tactical decisions about copy, scheduling, and media choices. Finally, advertisements are evaluated, and appropriate feedback is provided to management. There are two basic categories of advertising: product advertising and institutional advertising. Both categories can be further subdivided into informative, persuasive, and reminder advertising. One of the most vital decisions in developing an advertising strategy is the selection of the media to be employed.

The major tasks of advertising departments are advertising research, design, copywriting, media analysis, and sales promotion. Many advertisers use independent advertising agencies to provide the creativity and objectivity missing in their own organizations and to reduce the cost of advertising. The final step in the advertising process is developing and preparing the advertisement.

The principal methods of sales promotion are point-of-purchase advertising; specialty advertising; trade shows; samples, coupons, and premiums; contests; and trading stamps. Public relations and publicity also play major roles in developing promotional strategies.

Solving the Stop-Action Case

New York Penta Hotel

How could the Penta marketing executives rebuild their hotel's reputation when the hotel and travel industries would have no faith in anything they would promise? Spending millions on renovations and launching a huge advertising campaign when the job was done would be an effective way of handling the problem. Unfortunately, the New York Penta could not afford to halt operations while these renovations were made. Marketing executives had to attract a steady flow of customers while these improvements were being implemented. To accomplish this, they had to convince the travel and hotel industries that their promises were good.

The firm's marketing executives decided to use a humorous and completely honest approach to the hotel's image and their plans to correct it. "We plan on saying about ourselves what we know people are saying about us behind closed doors in cupped hands," said marketing director Graves. "Rather than have people ask who the fools are who bought the Statler, we figured we would bring the problem out in a tongue-in-cheek manner."

The result was a series of 18 one-page advertisements, each with a humorous headline that compelled readers to stop, look, and continue reading. "My analyst thought we had my masochism licked. Then I became vice-president of the former New York Statler," said one. The intention of such fun-poking was to induce people to read on so they could see what was being done to the Penta. "Our ads derive from a position of confidence in the abilities of our owners, who have a proven track record in Europe, and of our professional management team in New York to turn this hotel around and to operate it as a first-class business and meetings and convention hotel," stated Graves.

Several ads in the campaign were aimed at hotel guests. Some featured low-price weekend packages.

Photo Source: Courtesy of New York Penta Hotel.

Other price-oriented advertisements sought to attract Canadian travelers by announcing that the Penta would accept Canadian dollars as full payment for rooms, even though Canadian dollars were worth about 20 percent less than American dollars.

Since the advertising campaign began in early 1984, the Penta's image has undergone a dramatic change in the hotel and travel industries. "We created a new identity for ourselves," said Graves. "People are talking about us all over the place. Any ad campaign that brings that kind of attention is successful."

Source: Graves quotations from telephone interview, May 1, 1984.

Questions for Discussion

1. Explain the wide variation in advertising expenditures as a percentage of sales in the industries shown in Figure 15.1.

2. Trace the historical development of advertising.

3. Describe the primary objectives of advertising.

4. List and discuss the two basic types of advertising. Cite an example of the three subcategories for each type.

5. Discuss the relationship between advertising and the product life cycle.

6. Describe the process of advertising planning.

7. What are the advantages and disadvantages associated with using each of the advertising media?

8. Review the changes in the relative importance of the various advertising media during the past 35 years that are mentioned in the chapter. Suggest likely explanations for the changes that have occurred during the past three decades.

9. Develop an argument favoring the use of comparative advertising by a marketer who is currently preparing an advertising plan. Make any assumptions necessary.

10. Discuss the organization of the advertising function. Consider all the major activities associated with advertising.

11. Under what circumstances are celebrity spokespersons in advertising likely to be effective?

12. Sweden's business practices court ordered a U.S. advertising agency and its client, a Swedish insurance company, to stop using models identified in their commercials as other people. The court ruled that this practice misled buyers. Do you agree? Why or why not?

13. Why is retail advertising so important today? Relate cooperative advertising to the discussion of alternative promotional strategies in Chapter 15.

14. Cooperative advertising results in a sharing of advertising costs between the retailer and the manufacturer or vendor. From society's viewpoint, should this kind of advertising be prohibited on the grounds that it leads to manufacturer domination of the distribution channel? Defend your answer.

15. Several states now have government-operated lotteries. How should a state advertise lottery tickets?

16. List and discuss the principal methods of sales promotion.

17. What specialty advertising would be appropriate for the following?
    a. An independent insurance agent
    b. A retail furniture store
    c. An interior decorator
    d. A local radio station

18. Distinguish between:
    a. Product advertising and cooperative advertising
    b. Premiums and specialty advertising
    c. Trading stamps and coupons

19. What do most of your friends think about the role of advertising in contemporary society? Why do you think they hold these beliefs?

20. Choose a candidate who ran for political office during a recent election. Assume that you were in charge of advertising for this person's campaign. Develop an advertising strategy for your candidate. Select a campaign theme and the media to be employed. Finally, design an advertisement for the candidate.

Case: Prudential's New Approach to Advertising Life Insurance

Enough jokes. After three years of whimsical commercials for life insurance, Prudential Insurance Co. of America is turning joltingly serious. It believes people have overcome their squeamishness about the subject of death.

"I remember hearing somebody say I was . . . dead," whispers a man's voice as one of Prudential's new 30-second TV spots begins. Unseen, the man is lying on an operating table as doctors look down on him. The wavy green line of an oscilloscope monitoring his pulse goes flat. "I thought about Janice and Bobby," he says. "Who'd take care of them now?"

The doctors pump on his chest. As the patient responds, they are heard saying, "He's coming back. He's all right now."

The scene is the latest step in the evolution of life insurance advertising. Once so genteel that it never mentioned the word "death," it has slowly stopped skirting the reason why people buy the product. As Prudential did in its three-year campaign that just ended, some insurers have used humor to overcome viewers' anxiety about death.

The Prudential campaign was inspired by *Heaven Can Wait,* a 1978 movie comedy starring Warren Beatty. In the commercials, angels dressed in white, three-piece suits came to collect the deceased, generally young men who had died unexpectedly.

Those ads didn't stop working, says Connie Sartain, Prudential's advertising vice-president. Instead, the straightforward portrayal of death simply outscored humor in consumer tests. "You just keep trying to beat what you have on the air," she says.

Prudential has four commercials in the new campaign. In addition to the surgery patient, they feature a woman drowning, a volunteer fireman overcome by smoke in a burning building, and a man being rushed to a hospital in an ambulance. Each recovers from the close call.

After that moment of "resurrection," as Prudential's ad agency calls it, the scene shifts to the protagonist, fully revived and back in safer surroundings. The drowning woman, for example, is walking on a beach with her two young daughters. "I got a second chance to do all those things I meant to do," she says.

An off-camera announcer concludes the pitch: "At Prudential we know that most of us don't get a second chance." He recommends a chat with a Prudential agent.

The switch in campaigns comes amid increased media attention to death, near-death experiences, and what one news magazine calls a "gloom boom." "If we've timed it right, this campaign should exploit the trend," says Lee Hines, executive vice-president at Ted Bates Advertising, Prudential's agency.

Tests of viewers' reactions to Prudential's treatment of death in the "angels" campaign showed that about 15 percent of the audience objected to it. Preliminary tests of the new ads show that a slightly smaller number dislike the serious approach.

Both campaigns have the same purpose, says Mr. Hines. "The idea is to get people to stop procrastinating, to put a sharp stick in their eye," he explains. "It's human nature not to face up to your own mortality."

Source: Bill Abrams, "New Prudential Ads Portray Death as No Laughing Matter," *The Wall Street Journal* (November 10, 1983), p. 29. Reprinted by permission of *The Wall Street Journal,* © Dow Jones & Company, Inc., 1983.

Questions

1. Evaluate the Prudential Life Insurance advertising campaign.

2. Research on consumer reaction to the use of fear appeals in advertising indicates that consumers filter out those messages involving strong fear appeals. Is this likely to occur with the Prudential ads? Defend your answer.

3. What ethical issues are raised by the use of fear appeals in promoting a product, service, organization, idea, or person?

Computer Applications

Since advertising frequently represents a substantial portion of total marketing costs, marketers are continually seeking more efficient methods of accomplishing their promotional objectives. Advertisers not only seek to communicate with and persuade prospective customers, they also want to accomplish this at the least possible costs. In evaluating alternative advertising media, marketers seek to match the characteristics of their market target customers with the audiences attracted by radio and television programs, newspapers, magazines, or other media. But even when a specific advertising medium has been chosen, its advertising costs vary greatly depending upon such factors as market coverage, size or length of the advertisement, and location of the advertising message. Consequently, some common denominator is needed to compare available alternatives.

One commonly used method in comparing alternative vehicles within a single advertising medium is the *cost-per-thousand* criterion. Since M is the Roman numeral for 1,000, cost per thousand is frequently abbreviated as CPM. For magazines, the following formula is used:

$$\frac{\text{Cost Per}}{\text{Thousand (CPM)}} = \frac{\text{Magazine Page Cost} \times 1,000}{\text{Circulation}}.$$

For radio or television, the CPM formula is modified as follows:

$$\frac{\text{Cost Per}}{\text{Thousand (CPM)}} = \frac{\text{Cost of a Commercial} \times 1,000}{\text{Circulation}}.$$

Since circulation and program audience data are available from independent research sources, CPM calculations can be made easily and updated on a regular basis. Circulation data for magazines are available from such research specialists as Standard Rate & Data Service. Program audience data for television and radio can be obtained from such firms as A. C. Nielsen or Arbitron.

Assume that *Modern Maturity* has a circulation of 8 million and charges $75,000 for a one-page, full-color advertisement. The magazine's CPM would be calculated as follows:

$$\text{CPM} = \frac{\$75,000 \times 1,000}{8,000,000} = \frac{75,000,000}{8,000,000} = \$9.375.$$

In addition to the basic CPM calculation, the potential advertiser may be able to make a more precise eval-

uation of different advertising vehicles by focusing solely on the percentage of the magazine's readers, radio program's listeners, or television program's viewers who match the demographic and geographic profiles of the firm's market target. The denominator in the CPM formulation would be changed to include only the market target members in the advertising medium's audience. Should the advertiser feel that only one-eighth of the total circulation of *Modern Maturity* matches the precise profiles of the firm's market target, the CPM calculation would be made as follows:

$$\text{CPM} = \frac{\begin{array}{c}\text{Advertisement}\\\text{Cost} \times 1,000\end{array}}{\begin{array}{c}\text{Number of Market}\\\text{Target Members}\\\text{in Audience}\end{array}} = \frac{75,000,000}{1,000,000} = \$75.$$

CPM is of little use in comparing different *types* of advertising media. "You can't compare a CPM figure for a page in *Reader's Digest* with a CPM for a 30-second commercial on 'Laverne and Shirley' because there's no basis for comparing the value of a magazine ad to the value of a TV commercial. The communications approaches are totally different, as are audience attention and involvement."[1] However, such comparisons may be of major use in evaluating alternative vehicles within a single advertising medium.

After the CPMs provide the advertiser with a common denominator for making such comparisons, qualitative judgments can then be made about the relative merits of the leading candidates. One author suggests four considerations that should be made before deciding where to place the advertisements:

First, the measure should be adjusted for *audience quality*. For a baby lotion advertisement, a magazine read by one million young mothers would have an exposure value of one million, but if read by one million old men would have a zero exposure value. Second, the exposure value should be adjusted for the *audience attention probability*. Readers of *Vogue*, for example, pay more attention to ads than readers of *Newsweek*. Third, the exposure value should be adjusted for the *editorial quality* (prestige and believability) that one magazine [or broadcast program] might have over another. Fourth, the exposure value should be adjusted for the magazine's [or broadcaster's] *ad placement policies and extra services*.[2]

[1]Christopher Gilson and Harold W. Berkman, *Advertising: Concepts and Strategies* (New York: Random House, 1980), pp. 273–274.
[2]Philip Kotler, *Marketing Management* (Englewood Cliffs, N.J.: Prentice-Hall, 1984), p. 650.

Directions: Use menu item 14 titled "Advertising Evaluations" to solve each of the following problems.

Problem 1 Belinda Jacobson is senior brand manager for the snacks division of Daily Treats, of Richmond, Virginia. She is in the process of narrowing the number of magazines under consideration for the 1987 advertising campaign and has prepared the following table for eight magazines whose readership appears to best match the characteristics of Daily Treats' market target. Jacobson has also included her estimate of the percentage of each magazine's readers who precisely match the demographic characteristics of her firm's market.

Magazine	Four-Color Page Rate	Total Readers	Estimated Number of Magazine Readers Matching Daily Treats' Market Profile
Elan	$11,500	1,800,000	520,000
Family	17,500	2,200,000	440,000
Gotham Lady	13,000	1,900,000	380,000
Happy Home	36,000	8,500,000	850,000
Modern Homemaker	28,000	5,700,000	800,000
Single Parent	7,500	900,000	250,000
Suburban Garden	34,500	8,000,000	450,000
21st Century Homes	26,000	4,900,000	100,000

a. Which of the eight magazines has the lowest CPM if total readers are considered? Which has the highest CPM?

b. Which of the eight magazines has the lowest CPM if only market target readers are considered? Which has the highest CPM?

Problem 2 Joel DiPaoli is in charge of placing advertisements for ToyCorp of Philadelphia. He is currently in the process of comparing seven major magazines. The cost of a one-page, four-color advertisement is shown below.

Which of the seven magazines has the lowest CPM? Which has the lowest CPM for male readers? Which has the lowest CPM for female readers?

Magazine	Four-Color Page Rate	Total Readers	Male Readers	Female Readers
Contemporary Homes	$62,750	12,375,000	3,473,000	8,902,000
Amazing World	80,675	10,335,000	5,575,000	4,760,000
Weekly Facts	53,175	7,300,000	4,220,000	3,080,000
Sunday Digest	82,400	19,940,000	8,790,000	11,150,000
SportWeek	45,550	5,365,000	4,045,000	1,320,000
52	70,775	8,180,000	4,645,000	3,535,000
Viewer	70,000	16,650,000	7,590,000	9,060,000

Problem 3 After comparing the readership profiles of the seven magazines discussed in Problem 2, Joel DiPaoli developed the following estimates of the percentages of male and female readers for each magazine who match the profile of ToyCorp's market target customers:

Magazine	Readers in Market Target	
	Male Readers	Female Readers
Contemporary Homes	1,750,000	1,800,000
Amazing World	1,900,000	1,600,000
Weekly Facts	1,000,000	800,000
Sunday Digest	2,200,000	3,700,000
SportWeek	1,350,000	225,000
52	1,200,000	900,000
Viewer	1,900,000	2,300,000

a. Which of the seven magazines has the lowest CPM for male readers who match ToyCorp's market target profile? Which has the highest CPM?

b. Which of the seven magazines has the lowest CPM for female readers who match ToyCorp's market target profile? Which has the highest CPM?

Problem 4 Ed Maynard is in charge of advertising for Acme Video Rentals in New Orleans. He is targeting his advertising message at persons between the ages of 18 and 49 in the New Orleans metropolitan area and is planning to use radio during the morning and afternoon hours in which people are driving to and from work. He has assembled the following data concerning the four radio stations offering the blend of programming designed to attract his market target listeners.

Radio Station	Cost of 30-Second Commercial	Total Audience	Listeners Age 18–34	Listeners Age 35–49
WZZZ	$100	25,000	6,500	6,000
WNEL	90	28,000	5,600	7,000
WBBB	220	42,000	16,800	12,600
WZED	250	70,000	21,000	17,500

a. Which of the four radio stations has the lowest overall CPM? Which is the most expensive in terms of overall CPMs?

b. Which of the four stations has the lowest CPM for listeners between the ages of 18 and 34? Which is the most expensive for this age category?

c. Which of the four stations will reach Maynard's targeted customers at the lowest CPM?

Problem 5 George Vukovich is brand manager for SuperDrive golf balls, one of more than 50 brand names produced and marketed by Apollo Sporting Goods Com- pany of Kansas City. Vukovich has analyzed six likely magazines to use in advertising the SuperDrive brand. He has collected the following data:

Magazine	Black-and-White Page Rate	Total Readers	College Graduates	Managerial, Administrative
Golf Pro	$18,800	1,900,000	700,000	1,100,000
SportView	13,500	1,000,000	300,000	500,000
Modern Golf	16,300	2,600,000	400,000	1,300,000
Links	9,750	600,000	200,000	300,000
Golf Tips	38,200	4,000,000	800,000	900,000
18 Holes	12,960	2,200,000	400,000	600,000

a.   Which magazine has the lowest overall CPM? Which is most expensive in terms of overall CPMs?

b.   If Vukovich defines his market target as consisting only of college graduates, which of the six maga- zines would offer him the lowest CPM?

c.   If Vukovich decides to focus solely on persons hold- ing managerial or administrative positions, which magazine would allow him to reach this target at the lowest CPM? Which would be most expensive in terms of CPMs?

16 Personal Selling and Sales Management

Key Terms

personal selling
telephone selling
over-the-counter selling
field selling
order processing
creative selling
missionary sales
prospecting
qualifying
approach
precall planning
presentation
canned approach
closing
follow-up
selling up
suggestion selling
sales management
commission
salary
sales quota

Learning Goals

1. To explain the factors affecting the importance of personal selling in the promotional mix
2. To contrast telephone selling, over-the-counter selling, and field selling
3. To identify the three basic sales tasks
4. To list the characteristics of successful salespersons
5. To outline the steps in the sales process
6. To describe the major problems facing sales managers
7. To list the functions of sales management

Stop-Action Case

Xerox Corporation

There's no question about it. Many businesspeople use the Xerox name as a verb when they think about photocopying. The fact that Xerox's registered trademark has become a surrogate for the term *photocopy* could be considered a major asset to the firm's photocopy machine sales force. However, those same businesspeople who make the association between Xerox and photocopying rarely think of Xerox when they are considering the purchase of a personal computer or other high-tech office product. The lack of allure of the Xerox name in this area is ironic, since the company made pioneering efforts in developing one of the first personal computers and the first network connecting office machines scattered throughout an office building or company.

To many, the root of Xerox's dismal performance in the noncopier, high-tech market was its sales force. "It's one thing to have the technology and another thing to be able to sell it," remarked Donald J. Massaro, head of Metaphor Computer Systems and former president of Xerox's office products division.

Although Xerox's 4,000-member photocopier sales force has a proven track record, its high-tech sales force has often come up short. The high-tech group consisted of 1,000 salespersons and was subdivided into three different areas for personal computers, printers, and computer work stations. The result was a disjointed effort on the parts of sales representatives in the different areas. Worse yet, the copier and high-tech sales forces acted like archrivals, pulling apart rather than cooperating to maximize customer contacts and satisfy client needs. "We always had a lot of internal competition, and some of it was healthy," said John Robison, a Xerox regional account manager. "But it was very easy to get caught up with your own organization."

With a 1983 operating loss of nearly $57 million in its high-tech areas, Xerox had to take decisive action to turn the situation around. A new direction was needed immediately if Xerox's long-range plans were to be achieved. Although high-tech product sales accounted for less than 25 percent of Xerox's total revenue in 1983 (with the reprographics business, which includes copiers, providing most of the remaining 75 percent), top management wanted to achieve a 50/50 balance by 1989 and industry superiority in the high-tech areas by 1994.

Assignment: Use the materials in Chapter 16 to recommend a course of action for Xerox.

Photo Source: Courtesy of Xerox Corporation.

Source: Massaro and Robison quotations from Dennis Kneale, "Xerox Takes New Marketing Tack to Improve Poor Computer Sales," *The Wall Street Journal* (May 9, 1984), p. 31.

Chapter Overview

Personal Selling
Interpersonal influence process
involving a seller's promotional
presentation conducted on a person-
to-person basis with the buyer.

The first two chapters of this section focused on the concept of promotion, the promotional mix, and the use of advertising and other nonpersonal promotion in achieving marketing objectives. In this chapter, we turn our attention to the second major variable of the promotional mix: personal selling.

Personal selling was defined in Chapter 14 as an interpersonal influence process. Specifically, it involves a seller's promotional presentations conducted on a person-to-person basis with the buyer. It is an inherent function of any enterprise. Accounting, engineering, personnel, production, and other organizational activities are useless unless the firm's product or service matches the need of a client or customer. The 6 million salespeople currently employed full time in the United States bear witness to selling's importance in the late 1980s. While advertising expenses in the average firm may represent from 1 to 3 percent of total sales, selling expenses are likely to equal 10 to 15 percent of sales. In many firms, personal selling is the single largest marketing expense.

As Chapter 14 pointed out, personal selling is likely to be the primary component of a firm's promotional mix when consumers are concentrated geographically; when orders are large; when the products or services are expensive, technically complex, and require special handling; when trade-ins are involved; when channels are short; and when the number of potential consumers is relatively small. Figure 16.1 summarizes the factors influencing the importance of personal selling in the overall promotional mix.

Figure 16.1

Factors Affecting the Importance of Personal Selling in the Promotional Mix

	Personal Selling is likely to be more important when:	Advertising is likely to be more important when:
Consumer is 	geographically concentrated, relatively small in numbers	geographically dispersed, relatively large in numbers
Product is 	expensive, technically complex, custom-made, requires special handling, frequently involves trade-ins	inexpensive, simple to understand, standardized, does not require special handling, does not involve trade-ins
Price is 	relatively high	relatively low
Channels are 	relatively short	relatively long

How Personal Selling Evolved _____

Selling has been a standard part of business for thousands of years. The earliest peddlers were traders who had some type of ownership interest in the goods they sold after manufacturing or importing them. In many cases, these people viewed selling as a secondary activity.

Selling later became a separate function. The peddlers of the eighteenth century sold to the farmers and settlers of the vast North American continent. In the nineteenth century, salespeople called "drummers" sold to both consumers and marketing intermediaries. These early sellers sometimes used questionable sales practices and techniques and earned an undesirable reputation for themselves and their firms. Some of these negative stereotypes remain today. To some people the term *salesperson* conjures up unpleasant visions of Arthur Miller's antihero Willy Loman in *Death of a Salesman:*

You don't understand: Willy was a salesman . . . . He don't put a bolt to a nut. He don't tell you the law or give you medicine. He's a man way out there in the blue, riding on a smile and a shoeshine. And when they start not smiling back—that's an earthquake.[1]

But selling is far different from what it was in the early years. Far from the fast-talking, joke-telling, back-slapping caricatures in some novels and comic strips, today's salesperson is a professional. He or she is a problem solver, armed with product knowledge, and typically seeking mutually beneficial relationships with clients on a regular basis over an extended time period. The old stereotype of the salesperson has been replaced with the realization that personal selling is a vital, vibrant, dynamic process. It also represents an attractive career choice for today's college and university students. Approximately 60 percent of all marketing graduates choose sales as their first marketing position.

Telephone, Over-the-Counter, and Field Selling _____

Telephone Selling
Promotional presentation involving the use of the telephone on an "outbound" basis by salespeople or an "inbound" basis by customers who initiate such calls to obtain information and place orders.

The personal selling process may occur in a variety of environments. In some instances, telephone selling is used. This approach is used to reduce the substantial costs involved in maintaining a sales force to make personal calls at the customer's home or business. In some instances, telephone selling involves the combination of the telephone and computer hookups that provide printed data and other graphics to support the sales promotion. Inward-bound telephone selling typically involves a WATS number for customers who make free calls to obtain information and make purchases. This form of selling provides maximum convenience for customers who initiate the sales process.

Over-the-Counter Selling
Personal selling occurring in retail and some wholesale locations where customers come to the seller's place of business.

The second approach, over-the-counter selling, typically describes selling in retail locations. The customers take the initiative to come to the seller's location—sometimes in response to direct mail or personal letters of invitation from store personnel, or to take advantage of advertised sales, special events, or the introduction of new product lines. This type of selling typically involves provision of product information and arrangement for completion of the sales transaction.

Field Selling
Sales presentations made at the homes or businesses of prospective customers on a face-to-face basis by salespeople.

The final approach, field selling, involves sales calls to customers at their homes or businesses. In some instances, such as in-home sales of encyclopedias and insurance or industrial sales of a major computer installation, considerable creative selling is involved. In other cases, such as salespeople who call on already-established customers in such industries as food, textiles, or wholesaling, the processing of customer orders is the chief selling task.

Sales Tasks

The sales job has evolved into a professional occupation. Today's salesperson is more concerned with helping customers select the correct product to meet their needs than with simply selling whatever is available. Professional salespeople advise and assist customers in their purchase decisions. Where repeat purchases are common, the salesperson must be certain that the buyer's purchases are in his or her best interest or otherwise no future sales will be made. The interests of the seller are tied to those of the buyer in a symbiotic relationship.

Not all selling activities are alike. While all sales activities assist the customer in some manner, the exact tasks that are performed vary from one position to another. Three basic sales tasks can be identified: (1) order processing, (2) creative selling, and (3) missionary sales.

These tasks form the basis for a sales classification system. It should be observed, however, that most sales personnel do not fall into any single category. Instead, salespersons often perform all three tasks to a certain extent. A sales engineer for a computer firm may be doing 50 percent missionary sales, 45 percent creative selling, and 5 percent order processing. Most selling jobs, however, are classified on the basis of the primary selling task that is performed. We shall examine each of these tasks.

Order Processing

Order Processing
Selling at the wholesale and retail levels; specifically, identifying customer needs, pointing out the need to the customer, and completing the order.

Order processing, which can involve both field selling and telephone selling, is most often typified by selling at the wholesale and retail levels. Salespeople who perform this task must do the following:

1. *Identify customer needs.* For instance, a soft-drink route salesperson determines that a store that carries a normal inventory of 40 cases has only 7 cases left in stock.

2. *Point out the need to the customer.* The route salesperson informs the store manager of the inventory situation.

3. *Complete (or write up) the order.* The store manager acknowledges the situation. The driver unloads 33 cases and the manager signs the delivery slip.

Order processing is part of most selling positions and becomes the primary task where needs can be readily identified and are acknowledged by the customer. Even in such instances, salespersons whose primary responsibility involves order processing will devote some time in seeking to convince their wholesale or retail customers to carry a more complete inventory of the firm's products or to handle additional product lines. In addition, they are likely to try to motivate the purchaser to feature some of the firm's products, to increase the amount of shelf space devoted to their products, and to improve product location in the store.

Creative Selling

When a considerable degree of analytical decision making on the part of the consumer is involved in purchasing a product, the salesperson must skillfully solicit an order from a prospect. To do so, creative selling techniques must be used. New products often require a high degree of creative selling. The salesperson must first identify the needs of the customer and then provide a proposed solution, in the form of the product or service being offered, to solve the problem and fill the need. Creative selling, which may occur in telephone selling, over-the-counter selling, and field selling, may be the most demanding of the three tasks.

Missionary Sales

Missionary sales are an indirect type of selling: people sell the goodwill of a firm and provide the customers with technical or operational assistance. For example, a toiletries company salesperson may call on retailers to check on special promotions and overall stock movement, although a wholesaler is used to take orders and deliver merchandise. The medical detail salesperson seeks to persuade doctors, the indirect customers, to specify the pharmaceutical company's brand-name product for prescriptions. However, the company's actual sales are ultimately made through a wholesaler or direct to pharmacists who fill prescriptions. Missionary sales may involve both field selling and telephone selling. In more recent times, technical and operational assistance, such as that provided by a systems specialist, have also become a critical part of missionary selling.

Characteristics of Successful Salespeople

The saying "Salespeople are born, not made" is untrue. Most people have some degree of sales ability. At some time each of us is called upon to sell others his or her ideas, philosophy, or personality. However, while some individuals adapt to selling more easily than others, selling is not an easy job: it involves a great deal of practice and hard work.

Effective salespersons are self-motivated individuals who are well prepared to meet the demands of the competitive marketplace. The continuing pressure to solve buyers' problems requires that salespeople develop good work habits and exhibit considerable initiative.

Successful sales representatives are not only self-starters, they are knowledgeable businesspersons. Sales personnel are also in the peculiar position of having their knowledge tested almost continually. Sales success is often a function of how well a salesperson can handle questions. Salespeople must know their company, products, competition, customers, and themselves.

Feedback: The Responsibility of Every Salesperson

There is one function that all sales personnel perform—providing sales intelligence to the marketing organization.[2] Chapter 14 noted that sales reports are a part of the feedback generated within the marketing system. Since the sales force is close to the market, it is often the best (and most reliable) source of current marketing information upon which management decisions are based.

The marketing intelligence provided by sales personnel is copious and varied. Sales personnel can provide timely, current assessments of competitive efforts, new product launches, customer reactions, and the like. Marketing executives should nurture and implement this valuable information source.

The Sales Process

What, then, are the steps involved in selling? While the terminology may vary, most authorities agree on the following sequence: (1) prospecting and qualifying, (2) approach, (3) presentation, (4) demonstration, (5) handling objections, (6) closing, and (7) follow-up.

As Figure 16.2 indicates, the steps in the personal selling process follow the attention-interest-desire-action (AIDA) concept discussed in Chapter 14. Once a sales prospect has been qualified, an attempt is made to secure his or her attention. The presentation and demonstration steps are designed to generate interest and desire. Successful handling of buyer objections should further arouse desire, and action occurs at the close of the sale.

Prospecting and Qualifying

Prospecting

Function of identifying potential customers.

Prospecting, the identification of potential customers, is difficult work involving many hours of diligent effort. Prospects may come from many sources: previous customers, friends and neighbors, other vendors, nonsales employees in the firm, suppliers, and social and professional contacts. New sales personnel often find prospecting frustrating, because there is usually no immediate payback. But without prospecting, there are no future sales. For example, in the marketing of various types of adhesive tapes for industrial use, a representative of a tape manufacturing company, perhaps a manufacturers' agent, must seek out potential users of these specialty tapes. Prospecting is a continuous process because of loss of some customers over time, as well as the emergence of new potential customers or those who have never been contacted before. Many sales management experts consider prospecting to be the very essence of the sales process.

Qualifying

Determining that a prospect is actually a potential customer.

Qualifying—determining that the prospect is really a potential customer—is another important sales task. Not all prospects are qualified to become customers. Qualified customers are people with both money and the authority to make purchase decisions. A person with an annual income of $15,000 may wish to own a $75,000 house, but this person's ability to actually become a customer is questionable. Similarly, a parent with six children may strongly desire a two-seater sports car, but this would probably not be a practical purchase as the sole family vehicle. Both direct mail and telephone communications are utilized in prospecting and in setting up appointments with prospective customers.

Approach

Approach

Initial contact of a salesperson with a prospective customer.

Once the salesperson has identified a qualified prospect, he or she collects all available information relative to the potential buyer and plans an approach—the initial contact of the salesperson with the prospective customer. Collecting information is invaluable for telephone and field salespeople.

Precall Planning

Use of information collected during the prospecting and qualifying stages of the sales process and during previous contacts with the prospect to tailor the approach and presentation to match the needs of the customer.

This information-gathering component of personal selling makes precall planning possible. Salespeople who have gathered relevant information about their clients are prepared for the opening discussions that may ultimately result in a consumer purchase. Effective precall planning permits the

Figure 16.2

The AIDA Concept and the Steps in the Personal Selling Process

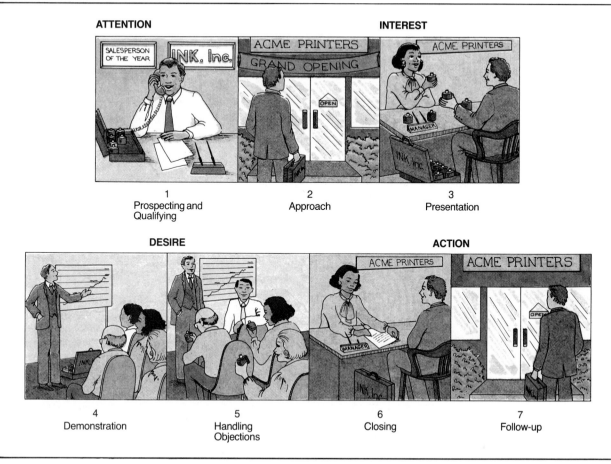

ATTENTION

1
Prospecting and
Qualifying

2
Approach

INTEREST

3
Presentation

DESIRE

4
Demonstration

5
Handling
Objections

ACTION

6
Closing

7
Follow-up

salesperson to make an initial contact, armed with knowledge about a client's purchasing habits; his or her attitudes, activities, and opinions; and commonalities shared by the salesperson and prospective customer.

Figure 16.3 illustrates the type of information that should be collected for use in precall planning. The Account-Impact Profile sorts customer data into buying-decision information, buyer's job-specific data, current account information, buyer demographics, outside activities, outside interests, and opinions. Such information should be updated on a regular basis.

Precall planning is used less frequently by retail salespeople, but they can compensate by asking leading questions to learn more about the prospect's purchase preferences. Industrial marketers have far more data available, and they should make use of it before scheduling the first sales contact.

Presentation

Presentation
Description of a product's major features and the relating of them to a customer's problems or needs.

When the salesperson gives the sales message to a prospective customer, he or she makes a presentation. The seller describes the product's major features, points out its strengths, and concludes by citing illustrative successes. The seller's objective is to talk about the product or service in terms meaning-

Figure 16.3
Account-Impact Profile (AIP)

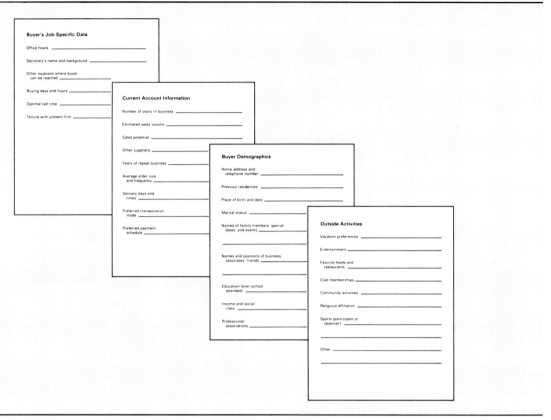

Source: Adapted by permission from *BUSINESS* Magazine, "Matching Profiles for Your Industrial Sales Force,"
by Robert J. Zimmer and James W. Taylor, March–April 1981. Copyright © 1981
by the College of Business Administration, Georgia State University, Atlanta.

ful to the buyer—benefits, rather than technical specifications. Thus the presentation is the stage in which the salesperson relates product features to customer needs.

The presentation should be clear and concise, and it should emphasize the positive. In an attempt to increase its significant share of the $1.5 billion retail market for sheet vinyl floor covering, Mannington Mills decided to assist retail salespeople by including an electronic pattern/color selector, as shown in Figure 16.4, as part of its most expensive consumer display system. The Mannington computerized selection aid emits beeps for attracting shoppers' attention. After it has been activated by the consumer pushing the "Go" button, it asks eight questions about room decor, color preference, foot traffic, etc. It then digests the consumer's answers and displays style numbers of between three and ten appropriate Mannington patterns. The salesperson and the customer are spared the task of searching through almost 300 samples of Mannington vinyl flooring in the surrounding display. The computer aid has proven more than satisfactory to both retail managers and to Mannington marketers, who are competing with large manufacturers such as Armstrong World Industries and Congoleum Corporation. Many stores have increased their sales of the Mannington line from 100 to 400 percent since obtaining the electronic unit. The stores use it to narrow the selection process with a customer

Figure 16.4
Mannington Mills: Applying Technology to the Sales Presentation

Source: Courtesy of Mannington Mills, Inc.

down to a workable number quickly or to "entertain" customers during busy periods while salespeople are assisting other customers. Almost always, the chosen pattern and color purchased by the customer is from among the computer's recommended choices, because the program is based on in-depth input from professional home decorators.

Canned Approach
Memorized sales talk used to ensure uniform coverage of the selling points that management has deemed important.

The traditional approach to sales presentations—the canned approach—was originally developed by John H. Patterson of National Cash Register Company during the late 1800s. It is a memorized sales talk used to ensure uniform coverage of the points deemed important by management. While canned presentations are still used in such areas as door-to-door *cold canvassing*, most sales forces have long since abandoned their use.[3] The attitude of today's professional salespeople is that flexible presentations are needed to match the unique circumstances of each purchase decision. Proper planning, of course, is an important part of tailoring a presentation to each particular customer.

Demonstration

Demonstrations can play a critical role in a sales presentation. A demonstration ride in a new automobile allows the prospect to become involved in the presentation. It awakens customer interest in a manner that no amount of verbal presentation can achieve. Demonstrations supplement, support, and reinforce what the sales representative has already told the prospect. The key to a good demonstration is planning. A unique demonstration is more likely to gain a customer's attention than a typical sales presentation. A demonstration must be well planned and executed if a favorable impression is to be made. One cannot overemphasize that the salesperson should check and recheck all aspects of the demonstration prior to its delivery.

Handling Objections

A vital part of selling involves handling objections. It is reasonable to expect a customer to say, "Well, I really should check with my family," or "Perhaps I'll stop back next week," or "I like everything except the color." A good salesperson, however, should use each objection as a cue to provide additional information to the prospect. In most cases an objection, such as "I don't like the bucket seats," is really a prospect's way of asking what other choices or product features are available. A customer's question reveals an interest in the product. It gives the seller an opportunity to expand a presentation by providing additional information.

Closing

Closing
Point in personal selling at which the salesperson asks the customer to make a purchase decision.

The moment of truth in selling is the closing, for this is when the salesperson asks the prospect for an order. A sales representative should not hesitate during the closing. If he or she has made an effective presentation based on applying the product to the customer's needs, the closing should be the natural conclusion.

A surprising number of sales personnel have difficulty in actually asking for an order. To be effective they must overcome this difficulty. Methods of closing a sale include the following:

1. The *alternative-decision technique* poses choices to a prospect where either alternative is favorable to the salesperson. "Will you take this sweater or that one?"

2. The *SRO (standing room only) technique* is used when a prospect is told that a sales agreement should be concluded now, because the product may not be available later or an important feature such as price will soon be changed.

3. *Emotional closes* attempt to get a person to buy through appeal to such factors as fear, pride, romance, or social acceptance.

4. *Silence* can be used as a closing technique since a discontinuance of a sales presentation forces the prospect to take some type of action (either positive or negative).

5. *Extra-inducement closes* are special incentives designed to motivate a favorable buyer response. Extra inducements may include quantity discounts, special servicing arrangements, or a layaway option.

Follow-up

Follow-up
Postsales activities that often determine whether an individual who has made a recent purchase will become a repeat customer.

The postsales activities that often determine whether a person will become a repeat customer constitute the sales follow-up. To the maximum extent possible, representatives should contact their customers to find out if they are satisfied with their purchases. This step allows the salesperson to psychologically reinforce the person's original decision to buy. It gives the seller an opportunity, in addition to correcting any sources of discontent with the purchase, to secure important market information and to make additional sales. Auto-

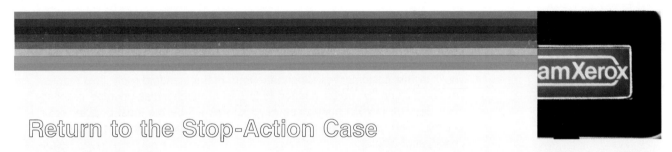

Return to the Stop-Action Case

Xerox Corporation

Even in instances where personal selling is the primary emphasis of a firm's promotional mix, advertising is frequently employed to assist the marketing efforts. In some instances, advertising aids sales representatives by informing potential customers of the market acceptance of a new product. In still other cases, advertising campaigns may be developed to enhance the overall image of the firm. The result may be more acceptance of the firm's salespeople and more serious consideration of their offerings.

Even though the Xerox promotional mix emphasizes personal selling to its customers, the firm spends over $100 million annually on advertising and in recent years has ranked as the 65th largest national advertiser in the United States. In some instances, advertising is directed toward new product introductions of such market entries as its Series 10 copiers and its Memorywriter electronic typewriters. In other instances, the focus is less on specific products than on the concept of teamwork—machines and people working together to meet customer needs. This focus is designed to match the changes that were occurring in Xerox's sales strategies.

mobile dealers often keep elaborate records of their previous customers so they can promote new models to individuals who have already shown a willingness to buy from them. One successful travel agency never fails to telephone customers upon their return from a trip. Proper follow-up is a logical part of the selling sequence.

Effective follow-up also means that the salesperson should conduct a critical review of every call that is made by asking "What was it that allowed me to close that sale?" or "What caused me to lose that sale?" Such continual review results in significant sales dividends.

Retail Selling

For the most part, the public is more aware of retail selling than of any other form of personal selling. In fact, many writers have argued that a person's basic attitude toward the sales function is determined by his or her impression of retail sales personnel.

Retail selling has some distinctive features that require its consideration as a separate subject. The most significant difference between retail selling and its counterparts is that the customer comes to the retail salesperson. This requires that retailers effectively combine selling with a good advertising and sales promotion program that draws the customer into the store. Another difference is that while store employees are sales personnel in one sense, they are also retailers in the broader dimension. Selling is not their only responsibility.

Retail sales personnel should be well versed in store policy and procedures. Credit, discounts, special sales, delivery, layaway, and return policies are examples of the type of information that the salesperson should know. One of the major complaints voiced by today's customer concerns uninformed sales personnel.

The area of retail selling that exhibits the greatest potential for improvement is the greeting. The standard "May I help you?" seems totally out of place in contemporary marketing, and yet it is interesting to observe the number of retail salespeople who still use this outdated approach. "May I help you?" invites customer rejection in the form of the standard reply, "No thanks, I'm just looking." A better method is to use a merchandise-oriented greeting such as "The fashion magazines say that this will be the most popular color this fall." The positive approach helps to orient the customer toward the merchandise or display.

Two selling techniques particularly applicable to retailing are selling up and suggestion selling. Selling up is the technique of convincing the customer to buy a higher-priced item than he or she originally intended. An automobile salesperson may convince a customer to buy a more expensive model than the person intended to buy. An important point is that the practice of selling up should always be used within the constraints of the customer's real needs. If the salesperson sells the customer something that he or she really does not need, the potential for repeat sales by that seller is substantially diminished.

Suggestion selling seeks to broaden the customer's original purchase with related items, special promotions, and/or holiday and seasonal merchandise. Here, too, suggestion selling should be based upon the idea of helping the customer recognize true needs rather than selling the person unwanted merchandise. Suggestion selling is one of the best methods of increasing retail sales and should be practiced by all sales personnel.

Selling Up
Retail sales technique of convincing a customer to buy a higher-priced item than he or she originally intended to buy.

Suggestion Selling
Form of retail selling that attempts to broaden the customer's original purchase with related items, special promotions, and holiday or seasonal merchandise.

Managing the Sales Effort

Sales Management
Activities of planning, organizing, staffing, motivating, compensating, and evaluating and controlling an effective sales force.

Contemporary selling requires that sales management efforts be exerted in the direction of planning, organizing, staffing, motivating, compensating, evaluating and controlling an effective field sales force. The sales manager is a boundary-spanning executive who links the salespeople, customers and prospects, and the firm's management.[4] The sales manager has professional responsibilities in both directions. Most sales management positions require some degree of both technical or sales-oriented skills and administrative or managerial skills. The higher one rises in the sales management hierarchy, the more administrative skills and the less technical skills are required to perform the job. Figure 16.5 diagrams this relationship.

Problems Faced by Sales Management

Sales executives face a variety of management problems. However, with few exceptions, these problems have remained largely the same over the years. Poor utilization of time and failure to plan sales efforts were reported as the leading problems in surveys conducted in 1959 and 1979. By contrast, failure to provide adequate sales training, the problem listed as the second most important deficiency in the early survey, did not even appear in the top 20 problem areas mentioned in the more recent study.[5]

Planning

As a line executive in the marketing department, the sales manager is closely and continuously engaged in the management function of planning. His or her responsibilities include analyzing markets and developing forecasts, develop-

Figure 16.5

Relative Importance of Sales-Oriented Skills and Administrative Skills
at Various Levels in the Sales Management Hierarchy

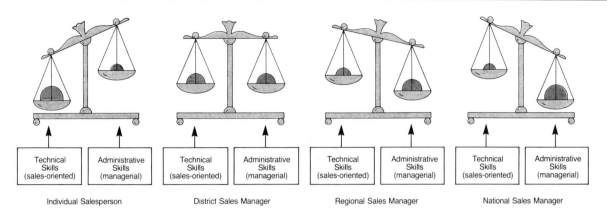

Technical Skills (sales-oriented)	Administrative Skills (managerial)	Technical Skills (sales-oriented)	Administrative Skills (managerial)	Technical Skills (sales-oriented)	Administrative Skills (managerial)	Technical Skills (sales-oriented)	Administrative Skills (managerial)
Individual Salesperson		District Sales Manager		Regional Sales Manager		National Sales Manager	

ing budgets and establishing sales quotas, analyzing competitive strategies, and establishing territories. Such plans are derived from overall marketing plans that are, in turn, the result of overall organizational objectives. Establishing an annual marketing goal of a 10 percent increase in total sales may be translated into sales plans to increase the number of salespeople in a territory, to enter new geographic markets, or to offer volume discounts to major customers to stimulate larger-size orders.

Organizing

The second responsibility of sales managers is organizing. To carry out plans and accomplish marketing objectives, sales managers must arrange people and physical resources in a formal organizational structure.

General organizational alignments, which are usually made by top marketing management, may be based upon geography, products, types of customers, or some combination of these factors. Figure 16.6 presents a simplified organization chart showing these alignments.

A product sales organization would have specialized sales forces for each major category of product offered by the firm. A customer organization would use different sales forces for each major type of customer served. For example, a plastics manufacturer selling to the automobile, small appliance, and defense industries might decide that each type of customer requires a separate sales force.

The individual sales manager then has the task of organizing the sales territories within his or her area of responsibility. Generally, the territory allocation decision should be based upon company objectives, personnel qualifications, workload considerations, and territory potential.

Staffing

The initial step in building an effective sales force involves recruiting and selecting qualified personnel. Sources of new salespeople include community colleges, trade and business schools, colleges and universities, sales person-

Figure 16.6

Basic Approaches to Organizing the Sales Force

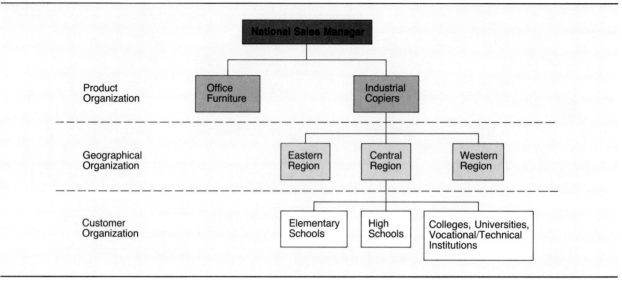

nel in other firms, people currently employed in nonselling occupations, and a company's own nonselling employees.

Not all of these areas are equally productive. One of the problem areas seems to be the reluctance of high-school guidance counselors to convey the advantages of a selling career to students. A successful career in sales offers satisfaction in all the five areas that a person generally looks for when deciding on a profession:

1. *Opportunity for advancement.* Studies have shown that successful sales representatives advance rapidly in most companies. Advancement can come either within the sales organization or laterally to a more responsible position in some other functional area of the firm.

2. *High earnings.* The earnings of successful salespersons compare favorably to the earnings of successful people in other professions. As Figure 16.7 indicates, the average senior salesperson now earns more than $30,000 per year.

3. *Personal satisfaction.* One derives satisfaction in sales from achieving success in a competitive environment and from helping people satisfy their wants and needs.

4. *Security.* Contrary to what many students believe, selling provides a high degree of job security. Experience has shown that economic downturns affect personnel in sales less than those in most other employment areas. In addition, there is a continuing need for good sales personnel.

5. *Independence and variety.* Most often salespersons really operate as independent businesspeople or as managers of sales territories. Their work is quite varied and provides an opportunity for involvement in numerous business functions.

The careful selection of salespeople is important for two reasons. First, it involves substantial amounts of money and management time. Second, selec-

Figure 16.7
Annual Compensation for Salespeople

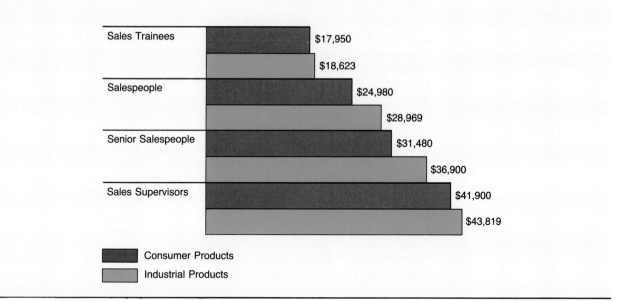

Sales Trainees $17,950
                      $18,623

Salespeople $24,980
                      $28,969

Senior Salespeople $31,480
                      $36,900

Sales Supervisors $41,900
                      $43,819

◼ Consumer Products
▢ Industrial Products

Source: Executive Compensation Service, Inc., a subsidiary of the Wyatt Co. Reported in
Sales & Marketing Management (February 20, 1984), p. 60.

tion mistakes will be detrimental to customer relations and sales force performance, as well as costly to correct.

In the selection process for sales personnel, an application screening is followed by an initial interview. If there is sufficient interest, in-depth interviewing is conducted. Next, the company may use testing in its selection procedure. This step could include aptitude, intelligence, interest, knowledge, or personality tests. References are then checked to guarantee that job candidates have represented themselves correctly. A physical examination is usually included before a final hiring decision is made.

Training   To shape new sales recruits into an efficient sales organization, management must conduct an effective training program. The principal methods used in sales training are lectures, role playing, and on-the-job training.

Sales training is also important for veteran salespeople. Most of this type of training is done in an informal manner by sales managers. A standard format is for the sales manager to travel with a field sales representative periodically and then compose a critique of the person's work. Sales meetings are also an important part of training for experienced personnel.

Motivating

The sales manager's responsibility for motivating the sales force cannot be glossed over lightly. Because the sales process involves problem solving, it often leads to considerable mental pressures and frustrations. Sales are often achieved only after repeated calls on customers and may, especially with new customers and complex technical products, occur over long periods of time. Motivation of salespeople usually takes the form of debriefing, information sharing, and both psychological and financial encouragement. Appeals to emotional needs, such as ego needs, recognition, and peer acceptance, are examples of psychological encouragement. Monetary rewards and fringe benefits, such as club memberships and paid travel arrangements, are appealing as financial incentives.

A source of constant debate among sales managers is the supervision of the sales force. It is impossible to pinpoint the exact amount of supervision that is correct in each situation because it varies with the individuals involved. However, there is probably a curvilinear relationship between the amount of supervision and organizational performance. Increases in supervision input increases sales output to some point, after which additional supervision tends to retard further sales growth.

One key to effective sales force motivation is clear, two-way communications. This, of course, involves effective listening on the part of the sales manager. Sales personnel who clearly understand messages from management and who have an opportunity to express their concerns and opinions to their supervisors are usually easier to supervise and motivate.

Compensating

Since monetary rewards are an important factor in motivating subordinates, compensating sales personnel is a critical matter to managers. Basically, sales compensation can be determined on a straight-salary plan, a commission plan, or some combination.

Commission
Incentive compensation directly related to the sales or profits achieved by a salesperson.

A commission is a payment directly tied to the sales or profits achieved by a salesperson. For example, a salesperson might receive a 5 percent commission on all sales up to a specified quota, then 7 percent on sales beyond the quota. Commissions provide a maximum selling incentive but may cause the sales force to shortchange nonselling activities, such as completing sales reports, delivering sales promotion materials, and normal account servicing.

Salary
Fixed compensation payments made on a periodic basis to employees, including some sales personnel.

A salary is a fixed payment made on a periodic basis to employees, including some sales personnel. A firm that has decided to use salaries rather than commissions might pay a salesperson a set amount every week, for example. There are benefits of using salaries for both management and sales personnel. A straight-salary plan allows management to have more control over how sales personnel allocate their efforts, but it reduces the incentive to expand sales. As a result, compensation programs combining features of both salary and commission plans have been accepted in many industries.

Evaluation and Control

Perhaps the most difficult tasks required of sales managers are evaluation and control. The basic problems are setting standards and finding an instrument to measure sales performance. Sales volume, profitability, and investment return are the usual means of evaluating sales effectiveness. They typically involve the use of a sales quota—a specified sales or profit target a salesperson is expected to achieve. A particular sales representative might be expected to sell $300,000 in Territory 414 during a given year, for example. In many cases, the quota is tied to the compensation system.

Sales Quota
Level of expected sales for a territory, product, customer, or salesperson against which actual results are compared.

Regardless of the key elements in the program for evaluating salespeople, the sales manager needs to follow a formal system of decision rules.[6] The purpose of this system is to supply information to the sales manager for action.

What the sales manager needs to know are the answers to three general questions. First, what are the rankings of the salesperson's performance relative to the predetermined standards? In determining this ranking, full consideration should be given to the effect of uncontrollable variables on sales performance. Preferably, each adjusted ranking should be stated in terms of a percentage of the standard. This simplifies evaluation and makes conversion of the various rankings into a composite index of performance easy.

Second, what are the strong points of the salesperson? One way to answer this question is to list areas of the salesperson's performance in which he or she has surpassed the respective standard. Another way is to categorize a salesperson's strong points in three areas of the work environment:

1. *Task,* or the technical ability of the salesperson. This is manifested in knowledge of the product (end uses), customer, and company, as well as selling skills.

2. *Process,* or the sequence of work flow. This pertains to the actual sales transaction—the salesperson's application of technical ability and interaction with customers. Personal observation is frequently used for measuring process performance. Other measures are sales calls and expense reports.

3. *Goal,* end results or output of sales performance. Usually this aspect of the salesperson's work environment is stated in terms of sales volume and profits.

The third question is, what are the weaknesses or negatives in the performance of the salesperson in question? These should be listed or categorized as much as the salesperson's strong points. An evaluation summary for a hypothetical salesperson appears in Figure 16.8.

Figure 16.8
Performance Evaluation Summary

Name: C. B. Admudson	
Territory: Southern California	
Time Period Covered: 1st Quarter 1986	
Salesperson's Ability	
Strong Points	Has extensive product knowledge, knows end uses. Keeps up to date on company pricing policies.
Weaknesses	Does not have in-depth knowledge of customer requirements.
Selling Proficiency	
Strong Points	Exceeded by 20 percent the standard for sales/calls. Exceeded by 12 percent the standard for sales calls/day. Exceeded by 8 percent the standard for invoice lines/order.
Weaknesses	Overspending of expense monies (14 percent). Overaggressive in selling tactics.
Sales Results	
Strong Points	Exceeded sales quota by 3 percent. Exceeded new account quota by 6 percent.
Weaknesses	Turnover of customers amounted to 5 percent. Repeated delay in report submission.

Source: Adapted from H. Robert Dodge, *Field Sales Management* (Dallas, Tex.: Business Publications, Inc., 1973), pp. 337–338.

In making the evaluation summary, the sales manager should follow a set procedure:

1.   Each aspect of sales performance for which there is a standard should be measured separately. This helps to avoid the halo effect, whereby the rating given on one aspect is carried over to other aspects.

2.   Each salesperson should be judged on the basis of actual sales performance rather than potential ability. This emphasizes the importance of rankings in evaluation.

3.   Each salesperson should be judged on the basis of sales performance for the entire period under consideration rather than for particular incidents. The sales manager as the rater should avoid reliance on isolated examples of the salesperson's success or failure.

4.   Each salesperson's evaluation should be reviewed for completeness and evidence of possible bias. Ideally, this review should be made by the immediate superior of the sales manager.

While the evaluation step includes both revision and correction, the attention of the sales manager must necessarily focus on correction. This is defined as the adjustment of actual performance to predetermined standards. Corrective action, with its obvious negative connotations, poses a substantial challenge to the typical sales manager.

Summary

Personal selling is an interpersonal influence process involving the seller's promotional presentation conducted on a person-to-person basis with the buyer. It is inherent in all business enterprises. Personal selling occurs in a number of different environments, ranging from telephone selling to over-the-counter retail selling and field selling.

The three basic selling tasks are order processing, creative selling, and missionary selling. The successful salesperson is self-motivated and prepared to meet the demands of the competitive marketplace.

The basic steps involved in selling are (1) prospecting and qualifying, (2) approach, (3) presentation, (4) demonstration, (5) handling of objections, (6) closing, and (7) follow-up. Precall planning improves the approach, presentation, demonstration, handling of objections, and closing phases of the sales process.

Retail selling is different from other kinds of selling, primarily because the customer comes to the salesperson. Also, salespeople in stores are concerned with responsibilities other than selling. Two selling techniques particularly applicable to retailing are selling up and suggestion selling.

Sales management involves six basic functions: (1) planning, (2) organizing, (3) staffing, (4) motivating, (5) compensating, and (6) evaluation and control. Sales compensation can be on a straight-salary plan, a commission plan, or a combination of the two. Each type of compensation has numerous advantages and disadvantages, and the most appropriate choice must be designed to meet the unique situation of each individual firm. Poor utilization of time and lack of planned sales effort rank as the leading problems faced by sales management today.

Photo Source: Courtesy of Xerox Corporation.

Solving the Stop-Action Case

Xerox Corporation

One of the major ways Xerox solved the problem of its high-tech sales woes was to merge the sales force with the larger sales team from the copier division. Under a long-term training program, all copier salespeople will be trained in computers and office systems. In addition, joint account teams were formed under the supervision of a single account manager who coordinates customer-contact efforts.

"Before, we had three separate showrooms in three separate areas," points out Patrick Crane, a Xerox branch manager. "We effectively had three separate branch managers. Nobody knew each other—because they didn't get paid for it."

When the Team Xerox approach was tested in 1983, Xerox managers reported "encouraging percentage increases" in orders. This team approach was at least partially responsible for the closing of a multimillion-dollar computer sales contract with the University of Pittsburgh. Paul Stieman, director of the university's computer center, explained the choice of Xerox over IBM in this way: "Xerox salespeople understand how to fit their products to our needs as well as a shoe. They know each other and know what one another's business is—they appear to be a team."

Team Xerox is also the theme of Xerox's advertising campaign—a campaign that stresses the unified voice of the Xerox sales force. One ad, called "Race Car," communicates the message in this way:

. . . . You're going to drive this thing at 160 miles per hour tomorrow. You've got the skill and coordination to win all right, but without an experienced team behind you, you won't even get out of the pit. And that's the thinking behind Team Xerox. An able team with a dazzling array of equipment for any size office. . . .

Xerox executives understand that, with competitors like IBM and AT&T, they will be involved in a long-term battle for a major Team Xerox success. "I would like to have the mindset of a long-distance runner," said Robert Adams, president of Xerox's high-tech group. "Although I'd like to be out in front of a race at every moment, I believe this race is going to be ten years long, and we've only seen the first couple of laps."

Sources: Crane, Stieman, and Adams quotations are from Dennis Kneale, "Xerox Takes New Marketing Tack to Improve Poor Computer Sales," *Wall Street Journal* (May 9, 1984), p. 31. Xerox advertising copy courtesy Xerox Corporation.

Questions for Discussion

1. Identify the factors affecting the importance of personal selling in the promotional mix.

2. Explain how the following factors affect the decision to emphasize personal selling or advertising:
    a. Geographic market concentration
    b. Length of marketing channels
    c. Degree of technical complexity of product
    d. Relative price of product
    e. Number of customers
    f. Whether trade-ins are customary

3. Explain how a sales manager's problems and areas of emphasis might change in dealing with each of the following:
    a. Telephone salespeople
    b. Over-the-counter retail salespeople
    c. Field sales representatives
    d. Missionary salespeople

4. Identify the three basic sales tasks and give an example of each.

5. What sales tasks are involved in selling the following products?
    a. Lanier office equipment
    b. Request for support of Easter Seals to a local Rotary Club
    c. A fast-food franchise
    d. Used automobiles
    e. Cleaning compounds to be used in plant maintenance

6. How would you describe the job of each of the following salespersons?
    a. A salesperson in a retail record store
    b. Century 21 real estate sales representative
    c. A route driver for Frito-Lay (sells and delivers to local food retailers)
    d. A sales engineer for Wang computers

7. What roles do flight crews play in an airline's promotional efforts?

8. Identify the characteristics of successful salespersons.

9. What are the steps in the sales process? Relate the AIDA concept to the process.

10. Under what conditions is the canned approach to selling likely to be used? What are the major problems with this approach?

11. Discuss how a sales representative could use the Account-Impact Profile shown in Figure 16.3.

12. How is retail selling different from field selling?

13. Discuss the benefits of a sales career.

14. As marketing vice-president of a large paper company, you are asked to talk to a group of college students about selling as a career. List the five most important points you would make in your speech.

15. Describe the major problems faced by sales managers.

16. Some critics advocate stringent regulations for telephone sales solicitations. What arguments can be made for and against such regulations?

17. What are the primary functions of sales management?

18. Compare the alternative sales compensation plans. Point out the advantages and disadvantages of each.

19. Suppose that you are the local sales manager for American Bell's Yellow Pages and you employ six representatives who call upon local firms. What type of compensation system would you employ?

20. How would you evaluate the sales personnel described in Question 19?

Case: Women in Selling

The sales field offers excellent career opportunities for women as well as men. Selling has been a nontraditional occupation for women, but the field is rapidly opening. According to a recent survey conducted by the National Association

Source: Barbara A. Pletcher, executive director, National Association for Professional Saleswomen, *1983 Successful Saleswomen Survey*, (December 1983).

for Professional Saleswomen, 40 percent of the survey respondents earned $30,000 or more a year, including 9 percent who earned more than $50,000. Sixty-three percent of the responding saleswomen also had company expense accounts to cover normal business expenses. The study confirmed that sales is a relatively new career field for women. With more than 70 percent of the survey participants in the 25- to 39-year age group and with only 33 percent in sales for more than five years, the future promises significant career growth.

Deborah Leuch was the first woman to join the 60-member sales force of Carnick Laboratories. Within seven months of joining the firm, she ranked as its leading salesperson and soon took on the responsibility of training 15 new sales representatives.

Questions

1.   Explain the relatively recent movement of women into professional selling careers. What advantages do female salespersons possess?

2.   Identify the primary problems women face in sales careers. Suggest specific methods for eliminating or minimizing each problem.

Computer Applications

Although a quality sales force may represent the difference between marketing success and failure, the salaries and direct expenses necessary to support a field sales force may be the largest single component of total marketing expenses. Consequently, an important marketing decision involves determining the optimal number of salespersons. The sales force size decision is most commonly made by using the *workload* method. It consists of the following steps:[1]

1. *Classify the firm's customers into categories.* Because customers vary greatly in terms of sales, servicing costs, and profitability, they should be divided into categories. One writer estimates that the top 15 percent of a firm's customers will account for 65 percent of its sales, the next 20 percent will account for 20 percent, and the remaining 65 percent will yield only 15 percent of sales.[2] The first group might be labeled *A accounts*, the second group *B accounts*, and the third group *C accounts*. A firm with 5,200 accounts might categorize them as follows:

---

800 Type A Accounts (high sales, high profitability)

1,400 Type B Accounts (medium sales, moderate profitability)

3,000 Type C Accounts (low sales, low profitability)

---

2. *Specify the desired number of annual calls for each account type and the average length of each call.* These specifications can be based upon analysis of sales call reports submitted by the field sales force. In addition, it is likely to involve the judgment and experience of sales management. Suppose that sales management decides on weekly contacts for Type A accounts, biweekly contacts for Type B accounts, and monthly contacts for Type C accounts. In addition, the desired length of an average sales call is set at 40 minutes for Type A accounts, 30 minutes for Type B accounts, and 20 minutes for Type C accounts. Finally, an additional 10 percent is included for emergency or other unplanned calls in each account category. The number of hours required for each type of account can be calculated in Table 1.

3. *Calculate the total hours required to contact all accounts.* This step is accomplished by multiplying the total number of hours required to service each account type by the number of customers in each category. In this example, the calculation would be:

$$
\begin{aligned}
800 \text{ Type A accounts} \times 38.13 \text{ hours} &= 30,504 \text{ hours} \\
1,400 \text{ Type B accounts} \times 14.30 \text{ hours} &= 20,020 \text{ hours} \\
3,000 \text{ Type C accounts} \times 4.40 \text{ hours} &= \underline{13,200 \text{ hours}} \\
\text{Total} &= \underline{\underline{63,724 \text{ hours.}}}
\end{aligned}
$$

4. *Calculate the time available for each salesperson.* This step is accomplished by multiplying the number of hours the typical salesperson works each week by the average number of weeks worked per year. If the typical salesperson works 40 hours per week for 46 weeks, the average number of hours per year is 1,840 (40 × 46).

5. *Allocate each salesperson's time to assigned tasks.* A considerable percentage of the typical salesperson's time is spent on activities other than making calls on established accounts. Some time is involved in traveling between accounts. In addition, the typical representative is responsible for such nonselling activities as preparing reports and attending sales meetings. Finally, additional time may be devoted to contacting potential customers to generate additional sales. For example, the salesperson working an average of 1,840 hours per year may divide his or her hours as shown in Table 2:

---

[1]The workload method was first described in Walter J. Talley, Jr., "How to Design Sales Territories," *Journal of Marketing*, January 1961, pp. 7–13. The steps are described in Richard R. Still, Edward W. Cundiff, and Norman A. P. Govoni, *Sales Management* (Englewood Cliffs, N.J.: Prentice-Hall, 1981), pp. 99–101; and Gilbert A. Churchill, Jr., Neil M. Ford, and Orville C. Walker, Jr., *Sales Force Management* (Homewood, Ill.; Richard D. Irwin, 1985), pp. 181–183.

[2]Porter Henry, "The Important Few—The Unimportant Many," 1980 *Portfolio of Sales and Marketing Plans* (New York: Sales and Marketing Management, 1980), pp. 34–37.

Table 1

Determination of the Total Number of Hours Required for Sales Calls for Each Type of Account

Type of Account	Number of Contacts per Year	X	Minutes per Sales Call	=	Time Required for Planned Calls	+	Time Required for Unplanned/ Emergency Calls*	=	Total Minutes	=	Total Hours
A	52		40		2,080		208		2,288		38.13
B	26		30		780		78		858		14.3
C	12		20		240		24		262		4.4

*Estimated by management at 10 percent of total time required for planned calls.

Table 2
Allocation of One Salesperson's Time to Assigned Tasks

Activity	Percentage of Available Time	Number of Hours per Year
Sales/Service Calls on Established Accounts	40%	736
Sales Calls on Potential Accounts	10	184
Travel	30	552
Other Nonselling Activities	20	368
Total	100%	1,840 hours

6. *Determine the required number of salespersons.* The final step can be accomplished by dividing the total number of hours required to service all accounts by the average number of hours each salesperson devotes to sales and service of established accounts. The formula is:

$$\text{Required Number of Salespersons} = \frac{\text{Total Number of Hours Required to Service Accounts}}{\text{Total Number of Hours Each Salesperson Devotes to Calling on Established Accounts}}$$

$$= \frac{63{,}724 \text{ hours}}{736 \text{ hours}}$$

$$= 86.6 \text{ or } 87 \text{ salespersons.}$$

Directions: Use menu item 15 titled "Sales Force Size Determination" to solve each of the following problems.

Problem 1 Jim Youngblood is vice-president of sales at Youngstown Industrial Supplies. Youngblood uses three classifications for his firm's 1,600 accounts: 220 Type A firms, 580 Type B firms, and 800 Type C firms. He estimates that Type A accounts should be called on 26 times per year, while Type B and Type C accounts should be contacted 20 and 15 times per year, respectively. The length of time for each sales call should be 30 minutes for Type A and Type B accounts, and 15 minutes for Type C accounts. Another 15 percent is to be added to each type account for unplanned/emergency calls. The typical Youngstown Industrial Supplies sales representative works a 40-hour work week for 48 weeks each year and devotes 50 percent of his or her time to calling on established accounts, 20 percent on potential accounts, 20 percent on travel, and 10 percent on nonselling activities. How many salespersons should Youngblood have in his department?

Problem 2 Sarah Halverson is a Dallas-based manufacturer's agent in the clothing industry. Over the years, the number of salespersons who work for her organization has grown to match the increase in the number of her firm's retail accounts. Halverson divides her 3,500 retail store accounts as follows: 525 Type A, 700 Type B, and 2,275 Type C. She expects each Type A account to be contacted once a month and the sales call to last 60 minutes. Type B accounts should be contacted every other month, with the average call lasting 45 minutes. The less profitable Type C accounts should be contacted once in the spring, summer, autumn, and winter, with each call lasting an average of 40 minutes. Unplanned/emergency calls add another 5 percent to the total. Halverson estimates that her average sales representative works 40 hours each week and 45 weeks each year. Approximately 40 percent of a sales representative's time is spent in contacting established accounts, 30 percent on potential accounts, 15 percent on travel, and 15 percent on nonselling activities. How many salespersons does Halverson need to cover her market?

Problem 3 Manuel Garcia has gradually increased the market coverage of his San Antonio-based wholesaling firm until it currently serves retail accounts throughout southeast and central Texas. His Type A accounts represent 15 percent (165) of the firm's 1,100 accounts. Another 25 percent (275) of his accounts are categorized as Type B, while the remaining 60 percent (660) are labeled Type C. Type A accounts are contacted weekly, Type B accounts are contacted biweekly, and Type C accounts are contacted every month. The average length of each of the sales calls are 40 minutes, 30 minutes, and 20 minutes, respectively. An additional 10 percent is added to the time spent on each type of account as a result of unplanned/emergency calls. Garcia's sales representatives work 40-hour weeks for an average of 46 weeks each year and spend approximately 35 percent of their time contacting established accounts, 25 percent on potential accounts, 20 percent on travel, and the remaining 20 percent on nonselling activities.

a. How many salespersons should Garcia employ?
b. Garcia is considering an increase in the number of sales calls on Type C retail customers from 12 to 24 in an attempt to stimulate additional orders. What impact would this have on the number of salespersons he needs?
c. Rather than attempting to stimulate purchases by Type C customers, Garcia is considering the use of his current sales force to contact prospective customers in an attempt to secure their business. To accomplish this, he would have to reallocate the current usage of time by his sales force. He estimates that he would have to reduce the time spent on established accounts from 35 percent to 25 percent. What impact would this change have on the number of salespersons needed?

Problem 4 Margaret Admundson's sales force calls on 4,000 beauty shops and hair styling salons throughout Missouri, Kansas, Oklahoma, and Nebraska from her Kansas City headquarters. She estimates that she currently has 800 Type A accounts for her firm's beauty supplies, 1,000 Type B accounts, and 2,200 Type C accounts. Each Type A account is contacted every other week for 30 minutes per call. Type B accounts are contacted monthly for 30 minutes per call, while Type C accounts are contacted every other month for 20 minutes per call. An additional 10 percent of the time involved in contacting established accounts is included for unplanned/emergency calls. Admundson's sales representatives work 48 weeks per year with an average work week of 40 hours. Each sales representative spends approximately 40 percent of his or her time contacting established accounts, 15 percent on potential accounts, 30 percent on travel, and 15 percent on nonselling activities.

a. How many sales representatives should Admundson employ to service her accounts?
b. What effect would reducing the number of weeks worked per year from 48 to 45 have on the size of her sales force?
c. What effect would a decision to increase the amount of time spent on a Type C account sales call from 20 minutes to 30 minutes and an increase in the number of contacts from 6 to 12 have on the size of Admundson's sales force?

Problem 5 Larry Jacobs is sales manager for a Pittsburgh-based industrial distributor. Jacobs categorizes 100 of his 600 accounts as Type A, another 125 as Type B, and the remaining 375 as Type C. Type A accounts are contacted every other week, and Type B and C accounts are contacted once a month. Average sales calls last 30 minutes for Type A and B accounts and 20 minutes for Type C accounts. An additional 15 percent of the time involved in contacting each account is included for unplanned/emergency calls. Jacobs's sales representatives work 40-hour weeks for an average of 47 weeks each year. He estimates that 35 percent of their time is spent in actual sales calls on established accounts, 20 percent on potential accounts, 15 percent on travel, and 30 percent on nonselling activities.

a. How many sales representatives does Jacobs need to service his accounts?

b. Jacobs is considering several methods of reducing sales expenses. Since the Type C accounts generate smaller sales and profits than do Type A and Type B accounts, he is considering reducing the number of contacts from 12 to 6 and lowering the average sales call time from 20 minutes to 15 minutes. What effect would these changes have on the number of sales representatives required?

c. One of Jacobs's senior sales representatives argued that the percentage of time spent in sales calls on established accounts could be increased from 35 percent to 50 percent by reducing the frequency and amount of reports and other paperwork each salesperson must prepare. Assuming the sales representative is correct, what effect would this change have on the number of sales representatives needed to service the firm's accounts?

PART SEVEN

Pricing Strategy

17 Introduction to Pricing

Key Terms

Learning Goals

1. To identify the major categories of pricing objectives
2. To explain the practical problems involved in applying price theory concepts to actual pricing decisions
3. To explain the major cost-plus approaches to price setting
4. To list the major advantages and shortcomings of using breakeven analysis in pricing decisions
5. To explain the superiority of modified breakeven analysis over the basic breakeven model

Remington Products, Inc.

Back in 1979, Victor K. Kiam II was thumbing through a copy of *Business Week* when an article caught his eye. Sperry Rand Corporation, a giant in industries ranging from computers and defense to agriculture, was trying to unload its Remington razor division—and for a very good reason. Remington had lost $30 million over the preceding three years, and Sperry Rand seemed unable to turn the situation around. "Sperry is a high-technology company," said Kiam. "Remington was the only real consumer product they had and they were uncomfortable with it. They didn't understand what to do with it."

When Kiam looked closer, he discovered that Remington had not always been a money loser. During the 1950s, the company had been the world's leading manufacturer of electric shavers—a position it held until the 1960s when the Dutch-made Norelco shaver was introduced in the United States. Remington's market position and profits shrank even further when a foreign firm was granted control of Remington's European market in the late 1960s and when twin-bladed razors were introduced in the early 1970s. At the time Kiam was contemplating the purchase, Remington held a meager 19 percent share of what had become a nongrowth market.

Despite these problems, Kiam decided to continue his investigation. "I went over to their headquarters and discovered they had operations in 26 countries. So I was given 26 separate books on the corporation plus literature on the history of the business, and I brought a lot of it to our apartment in Manhattan. I laid the stuff out on the dining room table and started organizing it."

"My wife Ellen came home for dinner," continued Kiam, "and she told me to clean off the table. I said, 'Oh, honey, I can't. It took me 40 minutes just to spread these pages out.' We argued about this for a few minutes until she finally asked, 'What's so important about this anyway? What are you looking at?' So I told her. She said, 'How can you even think about buying that company? You've never shaved electrically in your whole life. You can't do anything like this until you try it.' So she went out and bought me the shaver and I tried it," said Kiam, as he stroked his baby-smooth cheeks. "I thought the . . . thing was just marvelous. I said, 'Where . . . have I been all my life?' "

Convinced that the Remington was the best shaver on the market and merely lacking a competent marketing program to achieve success, Kiam purchased the company from Sperry for $25 million—an amount that bought him little more than the Remington name. He now faced

Photo Source: Courtesy of Remington Products, Inc.

the enormous challenge of convincing consumers that Remington shavers were better than Norelcos. If he failed, he would lose Remington to the Chase Manhattan Bank, which had provided much of the funds he needed to acquire Remington.

Assignment: Use the materials in Chapter 17 to recommend methods to be used by Victor Kiam to increase consumer acceptance and profitability of the Remington shaver.

Source: Victor Kiam quotation from Bill Zehme, "Victor Victorious," *Success* (September 1982), p. 45.

Chapter Overview _____

Three of the four variables in the marketing mix have been discussed in previous sections of *Contemporary Marketing*. Chapters 8 and 9 examined the first critical element of a firm's marketing mix: the determination of the products and services to offer the market target. The four chapters in Part Five focused on marketing channel decisions and physical distribution: the optimum method for getting products and services *to* the firm's market target. Chapters 14 through 16 discussed the third variable of the marketing mix: communicating with the firm's market target and attempting to persuade them through personal and nonpersonal selling. The final variable—price—is the subject of both this and the following chapter.

Although each of the marketing mix variables have been examined in considerable detail in separate sections of the text, they are all clearly interrelated. The decision by General Motors to include such options as a radio, a digital clock, power brakes, and reclining seats as standard items rather than separately priced options on the Chevrolet Cavalier affects not only the price of the auto, but also the promotional strategy and the profit margins of channel members. Since retail dealers had previously received a higher profit margin on auto options specified by purchasers than on the auto itself, the new practice prompted them to offer smaller price discounts from the posted sticker price of the auto. The actual price set for a product or service is influenced by dozens of factors including marketing objectives, consumer demand, costs, competition, channel profit requirements, and government regulations.

Price
Exchange value of a good or service.

The starting place for examining pricing strategy is to understand the meaning of the term *price*. **Price** is the exchange value of a good or service, and the value of an item is what it can be exchanged for in the marketplace. In earlier times the price of an acre of land might have been 20 bushels of wheat, three cattle, or a boat. Price is a measure of what one must exchange to obtain a desired good or service. When the barter process was abandoned in favor of a monetary system, price became the amount of funds required to purchase an item. As one writer has pointed out, contemporary society uses a number of names to refer to price:

Price is all around us. You pay *rent* for your apartment, *tuition* for your education, and a *fee* to your physician or dentist.

The airline, railway, taxi, and bus companies charge you a *fare;* the local utilities call their price a *rate;* and the local bank charges *interest* for the money you borrow.

The price for driving your car on Florida's Sunshine Parkway is a *toll,* and the company that insures your car charges you a *premium.*

The guest lecturer charges an *honorarium* to tell you about a government official who took a *bribe* to help a shady character steal *dues* collected by a trade association.

Clubs or societies to which you belong may make a special *assessment* to pay unusual expenses. Your regular lawyer may ask for a *retainer* to cover her services.

The "price" of an executive is a *salary;* the price of a salesperson may be a *commission;* and the price of a worker is a *wage.*

Finally, although economists would disagree, many of us feel that *income taxes* are the price we pay for the privilege of making money![1]

Determination of profitable and justified prices are the result of considering such factors as pricing objectives and alternative approaches to setting prices. These topics are discussed in this chapter. The following chapter focuses upon management of the pricing function and discusses pricing strategies, price–quality relationships, and both industrial pricing and pricing in the public sector.

Importance of Price in the Marketing Mix

Ancient philosophers recognized the importance of price to the functioning of an economic system. Some of their early written accounts refer to attempts to determine a fair or just price. However, their limited understanding of time, place, and possession utilities thwarted such efforts.

Price continues to serve as a means of regulating economic activity. Employment of any or all of the four factors of production (land, capital, human resources, and entrepreneurship) depends upon the prices received by each factor. For an individual firm, prices and the corresponding quantity to be purchased by its customers represent the revenue to be received. Prices, therefore, influence a firm's profit as well as its employment of the factors of production.

How Marketing Executives Rank the Price Variable

Over two decades ago, marketing professor Jon G. Udell conducted a survey of marketing executives to determine the relative importance of price as an element of their firms' marketing mixes. When the various factors included on the questionnaire were reorganized into the four major mix variables, price was ranked third—ahead only of distribution.[2]

But times have changed. A recent study of marketing executives revealed that price currently ranks as the single most important marketing mix variable.[3] Product planning and management is a close second, and distribution and promotion rank third and fourth, respectively. Figure 17.1 compares the Udell findings to those of the later study.

Pricing Objectives

Just as price is a component in the total marketing mix, so are pricing objectives a component of the overall objectives of the organization. As Chapter 3 explained, marketing objectives represent the desired outcomes that executives hope to attain. These objectives are based upon the overall objectives of the organization. Pricing objectives are also a critical component of the means–end chain extending from overall aims of the firm. The objectives of the firm and the marketing organization provide the basis for the development of pricing objectives, which are then used to develop and implement the more specific pricing policies and procedures.

A firm's major overall objective may be to become the dominant factor in the domestic market. Its marketing objective might then be to achieve maximum sales penetration in each region. The related pricing objective would be sales maximization. This means–end chain might lead to the adoption of a

Figure 17.1

Relative Importance of Marketing Variables: A 20-Year Perspective

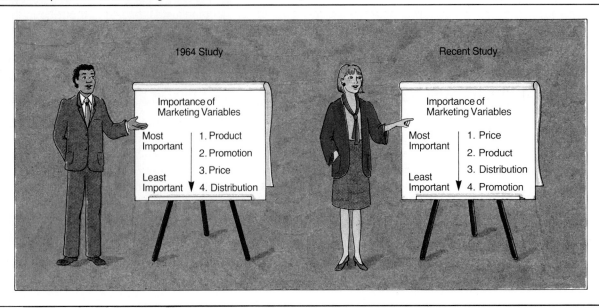

low-price policy implemented by the highest price discounts to channel members of any firm in the industry.

Pricing objectives vary from firm to firm. In a pioneering study of pricing objectives of major U.S. corporations, economist Robert F. Lanzillotti identified the primary pricing objectives of each firm.[4] As Figure 17.2 indicates, satisfactory return on investment, attainment of specified market shares, and meeting the actions of competitors are common objectives.

Pricing objectives can be classified into four major groups: (1) profitability objectives, (2) volume objectives, (3) meeting competition objectives, and (4) prestige objectives. Profitability objectives include profit maximization and target return goals. As Figure 17.2 indicates, Alcoa, Du Pont, and General Electric specify profitability objectives. Volume objectives can be categorized as either sales maximization or market-share goals. The objectives of American Can, Sears, and Standard Oil (Indiana) fall into this category.

A recent study of U.S. businesses asked marketers to identify both the primary and secondary pricing objectives of their firms. Meeting competitive prices was most often mentioned as a primary or secondary pricing objective. It was followed closely by two profitability-oriented objectives: a specified return on investment and specified total profit levels. These two objectives ranked first and second, respectively, as primary pricing objectives.[5] The findings are shown in Table 17.1.

Figure 17.2
Pricing Objectives of Eight Large Companies

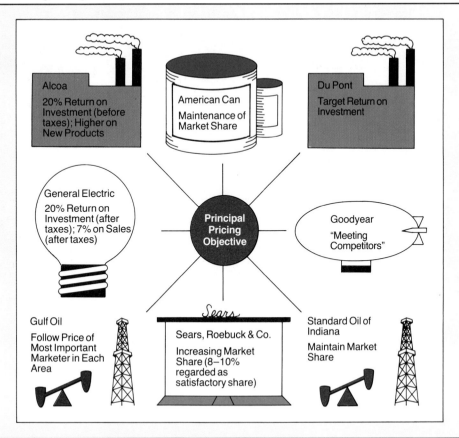

Source: Objectives reported in Robert E. Lanzillotti, "Pricing Objectives in Large Companies,"
American Economic Review (December 1958), pp. 924–926.

Profitability Objectives

In classical economic theory, the traditional pricing objective has been to maximize profits. The study of microeconomics is based on certain assumptions—that buyers and sellers are rational and that rational behavior constitutes an effort to maximize gains and to minimize losses. In terms of actual business practice, this means that profit maximization is assumed to be the basic objective of individual firms.

Profits are a function of revenue and expenses:

$$\text{Profits} = \text{Revenues} - \text{Expenses}.$$

Revenue is determined by the selling price and number of units sold:

$$\text{Total Revenue} = \text{Price} \times \text{Quantity Sold}.$$

Table 17.1

Primary and Secondary Pricing Objectives of U.S. Firms

Pricing Objective	Percentage of Respondents Ranking the Item[a]		
	As Primary Objective	As Secondary Objective	As Either Primary or Secondary Objective
Profitability Objectives			
Specified Rate of Return on Investment	61	17	78
Specified Total Profit Level	60	17	77
Increased Total Profits above Previous Levels	34	38	72
Specified Rate of Return on Sales	48	23	71
Volume Objectives			
Increased Market Share	31	42	73
Retaining of Existing Market Share	31	36	67
Serving of Selected Market Segments	27	39	66
Specified Market Share	16	41	57
Meeting Competition Objectives			
Meeting of Competitive Price Level	38	43	81
Prestige Objectives			
Creation of a Readily Identifiable Image for the Firm and/or Its Products	22	41	63

[a]Totals exceed 100 percent because most firms list multiple pricing objectives.
Source: Louis E. Boone and David L. Kurtz, *Pricing Objectives and Practices in American Industry: A Research Report*.

Profit Maximization
In pricing strategy, the point at which the additional revenue gained by increasing the price of a product equals the increase in total cost.

Target Return Objectives
Short-run or long-run pricing objectives of achieving a specified return on either sales or investment.

Price, therefore, should be increased to the point where it causes a disproportionate decrease in the number of units sold. A 10 percent price increase that results in only an 8 percent cut in volume adds to the firm's revenues. However, a 10 percent price hike that results in an 11 percent sales decline reduces revenues.

Economists refer to this approach as *marginal analysis*. They identify profit maximization as the point at which the addition to total revenue is just balanced by the increase in total cost. The basic problem is how to achieve this delicate balance between marginal revenue and marginal cost. Relatively few firms actually achieve the objective of profit maximization. A significantly larger number prefer to direct their efforts toward goals that are more reasonably implemented and measured.

Consequently, target return objectives have become common in industry, particularly among the larger firms where public pressure typically prohibits consideration of the profit maximization objective. Automobile companies are an example of this phenomenon. Target return objectives are either short-run or long-run goals usually stated as a percentage of sales or investment. A company may, for instance, seek a 15 percent annual rate of return on investment or an 8 percent rate of return on sales. A specified rate of return on investment was the most commonly reported primary pricing objective in Table 17.1. Goals of this nature also serve as useful guidelines in evaluating corporate activity. As one writer has aptly expressed: "For management consciously accepting less than maximum profits, the target rate can provide a measure of the amount of restraint. For firms making very low profits, the target rate can serve as a standard for judging improvement."[6]

Target return objectives offer several benefits to the marketer. As noted above, they serve as a means for evaluating performance. They also are designed to generate a "fair" profit, as judged by management, stockholders, and the general public as well.

Volume Objectives

Many business executives argue that a more accurate explanation of actual pricing behavior is that firms strive for *sales maximization* within a given profit constraint.[7] In other words, they set a minimum at what they consider the lowest acceptable profit level and then seek to maximize sales (subject to this profit constraint) in the belief that the increased sales are more important than immediate high profits to the long-run competitive picture. The companies continue to expand sales as long as their total profits do not drop below the minimum return acceptable to management.

Another volume-related pricing objective is the market share objective—the goal set for the control of a portion of the market for a firm's product or service. The company's specific goal may be to maintain or increase its share of a particular market, say, from 10 percent to 20 percent.

In Figure 17.2, Sears expressed its pricing objective as a market share growth rate of 8 to 10 percent annually. As Table 17.1 indicates, almost two-thirds of all responding firms list volume objectives as either a primary or secondary pricing objective.

Although *growth* is typically the end result of volume objectives, some firms with relatively high market shares may even prefer to reduce their share of specific markets at times due to possible government action in the area of monopoly control. Market share is a frequently used indicator in court evaluations of cases involving alleged monopolistic practices.

Profit Impact of Market Strategies (PIMS) Project
Major research study that discovered a strong positive relationship between a firm's market share and its return on investment.

The PIMS Studies Market share objectives may prove critical in the achievement of other organizational objectives. High sales, for example, often mean more profits. The extensive Profit Impact of Market Strategies (PIMS) project, conducted by the Marketing Science Institute, analyzed more than 2,000 firms and revealed that two of the most important factors influencing profitability were product quality and market share.

The linkage between market share and profitability is dramatically expressed by Figure 17.3. For firms enjoying more than 40 percent of a market, their pretax return on investment averages 32.3 percent. By contrast, firms with a minor market share (less than 10 percent) generate average pretax investment returns of 13.2 percent.

The underlying factor in explaining the positive relationship between profitability and market share appears to be the operating experience and lower overall costs of high-market-share firms as compared with competitors who possess smaller shares of the market. Accordingly, the segmentation strategies for astute marketers may involve focusing upon obtaining larger shares of smaller markets and less on smaller shares of a larger market. The financial returns may be enhanced by being a major competitor in several smaller market segments than by being a relatively minor competitor in a larger market.

Figure 17.3
Relationship of Market Share to Return on Investment

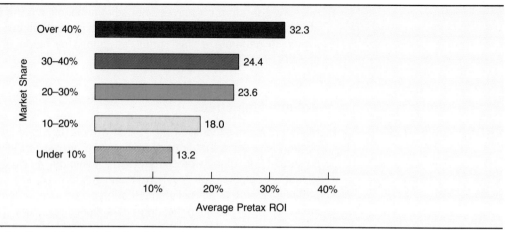

Meeting Competiton as a Pricing Objective

This third pricing objective is much less aggressive than profitability or volume objectives. Competing firms operationalize this pricing objective by simply matching the prices of the established industry price leader. In the Lanzillotti study of pricing objectives, Goodyear, Gulf, and National Steel specified meeting competitive prices as a primary pricing objective. As Table 17.1 indicates, 81 percent, or four of every five respondent firms, listed this as a primary or secondary objective, making meeting competition the pricing objective most often mentioned.

Frequently, the net result of this pricing objective is to deemphasize the price element of the marketing mix and to focus more strongly on nonprice competition. Although price is a highly visible mix component and an effective method of obtaining a differential advantage over competitors, a price reduction is also an easily duplicated move. The airline price competition of recent years exemplifies the actions and reactions of competitors for passenger and freight business. Because of the direct impact of such price changes on overall profitability, many firms attempt to promote stable prices by utilizing the objective of simply meeting competition and competing for market share by focusing upon product/service strategies, promotional decisions, and distribution—the nonprice elements of the marketing mix.

Prestige Objectives

A final category of pricing objectives, unrelated to either profitability or sales volume, is prestige objectives. Prestige objectives involve the establishment of relatively high prices to develop and maintain an image of quality and exclusiveness. Such objectives reflect marketers' recognition of the role of price in the creation of an overall image for the firm and its products and services.

For years Curtis Mathes used price as a surrogate indicator of quality for its television sets. The Curtis Mathes advertisements made this point with the line ". . .the highest-priced television set in America; and it's worth it." Nei-

Return to the Stop-Action Case

Remington Products, Inc.

Victor Kiam, the new owner of Remington Products, Inc., realized that his pricing objectives could be categorized as both volume and profitability. Consequently, one of his first priorities was to change the former management's marketing philosophy and pricing strategy. "The former management thought you could sell only so many electric shavers in this country," said Kiam, who strongly disagreed. "The market is not inelastic. Our marketplace is any male or female who shaves, anywhere in the world. That's a big universe."

To increase the number of Remington shavers sold, Kiam slashed prices nearly in half from $34.95, the price of the cheapest model in 1979, to $19.95. "I thought that [$34.95] was an awfully high price," said Kiam. "I wanted to see if we could bring out a shaver at a lower cost that would reach more people. We wanted to expand the market. And we wanted to do that without damaging the quality of the product."

To bring the price down to $19.95—a price that would undercut the least expensive Norelco by $15.00—

Kiam streamlined the entire company. He eliminated 70 executive positions at a savings of $2 million per year in salaries and closed three overseas plants, deciding to consolidate all manufacturing facilities in Bridgeport, Connecticut. To reduce production costs, Kiam also used his vision of what the public wanted in a shaver. He eliminated all unnecessary frills such as decorative chrome trim. "It was very nice, very pretty," said Kiam. "But by taking it off we eliminated the extra cost of the chrome as well as the cost of putting it on. We were able to reduce the price of the shaver that way."

He also decided to eliminate the handsome stainless steel case in which the shaver was stored. "The case weighed a ton and cost $2.50," said Kiam. "The first time I brought the shaver on a trip, I threw the case out. I didn't want to lug it around." In its place Kiam substituted a practical, lightweight leatherette pouch that added only pennies to each shaver's cost.

Source: Kiam quotations from Claudia M. Christie, "The Most Expensive Gift for a Husband a Wife Ever Bought," *New England Business* (June 20, 1983), pp. 45–46.

man-Marcus, the prestigious Dallas-based retailer, annually issues a catalog of luxuries for Christmas gift-giving. Recent examples of its offerings include a 24-piece set of custom linens, costing $900, which match customers' china; a $1.2 million condominium on the island of Kauai, Hawaii; and a $200 Iglu-Maker. While some marketers set relatively high prices to maintain a prestige image with their consumers, others prefer the opposite approach of developing a low-price image among customers.

In sharp contrast to the low-price strategies of newer airlines formed after deregulation, Regent Air decided to offer the ultimate in luxury for travelers between New York and Los Angeles. The fares are competitive with first-class tickets on many other airlines. But, as Figure 17.4 reveals, the service, meals, in-flight club rooms, and even private compartments are regal. For an added fee, Regent Class Deluxe service includes door-to-door limousine service for departure and arrival.

Price Determination

The determination of price may be viewed in two ways: the theoretical concepts of supply and demand and the cost-oriented approach that characterizes current business practice. During the first part of this century, most con-

Figure 17.4

Enhancement of a Prestige Image by Avoiding
Economy and Other Discount Air Fares

Source: Courtesy of Regent Air.

siderations of price determination emphasized the classical concepts of supply and demand. Since World War II, however, the emphasis has shifted to a cost-oriented approach. Hindsight allows us to see that both concepts have certain flaws.

Another concept of price determination—based on the impact of custom and tradition—is often overlooked. **Customary prices** are retail prices that consumers expect as a result of custom, tradition, and social habit. The candy makers' attempt to hold the line on the traditional $.10 candy bar led to considerable reduction in the product size. Similar practices have prevailed in the marketing of soft drinks as bottlers attempt to balance consumer expectations of customary prices with the realities of inflation.

Hershey Food Corporation approached the dilemma of rising product costs for a snack item by simultaneously increasing the product size and price. In 1982, Hershey increased the weight of its milk chocolate bar and Reese's Peanut Butter Cups between 33 and 38 percent to accompany a wholesale price increase of 20 percent. Even though the cost per candy bar increased, Hershey's marketers emphasized that the cost per ounce was actually less than in 1969.

Customary Prices
In pricing strategy, the traditional prices that customers expect to pay for certain products and services.

The division of the U.S. beer market into premium- and popular-price levels provides another example of a traditional pricing system. In the 1930s, several major brewers were faced with excess capacity that could not be absorbed by their local markets. These brewers began to ship their products to distant markets. The freight charges were covered by charging retail prices higher than those charged for local beers. The higher prices were justified by the marketers' claims that their beers were of higher quality than the local beers. The "imports," classified as premium by their marketers, often were better than many of the numerous local brands. Today, any difference in quality among beers is probably negligible, and there is little difference in the production costs of premium and popular beers. However, the traditional pricing system continues to exist.

At some point in time, someone has to set initial prices for products. Sustained inflation has also created a need for periodically reviewing firms' price structures. The remainder of this chapter discusses the traditional and current concepts of price determination. It also considers how best to integrate the concepts to develop a realistic pricing approach.

Price Determination in Economic Theory

The microeconomic approach to price determination assumes a profit maximization objective and leads to the derivation of correct equilibrium prices in the marketplace. This approach considers both supply and demand factors and, therefore, provides a more complete analysis than that typically utilized by business firms.

Demand
Schedule of the amounts of a firm's product or service that consumers will purchase at different prices during a specified time period.

Supply
Schedule of the amounts of a product or service that will be offered for sale at different prices during a specified time period.

Pure Competition
Market structure characterized by homogeneous products in which there are so many buyers and sellers that none has a significant influence on price.

Monopolistic Competition
Market structure involving a heterogeneous product and product differentiation among competing suppliers, allowing the marketer some degree of control over prices.

Oligopoly
Market structure involving relatively few sellers and, because of high start-up costs, significant entry barriers to new competitors.

Monopoly
Market structure involving only one seller of a product or service for which no close substitutes exist.

Demand refers to a schedule of the amounts of a firm's product or service that consumers will purchase at different prices during a specified period. Supply refers to a schedule of the amounts of a product or service that will be offered for sale at different prices during a specified time period. These schedules may vary for different types of market structures. Four types of market structures exist: pure competition, monopolistic competition, oligopoly, and monopoly. Pure competition is the market structure in which there are such a large number of buyers and sellers that none of them has a significant influence on price. Other characteristics of pure competition are a homogeneous product and ease of entry for sellers that results from low start-up costs.

This marketing structure is largely theoretical in contemporary society; however, the agricultural sector exhibits many of the characteristics of a purely competitive market and provides the closest example of this marketing structure.

Monopolistic competition, which typifies most retailing, is a market structure with large numbers of buyers and sellers. However, it involves a heterogeneous product and product differentiation, which allow the marketer some degree of control over prices. An oligopoly is a market structure in which there are relatively few sellers. Each seller may affect the market, but no one seller controls it. Because of high start-up costs, new competitors encounter significant barriers to entry. The demand curve facing each individual firm in an oligopolistic market contains a unique "kink" at the current market price. Because of the impact of a single competitor upon total industry sales, any attempt by one firm to reduce prices in an effort to generate additional sales is likely to be matched by competitors. The result of total industry price cutting is a reduction in total industry revenues. Oligopolies occur frequently in the steel, petroleum refining, automobile, and tobacco industries.

A monopoly is a market structure with only one seller of a product and no close substitutes for it. Antitrust legislation has nearly eliminated all but temporary monopolies, such as those provided by patent protection, and regulated monopolies, such as the public service utilities—telephone, electric, cable television—and natural gas companies. The government allows regulated monopolies in markets where competition would lead to an uneconomic duplication of services. In return for this license, government reserves the right to regulate the monopoly's rate of return.

Table 17.2 compares the four types of market structures on the following bases: number of competitors, ease of entry into the industry by new firms, similarity of competing products, degree of control over price by individual firms, and whether the demand curve facing the individual firm is elastic or inelastic. Elasticity, the degree of consumer responsiveness to changes in price, is affected by such factors as availability of substitute goods, whether the product or service is a necessity or a luxury, the portion of a person's budget being spent, and the time perspective under consideration.

Revenue and Cost Curves   The demand side of price theory is concerned with revenue curves. Average revenue *(AR)* is obtained by dividing total revenue *(TR)* by the quantity *(Q)* associated with these revenues:

$$AR = \frac{TR}{Q}.$$

The average revenue is actually the demand curve facing the firm. Marginal revenue *(MR)* is the change in total revenue *(ΔTR)* that results from selling an additional unit of output *(ΔQ):*

$$MR = \frac{\Delta TR}{\Delta Q}.$$

Table 17.2

Important Characteristics of the Four Market Structures

	Type of Market Structure			
Characteristics	Pure Competition	Monopolistic Competition	Oligopoly	Monopoly
Number of Competitors	Many	Few to Many	Few	No Direct Competitors
Ease of Entry into the Industry by New Firms	Easy	Somewhat Difficult	Difficult	Regulated by Government
Similarity of Products or Services Offered by Competing Firms	Similar	Different	Can Be Either Similar or Different	No Directly Competing Products or Services
Control over Price by Individual Firms	None	Some	Some	Considerable
Demand Curve Facing Individual Firms	Totally Elastic	Can Be Either Elastic or Inelastic	Kinked; Inelastic below Kink; More Elastic above	Can Be Either Elastic or Inelastic

The demand curves—average revenue lines—and marginal revenue curves for each market are shown later in Figure 17.6. Average variable cost *(AVC)* is simply the total variable costs *(TVC)* divided by the related quantity *(Q):*

$$AVC = \frac{TVC}{Q}.$$

Similarly, average fixed cost *(AFC)* is determined by dividing total fixed costs *(TFC)* by the related quantity *(Q):*

$$AFC = \frac{TFC}{Q}.$$

Marginal cost *(MC)* is the change in total cost *(ΔTC)* that results from producing an additional unit of output (ΔQ):

$$MC = \frac{\Delta TC}{\Delta Q}.$$

Marginal costs, therefore, are similar to marginal revenue—the change in total revenue resulting from the sale of an incremental unit. The point of profit maximization is where marginal costs are equal to marginal revenues. The cost curves of the equations shown above appear in Figure 17.5. The marginal cost *(MC)* curve intersects the average variable cost *(AVC)* curve and average total cost *(ATC)* curve at their minimum points.

In the short run, a firm will continue to operate even if the price falls below *ATC*, provided it remains above *AVC*. Why does this constitute rational market behavior? If the firm were to cease operations after the price fell below *ATC*, it would still have some fixed costs, but it would have *no* revenue. Any amount received above *AVC* can be used to cover at least part of the fixed costs. The manager is acting rationally by continuing to produce as long as

Figure 17.5
Cost Curves

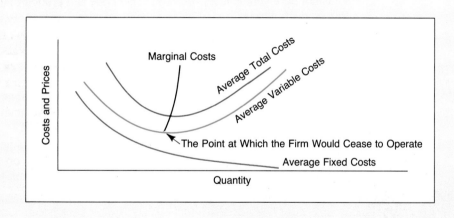

Figure 17.6
Price Determination in the Four Product Markets

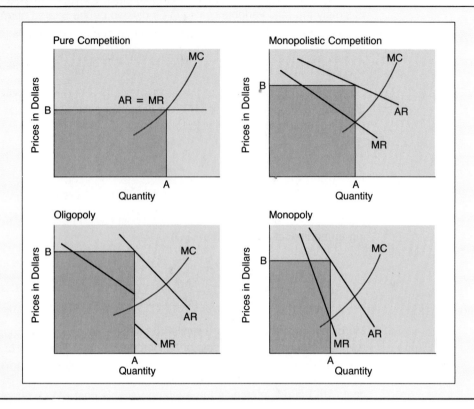

price exceeds *AVC*, since this minimizes losses. If price falls below *AVC*, the manager should cease operations because continued operation would *increase* the amount of losses. The supply curve, therefore, is the marginal cost curve above its intersection with *AVC*, since this is the area of rational pricing behavior for the firm.

How are the prices set in each of the product market situations? Figure 17.6 shows how prices are determined in each of the four product markets. The point of profit maximization *(MC = MR)* sets the equilibrium output (Point A), which is extended to the *AR* line to set the equilibrium price (Point B). In the case of pure competition, *AR = MR*, so price is a predetermined variable in this product market.

Practical Problems of Price Theory

From the viewpoint of the marketer, price theory concepts are sometimes difficult to apply in practice. What, then, are their practical limitations?

1.   *Many firms do not attempt to maximize profits.* Economic analysis is subject to the same limitations as the assumptions on which it is based—for example, the proposition that all firms attempt to maximize profits.

2. *It is difficult to estimate demand curves.* Modern accounting procedures provide managers with a clear understanding of cost structures. The managers can, therefore, readily comprehend the supply side of the pricing equation, but it is difficult to estimate demand at various price levels. Demand curves must be based on market research estimates that often are not as exact as cost figures. Over time, however, these problems may be eliminated by the use of advanced research methodology. Although the demand element can be identified, it is often difficult to measure in the real-world setting.

3. *Inadequate training and communication hinder price theory in the real world.* Many managers lack the formal training in economics to be able to apply its concepts to their own pricing decisions. On the other hand, many economists remain essentially theorists, devoting little interest or effort to real-world pricing situations. This dual problem significantly hinders the use of economic theory in actual pricing practice.

Price Determination in Practice

The practical limitations inherent in price theory have forced practitioners to turn to other techniques. The cost-plus approach is the most commonly used method of setting prices today. For many years, government contracts with suppliers called for payments of all expenses plus a set profit usually stated as a percentage of the cost of the project. These cost-plus contracts, as they were known, have been abandoned in favor of competitive bidding or specifically negotiated prices.

Cost-plus Pricing
In pricing strategy, the practice of adding a percentage or specified dollar amount (the markup) to the base cost of the product or service to cover unassigned costs and to provide a profit.

   Cost-plus pricing uses a base cost figure per unit and adds a markup to cover unassigned costs and to provide a profit. The only real difference in the multitude of cost-plus techniques is the relative sophistication of the costing procedures employed. For example, a local apparel shop may set prices by adding a 40 percent markup to the invoice price charged by the supplier. As pointed out in the Computer Applications section for Chapter 12, the markup is expected to cover all other expenses and permit the owner to earn a reasonable return on the sale of the clothes.

   Figure 17.7 shows how a residential home builder uses cost-plus pricing. For the typical $100,000 home in the suburbs of a large city, land costs would average $22,500. Construction costs would add another $52,500. Construction financing, closing costs, and other fees produce an additional $15,000 in costs. Approximately $5,000 would be included in the selling price for the real estate sales commission, which brings the total costs to $95,000. The builder then adds $5,000, or 5 percent of the sales price, for profit.

   In contrast to this rather simple pricing mechanism, a large manufacturer may employ a pricing formula that requires a computer to handle the necessary calculations. But advanced calculations are reserved for a sophisticated costing procedure. In the end, the formula still requires someone to make a decision about the markup. The apparel shop and the large manufacturer may be vastly different with respect to the cost aspect, but they are remarkably similar when it comes to the markup side of the equation.

   This discussion demonstrates one of the problems associated with cost-plus pricing: "Costs do not determine prices, since the proper function of cost in pricing is to determine the profit consequences of pricing alternatives."[8] Unfortunately, this point is not always understood by marketers.

Figure 17.7
The $100,000 House

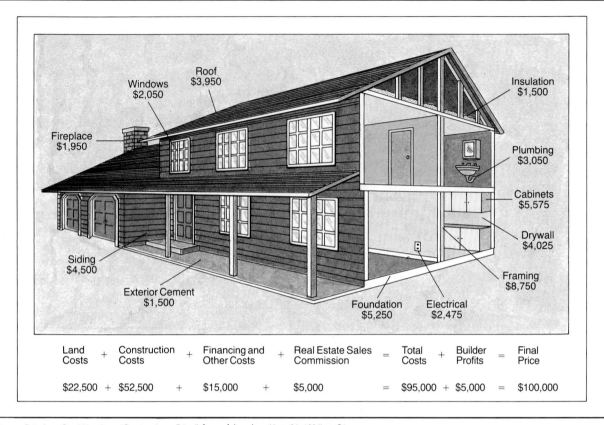

Land Costs	+	Construction Costs	+	Financing and Other Costs	+	Real Estate Sales Commission	=	Total Costs	+	Builder Profits	=	Final Price
$22,500	+	$52,500	+	$15,000	+	$5,000	=	$95,000	+	$5,000	=	$100,000

Source: Data from Carol Nanninga, "Constructing a Price," *Journal-American* (June 24, 1984), p. G1.

Full-Cost Pricing and Incremental-Cost Pricing   The two most common cost-oriented pricing procedures are the full-cost method and the incremental-cost method. *Full-cost pricing* uses all relevant variable costs in setting a product's price. In addition, it allocates those fixed costs that cannot be directly attributed to the production of the specific item being priced. Under the full-cost method, if job order 515 in a printing plant amounts to 0.000127 percent of the plant's total output, then 0.000127 percent of the firm's overhead expenses are charged to that job. This approach allows the marketer to recover all costs plus the amount added as a profit margin.

The full-cost approach has two basic deficiencies. First, there is no consideration of the competition or of the demand for the item. Perhaps no one wants to pay the price the firm has calculated! Second, any method of allocating overhead (fixed expenses) is arbitrary and may be unrealistic. In manufacturing, overhead allocations are often tied to direct labor hours. In retailing, the square footage of each profit center is sometimes the factor used in computations. Regardless of the technique, it is difficult to show a cause–effect relationship between the allocated cost and most products.

One way to overcome the arbitrary allocation of fixed expenses is by *incremental-cost pricing*, which attempts to use only those costs directly attributable to a specific output in setting prices. Consider a small manufacturer with the following income statement:

Sales (10,000 units at $10)		$100,000
Expenses:		
Variable	$50,000	
Fixed	40,000	90,000
Net profit		$ 10,000

Suppose the firm is offered a contract for an additional 5,000 units. Since the peak season is over, these items can be produced at the same average variable cost. Assume that the labor force would be idle otherwise. To get the contract, how low could the firm price its product?

Under the full-cost approach, the lowest price would be $9 per unit. This figure is obtained by dividing the $90,000 in expenses by an output of 10,000 units. The incremental approach, on the other hand, could permit a price of $5.10, which would significantly increase the possibility of securing the additional contract. This price would be composed of the $5.00 variable cost related to each unit of production plus a $.10-per-unit contribution to fixed expenses and overhead. The income statement now looks like this:

Sales (10,000 at $10; 5,000 at $5.10)		$125,000
Expenses:		
Variable (15,000 × $5)	$75,000	
Fixed	40,000	$115,000
Net profit		$ 10,500

Profits are increased under the incremental approach. Admittedly, the illustration is based on two assumptions: (1) the ability to isolate markets so that selling at the lower price will not affect the price received in other markets; and (2) the absence of legal restrictions on the firm. The example, however, does illustrate that profits can sometimes be enhanced by using the incremental approach.

Breakeven Analysis

Breakeven Analysis
Pricing technique used to determine the number of products or services that must be sold at a specified price to generate sufficient revenue to cover total costs.

The technique of **breakeven analysis** is a means of determining the number of products or services that must be sold at a given price to generate sufficient revenue to cover total costs. Figure 17.8 presents a graphical depiction of the breakeven point. The total cost curve includes both fixed and variable segments, and total fixed cost is represented by a horizontal line. Average variable cost is assumed to be constant per unit as it was in the earlier example for incremental pricing.

The breakeven point is the point at which total revenue *(TR)* just equals total cost *(TC)*. It can be found by using the following formula:

$$\text{Breakeven Point} \atop \text{(in Units)} = \frac{\text{Total Fixed Cost}}{\text{Per Unit Contribution to Fixed Cost}},$$

where the per unit contribution equals the price of the product less the variable costs per unit.

Figure 17.8
Breakeven Chart

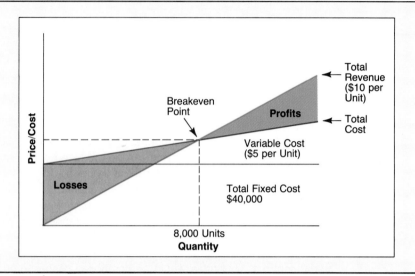

$$
\text{Breakeven Point (in Dollars)} = \frac{\text{Total Fixed Cost}}{1 - \dfrac{\text{Variable Cost per Unit}}{\text{Price}}}.
$$

In our earlier example, a selling price of $10 and an average variable cost of $5 resulted in a per-unit contribution to fixed costs of $5. This figure can be divided into total fixed costs of $40,000 to obtain a breakeven point of 8,000 units, or $80,000 in total sales revenue:

$$
\text{Breakeven Point (in Units)} = \frac{\$40,000}{\$5} = 8,000 \text{ units.}
$$

$$
\text{Breakeven Point (in Dollars)} = \frac{\$40,000}{1 - \dfrac{\$5}{\$10}} = \frac{\$40,000}{.5} = \$80,000.
$$

This data is shown plotted in Figure 17.8.

Target Returns Although breakeven analysis indicates the level of sales at which the firm will incur neither profits nor losses, management of most firms include some target profit in their analyses. In some instances, management sets a desired dollar return when considering a proposed new product or other marketing action. A retailer may set a desired profit of $250,000 in considering whether to expand to a second location. In other instances, the target return may be expressed in percentages, such as a 15 percent return on sales. These target returns can be included in the breakeven calculations.

In the case of a specified dollar target return, the return can be treated as an addition to total fixed costs in the breakeven equation. Using the example of the firm with total fixed costs of $40,000, a selling price of $10, and an average variable cost of $5, assume that management specifies a $15,000 return. In this case, the basic breakeven formula would be modified as follows:

$$\text{Breakeven Point (including specified dollar target return)} = \frac{\text{Total Fixed Costs} + \text{Profit Objective}}{\text{Per Unit Contribution}}$$

$$= \frac{\$40,000 + \$15,000}{\$5}$$

$$= 11,000 \text{ units.}$$

If the target return is expressed as a percentage of sales, it can be included in the breakeven formula as a variable cost. Suppose the marketing manager in the above example seeks a 10 percent return on sales. The desired return is $1 for each product sold (the $10 per unit selling price multiplied by the 10 percent return on sales). In this case, the basic breakeven formula would remain unchanged, although the variable costs per unit would be increased to reflect the target return. In this problem, the current variable costs of $5 would be increased by the $1-per-unit target return, and the per-unit contribution to fixed costs would be reduced to $4. As a result, the breakeven point would increase from 8,000 units to 10,000 units.

$$\text{Breakeven Point (in Units)} = \frac{\$40,000}{\$4} = 10,000 \text{ Units.}$$

Evaluation of Breakeven Analysis   Breakeven analysis is an effective tool for marketers in assessing the sales required to cover costs and achieve specified profit levels. It is easily understood by both marketing and nonmarketing executives and may assist in deciding whether required sales levels for a certain price are in fact realistic goals. However, it is not without shortcomings.

First, the model assumes that costs can be divided into fixed and variable categories. Some costs, such as salaries and advertising outlays, may be either fixed or variable depending upon the particular situation. In addition, the model assumes that per-unit variable costs do not change at different levels of operation. However, these may vary as a result of quantity discounts, more efficient utilization of the work force, or other economies resulting from increased levels of production and sales. Finally, the basic breakeven model does not consider demand. It is a cost-based model and does not directly address the crucial question of whether consumers will actually purchase the product at the specified price and in required quantities necessary to break even or to generate profits. The challenge of the marketer is to modify breakeven analysis and the other cost-oriented pricing approaches to introduce demand analysis. Pricing must be examined from the buyer's perspective. Such decisions cannot be made in a management vacuum in which only cost factors are considered.

Toward Realistic Pricing

Traditional economic theory considers both costs and demand in the determination of an equilibrium price. The dual elements of supply and demand are balanced at the point of equilibrium. In actual industry practice, however, most

Table 17.3

Revenue and Cost Data for Modified Breakeven Analysis

	Revenues			Costs		Breakeven Point (Number of Sales Required to Break Even)	Total Profit (or Loss)
Price	Quantity Demanded	Total Revenue	Total Fixed Cost	Total Variable Cost	Total Cost		
$15	2,500	$ 37,500	$40,000	$12,500	$ 52,500	4,000	$(15,000)
10	10,000	100,000	40,000	50,000	90,000	8,000	8,000
9	13,000	117,000	40,000	65,000	105,000	10,000	12,000
8	14,000	112,000	40,000	70,000	110,000	13,334	2,000
7	15,000	105,000	40,000	75,000	115,000	20,000	(10,000)

pricing approaches are largely cost oriented. Since purely cost-oriented approaches to pricing violate the marketing concept, modifications are required to add demand analysis to the pricing decision.

Consumer research on such issues as degree of price elasticity, consumer price expectations, existence and size of specific market segments, and perceptions of strengths and weaknesses of substitute products is necessary for developing sales estimates at different prices. Because much of the resultant data involves perceptions, attitudes, and future expectations, such estimates are likely to be less precise than cost estimates.

The Modified Breakeven Concept

In Figure 17.8, the breakeven analysis was based upon the assumption of a constant $10 retail price regardless of quantity. What happens when different retail prices are considered? Modified breakeven analysis combines the traditional breakeven analysis model with an evaluation of consumer demand.

Table 17.3 summarizes both the cost and revenue aspects of a number of alternative retail prices. The $5 unit variable costs and the $40,000 total fixed costs are based upon the costs utilized earlier in the basic breakeven model. The expected unit sales for each specified retail price are obtained from consumer research. The table contains the information necessary to calculate the breakeven point for each of the five retail price alternatives. These points are shown in the first part of Figure 17.9.

The data in the first two columns of Table 17.3 represent a demand schedule by indicating the number of units consumers are expected to purchase at each of a series of retail prices. As the second part of Figure 17.9 shows, this data can be superimposed onto a breakeven chart to identify the range of feasible prices for consideration by the marketing decision maker.

Figure 17.9 reveals that the range of profitable prices exists from a low of approximately $8 (TR_4) to a high of $10 (TR_2), with a price of $9 (TR_3) generating the greatest projected profits. Changing the retail price produces a new breakeven point. At a relatively high $15 retail price, the breakeven point is 4,000 units; at a $10 retail price the breakeven point is 8,000 units; and at the lowest price considered of $7, a total of 20,000 units must be sold to break even.

The contribution of modified breakeven analysis is that it forces the pricing decision maker to consider whether the consumer is likely to purchase the required number of units of a product or service to achieve breakeven at a given price. It demonstrates that a large number of units sold does not nec-

Modified Breakeven Analysis
Pricing technique used to consider consumer demand by comparing the number of products or services that must be sold at a variety of different prices to cover total costs with estimates of expected sales at the various prices.

Figure 17.9

Modified Breakeven Chart (A) Showing Different Sales Prices
and (B) Reflecting Consumer Demand

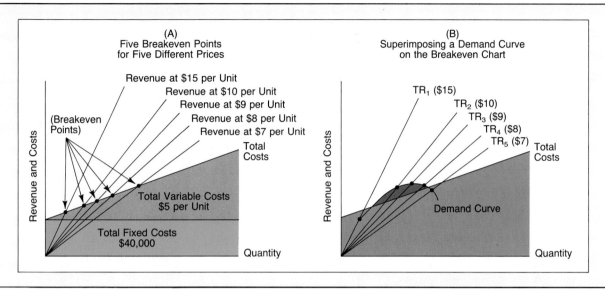

essarily produce added profits since—other things equal—lower prices are
necessary to stimulate added sales. Consequently, it necessitates careful consideration of both costs and consumer demand in determining the most appropriate price.

Summary

Price—the exchange value of a good or service—is important because it regulates economic activity as well as determines the revenue to be received by
an individual firm. As a marketing mix element, pricing is one of those gray
areas where marketers struggle to develop a theory, technique, or rule of
thumb on which they can depend. It is a complex variable because it contains
both objective and subjective aspects. It is an area where precise decision
tools and executive judgment meet.

Pricing objectives should be the natural consequence of overall organizational goals and more specific marketing goals. They can be classified into
four major groupings: (1) profitability objectives, including profit maximization
and target returns; (2) volume objectives, including sales maximization and
market share; (3) meeting competition objectives; and (4) prestige objectives.

Prices can be determined by theoretical or cost-oriented approaches.
Economic theorists attempt to equate marginal revenue and marginal cost.
Price determination in actual practice frequently emphasizes cost. Both breakeven analysis and the use of markups are essentially cost-plus approaches to
pricing.

A more realistic approach to effective price decisions is to integrate both
buyer demand and costs. Modified breakeven analysis is a method for accomplishing this task.

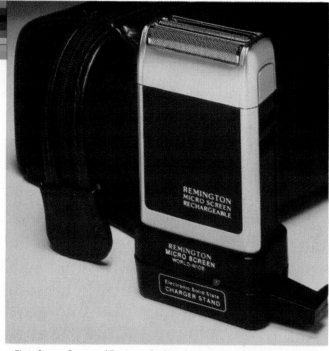

Photo Source: Courtesy of Remington Products, Inc.

Solving the Stop-Action Case

Remington Products, Inc.

Victor Kiam had a lot of marketing and pricing ideas, but he didn't implement them in a vacuum. To make certain that he was on target, he began talking to retailers to learn their opinions of the Remington shaver. Many shared the same complaint: Remington was introducing too many new models each year—a practice that made retailers reluctant to order large quantities. To eliminate the problem, Kiam began marketing essentially the same model year after year, adding improvements with little or no fanfare. As a result, retailers are much more willing to stock larger numbers of Remington shavers.

Kiam's belief in the product continues to be demonstrated in a series of television commercials that feature him. These commercials, which appear in 32 countries, tell the story of why he bought Remington: "I was a dedicated blade shaver until my wife bought me this Remington Micro-Screen shaver," says the bathrobe-garbed Kiam. "I was so impressed I bought the company." He also backs his claim: ". . . shaves close as a blade or your money back."

Although the commercials have made Kiam one of the world's most recognized executives, he does not attribute the company's turnaround to the advertisements. "I say they may have influenced some people to buy our product," he states. "But what we first did was bring the prices down, so our product is within reach of more people."

The success of Remington's pricing decisions is evident from sharp increases in sales and profits. Remington's current sales exceed $150 million. In addition, the company's U.S. market share more than doubled over a four-year period to 40 percent, and its worldwide share is now 25 percent.

Part of the reason Kiam pushes so hard is his pride in manufacturing the only electric shaver made in America and in operating a company that employs some 800 people. Kiam proudly points out that the Remington shaver is the only American-made, small electrical product in Mitsukoshi, Tokyo's department store equivalent to Macy's. "Sure, you'll find American brand names, but flip them over, and they'll say 'Made in Taiwan'. "

Sources: Kiam quotation in paragraph 3 is from Claudia M. Christie, "The Most Expensive Gift for a Husband a Wife Ever Bought," *New England Business* (June 20, 1983), p. 47. Kiam quotation in final paragraph is from Jim Powell, "Made in America," *United Airlines Magazine* (January 1984), p. 45.

Questions for Discussion

1. Identify the four major categories of pricing objectives.
2. Categorize each of the following into a specific type of pricing objective:
    a. 8 percent increase in market share
    b. 5 percent increase in profits over previous year
    c. Prices no more than 5 percent higher than prices quoted by independent dealers
    d. 20 percent return on investment (before taxes)

    e.   Highest prices in product category to maintain favorable brand image
    f.   Follow price of most important competitor in each market segment

3.   What are the major price implications of the PIMS studies? Suggest possible explanations for the relationships discovered by the studies.

4.   Why do many firms choose to deemphasize pricing as a marketing tool and instead use the other marketing mix variables in seeking to achieve a differential advantage?

5.   What do economists mean by the term *marginal analysis?*
Discuss.

6.   Why would a firm choose to have a reduced market share? What are the policy implications of this situation?

7.   What market situations exist for the following products:

a.	Telephone service	e.	Soybeans
b.	U.S.-made cigars	f.	Dishwashers
c.	Golf clubs	g.	Tape recorders
d.	Steel	h.	Skis

8.   What are the practical problems involved in attempting to apply price theory concepts to actual pricing decisions?

9.   Explain the advantages of using incremental-cost pricing rather than full-cost pricing. What potential drawbacks exist?

10.   How are the following prices determined and what do they have in common?

a.	A ticket to a movie theater	c.	The local property tax rate
b.	Your college tuition fee	d.	The printing of graduation announcements

11.   Distinguish between the following:
    a.   Variable costs and fixed costs
    b.   Average revenue and marginal revenue
    c.   Total costs and total revenue
    d.   Average variable costs and average fixed costs
    e.   Marginal costs and marginal revenue

12.   How can determining the breakeven point assist in price determination?

13.   Explain the primary benefits of using breakeven analysis in price determination. What are the shortcomings of the basic breakeven model?

14.   What is the breakeven point for a product with a selling price of $35, average variable cost of $18, and related fixed costs of $25,500?

15.   What is the breakeven point in dollars and units for a product with a selling price of $25, related fixed costs of $126,000, and per-unit variable costs of $16?

16.   Total fixed costs of a firm are $120,000, variable costs total $2 per unit, and the product's proposed price is $4. The firm's marketing manager has decided that $10,000 must be earned each month to justify the investment. How many products must be sold the first month to meet the specified criteria?

17.   Refer to Question 16 above. How many products must be sold if the proposed price can be increased to $5 and an $8,000 earnings minimum is used?

18.   "Firms whose sales reach the magic breakeven analysis should increase their promotional budgets to earn greater and greater amounts of above-breakeven point profits." Do you agree? Defend your answer.

19.   In what ways is modified breakeven analysis superior to the basic model?

20. A firm has total fixed costs of $100,000, and its variable costs are $10 per unit. Preliminary marketing research studies indicate the following sales projections at the following prices:

    40,000 units at $12
    22,000 units at $15
    15,000 units at $18
    10,000 units at $20
     3,000 units at $25

Draw the breakeven chart showing the various prices. Indicate the feasible range of prices.

Case: Automobile Pricing — Detroit Style

Probably nothing Detroit does today makes less sense to consumers than the way it sets car prices. If Detroit persists in its contention that its pricing structure is a function of the need to calculate costs five years before production, it is unlikely that the Byzantine pricing structure will change much. However, consumer rebellion is forcing auto makers to take a new look at their manufacturing costs and marketing assumptions before affixing a model's price. Two factors complicate the search for a solution to the problem of reducing car prices: persistent inflation and the domestic auto makers' need to pay for an $80 billion retooling switch to small vehicles.

Traditionally, the domestic auto makers keyed their prices to General Motors Corporation, because that company controls more than 60 percent of the market for U.S.-built cars. The process got more complicated when imports, mainly from Japan, began infiltrating the United States. Foreign auto makers pay different labor rates, make different assumptions about investment paybacks for new tooling, and even manage their factories differently. Several studies say the difference in production costs between U.S. and Japanese auto makers is at least $1,500 per car. That difference would give Japanese

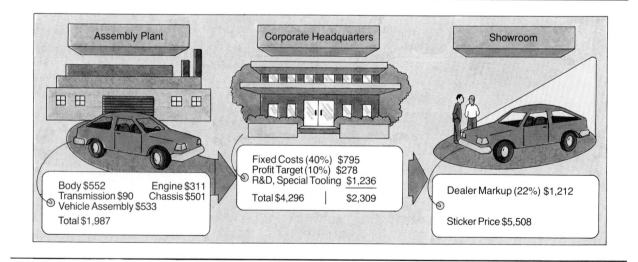

Source: "Why Detroit Can't Cut Prices." Reprinted from the March 1, 1982 issue of *Business Week* by special permission, pp. 110–111. Copyright 1982 by McGraw-Hill, Inc.

companies a huge cushion from which to react to permanent price cuts from Detroit. Robert J. Orsini, vice-president for strategic management consulting with William C. Roney & Co., estimates that domestic car makers must find a way to cut production costs a staggering $2,200 per car if they expect to compete fully with the Japanese. Analysts suggest Detroit could give up its determination to break even on a new car model within four or five years and stretch the payback period to perhaps eight years as the Japanese do. This would reduce costs per year by altering the way the auto makers account for such expenses.

But LeRoy H. Lindgren, a vice-president and industrial cost consultant with Rath & Strong, Inc., believes that much of the $1,500 difference comes from the production snags that accompany Detroit's conversion to front-wheel drive and new body designs. "We're going through a tremendous conversion, and the Japanese aren't," he says. Lindgren figures it takes a plant about two years after such sweeping changes in tooling and manufacturing methods to achieve output efficiencies. In the meantime, he says, many U.S. auto plants are running up costs per car two or three times their eventual levels.

Questions

1. Categorize the pricing method shown in the case figure.
2. Summarize the reasons described in the case for the price discrepancies between many U.S. automobiles and comparable imports. Which of the discrepancies would be easiest to reduce? How can it be accomplished?

Computer Applications

Breakeven analysis, described on pages 479–483, is a useful technique for determining the sales volume (either in dollars or units) that must be achieved at a specified price to generate sufficient revenues to cover total production and marketing costs. Target profit returns, either in absolute dollar amounts or in percentages of sales, can also be included in the breakeven model. *Modified breakeven analysis* is a technique for including assessments of consumer demand into the basic breakeven model. By considering estimated sales at several different possible prices, modified breakeven analysis aids the marketing decision maker in determining the required volume needed to break even at various prices. It also shows whether such sales can be achieved.

Directions: Use menu item 16 titled "Breakeven Analysis" to solve each of the following problems.

Problem 1 Long Island Industries, of Jamaica, New York, is considering the possible introduction of a new product proposed by its research and development staff. The firm's marketing director estimates that the product could be marketed at a price of $25. Total fixed costs are $132,000, and average variable costs are calculated to be $19.

a. What is the breakeven point in units for the proposed product?
b. The firm's president has suggested a target profit return of $100,000 for the proposed product. How many units must be sold to break even *and* achieve this target return?
c. The marketing director at Long Island Industries made a counterproposal of a 10 percent return on sales as a realistic expectation for the proposed new product. How many units must be sold to break even *and* achieve the return specified by the marketing director?
d. How would your answers to Questions a, b, and c change if the proposed price is increased to $28?

Problem 2 Water World, Inc., of Houston, manufactures a line of women's swimsuits. The swimsuits wholesale for $15. Variable costs per unit are $4. Total fixed costs for the line are $180,000.

a. How many swimsuits must be produced and sold to break even?
b. How much revenue must be generated from the Water World product line to reach the breakeven point?
c. Water World marketing director Mary Beth Smithers would like to generate profits equal to 12 percent of sales for the swimsuit line. How many units must be produced and sold to break even *and* achieve this target return?
d. Smithers is also considering the use of a cooperative advertising allowance of $1 per women's swimsuit to motivate retailers to push the Water World brand. What impact, if any, would Smithers's proposal have on the breakeven point for the women's swimwear if the target return is *not* included?

Problem 3 Hoosier Foods, of Indianapolis, is in the process of evaluating the feasibility of introducing Canine Delight, a new canned dog food. Variable cost estimates include the following:

Labor	$.24
Materials	.32
Transportation	.02
Packaging	.06
Sales Commissions	.08
Other	.04

Fixed costs include $50,000 for such manufacturing overhead outlays as salaries, general office expenses, rent, utilities, interest charges, and depreciation; $200,000 on marketing, which includes such expenditures as salaries and advertising expenditures contracted at the beginning of the operating period; and $50,000 for research and development on the product. The proposed sales price to the firm's channel customers is $.92.

a. What is the breakeven point (in units) for Canine Delight? How much sales in dollars are required to break even?
b. A compromise has been reached by the various members of top management at Hoosier Foods concerning target profit returns for the proposed dog food. Rather than adhering to a specific dollar profit return recommended by the firm's chief financial officer, a decision has been reached to use 10 percent of sales as the target return. How many units of Canine Delight must be sold to break even *and* achieve the specified target return?

Problem 4 The marketing research staff at Newark-based Consolidated Novelties has developed the following sales estimates for a proposed new adult toy item designed to be marketed through direct-mail sales:

Proposed Selling Price	Sales Estimates (in units)
$ 8	55,000
10	22,000
15	14,000
20	5,000
24	2,800

The new product has total fixed costs of $60,000 and a $7 variable cost per unit.

a. Which of the proposed selling prices would generate a profit for Consolidated Novelties?
b. Consolidated Novelties' director of marketing also estimates that an additional $.50 per unit allocation for extra promotion would produce the following increases in sales estimates: 69,000 units at an $8 selling price, 28,000 units at $10, 17,000 units at $15, 6,000 units at $20, and 3,500 units at a selling price of $24 per unit. Indicate the feasible range of prices if this proposal is implemented and it results in the predicted sales increases.
c. Indicate the feasible price or prices if the $.50 per unit additional promotion proposal is not implemented, but management insists upon a $25,000 target return.

Problem 5 Don Ingram, vice-president of marketing at Sun Belt Manufacturing of Atlanta, has assembled the following estimates of per unit variable costs for a proposed new product:

Labor	$2.52
Materials	3.60
Packaging	.08
Sales Commissions	1.00
Transportation	.18
Other	.62

His calculations of fixed costs include $30,000 for manufacturing overhead, $112,000 for marketing, and $58,000 for miscellaneous fixed costs. Sales estimates for each of the possible prices are as follows:

Proposed Selling Price	Sales Estimates (in units)
$ 9	150,000
12	55,000
15	40,000
18	25,000
20	18,000
25	8,000

a. Indicate the range of feasible prices for the new product.
b. Which price or prices are feasible if a target return of 10 percent of sales is included?
c. Which price or prices are feasible if a $40,000 target return is included?

18 Elements of Pricing Strategy

Key Terms

skimming pricing strategy
penetration pricing strategy
competitive pricing strategy
list price
market price
cash discounts
trade discounts
quantity discounts
trade-ins
promotional allowances
rebates
FOB plant
freight absorption
uniform delivered price
zone pricing
basing point system
pricing policy
psychological pricing
odd pricing
unit pricing
price flexibility
product-line pricing
promotional price
loss leaders
escalator clause
transfer price
profit centers

Learning Goals

1. To explain the organization for pricing decisions
2. To compare the alternative pricing strategies and explain when each strategy is most appropriate
3. To describe how prices are quoted
4. To identify the various pricing policy decisions that must be made by marketers
5. To relate price to consumer perceptions of quality
6. To contrast negotiated prices and competitive bidding
7. To explain the importance of transfer pricing
8. To describe pricing in the public sector

Coca-Cola versus Pepsi Cola

A war is raging among soft-drink companies to capture larger and larger chunks of the $26 billion a year soft-drink market. Not surprisingly, the Coca-Cola Company is dominating the competition with four of the nation's ten leading soft-drink brands. Coke, the market leader, holds a 24.5 percent market share, while number 5 Diet Coke holds a 4.6 percent share. Tab, at number 6, is the third Coca-Cola brand in the top ten, and Sprite occupies the eighth position in the industry.

The explosive success of Diet Coke cemented Coca-Cola Company's lead. With 275 million cases sold in 1983, Diet Coke had the most successful soft-drink product launch in history. Although these sales figures brought cheers from Coca-Cola executives, they were somewhat subdued by the fact that at least part of Diet Coke's gain came at the expense of Tab. Tab, Coca-Cola's original diet drink, lost 20 percent of its pre–Diet Coke era sales following the new brand's market introduction.

Pepsi Cola, the nation's second largest soft-drink company, is fighting hard to catch up. Its Pepsi Cola brand ranks second in soft-drink sales with an 18.2 percent market share. Another Pepsi brand, Mountain Dew, is in seventh place with a 2.8 percent share; and number 9 Diet Pepsi has a 2.5 percent market share. Unfortunately for Pepsi, its game of catch-up has proven somewhat disappointing. In a single year of intense competition between 1983 and 1984, case sales for Pepsi declined by 2 percent. Moreover, Mountain Dew sustained an 8 percent loss, and Diet Pepsi case sales declined by a whopping 19 percent. In addition to competing with the brands of number 1 Coca-Cola Company, Pepsi also contends with third place 7-Up, which experienced a 14 percent volume gain, fourth place Dr. Pepper, and tenth place Royal Crown Cola.

Soft-drink case sales exceeded the 6 billion mark for the first time ever in 1983. This market growth prompted prime competitors Coca-Cola and Pepsi Cola to double their efforts toward a single goal: to increase case volume even more. Accomplishing this goal is critical to the success of each of their individual brands and to both corporations.

Assignment: Use the materials in Chapter 18 to recommend methods that could be used by Coca-Cola Company and Pepsi Cola to increase sales of their soft-drink brands.

Photo Source: Copyright 1983 by George Lange.

Source: Soft-drink market shares are listed in "Turning Red with Proliferation," *Beverage World*, March 1984, pp. 32–33.

Chapter Overview

The pricing variable can significantly affect the success of any firm's marketing program. The previous chapter introduced the concept of price and its role in the economic system and in marketing strategy. This chapter considers who should be responsible for the pricing decision and the sequential approach to such decisions. It examines alternative pricing strategies and the administration of price structures. Finally, other pricing practices such as negotiated prices, competitive bidding, and pricing in the public sector are considered.

Organization for Pricing Decisions

In translating pricing objectives into pricing decisions, there are two major steps to follow. First, someone must be assigned responsibility for making pricing decisions and administering the pricing structure. Second, the overall pricing structure—that is, the selected price and the appropriate discounts for channel members as well as for various quantities and for geographic and promotional considerations—must be set.

A recent survey of marketing executives found that the people or groups most commonly chosen to set price structures were (1) a pricing committee composed of top executives, (2) the president of the company, and (3) the chief marketing officer. According to the same survey, the pricing structure is administered most often by marketers. As Figure 18.1 indicates, the chief marketing officer was the person responsible for pricing in 51 percent of the firms surveyed. In all, marketers administered the pricing structure in over 68 percent of the companies. These results seem consistent with industry's attempt to implement the marketing concept.

Figure 18.1
Executives Responsible for Setting and Administering Price Structures

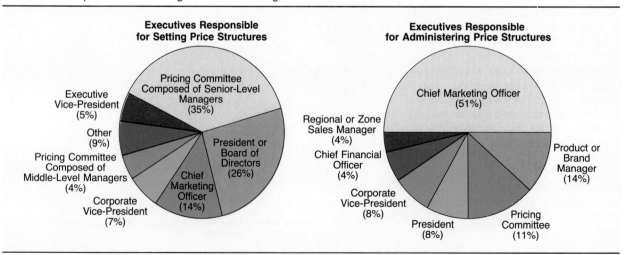

Alternative Pricing Strategies

The specific strategies used by firms in pricing their products and services are the result of the marketing strategies formulated to assist in accomplishing overall organizational objectives. A firm such as MCI Telecommunications that seeks to gain consumer acceptance and to attract a large share of the long-distance telephone market against a well-known, highly regarded firm such as American Telephone & Telegraph may decide to pursue these objectives through emphasizing low prices as a competitive tool. As Figure 18.2 shows, MCI's advertisements use AT&T's "Reach out and touch someone" headline, but they emphasize in the ad copy their price advantages with the statement, "You haven't been talking too much. You've just been paying too much."

By contrast, a firm such as S.T. Dupont, a French subsidiary of Gillette, aims at a smaller segment of the market and uses price to enhance its image of prestige and exclusivity. Dupont makes items such as lighters and writing pens. Its pens are crafted from solid brass and treated with five layers of lacquer made from the sap of the rhus tree found in China. The sap is shipped to France in special slosh-proof containers. Dupont spends three months producing each pen and still rejects 20 percent in a rigid series of quality-control inspections. This quality image is conveyed to Dupont's wealthy clientele not only through product design, choice of retail outlets, and advertising design

Figure 18.2
Using a Low-Price Marketing Strategy as a Competitive Tool

Source: Reprinted by permission of MCI Telecommunications Corporation, Washington, D.C.

and media, but also through price. The writing pens are priced in the $380 to $410 range, while Dupont's lighters sell for $150 to $400.

The MCI Telecommunications and S.T. Dupont examples illustrate two of the three major pricing strategies. MCI uses a penetration pricing strategy, while S.T. Dupont favors a skimming pricing strategy. The third pricing strategy alternative is one of simply meeting competition by pricing the firm's products at a comparable level with those of primary competitors.

Skimming Pricing Strategy

Skimming Pricing Strategy
Pricing strategy involving the use of a relatively high price compared to competitive offerings.

A skimming pricing strategy is sometimes referred to as a "market-plus" approach to pricing because it involves the use of a relatively high price compared to prices of competing products or services. The name is derived from the expression "skimming the cream." Although some firms continue to utilize a skimming strategy throughout most stages of the product life cycle, it is more commonly used as a market entry price for distinctive products or services with little or no initial competition.

One purpose of the skimming strategy is to allow the firm to recover its research and development costs quickly. The assumption is that competition will eventually drive the price to a lower level. Such was the case with video cassette recorders, electric toothbrushes, and personal computers. A skimming strategy for many new products, therefore, attempts to maximize the revenue received from the sale of a new product before the entry of competition.

A skimming strategy is also useful in segmenting the overall market on a price basis. In the case of new products that represent significant innovations, relatively high prices convey an image of distinction and appeal to buyers who are less sensitive to price. Ballpoint pens were introduced shortly after World War II at a price of about $20. Today the best-selling ballpoint pens are priced at less than $1. Other examples of products that were introduced using a skimming strategy include television sets, Polaroid cameras, digital watches, and pocket calculators. Subsequent price reductions allowed the marketers of these products to appeal to additional market segments that are more price sensitive.

A third advantage of a skimming strategy is that it permits the marketer to control demand in the introductory stages of the product's life cycle and adjust its productive capacity to match demand. A danger of low initial prices for a new product is that demand may outstrip the firm's production capacity, resulting in consumer and intermediary complaints and possibly permanent damage to the product's image. Excess demand occasionally results in poor-quality products because the firm strives to satisfy consumer desires but lacks adequate production facilities.

During the late growth and early maturity stages of the product life cycle, the price is typically reduced for two reasons: (1) the pressure of competition and (2) the desire to expand the product's market. Figure 18.3 shows that 10 percent of the market for Product X would buy the item at $20, while another 20 percent would be attracted into the market at $17. Successive price declines will expand the firm's market as well as meet new competition.

A skimming strategy has one chief disadvantage: it attracts competition. Potential competitors see that the innovating firms make large financial returns and also enter the market. This forces the price even lower than where it might be under a sequential skimming procedure. However, if a firm has a patent protection, as Polaroid had, or a proprietary ability to exclude competition, it

Figure 18.3

Use of Price Reductions to Expand Total Markets

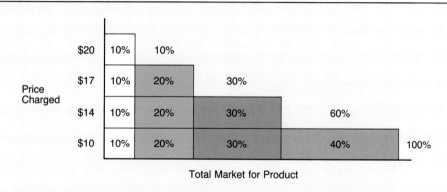

Price Charged

$20	10%	10%			
$17	10%	20%	30%		
$14	10%	20%	30%	60%	
$10	10%	20%	30%	40%	100%

Total Market for Product

may use a skimming policy for a relatively long period. Figure 18.4 indicates that about 16 percent of the respondents in a recent pricing study used a skimming strategy. Skimming appears to be more common in industrial markets than in consumer markets.

Penetration Pricing

Penetration Pricing Strategy
Pricing strategy involving the use of a relatively low price as compared with competitive offerings.

A **penetration pricing strategy** uses price as a major marketing weapon. Products or services are priced noticeably lower than the prices of competing offerings. In some instances, penetration pricing is used as a method of intro-

Figure 18.4

Relative Usage of Alternative Pricing Strategies

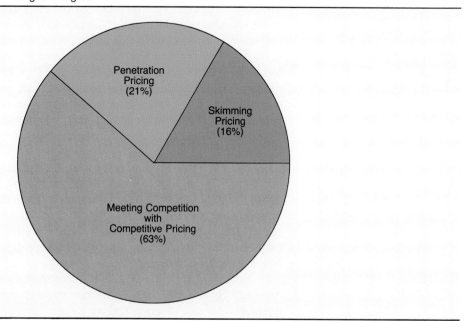

Penetration Pricing (21%)

Skimming Pricing (16%)

Meeting Competition with Competitive Pricing (63%)

ducing new products in industries characterized by dozens of competing brands. Once the product has achieved some market recognition as a result of consumer trial purchases stimulated by the lower prices, marketers may then increase the price to the level of competitive products. Consumer products such as toothpastes and detergents often use this strategy. In other cases, a penetration pricing strategy may be used throughout several stages of the product life cycle as the firm seeks to maintain a reputation as a low-price competitor.

The penetration pricing strategy is sometimes called a "market-minus" approach and is based upon the premise that a lower-than-market price will attract buyers and convert the brand from the unknown category to at least the brand recognition stage—or even the brand preference stage. Since in many instances the firm intends to increase the price at a later time, large numbers of consumer trial purchases are critical to the success of a penetration strategy. One advantage of this strategy is that it discourages competition, since the prevailing low price does not suggest the attractive financial returns associated with a skimming strategy.

Penetration pricing is likely to be used in instances where demand for the product or service is highly elastic. In such instances, large numbers of consumers are highly price sensitive. In addition, it is more likely to be used in instances where large-scale operations and long production runs result in substantial reductions in the firm's production and marketing costs. Finally, penetration pricing may be appropriate in instances where a new product is likely to attract strong competitors when it is introduced. Such a strategy may allow it to reach the mass market quickly and capture a large share of the market prior to entry by competitors.

Competitive Pricing

Competitive Pricing Strategy
Pricing strategy designed to deemphasize price as a competitive variable by pricing a product or service at the general level of comparable offerings.

Although a number of organizations make extensive use of price as a competitive weapon, an even larger number prefer to use a competitive pricing strategy. This approach emphasizes nonprice competition by concentrating marketing efforts on the product, distribution, and promotional elements of the marketing mix. As pointed out earlier, price is not only a dramatic means of achieving a competitive advantage, it is also the easiest variable for competitors to match. In industries where the offerings of competitors are relatively homogeneous, competitors are forced to match price reductions to maintain market share and to remain competitive. When competitors began to lower prices of truck and trailer rentals, the industry leader U-Haul matched the price reductions with advertisements announcing "U-Haul Will Not Be Undersold."

Even in instances where product offerings are relatively heterogeneous, competitors analyze the prices of major competing offerings so that their own prices will not be markedly different. When IBM moved into the personal computer market with the IBM PC, PC-XT, and PC-AT, its marketing efforts emphasized the versatility and power of its computer line. However, the firm's marketers were quick to point out that each product in the personal computer line is competitively priced.

What happens when a price reduction is matched by other firms in the industry? Unless the lower prices can expand the overall market enough to offset the per-unit revenue lost as a result of the lower prices, the result is less revenue for all competitors. As Figure 18.4 reveals, nearly two-thirds of all firms surveyed used pricing at the level of comparable products as their primary pricing strategy.

By pricing their products or services at the general levels of competitive offerings, marketers are to a large extent negating the price variable in their marketing strategies. They then emphasize nonprice variables in seeking to develop areas of distinctive competence and in attracting customers.

Price Quotations

The method for quoting prices depends on many factors, such as cost structures, traditional practices in the particular industry, and the policies of individual firms. In this section we examine the reasoning and methodology behind price quotations.

Movie-goers accustomed to a $4 ticket price have been paying more in recent years—$5 and even $6 for new movies. The decision of how much to charge ticket buyers is affected by many variables: prices at competing theaters; prices at alternative entertainment outlets, such as concerts; consumer price elasticity of demand; and costs. Consider the case of the movie *Summer Lovers*. The movie, a story of R-rated romance set in Greece, cost $5.3 million to produce. As Figure 18.5 reveals, finance and marketing expenses add another $15 million, requiring $20 million in box-office income to break even. For this film, the price charged at the box office must be sufficient to cover the theater owner's costs and generate revenues greater than the overall $20 million cost.

List Price
Established price normally quoted to potential buyers.

The basis upon which most price structures are built is the list price, the rate normally quoted to potential buyers. List price is usually determined by one or a combination of the methods discussed in the preceding chapter. The sticker prices on new automobiles are good examples: they show the list price for the basic model and then add the list price for the options that are included.

Discounts, Allowances, and Rebates

Market Price
Price a consumer or intermediary actually pays for a product or service after subtracting any discounts, allowances, or rebates from the list price.

The amount that a consumer pays—the market price—may or may not be the same as the list price. In some cases discounts or allowances reduce the list price. List price is often used as the starting point from which discounts that set the market price are taken. Discounts can be classified as cash, quantity, or trade.

Cash Discounts
Price reductions offered to a consumer, industrial user, or marketing intermediary in return for prompt payment of a bill.

Cash Discounts   Reductions in price that are offered to consumers, industrial purchasers, or channel members for prompt payment of a bill are known as cash discounts. They are probably the most commonly used variety. Cash discounts usually specify an exact time period, such as 2/10, net 30. This means that the bill is due within 30 days, but if it is paid in 10 days, the customer may subtract 2 percent from the amount due. Cash discounts have become a traditional pricing practice in many industries. They are legal provided they are granted to all customers on the same terms. Such discounts were originally instituted to improve the liquidity position of sellers, to lower bad-debt losses, and to reduce the expenses associated with the collection of bills. Whether these advantages outweigh the relatively high cost of capital involved in cash discounts depends upon the seller's need for liquidity as well as alternative sources (and costs) of funds.

Figure 18.5
Cost Components of the Movie *Summer Lovers*

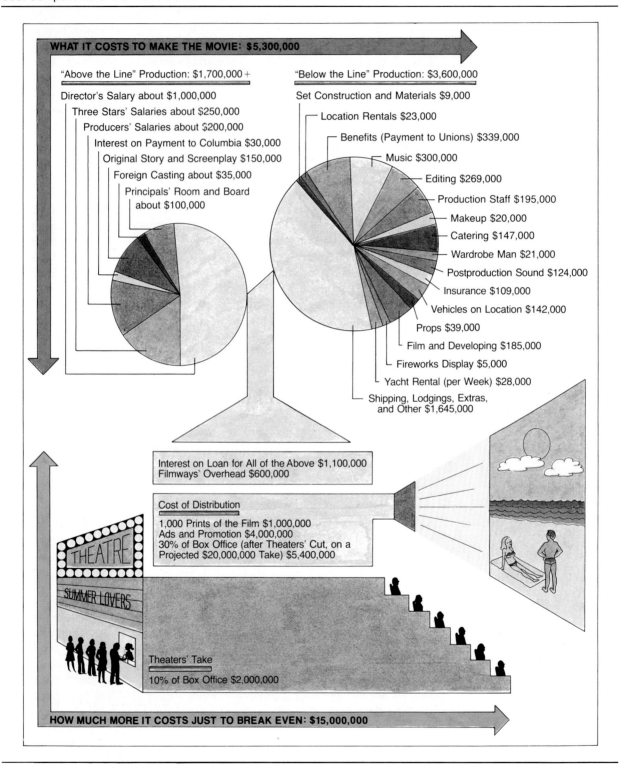

WHAT IT COSTS TO MAKE THE MOVIE: $5,300,000

"Above the Line" Production: $1,700,000+

Director's Salary about $1,000,000
Three Stars' Salaries about $250,000
Producers' Salaries about $200,000
Interest on Payment to Columbia $30,000
Original Story and Screenplay $150,000
Foreign Casting about $35,000
Principals' Room and Board about $100,000

"Below the Line" Production: $3,600,000

Set Construction and Materials $9,000
Location Rentals $23,000
Benefits (Payment to Unions) $339,000
Music $300,000
Editing $269,000
Production Staff $195,000
Makeup $20,000
Catering $147,000
Wardrobe Man $21,000
Postproduction Sound $124,000
Insurance $109,000
Vehicles on Location $142,000
Props $39,000
Film and Developing $185,000
Fireworks Display $5,000
Yacht Rental (per Week) $28,000
Shipping, Lodgings, Extras, and Other $1,645,000

Interest on Loan for All of the Above $1,100,000
Filmways' Overhead $600,000

Cost of Distribution

1,000 Prints of the Film $1,000,000
Ads and Promotion $4,000,000
30% of Box Office (after Theaters' Cut, on a Projected $20,000,000 Take) $5,400,000

THEATRE

SUMMER LOVERS

Theaters' Take

10% of Box Office $2,000,000

HOW MUCH MORE IT COSTS JUST TO BREAK EVEN: $15,000,000

Source: Stan Berkowitz and David Lees, "What Price Romance?" *Esquire* (July 1982), p. 107.

Trade Discounts   Payments to channel members for performing a marketing function are known as trade discounts, or functional discounts. The discussion of wholesalers and retailers in Chapters 11 and 12 included a listing of services performed by the various channel members and the related costs. A manufacturer's list price must take into consideration the costs incurred by channel members in performing required marketing functions and expected profit margins for each member. Trade discounts were initially based on the operating expenses of each category, but they have now become more of a matter of custom in some industries. They are legal under the Robinson-Patman Act as long as all buyers in the same category, such as wholesalers and retailers, receive the same discount privilege.

Figure 18.6 shows how a chain of trade discounts works. In the first instance, the trade discount is "40 percent, 10 percent off list price" for wholesalers. In other words, the 40 percent discount on the $40 product is the trade discount received by the retailer to cover operating expenses and to earn a profit. The wholesaler receives 10 percent of the $24 price to retailers to cover expenses and to earn a profit. The manufacturer receives $21.60 from the wholesaler for each order.

In the second example, the manufacturer and retailer bypass the wholesaler, and a trade discount of 45 percent is offered to the retailer. In this in-

Figure 18.6
Chain of Trade Discounts

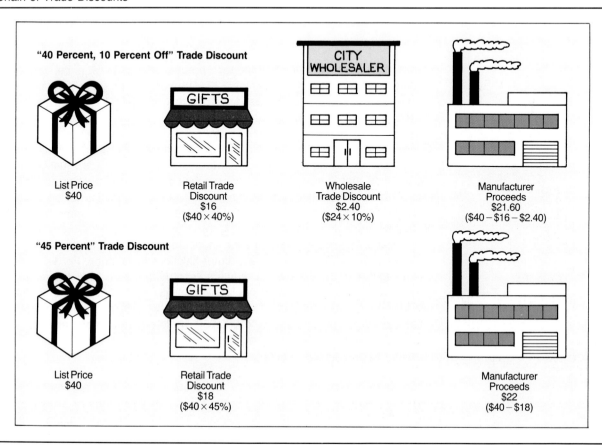

"40 Percent, 10 Percent Off" Trade Discount

List Price $40

Retail Trade Discount $16 ($40 × 40%)

Wholesale Trade Discount $2.40 ($24 × 10%)

Manufacturer Proceeds $21.60 ($40 − $16 − $2.40)

"45 Percent" Trade Discount

List Price $40

Retail Trade Discount $18 ($40 × 45%)

Manufacturer Proceeds $22 ($40 − $18)

Figure 18.7
A Noncumulative Quantity Discount Schedule

Best Suppliers
3343 Grand Avenue
Denver, Colorado 80956
555–0678

Price per Unit	$1,000

Discount Schedule:
(noncumulative)

1 Unit	$1,000
2–5 Units	List Less 10%
6–10 Units	List Less 20%
Over 10 Units	List Less 25%

stance, the retailer receives $18 for each product sold at its list price, and the manufacturer receives the remaining $22. The services previously performed by the wholesaler are either assumed by the retailer or manufacturer or shared by the two channel members.

Quantity Discounts   Price reductions granted because of large-volume purchases are known as quantity discounts. These discounts are justified on the grounds that large-volume purchases reduce selling expenses and may shift a part of the storing, transporting, and financing functions to the buyer. Quantity discounts are lawful provided they are offered on the same basis to all customers.

Quantity discounts may be either noncumulative or cumulative. *Noncumulative quantity discounts* are one-time reductions in list price. For example, a firm might offer the discount schedule presented in Figure 18.7. *Cumulative quantity discounts* are reductions determined by purchases over a stated time period. Annual purchases of $25,000 might entitle the buyer to an 8 percent rebate, while purchases exceeding $50,000 would mean a 15 percent refund. These reductions are really patronage discounts since they tend to bind the customer to one source of supply.

Allowances   Allowances are similar to discounts in that they are deductions from the price the purchaser must pay. The major categories of allowances are trade-ins and promotional allowances. Trade-ins are often used in the sale of durable goods such as automobiles. They preserve the basic list price of the new item while reducing the amount the customer has to pay by allow-

Quantity Discounts
Price reductions granted for large-volume purchases.

Trade-ins
Credit allowances given for an old item when a customer purchases a new item.

Return to the Stop-Action Case

Coca-Cola versus Pepsi Cola

With the goal of constantly improving their market performance, both Coca-Cola Company and Pepsi Cola have turned to price discounting to promote sales. By 1986, discounting had become a universal weapon used by all the soft-drink companies. Industry analysts estimate that up to 90 percent of all soft-drink sales involve some form of discounting. Martin Romm, vice-president of equity research for the New York-based First Boston Corporation, believes discounting is here to stay. "The very structure of the soft-drink industry," said Romm, "is volume-directed, and the major franchise companies are encouraging their bottlers—through underlying support programs—to continue to perpetuate discounting."

Discounting has been especially useful in stimulating consumer demand during economic downturns. Sensing that the time was right for such a move in 1980, Coca-Cola initiated an intensely competitive discounting environment. As the economy weakened over the next couple of years, Coca-Cola's discounting practices intensified. These practices resulted in similar matching discounts by competitors. Although the discounting battle was heaviest between Coke and Pepsi, smaller brands were forced to respond in kind or face being driven out of the market.

Source: Romm quotation is from "Soft Drinks '84: Keeping the Faith," *Beverage World* (January 1984), p. 23.

Promotional Allowances
Advertising or sales promotion funds provided by a manufacturer to other channel members in an attempt to integrate promotional strategy in the channel.

ing credit on a used object, usually the kind being purchased. **Promotional allowances** are attempts to integrate promotional strategy in the channel. For example, manufacturers often provide advertising and sales-support allowances for other channel members. Automobile manufacturers have offered allowances to retail dealers several times in recent years so the dealers could reduce prices to stimulate sales.

These promotional allowances are the secrets behind the specials run by the local supermarket or variety store. In Figure 18.8, an advertising flyer distributed by a New York City supermarket shows specials offered by the store. The price specials reflect the promotional allowances that the manufacturer gave the retailer to push the product. The retailer ordinarily pays $1.15 a can for Bumble Bee white tuna; the allowance brought his net cost to $.96. In this instance the product was marked up $.03 per can. The tuna was recently selling at this store for $1.39, the spaghetti sauce for $1.05, and the instant coffee for $4.79.[1]

Rebates
Refunds for a portion of the purchase price, usually granted by the manufacturer of a product.

Rebates are refunds of a portion of the purchase price, given by the seller. They have been used most prominently by automobile manufacturers eager to move models during periods of slow sales. Faced with intense competition in the home-computer market, Texas Instruments once decided to reduce the price of its lowest-priced computer by one-third with a $100 rebate offer.

In recent years, General Electric has held the title of the leading rebater in the United States. The firm, which began using rebates in 1974 with offers on radios and tape recorders, has offered shoppers rebates on 62 small appliances, 23 refrigerators and ovens, 4 lighting fixtures, and some televisions and stereos in a single 12-month period. However, the extensive use of re-

Figure 18.8
Promotional Allowances Permit Retail Price Reductions

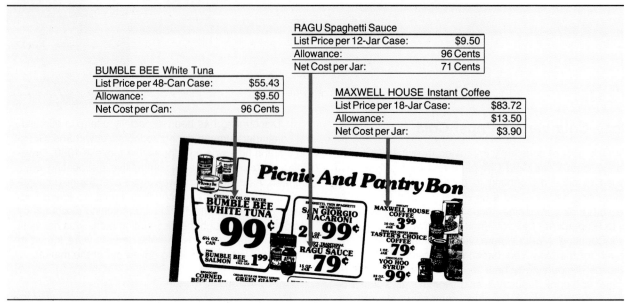

RAGU Spaghetti Sauce	
List Price per 12-Jar Case:	$9.50
Allowance:	96 Cents
Net Cost per Jar:	71 Cents

BUMBLE BEE White Tuna	
List Price per 48-Can Case:	$55.43
Allowance:	$9.50
Net Cost per Can:	96 Cents

MAXWELL HOUSE Instant Coffee	
List Price per 18-Jar Case:	$83.72
Allowance:	$13.50
Net Cost per Jar:	$3.90

bates by other firms and the problems involved in processing rebates led GE marketers to reduce rebates to about 30 items the following year. As GE's vice-president in charge of hard goods pointed out, "The novelty and freshness have worn off. I don't think any product was ever rebated into a No. 1 position or into consumer recognition."[2]

Geographical Considerations

Geographical considerations are important in pricing when the shipment of heavy, bulky, low-unit-cost materials is involved. The transportation component of a product's price may be handled in several ways: (1) the buyer pays all transportation charges, (2) the seller pays all transportation charges, or (3) both the buyer and the seller share the charges. This is particularly important in the case of firms seeking to expand their geographic coverage to distant markets. How can they compete when local suppliers in the distant markets are able to avoid the considerable shipping costs facing them? The seller has several alternatives in handling transportation costs.

FOB Plant
"Free on board," a price quotation that does not include shipping charges; the buyer is responsible for paying them. Also called *FOB origin*.

FOB plant or *FOB origin*, pricing provides a price that does not include any shipping charges. The buyer must pay all the freight charges. The seller pays only the cost of loading the merchandise aboard the carrier selected by the buyer. The abbreviation FOB means "free on board." Legal title and responsibility pass to the buyer after the purchase is loaded and a receipt is obtained from the representative of the common carrier.

Prices may also be shown as FOB origin—freight allowed. The seller permits the buyer to subtract transportation expenses from the bill. The amount the seller receives varies with the freight charged against the invoice. This alternative, called freight absorption is commonly used by firms with high fixed costs because it permits a considerable expansion of their market since the same price is quoted regardless of shipping expenses.

Freight Absorption
System for handling transportation costs under which the buyer of goods may deduct shipping expenses from the cost of the goods.

Uniform Delivered Price
System for handling transportation costs under which all buyers are quoted the same price, including transportation expenses.

The same price, including transportation expenses, is quoted to all buyers when a **uniform delivered price** is the firm's policy. Such pricing is the exact opposite of FOB pricing. This system is often compared to the pricing of mail service, hence, it is sometimes called *postage-stamp pricing*. The price that is quoted includes an average transportation charge per customer, which means that distant customers are actually paying a lesser share of shipping costs while customers near the supply source pay what is known as *phantom freight* (the amount by which the average transportation charge exceeds the actual cost of shipping).

Zone Pricing
System for handling transportation costs under which the market is divided into geographic regions and a different price is set in each region.

In **zone pricing**, which is simply a modification of a uniform delivered pricing system, the market is divided into different zones, and a price is established within each zone. By including average transportation costs for shipments within each zone as part of the delivered price of goods sold within the zone, phantom freight is reduced but not eliminated. The U.S. Postal Service's package rates depend upon zone pricing. The primary advantage of zone pricing is that it is easy to administer and enables the seller to be more competitive in distant markets. Figure 18.9 shows how a marketer located in Kansas City might divide its market into geographic segments. All customers in Zone 1 would be charged $10 per unit freight, while more distant customers would pay freight costs based upon the zone in which they are located.

Basing Point System
System for handling transportation costs in which the buyer's costs include the product price plus freight charges from the basing point city nearest the buyer.

In a **basing point system**, the price to the customer includes the price at the factory plus freight charges from the basing point city nearest the buyer. The basing point is the point from which freight charges are determined; it is not necessarily the point from which the goods are shipped. Both single and multiple basing point systems are used. In either case, the actual shipping point is not considered in the price quotation. The intent of this novel approach to handling shipping charges is to permit distant marketers to compete, since all competitors will quote identical transportation rates.

During the 1940s, several legal cases involving the steel, glucose, and cement industries were brought against users of basing point pricing systems. The outcomes of the proceedings themselves were confusing, but the result was a reduction in the use of these systems as a basis for pricing.

Figure 18.9
Zone Pricing for a Kansas City Firm

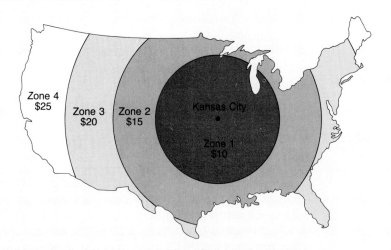

The best-known basing point system was the *Pittsburgh-plus pricing* procedure that was used in the steel industry for many years. Steel price quotations contained freight charges from Pittsburgh regardless of where the steel was produced. As the industry matured, other steel centers emerged in Chicago, Gary, Cleveland, and Birmingham. Pittsburgh, however, remained the basing point for steel pricing. This meant that a buyer in Terre Haute, Indiana, who purchased steel from a Gary mill had to pay phantom freight from Pittsburgh.

Price Policies

Pricing Policy
General guideline based upon pricing objectives and intended for use in specific pricing decisions.

Price policies are an important ingredient in the firm's total image. They provide the overall framework and consistency needed in pricing decisions. A pricing policy is a general guideline, based upon pricing objectives, that is intended for use in specific pricing decisions.

Decisions concerning price structure generally tend to be more technical than decisions concerning price policies. Price structure decisions take the selected price policy as a given and use it to specify the discount structure details. Price policies have a greater strategic importance, particularly in relation to competitive considerations. They are the bases on which pricing decisions are made.

Pricing policies must deal with varied competitive situations. The type of pricing policy used depends upon the environment within which the pricing decision must be made. The types of policies to consider are psychological pricing, unit pricing, one-price policy versus price flexibility, product-line pricing, and promotional prices.

Psychological Pricing

Psychological Pricing
Pricing policy based on the belief that certain prices or price ranges are more appealing than others to buyers.

Psychological pricing is based upon the belief that certain prices or price ranges are more appealing to buyers than others. There is, however, no consistent research foundation for such thinking, and studies often report mixed findings. Prestige pricing, mentioned in Chapter 17, is one of many forms of psychological pricing.

Odd Pricing
Pricing policy based on the belief that a price with an uncommon last digit is more appealing than a round figure. An example would be a price of $9.99 rather than $10.

Odd pricing is a good example of the application of psychological pricing. Prices are set ending in numbers not commonly used for price quotations. A price of $16.99 is assumed to be more appealing than $17, supposedly because it is a lower figure.

Originally, odd pricing was used to force clerks to make change, thus serving as a cash-control device within the firm.[3] Now it has become a customary feature of contemporary price quotations. For instance, one discounter uses prices ending in 3 and 7 rather than 5, 8, or 9, because of a belief that customers regard price tags of $5.95, $6.98, and $7.99 as *regular* retail prices, while $5.97 and $6.93 are considered *discount* prices.

Unit Pricing

Consumer advocates have often pointed out the difficulty of comparing consumer products that are available in different-size packages or containers. Is a 28-ounce can selling for $.75 a better buy than two 16-ounce cans priced at $.81 or another brand that sells three 16-ounce cans for $.99? The critics argue that there should be a common way to price consumer products.

Unit pricing is a response to this problem. Under unit pricing, all prices are stated in terms of some recognized unit of measurement (such as grams and liters) or a standard numerical count. There has been considerable discussion about legislating mandatory unit pricing. The American Marketing Association's board of directors has endorsed unit pricing, and many of the major food chains have adopted it.

Some supermarket chains have come to regard the adoption of unit pricing as a competitive tool upon which to base extensive advertising. However, unit pricing has not been particularly effective in improving the shopping habits of the urban poor; research studies have shown that it is most likely to be used by better-educated consumers with higher incomes.

The real question, of course, is whether unit pricing improves consumer decisions. One study found that shoppers who used unit-price information paid on average 9 percent less.[4] Another study found that the availability of unit prices resulted in consumer savings and that retailers also benefited when unit pricing led to greater purchases of store brands. The study concluded that unit pricing was valuable to both buyer and seller and that it merited full-scale usage.[5] Unit pricing is a major pricing policy issue that must be faced by many firms.

Price Flexibility Policies

Marketing executives must also determine company policy with respect to price flexibility. Is the firm going to have just one price or pursue a variable price policy in the market? Generally, *one-price policies* characterize situations where mass selling is employed, whereas *variable pricing* is more common where individual bargaining typifies market transactions.

A one-price policy is common in retailing because it facilitates mass merchandising. For the most part, once the price is set, the manager can direct attention to other aspects of the marketing mix. Variable pricing, by contrast, is found more in wholesaling and industrial markets. This does not mean that price flexibility exists only in manufacturing industries. A study of the retail home-appliance market concluded that persons who purchased identical products from the same dealer often paid different prices for them. The primary reasons for the differences were customer knowledge and bargaining strength.[6]

While variable pricing has the advantage of flexibility in selling situations, it may conflict with the Robinson-Patman Act provisions. It may also lead to retaliatory pricing by competitors, and it is not well received by those who have paid the higher prices.

Product-Line Pricing

Since most firms market several different lines of products or services, an effective pricing strategy must consider the relationship among all of these products or services instead of viewing each in isolation. Product-line pricing is the practice of marketing merchandise at a limited number of prices.[7] For example, a clothier might have three lines of men's suits: one priced at $225, a second line priced at $350, and the most expensive line priced at $450. These price points are important factors in achieving product-line differentiation and for trading up and trading down by the firm's customers.

Product-line pricing is used extensively in retail marketing; the old five-and-dime variety stores were operated using this approach. It can be an advantage to both retailer and customer. Shoppers can choose the price range they wish to pay, then concentrate on other product variables such as color, style, and material. The retailer can purchase and offer specific lines at a limited number of price categories instead of a more general assortment with dozens of different prices.

Product-line pricing requires identifying the market segment or segments to which the firm is appealing. For example, "Samsonite sees its market not as all luggage, but as the 'medium-priced, hard-side' portion of the luggage trade."[8] The firm must decide how to line its product prices. A dress manufacturer might have lines priced at $69.95, $99.95, and $129.95. Product-line pricing not only simplifies the administration of the pricing structure, but also alleviates the confusion that can occur when all products are priced separately. Product-line pricing is really a combined product/price strategy.

One problem with a product-line pricing decision is that once it is made, retailers and manufacturers have difficulty in adjusting it. Rising costs, therefore, put the seller in the position of either changing the price lines, with the resulting confusion, or reducing costs by production adjustments, which opens the firm to the complaint that "XYZ Company's merchandise certainly isn't what it used to be!"

Promotional Pricing

Promotional Price
Lower-than-normal price used as a temporary ingredient in a firm's marketing strategy.

A promotional price is a lower-than-normal price used as a temporary ingredient in a firm's selling strategy. In some cases, promotional prices are recurrent, such as the annual shoe store "buy one pair of shoes, get the second pair for one cent" sale. Another example is a new pizza restaurant which has an opening special to attract customers. In other situations, a firm may introduce a promotional model or brand to allow it to compete in another market.

Loss Leaders
Products offered to consumers at less than cost to attract them to retail stores where they are likely to buy other merchandise at regular prices.

Most promotional pricing is done at the retail level. One type is loss leaders goods priced below cost to attract customers who, the retailer hopes, will then buy other regularly priced merchandise. The use of loss leaders can be effective. However loss-leader pricing is not permitted in those states with unfair trade practices acts, which were discussed in Chapter 2.

One of the best innovators of loss-leader pricing was Cal Mayne. He was one of the first marketers to systematically price specials and to evaluate their effect on gross margins and sales. Mayne increased sales substantially by featuring coffee, butter, and margarine at 10 percent below cost. Ten other demand items were priced competitively, and at a loss when necessary, to undersell competition. Still another group of so-called secondary demand items were priced in line with competition. Mayne based his pricing policy on the theory that a customer can only remember about 30 prices. Keep prices down on these items, he reasoned, and the customer will stay with you.[9]

Some studies, however, have reported considerable price confusion on the part of consumers. One study of consumer price recall reported that average shoppers misquoted the price they last paid for coffee by over 12 percent. While some people named the prices exactly, others missed by several hundred percent.[10]

Three potential pitfalls should be considered when facing a promotional pricing decision:

1.   Promotional prices may violate unfair trade practices acts in some states.
2.   Some consumers are little influenced by price appeals, so promotional pricing will have little effect on them.

3. Continuous use of an artificially low rate may result in it being accepted as customary for the product. For example, poultry, which was used as a loss leader during the 1930s and 1940s, has suffered from such a phenomenon in the United States.

Price–Quality Relationships

One of the most researched aspects of pricing is the relationship between price and the consumer's perception of the product's quality. In the absence of other cues, price is an important indication of the way the consumer perceives the product's quality.[11] Many buyers believe the higher the price, the better the quality of the product. One study asked 400 people what terms they associated with the word *expensive*. Two-thirds of the replies were related to high quality, with words such as *best* and *superior*. The relationship between price and perceived quality is a well-documented fact in contemporary marketing.

The extremely high prices paid by purchasers of one of the 2,000 new Rolls-Royces offered for sale in 1986 contribute to the image of exclusiveness and quality. Although the advertisement shown in Figure 18.10 emphasizes

Figure 18.10
The Rolls-Royce Image: The Result of Both Price and Quality

the quality workmanship that permits the firm to characterize its product as "simply the best motor car in the world," price is also a significant ingredient in the overall Rolls-Royce image.

Probably the best price–quality conceptualization is the idea of *price limits*.[12] It is argued that consumers have limits within which product-quality perception varies directly with price. A price below the lower limit is regarded as too cheap, whereas a price above the higher limit means it is too expensive.

This concept provides a reasonable explanation of the price–quality relationship. Most consumers do tend to set an acceptable price range when purchasing goods and services. The range, or course, varies among consumers depending upon their socioeconomic characteristics and buying dispositions. Consumers, nonetheless, should be aware that price is not necessarily an indicator of quality. In Canada, the Alberta Department of Consumer and Corporate Affairs summarized seven price–quality research studies, six covering *Consumer Reports* analyses of 932 products between 1940 and 1977, and one for 43 products tested by *Canadian Consumer* between 1973 and 1977. Findings indicated that while there was a positive relationship between price and quality, the correlation was a relatively low 0.25 (1.0 is perfect correlation; 0.0 represents no correlation). About 25 percent of the products tested had a negative price–quality relationship; that is, products which were ranked lower in performance had higher prices than products deemed superior by the U.S. and Canadian consumer testing organizations.[13]

Negotiated Prices and Competitive Bidding

Many situations involving government and industrial procurement are not characterized by set prices, particularly for nonrecurring purchases such as a defense system for the armed forces. Markets such as these are growing at a fast pace. In the United States, government purchases now exceed 20 percent of the nation's gross national product; in Canada, the various government units spend almost one-half of the total GNP.

Competitive bidding is a process by which buyers ask potential suppliers to make price quotations on a proposed purchase or contract. *Specifications* give a description of the item (or job) that the government or industrial firm wishes to acquire. One of the most important tasks in modern purchasing management is to describe adequately what the organization seeks to buy. This generally requires the assistance of the firm's technical personnel such as engineers, designers, and chemists.

In some cases industrial and governmental purchasers use *negotiated contracts* instead of inviting competitive bidding for a project. In these situations, the terms of the contract are set through talks between the buyer and the seller.

Where there is only one available supplier or where contracts require extensive research and development work, negotiated contracts are likely to be employed. In addition, some state and local governments permit their agencies to negotiate purchases under a certain limit, say $500 or $1,000. This policy is an attempt to eliminate the economic waste involved in obtaining bids for relatively minor purchases.

One response to inflation has been the use of escalator pricing. An **escalator clause** allows the seller to adjust the final price based upon changes in the costs of the product's ingredients between the placement of the order

Escalator Clause
In pricing, part of many bids allowing the seller to adjust the final price, based upon changes in the costs of the product's ingredients, between the placement of the order and the completion of construction or delivery of the product.

and the completion of construction or delivery of the product. Such clauses typically base the adjustment calculation on the cost-of-living index or a similar indicator. While an estimated one-third of all industrial marketers use escalator clauses in some of their bids, they are most commonly used with major projects involving long time periods and complex operations.

The Transfer Pricing Dilemma

Transfer Price
Costs assessed when products are moved from one profit center in a firm to another center in the same firm.

Profit Centers
Any part of an organization to which revenue and controllable costs can be assigned.

One pricing problem peculiar to large-scale enterprises is that of determining an internal transfer price—the price for sending goods from one company profit center to another. As companies expand, they tend to decentralize management. Profit centers are set up as a control device in the new decentralized operation. Profit centers are any part of the organization to which revenue and controllable costs can be assigned, such as a department.

In large companies, the centers can secure many of their resource requirements from within the corporate structure. The pricing problem becomes: What rate should Profit Center A (maintenance department) charge Profit Center B (sales department) for the cleaning compound used on B's floors? Should the price be the same as it would be if A did the work for an outside party? Should B receive a discount? The answers to these questions depend upon the philosophy of the firm involved.

The transfer pricing dilemma is an example of the variations that a firm's pricing policy must deal with. Consider the case of UDC-Europe, a Universal Data Corporation subsidiary that has ten subsidiaries. Each of the ten is organized on a geographic basis, and each is treated as a separate profit center. Intercompany transfer prices are set at the annual budget meeting. Special situations, like unexpected volume, are handled through negotiations by the subsidiary managers. If complex tax problems arise, UDC-Europe's top management may set the transfer price.[14]

Pricing in the Public Sector

The pricing of public services has also become an interesting, and sometimes troublesome, aspect of contemporary marketing. Traditionally, government services were very low cost or were priced using the full-cost approach: users paid all costs associated with the service. In more recent years, there has been a move toward incremental or marginal pricing, which considers only those expenses specifically associated with a particular activity. However, it is often difficult to detemine the costs that should be assigned to a particular activity or service. Governmental accounting problems are often more complex than those of private enterprises.

Another problem in pricing public services is that taxes act as an *indirect* price of a public service. Someone must decide the relationship between the direct and indirect prices of such a service. A shift toward indirect tax charges (where an income or earnings tax exists) is pricing based on the *ability-to-pay* principle rather than on the *use* principle.

The pricing of any public service involves a basic policy decision to determine whether the price is an instrument to recover costs or a technique to accomplish some other social or civic objective. For example, public health services may be priced near zero to encourage their use. On the other hand, parking fines in some cities are high to discourage the use of private automobiles in the central business district. Pricing decisions in the public sector are difficult because political and social considerations often outweigh the economic aspects.

Summary

The main elements to consider in setting a price strategy are the organization for pricing decisions, pricing policies, price–quality relationships, negotiated prices, competitive bidding, transfer pricing, and pricing in the public sector. Alternative pricing strategies include price skimming, penetration pricing, and meeting competition by pricing at the level of comparable products. Methods for quoting prices depend on factors such as cost structures, traditional practices in a particular industry, and policies of individual firms. Prices quoted can involve list prices, market prices, cash discounts, trade discounts, quantity discounts, and allowances such as trade-ins, promotional allowances, and rebates.

Shipping costs often figure heavily in the pricing of goods. A number of alternatives exist for dealing with these costs: FOB plant, when price does not include any shipping charges; freight absorption, when the buyer can deduct transportation expenses from the bill; uniform delivered price, when the same price—including shipping expenses—is charged to all buyers; and zone pricing, when a set price exists within each region.

Pricing policies vary among firms. Among the most common are psychological pricing, unit pricing, price flexibility, product-line pricing, and promotional pricing.

The relationship between price and consumer perception of quality has been the subject of much research. A well-known and accepted concept is that of price limits—limits within which the perception of product quality varies directly with price.

Sometimes, prices are negotiated through competitive bidding, a situation in which several buyers quote prices on the same service or good. At other times, prices depend on negotiated contracts, a situation in which the terms of the contract are set through talks between a particular buyer and seller.

A phenomenon of large corporations is transfer pricing, in which a company sets prices for transferring goods or services from one company profit center to another.

Pricing in the public sector has become a troublesome aspect of marketing. It involves decisions on whether the price of a public service serves as an instrument to recover costs or as a technique for accomplishing some other social or civic purpose.

Solving the Stop-Action Case

Coca-Cola versus Pepsi Cola

In recent years, promotional allowances have represented the most widely used pricing tool by both Coca-Cola and Pepsi Cola. These allowances provide retailers with the financial incentive they need to push the bottlers' products. Alternative forms of this special treatment include special store displays, store newspaper ads featuring the product, and consumer discounts.

In-store displays have become an area of fierce competition due to their potential for increasing sales. Soft-drink bottlers are well aware of the potential for a single display in the front of a store to increase a brand's sales sixfold. Buyers from one of the nation's largest supermarket chains play Coke against Pepsi to secure the largest allowance for their prime-location store displays. After receiving Coca-Cola's discount offer, store buyers have been known to call Pepsi Cola marketers with this message: "You have a half hour to get back to us [with a counteroffer]."

While these price competition practices increase sales volume, they also create longer-range problems for Coca-Cola and Pepsi Cola. Consumers begin to think of soft drinks as a commodity rather than as separate brands. According to Allan Kaplan, industry analyst for Merrill Lynch, "Price promotions have really hurt the brand image of the soft-drink business. It has reached a point where the consumer will go into the supermarket and just buy whichever soft drink is on sale, whether it be Pepsi, or Coke, or other brands. This demeans the brand names of all soft-drink products."

Photo Source: Courtesy of PepsiCo, Inc.

Large-scale discounting and promotional allowances can backfire in other ways. Most chains buy more inventory than they currently need when attractive discounts are offered. Many try to buy enough to carry them to the next discount offer. As a result, the retailer's warehouse and distribution costs increase, and the bottler receives no new orders until this stock is sold. The result for the bottler is uneven demand on production and distribution.

Despite these problems, discounting appears to be an entrenched pricing practice in the continuing battle between Coca-Cola and Pepsi Cola. And with new brands like Diet Coke entering the market to challenge the positions of established leaders, the practice seems certain to continue in the years ahead.

Source: Kaplan quotation is from " '83: More Trench Warfare," *Business Week* (January 1983), p. 23.

Questions for Discussion

1. Who in the organization is most likely to be responsible for setting a price structure? Who is most likely to administer a price structure?

2. What are the benefits derived from utilizing a skimming approach to pricing?

3. Under what circumstances is penetration pricing most likely to be used?

4. Explain why most marketing executives choose meeting competitors' prices as a pricing strategy.

5. What type of new product pricing would be appropriate for the following items?
   a. New deodorant
   b. Fuel additive that increases mileage by 50 percent

c.   New pattern of fine china
d.   New ultrasensitive burglar, smoke, and fire alarm
e.   New video game

6.   How are prices likely to be quoted?

7.   How are prices quoted for each of the following:
a.   Eastern Airlines ticket to Toronto
b.   Aluminum siding installation by a local contractor
c.   New jogging suit from a sportswear retailer
d.   New Nissan Stanza

8.   Contrast the freight absorption and uniform delivered pricing systems.

9.   Assume that a product sells for $100 per ton and that Pittsburgh is the basing-point-system city. Per-ton shipping from Pittsburgh to a potential customer in Baltimore costs $10 per ton. Actually, the shipping costs from suppliers in three other cities are $8 per ton for supplier A, $11 per ton for supplier B, and $10 per ton for supplier C. Using this information, answer the following questions.
a.   What delivered price would a salesperson for supplier A quote to the customer?
b.   What delivered price would a salesperson for supplier B quote to the customer?
c.   What delivered price would a salesperson for supplier C quote to the customer?

10. Prepare a list of arguments that might be used in justifying a basing point pricing system.

11. List and discuss the reasons for establishing price policies.

12. A manufacturer markets a product with a retail list price of $100 with trade discounts of 40, 20, and 5. How much will the manufacturer receive for each product sold?

13. Refer to Question 12 above and identify the likely intermediaries involved in the marketing channel for the $100 product.

14. When does a price become a promotional price? What are the pitfalls in promotional pricing?

15. What is the relationship between prices and consumer perceptions of quality?

16. Interview three friends and determine their acceptable price ranges for a common consumer good or service, such as toothpaste, a haircut, or mouthwash. Ask them the price below which they would doubt the product's quality and the highest price they would pay for the product. Relate your findings to product–quality relationships and pricing strategies.

17. Comment on the following statement: Unit pricing is not only expensive for retailers, but also useless because everyone ignores it.

18. Contrast negotiated prices and competitive bidding.

19. What criteria should be considered for transfer pricing in a large corporation like Westinghouse Electric?

20. What types of decisions must be made in the pricing of public services? What role could escalator clauses play in this area?

Case: The Ten-Dollar Light Bulb

General Electric's steering wheel-shaped answer to the often-heard complaint that light bulbs burn out all too frequently is Circlite, a fluorescent lamp that fits incandescent sockets. As the accompanying photo indicates, one 44-watt Circlite fluorescent produces the light output of a 100-watt incandescent bulb but has the rated life of ten 100-watt light bulbs. Priced at about $10, Circlite fluorescents will generate energy savings of $20 over their 5-year life expectancy.

Even though GE marketers face a significant challenge in enticing consumers to spend more than 10 times as much as ordinary bulbs on the new fluorescent lamps, a number of competitors have already entered the market. Both North American Philips Lighting Corporation and Westinghouse Electric currently market similar long-life fluorescent lamps. All three firms are seeking ways to expand the market. As the manager of product planning for Westinghouse's Lamp Division stated, "We face an enormous education process."

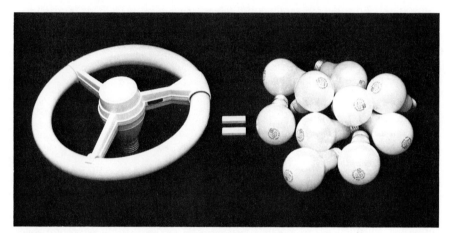

Sources: "The Race to the $10 Light Bulb," *Business Week* (May 19, 1980), p. 124; phone interview with Jim Jensen, General Electric Company, Lighting Business Group. Photo courtesy of General Electric Company, Lighting Business Group.

Questions

1. What pricing strategy is being used by General Electric and its competitors for the long-life fluorescent lamps? Justify the choice of this strategy.

2. Suggest a marketing strategy designed to increase the market for the new fluorescent lamps. Consider each marketing mix variable in your potential recommendations.

Computer Applications

Problems 1 through 4 deal with situations involving competitive bidding by firms offering products and services to industrial purchasers or government organizations. The description of the *expected net profit* (ENP) approach to competitive bidding on page 206 should be reviewed before attempting to solve these problems.

Problems 5 and 6 focus upon the application of two pricing strategies discussed earlier in the chapter: skimming strategies and penetration pricing. The discussion of breakeven analysis on pages 479–483 should be reviewed before attempting to solve these problems.

Directions: Use menu item 7 titled "Competitive Bidding" to solve Problems 1–4. Use menu item 16 titled "Breakeven Analysis" to solve Problems 5 and 6.

Problem 1 John Johannsen, marketing manager at Minneapolis-based Northern States Construction, wants to submit a bid for a job that he estimates will cost $80,000. He has prepared two preliminary proposals: (1) a bid for $120,000 and (2) a bid for $105,000. If Johannsen estimates that there is a 50 percent chance of the buyer accepting the first bid and a 60 percent chance of his accepting the second bid, which of the two bids would yield the higher expected net profit?

Problem 2 Toledo Suppliers' marketing executive Ed Sodek has spent a number of days developing a bidding strategy for two bid invitations his firm recently received from the Cuyahoga County Commission.

a.   The cost of the first job is estimated to be $18,000. What bid should Sodek submit to assure an expected net profit of $15,000 if he estimates the expected probability of acceptance at 60 percent?
b.   Sodek also estimates that the second bid will cost $18,000. However, the owner of Toledo Suppliers has specified a minimum acceptable expected net profit of $12,500. Sodek estimates the probability of acceptance to be 55 percent. What bid should he submit?
c.   What bid should Sodek submit if the Toledo Suppliers' owner requires a minimum acceptable expected net profit of $12,500 and also asks Sodek to lower the probability of the second bid's acceptance to 45 percent?

Problem 3 The manager of Rochester-based Erie Construction would like to earn an expected net profit (ENP) of $9,000 on a job with an estimated cost of $3,500.

a.   What probability of acceptance is being assigned if the manager submits a bid of $20,000?
b.   What probability of acceptance is being assigned if the manager submits a bid of $14,000?

Problem 4 Marjorie Abernathy is owner/manager of Jayhawk Contractors based in Wichita, Kansas. She has estimated the probability for acceptance of her firm's bid on a state contract at 70 percent. Since her planned bid is $60,000 and the estimated cost of completing the project is $36,000, Abernathy has calculated the expected net profit to be $16,800.

a.   What would the expected net profit be if the cost estimate turns out to be $1,500 too low?
b.   What would the expected net profit be if total costs could be held to only $34,000?

Problem 5 Ed Whiting is marketing vice-president of Boston-based Viking Manufacturing, a major appliance manufacturer with its own chain of retail outlets. Whiting is evaluating a product development department proposal for a new portable washer. Fixed costs are estimated at $1.2 million, variable costs are expected to be $50 per unit, and typical retail prices on similar products are $125.

a.   What is the breakeven point for Viking Manufacturing if Whiting decides to meet competition by choosing the $125 price for the portable washer?

b.   Whiting is also considering a skimming strategy for the new washer and is considering pricing it at $160. This strategy will aid in improving the image for other Viking appliances and will assist him in adjusting his production level to match consumer demand. However, he feels that the firm would have to spend an additional $500,000 on advertising, store displays, and other promotional materials to ensure the success of the new washer if he decides to implement the price skimming strategy. Determine the breakeven point if these expenditures are made and the skimming strategy is used.

c.   Whiting's national sales manager feels that a penetration pricing strategy might prove effective in gaining quick consumer acceptance for the new product and in attracting customers to the firm's retail stores who might purchase additional appliances with higher margins. He suggests $100 as a retail price. How many units of the new portable washer would have to be sold to break even if the firm chooses the penetration strategy?

d.   Suppose that Viking Manufacturing selects the penetration strategy but also establishes a minimum target return of 15 percent of sales. How many units must be sold to break even *and* achieve the target return?

Problem 6 Wolverine Industries of Milwaukee is considering the possible introduction of a new service. Focus group research has revealed that consumers expect the service to be priced at approximately $50. Total fixed costs are $620,000, and average variable costs are calculated to be $22.

a.   What is the breakeven point (in units) for the proposed service?

b.   The firm's director of marketing has suggested a target profit return of $100,000 for the service. How many units must be sold to break even *and* achieve the target return?

c.   Another proposal is to use 12 percent return on sales as a target return instead of a fixed dollar amount. How many units must be sold to break even *and* achieve the 12 percent return?

d.   How would your answers to Questions a, b, and c change if the firm's marketing director decided to implement a skimming strategy and price the service at $85?

e.   How would your answers to Questions, a, b, and c change if the firm's marketing director decided to implement a penetration strategy and price the service at $35?

PART EIGHT

Further Perspectives

Global Dimensions of Marketing

Key Terms

exporting
importing
tariffs
General Agreement on
  Tariffs and Trade (GATT)
import quota
embargo
exchange control
dumping
friendship, commerce, and
  navigation (FCN) treaties
foreign licensing
joint venture
global marketing strategy
multinational corporation

Learning Goals

1. To describe the importance of international marketing from the perspective of the individual firm and the nation

2. To relate marketing environmental variables to international marketing

3. To identify the various levels of involvement in international marketing

4. To evaluate the strengths and weaknesses of utilizing a global marketing strategy

5. To explain each of the alternative product/promotion strategies in international marketing

6. To explain the underlying reasons for the attractiveness of the United States as a market target for foreign marketers

Dresser Industries

Dresser Industries is one of those giant firms that comes to mind when the word *multinational* is mentioned. The Dallas-based giant has built production facilities in 29 countries on six continents to serve world markets for technology, products, and services used by the energy industries in the development of petroleum, natural gas, and coal. A recent annual report showed that the firm's $1 billion-plus annual sales were produced on a global basis. U.S. purchasers were the firm's largest customers, accounting for 56 percent of total sales. In second place were European buyers (17 percent), followed by purchasers from Africa and the Middle and Far East (14 percent). Latin American purchasers represented 7 percent of Dresser's total sales, and Canadian buyers accounted for the final 6 percent.

In September 1981, the firm's French-based subsidiary, Dresser-France, received an order from the Soviet Union for twenty-one 60-ton compressors to be used in a giant 3,500-mile gas pipeline project designed to carry natural gas from Siberia to Western Europe. Dresser-France immediately notified the U.S. Department of Commerce (a requirement of U.S. law) and received approval to proceed.

Less than a year later, however, just prior to the scheduled delivery of the first three compressors, the project was halted. On June 18, 1982, President Reagan issued an executive order banning the delivery of oil and gas equipment to the Soviet Union from foreign firms that were either owned or controlled by U.S. firms. (A December 1981 order had already banned the shipment of similar goods manufactured in the United States.) The Reagan Administration declared these embargoes under provisions of the Export Administration Act of 1979, which was designed to control the shipment of high-technology material considered vital to U.S. security. President Reagan took these dramatic steps to protest the imposition of martial law in Poland and to pressure the Soviets to ease their hold on the Polish people.

Despite serious questions over the legality of the export ban, Dresser-France immediately complied by suspending work on 18 unfinished compressors. Although these moves satisfied U.S. government officials, they enraged European leaders who were determined to see the pipeline proceed. Feeling the tightening grip of a severe economic recession, France, Britain, West Germany, and Italy needed the $3.5 billion in pipeline material orders as well as the thousands of jobs and continuing supplies of fuel associated with the pipeline project. European lead-

Photo Source: Courtesy of NASA.

ers were also reluctant to undermine their countries' positions as reliable foreign trade partners. "I feel strongly that once you have made a deal you have got to keep it, short of war. . . .," said British Prime Minister Margaret Thatcher. Clearly, Dresser Industries was in the middle of a sticky situation.

Assignment: Use the materials in Chapter 19 to recommend a course of action for Dresser Industries.

Source: Thatcher quotation is from "The Nasty Pipeline Mess: Any Way Out?" *U.S. News & World Report* (September 13, 1982), p. 28.

Chapter Overview _____

Although international examples have been included in earlier chapter discussions of such concepts as marketing planning, segmentation, and elements of the marketing mix, most of the previous discussions have focused upon domestic marketing. Increasingly, U.S. organizations are crossing national boundaries in search of markets and profits. At the same time, foreign marketers are appearing in America to provide new competition for domestic firms.

Coca-Cola is one of the most readily identifiable products in the world. The Atlanta-based firm is one of the nation's most successful global marketers. Coca-Cola operates in 155 foreign countries, receiving 40 percent of its sales and 53 percent of its profits from abroad. Kiosks located inside Japan's Seibu department stores feature a familiar sight for the American tourist: an Allstate Insurance representative. The insurance company and the Japanese retailer have joined forces to market life insurance in much the same manner that Allstate operates at U.S. stores of its parent, Sears, Roebuck & Company. The results are impressive. Today, 100,000 Allstate insurance policies are in force in Japan, with total coverage of about $4 billion.

International marketing is obviously of considerable importance to Coca-Cola and Allstate Insurance. It is also important to Caterpillar Tractor, since it accounts for 41 percent of total company sales and over half of total earnings. In fact, such well-known firms as Colgate–Palmolive, Exxon, Heinz, Hoover, and NCR generate more than 50 percent of their annual earnings from international operations.

Figure 19.1 shows the major trading partners of the United States. Foreign purchasers are most likely to buy such American products as grain, aircraft, motor vehicles and parts, metals and manufactures, and power-generating machinery. By comparison, the foreign products most often purchased by U.S. firms are petroleum, machinery, transport equipment, automobiles and parts, and metals and manufactures.

Just as some firms depend on foreign sales, others depend on purchasing raw materials to use in their manufacturing operations at home. A furniture company's purchase of South American mahogany is an example.

International marketing is valuable to the individual firm for other reasons. In some instances, the company may discover significant product innovations being offered by competitors in foreign markets. These improved offerings may be adapted for the firm's product line currently being offered in its home country, thereby serving as a means of generating profitable new-product ideas.

Another reason why international marketing is important is that the global marketer may be able to meet foreign competition abroad before it infringes on home markets. After Japan's Makita Electric Works succeeded in capturing a 20 percent market share in professional tools in Europe over a three-year period by offering a highly standardized product line at low prices, Black & Decker executives responded with a crash program designed to cut costs and tighten quality control to match the Japanese firm's retail prices. These corrective measures prevented Makita from expanding its European successes to the United States.[1]

Dominant U.S. firms are not always the most successful enterprises in foreign markets. General Motors has a 46 percent share in the United States, but only 8.5 percent worldwide. In fact, GM rates behind Toyota, Nissan, and Ford in overseas markets. The Detroit giant is currently altering its marketing strategy to become a more formidable competitor in foreign markets.

Figure 19.1
Major U.S. Consumer and Supplier Nations

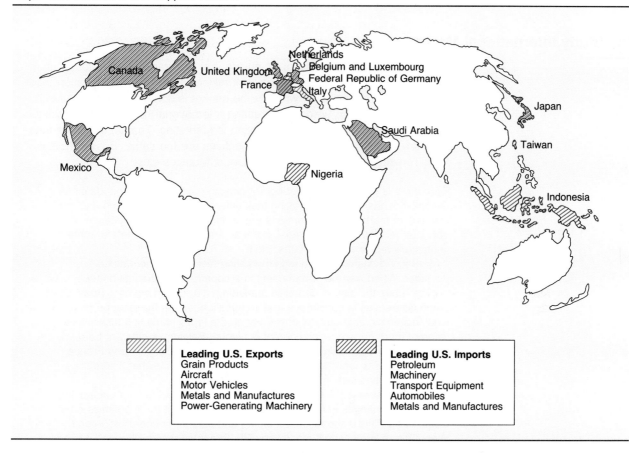

	Leading U.S. Exports		**Leading U.S. Imports**
	Grain Products		Petroleum
	Aircraft		Machinery
	Motor Vehicles		Transport Equipment
	Metals and Manufactures		Automobiles
	Power-Generating Machinery		Metals and Manufactures

Conversely, foreign marketers are becoming increasingly attracted to the huge U.S. market. Foreign product invasions are no longer limited to industries such as automobiles, electronics, and steel. Yoshinoya & Company of Japan is opening over 200 fast-food outlets in the United States.

International trade is vital to a nation and its marketers for several reasons. It expands the market and makes production and distribution economies feasible. It can also mean more jobs at home. From 30,000 to 40,000 new jobs are supported by each billion dollars of exports.[2]

Exporting
Marketing goods and services in foreign countries.

Importing
Purchasing of foreign products and raw materials.

Foreign trade can be divided into exporting—selling goods abroad—and importing—buying foreign goods and raw materials. While the United States is the world's largest exporter and importer, foreign trade is still less critical to it than to many other nations. In fact, U.S. exports account for a modest 6.9 percent of the nation's gross national product. The leading U.S. exporters in total volume are General Motors, General Electric, Boeing, Ford, and Caterpillar Tractor.

Although international marketing requires implementation of marketing strategies consisting of identification of market targets, analyses of environmental influences, and development of marketing mixes, both similarities and differences exist between international and domestic marketing. This chapter examines characteristics of the international marketplace, environmental influences on marketing, and the development of an international marketing mix.

It also discusses the sequential steps used by most firms in entering the international marketplace.

Why Study International Marketing?

Since the marketing functions of buying, selling, transporting, storing, standardization and grading, financing, risk-taking, and market information must be performed regardless of whether the market is domestic or global, a question arises about the wisdom of treating international marketing as a unique subject. After all, international marketing is marketing. That is, the same functions are performed and the firm's objectives are the same. But as Professor Vern Terpstra points out, three important differences exist:

First, there is the inter-nation or border-crossing aspect. When goods cross national boundaries, the marketing task differs. Marketing research and the blending of marketing mix elements are conducted differently because of the new international economic, legal, political, and cultural parameters (tariffs, quotas, exchange rates, boycotts, etc.).

Second, there is the foreign marketing task of the international marketer. Whenever the firm markets in a country other than its home market, it has the task of domestic marketing in a foreign country. Because of the differences in consumers and competition, and in the local political, legal, economic, and cultural environment, the firm's marketing task will be different. Furthermore, each country is unique: Belgium is different from Brazil; France is different from Japan; and neighbors Belgium and France are different. The international marketer thus has a somewhat different foreign marketing task in each country entered.

Third, there is the multinational marketing task of the international firm. When a firm markets in many foreign countries, it must try to optimize on a global basis. This is the task of planning and control, or coordination and integration of international marketing. The firm must recognize when it has to go native in its marketing and when it can standardize and get the leverage and economies of scale that make a successful international marketer. It must find the right blend of standardization and adaptation in its international marketing programs.[3]

Each of these differences is discussed in this chapter.

The International Marketplace

Many U.S. firms never venture outside their own domestic market. They feel they do not have to because the U.S. market is huge. Even today, only about 10 percent of all domestic manufacturing firms export their products, and only 250 of these manufacturers account for 80 percent of all U.S. exports.[4] Those that do venture abroad find the international marketplace far different from the one to which they are accustomed. Market sizes, buyer behavior, and marketing practices all vary, which means international marketers must carefully evaluate all market segments in which they expect to compete.

Market Size

In 1976, the world population passed the 4 billion mark. Only 15 years had passed since the 3 billion mark had been reached in 1961. It took 31 years to reach 3 billion from the 2 billion mark and over 300 years to reach 2 billion from the 1 billion mark. In contrast, forecasters predict the world population will reach 5 billion in 1989—just 13 years after the 4 billion mark was reached.

The United States has attained one of the highest standards of living in the history of the world, but its population size is insignificant when compared with the rest of the world. Figure 19.2 shows how the United States is dwarfed by the tremendous populations of countries such as India and China. While one-fifth of the world's population lives in China, less than 6 percent resides in the United States.

A prime ingredient of market size is population growth, and every day the world's population increases by about 213,000 people. By the year 2000, the world's population is expected to be 6.1 billion. A review of these projections produces some important contrasts. Average birthrates are dropping, but death rates are declining even faster. Population growth has fallen in industrialized nations, but it has increased in the less-developed countries. Nearly 80 percent of the population in 2000 will live in less-developed nations.

Many of the world's new inhabitants live in large cities. By the year 2000, these urban dwellers are expected to account for half the world population instead of the current 41 percent. Today, 41 cities have a population of 4 million or more. In 2000, 66 such cities will exist. Mexico City, which now ranks third in population with nearly 9 million people, is expected to grow to 26.3 million, making it the world's largest city.

Statistical data indicates that the international marketplace will continue to grow in size and that it will become increasingly urbanized. This does not mean, however, that all foreign markets will have the same potential. Income differences, for instance, vitally affect any nation's market potential. India has a population of nearly 750 million, but its per-capita income is very low. Can-

Figure 19.2
The World in Proportion to Population

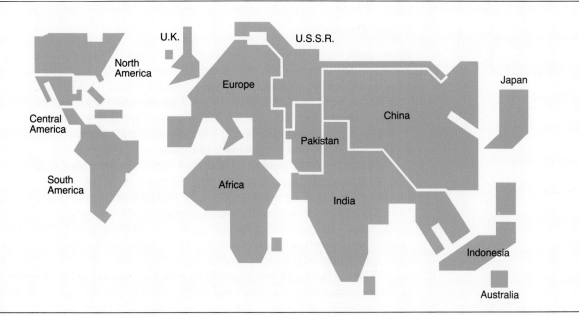

ada, on the other hand, has only a small fraction of India's population, but its per-capita income is higher than that of the United States. The following is a useful method of classifying the stages of market development of different nations:

1. *Subsistence economies.* In a subsistence economy the vast majority of people engage in simple agriculture. They consume most of their output and barter the rest for simple goods and services. They offer few opportunities for exporters.

2. *Raw material exporting countries.* These economies are rich in one or more natural resources but poor in other respects. Much of their revenue comes from exporting these resources. Examples are Chile (tin and copper), Zaire (copper), and Saudi Arabia (oil). These countries are good markets for extractive equipment, tools and supplies, materials-handling equipment, and trucks. Depending on the number of foreign residents and wealthy local rulers and landholders, they are also a market for Western-style commodities and luxury goods.

3. *Industrializing economies.* In an industrializing economy, manufacturing is beginning to account for between 10 to 20 percent of the country's gross national product. Examples include Egypt, the Philippines, India, and Brazil. As manufacturing increases, the country relies more on imports of textile raw materials, steel, and heavy machinery and less on imports of finished textiles, paper products, and automobiles. The industrialization creates a new rich class and a small but growing middle class, both demanding new types of goods, some of which can be satisfied only by imports.

4. *Industrial economies.* Industrial economies are major exporters of manufactured goods and investment funds. They trade manufactured goods among themselves and also export them to other types of economies in exchange for raw materials and semifinished goods. The large and varied manufacturing activities of these industrial nations and their sizable middle class make them rich markets for all sorts of goods.[5]

Buyer Behavior

Buyer behavior differs from one country to another. Therefore, marketers should carefully study each market before implementing a marketing strategy. Not all successful domestic marketing strategies can be exported to other parts of the world. Improved U.S.–Chinese relations will open up new markets for both nations. But the Chinese would be well advised to change some of their brand names before entering the American market: for example, White Elephant batteries and Pansy men's underwear.

Marketers must also be careful that their marketing strategies comply with local customs, tastes, and buying practices. In some cases, even the product itself has to be modified. General Foods, for instance, offers different blends of coffee for each of its overseas markets. One variety goes to British consumers, who prefer considerable quantities of milk in their coffee; another goes to the French, who usually drink coffee black; still another mix goes to Latin Americans, who prefer a chicory taste.[6]

Different buying patterns mean that marketing executives should do considerable research before entering a foreign market. Sometimes the research

Figure 19.3

Independent Marketing Research Firm Specializing
in Research in Arab Countries

CALL US TODAY. WE WILL BE GLAD TO ASSIST YOU.

PAN ARAB RESEARCH CENTER
P.O. Box 921 Safat, Kuwait.
Phone. 442100 442107
Telex : 2901 PACC KT

Source: Reprinted by permission of Pan Arab Research Center.

can be done by the marketer's own organization or a U.S.-based research firm. In other cases, a foreign-based marketing research organization should be used. The advertisement shown in Figure 19.3 is an example of a marketing research firm that specializes in Arab countries.

Foreign research firms are often innovative. For example, Audits, Ltd., of Great Britain, pioneered in the field of home audits of package goods. The British firm provided its respondents with a special trash container rather than relying on a diary of purchases. Discarded packages were then studied to determine consumer buying patterns.[7]

The Environment for International Marketing

Various environmental factors can influence international marketing strategy. Marketers should be as aware of these influences as they are of those in domestic markets.

Cultural, Economic, and Societal Factors

International marketing is often influenced by cultural, economic, and societal factors. The economic status of some countries makes them less or more likely candidates for international business expansion. Nations with low per-

Table 19.1

Marketing Miscommunications

What the Message Said	How the Message Was Interpreted (Language in Parentheses)
"You could use no finer napkin at your dinner table."	"You could use no finer diaper at your dinner table." *(U.K. English)*
"Body by Fisher"	"Corpse by Fisher" *(Flemish)*
"Schweppes tonic water"	"Schweppes bathroom water" *(Italian)*
"Misair Airlines" (Egypt)	"Misery Airlines" *(French)*
"Rendezvous lounges" (private airline lounges in U.S. airports)	"Rooms for lovemaking" *(Portuguese)*
"Come Alive with Pepsi"	"Come Alive out of the Grave" *(German)*

Source: Examples reported in David Ricks, "How to Avoid Business Blunders Abroad."
Business (April–June 1984), pp. 3–11.

capita income may be poor markets for expensive industrial machinery but good markets for agricultural hand tools. These nations cannot afford the technical equipment necessary in an industrialized society. Wealthier countries may be prime markets for the products of many U.S. industries, particularly those involved with consumer goods and advanced industrial products.

Many products have failed abroad simply because the producing firm tried to use the same marketing strategy that was successful in the United States. Consider, for example, an advertising strategy based primarily on the use of print media and featuring testimonials. Such a campaign would offer dim prospects in a less-developed nation with a high degree of illiteracy.

U.S. products sometimes face consumer resistance abroad. American automobiles, for example, have traditionally been rejected by European drivers who complain of poor styling, low gasoline mileage, and poor handling. But the new, smaller cars from Detroit are making moderate inroads into European markets. This reversal suggests that it is not always possible to determine the precise impact of cultural, economic, or societal factors prior to entering a foreign market. Japanese tea drinkers for centuries have preferred natural tea, but Boston Tea Company's blended, spiced, and herbal teas are now selling well in Japan.

Because languages are frequently different in international markets, care must be taken to ensure that the firm's communications are translated correctly and convey the intended meanings. Table 19.1 shows a number of classic examples of international communication failures.

Trade Restrictions

Tariffs
Taxes levied on imported products.

Assorted trade restrictions also affect global marketing. These restrictions are most commonly expressed through tariffs—taxes levied against imported products. Some tariffs are based on a set tax per pound, gallon, or unit; others are figured on the value of the imported product. They can be classified as either revenue or protective tariffs. Revenue tariffs are designed to raise funds for the government. Most of the revenue of the early U.S. government came from this source. Protective tariffs are designed to raise the retail price of an imported product to match or exceed a similar domestic product. Protective tariffs are usually higher than revenue tariffs. In the past, it was believed that a country should protect its infant industries by using tariffs to keep out foreign-made products. Some foreign goods entered, but the addition of a high tariff payment made domestic products competitive in price. Recently, it has been argued that tariffs should be raised to protect employment and profits in domestic U.S. industry.

General Agreement on Tariffs and Trade (GATT)
International trade agreement that has helped to reduce world tariffs.

The **General Agreement on Tariffs and Trade (GATT)**, an international trade accord, has sponsored several tariff negotiations that have reduced the overall level of tariffs throughout the world. The latest series, the so-called Tokyo Round, began in 1974 and concluded in 1979. The Tokyo Round reduced tariffs by about 33 percent over an eight-year period. The agreement also lessened nontariff barriers, such as government procurement regulations, that discriminated against foreign marketers.

Import Quota
Trade restriction that limits the amount of certain products that can enter a country for resale.

Embargo
Complete ban on the import of specified products.

There are also other forms of trade restrictions. An **import quota** sets limits on the amount of products in certain categories that can be imported. Import quotas seek to protect domestic industry and employment and to preserve foreign exchange. The ultimate quota is the **embargo**, the complete ban on the import of certain products. In the past, the United States has prohibited the import of products from some communist countries. The United States has also used export quotas. In 1984, for example, President Reagan enforced trade sanctions against Nicaragua.

Exchange Control
Method used to regulate the privilege of international trade among importing organizations by controlling access to foreign currencies.

Foreign trade can also be regulated by exchange control through a central bank or government agency. **Exchange control** means that firms gaining foreign exchange by exporting must sell this exchange to the central bank, or other agency, and importers must buy foreign exchange from the same organization. The exchange control authority can then allocate, expand, or restrict foreign exchange according to existing national policy.

Dumping: A Contemporary Marketing Problem   The practice of selling a product at a lower price in a foreign market than it sells for in the producer's domestic market is called **dumping**. In the late 1970s, Bethlehem Steel ran advertisements to protest what it viewed as dumping in the steel industry. It is often argued that foreign governments give substantial export support to their own companies. Such support may permit these firms to extend their export markets by offering lower prices abroad.

Dumping
Controversial practice of selling a product in a foreign market at a lower price than it would receive in the producer's domestic market.

Products that have been dumped on U.S. markets can be subject to additional import tariffs to bring their prices in line with domestically produced products. For instance, a 32 percent dumping duty was assessed against five Japanese steel sellers. However, businesses often complain that charges of alleged dumping must go through a lengthy investigative and bureaucratic procedure before duties are assessed. In an attempt to speed up the process in the steel industry, a trigger pricing system, which established a set of minimum steel prices, has been used. Japanese production costs, the world's lowest, were used in these calculations. Any imported steel selling at less than these rates triggers an immediate Treasury Department investigation. If dumping is substantial, additional duties are imposed.

Steel is not the only product to involve allegations of dumping. Similar allegations have been leveled against foreign makers of products as diverse as hockey sticks, cement, and motorcycles.

Demands for protection against foreign imports are common in all countries, particularly during periods of economic uncertainty. Firms ask for protection against sales losses, and unions seek to preserve their members' jobs. Overall, however, the long-term trend is in the direction of free trade among nations.

Political and Legal Factors

Political factors greatly influence international marketing. Political turmoil in the Philippines, Lebanon, Nicaragua, El Salvador, and Iran suggests how volatile this factor can be in international markets. In fact, many U.S. firms have set up internal political risk assessment (PRA) units or turned to outside consulting services to evaluate the political risks of the marketplace in which they operate. Sometimes marketing strategies have to be adjusted to reflect the new situation. For example, when Colgate–Palmolive introduced Irish Spring in England, it marketed the soap as Nordic Spring.

Many nations try to achieve political objectives through international business activities. Japan, for instance, has openly encouraged its firms' involvement in international marketing because much of the nation's economy is dependent on overseas sales.

Legal requirements complicate world marketing. Indonesia has banned commercial advertisements from the nation's only television channel. It was feared that the advertisements would cause the 80 percent of the population living in rural areas to envy those who resided in cities. All commercials in the United Kingdom and Australia must be cleared in advance. In the Netherlands, ads for candy must also show a toothbrush. Some nations have local content laws that specify the portion of a product that must come from domestic sources. These examples suggest that managers involved in international marketing must be well versed in legislation affecting their specific industry.

In some cases, the intricacies of customs regulations, documentation, and the complexity of foreign transportation systems create an opportunity for successful marketers. Figure 19.4 shows how the Netherlands markets its abilities to handle U.S. goods being exported to Europe.

The legal environment for U.S. firms operating abroad can be divided into three dimensions: (1) U.S. law, (2) international law, and (3) legal requirements of host nations. International law can be found in the treaties, conventions, and agreements that exist among nations. The United States has many friendship, commerce, and navigation (FCN) treaties—agreements that deal with many aspects of commercial relations with other countries, such as the right to conduct business in the treaty partner's domestic market.

Friendship, Commerce, and Navigation (FCN) Treaties
International agreements that deal with many aspects of commercial relations with other nations.

Other international business agreements concern international standards for various products, patents, trademarks, reciprocal tax treaties, export control, international air travel, and international communication. The International Monetary Fund has been set up to lend foreign exchange to nations that require it to conduct international trade. These agreements facilitate the whole process of world marketing.

The legal requirements of host nations affect foreign marketers. For example, some nations limit foreign ownership in their business sectors. International marketers in general recognize the importance of obeying the laws and regulations of the countries within which they operate. Even the slightest violations of these legal requirements are setbacks for the future of international trade.

International marketing is subject to various trade regulations, tax laws, and import/export requirements. One of the best-known U.S. laws is the Webb-Pomerene Export Trade Act (1918), which exempted various combinations of U.S. firms acting together to develop foreign markets from antitrust laws. The intent was to give U.S. industry economic power equal to that possessed by cartels, the monopolistic organizations of foreign firms. Companies operating under the Webb-Pomerene Act cannot reduce competition within the

Figure 19.4
Creating a Market by Uncomplicating Legal
Requirements in International Marketing

Source: Courtesy of Consulate General of the Netherlands.

United States and cannot use "unfair methods of competition." Generally, Webb-Pomerene associations have not been significant in the growth of U.S. trade.

The Foreign Corrupt Practices Act   A recently enacted legislation with a major impact on international marketing is the Foreign Corrupt Practices Act, which makes it illegal to bribe a foreign official in an attempt to solicit new or repeat sales abroad. The act also specifies that adequate accounting controls be installed to monitor internal compliance. Violations can result in a $1 million fine for the firm and a $10,000 fine and five years' imprisonment for individuals involved. This law has been quite controversial since several companies have reported that the paperwork involved has caused them to lose overseas sales.

Methods of Entering International Markets

Although about one in ten U.S. firms is currently engaged in international marketing, thousands of other potentially successful international firms continue to operate as domestic producers and marketers. In some cases, their reluctance to begin international marketing operations stems from misconceptions

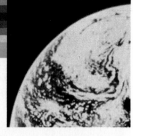

Return to the Stop-Action Case

Dresser Industries

The U.S. ban on the shipment of the compressors by Dresser-France, the French subsidiary of parent firm Dresser Industries, infuriated the French. The conflict reached the boiling point when France's minister of state served a *Requisition Order for Services* on the president of Dresser-France. The order, which had the authority of French law and carried with it civil and criminal penalties, directed Dresser-France "to complete the manufacture and delivery of all compressors and other equipment provided for" in the company's contract with the Soviet Union. Disobeying this order might mean French nationalization of the $50 to $100 million Le Havre production facility.

Finding itself between the proverbial rock and a hard place in a territory uncharted by U.S. or international law, Dresser-France had to decide whether to disobey the laws of France or those of the United States. "We talked about everything," said Edward R. Luter, Dresser's senior vice-president for finance. "In

fact, our president of Dresser-France considered resigning and just walking away from it. The attorneys said it would be a futile act because you're not going to stop the shipments whatever you do. Had he gone to jail they would have taken the compressors and shipped them anyway."

Luter said appeals to Washington for help were unanswered. "We called the State [Department], Commerce [Department], everyone in Washington who was working on this. They did nothing. We asked them what we could do—'Do you want us to ask the French Government to delay this thing while you discuss it?' and they said no." With no help from Washington and with France continuing to press for action, Dresser-France was forced to make a decision that could have a major impact on its ability to market its products and services in the United States and abroad.

Source: Luter quotation is from Michael Blumstein, "Dresser Says Unit Can Finish Order," *New York Times* (August 30, 1982), p. D2.

concerning such trade. Table 19.2 identifies six major myths about international marketing.

Several levels of involvement in international marketing can be identified: casual or accidental exporting, active exporting, foreign licensing, overseas marketing, and foreign production and marketing.[8] As Figure 19.5 indicates, the level of risk involved and the degree of control over international marketing by the firm increase with increased involvement.

Casual or accidental exporting is a passive level of involvement in international marketing. A U.S. company may export goods without even knowing it if its goods are bought by resident buyers for foreign companies. In other cases, a firm may export only occasionally when surplus or obsolete inventory is available.

When a firm actually makes a commitment to seek export business, it engages in active exporting. While the exact extent of the commitment may vary, the term implies that the firm is making a continuing effort to sell its merchandise abroad.

Foreign licensing occurs when a firm permits a foreign company to produce and distribute its merchandise or use its trademark or patent under a formal agreement. Licensing has several advantages over exporting: among them are the availability of local marketing information and distribution channels and protection from various legal barriers. Sometimes it is the best way

Foreign Licensing
Agreement in which a domestic firm permits a foreign company to either produce or distribute the firm's goods in the foreign country or to receive the right to utilize the firm's trademark, patent, or processes in a specified geographic area.

Table 19.2
Six Myths of International Marketing

International Marketing Myths	International Marketing Facts
Only large firms can export successfully.	Small size is no barrier to entering the export field.
Payment by foreign buyers is uncertain.	Fewer credit losses occur in international sales than are experienced domestically.
Unfamiliarity with foreign currencies leads to financial loss.	The U.S. dollar has become the primary currency of international trade: about 90 percent of world trade is transacted in dollars.
Overseas markets represent only minor sales opportunities.	Approximately 95 percent of the world's population and two-thirds of its purchasing power lie off U.S. shores.
American products are unsuitable for foreign markets.	American products command a reputation for high quality, durability, style, and "state of the art" technological superiority. (Some typical "Made in U.S.A." products, such as jeans and surf boards, are in demand overseas because of their American-ness.)
Export start-up costs are high.	The beginning exporter can choose to sell products outright to an exporting intermediary at no real cost or through low-cost participation in world trade shows.

Source: Adapted by permission from Dennis H. Tootelian and Ralph M. Gaedeke, *Small Business Management*
(Santa Monica, Calif.: Goodyear Publishing Co., 1978), pp. 179–180.

Figure 19.5
Levels of Involvement in International Marketing

Low	Degree of Risk			High
Level 1 Casual or Accidental Exporting	Level 2 Active Exporting	Level 3 Foreign Licensing	Level 4 Overseas Marketing	Level 5 Foreign Production and Foreign Marketing

Degree of Control

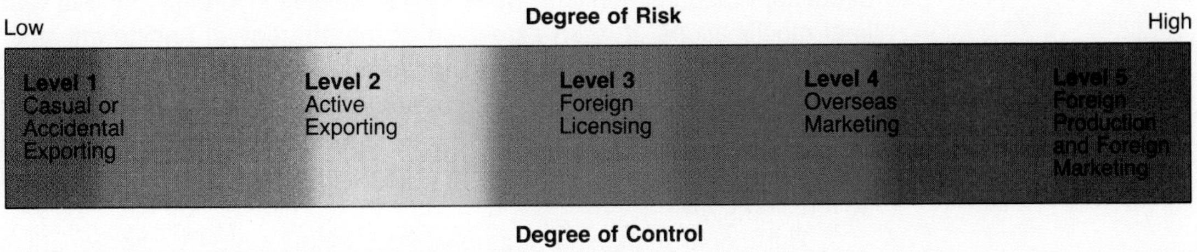

to get into a particular market. For instance, Hughes Tool Company of Houston has negotiated a licensing agreement that will provide drill bits to the People's Republic of China.

A firm that maintains a separate marketing or selling operation in a foreign country is involved in overseas marketing. Examples are foreign sales offices and overseas marketing subsidiaries. The product may be produced by domestic factories, foreign licensees, or contract manufacturers, but the company always directly controls foreign sales.

Foreign production and foreign marketing, the ultimate degree of company involvement in the international market arena, may be accomplished in the following ways:

1. The firm may set up its own production and marketing operation in the foreign country.

2.   It may acquire an existing firm in the country in which it will do business.

3.   It may form a joint venture, in which the risks, costs, and management of the foreign operation are shared with a partner who is usually a national of the host country.

Joint Venture
Agreement between business partners in two or more nations whereby the firms establish a foreign operation, sharing risks, costs, and management responsibilities with the other partner or partners who are usually citizens of the host country.

Recent joint ventures have involved a General Motors–Toyota agreement to manufacture a Toyota-designed subcompact in a Fremont, California, GM plant. McDonald's 350 Japanese restaurants involve a joint venture partnership. One suggestion of the Japanese partner was to change the firm's trademark character, known as Ronald McDonald in the United States, to Donald McDonald because it is easier for the Japanese to pronounce.[9]

Designing Marketing Mixes for International Markets

Marketing practices vary throughout the world. These differences must be taken into consideration when any firm decides to expand its marketing horizons to include foreign nations. A high illiteracy rate, for example, may substantially limit the types of advertising campaigns employed. Aggressive sales efforts may be regarded negatively in some foreign cultures. Business customs and traditions may restrict a firm's distribution strategy to certain marketing channels.

Evaluating Global Marketing Strategies

In an attempt to realize economies of scale from their production and marketing efforts, a number of firms approach international marketing as an extension of their domestic marketing efforts. This global marketing strategy is a direct application of domestic marketing strategies in foreign markets with minimal modifications. It is an extension of the strategy of undifferentiated marketing to other countries. The Japanese advertisement for Audemars Piguet watches in Figure 19.6 illustrates this approach. The firm's marketing strategy focuses upon product quality and the exclusive image of the expensive Swiss watch; the only marketing modification is a Japanese translation of the firm's advertising copy.

Global Marketing Strategy
Direct application of a domestic marketing strategy in foreign markets with little or no modifications.

But global marketing strategies may ignore marketplace variables that are likely to impact negatively upon a domestic marketing strategy. Executives at Grey Advertising, Inc., a large advertising agency with 88 offices worldwide, suggest that firms should ask themselves three questions before choosing a single global strategy. A negative answer to even one question indicates that such a strategy is likely to fail.

1.   *Has the market developed in the same way from country to country?*
       Grey notes that Kellogg's Pop-Tarts failed in Britain because toasters weren't widely used. The continued popularity of clotheslines in Europe similarly meant little demand for fabric softener sheets used in dryers.

2.   *Are the consumer targets similar in different nations?*
       Canon found that in advertising 35mm cameras in the United States, they had to appeal to people who are fearful about complex technological products. Many Japanese consumers, on the other hand, seek sophisticated, high-tech products.

3.   *Do consumers share the same wants and needs around the world?*
       In the United States, General Foods Corporation successfully positioned

Figure 19.6
Audemars Piguet: Following a Global Marketing Strategy

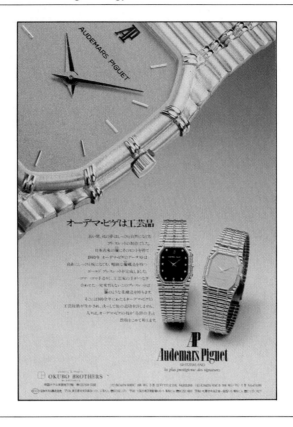

Source: Courtesy of Audemars Piguet.

Tang as a substitute for orange juice at breakfast but discovered that in France people drink little orange juice and almost none at breakfast. General Foods had to create a totally different advertising approach promoting Tang as a refreshment for any time of day.[10]

Consideration of each marketing strategy component is necessary to determine whether the differences that exist in markets and marketing practices overseas are sufficiently different from domestic marketing to require a unique marketing program for different markets.

Product Strategy

Although baseball may be known as an American pastime, Mizuno Corporation, of Osaka, Japan, has developed an innovative product strategy for the U.S. market. About 400 professional baseball players in the United States now use custom-fitted Mizuno baseball gloves. Mizuno imports leather from the United States, then tans, cures, and shapes it into a baseball glove that does not need to be broken in. Mizuno has spent $3 million on research and development of an entire line of baseball equipment. The line includes plexiglass catcher's masks, an electronic umpire-to-scoreboard relay system, strike-zone sensors, and electronic foul lines.[11]

Mizuno has chosen to offer an innovative product mix to the market-place, but sometimes existing products can be modified to meet consumer needs. Successful adaptation can significantly extend the market for a product. Sometimes the product itself has to be modified; in other cases, it is the packaging; in still others, it is the product's identification. Consider the many products that use the word *mist* as part of their name. But imagine the difficulty of marketing such a product in Germany where mist means "manure."

Alternative Product/Promotion Strategies for International Marketing

The marketer can choose from five alternative strategies in selecting the most appropriate product/promotion strategy for a specific foreign market. As Figure 19.7 indicates, the strategies revolve around whether to extend a domestic product and promotional strategy into international markets, or to adapt one or both to meet the unique requirements of the market.

The one-product, one-message strategy is typical of firms employing a global marketing strategy. The photograph in Figure 19.8 of the German couple enjoying Coca-Cola is typical of the firm's uniform approach in each market. This strategy permits economies of scale in production and marketing and a universally recognized product for consumers traveling from country to country.

Other strategies call for modification of the product, the promotional strategy, or both. While products such as bicycles, motorcycles, and outboard motors are primarily recreational vehicles in the United States, they may represent important transportation modes in other nations. Consequently, the promotional message may be adapted, even though the product remains unchanged. By contrast, a promotional theme such as Exxon's "Put a tiger in your tank" may be successfully used in dozens of nations, even though Exxon gasoline is reformulated to meet different weather conditions and varying engine specifications in different countries. In still other instances, both the product and the promotional message may require adaptation to meet unique needs of specific international markets. Marketers of coffee, such as Nescafé, develop different blends and different promotional campaigns to match consumer preferences in different countries.

The final strategy can be labeled invention. In such cases, the firm may decide to develop an entirely different product to take advantage of unique foreign market opportunities. For example, to match dissimilar foreign needs in developing nations, an appliance manufacturer might develop a hand-pow-

Figure 19.7
Alternative Product-Promotional Strategies

Product Strategy	Promotional Strategy	Example of Application of This Strategy
Same Product	Same Message	Wrigley's Gum, Coca-Cola, Eastman Kodak
Same Product	Different Message	Bicycles/Motorcycles, Outboard Motors
Different Product	Same Message	Campbell Soup, Exxon
Different Product	Different Message	Coffee, Clothing
Product Invention	New Message	Nonelectric Sewing Machine, Manually Operated Washing Machine

Source: Adapted from Warren Keagan, "Multinational Product Planning: Strategic Alternatives," *Journal of Marketing* (January 1969), pp. 58–62.

Figure 19.8
Coca-Cola in West Germany: Using a Global Marketing Strategy

Source: Courtesy of The Coca-Cola Company.

ered washing machine even though such products have been obsolete in the United States for many years.

Promotional Strategy

As these alternative strategies reveal, no one best product and promotional strategy for international marketing exists. In some cases, domestic promotional strategies will be extended to international markets. In other instances, substantial modifications or even an entirely different message will be required. The choice depends upon market characteristics, the product strategy employed, and the interaction of the other mix elements.

While effective personal selling continues to be vital in foreign markets, advertising has gained in importance. The wider availability of media such as radio and television has enhanced advertising's contribution to the overall promotional effort. However, many U.S. advertising approaches are not really adaptable overseas. Promotional strategies tend to be strictly regulated in many foreign marketplaces.

Distribution Strategy

Distribution is a vital aspect of overseas marketing. Proper channels must be set up and extensive physical distribution problems handled. Transportation systems and warehousing facilities may be unavailable or of poor quality. International marketers must adapt speedily and efficiently to these situations if they are to profit from overseas sales.

Distribution decisions involve a two-step sequence. First, the firm must make decisions concerning its method of entry into foreign markets. Will a foreign trade intermediary such as an export trading company be used? In Japan, distribution decisions frequently involve such general trading companies as Mitsubishi, Mitsui, C. Itoh, Marubeni, Sumitoma, and Inssho-Iwai. The nine major Japanese trading companies account for 50 percent of total Japanese exports and 60 percent of imports.

Powerful Japanese trading companies *(sogo shosha)* stand ready to help U.S. exports enter the Japanese market. . . . They have enormous capabilities in international trade, in that they collect and process information, and organize business projects. However, *sogo shosha* generally have dealt in bulk commodities; they only recently have started to emphasize consumer goods imports and now are organizing operations aimed at handling such goods, which normally involve small lot shipments of a great variety of merchandise.[12]

The second decision involves how to distribute the product within the foreign market once an appropriate channel has been chosen to gain entry into that market. The choice of whether the firm should use direct or indirect channels and the degree of intensity of market coverage must be made.

Sears, one of the most effective retailers in the United States, met its match in Seibu, a large Japanese retailer with 600 outlets. So Sears turned to Seibu to sell its catalog merchandise in Japan.

Nissan automobiles are the leading seller in oil-rich Saudi Arabia, where gasoline sells for 23 to 25 cents per gallon. Its large market share is credited to the excellent organization of local distributors who were recruited in the early 1960s. The Japanese firm sought out Saudi entrepreneurs who had sufficient investment capital and who were skilled managers and marketers. The strategy was obviously effective.

Pricing Strategy

Pricing in foreign markets can be a critical ingredient in overall marketing strategy. Pricing practices in overseas markets are subject to considerable competitive, economic, political, and legal constraints. International marketing managers must clearly understand these requirements if they are to succeed.

The most significant development in pricing strategy for international marketing has been the emergence of commodity marketing organizations that seek to control prices through collective action. OPEC (the Organization of Petroleum Exporting Countries) is the best example of these collective export organizations, but a variety of others exist.

The Multinational Corporation

Switzerland's Nestlé now operates in over 50 markets with 140,000 employees and 280 plants. Sales total approximately $13 billion. Nestlé gets 40 percent of its revenue from Europe, 28 percent from Third World nations, and the remainder primarily from the United States and Japan.

A **multinational corporation** is a firm that has significant operations and marketing activities outside its home country. Examples of multinationals in-

Multinational Corporation
Company that operates in several nations and literally views the world as its market.

clude General Electric, Siemens, and Mitsubishi in the heavy electrical equipment industry; Caterpillar and Komatsu in large construction equipment; and Timex, Seiko, and Citizen in watches. Although the United States ranks first in the number of multinational corporations, its lead has diminished in the past two decades. Today only 40 percent of the world's largest corporations are based in the United States, down from 58 percent in 1971 and 67 percent in 1963. The second most popular home base for multinational marketers is Japan, followed by Great Britain, Germany, and France.

Hewlett-Packard provides an illustration of how a multinational firm can operate effectively. The California-based electronics company sells nearly as much abroad as it does in the United States. How does Hewlett-Packard do it? The company encourages its European subsidiaries to operate autonomously with European management. Subsidiaries are told to use local technical talent to produce export products. Hewlett-Packard's German subsidiary has been particularly successful, deriving more than half of its revenues from non-German markets. Some German executives now manage Hewlett-Packard operations in California.

Multinationals have been the subject of considerable public scrutiny both in the United States and abroad. Accusations ranging from excess market channel control to exploitation and bribery have been levied on occasion. Some nations—Australia and Canada, for example—have expressed concern about the multinationals' domination of some domestic markets. Similar complaints have been voiced in the United States about the inroads made by Japanese automobile firms. While criticism of multinational practices is likely to continue, it is obvious that multinational corporations have become fixtures in the international marketplace.

Multinational Economic Integration and World Marketing

A noticeable trend toward multinational economic integration has developed since the end of World War II. The Common Market, or European Economic Community (EEC), is the best known multinational economic community.

Multinational economic integration can be set up in several ways. The simplest approach is a free trade area, where participating nations agree to free trade of goods among themselves. All tariffs and trade restrictions are abolished between the nations involved. A customs union establishes a free trade area plus a uniform tariff for trade with nonmember nations. The EEC is the best example of a customs union. A true common market or economic union involves a customs union and also seeks to bring all government regulations affecting trade into agreement. The EEC has been moving in the direction of an economic union.

Multinational economic communities have played a significant part in international business. U.S. firms invested heavily in Western Europe in the 1960s basically because of the attraction of larger markets offered by the EEC. Such multinational economic integration is forcing management of international firms throughout the world to adapt their operations abroad.

The United States as a Market for International Marketers

The United States has become an increasingly inviting target for foreign marketers. It has a large population, high levels of discretionary income, political stability, an attitude generally favorable to foreign investment, and economic

Figure 19.9
U.S. Goods and Services Produced by Foreign-Owned Companies

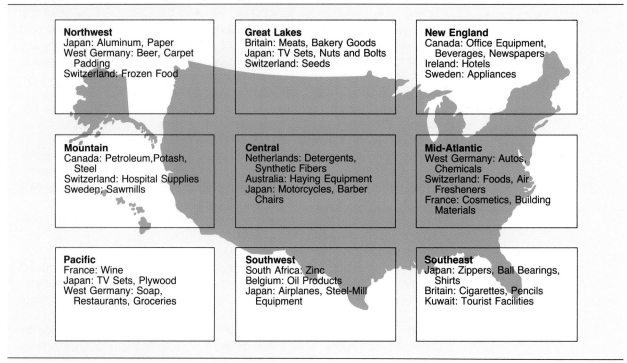

Northwest
Japan: Aluminum, Paper
West Germany: Beer, Carpet
    Padding
Switzerland: Frozen Food

Great Lakes
Britain: Meats, Bakery Goods
Japan: TV Sets, Nuts and Bolts
Switzerland: Seeds

New England
Canada: Office Equipment,
    Beverages, Newspapers
Ireland: Hotels
Sweden: Appliances

Mountain
Canada: Petroleum, Potash,
    Steel
Switzerland: Hospital Supplies
Sweden: Sawmills

Central
Netherlands: Detergents,
    Synthetic Fibers
Australia: Haying Equipment
Japan: Motorcycles, Barber
    Chairs

Mid-Atlantic
West Germany: Autos,
    Chemicals
Switzerland: Foods, Air
    Fresheners
France: Cosmetics, Building
    Materials

Pacific
France: Wine
Japan: TV Sets, Plywood
West Germany: Soap,
    Restaurants, Groceries

Southwest
South Africa: Zinc
Belgium: Oil Products
Japan: Airplanes, Steel-Mill
    Equipment

Southeast
Japan: Zippers, Ball Bearings,
    Shirts
Britain: Cigarettes, Pencils
Kuwait: Tourist Facilities

Source: "Foreign Firms: Covering the U.S." Reprinted from *U.S. News & World Report*
(July 24, 1978), p. 54. Copyright 1978, U.S. News & World Report, Inc.

ills that are relatively controlled in comparison to those in many other countries. Figure 19.9 shows U.S. goods and services produced by foreign-owned companies.

A number of foreign-owned competitors have found the United States an attractive market. The retailing industry has been a recent market target of foreign companies. All of the following U.S. retailers are owned in full or in part by an overseas firm: A&P (Germany), Grand Union (France), Gimbel Brothers (United Kingdom), Fed Mart (Germany), Bi-Lo (Netherlands), Kohl (United Kingdom), Fuir's (Germany), Dillard Department Stores (Netherlands), and Winn's Stores (Germany).

Some buyers have shown a preference for foreign products over the products of domestic firms. Foreign sports cars, English china, and French wine all hold sizable shares of the U.S. market. Some foreign products, such as Porsche sports cars, are sold in the United States because of the quality image. Others sell on the basis of price advantage over domestic competition.

U.S. marketers must expect to face substantial foreign competition in the years ahead. The United States' high level of buying power is sure to continue its considerable appeal abroad, and the reduction of trade barriers and expanded international marketing appear to be long-run trends. U.S. marketers no longer face the choice of whether to compete with foreign firms; their continued long-term success depends to a great extent on their ability to compete.

Summary

Global marketing has become increasingly important to the United States. Many U.S. firms depend on their ability to market their goods abroad, while others depend on buying raw materials from other countries.

Competing in overseas markets is often considerably different from competing in domestic markets. Market size, buyer behavior, and marketing practices may all differ. International marketers may have to make significant adaptations in their product, distribution, promotional, and pricing strategies to fit different markets abroad.

Several levels of involvement in international marketing can be identified: casual or accidental exporting, active exporting, foreign licensing, overseas marketing, and foreign production and foreign marketing. The world's largest firms are usually multinational in their orientation. Such companies operate in several countries and view the world as their market.

Various environmental factors that can influence international marketing strategy include cultural, economic, and societal factors; various trade restrictions; and political and legal factors.

Since the end of World War II, there has been a noticeable trend toward multinational economic integration. Three basic formats for integration are free trade areas, customs unions, and common markets.

The United States is now viewed as an attractive market for marketers from abroad. U.S. firms can expect to face growing foreign competition in the domestic market.

Solving the Stop-Action Case

Dresser Industries

Convinced that it had no choice but to comply with the French directive, Dresser-France shipped three completed compressors to the Soviet Union from Le Havre, France, on August 26, 1982. Within 35 minutes of this action, the U.S. government placed temporary trade sanctions on Dresser-France, prohibiting the company from importing goods or services from the United States. Although these sanctions would not affect the firm's ability to complete the Soviet order for the additional compressors, they would make it impossible for the company to continue its future operations. Without the necessary technological and engineering assistance it receives from its U.S. parent, Dresser-France would be forced to shut down.

Photo Source: "The Nasty Pipeline Mess: Any Way Out?" Reprinted from *U.S. News & World Report* (September 13, 1982), p. 28. Copyright 1982 U.S. News & World Report, Inc.

In a motion to the Department of Commerce's International Trade Administration to set aside the denial order, Dresser-France described its plight in this way: ". . . .The prospects for Dresser-France are bleak. Under normal circumstances, the prospect of such severe injury might be expected to ensure strict export control compliance. Such is not the case here. So long as the French requisition order remains in effect, a matter en-

(continued)

tirely beyond the control of Dresser-France, it is quite apparent that the performance of the Soviet contract will go through to its completion, whatever the cost, including even the bankruptcy or forced sale of the company. The likely effect of the denial order on Dresser-France is that the work on the Soviet contract will be carried through to completion, whereas the balance of its business operations will be in severe jeopardy."

Realizing that the issue was escalating into a full-scale confrontation with the NATO allies, who were encouraging European firms to defy the U.S. ban on shipping embargoed goods to the Soviet Union, the Reagan Administration finally agreed to a face-saving compromise. In exchange for relaxing the embargo and allowing Dresser-France to continue its ties with its U.S. parent, Washington received a commitment from its European allies to tighten future technology transfers to the Soviet Union.

Although Dresser-France came away from the confrontation with its business intact, the experience added even more recognition to the precarious nature of its position as a multinational marketer with ties to two countries. It also drove home the importance of environmental factors in the success of an international marketing mix. "These are uncharted waters," said Washington attorney Stanley Marcuss. "The United States is asserting extraterritorial rights that no foreign government has ever asserted over us."

Sources: Quotation in paragraph two is from *Motion to Vacate Temporary Denial of Export Privileges Before the United States Department of Commerce International Trade Administration* (August 27, 1982), pp. 14–15. Marcuss quotation in paragraph four is from Leslie H. Gelb, "Pipeline: An Impasse with No End in Sight," *New York Times* (August 31, 1982), p. D1.

Questions for Discussion

1. Why is international marketing important to U.S. firms? To the U.S. economy?

2. Comment on the following statement: It is sometimes dangerous for a firm to attempt to export its marketing strategy.

3. What types of products are most often marketed abroad by U.S. firms?

4. In what ways is the international marketing mix likely to be different from a marketing mix used in the domestic country?

5. Describe the environment for international marketing.

6. Identify the various levels of involvement in international marketing.

7. Give an example—hypothetical or actual—of a firm operating at each level of international marketing:
   a. Casual or accidental exporting
   b. Active exporting
   c. Foreign licensing
   d. Overseas marketing
   e. Foreign production and foreign marketing

8. Explain how trade restrictions may be employed to restrict or to stimulate international marketing activities.

9. Distinguish between import quotas and embargoes.

10. Explain the international marketing practice of dumping. Why does dumping sometimes occur?

11. Identify and briefly explain the three basic formats for economic integration.

12. Relate specific international environmental considerations to each of the following aspects of a firm's marketing mix:
    a. Brands and warranties
    b. Advertising
    c. Distribution channels
    d. Discounts to marketing intermediaries
    e. Use of comparative advertising

13. Outline the basic premises behind the operation of a multinational corporation. Why do you think the term has a negative connotation?

14. Describe the existing trends in world population. How do these trends affect international marketing?

15. Describe the types of adaptations that international business forces firms to make in their marketing strategies.

16. What is your opinion of existing U.S. policy toward dumping?

17. Satra Corporation of New York imports the Lada—a Soviet-built car—into the United States. What type of marketing strategy would you suggest Satra use? What problems do you expect the importer to encounter?

18. Do you agree with the general movement toward reduced trade restrictions among nations? Explain.

19. Why is the United States such an attractive market target for foreign markets? What does this mean for U.S. firms?

20. Some people argue that foreign investment in the United States should be limited. Would you agree with a plan that would limit such investment in a particular firm to some specified amount? Explain.

Case: Snow-Way International

International marketing saved Jim Blau's company. His firm, Snow-Way International, of Milwaukee, Wisconsin, marketed a $1,300 snowplow designed to be attached to subcompact, front-wheel-drive cars like the Volkswagen Rabbit. However, a relatively snow-free winter made Blau realize the need to broaden his consumer base.

"We had to have a broader marketing base, so I took a $10,000 gamble. I flew to a trade show in Germany, taking a plow with me. I spent $2,000 for a booth. I didn't know what to expect."

He wasn't in doubt for long. Blau's patented design, which does not require remodeling of a car's front end, was an instant success. "The reception was wild," he said. "The plow was perfect for the European market, fitting in with the narrow streets. They had never seen anything like it." After he took $150,000 in orders, and even sold the plow on display, local auto dealers flocked to his hotel room. Blau, a Subaru and Volvo dealer himself, signed up eleven distributors.

Unfortunately, Blau returned to the U.S. without the vaguest idea of how to ship those orders. "I started picking brains," he said. He called friends who had export experience, the local Commerce Department office for advice and recommendations, and several freight forwarders. They all helped.

Today Blau's snowplows are sold from Australia, where they clear mudslides, to Saudi Arabia, where they are used to clear sand from driveways. Foreign sales were such a snap—"Using containers, it is as easy and inexpensive ($100) to ship a plow to Switzerland as to Portland," said Blau—that he now prefers the overseas business. About 75 percent of Snow-Way's estimated $2 million annual revenues came as a result of exports.

"It's a cleaner business. You get your money up front with the letter of credit, no worries about collections," said Blau, who spent years tinkering with

Source: "Snowplows to Saudis," *Forbes* (April 13, 1981), p. 84. Reprinted by permission.

other projects, including less than instant winners, such as a kit to convert motorcycles into snowmobiles, before hitting upon the successful snowplow.

He has little time to tinker these days. A recent free ad in a Commerce Department magazine produced an 8-inch stack of inquiries. Snow-Way's six employees (25 subcontractors produce parts for the plow) are hard pressed to handle the volume of incoming mail and outgoing shipments. "I'm keeping 200 to 300 people busy," said Blau, still a little awed at the profitable results of that desperation trip to Germany.

Questions

1. Relate Snow-Way International's current operations to the levels of involvement in international marketing. What is necessary for them to move to the next level?

2. How could government assistance be used to increase international marketing by other small firms? What barriers exist to increasing the level of such assistance?

3. Is Snow-Way International implementing a global marketing strategy? Discuss the merits and weaknesses of their current marketing activities.

Computer Applications

A total of 16 analytical techniques have been introduced in the Computer Applications sections of previous chapters. These techniques have been applied to decisions involving large and small firms; industrial marketers and consumer-goods firms; service producers, retailers, and wholesaling intermediaries; profit-seeking firms and non-profit organizations. Versatility of these analytical techniques in solving different types of marketing problems has been demonstrated by the application of *decision*

tree analysis (menu item 2) in Chapters 2 and 10 and the *expected net profit (ENP)* technique for evaluation of competitive bids (menu item 7) in Chapters 7 and 18.

While this chapter focuses on global dimensions of marketing and compares domestic and international marketing decisions, the problems and decisions concerning international market target analysis and appropriate blending of marketing mix elements can benefit from the application of the analytical techniques discussed earlier for use by domestic marketers. The following problems can be solved by applying five techniques introduced in earlier chapters.

Directions: Use menu item 2 titled "Decision Tree Analysis" to solve Problem 1. Use menu item 3 titled "Sales Forecasting" to solve Problem 2. Use menu item 8 titled "Return on Investment" to solve Problem 3. Use menu item 10 titled "Markups" to solve Problem 4. Use menu item 12 titled "Economic Order Quantity" to solve Problem 5.

Problem 1 Omaha Standard Industries is currently involved in international marketing through a licensing agreement signed five years ago with Societé Europe, Ltd. The agreement expires at the end of this year, and the firm's management is considering the establishment of its own international marketing organization. Such a move would be particularly profitable if demand continues to grow for the firm's products. The following international demand estimates have been developed to aid the marketing decision makers at Omaha Standard:

High Demand:	Probability = 60 percent
Moderate Demand:	Probability = 40 percent

Forecasts for next year total $40 million in sales and a 10 percent earnings rate for a high demand environment if

the licensing agreement is renewed, and $30 million in sales and an 8 percent earnings rate for a moderate demand environment with the licensing agreement. By contrast, should Omaha Standard establish its own international marketing organization and high demand occur next year, sales are expected to rise to $70 million and earnings to 8 percent of sales. However, should a moderate demand environment exist, the cost of the new marketing organization would reduce profits to 2 percent of estimated sales of $30 million.

a.   Review the discussion of decision tree analysis on page 58. Then use menu item 2 titled "Decision Tree Analysis" to recommend a course of action for Omaha Standard Industries.

b.   Would your recommendation change if the likelihood of high demand were reduced to 50 percent?

Problem 2 International marketing is a major component of the total corporate sales and profits for Los Angeles-based International Brands. One geographical region that has enjoyed sustained growth since 1978 is the Far East Division. Annual sales revenues for this division are shown below:

1978	$ 50 million
1979	110 million
1980	170 million
1981	290 million
1982	310 million
1983	360 million
1984	480 million
1985	610 million
1986	750 million

Review the discussion on page 87 of sales forecasting using trend extension. Then use menu item 3 titled "Sales Forecasting" to forecast International Brands' sales revenues for 1987 and 1988.

Problem 3 Heidrich Manufacturers, of Oshkosh, Wisconsin, is considering the introduction of its product line in Australia. The firm's marketers estimate that sales of $18 million can be achieved, generating a profit of $3 million. However, the cost estimates for entering the Australian market amount to $4 million.

Review the discussion of the return on investment (ROI) model on page 235. Then use menu item 8 titled "Return on Investment" to determine the ROI associated with entering the Australian market.

Problem 4 In his article "Cumbersome Japanese Distribution System Stumps U.S. Concerns," author William D. Harley provides this description:

Consider a can of Del Monte peach halves and its Japanese odyssey. The peaches land in Yokohama at 26 cents a can. Immediately, customs and handling charges add nine cents to the price. Then the importer sticks on a bit more than a penny. He sells it to a wholesaler, who adds another three cents. The wholesaler sells it to another wholesaler, who adds a further two cents. He sells it to a grocery store, which adds an additional 11 cents. The retail price: 52 cents a can. . . .[1]

a.   Review the discussion of markups on page 347. Then use menu item 10 titled "Markups" to determine the markup percentage on selling price and the markup percentage on cost for the can of peaches.
b.   What is the markup percentage on selling price for the retailer in this example?

[1]Quoted in Louis E. Boone and James C. Johnson, *Marketing Channels*, 2nd ed. (Tulsa, Okla.: PennWell Books, 1977), p. 340.

Problem 5 The manager of the Tokyo office of Orion Products Corporation wants to calculate the economic order quantity for placing orders with the firm's home office and warehousing facility in St. Louis. Each product ordered costs the Tokyo office $40 and must be ordered in multiples of one dozen. Order placement costs total $50. Annual sales total 3,500 units, and inventory carrying costs are 25 percent.

Review the discussion of the economic order quantity (EOQ) model on pages 366 and 372. Then use menu item 12 titled "Economic Order Quantity" to determine the EOQ for the Tokyo office.

20 | Societal Issues and Nonprofit Applications

Key Terms

consumerism
consumer rights
marketing ethics
social responsibility
ecology
planned obsolescence
pollution
recycling
nonprofit organization
broadening concept
person marketing
idea marketing
organization marketing

Learning Goals

1. To describe the contemporary environment of marketing
2. To explain the need for better measures of marketing performance
3. To identify the three major current societal issues in marketing
4. To identify the primary characteristics of nonprofit organizations that distinguish them from profit-seeking organizations
5. To describe the evolution of the broadening concept
6. To explain the types of nonprofit organizations
7. To explain how a marketing mix might be developed in a nonprofit setting

Photo Source: Courtesy of St. Joseph Hospital.

Stop-Action Case

St. Joseph Hospital

Like many other community hospitals across the nation, St. Joseph Hospital, of Flint, Michigan, saw its patient load drop during the early 1980s. This decline was especially acute in the area of obstetrical services. During the mid-1970s, more babies were delivered at St. Joseph than at any other hospital in Flint. By 1980, however, the number of recorded births had dropped to 1,300—well below the number needed to meet minimum federal guidelines. Hospital administrators were faced with the dilemma of either increasing the number of babies born at their hospital to at least 1,500 a year or closing their obstetrical unit to comply with the federal government's directive to reduce the number of unneeded community hospital beds.

Closing the unit or consolidating it with the obstetrical unit of another hospital would have a serious adverse impact on the entire St. Joseph medical system. Hospital administrators considered the obstetrical unit a key element in their family-practice and medical-education programs. Moreover, according to a hospital report, "The hospital's board felt a special responsibility to continue providing obstetrical care based upon its philosophies and mission as the only religiously sponsored hospital in the community."

To discover why St. Joseph was losing more than its share of the market, hospital officials commissioned an extensive marketing research study. Although patients using the obstetrical facility cited significant strengths (many referred to the hospital as the place they always used when they needed health services—a "family" hospital), they also complained about unappealing physical facilities, lack of rest and privacy during their hospital stay, poor food, lack of consideration for spouses, and an inadequate physician referral system. Hospital administrators also realized that price was a key factor in the reduced patient load. Many families in Flint simply could not afford St. Joseph's standard labor and delivery fees.

To attract larger numbers of expectant mothers, St. Joseph's marketing director had to satisfy these complaints and offer prospective patients additional incentives they could not obtain at other hospitals.

Assignment: Use the materials in Chapter 20 to recommend a course of action for St. Joseph Hospital.

Source: Information on the St. Joseph Hospital marketing program was provided by Dennis Archambault, manager of marketing communications at St. Joseph. Additional information from *Obstetrical Services Marketing* (Flint, Michigan: St. Joseph Hospital, n.d.), p. 1.

Chapter Overview _____

This chapter examines two of the most significant factors in today's economy as marketing moves toward the final decade of the twentieth century. First, there is the expanded role of marketing within the societal context. People simply expect more of marketers than they did a few decades ago. Secondly, marketing's pervasive application has expanded into many nontraditional areas.

It should be clear by now that the marketing decision maker develops a marketing mix based on an analysis of a specified market target and the environmental factors that affect the consumer and the marketing mix. Chapter 2 outlined the key environmental considerations from that perspective.

There is another environmental dimension that goes beyond the previous considerations—the role that marketing plays in society itself and the consequent effects and responsibilities of marketing activities. Marketing's relationship to society in general and to various public issues is subject to constant scrutiny by the public. It may, in fact, be reasonably argued that marketing typically mirrors changes in the entire business environment. Because marketing is the final interface between the business enterprise and the society in which it operates, marketers often carry much of the responsibility for dealing with various social issues affecting their firms.

The first part of this chapter provides a framework within which the marketing system can be constructively evaluated. The second part of Chapter 20 analyzes the extension of marketing concepts and practices to such nontraditional areas as nonprofit organizations, political candidates and celebrities, and the marketing of ideas and causes. In Chapter 1, marketing was defined as the process of planning and executing the conception, pricing, promotion, and distribution of ideas, goods, and services to create exchanges that satisfy individual and organizational objectives. Although much of the text concentrated on organizations that operate for profit, the activities of the San Diego Zoo and St. Joseph Hospital are as representative of modern marketing activities as the marketing programs of Pizza Hut, Kmart, and Eastern Airlines. The definition of marketing encompasses both nonprofit and profit-seeking organizations.

The Contemporary Environment of Marketing _____

Marketing operates in an environment external to the firm. It reacts to its environment and is, in turn, acted upon by it. These environmental relationships exist with customers, employees, the government, vendors, and society as a whole. While they are often a product of the exchange process, these relationships are coincidental to the primary sales and distribution functions of marketing.

External relationships form the basis of the societal issues confronting contemporary marketing. Marketing's relationship to its external environment has a significant effect on the relative degree of success achieved by the firm. Marketing must continually find new ways to deal with the social issues facing our competitive system.

Historically, marketing has neglected some environmental relationships. Various regulations and license requirements have been enacted to limit door-to-door selling, which had become excessive in some areas. The government has banned some children's toys because they were unsafe.

The Federal Trade Commission has accused numerous firms of using misleading advertising and, as discussed in Chapter 2, has occasionally required them to use corrective advertising to inform consumers of the misrepresentation. For 50 years, Warner-Lambert promoted Listerine mouthwash as a cold and sore-throat remedy. During the 1970s, the FTC ruled that the product would not relieve sore throats or colds and required the firm to spend more than $10 million in advertising to make the statement "Listerine will not help prevent colds or lessen their severity."

The competitive marketing system is a product of our drive for materialism, but it is important to note that materialism developed from society itself. Most U.S. culture, with its acceptance of the work ethic, has viewed the acquisition of wealth favorably. The motto of this philosophy seems to be "More equals better." A better life has been defined in terms of more physical possessions, although that definition may be changing.

Evaluating the Quality of Life

One theme runs through the arguments of marketing's critics: materialism (as exemplified by the competitive marketing system) is concerned only with the quantities of life and ignores the quality aspect. Traditionally, a firm was considered socially responsible in the community if it provided employment to its residents, thereby contributing to its economic base. Employment, wages, bank deposits, and profits—the traditional measures of societal contributions—are quantity indicators. But what about air, water, and cultural pollution? The boredom and isolation of mass assembly lines? The depletion of natural resources? The charges of neglect in these areas go largely unanswered simply because we have not developed reliable indices to measure a firm's contribution to the quality of life.

An Indictment of the Competitive Marketing System

An indictment of the competitive marketing system would contain at least the following:

1. Marketing costs are too high.
2. The marketing system is inefficient.
3. Marketers (the business system) are guilty of collusion and price fixing.
4. Product quality and service are poor.
5. Consumers receive incomplete and/or false and misleading information.
6. The marketing system has produced health and safety hazards.
7. Unwanted and unnecessary products are promoted to those who least need them.

Almost anyone could cite specific examples where these charges have been proven. Because each of us has a somewhat different set of values, it should be recognized that we all evaluate the performance of the marketing system we experience within our own frames of reference.

Bearing this in mind and taking the system as a whole, we can evaluate the success or failure of the competitive marketing system in serving the needs of consumers. Most of us will likely arrive at the uncomfortable and not entirely satisfying conclusion that the system usually works quite adequately, although there are some aspects of it that we would like to see changed.

Current Issues in Marketing

Marketing faces many diverse social issues. The current issues in marketing can be divided into three major subjects: consumerism, marketing ethics, and social responsibility. While the overlap and classification problems are obvious, the framework provides a foundation for systematically studying the issues.

Consumerism

Consumerism
Social force within the environment designed to aid and protect the consumer by exerting legal, moral, and economic pressure on business and government.

Despite factors that tend to inhibit development of strong consumer groups, business practices and changing societal values have led to the consumerism movement. Today, everyone—marketers, industry, government, and the public—is acutely aware of the impact of consumerism on the nation's economy and general well-being. Consumerism has been defined as a social force within the environment designed to aid and protect the consumer by exerting legal, moral, and economic pressure on business.[1] Professors George Day and David Aaker argue that consumerism includes "the widening range of activities of government, business, and independent organizations that are designed to protect individuals from practices that infringe upon their rights as consumers."[2] It is a societal demand that organizations apply the marketing concept.

The Consumer's Rights

Consumer Rights
As stated by President John F. Kennedy in 1962, the consumer should have the following rights: to choose freely, to be informed, to be heard, and to be safe.

Not all consumer demands are met. A competitive marketing system is based upon the individualistic behavior of competing firms. Our economic system requires that reasonable profit objectives be achieved. Business cannot meet all consumer demands if it is to generate the profits necessary to remain viable. This selection process is one of the most difficult dilemmas facing society today. Given these constraints, what should the consumer have the right to expect from the competitive marketing system?

The most frequently quoted statement of consumer rights was made by President John F. Kennedy in 1962. While it was not a definitive statement, it is a good rule of thumb to explain basic consumer rights:

1. The right to choose freely
2. The right to be informed
3. The right to be heard
4. The right to be safe

These rights, described in Figure 20.1, have formed the conceptual framework of much of the consumer legislation passed in the last two decades. However, the question of how best to guarantee these rights remains unanswered.

Marketing Ethics

Marketing Ethics
The marketer's standards of conduct and moral values.

Environmental considerations have led to increased attention on the subject of marketing ethics. Marketing ethics are the marketer's standards of conduct and moral values. They are concerned with matters of right and wrong: the decision of the individual and the firm to do what is morally right. A discussion

Figure 20.1
Four Consumer Rights

of marketing ethics highlights the types of problems faced by individuals in their role as marketers. Such problems must be considered before we suggest possible improvements in the marketing system.

People develop standards of ethical behavior based upon their own systems of values. Their individual ethics help them deal with the various ethical questions in their personal lives. However, when they are put into a work situation, a serious conflict may materialize. Individual ethics may differ from the organizational ethics of the employer. An individual may believe that industry participation in developing a recycling program for industrial waste is highly desirable, but the person's firm may take the position that such a venture would be unprofitable. Similar conflicts are not difficult to imagine.

How can these conflicts be resolved? The development of and adherence to a professional ethic may provide a third basis of authority. This ethic should be based on a concept of professionalism that transcends both organizational and individual ethics. It depends on the existence of a professional peer association that can exercise collective sanctions over a marketer's individual behavior.

A variety of ethical problems face the marketer every day. While promotional matters have received the greatest attention recently, ethical questions concerning the research function, product management, channel strategy, and pricing also arise.

Ethical Problems in Marketing Research

Marketing research has been castigated because of its alleged invasion of personal privacy. Citizens of today's urban, mechanized society seek individual identity to a greater degree. Personal privacy is important to most consum-

Figure 20.2
A Marketing Code of Ethics

Code of Conduct

1. Deceptive or Unlawful Consumer Practices
No member company of the Association shall engage in any deceptive or unlawful consumer practice.

2. Products or Services
The offer of products or services for sale by member companies of the Association shall be accurate and truthful as to price, grade, quality, make, value, performance, quantity, currency of model, and availability.

3. Terms of Sale
A written order or receipt shall be delivered to the customer at the time of sale, which sets forth in language that is clear and free of ambiguity:

    a. all the terms and conditions of sale, with specification of the total amount the customer will be required to pay, including all interest, service charges, and fees, and other costs and expenses as required by federal and state law;
    b. the name and address of the salesperson or the member firm represented.

4. Warranties and Guarantees
The terms of any warranty or guarantee offered by the seller in connection with the sale shall be furnished to the buyer in a manner that fully conforms to federal and state warranty and guarantee laws and regulations. The manufacturer, distributor, and/or seller shall fully and promptly perform in accordance with the terms of all warranties and guarantees offered to consumers.

5. Pyramid Schemes
For the purpose of this Code, pyramid or endless chain schemes shall be considered consumer transactions actionable under this Code. The Code Administrator shall determine whether such pyramid or endless chain schemes constitute a violation of this Code in accordance with applicable federal, state, and/or local law or regulation.

Source: Reprinted courtesy of Direct Selling Association, 1730 M Street, N.W., Washington, D.C. 20036.

ers and has, therefore, become a public issue. Because direct salespeople are guests in the homes of their customers, the members of the Direct Selling Association felt it appropriate that their industry draw up a Code of Ethics that demanded adherence to high standards of marketplace ethics and courtesy. The DSA Code, shown in Figure 20.2, is enforced by a set of procedures for violations. In the case of serious or repeated code violations, the DSA can demand voluntary contributions of as much as $500 and can even report probable law violations to the appropriate government agency.

Today, the average person's name and some part of his or her life appear in an estimated 39 federal, state, and local-government data banks plus an additional 40 private-sector files. On a typical day, every name passes from one computer to another five times. Agencies with such files include selective service (11 million young men), the Medical Information Bureau (12 million patients), private investigative agencies (14 million reports annually), credit bureaus (150 million subjects), state motor-vehicle agencies (152 million licensed drivers), and various U.S. government agencies (3.8 billion names).[3]

Ethical Problems in Product Strategy

Product quality, planned obsolescence, brand similarity, and packaging questions are significant concerns of consumers, management, and governments. Competitive pressures have forced marketers into packaging practices that may be considered misleading, deceptive, and/or unethical in some quarters. Larger-than-necessary packages are used to gain shelf space and customer exposure in the supermarket. Odd-size packages make price comparisons difficult. Bottles with concave bottoms give the impression that they contain more liquid than is actually the case. The real question seems to be whether these practices can be justified in the name of competition. Growing regulatory mandates appear to be narrowing the range of discretion in this area.

Ethical Problems in Distribution Strategy

A firm's channel strategy is required to deal with two kinds of ethical questions:

1.   What is the appropriate degree of control over the channel?
2.   Should a company distribute its products in marginally profitable outlets that have no alternative source of supply?

The question of control typically arises in the relationship between a manufacturer and franchised dealers. Should an automobile dealership, a gas station, or a fast-food outlet be required to purchase parts, materials, and supplementary services from the parent organization? What is the proper degree of control in the channel of distribution?

Furthermore, should marketers serve unsatisfied market segments even if the profit potential is slight? What is marketing's ethical responsibility to serve retail stores in low-income areas, users of limited amounts of the firm's product, or a declining rural market?

These problems are difficult to resolve because they often involve individuals rather than broad segments of the general public. An important first step would be to assure that channel policies are enforced on a consistent basis.

Ethical Problems in Promotional Strategy

Promotion is the component of the marketing mix where the majority of ethical questions arise. Personal selling has always been the target of ethically based criticism. Early traders, pack peddlers, greeters, drummers, and the twentieth century used-car salesperson, for example, have all been accused of marketing malpractice ranging from exaggerating product merits to outright deceit. Gifts, bribes, and the like were identified as the primary ethical abuses in studies conducted in 1961 and 1976.[4]

Advertising, however, is even more maligned than the salesperson. It is impersonal and hence easier to criticize. In fact, a study by the American Association of Advertising Agencies showed that advertising ranked second (along with clothing and fashion) in a list of "things in life that we enjoy complaining about but we may not really be serious about our complaints."[5]

While this study may suggest that much of the criticism of advertising is overstated, there is ample evidence and legitimate concern regarding advertising. Charges of overselling, uses of fear-based advertising messages (of social rejection, of growing old), sexism, and the like are common.

The portrayal of women in advertising has been of particular concern to marketers. Too often, it is argued, women have been portrayed as frivolous individuals or assigned stereotyped housewife roles in radio and television commercials and other media. Advertisers are making a concerted effort to show women in varied situations, especially in nontraditional work roles, such

Figure 20.3
Award-Winning Advertisement Featuring Nontraditional Role for Women

as bus drivers, bank officers, and heavy equipment operators. Every year the Manhattan-based Women Against Pornography awards a plastic pig to advertisements they consider offensive. This dubious award was recently given to a Gillette Daisy razor ad showing a policewoman in hot pants dancing out of her precinct house. The group honored the *FORTUNE* advertisement shown in Figure 20.3 portraying a girl baseball player determined to be a winner for its promotion of "realistic and positive images of women."[6]

Another ethical concern surrounds advertising to children. Some critics fear that television advertising exerts an undue influence on children. They believe children are easily influenced by toy, cereal, and snack-food commercials. Correspondingly, there is the assumption that children then exert substantial pressure on their parents to acquire these items. In recognition of this concern, the Canadian Association of Broadcasters has formulated a comprehensive broadcast code restricting advertising to children. No similar code exists in the United States.

Ethical Problems in Pricing

Pricing is probably the most regulated aspect of a firm's marketing strategy. As a result, most unethical price behavior is also illegal. When asked to identify unethical practices they wanted eliminated, fewer executives specified issues such as price collusion, price discrimination, and unfair pricing in a 1976 survey than a similar group had in a 1961 study. This suggests that tighter government regulations exist in these areas now than in the past.[7]

There are, however, some gray areas in the matter of pricing ethics. For example, should some customers pay more for merchandise if distribution costs are higher in their areas? Do marketers have an obligation to warn customers of impending price, discount, or returns policy changes? All these questions must be dealt with in developing a professional ethic for marketing.

Social Responsibility

Social Responsibility
Marketing philosophies, policies, procedures, and actions that have the advancement of society's welfare as one of their primary objectives.

Another major issue affecting marketing is the question of social responsibility. In a general sense, social responsibility is the marketer's acceptance of the obligation to consider profit, consumer satisfaction, and societal well-being of equal value in evaluating the performance of the firm. It is the recognition that marketers must be concerned with the more qualitative dimensions of consumer and societal benefits as well as the quantitative measures of sales, revenue, and profits by which marketing performance is traditionally measured.

As Professors Engel and Blackwell point out, social responsibility is a more easily measured concept than marketing ethics:

Actions alone determine social responsibility, and a firm can be socially responsible even when doing so under coercion. For example, the government may enact rules that *force* firms to be socially responsible in matters of the environment, deception, and so forth. Also, consumers, through their power to repeat or withhold purchasing, may *force* marketers to provide honest and relevant information, fair prices, and so forth. To be ethically responsible, on the other hand, it is not sufficient to act correctly; ethical intent is also necessary.[8]

The locus for socially responsible decisions in organizations has always been an important question. Who should be specifically accountable for the social considerations involved in marketing decisions? The district sales manager? The marketing vice-president? The firm's president? The board of directors? Probably the most valid assessment is to say that *all marketers*, regardless of their stations in the organization, are accountable for the societal aspects of their decisions.

Marketing's Responsibilities

The concept of business responsibility has traditionally concerned the relationships between the manager and customers, employees, and stockholders. Management had the responsibility of providing customers with a quality product at a reasonable price, the responsibility of providing adequate wages and a decent working environment for employees, and the responsibility for providing an acceptable profit level for stockholders. Only on occasion did the concept involve relations with the government and rarely with the general public.

Today, the responsibility concept has been extended to the entire societal framework. A decision to continue operation of a profitable but air-polluting plant may be responsible in the traditional sense. Customers receive an uninterrupted supply of the plant's products, employees do not face layoffs, and stockholders receive a reasonable return on their investment in the plant. But from the standpoint of contemporary business ethics, this is not a socially responsible decision.

Similarly, a firm that markets foods with low nutritional value may satisfy the traditional concept of responsibility, but such behavior is questionable in the contemporary perspective. This is not to say that firms should distribute only foods of high nutritional value; it means only that the previous framework for evaluation is no longer considered comprehensive in terms of either scope or time.

Contemporary marketing decisions must include consideration of the external societal environment. These decisions must also account for eventual, long-term effects. Socially responsible decisions must consider future generations as well as existing society.

Marketing and Ecology

Ecology
Relationship between organisms and their environment.

Ecology is an important aspect of marketing. The concept of ecology—the relationship between organisms and their environments—appears to be in a constant state of evolution. There are several aspects of ecology that marketers must deal with: planned obsolescence, pollution, recycling waste materials, and preservation of resources.

Planned Obsolescence
Deliberate production of an item with limited durability.

The original ecological problem facing marketing was planned obsolescence—a situation where the manufacturer produced items with limited durability. In some instances, products are made obsolete by technological improvements. In other cases, physical obsolescence is intentional when products are designed so they will wear out within a short time period. In still other situations, rapid changes in design produce a type of fashion obsolescence. Planned obsolescence has always represented a significant ethical question for the marketer. On one side is the need for maintaining sales and employment; on the other is the need for providing better quality and durability.

A practical question is whether the consumer really wants or can afford increased durability. Many consumers prefer to change styles often and accept less durable items. Increased durability has an implicit cost. It may mean fewer people can afford the product.

Pollution
Spoiling or making unclean of natural resources.

Pollution is a broad term that can be applied to a number of circumstances. It usually means making unclean. The concern of polluting such natural resources as the water and the air has reached critical proportions in some areas.

Recycling
Reprocessing of used materials for their reuse.

Recycling—the reprocessing of used materials for reuse—is another important aspect of ecology. The marketing system annually generates billions of tons of packaging materials, such as glass, metal, paper, and plastics, that add to the nation's growing piles of trash and waste. The underlying rationale of recycling is that reprocessed materials can benefit society by saving natural resources and energy as well as by alleviating a major factor in environmental pollution.

Tire manufacturers have built artificial fish reefs out of used tires. Minnesota Mining and Manufacturing Company has printed outlines for splints on the corrugated shipping cartons destined for hospitals. The cartons are then used by emergency and rescue teams for temporary splints. The beverage industry is using more aluminum cans because of the relative ease of recycling aluminum.

Recovery rates for reusable materials vary by industry. For example, the recovery rate for copper is 50 percent, for iron and steel 30 percent, for paper and paper products 20 percent, and for glass only 4 percent. In many instances, the recovery rates are now less than they were in the mid-1950s. Yet

Return to the Stop-Action Case

St. Joseph Hospital

Attracting an increased number of paying patients to St. Joseph Hospital is especially important because of the hospital's humanitarian mission to provide free or low-cost health care to the poor. This mission was put to the test during the national economic recession of the early 1980s when joblessness rose sharply in the Flint area and Medicaid medical insurance benefits dropped. To meet the expanded patient-care burden, the Sisters of St. Joseph operated a variety of health-care programs, both inside and outside the hospital. These included:

- A special tiered pricing policy for emergency services that adjusts the cost of minor and more traumatic emergencies to reflect the care provided. Prices, which do not include physician's fees, range

from $15 to $150. Indigent patients are treated without charge.

- The McCree and Hamilton Avenue Family Health Centers, located outside the hospital, provide the poor with a complete range of health-care services. Fees are based on the ability to pay. St. Joseph cooperates with the federal government, various charitable foundations, and community agencies to provide these services.

While the organizational objectives of St. Joseph involve the needs to survive and prosper, its mission as a health-care provider to the poor means that it receives no reimbursement for many of its services. This outflow of funds increases the hospital's need for the effective marketing of services to patients who can afford to pay.

it is estimated that extensive recycling could produce 40 percent of the materials needed by manufacturers.

The biggest problem in recycling is getting the used materials from the consumer back to the manufacturer who will handle the technological aspects of recovery. These "backward" channels are limited, and those that do exist are primitive and lack adequate financial incentives. Marketing can play an important role by designing appropriate channel structures.

Another ecological problem concerns the preservation of natural resources. The natural gas and fuel oil shortages during the 1970s illustrate the urgent need for effective policies for both conserving and finding new sources of these resources.

Some critics claim that business spends more money publicizing its ecological expenditures than it does meeting specific ecological problems. In many cases, the criticism is valid, but experience has shown that consumers are also at fault because they sometimes fail to support ecology-inspired efforts.

Controlling the Marketing System

When the marketing-economic system does not perform as well as we would like, we attempt to change it. We hope to make it serve us better by producing and distributing goods and services in a fairer way. Most people believe that the system is working sufficiently well to require no changes and that relatively minor adjustments can achieve a fair distribution.

Four ways in which we control or influence the direction of the marketing system and try to rid it of imperfections are (1) by assisting the competitive market system to operate in a self-correcting manner, as Adam Smith suggested; (2) by educating the consumer; (3) by increasing regulation; and (4) by encouraging political action. The competitive market system operates to allocate resources and to provide most of the products we purchase to satisfy felt needs. While we may hear many complaints against the system, most of the goods and services we purchase or use flow through the system with little difficulty. Competition works if the conditions of many buyers and sellers and other technical requirements of the free market economic model allow it. We have attempted, sometimes with limited success, to restore competition where monopolies have reduced it.

Combined with the free market system, consumer education can lead to wise choices. As products become more complex, diverse, and plentiful, the consumer's ability to make wise decisions must also expand. Educational programs and efforts by parents, schools, business, government, and consumer organizations all contribute to a better system.

A responsible marketing philosophy should encourage consumers to voice their opinions. These comments can result in significant improvements in the products and services offered by the seller. One company with a responsible attitude toward consumer complaints featured its critics in television advertisements. The critics and the company spokesperson discussed the various issues surrounding the company and its service area. Surveys showed that the public adopted a more favorable attitude toward the company's position on these matters after seeing the advertisements.

The marketing concept must include social responsibility as a primary function of the marketing organization. Social and profit goals are compatible, but they require the aggressive implementation of an expanded marketing concept. Explicit criteria for responsible decision making must be adopted in all companies. This is truly marketing's greatest challenge.

Marketing in Nonprofit Settings

Nonprofit Organization
Firm whose primary objective is something other than the return of a profit to its owners.

The late 1980s are expected to be years in which marketing plays an expanded role in nonprofit settings. A substantial portion of the U.S. economy is made up of nonprofit organizations—those whose primary objective is something other than returning a profit to its owners. An estimated one of every ten service workers and one of six professionals in the United States is employed in the nonprofit sector. The nonprofit sector includes 350,000 religious organizations, 37,000 human service organizations, 6,000 museums, 5,800 private libraries, 4,600 secondary schools, 3,500 hospitals, 1,500 colleges and universities, 1,100 symphony orchestras, and thousands of other organizations such as government agencies, political parties, and labor unions.[9] Figure 20.4 illustrates a portion of the marketing efforts of two of these organizations. The Statue of Liberty-Ellis Island Foundation raised $230 million from private donations to restore two of the most important landmarks in America's heritage in time for the Statue of Liberty's 100th birthday. The National Council on Alcoholism used well-known individuals such as Los Angeles Dodger pitcher Bob Welch and actor Jason Robards in an attempt to eliminate the stigma associated with alcoholism—the ignorance, guilt, shame, and fear that prevent so many alcoholics from receiving treatment.

Nonprofit organizations can be found in both public and private sectors of society. Federal, state, and local governmental units and agencies whose

Figure 20.4
Illustrations of the Marketing Efforts of Two Nonprofit Organizations

Source: Courtesy of The Advertising Council Inc. and the National Council on Alcoholism, Inc.

revenues are derived from tax collection have service objectives not keyed to profitability targets. The Department of Defense provides protection. A state's department of natural resources regulates conservation and environmental programs. The local animal control officer enforces ordinances that protect both persons and animals.

The private sector offers an even more diverse array of nonprofit settings. Art institutes, the University of Southern California's football team, labor unions, hospitals, private schools, the March of Dimes, the Rotary Club, and the local country club all serve as examples of private-sector, nonprofit organizations. Some, like USC's football team, may return a surplus to the university that can be used to cover other activities, but the organization's primary goal is to win football games. The diversity of these settings suggests how pervasive organizational objectives—other than profitability—really are in a modern economy.

The market offering of the nonprofit organization is frequently more nebulous than the tangible goods or service provisions of profit-seeking firms. Examples of such social issues and ideas offered by nonprofit groups include:

Birth defects	Forest fire prevention	Physical fitness
Cancer research	Gun control	Prayer in schools
Capital punishment	Prevention of littering	Prison reform
Child abuse	Metric system	Suicide Hot Line
Drunk driving	Motorcycle helmets	United Way
Equal Rights Amendment	Peace Corps	55-mph speed limit

The diversity of these issues suggests the size of the nonprofit sector and the marketing activities involved in accomplishing their objectives. What makes them different from their profit-seeking counterparts?

Characteristics of Nonprofit Organizations

Nonprofit organizations have a special set of characteristics that impact their marketing activities. Like the profit-oriented service offerings discussed in Chapter 8, the product offered by a nonprofit organization is often intangible. A hospital's diagnostic services exhibit marketing problems similar to those inherent in marketing a life insurance policy.

A second feature of nonprofit organizations involves multiple publics. As one writer points out:

Nonprofit organizations normally have at least two major publics to work with from a marketing point of view: their clients and their funders. The former pose the problem of *resource allocation* and the latter, the problem of *resource attraction*. Besides these two publics, many other publics surround the nonprofit organization and call for marketing programs. Thus a college can direct marketing programs toward prospective students, current students, parents of students, alumni, faculty, staff, local business firms, and local government agencies. It turns out that business organizations also deal with a multitude of publics, but their tendency is to think about marketing only in connection with one of these publics, namely their customers.[10]

A customer or service user may wield less control over the destiny of a nonprofit organization. A government employee may be far more concerned with the opinion of a member of the legislature's appropriations committee than of a service user. Furthermore, nonprofit organizations often possess some degree of monopoly power in a given geographical area. An individual might object to the United Fund's inclusion of a crisis center among its beneficiary agencies. But a contributor who accepts the merits of the United Fund appeal recognizes that a portion of total contributions will go to the agency in question.

Another problem involves the resource contributor, such as a legislator or a financial backer, who interferes with the marketing program. It is easy to imagine a political candidate harassed by financial supporters who want to replace an unpopular campaign manager (the primary marketing position in a political campaign).

Perhaps the most commonly noted feature of the nonprofit organization is its lack of a *bottom line*—business jargon referring to the overall profitability measure of performance. While nonprofit organizations may attempt to maximize their return from a specific service, less exact goals such as service level standards are the usual substitute for an overall evaluation. The net result is that it is often difficult to set marketing objectives that are aligned specifically with overall organizational goals.

A final characteristic is the lack of a clear organizational structure. Nonprofit organizations often refer to constituencies that they serve, but these are often considerably less exact than, for example, the stockholders of a profit-oriented corporation. Nonprofit organizations often have multiple organizational structures. A hospital might have an administrative structure, the professional organization consisting of medical personnel, and a volunteer organization that dominates the board of trustees. These people may sometimes work at cross-purposes and not be totally in line with the marketing strategy that has been devised.

While the above factors may also characterize some profit-oriented organizations, they are certainly prevalent in nonprofit settings. These characteristics impact the implementation of marketing efforts in such organizations and must be considered in the development of an overall strategy.

The Broadening Concept

The current status of nonprofit marketing is largely the result of an evolutionary process that began in the early 1960s, when several writers suggested that marketing should be concerned with issues beyond the traditional profit-oriented domain. Marketing was beginning to be perceived as having wider application than was normally the case.

A major breakthrough came in 1969 with the publication of Kotler and Levy's classic article that argued that the marketing concept should be broadened to include the nonprofit sector of society.[11] The theoretical justification for this view was that marketing was a generic activity for all organizations. In other words, marketing was a function to be performed by any type of organization. Thus, the broadening concept was an extension of the marketing concept to nontraditional exchange processes.

Broadening Concept
Expanded view of marketing as a generic function to be performed by all organizations—profit-seeking or nonprofit.

The broadening concept was not unanimously accepted by marketers. Luck argued that it was an unwarranted extension of the marketing concept.[12] More recently, Laczniak and Michie argued that a broadened marketing concept could be responsible for undesirable social changes and disorder.[13] Despite some dissent, the broadening concept is enjoying wide acceptance among nonprofit organizations and various students of marketing.

Types of Nonprofit Marketing

Nonprofit marketing is as varied as profit-oriented marketing. The marketing focus of nonprofit organizations can be categorized into three major areas: person marketing, idea marketing, and organization marketing.

Person Marketing

Person marketing refers to efforts designed to cultivate the attention, interest, and preference of a market target toward a person.[14] This type of marketing is typically employed by political candidates and celebrities.

The instant celebrity status of Mr. T, a hulk of a man with a fierce-looking Mandinka hair style, is a case in point. Mr. T, whose real name is Lawrence Tureaud, is a former bodyguard who was discovered by actor Sylvester Stallone and cast in the film *Rocky III* before achieving national recognition on the television series "The A Team."

As tens of millions of viewers tuned in to the 1983 Super Bowl, a scowling face appeared and said, "Listen up. The A Team is looking for a few bad men. If you think you're tough enough, see us right after the Super Bowl."

This routine was repeated three times during the NBC telecast, and it worked. Today Mr. T, little known before the Super Bowl, is a household word, and "The A Team" is one of television's top-rated programs. Mr. T's unusual attire—combat boots, chest-baring vests, sweat pants, and heavy jewelry— quickly earned him several worst-dressed awards, but additional media coverage. As a *U.S. News & World Report* article points out:

Though critics decry "The A Team" as violent, Mr. T apparently has caught the fancy of youngsters. For him, success is building on success. NBC has developed a Saturday morning cartoon around him, and the market is awash in Mr. T lunch kits, dolls, clocks and watches, beach towels, sleeping bags, puzzles, and coloring books.[15]

Idea Marketing

The second type of nonprofit marketing deals with causes and social issues rather than an individual. Idea marketing refers to the identification and marketing of a cause to chosen consumer segments. A highly visual marketing mix element frequently associated with idea marketing is the use of *advocacy advertising,* discussed in Chapter 15. The importance of wearing seat belts is currently being marketed by the American Insurance Association. The National Organization for the Repeal of Marijuana Laws (NORML) is attempting to affect voter and legislative attitudes to legalize marijuana.

Different organizations may use advocacy advertising in marketing different viewpoints on the same product, service, or social issue. For example, an advertisement by R.J. Reynolds Tobacco Co. requests that the general public maintain an open-minded attitude toward the impact of "second-hand smoke" until definitive research studies are concluded. A different viewpoint— advocating nonsmoking—is presented in advertisements by the American Cancer Society as part of its continuing campaign to reduce the number of smokers in the United States.

Organization Marketing

The third type of nonprofit marketing, organization marketing, attempts to influence others to accept the goals of, receive the services of, or contribute in some way to an organization. Included in this category are *mutual benefit* organizations, such as churches, labor unions, and political parties; *service* organizations, such as colleges and universities, hospitals, and museums; and *government* organizations, such as military services, police and fire departments, and the post office. Figure 20.5 illustrates the efforts of the U.S. Postal

Figure 20.5
Some of the Services Provided by the U.S. Postal Service

Source: Courtesy of United States Postal Service.

Service to serve some of its clients through a broadened product and service mix. Other recent innovations include self-service stamp vending machines in shopping centers and office buildings, Express Mail for overnight delivery, and promotional efforts designed to encourage ZIP code usage.[16]

Defining Marketing in Nonprofit Settings

One of the most pervasive problems in nonprofit marketing is the way in which marketing is defined. Often, marketing is perceived only in terms of promotion. Other components of the marketing mix—product/service development, distribution, and pricing strategies—are largely ignored. Marketing, when defined only as aggressive promotion, is a short-lived, surface-level solution for a variety of organizational problems and objectives.

An important factor in such a narrow, incomplete view of the scope of marketing is the fact that marketing was a late arrival to the management of nonprofit organizations. The practices of improved accounting, financial control, personnel selection, and planning all were implemented before marketing.[17] Nevertheless, nonprofit organizations have accepted it enthusiastically. Dozens of articles and speeches attest to marketing's popularity. Meanwhile, university administrators attend seminars and conferences to learn how to better market their own institutions.

Marketing's rise in the nonprofit sector could not be continued without a successful track record. While it is often more difficult to measure results in nonprofit settings, marketing can already point to examples of success. The Presbyterian-affiliated Church of the Covenant in Cleveland credits a 10 percent increase in average attendance to a series of radio commercials, which begin with voice-over-music and are spoken by the church's regular Sunday morning announcer. And a Midwestern hospital's marketing analysis allowed it to reposition itself as a provider of tertiary care services rather than as a community hospital. Marketing is now an accepted part of the operational environment of most successful nonprofit organizations.

Developing a Marketing Strategy _____

The need for a comprehensive marketing strategy rather than merely increasing promotional expenditures was noted earlier. Substantial opportunities exist for effective, innovative strategies since there has been little previous marketing effort in most nonprofit settings.

Marketing Research

Many decisions in nonprofit settings are based on little, if any, research. An Illinois hospital opened an adult day-care center for elderly people requiring ongoing attention and personal services, based solely on the observation that many seniors lived within a three-mile radius. Only two patients were admitted at the daily fee set by hospital administrators.[18]

Adequate marketing research can be extremely important in a variety of nonprofit settings. Resident opinion surveys in many cities have proven valuable to public officials. Consumer surveys currently play an important role in product liability lawsuits. The analysis of projected population trends has led to tentative decisions to close obstetric units at some hospitals.

Product Strategy

Nonprofit organizations face the same product decisions as profit-seeking firms. They must choose a product, service, person, idea, or social issue to be offered to their market target. They must decide whether to offer a single product or a mix of related products. They must make product identification decisions. The United Way symbol and the Red Cross trademark illustrate the similarity in the use of product identification methods.

A common failure among nonprofit organizations is the assumption that heavy promotional efforts can overcome a poor product strategy or marketing mix. Consider the number of liberal arts colleges that tried to use promotion to overcome their product mix deficiencies when students became increasingly career-oriented. Successful institutions adjust their product offerings to reflect customer demand.

Distribution Strategy

Distribution channels for nonprofit organizations tend to be short, simple, and direct. If marketing intermediaries are present in the channel, they are usually agents such as an independent ticket agency or a specialist in fund raising. A major distribution decision involves the specific location of the nonprofit organization.

Nonprofit organizations often fail to exercise caution in the planning and execution of the distribution strategy. Organizers of recycling centers sometimes complain about lack of public interest, but their real problem is an inconvenient location or lack of adequate drop-off points. Urban hospitals located in declining areas sometimes find it difficult to attract suburban patients. By contrast, some public agencies like health and social welfare departments have set up branches in neighborhood shopping centers to be more accessible to their clientele.

Promotional Strategy

It is common to see or hear advertisements from nonprofit organizations such as educational institutions, churches, and public service organizations. A striking example of nonprofit advertising is Figure 20.6, a magazine advertisement for the United Negro College Fund.

The effectiveness of marketing communications and promotional strategy is impacted by a variety of factors including relative involvement in the nonprofit setting, pricing, and perceived benefits. But overall, promotion is seen by many nonprofit managers as the primary solution to their marketing

Figure 20.6
An Advertisement for the United Negro College Fund

Source: Courtesy of United Negro College Fund, Inc.

problems. As noted earlier, this view is often naive, but it does not diminish the importance of promotion in nonprofit marketing.

Pricing Strategy

Pricing is typically a very important element of the marketing mix for nonprofit organizations. Pricing strategy can be used to accomplish a variety of organizational goals in nonprofit settings. These include:

1. *Profit maximization.* While nonprofit organizations by definition do not cite profitability as a primary goal, there are numerous instances in which they do try to maximize their return on a single event or a series of events. The $1,000-a-plate political fund raiser is a classic example.

2. *Cost recovery.* Some nonprofit organizations attempt only to recover the actual cost of operating the unit. Mass transit, publicly supported colleges, and bridges are common examples. The amount of recovered costs is often dictated by tradition, competition, and/or public opinion.

3. *Providing market incentives.* Other nonprofit groups follow a penetration pricing policy or offer a free service to encourage increased usage of the product or service. Seattle's bus system charges no fare in the downtown area to reduce traffic congestion, encourage retail sales, and minimize the effort required to use downtown public services.

4. *Market suppression.* Price is sometimes used to discourage consumption. In other words, high prices are used to accomplish societal objectives and are not directly related to the costs of providing the product or service. Illustrations include tobacco and alcohol taxes, parking fines, tolls, and gasoline excise taxes.[19]

The Future of Nonprofit Marketing

While marketing has gained increasing acceptance in the nonprofit sector, it is still viewed with suspicion by many of the people involved. The heavy emphasis on promotion is one reason. But, in a broader sense, marketing efforts in nonprofit organizations often lack the sophistication and integration found in the marketing of profit-oriented businesses. Marketing is too often seen as the quick-fix solution to a more basic problem. To combat this, marketers must market their discipline in a realistic and socially responsible manner. The client must be made to understand the opportunities, benefits, behavior modifications, and commitments involved in the adoption of the marketing concept in a nonprofit setting.

Summary

At the interface between business and society, the marketer often takes the brunt of criticisms of the operation of the market system. There are many important issues in contemporary marketing's societal environment. Marketing's environmental relationships have expanded in scope and importance. The current issues in marketing can be categorized as consumerism, marketing ethics, and social responsibility.

Criticisms of the marketing system are often justified and result from a broad range of ideas about what is and what is not ethical business activity. It is much too easy to point the finger at marketers or at business as the perpetrators of the evils of the system rather than to recognize that the system is *us*. The system is what its members want it to be, and when the system does not respond as we would like it to, the result is government-instituted regulations and controls to correct the situation.

Attempts to make the system more responsive to the desires of society have resulted in increased regulation and the emergence of groups representing consumer interests. Basic consumer rights to choice, to information, to be heard, and to safety and health, and consumers' interests in maintaining these rights are most commonly ensured by competition in the marketplace. When the marketplace has inadequately ensured the consumer rights and interests, government has responded to public pressure and intervened to improve the situation. Consumer groups have developed to spur business and government in this action and to counteract the natural advantage that special interest groups have in representing their interests in the political process at the expense of more broadly based consumer interests.

Increased regulation, better public information, and a more responsible marketing philosophy are possible avenues for resolving these issues. All are expected to play a greater role in the years ahead.

The adoption of marketing strategies and marketing philosophies in nonprofit settings is another important aspect of marketing in the late 1980s. Nonprofit organizations are those enterprises whose primary objective is something other than returning a profit to the owners. Nonprofit organizations are often characterized by the intangible nature of many of their services; multiple publics; minimal control by customers; professional rather than organizational orientation of their employees; involvement of resource contributors; lack of an overall bottom line; and the lack of a clear organizational structure. Person, idea, and organization marketing are the three types of nonprofit marketing.

The introduction of marketing into nonprofit settings has been associated with the broadening concept, which extends the marketing concept to nontraditional exchange processes. The broadening concept was introduced by Philip Kotler and Sidney J. Levy in 1969.

Marketing is now viewed as integral to many nonprofit settings, although it is too often defined largely in terms of promotional strategy. Nonprofit organizations require a comprehensive marketing mix based upon accurate marketing research.

Solving the
Stop-Action Case

St. Joseph Hospital

Findings from the marketing research study prompted St. Joseph Hospital administrators to implement several programs aimed at attracting greater numbers of obstetrical patients. Two homelike birthing centers were added to the hospital's labor and delivery area; new staffing guidelines were adopted requiring staff members to pay more attention to the families of patients by providing them with explanations of procedures and involving them in patient care; and the physician referral system was strengthened.

Although these changes were significant, administrators also realized that the hospital must significantly alter its price and product strategies to attract greater numbers of patients. Decisions were made to offer mothers the option of having their babies in low-technology birthing centers and to compete for the private-pay market comprised of people with no health insurance coverage. This market was especially large in Flint as a result of the severe unemployment problem that placed families in the precarious position of having too much money to qualify for public assistance and too little to pay the standard cost of obstetrical care.

The cornerstone of St. Joseph's new marketing program was a reduced-price labor and delivery program featuring a 24-hour hospital stay in a homelike hospital setting. Dubbed "Special Delivery," this program offered patients a complete package of prenatal care, childbirth classes, hospital delivery, postnatal care, home visit after delivery, and a final clinic checkup. The $799 fee was about half the amount charged by other hospitals and doctors in the Flint area.

An extensive marketing program was used to launch the new marketing strategy. It was determined that the best way to reach the marketing effort's target audience—women between the ages of 18 and 35—was radio. One of the two radio commercials prepared for the marketing program was aimed at black women and was aired on a radio station with a large black audience. A one-half page newspaper ad as well as a direct-mail brochure were other components of the marketing effort.

After 18 months, the marketing program's results were measured. "Special Delivery" had brought 500 expectant mothers into the St. Joseph obstetrical system—a number that far exceeded the hospital's initial projections of 50 patients a year. Six of every ten patients

a bundle of joy...
a bundle of
money

St. Joseph Hospital has a new answer for expecting mothers worried about how to pay for their baby's delivery—it's called **SPECIAL DELIVERY.**

Although not for everyone, **SPECIAL DELIVERY** is an alternative to traditional maternity services.

And it costs just $799. Complete.

Here's what you get:
- Prenatal classes and clinic visits.
- Nutritional counseling.
- Medical care by Family Practitioners in our obstetrics clinics.
- Complete labor, delivery and postnatal care in St. Joseph's Maternity Center.
- You go home, with your baby, within 24 hours after delivery.
- A nurse comes to see you and your baby at home within 2 days.
- A clinic visit for you and your baby within 2 weeks after delivery.

This service may be for you if you don't have insurance to cover the total cost of your maternity care.

Unfortunately, not everyone qualifies for this service for medical reasons, but if you need help, you probably can.

If you want your bundle of joy without a bundle of cost, call 762-8552 for more information.

Another innovative service of:

Saint Joseph Hospital
Maternity Center
302 Kensington, Flint

Photo Source: Courtesy of St. Joseph Hospital.

attributed their selection of St. Joseph to the 24-hour, short-stay program. The success of "Special Delivery" combined with other patients increased total deliveries to almost 1,700 a year—well above the 1,500 births needed to stay in operation.

Despite the program's success, "Special Delivery" has not proven profitable for the hospital. But Polly Piepenbrink, the hospital's vice-president of marketing, views the program as a type of loss leader. Piepenbrink believes that mothers who are satisfied with St. Joseph's obstetrical care are more likely to return to the hospital when they, their spouse, or their children require hospital care. For them, St. Joseph is likely to become even more of a family hospital.

St. Joseph is one of many healthcare institutions across the nation that have turned to marketing to attract new patients. It is not uncommon to find hospitals allocat-

Source: Information on the St. Joseph Hospital marketing program was provided by Dennis Archambault, Manager of Marketing Communications at St. Joseph.

ing $500,000 or more annually for promotion and advertising outlays—ten times the amount spent a few years ago. An estimated 50 to 60 percent of the nation's hospitals currently have a marketing expert on their staffs, as compared to only 5 to 10 percent three years ago.

In what is perhaps the most unusual example of healthcare marketing, Sunrise Hospital in Las Vegas, Nevada, offered patients who checked in on the weekend—a normally slow time at hospitals—a chance to participate in a special lottery with a grand prize of a cruise for two. Within 18 months, weekend check-ins soared by 60 percent.

Questions for Discussion

1. Evaluate consumerism's indictment of the competitive marketing system.

2. Should the United States ban advertising aimed at children?

3. Discuss the problems involved in setting up "backward" channels of distribution for recycling used packages.

4. Distinguish among individual, organizational, and professional ethics.

5. Describe the ethical problems related to:
    a. Marketing research
    b. Product management
    c. Distribution strategy
    d. Promotional strategy
    e. Pricing

6. Henry Ford II has argued that in a competitive market system, a firm cannot afford to meet the expense of environmental improvements unless competitors are also legally required to follow the same standards. Discuss.

7. Some have suggested that a national law be passed requiring a deposit on all beverage containers in an attempt to reduce roadside litter. Do you agree? Defend your position.

8. Describe the major avenues open for the resolution of contemporary issues facing the marketing system.

9. What are the primary characteristics of nonprofit organizations that distinguish them from profit-seeking organizations?

10. Describe the evolution of the broadening concept.

11. What type of nonprofit organization does each of the following represent:
    a. United Steelworkers
    b. Kennedy for President committee
    c. Art Institute of Chicago
    d. Oklahoma City Zoo
    e. Mothers Against Drunk Drivers (MADD)
    f. U.S. Girl Scouts
    g. Easter Seals

12. What is person marketing? Contrast it with marketing of a consumer good such as magazines.

13. Why is idea marketing more difficult than organization marketing?

14. Identify the types of organization marketing and give examples of each.

15. Why is marketing sometimes defined inaccurately in a nonprofit organization?

16. Contrast the product strategy of nonprofit marketing with that of marketing for profit.

17. Identify the pricing goals that are commonly used by nonprofit enterprises.

18. Cite several examples of circumstances in which penetration pricing might be practiced by public utilities.

19. Compare distribution and promotional strategies of nonprofit organizations with profit-seeking enterprises.

20. Outline the marketing program of your college or university. Make any reasonable assumptions necessary. Where are the major strengths and weaknesses of the current program? What recommendations would you make for improving it?

Case: Chelsea—The Baby Beer Controversy

Anheuser-Busch wanted to introduce a premium-priced soft drink to appeal to the sophisticated adult. The product it developed had a ginger, lemon, and apple flavoring and a malt-type base. It also had a 0.4 percent alcohol content, compared to 5 percent in most beers. The new product, Chelsea, was to be priced at about $2 per six-pack. Because of its lower alcohol content, the FDA classified Chelsea as a soft drink.

Chelsea was test-marketed in Virginia, Massachusetts, Louisiana, Illinois, Colorado, and California. Its introduction led to widespread protests by church groups, nurses, and educators. It was labeled "Baby Beer" by its critics, who claimed it would condition children to drink beer when they became older. They pointed out that Chelsea was advertised as the "not-so-soft soft drink" and was packaged more like beer than like soft drinks. The amber-colored product, sold in clear bottles, also looked like beer.

Anheuser-Busch quickly stopped marketing Chelsea because of the protests. The product had by then exceeded the 1 percent market share figure commonly used in the soft-drink industry to assess new product viability.

After consulting with the many critics of the original product, Anheuser-Busch developed a new version of Chelsea. The new Chelsea had only a trace of alcohol, was similar to other citrus-flavored beverages, and no longer foamed. It was sold in green bottles to mask the product's amber color. The advertising slogan was changed to "the natural alternative," capitalizing on the fact that Chelsea had all natural flavors and no preservatives. However, consumer acceptance of the new Chelsea was disappointing, and test marketing was suspended in 1979.

Questions

1. What went wrong? Why did Chelsea prove to be a marketing failure? Refer to the description of the steps in the marketing research process in Chapter 4 and indicate actions or tests that should have provided Anheuser-Busch with an earlier warning concerning the problem with Chelsea.

2. The market share achieved by Chelsea during its brief existence provides some indication of its viability in some market segments. Briefly outline a marketing program that could increase the probability of success for such a product.

Computer Applications

In the previous chapter, five of the sixteen analytical techniques introduced earlier were used to aid in decisions and to solve problems affecting international marketers. The focus of this chapter is on societal issues and the not-for-profit sectors of the economy. Accordingly, the an-

alytical techniques focus upon problems and decisions affecting organizations ranging from a university purchasing department and a recycling center to two fund-raising organizations and a Red Cross plasma donation center. The problems illustrate the marketing issues facing a diverse array of organizations and the applicability of these analytical techniques for nonprofit organizations as well as profit-seeking firms.

Directions: Use menu item 2 titled "Decision Tree Analysis" to solve Problem 1. Use menu item 3 titled "Sales Forecasting" to solve Problem 2. Use menu item 15 titled "Sales Force Size Determination" to solve Problem 3. Use menu item 12 titled "Economic Order Quantity" to solve Problem 4. Use menu item 16 titled "Breakeven Analysis" to solve Problem 5.

Problem 1 The manager of the Los Angeles Recycling Center has been pleased that recent publicity emphasizing the importance of recycling has greatly increased the amount of materials brought to the center. In fact, she is giving serious consideration to adding two suburban locations in addition to the central center. She estimates a 60 percent likelihood of high growth in the sale of materials for recycling over the next year and a 40 percent chance of moderate growth. Although the expenses associated with operating the proposed new recycling locations would reduce her profits earned on a per-pound basis, the added convenience is certain to generate additional recyclable materials. The manager summarized her two alternatives as follows:

A.   *Continuing operating at one central location*
  1.   A high-growth environment will result in 25,000 pounds of materials and generate profits of $.10 per pound.

  2.   A moderate-growth environment will result in 15,000 pounds of materials and profits of $.06 per pound.

B.   *Open two suburban locations*
  1.   A high-growth environment will result in 40,000 pounds of materials and generate profits of $.06 per pound.
  2.   A moderate-growth environment will result in 24,000 pounds of materials and profits of $.01 per pound.

a.   Review the discussion of decision tree analysis on page 58. Then use menu item 2 titled "Decision Tree Analysis" to recommend a course of action for the Los Angeles Recycling Center.

b.   Would your recommendation change if the likelihood of high growth were increased to 80 percent?

Problem 2 Annual operations of the Cancer Fund of Hartford, Connecticut, are funded entirely from contributions from area residents and businesses. A substantial portion of these contributions results from an annual telethon conducted by a local television station. The Cancer Fund board of directors bases the annual operating budget on estimated contributions. Contributions for the past eight years are shown below:

1979	$ 370,000
1980	650,000
1981	880,000
1982	1,200,000
1983	1,600,000
1984	2,100,000
1985	2,750,000
1986	3,500,000

Review the discussion of sales forecasting using trend extension on page 87. Then use menu item 3 titled "Sales Forecasting" to forecast Cancer Fund contributions for 1987.

Problem 3 George Jensen, director of the Florida office of the Mothers' March Against Heart Disease, is attempting to use more scientific techniques in determining the number of collectors needed for the annual fund drive. Jensen has labeled several neighborhoods containing 30,000 of the 220,000 Miami households as Type A *(high-contribution households);* another group of neighborhoods containing 60,000 households as Type B *(moderate-contribution households);* and a third group of neighborhoods containing 130,000 households as Type C *(low-contribution households).* A Mothers' March volunteer collector will personally contact each household once during the eight-week fund drive. A stamped, addressed contribution envelope will be left if no one is at home. Jensen estimates the desired length of an average contact at 15 minutes for Type A households, 10 minutes for Type B households, and 5 minutes for Type C households. All contacts by Mothers' March collectors will be planned contacts. He estimates that the average volunteer collector will work 10 hours per week for the eight-week period. Each volunteer will spend 40 percent of available time in calling on specifically designated accounts, 30 percent on travel, and the remaining 30 percent on nonselling activities (training and reports).

Review the discussion of the workload method for determining the required sales force size on pages 456 and 457. Then use menu item 15 titled "Sales Force Size Determination" to specify the number of collectors needed in Miami by the Mothers' March Against Heart Disease.

Problem 4 Dorothy Mayfield is director of purchasing at Kendall University. Since copier-quality paper is one of her university's most frequent and routine purchases, Mayfield is attempting to systemize the process of reordering. Current prices of the paper average $60 per case, and the university is expected to use 8,000 cases per year. She estimates the cost of placing an order to be $7.50. Annual inventory carrying costs are 10 percent.

Review the discussion of the economic order quantity (EOQ) model on pages 366, 367, and 372. Then use menu item 12 titled "Economic Order Quantity" to determine the EOQ for paper purchases at Kendall University.

Problem 5 A small town of 10,000 is currently under consideration for the location of a Red Cross plasma donation center. Donations generate an average revenue of $30 per pint for the office. Estimated total fixed costs for the center are $60,000, and per-unit variable costs, including cash payments to some of the plasma donors, are expected to total $12.

a. Review the discussion of breakeven analysis on pages 479–483. Then use menu item 16 titled "Breakeven Analysis" to determine the number of pints of plasma that must be collected for the proposed donation center to break even.

b. The area director of the Red Cross has recommended the inclusion of a $10,000 target surplus for the proposed center to cover unexpected expenses that might arise. How many units must be collected to break even *and* achieve this target return?

c. How would your answer to Question a change if the average variable costs could be reduced to $9?

d. How would your answer to Question b change if the average variable costs could be reduced to $9?

Appendix
Careers in Marketing

Seventeen-year-old Nicholas DiBari had to make a decision. The Boston Red Sox had offered the young pitcher a minor league contract. But DiBari picked a second option. He became a marketing major at the University of Dayton. As it turned out, he clearly made the right decision.

Prior to his retirement at age 38, DiBari was marketing vice-president at Comdisco, an Illinois-based computer leasing company. He was the best-paid sales executive in the country, earning in excess of $1.5 million. DiBari is now a consultant based in Deerfield Beach, Florida.[1]

DiBari is not cited as illustrative of what every marketing student can expect to earn, but only as an example of how far one can reach in this most vital of all business disciplines.

A marketing career is also an excellent preparation for top management. Heidrick and Struggles, Inc., a worldwide executive search organization, reports that almost one-third of the chief executive officers (CEOs) they surveyed had been promoted from sales/marketing positions. The next most likely background for a CEO was finance/accounting. The survey also noted that sales/marketing's lead over other functions had increased since 1980.[2]

This appendix focuses on careers in marketing. The following aspects are considered:

1. The kinds of positions available, with brief descriptions of the responsibilities attached to each
2. The academic training and other preparation needed for marketing employment
3. Marketing employment trends and opportunities
4. Marketing employment for women and minorities

Marketing Positions

The text has examined the great extent and diversity of the components of the marketing function. The types of marketing occupations required to fulfill these tasks are just as numerous and diverse. In fact, marketing is the single largest employer in our civilian labor force. Students intending to pursue a marketing

The original draft of the Appendix was developed with the assistance of Professor Dinoo J. Vanier of San Diego State University.

career may be bewildered at the range of employment opportunities in marketing. How can they find their way through the maze of marketing occupations and concentrate on the ones that best match their interests and talents? A convenient starting point is an understanding of the different positions and the duties required of each.

Marketing personnel are classified as either sales force personnel or marketing staff personnel who are employed in functions such as advertising, product planning, marketing research, purchasing, and public relations. The precise nature of their responsibilities and duties varies among organizations and industries. Marketing tasks may be undertaken in-house by company marketing personnel or subcontracted to outside sources. Indeed, a large number of agencies are available to support in-house marketing efforts. Among them are advertising agencies, public relations firms, and marketing research agencies. Marketing employment can be found in a variety of organizations: manufacturing firms, distributive enterprises such as retailers and wholesalers, service suppliers, and research agencies.

All of these organizations have managerial positions in marketing. The specific duties of the positions vary with the size of the organization, the nature of its business, and the extent to which marketing operations are departmentalized or centralized. Marketing management jobs generally require the individual to assist in the formulation of the organization's marketing policies and to plan, organize, coordinate, and control marketing operations and resources. Some of the typical marketing management positions and descriptions of their responsibilities follow. Specific titles of positions may vary among companies.

The Chief Marketing Executive   The person who oversees all the marketing activities and is ultimately responsible for the success of the marketing function is the chief marketing executive. All other marketing executives report through channels to this person.

The Marketing Research Director   The marketing research director determines the marketing research needs of the organization and plans and directs various stages of the marketing research projects. These stages include formulation of the problem, research design, data collection, analysis, and interpretation of results. On the basis of marketing research, the director also helps formulate marketing policy and strategies pertinent to any of the marketing variables.

The Product Manager   The person in charge of marketing operations for a particular type of product—such as clothing, building materials, or appliances—is the product manager. This person also assumes responsibility for some or all of the functions of the marketing executive, but only as they pertain to particular products.

The Brand Manager   The brand manager performs functions similar to those of the product manager, but only with regard to a specific brand.

The Sales Manager   The person responsible for managing the sales force is the sales manager. Some of the manager's specific duties are establishing sales territories; deploying the sales force; recruiting, hiring, and training salespeople; and setting sales quotas.

The Advertising Manager   The person who plans and arranges for the promotion of the company's products or services is the advertising manager. Among that person's duties are formulating advertising policy, selecting advertising agencies, evaluating creative promotional ideas, and setting the advertising budget.

The Public Relations Officer   The public relations officer directs all the activities that project and maintain a favorable image for the organization. This person arranges press conferences, exhibitions, news releases, and the like.

The Purchasing or Procurement Manager   The purchasing manager controls all purchasing and procurement activities involved in acquiring merchandise, equipment, and materials for the organization.

The Retail Buyer   The retail buyer is responsible for the purchase of merchandise from various sources—manufacturers, wholesalers, and importers, among others—for resale through retail outlets.

The Wholesale Buyer   The person who buys products from manufacturers, importers, and others for resale through wholesale outlets is the wholesale buyer. This buyer's duties are similar to those for the retail buyer, but they are within the specific context of wholesale distribution.

The Physical Distribution Manager   The trend for firms to consolidate physical distribution activities under a single managerial hierarchy has resulted in a significant increase in the importance of the physical distribution manager. This person is involved with activities such as transportation, warehousing, inventory control, order processing, and materials handling.

The discussion so far has spotlighted the top management level of each type of work. Depending on company size, however, there may be several other levels within each of the categories described. For every management position, there are several other marketing occupations that involve the "doing" of specific tasks that are supervised and controlled by the managers; their exact number varies considerably from organization to organization. In the area of marketing research, for instance, employees engage in field work, information collection, editing, coding, tabulation, and other statistical analyses of data.

In advertising, the copywriter assimilates information on the products and customers or likely customers and then writes copy, creating headlines, slogans, and text for the advertisements. The media planner is often a time and space buyer who specializes in determining which advertising media will be most effective. The advertising layout person decides the exact layout of illustrations and copy that comprise the finished advertisement.

The majority of people in marketing are in the area of sales. Sales representatives sell at the manufacturing, wholesale, or retail level. Their job descriptions vary somewhat with the types of products and customers. Sales positions are a common entry point for people desiring promotion to marketing management positions.

Preparing for a Marketing Career

What are the requirements for obtaining a marketing job? What are the typical positions at which marketing careers begin? What are the usual patterns of progression to the top spots in marketing management?

The starting point should be a sound education. Certainly, collegiate course work does not guarantee entry into any career field. But the more one knows about business, careers, employment trends, and the like, the better prepared he or she will be when entering the labor force. In fact, business administration is now the most popular major on many U.S. campuses.

Trends and Opportunities

Table 1 reports the Bureau of Labor Statistics employment projections to 1995 for selected marketing occupations. Some sales positions are forecasted to do particularly well through 1995.

Table 1
Marketing Employment Projections through 1995

Marketing Occupation	Recent Employment	Projected Employment Growth through 1995
Buyers, Retail and Wholesale Trade	256,000	About as Fast as Average
Insurance Agents and Brokers	361,000	About as Fast as Average
Manufacturers' Sales Workers	414,000	More Slowly Than Average
Public Relations Workers	90,000	About as Fast as Average
Purchasing Agents	191,000	About as Fast as Average
Real Estate Agents and Brokers	337,000	Faster Than Average
Reservation Agents and Ticket Clerks (air travel)	88,000	Little Change
Retail Trade Sales Workers	3,367,000	About as Fast as Average
Securities Sales Workers	78,000	Faster Than Average
Wholesale Trade Sales Workers	1,093,000	Faster Than Average

Source: U.S. Department of Labor, Bureau of Labor Statistics, *Occupational Outlook Handbook, 1984–1985 Edition* (Washington, D.C.: U.S. Government Printing Office, Bulletin 2205, April 1984), pp. 28, 40, 154, 188–201, 210.

Marketing Salaries

Table 2 depicts the typical annual salaries for marketing management positions. The total compensation of these executives is not entirely reflected by this information, since executives usually receive bonuses and participate in corporate profit sharing. The data does, however, illustrate the earnings potential in marketing careers. A more pertinent question, perhaps, from the student's viewpoint is what are the beginning salary levels in marketing? During 1984, most marketing and sales graduates were hired at about $19,620.[3]

Table 2

Average Salary for Marketing Positions

Job Title	Salary
Chairman/President	$198,400
Executive Vice-President	150,000
General Manager	120,000
Vice-President/Director of Marketing	61,400
Vice-President/Director of Advertising	47,214
Vice-President/Director of Marketing Services	60,667
Vice-President/Director of Public Relations	69,964

Source: *The Gallagher Report*, vol. 32, second supplement to February 29, 1984,
© 1984 The Gallagher Report, Inc. All rights reserved. Reprinted by permission.

The Status of Women and Minorities in Marketing

In recent years companies have been actively attempting to fill positions with qualified women and minorities. These efforts have produced marked increases in the employment options available to women and minorities. Advertising, marketing research, and retailing are marketing occupations in which women have traditionally held jobs. Women often enter these fields by way of retail sales, where they outnumber men by a ratio of more than two to one, as shown in Table 3. Women also account for a high percentage of the total employees in real estate sales and service and construction sales.

Although there have been gains in women's employment in recent years, an earnings gap between men and women employees still exists. The average pay for a woman is still lower than that for a man in most fields. But there are signs of progress.

A similar situation confronts minorities. Employment of blacks in marketing is usually less than 5 percent of any particular marketing job category, as illustrated in Table 3. Similar to the female marketing employment situation, a higher proportion of blacks are employed as retail sales clerks (5.1 percent). Few blacks hold marketing management positions, but, as is the case with women, black participation in marketing employment is expected to grow.

Table 3

Female and Minority Employment in Marketing

Occupation	Percentage of Females	Percentage of Blacks
Buyers, Wholesale and Retail Trade	43.1	2.6
Purchasing Agents and Buyers	35.7	3.2
Sales Managers	25.9	3.6
Real Estate Agents and Brokers	50.2	0.7
Stock and Bond Sales Agents	19.8	4.1
Sales Representatives, Manufacturing Industries	21.4	2.6
Sales Representatives, Wholesale Trade	13.9	1.6
Sales Clerks, Retail Trade	70.0	5.1
Sales Workers (except Clerks) Retail Trade	19.2	3.3
Sales Workers, Services and Construction	42.5	3.4

Source: U.S. Bureau of the Census, *Statistical Abstract of the United States: 1984*
(104th edition), Washington, D.C., 1983, p. 419.

Notes

Chapter 1

[1]Peter F. Drucker, *The Practice of Management* (New York: Harper & Row, 1954), p. 37.

[2]Joseph P. Guiltinan and Gordon W. Paul, *Marketing Management* (New York: McGraw-Hill, 1982), pp. 3–4.

[3]"AMA Board Approves New Marketing Definition," *The Marketing News* (March 1, 1985), p. 1.

[4]Wroe Alderson, *Marketing Behavior and Executive Action* (Homewood, Ill.: Richard D. Irwin, 1957), p. 292.

[5]Robert J. Keith, "The Marketing Revolution," *Journal of Marketing* (January 1960), p. 36.

[6]The company's experience is described in Chester M. Woolworth, "So We Made a Better Mousetrap," *The President's Forum* (Fall 1962), pp. 26–27.

[7]Robert J. Keith, "The Marketing Revolution," *Journal of Marketing* (January 1960), p. 38.

[8]Theodore Levitt, *Innovations in Marketing* (New York: McGraw-Hill, 1962), p. 7.

[9]*Annual Report* (New York: General Electric, 1952), p. 21.

[10]Theodore Levitt, "Marketing Myopia," *Harvard Business Review* (July–August 1960), pp. 45–56.

[11]Bill Abrams, "Selling Wine Like Soda Pop, Riunite Uncorks Huge Market," *The Wall Street Journal* (July 2, 1981). Updated statistics from "Villa Banfi: Aspiring to World-Class Wines," *Business Week* (October 15, 1984), pp. 93–97.

Chapter 2

[1]E. J. McCarthy and William D. Perrault, Jr., *Basic Marketing* (Homewood, Ill.: Richard D. Irwin, Inc., 1984), Chapter 4.

[2]"Rethink the Marketing Concept," *Marketing News* (September 14, 1984), pp. 1, 22, 24.

[3]S. M. Scherer, *Industrial Market Structure and Economic Performance* (Chicago: Rand McNally, 1980), p. 470.

[4]"AMF Will Produce TV Ads Featuring Safety in Bicycling," *The Wall Street Journal* (July 9, 1979), p. 5.

[5]William L. Wilkie, Dennis L. McNeil, and Michael B. Mazis, "Marketing's 'Scarlet Letter': The Theory and Practice of Corrective Advertising," *Journal of Marketing* (Spring 1984), pp. 11–31.

[6]The fair trade concept is reviewed in such articles as James C. Johnson and Louis E. Boone, "Farewell to Fair Trade," *MSU Business Topics* (Spring 1976), pp. 22–30, and L. Louise Luchsinger and Patrick M. Dunne, "Fair Trade Laws—How Fair?" *Journal of Marketing* (January 1978), pp. 50–54.

[7]Lawrence Stessin, "Incidents of Culture Shock Among American Businessmen Overseas," *Pittsburgh Business Review* (November–December 1971), p. 3.

Chapter 3

[1]Alfred D. Chandler, *Strategy and Structure* (Cambridge, Mass.: MIT Press, 1962), p. 13. See also Paul F. Anderson, "Marketing, Strategic Planning, and the Theory of the Firm," *Journal of Marketing* (Spring 1982), pp. 15–26.

[2]"Strategic Planning Should Occupy 30 to 50 Percent of CEO's Time: Schanck," *Marketing News* (June 1, 1979), p. 1.

[3]Derek F. Abell, "Strategic Windows," *Journal of Marketing* (July 1978), pp. 21–26.

[4]This strategy has also been called product differentiation. See Wendell R. Smith, "Product Differentiation and Market Segmentation as Alternative Marketing Strategies," *Journal of Marketing* (July 1956), pp. 3–8. The terms undifferentiated marketing, differentiated marketing, and concentrated marketing were suggested by Philip Kotler. See his *Marketing Management* (Englewood Cliffs, N.J.: Prentice-Hall, 1984), pp. 267–271.

[5]Bernie Whalen, "Tiny Saab Drives Up Profits with Market-Niche Strategy, Repositioning," *Marketing News* (March 16, 1984), pp. 14–15.

[6]Martin Love, "The Man in the Doubleknit Suit," *Forbes* (October 24, 1983), p. 100.

[7]See R. William Kotrba, "The Strategy Selection Chart," *Journal of Marketing* (July 1966), pp. 22–25.

[8]"GE's New Strategy for Faster Growth," *Business Week* (July 8, 1972), pp. 52–58. Quoted in Lester A. Neidell, *Strategic Marketing Management* (Tulsa: PennWell Books, 1983), p. 92.

[9]Neidell, p. 93.

[10]Philippe Haspeslagh, "Portfolio Planning: Uses and Limitations," *Harvard Business Review* (January–February 1982), pp. 58–73.

[11]Quoted in Arthur R. Roolman, "Why Corporations Hate the Future," *MBA* (November 1975), p. 37.

[12]David T. Kollat, Roger D. Blackwell, and James F. Robeson, *Strategic Marketing* (New York: Holt, Rinehart & Winston, 1972), p. 498.

[13]Ed Roseman, "An Audit Can Make the 'Accurate' Difference," *Product Marketing* (August 1979), pp. 24–25.

[14]Louis R. Capella and William S. Sekely, "The Marketing Audit: Usage and Applications," in Robert S. Franz, Robert M. Hopkins, and Alfred G. Toma, eds., *Proceedings of the Southern Marketing Association* (New Orleans, 1979), p. 412.

Chapter 4

[1]Committee on Definitions, *Marketing Definitions: A Glossary of Marketing Terms* (Chicago: American Marketing Association, 1960), p. 17.

[2]"Include Marketing Research in Every Level of Corporate Strategic Planning," *Marketing News* (September 18, 1981), Sec. 2, p. 8.

[3]This story is told in the following source and elsewhere: Eric Scigliano, "Research Hinges on Human Factors," *Monthly* (October 1981), p. 9.

[4]For a detailed treatment of the historical development of marketing research, see Robert Bartels, *The Development of Marketing Thought* (Homewood, Ill.: Richard D. Irwin, 1962), pp. 106–124.

[5]Reported in Priscilla A. La Barbera and Larry J. Rosenberg, "How Marketers Can Better Understand Consumers," *MSU Business Topics* (Winter 1980), p. 29.

[6]"Marketing Oriented Lever Uses Research to Capture Bigger Dentifrice Market Shares," *Marketing News* (February 10, 1978), p. 9.

[7]"Marketing Research Needs Right Organization People to Fulfill Its Strategic Planning Potential," *Marketing News* (September 18, 1981), Sec. 1, p. 14.

[8]"Marquee," *The Seattle Times* (May 16, 1982), p. H 4.

[9]"Let a Data Base Get You the Facts," *Changing Times* (October 1984), pp. 47, 49.

[10]Bertram Schoner and Kenneth P. Uhl, *Marketing Research: Information Systems and Decision Making* (New York: John Wiley & Sons, Inc., 1975), p. 199.

[11]Eileen Norris, "Product Hopes Tied to Cities with the 'Right Stuff'," *Advertising Age* (February 20, 1984), p. M 10.

[12]"Marketing Research Industry Survey Finds Increase in Phone Interviewing," *Marketing News* (January 9, 1981), p. 20.

[13]Reported in A. B. Blankenship, "Listed Versus Unlisted Numbers in Telephone-Survey Samples," *Journal of Advertising Research* (February 1977), pp. 39–42.

[14]Mail questionnaire response rate variables have been researched extensively. See recent papers like Julie Yu and Harris Cooper, "A Quantitative Review of Research Design Effects on Response Rates to Questionnaires," *Journal of Marketing Research* (February 1983), pp. 36–44; and Curt J. Dommeyer, "Will Offering Respondents A Summary of the Results Affect the Responses to a Mail Survey?" edited by Stephen H. Achtenhagen, *Proceedings of the 1982 Western Marketing Educators' Conference*, pp. 35–36.

[15]"About that Cow," *The Wall Street Journal* (June 28, 1972), p. 1.

[16]Cathy Reiner, "Seattle-Area Pop Drinkers to Test Decaffeinated Pepsi," *The Seattle Times* (August 3, 1982), p. E 4.

[17]William G. Zikmund, *Exploring Marketing Research* (Hinsdale, Ill.: The Dryden Press, 1982), pp. 377–393.

[18]Donald F. Cox and Robert E. Good, "How to Build a Marketing Information System," *Harvard Business Review* (May–June 1967), p. 147. See also Charles D. Schewe and William R. Dillon, "Marketing Information Systems Utilization: An Application of Self-Concept Theory," *Journal of Business Research* (January 1978), pp. 67–69.

[19]"Marketing Intelligence Systems: A DEW Line for Marketing Men," *Business Management* (January 1966), p. 32.

[20]Information from "Marketing Management and the Computer," *Sales Management* (August 20, 1965), pp. 49–60. See also Leon Winer, "Effective Computer Use in Marketing Information Systems and Model Building," in *Marketing: 1776–1976 and Beyond*, edited by Kenneth L. Bernhardt (Chicago: American Marketing Association, 1976), pp. 626–629.

Chapter 5

[1]U.S. Department of Commerce, Bureau of the Census, *Current Population Reports: Population Estimates and Projections*, Series P–25, No. 944 (issued January 1984), p. 2.

[2]"Prediction: Sunny Side Up," *Time* (September 19, 1983), p. 28.

[3]"Americans Don't Move as Often, Report Says," *Journal-American* (March 5, 1984), p. A 5 (AP story).

[4]The new designations are outlined in U.S. Bureau of the Census, *Statistical Abstract of the United States: 1984* (104th edition), Washington, D.C., pp. 895–896.

[5]Kenneth Runyon, *Consumer Behavior*, 2nd ed. (Columbus, Ohio: Charles E. Merrill, 1980), p. 35.

[6]"Briefs," *Wealthbuilding* (March 1984), p. 5.

[7]"U.S. Median Age Nears a Record 31," *Journal-American* (May 21, 1984), p. A 8.

[8]"The Way U.S. Looks Now—Official Profile," *U.S. News & World Report* (May 28, 1984), p. 56.

[9]These examples are from an earlier life cycle study. See William D. Wells and George Gubar, "Life Cycle Concept in Marketing Research," *Journal of Marketing Research* (November 1966), p. 362. See also Frederick W. Derrick and Alane K. Lehfeld, "The Family Life Cycle: An Alternative Approach," *Journal of Consumer Research* (September 1980), pp. 214–217.

[10]Ralph Gray, "Ford Puts Two-Seater into Drive," *Advertising Age* (February 23, 1981), p. 10.

[11]Reported in "Research on Food Consumption Values Identifies Four Market Segments: Finds Good Taste Still Tops," *Marketing News* (May 15, 1981), p. 17. Used by permission of the American Marketing Association.

[12]See "Lifestyle Research: A Lot of Hype Versus Little Performance," *Marketing News* (May 14, 1982), Sec. 2, p. 3.

[13]Sharon Pavishall, "Greeting Card Business Comes of Age," *Journal-American* (April 30, 1984), pp. C 1, C 2.

[14]Reported in David T. Kollat, Roger D. Blackwell, and James F. Robeson, *Strategic Marketing* (New York: Holt, Rinehart and Winston, 1972), p. 192.

[15]Dik Warren Twedt, "How Important to Marketing Strategy is the 'Heavy User'," *Journal of Marketing* (January 1962), pp. 71–72.

[16]These methods are suggested in Martin L. Bell, *Marketing: Concepts and Strategy* (Boston: Houghton-Mifflin, 1979), p. 129.

[17]Daniel Yankelovich, "New Criteria for Market Segmentation," *Harvard Business Review* (March–April, 1964), pp. 83–90.

[18]Alfred E. Goldman, "Market Segmentation Analysis Tells What to Say to Whom," *Marketing News* (January 22, 1982), Sec. 1, p. 10.

[19]Myron Magnet, "How to Compete with IBM," *FORTUNE* (February 6, 1984), p. 58.

[20]"Lite Bite," *Time* (October 24, 1983), p. 74.

[21]A similar analysis is suggested in Robert M. Fulmer, *The New Marketing* (New York: Macmillan, 1976), pp. 34–37; Philip Kotler, *Marketing Management* (Englewood Cliffs, N.J.: Prentice-Hall, 1976), pp. 141–151; and E. Jerome McCarthy, *Basic Marketing* (Homewood, Ill.: Richard D. Irwin, 1975), pp. 111–126.

Chapter 6

[1]This definition is adapted from James F. Engel and Roger D. Blackwell, *Consumer Behavior*, 4th edition (Hinsdale, Ill.: The Dryden Press, 1982), p. 9.

[2]See Kurt Lewin, *Field Theory in Social Science* (New York: Harper & Row, 1951), p. 62. See also C. Glenn Walters, "Consumer Behavior: An Appraisal," *Journal of the Academy of Marketing Science* (Fall 1979), pp. 237–284.

[3]"Learning How to Please the Baffling Japanese," *FORTUNE* (October 5, 1981), p. 122.

[4]Engel and Blackwell, *Consumer Behavior*, 4th edition, p. 72.

[5]The discussion of the baby boom generation is adapted from Connie Lauerman, "Where Have All the Flower Children Gone?" *Florida* (November 8, 1981), pp. 6–7.

[6]Daniel Yankelovich, "New Rules," *The Seattle Times* (November 1, 1981), pp. F 1, F 4. Excerpted from the book, *New Rules: Searching for Self-Fulfillment in a World Turned Upside Down*, by Daniel Yankelovich. Copyright 1981, Daniel Yankelovich. Distributed by Los Angeles Times Syndicate.

[7]This is noted in Engel and Blackwell, *Consumer Behavior*, 4th edition, p. 75.

[8]"Learning How to Please the Baffling Japanese," p. 122.

[9]Robert Linn, "Americans Turn Deaf Ear to Foreign Tongues," *Orlando Sentinel Star* (November 1, 1981).

[10]"Chinese Commit Faux Pas, Too, in Export Marketing," *Marketing News* (October 14, 1983), p. 13.

[11]See "Counting Up Blacks and Hispanics," *Sales & Marketing Management* (April 6, 1981), p. 24.

[12]These statistics are from *Ibid.*, p. 24; and Theodore J. Gage, "RSVP: An Invitation to Buy," *Advertising Age* (May 18, 1981), Sec. 2, p. 51.

[13]U.S. Bureau of the Census, *Statistical Abstract of the United States: 1984* (104th edition) Washington D.C., 1983, pp. 32, 37, 38.

[14]These findings are summarized in Engel and Blackwell, pp. 91–92.

[15]Alphonzia Wellington, "Traditional Brand Loyalty," *Advertising Age* (May 18, 1981), Sec. 2, p. 52.

[16]Gage, "RSVP: An Invitation to Buy," pp. 5–9.

[17]U.S. Department of Commerce, Bureau of the Census, *Standard Metropolitan Statistical Areas and Standard Consolidated Statistical Areas: 1980* (PC 80–S1-5) issued October 1981.

[18]"Learning the Hispanic Hustle," *Newsweek* (May 17, 1982), p. 83.

[19]Reported in a table in "Views from the Inside," *Advertising Age* (April 6, 1981), Sec. 2, pp. 5–8.

[20]These statistics are reported in *U.S. News & World Report* (August 24, 1981), p. 63.

[21]"Learning the Hispanic Hustle," p. 84.

[22]Del I. Hawkins, Kenneth A. Coney and Roger J. Best, *Consumer Behavior: Implications for Marketing Strategy*, revised edition (Plano, Texas: Business Publications, 1983), p. 214. The quotation is adapted from S. E. Asch, "Effects of Group Pressure Upon the Modification and Distortion of Judgments," in *Readings in Social Psychology*, edited by E. E. MacCoby et al. (New York: Holt, Rinehart and Winston, 1958), pp. 174–183.

[23]See Richard P. Coleman, "The Significance of Social Stratification in Selling," and "Retrospective Comment," edited by Louis E. Boone, *Classics in Consumer Behavior* (Tulsa, Oklahoma: PPC Books, 1977), pp. 288–302; and Richard P. Coleman and Lee Rainwater, *Social Standing in America: New Dimensions of Class* (New York: Basic Books, 1978).

[24]Charles M. Schaninger, "Social Class Versus Income Revisited: An Empirical Investigation," *Journal of Marketing Research* (May 1981), pp. 192–208.

[25]See Danny N. Bellenger and Elizabeth C. Hirschman, "Identifying Opinion Leaders by Self-Report," in *Contemporary Marketing Thought*, edited by Barnett A. Greenberg and Danny N. Bellenger (Chicago: American Marketing Association, 1977), pp. 341–344.

[26]Elihu Katz and Paul F. Lazarsfeld, *Personal Influence* (New York: Free Press, 1957), p. 32.

[27]"Marriage Binds Fewer than 60% of U.S. Households," *Orlando Sentinel Star* (November 16, 1981), p. 6-A.

[28]Carmaron L. Smith and Beverly M. Barry, "Analyze Consumer Behavior, Social Trends to Determine Potential of New Food Products," *Marketing News* (April 6, 1982), p. 6.

[29]Bill Abrams, "TV Ad Shows Struggles to Replace Bygone Images of Today's Mother," *The Wall Street Journal* (October 5, 1984), p. 35.

[30]Engel and Blackwell, *Consumer Behavior*, 4th edition, pp. 176–182. See also Wilson Brown, "The Family and Consumer Decision Making," *Journal of the Academy of Marketing Science* (Fall 1979), pp. 335–343.

[31]Rand Youth Poll, "Teenage Economic Power." Survey findings received in a letter from Robert Williams, executive director of the Youth Research Institute, May 17, 1984.

[32]Mark N. Dodosh, "Widely Ignored Teen Market Has A Lot of Spending Power," *The Wall Street Journal* (June 17, 1982), p. 23; Richard Kreisman, "Teens' Role Grows in Family's Grocery Purchases," *Advertising Age* (May 17, 1982), p. 68; and an advertisement for *Seventeen* magazine that appears in *Advertising Age* (May 3, 1982), p. 33.

[33]A. H. Maslow, *Motivation and Personality* (New York: Harper & Row, 1954).

[34]See Robert H. Bloom, "Production Redefinition Begins With Consumer," *Advertising Age* (October 26, 1981), p. 51.

[35]Maslow, *Motivation and Personality*, p. 382. See also George Brooker, "The Self-Actualizing Socially Conscious Consumer," *Journal of Consumer Research* (September 1976), pp. 107–112.

[36]Burt Schorr, "The Mistakes: Many New Products Fail Despite Careful Planning, Publicity," *The Wall Street Journal* (April 5, 1961), pp. 1, 22.

[37]These examples are reported in Henry Assael, *Consumer Behavior and Marketing Action* (Boston: Kent Publishing Company, 1984), p. 124.

[38]See James H. Myers and William H. Reynolds, *Consumer Behavior and Marketing Management* (Boston: Houghton-Mifflin, 1967), p. 14; J. Steven Kelly and Barbara M. Kessler, "Subliminal Seduction: Fact or Fantasy?" in *Proceedings of the Southern Marketing Association* (November 1978), pp. 112–114; and Joel Saegert, "Another Look at Subliminal Perception," *Journal of Advertising Research* (February 1979), pp. 55–57.

[39]C. E. Osgood, G. J. Suci, and P. H. Tannenbaum, *The Measurement of Meaning* (Urbana: University of Illinois Press, 1957). For a comparison of the semantic differential Likert Scale, and the Stapel Scale, see Dennis Menezes and Norbert F. Elbert, "Alternative Semantic Scaling Formats for Measuring Store Image: An Evaluation," *Journal of Marketing Research* (February 1979), pp. 80–87.

[40]Frederick E. Webster, Jr., and Frederick Von Pechmann, "A Replication of the 'Shopping List' Study," *Journal of Marketing* (April 1970), pp. 61–63. See also George S. Lane and Gayne L. Watson, "A Canadian Replication of Mason Haire's 'Shopping List' Study," *Journal of the Academy of Marketing Science* (Winter 1975), pp. 48–59.

[41]This section is based on Michael L. Rothschild and William C. Gaidis, "Behavioral Learning Theory: Its Relevance to Marketing and Promotion," *Journal of Marketing* (Spring 1981), pp. 70–78.

[42]John Koten, "For Kellogg, the Hardest Part is Getting People Out of Bed," *The Wall Street Journal* (May 27, 1982), p. 27.

[43]B. M. Campbell, "The Existence of Evoked Set and Determinants of Its Magnitude in Brand Choice Behavior," in *Buyer Behavior and Empirical Foundations*, edited by John A. Howard and Lonnie Ostrom (New York: Alfred A. Knopf, Inc., 1973), pp. 243–244.

[44]Engel and Blackwell, *Consumer Behavior*, 4th edition, p. 418.

[45]For a thorough discussion of purchase location, see David L. Loudon and Albert J. Della Bitta, *Consumer Behavior: Concepts and Applications* (New York: McGraw-Hill, 1979), pp. 483–511.

[46]Leon Festinger, *A Theory of Cognitive Dissonance* (Stanford, Calif.: Stanford University Press, 1958), p. 3.

[47]See Robert J. Connole, James D. Benson, and Inder P. Khera, "Cognitive Dissonance Among Innovators," *Journal of the Academy of Marketing Science* (Winter 1977), pp. 9–20; David R. Lambert, Ronald J. Dornoff, and Jerome B. Kernan, "The Industrial Buyer and Postchoice Evaluation Process," *Journal of Marketing Research* (May 1977), pp. 246–251; and William H. Cummings and M. Venkatesan, "Cognitive Dissonance and Consumer Behavior: A Review of the Evidence," *Journal of Marketing* (August 1976), pp. 303–308.

[48]These categories were originally suggested in John A. Howard, *Marketing Management: Analysis and Planning* (Homewood, Ill.: Richard D. Irwin, Inc., 1963). The discussion here is based on Donald R. Lehmann, William L. Moore, and Terry Elrod, "The Development of Distinct Choice Process Segments Over Time: A Stochastic Modeling Approach," *Journal of Marketing* (Spring 1982), pp. 48–50.

Chapter 7

[1]The similarities between consumer and industrial goods marketing are discussed in Edward F. Fern and James R. Brown, "The Industrial/Consumer Marketing Dichotomy: A Case of Insufficient Justification," *Journal of Marketing* (Spring 1984), pp. 68–71.

[2]Quoted in James D. Hlavacek, "Business Schools Need More Industrial Marketing," *Marketing News* (April 4, 1980), p. 1.

[3]*Statistical Abstract of the United States* (Washington, D.C.: U.S. Government Printing Office, 1984), p. 764.

[4]Sales & Marketing Management's 1984 Survey of Industrial and Commercial Buying Power, *Sales & Marketing Management* (April 23, 1984), p. 22.

[5]Executive Office of the President, Office of Management and Budget, *Standard Industrial Classification Manual: 1972*, pp. 71–77; U.S. Department of Commerce, Bureau of the Census, *1977 Census of Manufacturers*, Part 1: SIC Major Groups 20–26, Vol. II, Industry Statistics, p. 22E-19.

[6]"Paper Mate's Broader Outlook," *Business Week* (January 28, 1980), p. 69.

[7]These characteristics are suggested in Robert W. Haas, *Industrial Marketing Management* (New York: Petrocelli/Charter, 1976), pp. 21–26; and Richard M. Hill, Ralph S. Alexander, and James S. Cross, *Industrial Marketing*, 4th ed. (Homewood, Ill.: Richard D. Irwin, Inc., 1975), pp. 46–47.

[8]The development of the new type of pole and the problems involved in its adoption are described in Arch G. Woodside, "Marketing Anatomy of Buying Process Can Help Improve Industrial Strategy," *Marketing News* (May 1, 1981), Section 2, p. 11.

[9]These are suggested in Patrick J. Robinson, Charles W. Farris, and Yoram Wind, *Industrial Buying and Creative Marketing* (Boston: Allyn and Bacon, 1967), Chapter 1. The discussion here follows Michael D. Hutt and Thomas W. Speh, *Industrial Marketing Management*, 2nd ed. (Hinsdale, Ill.: The Dryden Press, 1985), pp. 65–69.

[10]This section is based on Hutt and Speh, *Industrial Marketing Management*, 2nd edition, pp. 97–105.

[11]Hutt and Speh, *Industrial Marketing Management*, 2nd edition, p. 97 cite the following sources for their statistics: "Industrial Salespeople Report 4.1 Buying Influences in Average Company," *LAP Report* 1042.2 (McGraw-Hill Research, October 1977); and G. Van der Most, "Purchasing Process: Researching Influence Is Basic to Marketing Plan," *Industrial Marketing* (October 1976), p. 120.

[12]These price cuts are described in Thomas F. O'Boyle, "Price Cutting Being Forced on Suppliers," *The Wall Street Journal* (May 14, 1982), p. 27.

[13]The history of reciprocity agreements is summarized in E. Robert Finney, "Reciprocity: Gone But Not Forgotten," *Journal of Marketing* (January 1978), pp. 54–59.

[14]"Out of the Maze," *Sales & Marketing Management* (April 9, 1979), p. 45. Material updated on June 14, 1984 by Allan Beres of the GSA.

[15]This section is based on "Out of the Maze," pp. 44–46, 48, 50, 52.

[16]*Ibid.*, pp. 46, 48, 50, 52.

[17]Phone conversation with Bud Maraist, Office of Management and Budget, Federal Procurement Policy, May 10, 1984.

[18]"GSA and Life Cycle Costing: A Formula for Success," *Government Executive* (April 1984).

Chapter 8

[1]Janet Marr, "The Magnuson-Moss Warranty Act," *Family Economics Review* (Summer 1978), pp. 3–7.

[2]Future Computing Company, Richardson, Texas (May 2, 1984).

[3]Students of economics will recognize this situation as exemplifying price elasticity of demand. For a discussion of the concept of elasticity, see Edwin G. Dolan, *Basic Economics* (Hinsdale, Ill.: The Dryden Press, 1983). Also an excellent discussion of the management of firms with mature products is found in Roger C. Bennett and Robert G. Cooper, "The Product Life Cycle Trap," *Business Horizons* (September–October, 1984), pp. 7–16.

[4]Fashion cycles are discussed in Raymond A. Marquardt, James C. Makens, and Robert G. Roe, *Retail Management*, 3rd edition. (Hinsdale, Ill.: The Dryden Press, 1983), pp. 98–99. Also see George B. Sproles, "Analyzing Fashion Life Cycles—Principles and Perspectives," *Journal of Marketing* (Fall 1981), pp. 116–124.

[5]Stephen Grover, "Record Business Slumps as Taping and Video Games Take Away Sales," *The Wall Street Journal* (Feb. 18, 1982), p. 25.

[6]See David R. Rink and John E. Swan, "Product Life Cycle Research: A Literature Review," *Journal of Business Research* (September 1979), pp. 219–242.

[7]Everett M. Rogers and F. Floyd Shoemaker, *Communication of Innovation* (New York: The Free Press, 1971), pp. 135–157.

[8]"Gillette Spends $17.4 Million to Introduce Aapri, Gain Foothold in Skin Care Market," *Marketing News* (May 29, 1981), p. 6. For a discussion of the use of marketing techniques to facilitate trial purchases, see James W. Taylor and Paul S. Hugstad, " 'Add-on' Purchasing: Consumer Behavior in the Trial of New Products," *Journal of the Academy of Marketing Science* (Winter 1980), pp. 294–299.

[9]Ronald Marks and Eugene Hughes, "Profiling the Consumer Innovator," edited by John H. Summey and Ronald D. Taylor, *Evolving Marketing Thought for 1980* (New Orleans: Southern Marketing Association, 1980), pp. 115–118; Elizabeth Hirschman, "Innovativeness, Novelty Seeking and Consumer Creativity," *Journal of Consumer Research* (December 1980), pp. 283–295; and Richard W. Olshavsky, "Time and the Rate of Adoption of Innovations," *Journal of Consumer Research* (March 1980), pp. 425–428.

[10]For a more thorough discussion of the speed of the adoption process, see Rogers and Shoemaker, *Communication of Innovations*, pp. 135–157.

[11]This three-way classification of consumer goods was first proposed by Melvin T. Copeland. See his *Principles of Merchandising* (New York: McGraw-Hill, 1924), chapters 2–4. For a more recent discussion of this classification scheme, see Marvin A. Jolson and Stephen L. Proia, "Classification of Consumer Goods—A Subjective Measure?" in *Marketing: 1776–1976 and Beyond* (Chicago: American Marketing Association, 1976), pp. 71–75.

[12]For an early discussion of the distinctions between homogeneous and heterogeneous shopping goods, see E. J. McCarthy, *Basic Marketing* (Homewood, Ill.: Richard D. Irwin, 1964), pp. 398–400. See also Harry A. Lipson and John R. Darling, *Marketing Fundamentals* (New York: Wiley, 1974), p. 244.

[13]A similar classification scheme has been proposed by Leo Aspinwall, who considers five product characteristics in classifying consumer goods—*replacement rate*, *gross margin* (the difference between cost and selling price), *adjustment* (the necessary changes made in a goal to satisfy precisely the consumer's needs), *time of consumption* (the time interval during which the product provides satisfaction), and *length of consumer search time*. See Leo V. Aspinwall, "The Characteristics of Goods Theory," in *Four Marketing Theories* (Boulder: Bureau of Business Research, University of Colorado, 1961).

[14]Some of the information in this section is from Eugene Johnson, "The Selling of Services," in *Handbook of Modern Marketing*, edited by Victor P. Buell (New York: McGraw-Hill, 1970), pp. 12-110 to 12-120.

[15]Carol Smith Monkman, "Is It a Product or Service? Software Is Taxing Issue," *Journal-American* (July 25, 1984), pp. D-1, D-2.

[16]A goods-services continuum is suggested in G. Lynn Shostack, "Breaking Free From Product Marketing," *Journal of Marketing* (April 1977), p. 77. See also John M. Rathmell, "What is Meant by Services?" *Journal of Marketing* (October 1966), pp. 32–36.

[17]An excellent discussion of the literature on classifying services is found in Christopher H. Lovelock, "Classifying Services to Gain Strategic Marketing Insights," *Journal of Marketing* (Summer 1983), pp. 9–20.

Chapter 9

[1]The width and depth of assortment is described in Raymond A. Marquardt, James C. Makens, and Robert G. Roe, *Retail Management*, 3rd ed. (Hinsdale, Ill.: The Dryden Press, 1983), pp. 95–96.

[2]"Name Game," *Time* (August 31, 1981), p. 42.

[3]Nancy Giges, "Nestlé's Chief's Mission: Pick Winners, Ax Losers," *Advertising Age* (September 7, 1981), p. 64.

[4]Polaroid's product development strategies are described in "Polaroid: Turning Away from Land's One-Product Strategy," *Business Week* (March 2, 1981), pp. 108–112.

[5]Booz, Allen & Hamilton, Inc., *New Products Management for the 1980s*, (1982), p. 4.

[6]Douglas R. Scase, "Chrysler Is Upbeat as Market Share Rises, but Some Doubt It Can Maintain Success," *The Wall Street Journal* (April 22, 1982), p. 33.

[7]Howard Rudnitakey, "Snap Judgments Can Be Wrong," *Forbes* (April 12, 1982).

[8]Carol J. Loomis, "P & G Up Against Its Wall," *FORTUNE* (February 23, 1981), pp. 49–54.

[9]Eileen Norns, "Product Hopes Tied to Cities with the 'Right Stuff'," *Advertising Age* (February 20, 1984), p. M-10.

[10]Product positioning maps are discussed in a variety of sources. See, for example, Henry Assae, *Consumer Behavior and Marketing Action*, 2nd ed. (Boston: Kent Publishing Company, 1984), pp. 499–516.

[11]John Koten, "Giving Buyers Wide Choices May Be Hurting Auto Makers," *The Wall Street Journal* (December 15, 1983), p. 33.

[12]Edward M. Tauber, "New Roles for Old Items," (An MT Forum) *Marketing Times* (July–August 1981), p. 40.

[13]Abrams, "Despite Mixed Record, Firms Still Pushing for Products," p. 25.

[14]Reported in Ann M. Morrison, "The General Mills Brand of Manager," *FORTUNE* (January 12, 1981), pp. 99–107. Another interesting discussion appears in "Brand Management System Is Best, but Refinements Needed," *Marketing News* (July 9, 1982), p. 12.

[15]Jacob M. Duker and Michael V. Laric, "The Product Manager: No Longer on Trial," in *The Changing Marketing Environment: New Theories and Applications*, edited by Kenneth Bernhardt, Ira Dolich, Michael Etzel, William Kehoe, Thomas Kinnear, William Perrault, Jr., and Kenneth Roering (Chicago: American Marketing Association, 1981), pp. 93–96; and Peter S. Howsam and G. David Hughes, "Product Management System Suffers from Insufficient Experience, Poor Communication," *Marketing News* (June 26, 1981), Sec. 2, p. 8.

[16]William S. Sachs and George Benson, *Product Planning and Management* (Tulsa, Okla.: PennWell Books, 1981), p. 164.

[17]See William B. Locander and Richard W. Scamell, "Screening New Product Ideas—A Two-Phase Approach," *Research Management* (March 1976), pp. 14–18.

[18]Reported in Edward Buxton, *Promise Them Anything* (New York: Stein & Day, 1972), p. 101.

[19]Quoted in Mary McCabe English, "Marketers: Better Than A Coin Flip," *Advertising Age* (February 9, 1981), p. S-15.

[20]Dylan Landis, "Durable Goods for a Test?" *Advertising Age* (February 9, 1981), pp. S-18.

[21]B. G. Yovovich, "Competition Jumps the Gun," *Advertising Age* (February 9, 1981), pp. S-18.

[22]Reported in "Polaroid: Turning Away from Land's One-Product Strategy," *Business Week* (March 2, 1981), p. 111.

[23]Committee on Definitions, *Marketing Definitions: A Glossary of Marketing Terms* (Chicago: American Marketing Association, 1960), pp. 9–10.

[24]The registration of trademarks and related issues are discussed in Louis E. Boone and James C. Johnson, "Trademark Protection: What's in A Name?" *Business* (April–June 1982), pp. 12–17.

[25]Bernice Kanner, "The Game of the Name," *New Yorker* (August 23, 1983), p. 32.

[26]"A Worldwide Brand for Nissan," *Business Week* (August 24, 1981), p. 104.

[27]"No More Monopoly on Monopoly," *The Seattle Times* (February 22, 1983), p. A 6.

[28]John Koten, "Mixing With Coke over Trademarks Is Always a Fizzle," *The Wall Street Journal* (March 9, 1978). For a thorough discussion of the brand name decision, see James U. McNeal and Linda M. Zeren, "Brand Name Selection for Consumer Products," *MSU Business Topics* (Spring 1981), pp. 35–39.

[29]Meir Statman and Tyzoon T. Tyebjee, "Trademarks, Patents, and Innovation in the Ethical Drug Industry," *Journal of Marketing* (Summer 1981), pp. 71–81.

[30]Bill Abrams, "Brand Loyalty Rises Slightly, but Increase Could Be Fluke," *The Wall Street Journal* (February 7, 1982), p. 21.

[31]Ronald Alsop, "Fisher Price Banks on Name, Design In Foray into Playwear," *The Wall Street Journal* (August 2, 1984), p. 23.

[32]"Name Game," *Time* (August 31, 1981), p. 41.

[33]Bill Abrams, "Shoppers Are Often Confused by All The Competing Brands," *The Wall Street Journal* (April 22, 1982), p. 33.

[34]Norman Seigle, "Generic Foods—A Further Report," *Nargus Merchandising Letter* (May 1980); Robert Dietrich, "Still Rooted in the Basics, Generics Sprout New Buds Too," *Progressive Grocer* (May 1980), p. 119. Generics are also discussed in Martha R. McEnally and Jon M. Hawes, "The Market for Generic Brand Grocery Products: A Review and Extension," *Journal of Marketing* (Winter 1984), pp. 75–83.

[35]Rubber Manufacturing Association, April 1, 1984; American Petroleum Institute, *Gasoline Marketing In the United States Today* (September 1983), p. 18.

[36]John Koten, "Why Do Hot Dogs Come in Packs of 10 and Buns in 8s or 12s," *The Wall Street Journal* (September 21, 1984), p. 1.

[37]"Packaging Linked to Ad's Effect," *Advertising Age* (May 3, 1982), p. 63.

[38]Bill Abrams and David P. Garino, "Package Gains Stature as Visual Competition Grows," *The Wall Street Journal* (August 6, 1981).

[39]The National Confectioners Association of the United States.

[40]Robert Ball, "Warm Milk Wakes Up the Packaging Industry," *FORTUNE* (August 7, 1982), pp. 78–82.

[41]"Shift to Metrics Moving Ahead in Millimeters," *U.S. News & World Report* (June 7, 1982), p. 77.

[42]This section is based on Raymond A. Marquardt, James C. Makens, and Robert G. Roe, *Retail Management*, 3rd edition (Hinsdale, Ill.: The Dryden Press, 1983), pp. 280–283; Edward M. Cooper and Harvey H. Sundel, "Attitudes of Users and Non-Users of Scanner Equipped Retail Food Stores: An Empirical Study," in *Progress in Marketing and Practice*, edited by Ronald D. Taylor, John S. Summey, and Blaise J. Bergiel (Proceedings of the Southern Marketing Association), pp. 186–190; and "Store Scanners: Not A Super Market," *Newsweek* (June 22, 1981), p. 14.

Chapter 10

[1]Wilke English, Dale M. Lewison, and M. Wayne DeLozier, "Evolution in Channel Management: What Will Be Next?" in *Proceedings of the Southwestern Marketing Association*, edited by Robert H. Ross, Frederic B. Kraft, and Charles H. Davis (Wichita, Kansas: 1981), pp. 78–81.

[2]News release, The Reynolds Metals Company, April 24, 1984.

[3]Bruce J. Walker and Donald W. Jackson, Jr., "The Channels Manager: A Needed New Position," in *Proceedings of the Southern Marketing Association*, edited by Robert S. Franz, Robert M. Hopkins, and Al Toma (New Orleans, La.: November 1978), pp. 325–328. See also R. Kenneth Teas and Stanley D. Sibley, "An Examination of the Moderating Effect on Channel Member Size of Perceptions of Preferred Channel Linkages," *Journal of the Academy of Marketing Science* (Summer 1980), pp. 277–293.

[4]Letter from Leah F. Colihan, manager of Public Relations, Bic Corporation, April 24, 1984.

[5]Paul A. Allen, "Why Distributors Sue Manufacturers," *Inc.* (November 1981), p. 157.

[6]Exclusive distribution is described in more detail in Bert Rosenbloom, *Marketing Channels* (Hinsdale, Ill.: The Dryden Press, 1983), pp. 147–150.

[7]Michael B. Metzger, "Schwinn's Swan Song," *Business Horizons* (April 1978), pp. 52–56.

[8]This section is based on Bert C. McCammon, Jr., "The Emergence and Growth of Contractually Integrated Channels in the American Economy," in *Marketing and Economic Development* (Chicago: American Marketing Association, 1965), pp. 496–515.

[9]*Ibid.*, p. 496.

[10]Thomas G. Marx, "Distribution Efficiency in Franchising," *MSU Business Topics* (Winter 1980), p. 5.

[11]National Restaurant Association, May 8, 1984.

[12]Telephone conversation with the National Restaurant Association, May 8, 1984, and Burger King Corporation Franchising Brochure.

[13]See Donald W. Hackett, "U.S. Franchise Systems Abroad—The Second Boom," in *Marketing: 1776–1976 and Beyond*, edited by Kenneth L. Bernhardt (Chicago: American Marketing Association, 1976), pp. 253–256.

[14]U.S. Department of Commerce, Bureau of Industrial Economics, *Franchising in the Economy, 1982–1984*, Table 25, p. 45.

[15]Channel conflict is examined in James R. Brown and Ralph L. Day, "Measures of Manifest Conflict in Distribution Channels," *Journal of Marketing Research* (August 1981), pp. 263–274.

[16]Bruce Mallen, "A Theory of Retailer–Supplier Conflict, Control, and Cooperation," *Journal of Retailing* (Summer 1963), p. 26. Reprinted with permission. See also F. Robert Dwyer, "Channel–Member Satisfaction: Laboratory Insights," *Journal of Retailing* (Summer 1980), pp. 45–65.

[17]*Educators Conference Proceedings*, edited by Neil Beckwith, Michael Houston, Robert Mittelstaedt, Kent B. Monroe, and Scott Ward (Chicago: American Marketing Association, 1970), pp. 495–499; Michael Etgar, "Sources and Types of Intra Channel Conflict," *Journal of Retailing* (Spring 1979), pp. 61–78; and Louis W. Stern and Torger Reve, "Distribution Channels as Political Economies," *Journal of Marketing* (Summer 1980), pp. 52–64.

Chapter 11

[1]Marilyn Wellemeyer, "Middlemen of Metal," *FORTUNE* (March 1977), pp. 163–165.

[2]James R. Moore, "Wholesaling: Structural Changes and Manufacturers' Perceptions," in *Foundations of Marketing Channels*, edited by Arch G. Woodside, J. Taylor Sims, Dale M. Lewison, and Ian F. Wilkinson (Austin, Texas: Austin Press, 1978), pp. 118–131.

[3]Louis P. Bucklin, *Competition and Evolution in the Distributive Trades* (Englewood Cliffs, N.J.: Prentice-Hall, 1972), p. 214.

[4]"Surveys Find Trade Shows Cost-Effective, Productive," *Marketing News* (October 3, 1980), p. 4. See also Steven Kelly and James M. Comer, "Trade Show Exhibiting: A Managerial Perspective," in *Evolving Marketing Thought for 1980*, edited by John H. Summey and Ronald D. Taylor (Southern Marketing Association, 1980), pp. 11–13.

[5]Mart Center Chicago, "The Mart Center Fact Sheet."

[6]Benson Shapiro, "Improve Distribution with Your Promotional Mix," *Harvard Business Review* (March–April 1977), p. 116.

[7]Manufacturers' Agents National Association, "MANA's 1983 Survey of Sales Commissions."

Chapter 12

[1]For a complete discussion on the wheel of retailing hypothesis, see Stanley C. Hollander, "The Wheel of Retailing," *Journal of Marketing* (July 1960), pp. 37–42.

[2]Mervyn's News, a 1984 media release.

[3]Barbara Oman, "Department Stores Start Adding Seminars and Services to Attract Working Women," *The Wall Street Journal* (July 19, 1982), p. 19.

[4]"Quaker Oats Tailors for Growth," *Business Week* (July 26, 1982), p. 79.

[5]Bill Abrams, "New Worry for Manufacturers: Growth of Warehouse Outlets," *The Wall Street Journal* (May 28, 1981), p. 29.

[6]See "Ward's Latest Formula: Hybrid Discounting," *Business Week* (November 2, 1981), pp. 77, 80, 81, 83; and Steven Weiner, "Much of Old Montgomery Ward May Go As Pistner Seeks Profitability, New Image," *The Wall Street Journal* (June 15, 1981), p. 25.

[7]George Salman, "IC Places Pet on Profitable Diet," *St. Louis Business Journal* (June 6, 1982), p. 18.

[8]Lawrence Rout, "Shopping Center Glut Forces Investors to Look Elsewhere," *The Wall Street Journal* (August 12, 1981), p. 25.

[9]The Woodfield Mall is described in "Shopping Centers Will Be America's Towns of Tomorrow," *Marketing News* (November 28, 1980), p. 1.

[10]"Ward's Latest Formula: Hybrid Discounting," *Business Week* (November 2, 1981), p. 83.

[11]"A New Twist: Supermarket with All the Frills," *Business Week* (August 17, 1981), p. 122.

[12]"Due to Parity of Offerings, Retail Ads Should Emphasize Employee Pride, Customer Service," *Marketing News* (October 5, 1981), pp. 5, 8.

[13]This section is adapted from Louis P. Bucklin, "Retail Strategy and the Classification of Consumer Goods," *Journal of Marketing* (January 1963), pp. 50–55, published by the American Marketing Association.

[14]See Thomas J. Stanley and Murphy A. Sewell, "Predicting Supermarket Trade: Implications for Marketing Management," *Journal of Retailing* (Summer 1978), pp. 13–22. See also Danny N. Bellenger, Thomas J. Stanley, and John W. Allen, "Trends in Food Retailing," *Atlanta Economic Review* (May–June 1978), pp. 11–14.

[15]U.S. Bureau of the Census, *Statistical Abstract of the United States: 1982–1983*, 103rd ed., (Washington, D.C.: U.S. Government Printing Office, 1983), p. 802.

[16]*Ibid.*

[17]Ann M. Morrison, "The Upshot of Off-Price," *FORTUNE* (June 13, 1983), p. 122.

[18]Superstores are discussed in Myron Gable and Ronald D. Michman, "Superstores—Revolutionizing Distribution," *Business* (March–April 1981), pp. 14–18.

[19]Leonard Berry, "The Time-Buying Consumer," *Journal of Retailing* (Winter 1979), pp. 58–69.

[20]John A. Quelch and Hirotaka Takeuchi, "Nonstore Marketing: Fast Track or Slow?" *Harvard Business Review* (July–August 1981), p. 75.

[21]Estimated by Paul Muchnick, National Mail Order Association, 1982.

[22]This situation was updated by Walter W. Reed of the National Automatic Merchandising Association, April 25, 1984.

[23]Tom Bayer, "7-Eleven Takes Steps to Move Beyond Image," *Advertising Age* (December 7, 1981), pp. 4, 78.

[24]"Those Mom-and-Pop Stores Are Still Going Strong," *U.S. News & World Report* (July 28, 1978), pp. 59–62; and Gerald Albaum, Roger Best, and Del Hawkins, "Retailing Strategy for Customer Growth and New Customer Attraction," *Journal of Business Research* (March 1980), pp. 7–20.

[25]Julie Emery, "Gas Stations Offer Video Games, Groceries—and Service," *The Seattle Times* (May 2, 1982), p. A 25.

[26]Information provided by the National Association of Chain Drug Stores from *Drug Store News*.

[27]Information provided by Montgomery Ward, May 30, 1984.

[28]"What TV Revolution Will Bring into Your Home," *U.S. News & World Report* (September 14, 1981), pp. 67–68.

[29]"Only 10% of Consumers Interested in Shopping At Home Via 2-Way TV," *Marketing News* (May 29, 1981), pp. 1, 3.

[30]Malcolm P. McNair and Eleanor G. May, "The Next Revolution of the Retailing Wheel," *Harvard Business Review* (September–October 1978), pp. 81–91. Another interesting article is Larry J. Rosenberg and Elizabeth C. Hirschman, "Retailing without Stores," *Harvard Business Review* (July–August 1980), pp. 103–112.

[31]"Food Shoppers Rate Speed No. 1," *USA Today* (May 9, 1984), p. A 1.

Chapter 13

[1]National Council of Physical Distribution Management, *Measuring and Improving Productivity in Physical Distribution: 1984*, p. 7.

[2]Warren Rose, *Logistics Management* (Dubuque, Iowa: Wm. C. Brown, 1979), p. 4.

[3]James M. Daley and Zarrell V. Lambert, "Toward Accessing Trade-Offs by Shippers in Carrier Selection Decisions," *Journal of Business Logistics* Vol. 2, no. 1 (1980), pp. 35–54.

[4]Robert E. Sabath, "How Much Service Do Customers Really Want?" *Business Horizons* (April 1978), pp. 26–32. See also Arthur S. Graham, Jr., "Customer Service Measurement and Management in the 1980s," *Annual Proceedings of the National Council of Physical Distribution Management* (1980), pp. 265–275.

[5]Jeremy Main, "Toward Service Without a Snarl," *FORTUNE* (March 23, 1981), p. 61. © 1981 Time Inc. All rights reserved.

[6]Jack W. Farrell, "Boise-Cascade Transportation: An Active Partner in Business," *Traffic Management* (July 1983), p. 42.

[7]"Deregulation Watch," *Traffic Management* (February 1984), p. 94.

[8]The deregulation issue is discussed in Donald F. Wood and James C. Johnson, *Contemporary Transportation*, 2nd edition (Tulsa: PennWell Books, 1983), chapters 3–5. See also L. L. Waters, "Deregulation—For Better or For Worse?" *Business Horizons* (January–February 1981), pp. 88–91.

[9]"Court Affirms ICC's Toto Policy, Backs Private Trucks in For-Hire Moves," *Traffic World* (July 6, 1981), pp. 129–131.

[10]Gus Welty, "The Era of the Giants: Union Pacific, Missouri Pacific, and Western Pacific," *Railway Age* (April 27, 1981), pp. 20–26.

[11]Statistical data from Transportation Policy Associates, *Transportation in America—A Statistical Analysis of Transportation in the U.S.*, 2nd edition, March, 1984.

[12]*1983 Consolidated Freightways Annual Report.*

[13]*Transportation in America—A Statistical Analysis of Transportation in the U.S.*, March, 1984.

[14]Martin T. Farris and David L. Schrock, "The Economics of Coal Slurry Pipelines: Transportation and Non-Transportation Factors," *Transportation Journal* (Fall 1978), pp. 45–57. See also James C. Johnson and Kenneth C. Schneider, "Coal Slurry Pipelines: An Economic and Political Dilemma," *ICC Practitioners' Journal* (November–December 1980), pp. 24–37.

[15]*Transportation in America—A Statistical Analysis of Transportation in the U.S.*, March, 1984.

[16]Peter Nulty, "Friendly Skies for Little Airlines," *FORTUNE* (February 9, 1981), pp. 45–53; "Upstarts in the Sky: Here Comes a New Kind of Airline," *Business Week* (June 15, 1981), pp. 78–84; and Subrata N. Chakravarty, "Power Dive," *Forbes* (June 22, 1981), pp. 64–66.

[17]*Transportation in America—A Statistical Analysis of Transportation in the U.S.*, March, 1984.

[18]"ICC Adopts Rules Exempting Railroad Piggyback Service From Regulation," *Traffic World* (March 2, 1981), pp. 50–51.

[19]"Total Transportation: Just Around the Corner," *Traffic Management* (August 1983), pp. 70–71.

[20]The impact of effective inventory control systems on company profitability is discussed in Lewis Berman, "A Big Payoff from Inventory Controls," *FORTUNE* (July 27, 1981), pp. 76–80.

[21]"Kanban? Can Do!" *Forbes* (January 2, 1984), p. 113.

[22]For a discussion of materials handling innovations, see "Materials Handling Trends: One Expert's Viewpoint," *Traffic Management* (March 1981), pp. 36–38.

Chapter 14

[1]"The Nature of Communication between Humans," *The Process and Effects of Mass Communication*, rev. ed. (Urbana: University of Illinois Press, 1971), pp. 3–53.

[2]Watson Dunn and Arnold M. Barban, *Advertising: Its Role in Modern Marketing* (Hinsdale, Ill.: The Dryden Press, 1982), p. 7.

[3]Committee on Definitions, *Marketing Definitions: A Glossary of Marketing Terms* (Chicago: American Marketing Association, 1960), p. 20.

[4]See Michael Levy and George W. Jones, Jr., "The Effect of Changes in a 'Push' Strategy in a Marketing Channel Context," *Journal of the Academy of Marketing Science* (Winter 1984), pp. 85–105.

[5]Charles G. Burck, "While the Big Brewers Quaff, the Little Ones Thirst," *FORTUNE* (November 1972), p. 107.

[6]See J. Edward Russo, Barbara L. Metcalf, and Debra Stephens, "Identifying Misleading Advertising," *Journal of Consumer Research* (September 1981), pp. 119–131.

[7]Francis X. Callahan, "Does Advertising Subsidize Information?" *Journal of Advertising Research* (August 1978), pp. 19–22.

Chapter 15

[1]"The Average American," *Detroit News Magazine* (December 2, 1979), p. 13.

[2]David A. Aaker and J. Gary Shansby, "Positioning Your Product," *Business Horizons* (May/June 1982), p. 62.

[3]*Controversy Advertising: How Advertisers Present Points of View in Public Affairs; A Worldwide Study by the International Advertising Association* (New York: Communication Arts Books, 1977), p. 18.

[4]The discussion of various advertising media is adapted from material in Dunn and Barban, *Advertising*, pp. 512–591.

[5]Ruth Stroud, "A 43-Year Love Affair with the Great Outdoors," *Advertising Age* (August 8, 1983), p. M-10.

[6]William M. Carley, "Gillette Co. Struggles as Its Rivals Slice at Fat Profit Margin," *The Wall Street Journal* (February 2, 1972), p. 1.

[7]Joseph N. Fry and Gordon H. McDougall, "Consumer Appraisal of Retail Price Advertisements," *Journal of Marketing* (July 1974), pp. 64–67.

[8]Committee on Definitions, *Marketing Definitions: A Glossary of Marketing Terms* (Chicago: American Marketing Association, 1960), p. 20.

[9]Walter A. Gaw, *Specialty Advertising* (Chicago: Specialty Advertising Association, 1970), p. 7.

[10]*Specialty Advertising Report*, second quarter 1979, pp. 1–2.

[11]Alvin P. Sanoff, "Image Makers Worry about Their Own Images," *U.S. News & World Report* (August 13, 1979), pp. 57–59.

[12]Committee on Definitions, *Marketing Definitions: A Glossary of Marketing Terms* (Chicago: American Marketing Association, 1960), p. 18.

Chapter 16

[1]Arthur Miller, *Death of a Salesman* (New York: Viking, 1949).

[2]Joel Saegert and Robert J. Hoover, "Sales Managers and Sales Force Feedback: Information Left in the Pipeline," *Journal of the Academy of Marketing Science* (Winter/Spring 1980), pp. 33–39.

[3]Cold canvassing refers to unsolicited sales calls upon a random group of people; that is, the prospecting and qualifying effort is minimal.

[4]See Bert Rosenbloom and Rolph E. Anderson, "The Sales Manager: Tomorrow's Super Marketer," *Business Horizons* (March/April 1984), pp. 50–63; and Robert W. Eckles, "The Seven S's of Successful Sales Management," *Business Horizons* (March–April 1983), pp. 14–17.

[5]"Significant Trends," *Sales & Marketing Management* (October 15, 1979), p. 102.

[6]This section is adapted from H. Robert Dodge, *Field Sales Management* (Dallas, Tex.: Business Publications, Inc., 1973), pp. 337–338.

Chapter 17

[1]Abridged and adapted from *Marketing Today*, Third Edition, by David J. Schwartz, copyright © 1981 by Harcourt Brace Jovanovich, Inc. Reprinted by permission of the publisher.

[2]Jon G. Udell, "How Important Is Pricing in Competitive Strategy?" *Journal of Marketing* (January 1964), pp. 44–48.

[3]Louis E. Boone and David L. Kurtz, *Pricing Objectives and Practices in American Industry: A Research Report*. All rights reserved. These findings are consistent with those of Professor Robert A. Robicheaux. See "How Important Is Pricing in Competitive Strategy? Circa 1975," in *Proceedings of the Southern Marketing Association*, edited by Henry W. Nash and Donald Robin (Atlanta: November 1976), pp. 55–57.

[4]Robert F. Lanzillotti, "Pricing Objectives in Large Companies," *American Economic Review* (December 1958), pp. 921–940.

[5]Research by Saeed Samiee ranked "satisfactory return on investment" first among a similar list of objectives. Samiee correctly points out the difficulties in making the "meeting competition" objective operational. See "Pricing Objectives of U.S. Manufacturing Firms," in *Proceedings of the Southern Marketing Association*, edited by Robert S. Franz, Robert M. Hopkins, and Alfred G. Toma (New Orleans, 1978), pp. 445–447.

[6]Robert A. Lynn, *Price Policies and Marketing Management* (Homewood, Ill.: Richard D. Irwin, 1967), p. 99. See also Stuart U. Rich, "Firms in Some Industries Should Use Both Target Return and Marginal Cost Pricing," *Marketing News* (June 25, 1982), Sec. 2, p. 11.

[7]William J. Baumol, "On the Theory of Oligopoly," *Economica* (August 1958), pp. 187–198. See also William J. Baumol, *Business Behavior, Value and Growth* (New York: Macmillan, 1959).

[8]Theodore E. Wentz, "Realism in Pricing Analysis," *Journal of Marketing* (April 1966), p. 26.

Chapter 18

[1]"Secrets Behind the Specials," *FORTUNE* (July 11, 1983), p. 94.

[2]Robert Johnson, "Rebating Rises, but Unhappy Firms Can't Think of a Good Alternative," *The Wall Street Journal* (December 9, 1982), p. 31.

[3]See David M. Georgoff, "Price Illusion and the Effect of Odd-Even Retail Pricing," *Southern Journal of Business* (April 1969), pp. 95–103. See also Dik W. Twedt, "Does the 9 Fixation in Retailing Really Promote Sales?" *Journal of Marketing* (October 1965), pp. 54–55; Benson P. Shapiro, "The Psychology of Pricing," *Harvard Business Review* (July–August 1968), pp. 14–16; and Zarrel V. Lambert, "Perceived Prices as Related to Odd and Even Price Findings," *Journal of Retailing* (Fall 1975), pp. 13–22, 78.

[4]Valeria A. Zeithaml, "Consumer Response to In-Store Price Information Environments," *Journal of Consumer Research* (March 1982), pp. 357–369.

[5]J. Edward Russo, "The Value of Unit Price Information," *Journal of Marketing Research* (May 1977), pp. 193–201.

[6]Walter J. Primeaux, Jr., "The Effect of Consumer Knowledge and Bargaining Strength on Final Selling Price: A Case Study," *Journal of Business* (October 1970), pp. 419–426. Another excellent article is James R. Krum, "Variable Pricing as a Promotional Tool," *Atlanta Economic Review* (November–December 1977), pp. 47–50.

[7]See Alfred R. Oxenfeldt, "Product Line Pricing," *Harvard Business Review* (July–August 1966), pp. 137–144.

[8]Robert A. Lynn, *Price Policies and Marketing Management* (Homewood, Ill.: Richard D. Irwin, 1967), p. 143.

[9]Bernie Faust, William Gorman, Eric Oesterle, and Larry Buchta, "Effective Retail Pricing Policy," *Purdue Retailer* (Lafayette, Ind.: Department of Agricultural Economics, 1963), p. 2.

[10]Karl A. Shilliff, "Determinants of Consumer Price Sensitivity for Selected Supermarket Products: An Empirical Investigation," *Akron Business & Economic Review* (Spring 1975), pp. 26–32.

[11]J. Douglass McConnell, "An Experimental Examination of the Price–Quality Relationship," *Journal of Business* (October 1968), pp. 439–444. A recent exchange on this issue appears in the May 1980 issue of the *Journal of Marketing Research*. See Peter C. Riesz, "A Major Price-Perceived Quality Study Re-Examined," pp. 259–262; and J. Douglass McConnell, "Comment on a Major Price-Perceived Quality Study Re-Examined," pp. 263–264.

[12]Kent B. Monroe and M. Venkatesan, "The Concepts of Price Limits and Psychological Measurement: A Laboratory Experiment," in *Marketing in Society and the Economy: Proceedings of the American Marketing Association*, edited by Phillip R. McDonald (Cincinnati: American Marketing Association, 1969), pp. 345–351.

[13]*Market Spotlight* (Edmonton: Alberta Department of Consumer and Corporate Affairs, March 1979).

[14]M. Edgar Bennett, "Case of the Tangled Transfer Price," *Harvard Business Review* (May–June 1977), p. 22.

Chapter 19

[1]Bill Saporita, "Black & Decker's Gamble on 'Globalization'," *FORTUNE* (May 14, 1984), pp. 40, 42.

[2]"Trying to Right the Balance," *Time* (October 9, 1979), p. 84.

[3]Personal correspondence, May 7, 1984. See also Vern Terpstra, *International Marketing* (Hinsdale, Ill.: The Dryden Press, 1983).

[4]Sharon Nelton, "Doing Business Overseas," *Working Woman* (March 1984), p. 129.

[5]Philip Kotler, *Marketing Management: Analysis, Planning and Control*, 5th ed., © 1984, p. 447. Reprinted by permission of Prentice-Hall, Inc. Englewood Cliffs, N.J.

[6]David A. Ricks, Marilyn Y. C. Fu, and Jeffrey S. Arpan, *International Business Blunders* (Columbus, Ohio: Grid, 1974), pp. 17–18.

[7]Ralph Z. Sorenson, II, "U.S. Marketers Can Learn from European Innovators," *Harvard Business Review* (September–October 1972), p. 97.

[8]These levels are suggested in Vern Terpstra, *International Marketing*, 3rd ed. (Hinsdale, Ill.: The Dryden Press, 1983).

[9]"Ways Some U.S. Firms Crack Japan's Market," *U.S. News & World Report* (August 29, 1983), p. 33.

[10]Ronald Alsop, "Efficacy of Global Ad Projects Is Questioned in Firm's Survey," *The Wall Street Journal* (September 13, 1984), p. 29.

[11]"Japanese Company Invades U.S. Sporting Goods Market with Futuristic Baseball Gear," *Marketing News* (March 20, 1981), p. 18.

[12]Frank Meissner, "Americans Must Practice the Marketing They Preach to Succeed in Japan's Mass Markets," *Marketing News* (October 17, 1980), p. 5.

Chapter 20

[1]David W. Cravens and Gerald G. Hills, "Consumerism: A Perspective for Business," *Business Horizons* (August 1970), p. 21.

[2]George S. Day and David A. Aaker, "A Guide to Consumerism," *Journal of Marketing* (July 1970), p. 12.

[3]"How Your Privacy Is Being Stripped Away," *U.S. News & World Report* (April 30, 1984), p. 46.

[4]Steven N. Brenner and Earl A. Mollander, "Is the Ethics of Business Changing?" *Harvard Business Review* (January–February 1977), p. 62.

[5]*Rebuttal to Some Unfounded Assertions about Advertising* (New York: American Advertising Foundation, 1967), p. 13.

[6]"It's a Pig Award for 9 Ads," *USA Today* (February 28, 1984), p. B2.

[7]See Steven N. Brenner and Earl A. Mollander, "Is the Ethics of Business Changing?" *Harvard Business Review* (January–February 1977), pp. 61–62; and Jeffrey Sonnenfeld and Paul R. Lawrence, "Why Do Companies Succumb to Price Fixing?" *Harvard Business Review* (July–August 1978), pp. 145–157.

[8]James F. Engel and Roger D. Blackwell, *Consumer Behavior*, 4th ed. (Hinsdale, Ill: The Dryden Press, 1982), p. 668.

[9]Don Bates, "Special Demand on Nonprofit PR," *Public Relations Journal* (August 1976), p. 24.

[10]Philip Kotler, *Marketing for Nonprofit Organizations* (Englewood Cliffs, N.J.: Prentice-Hall, 1982), p. 9.

[11]Philip Kotler and Sidney J. Levy, "Broadening the Concept of Marketing," *Journal of Marketing* (January 1969), pp. 10–15. For a description of this evolution, see Philip D. Cooper and William J. Kehoe, "Marketing's Status, Dimensions, and Directions," *Business* (July–August 1979), pp. 14–15.

[12]David J. Luck, "Broadening the Concept of Marketing—Too Far," *Journal of Marketing* (July 1969), pp. 53–55.

[13]This interesting series of exchanges appears in the *Journal of Academy of Marketing Science* (Summer 1979). See Gene R. Laczniak and Donald A. Michie, "The Social Disorder of the Broadened Concept of Marketing," pp. 214–232; Sidney J. Levy and Philip Kotler, "Toward a Broader Concept of Marketing's Role in Social Order," pp. 232–238; and Laczniak and Michie, "Broadened Marketing and Social Order: A Reply," pp. 239–242.

[14]Philip Kotler, *Marketing for Nonprofit Organizations* (Englewood Cliffs, N.J.: Prentice-Hall, 1982), p. 482.

[15]"In Today's Marketplace, It's Hype, Hype, Hype," *U.S. News & World Report* (December 5, 1983), p. 52.

[16]David J. Rachman and Elaine Romano, *Modern Marketing* (Hinsdale, Ill.: The Dryden Press, 1980), p. 576. The delineation of person, idea, and organization marketing is proposed by Professors Rachman and Romano.

[17]This section is based on and used with permission from Philip Kotler, "Strategies for Introducing Marketing into Nonprofit Organizations," *Journal of Marketing* (January 1979), pp. 37–44, published by the American Marketing Association.

[18]Kotler, "Strategies for Introducing Marketing into Nonprofit Organizations," p. 40.

[19]This section is based on Philip Kotler, *Marketing for Nonprofit Organizations*, 1982, pp. 306–309. Adapted by permission of Prentice-Hall, Inc., Englewood Cliffs, N.J.

Appendix

[1]Nick DiBari, "Your Business Success Can Be Planned," *Sales & Marketing Management* (December 3, 1984), p. 53.

[2]"What Is the Fastest Track to the Executive Suite?" *Sales & Marketing News* (July 6, 1984), p. 7.

[3]"1984 Survey of Selling Costs," *Sales & Marketing Management* (February 20, 1984), p. 68.

[4]Al Urbanski, "Annual Survey of Executive Compensation," *Sales & Marketing Management* (August 15, 1983), p. 41.

Glossary

accessory equipment category of industrial products consisting of capital items that are usually less expensive and shorter-lived than installations; includes such items as typewriters, hand tools, and small computers (p. 225)

active exporting in international marketing, the activities of a firm that has made a commitment to seek export business (p. 530)

adoption process series of stages in the consumer decision process regarding a new product, including awareness, interest, evaluation, trial, and rejection or adoption (p. 217)

advertising paid, nonpersonal communication through various media by business firms, nonprofit organizations, and individuals who are identified in the advertising message and who hope to inform or persuade members of a particular audience (pp. 382, 404)

advertising agency independent businesses used to assist advertisers in planning and implementing advertising programs (p. 416)

advocacy advertising paid, public communication or message that presents information on a point of view bearing on a publicly recognized controversial issue (p. 410)

agents marketing intermediaries who perform wholesaling functions but do not take title to the goods handled (p. 311)

agents and brokers independent wholesaling intermediaries who may or may not take possession to the products they represent, but who never take title to them (p. 311)

AIDA concept acronym for attention-interest-desire-action; the traditional explanation of the steps an individual must go through prior to making a purchase decision (p. 379)

AIO statements collection of statements contained in a psychographic study to reflect activities, interests, and opinions of the respondents (p. 135)

approach initial contact of a salesperson with a prospective customer (p. 440)

Asch phenomenon occurrence first documented by psychologist S. E. Asch, which illustrates the effect of the reference group on individual decision making (p. 155)

aspirational group subcategory of a reference group where the individual desires to be associated with a group (p. 156)

atmospherics combination of physical store characteristics and amenities provided by the retailer that results in developing a retail image and attracting customers (p. 329)

attitudes one's enduring favorable or unfavorable evaluations, emotional feelings, or pro or con action tendencies (p. 166)

auction houses establishments that bring buyers and sellers together in one location for the purpose of permitting buyers to examine merchandise before purchasing it (p. 311)

basing point system system for handling transportation costs used in some industries during the early years of the twentieth century in which the buyer's costs included the factory price plus freight charges from the basing point city nearest the buyer (p. 503)

BCG matrix *See* market share/market growth matrix.

benefit segmentation dividing a population into homogeneous groups on the basis of benefits consumers expect to derive from a product or service (p. 136)

bids written sales proposals from vendors (p. 200)

bottom line business jargon referring to the overall profitability measure of performance (p. 561)

brand a name, term, sign, symbol, design, or some combination used to identify the products of one firm and differentiate them from competitive offerings (p. 252)

brand extension decision to use a popular brand name for a new product entry in an unrelated product category (p. 255)

brand insistence consumer preference for a specific brand to the point where the buyer will accept no alternatives and will search extensively for the product or service. Also known as brand requirement (p. 255)

brand name part of the brand consisting of words or letters that comprise a name used to identify and distinguish the firm's offerings from those of competitors (p. 252)

brand preference stage of brand acceptance at which the consumer will select one brand over competitive offerings, based upon previous experience with the product or service (p. 255)

brand recognition stage of brand acceptance at which the consumer is aware of the existence of a brand but does not prefer it to competing offerings (p. 255)

break-bulk center facility at which large shipments are divided into many smaller ones and delivered to individual customers in the area, in the interest of reducing transportation expenses (p. 364)

breakeven analysis pricing technique used to determine the number of products or services that must be sold at a specified price to generate sufficient revenue to cover total costs (p. 479)

broadening concept expanded view of marketing as a generic function to be performed by all organizations—profit-seeking or nonprofit (p. 561)

brokers agent wholesaling intermediaries who do not take title or possession to goods and whose primary function is bringing buyers and sellers together (p. 311)

buyer's market marketplace characterized by an abundance of goods and/or services in relation to the level of consumer demand (p. 12)

buying center refers to everyone who participates in an organizational buying action (p. 198)

canned approach memorized sales presentation used to ensure uniform coverage of selling points that management has deemed important (p. 443)

cannibalizing product that takes sales from another offering in a product line (p. 240)

capital items long-lived business assets that must be depreciated over time (p. 194)

cash-and-carry wholesaler limited-function merchant wholesaler who performs most wholesaling functions except financing and delivery (p. 309)

cash discounts price reductions offered to a consumer, industrial user, or marketing intermediary in return for prompt payment of a bill (p. 497)

casual exporting activities of a firm that takes a passive level of involvement in international marketing (p. 530)

catalog retailer retail merchant who operates from a showroom displaying samples of the product line. Customers place orders for displayed products or items in the store's catalog, and these orders are filled from a warehouse, usually on the store premises (p. 335)

Celler-Kefauver Antimerger Act (1950) federal legislation amending the Clayton Act to include restrictions on the purchase of assets, where such purchase would decrease competition. Previously, only "acquiring the stock" of another firm was prohibited if it lessened competition (p. 39) *See also* Clayton Act.

census collection of data from all possible sources in a population or universe (p. 108)

chain stores groups of retail stores that are centrally owned and managed and handle essentially the same product lines (p. 338)

channel captain the dominant and controlling member of a marketing channel (p. 283)

class rate standard transportation rate established for shipping various commodities (p. 256)

Clayton Act (1914) federal statute that strengthened antitrust legislation by restricting such practices as price discrimination, exclusive dealing, tying contracts, and interlocking boards of directors (p. 39)

closed sales territories restricted geographic selling regions specified by a manufacturer for its distributors (p. 289)

closing step in a personal sales presentation at which the salesperson asks the customer to make a purchase decision (p. 444)

cluster sample sampling technique in which geographic areas or clusters are selected, and then all subjects of interest located within the area (or a sample of respondents from within the area) are used as respondents (p. 108)

cognitions an individual's knowledge, beliefs, and attitudes about certain events (p. 175)

cognitive dissonance postpurchase anxiety that results when an imbalance exists among an individual's cognitions (knowledge, beliefs, and attitudes) (p. 175)

commission incentive compensation directly related to the sales or profits achieved by a salesperson (p. 450)

commission merchant agent wholesaling intermediary who takes possession of goods when they are shipped to a central market for sale, acts as the producer's agent, and collects an agreed-upon fee at the time of sale (p. 311)

commodity rate special transportation rate granted by carriers to shippers as a reward for either regular use or large quantity shipments (p. 256)

common carrier freight transporters that offer shipping service to the public at large (p. 357)

Common Market in international marketing, a format for multinational economic integration involving a customs union and continuing efforts to standardize trade regulations of all governments (p. 537) *See also* customs unions.

community shopping center a group of 15 to 50 retail stores, often including a branch of a department store as the primary tenant. This type of center typically serves 20,000 to 100,000 persons within a radius of a few miles (p. 328)

comparative advertising nonpersonal selling efforts that make direct promotional comparisons with leading competitive brands (p. 417)

competitive bidding process in which potential suppliers submit price quotations to a buyer for a proposed purchase or contract (p. 508)

competitive environment interactive process that occurs in the marketplace among marketers of directly competitive products, marketers of products that can be substituted for one another, and among marketers competing for the consumer purchase dollar (p. 33)

competitive pricing strategy pricing strategy designed to deemphasize price as a competitive variable by pricing a product or service at the general level of comparable offerings (p. 496)

component parts and materials finished industrial goods that actually become part of the final product. Also known as fabricated parts and materials (p. 225)

concentrated marketing marketing strategy that directs all of a firm's marketing resources toward serving a small segment of the total market (p. 72)

concept testing consideration of a product idea prior to its actual development (p. 248)

Consolidated Metropolitan Statistical Areas (CMSAs) major population concentrations, including the 25 or so urban giants like New York, Chicago, and Los Angeles (p. 127)

consumer behavior acts of an individual in obtaining and using goods or services, including the decision processes that precede and determine these acts (p. 150)

consumer goods products purchased by the ultimate consumer for personal use (p. 124)

Consumer Goods Pricing Act (1975) federal legislation that halted all interstate usage of resale price maintenance agreements (p. 41)

consumer innovators first purchasers of new products and services (p. 219)

consumerism social force within the environment designed to aid and protect the consumer by exerting legal, moral, and economic pressure on business and government (p. 550)

consumer orientation business philosophy incorporating the marketing concept of first determining unmet consumer needs and then designing a system for satisfying those needs (p. 12)

Consumer Product Safety Act (1972) federal statute that set up the Consumer Product Safety Commission to specify safety standards for most consumer products (pp. 42, 550)

consumer rights as stated by President John F. Kennedy in 1962, the consumer should have the following rights: to choose freely, to be informed, to be heard, and to be safe (p. 550)

containerization combination of several unitized loads of products into a single load to facilitate intertransport changes in transportation modes (p. 368)

contract carriers freight transporters who are contracted to certain firms and operate exclusively for a particular industry (p. 357)

convenience goods products that consumers want to purchase frequently, immediately, and with a minimum of effort (p. 222)

convenience retailer one who sells to the ultimate consumer and focuses chiefly on a central location, long store hours, rapid checkout, and adequate parking facilities (p. 331)

convenience sample nonprobability marketing research sample based on the selection of readily available respondents (p. 108)

cooperative advertising sharing of advertising costs between a retailer and the manufacturer of a good or service (p. 419)

corporate advertising form of institutional advertising consisting of nonproduct advertising sponsored by profit-seeking firms (p. 409)

corrective advertising policy of the Federal Trade Commission, under which companies found to have used deceptive promotional messages are required to correct their earlier claims with new messages (p. 39)

cost-plus pricing in pricing strategy, the practice of adding a percentage or specified dollar amount (the markup) to the base cost of the product or service to cover unassigned costs and to provide a profit (p. 477)

cost trade-offs concept in physical distribution whereby some functional areas of the firm will experience cost increases while others will have cost reductions, but the result will be that total physical distribution costs will be minimized (p. 354)

coupons sales promotional tool in which a specially marked slip of paper entitles the bearer to a discount on the purchase of a particular product (p. 423)

creative selling personal selling involving situations where a considerable degree of analytical decision making on the part of the buyer results in the need for skillful proposals of solutions to the buyer's needs (p. 439)

cues objects existing in the environment that determine the nature of the response to a drive (p. 169)

culture complex of values, ideas, attitudes, and other meaningful symbols created by people to shape human behavior and the artifacts of that behavior as they are transmitted from one generation to the next (p. 152)

customary prices in pricing strategy, the traditional prices that customers expect to pay for certain products and services (p. 472)

customer service standards quality of service that a firm's customers will receive (p. 354)

customs union in international marketing, a format for multinational economic integration that sets up a free trade area for member nations and a uniform tariff for nonmember nations (p. 537)

data statistics, opinions, facts, or predictions categorized on some basis for storage and retrieval (p. 110)

data base any collection of data that is retrievable through a computer (p. 100)

decoding in marketing communications, the receiver's interpretation of a message (p. 379)

demand schedule of the amounts of a firm's product or service that consumers will purchase at different prices during a specified time period (p. 473)

demarketing process of reducing consumer demand for a product or service to a level that can be supplied by the firm (p. 49)

demographics characteristics such as age, sex, and income level of potential buyers (pp. 129, 406)

demographic segmentation dividing a population into homogeneous groups based on characteristics such as age, sex, and income level (p. 129)

department store large retail firm handling a variety of merchandise, including clothing, household goods, appliances, and furniture (p. 333)

derived demand demand for an industrial product that is linked to demand for a consumer good (p. 193)

differentiated marketing marketing strategy employed by organizations that produce numerous products or services with different marketing mixes designed to satisfy numerous market segments (p. 72)

diffusion process acceptance of new products and services by the members of a community or social system (p. 219)

direct-sales-results test technique for measuring the effectiveness of promotional expenditures by ascertaining the increase in revenue per dollar spent (p. 392)

disassociative group type of reference group with which an individual does not want to be identified by others (p. 156)

discount house retail store that charges lower-than-normal prices but may not offer many typical retail services such as credit, sales assistance, or home delivery (p. 334)

distribution channels marketing institutions and their interrelationships responsible for the physical and title flow of goods and services from producer to consumer or industrial user (p. 276)

distribution strategy element of marketing decision making comprising activities and marketing institutions involved in getting the right product or service to the firm's customers; involves physical handling of goods and selection of appropriate marketing channels (p. 15)

distribution warehouse facility designed to assemble and then redistribute products to facilitate rapid movement of products to purchasers (p. 364)

drive strong stimulus that impels action (p. 169)

drop shipper limited-function merchant wholesaler who receives orders from customers and forwards them to producers who ship directly to the customers (p. 310)

dumping controversial practice of selling a product in a foreign market at a lower price than it would receive in the producer's domestic market (p. 527)

ecology relationship between organisms and their environment (p. 556)

economic environment component of the marketing environment consisting of a setting of complex and dynamic business fluctuations that historically tend to follow a four-stage pattern: recession, depression, recovery, and prosperity (p. 45)

embargo complete ban on the import or export of specified products (p. 527)

encoding in marketing communications, the translation of a message into understandable terms and its transmittal through a communication medium (p. 379)

end-use application segmentation dividing an industrial market into homogeneous groups on the basis of precisely how different industrial purchasers will use the product (p. 139)

Engel's laws statements on spending behavior, comprised of three generalizations: as household income increases, (1) a smaller percentage of income goes for food; (2) the percentage spent on household operations, housing, and clothing remains constant; and (3) the percentage spent on other items increases (p. 132)

environmental forecasting broad-based economic forecasting focusing upon the impact of external factors that affect a firm's markets (p. 82)

environmental management accomplishment of organizational objectives by predicting and influencing the competitive, political and legal, economic, technological, and societal/cultural environments (p. 33)

Environmental Protection Act (1970) federal legislation establishing the Environmental Protection Agency and giving it the power to deal with pollution issues (p. 42)

EOQ (economic order quantity) model technique devised to determine the optimal order quantity of each product; the optimal point is determined by balancing the costs of holding inventory and the costs involved in placing orders (p. 366)

Equal Credit Opportunity Act (1975–1977) federal legislation banning discrimination in lending practices based on sex, marital status, race, national origin, religion, age, or receipt of payments from a public assistance program (p. 42)

escalator clause in industrial pricing, a component of many bids that allows the seller to adjust the final price based upon changes in the costs of the product's ingredients, between the placement of the order and the completion of construction or delivery of the product (p. 508)

ethics *See* marketing ethics.

evaluative criteria in consumer decision making, the features considered in a consumer's choice of alternatives (p. 175)

evoked set in consumer decision making, the number of brands that a consumer actually considers before making a purchase decision (p. 174)

exchange control method used to regulate the privilege of international trade among importing organizations by controlling access to foreign currencies (p. 527)

exchange process process by which two or more parties give something of value to one another to satisfy felt needs (p. 8)

exclusive dealing agreement understanding between a manufacturer and a marketing intermediary that prohibits the intermediary from handling the product lines of the manufacturer's competitors (p. 288)

exclusive distribution policy under which a firm grants exclusive rights to a wholesaler or retailer to sell in a particular geographic area (p. 287)

expense item industrial products and services that are used within a short period of time (p. 194)

experiment scientific investigation in which a researcher controls or manipulates a test group (or groups) and compares those results with the results of a group (or groups) that did not receive the controls or manipulations (p. 107)

exploratory research preliminary discussion of a marketing problem with informed sources within a firm as well as with wholesalers, retailers, customers, and others outside the firm and an examination of secondary sources of information (p. 95)

exporting marketing goods and services in foreign countries (p. 521)

external data in marketing research, the type of secondary data that comes from sources outside a firm (p. 100)

fads fashions with abbreviated life cycles such as disco, punk, and new wave music (p. 216)

Fair Credit Reporting Act (1970) federal legislation providing for individuals' access to credit reports about them and the opportunity to change information that is incorrect (p. 42)

Fair Debt Collection Practices Act (1978) federal legislation prohibiting harassing, deceptive, or unfair collection practices by debt-collecting agencies (p. 42)

Fair Packaging and Labeling Act (1967) federal statute requiring disclosure of product identity, name and address of the manufacturer or distributor, and information on the quality of the contents (pp. 42, 259)

fair trade laws statutes enacted in most states that permitted manufacturers to stipulate a minimum retail price for a product (p. 41)

family brand name used for several related products, such as the Johnson & Johnson line of baby products (p. 255)

family life cycle process of family formation and dissolution which includes many subcategories and five major stages: (1) young single; (2) young married without children; (3) other young; (4) middle-aged; and (5) older (p. 130)

fashions currently popular products that tend to follow recurring life cycles (p. 216)

Federal Trade Commission Act (1914) federal legislation that prohibited unfair methods of competition and established the Federal Trade Commission to oversee the various laws dealing with business (p. 39)

feedback in marketing communications, the receiver's response to a message (p. 379)

field selling sales presentations made at the homes or businesses of prospective customers on a face-to-face basis by salespeople (p. 437)

fixed-sum-per-unit method promotional budget allocation method in which promotional expenditures are a predetermined dollar amount for each sales or production unit (p. 391)

Flammable Fabrics Act (1953) federal legislation prohibiting the interstate sale of flammable fabrics (p. 42)

FOB plant "free on board," a price quotation that does not include shipping charges; the buyer is responsible for paying them. Also called FOB origin (p. 502)

focus group interview information-gathering procedure in marketing research that typically brings eight to twelve individuals together in one location to discuss a given subject (p. 107)

follow-up postsales activities that often determine whether an individual who has made a recent purchase will become a repeat customer (p. 444)

Food, Drug, and Cosmetic Act (1938) federal legislation strengthening the Pure Food and Drug Act to prohibit the adulteration and misbranding of food, drugs, and cosmetics (pp. 42, 259)

foreign freight forwarders transportation intermediaries who consolidate international shipments in order to reduce global transportation costs (p. 368)

foreign licensing agreement in which a domestic firm permits a foreign company to either produce or distribute the firm's goods in the foreign country or to receive the right to utilize the firm's trademark, patent, or processes in a specified geographic area (p. 530)

form utility want-satisfying power created by the conversion of raw materials into finished products (p. 6)

franchise contractual arrangement in which a wholesale or retail dealer agrees to meet the operating requirements of a manufacturer (p. 291)

free trade area in international marketing, economic integration between participating nations, without any tariff or trade restrictions (p. 537)

freight absorption system for handling transportation costs under which the buyer of goods may deduct shipping expenses from the cost of the goods (p. 502)

freight forwarders transportation intermediaries who consolidate shipments to reduce shipping costs for their customers (p. 361)

friendship, commerce, and navigation (FCN) treaties international agreements that deal with many aspects of commercial relations with other nations (p. 528)

full-cost pricing pricing procedure in which all costs are considered in setting a price, allowing the firm to recover all of its costs and realize a profit (p. 478)

functional accounts income statement expense categories representing the purpose for which an expenditure is made (p. 98)

Fur Products Labeling Act (1951) federal statute requiring that the name of the animal from which a fur garment was derived be identified (p. 42)

General Agreement on Tariffs and Trade (GATT) international trade agreement that has helped to reduce world tariffs (p. 527)

general merchandise retailer establishment carrying a wide variety of product lines, all of which are stocked in some depth (p. 333)

generic name brand name that has become a generally descriptive term for a product (for example, nylon, zipper, and aspirin). When this occurs, the original owner may lose exclusive claim to the name (p. 253)

generic products food or household items characterized by plain labels, little or no advertising, and no brand name (p. 257)

geographic segmentation dividing a population into homogeneous groups on the basis of location (p. 126)

global marketing strategy direct application of a domestic marketing strategy in foreign markets with little or no modifications (p. 532)

goods-services continuum method for visualizing the differences and similarities of goods and services (p. 227)

hypermarket a giant retailing mass merchandiser who operates on a low-price, self-service basis and carries lines of soft goods and groceries (p. 335)

hypothesis tentative explanation about some specific event; statement about the relationship between variables that also includes clear implications for testing this relationship (p. 99)

iceberg principle concept emphasizing the likelihood that collected data in summary form often obscures important evaluative information; derived from the analogy of the 80 percent of the iceberg that lies hidden beneath the surface of the water (p. 97)

idea marketing identification and marketing of a cause to chosen consumer segments (p. 562)

importing purchase of foreign products and raw materials (p. 521)

import quota trade restriction that limits the amount of certain products that can enter a country for resale (p. 527)

impulse goods products for which the consumer spends little time in conscious deliberation prior to making a purchase decision (p. 222)

incremental-cost pricing pricing procedure in which only the costs directly attributable to a specific output are considered in setting a price (p. 478)

individual brands strategy of giving each item in a product line its own brand name rather than identifying it by a single family brand name used for all products in the line (p. 256)

individual offerings primary component of a product mix consisting of single products (p. 240)

industrial distributor wholesaling intermediary who operates in the industrial goods market and typically handles small accessory equipment and operating supplies (p. 225)

industrial goods products purchased for use either directly or indirectly in the production of other goods for resale (p. 124)

industrial market marketplace made up of buyers who purchase goods and services for use in producing other goods for resale (p. 188)

inflation rising price level that results in reduced purchasing power for the consumer (p. 45)

information data relevant to the marketing manager in making decisions (p. 110)

informative advertising promotions used during the introductory stages of the product life cycle that seek to announce the availability of and develop initial demand for a product, service, organization, person, idea, or cause (p. 409)

input-output models quantitative forecasting techniques that show the impact on supplier industries of production changes in a given industry and that can be utilized in measuring the impact of changing demand in any industry throughout the economy (p. 82)

installations major capital assets such as factories and heavy machinery; they are expensive and relatively long-lived, and their purchase represents a major decision for the company (p. 225)

institutional advertising promoting a concept, an idea, a philosophy, or the goodwill of an industry, company, organization, or person (p. 409)

intensive distribution policy under which a manufacturer of a convenience good attempts to saturate the market with the product (p. 287)

internal secondary data in marketing research, the type of information that is found in records of sales, product performances, sales force activities, and marketing costs (p. 100)

joint demand demand for an industrial good as related to the demand for another industrial good that is necessary for the use of the first item (p. 194)

joint venture in international marketing, an agreement between business partners in two or more nations whereby the firms establish a foreign operation, sharing risks, costs, and management responsibilities with the other partner or partners who are usually citizens of the host country (p. 532)

jury of executive opinion qualitative sales forecasting method which combines and averages the future business and sales expectations of executives in such functional areas as financing, production, marketing, and purchasing (p. 80)

just-in-time (JIT) inventory control system inventory control system designed to minimize inventory at production facilities. Also called *kan-ban* inventory system (p. 366)

Kefauver-Harris Drug Amendments (1962) amendments to the Pure Food and Drug Act requiring generic labeling of drugs and a summary of adverse side effects (p. 42)

label descriptive part of a product's package listing brand name or symbol, name and address of the manufacturer or distributor, ingredients, size or quantity of the product, and/or recommended uses, directions, or serving suggestions (p. 259)

Lanham Act (1946) federal statute providing for federal registration of all trademarks and requiring that registered trademarks not contain words in general use. Such *generic words* are descriptive of a particular type of product, such as "automobile" or "suntan lotion," and thus cannot be given trademark protection (p. 253)

learning changes in behavior, immediate or expected, that occur as a result of experience (p. 169)

life-style the way people decide to live their lives, including family, job, social activities, and consumer decisions (p. 134)

limited-line store retail establishment that offers a large assortment of a single product line or a few related product lines (p. 332)

line extension new product that is closely related to other products in the firm's existing product lines (p. 241)

list price established price normally quoted to potential buyers (p. 497)

logistics *See* physical distribution.

loss leader products offered to consumers at less than cost to attract them to retail stores where they are likely to buy other merchandise at regular prices (p. 506)

Magnuson-Moss Warranty Act (1975) federal statute authorizing the Federal Trade Commission to develop regulations on warranty practices (p. 212)

mail-order wholesaler limited-function merchant wholesaler who utilizes catalogs instead of a sales force to contact customers in an attempt to reduce operating expenses (p. 310)

make-bulk center facility at which several small shipments are consolidated into a large shipment and delivered to a central destination in an attempt to reduce transportation costs (p. 364)

manufacturers' agents agent wholesaling intermediaries who represent a number of manufacturers of related but noncompeting products, and who receive a commission based on a specified percentage of sales (p. 311)

manufacturer's brand brand name owned by a manufacturer or other producer. Also called a national brand (p. 256)

market group of people who possess purchasing power and the authority and willingness to purchase (p. 124)

marketing process of planning and executing the conception, pricing, promotion, and distribution of ideas, goods, and services to create exchanges that satisfy individual and organizational objectives (p. 8)

marketing audit thorough, objective evaluation of an organization's marketing philosophy, goals, policies, tactics, practices, and results (p. 79)

marketing channels route taken by a product or service and/or title to the product or service as it moves from producer to final purchaser; includes producer, consumer or industrial user, and any marketing intermediaries involved in the channel (p. 16)

marketing communications transmission from a sender to a receiver of messages dealing with buyer-seller relationships (p. 378)

marketing concept companywide consumer orientation with the objective of achieving long-run success (p. 13)

marketing cost analysis evaluation of such items as selling costs, billing, and advertising to determine the profitability of particular customers, territories, or product lines (p. 98)

marketing ethics marketers' standards of conduct and moral values (p. 550)

marketing information system (MIS) set of procedures and methods designed to generate an orderly flow of pertinent information for use in making decisions, providing management with the current and future states of the market and indicating market responses to company and competitor actions (p. 110)

marketing intermediary business firm, either wholesale or retail, that operates between the producer of the goods and the consumer or industrial user. Sometimes called a middleman (p. 276)

marketing mix blending the four strategy elements of marketing decision making—product, distribution, promotion, and pricing—to satisfy chosen consumer segments (p. 17)

marketing myopia term coined by Theodore Levitt in his argument that executives in many industries fail to recognize the broad scope of their business. According to Levitt, future growth is endangered because these executives lack a marketing orientation (p. 13)

marketing planning the process of anticipating the future and determining the courses of action designed to achieve marketing objectives (p. 66)

marketing research systematic gathering, recording, and analysis of data about problems and opportunities relating to the marketing of goods and services (p. 92)

marketing strategy overall company program for selecting a particular market target and then satisfying those target consumers through a blending of the elements of the marketing mix (p. 71)

market price price a consumer or marketing intermediary actually pays for a good or service after subtracting any discounts, allowances, or rebates from the list price (p. 497)

market segmentation process of dividing the overall market into smaller, more homogeneous groups with similar product or service interests based upon such factors as demographic or psychographic characteristics, geographic locations, or perceived product benefits (p. 125)

market share/market growth matrix matrix developed by the Boston Consulting Group that enables a firm to classify its products and services in terms of industry growth rate and its market share relative to competitive products. The matrix is comprised of four segments: *cash cows* (high market share, low market growth); *stars* (high market share, high market growth); *dogs* (low market share, low market growth); and *question marks* (low market share, high market growth) (p. 76)

market share objectives pricing objectives linked to achieving and maintaining a stated percentage of the market for a firm's product or service (p. 469)

market target decision analysis evaluation of potential market segments by dividing the overall market into homogeneous groups. Cross classifications may be based on variables such as type of market, geographic location, frequency of use, or demographic characteristics (p. 139)

market test quantitative forecasting technique in which a new product, price, promotional campaign, or other marketing variable is introduced in a relatively small test market location to assess consumer reactions under realistic market conditions (p. 81)

mass merchandiser retail merchant who stocks a wider line of goods than that offered by a department store, but who typically does not offer the same depth of assortment (p. 334)

materials handling all activities involved in moving products within a manufacturer's production facilities, warehouses, and transportation company terminals (p. 367)

membership group type of reference group in which the reference group members are members of a formal group such as a country club, church group, or other organization (p. 156)

merchandise mart permanent exhibition facility where manufacturers rent showrooms to display products for visiting retail and wholesale buyers, designers, and architects (p. 307)

merchant wholesaler wholesaling intermediary who takes title to the goods handled (p. 308)

Metropolitan Statistical Areas (MSAs) large, freestanding urban areas such as Sheboygan, Wisconsin, and Syracuse, New York, for which detailed marketing-related data is collected by the U.S. Census Bureau (p. 127)

middleman *See* marketing intermediary.

Miller-Tydings Resale Price Maintenance Act (1937) federal legislation that exempted interstate fair trade contracts from compliance with antitrust requirements (p. 41)

missionary sales indirect type of selling in which specialized salespeople promote the goodwill of the firm, often by providing the customer with assistance on product use (p. 439)

modified breakeven analysis pricing technique used to consider consumer demand by comparing the number of products or services that must be sold at a variety of different prices to cover total costs, with estimates of expected sales at the various prices (p. 482)

modified rebuy situation where industrial purchasers are willing to reevaluate available options in a repurchase of the same product or service. Lower prices, faster delivery, or higher quality may be buyer desires in this type of purchase situation (p. 198)

monopolistic competition market structure involving a heterogeneous product and product differentiation among competing suppliers, allowing the marketer some degree of control over prices (p. 473)

monopoly market structure involving only one seller of a product or service for which no close substitutes exist (p. 473)

motive inner state that directs people toward the goal of satisfying a felt need (p. 161)

MRO items supplies for an industrial firm categorized as maintenance items, repair items, or operating supplies (p. 226)

multinational corporation company that operates in several nations and literally views the world as its market (p. 536)

national brand *See* manufacturer's brand.

natural accounts expense categories traditionally listed on an organization's income statement. An example is salary expenses (p. 98)

need lack of something useful; a discrepancy between a desired state and the actual state (p. 161)

neighborhood shopping center geographical cluster of stores, usually consisting of a supermarket and about 5 to 15 smaller stores. The center provides convenient shopping for 5,000 to 15,000 shoppers in its vicinity (p. 328)

new task buying refers to first-time or unique industrial purchase situations that require considerable effort on the part of the decision makers (p. 198)

noise in marketing communications, interference in a transmitted message (p. 380)

nonprobability sample arbitrary marketing research sample in which most standard statistical tests cannot be applied to the collected data (p. 108)

nonprofit organization firm whose primary objective is something other than the return of a profit to its owners (p. 558)

odd pricing pricing policy based on the belief that a price with an uncommon last digit is more appealing than a round figure; an example would be a price of $9.99 rather than $10.00 (p. 504)

off-price retailer retailer who sells designer labels or well-known brand name clothing at less than typical retail prices (p. 335)

oligopoly market structure involving relatively few sellers and, because of high start-up costs, significant entry barriers to new competitors (p. 473)

operating supplies *See* MRO items.

opinion leaders individuals in a group who serve as information sources for other group members (p. 156)

order processing selling at the wholesale and retail levels; specifically, identifying customer needs, pointing out the need to the customer, and completing the order (p. 438)

organizational market marketplace made up of producers, trade industries (wholesalers and retailers), institutions, and governments at the federal, state, and local levels (p. 188)

organization marketing marketing by *mutual benefit organizations* (churches, labor unions, and political parties), *service organizations* (colleges, universities, hospitals, museums), and *government organizations* (military services, police and fire departments, U.S. Postal Service) that seek to influence others to accept the goals of, receive the services of, or contribute in some way to that organization (p. 562)

outlet mall shopping center consisting entirely of off-price retailers (p. 335)

overseas marketing in international marketing, a firm's maintenance of a separate selling operation in a foreign country (p. 531)

over-the-counter selling personal selling occurring in retail and some wholesale locations where customers come to the seller's place of business (p. 437)

ownership utility want-satisfying power created by marketers when title to a product is transferred to the customer at the time of purchase. Also known as possession utility (p. 277)

party selling retail distribution strategy under which a company's representative makes a presentation of the product(s) in a party setting. Orders are taken and the host or hostess receives a commission or gift based on the amount of sales (p. 336)

penetration pricing strategy pricing strategy involving the use of a relatively low entry price as compared with competitive offerings; based on the theory that this initial low price will help secure market acceptance (p. 495)

percentage-of-sales method promotional budget allocation method in which the funds allocated for promotion during a time period are based upon a specified percentage of either past or forecasted sales (p. 391)

perception manner in which an individual interprets a stimulus; the often highly subjective meaning that one attributes to an incoming stimulus or message (p. 163)

perceptual screens perceptual filters of individuals through which messages must pass to be consciously perceived (p. 164)

personal selling interpersonal influence process involving a seller's promotional presentation conducted on a person-to-person basis with the buyer (pp. 382, 424)

person marketing marketing efforts designed to cultivate the attention, interest, and preference of a market target toward a person (typically, a political candidate or celebrity) (p. 562)

persuasive advertising competitive promotions used during the growth and early maturity stages of the product life cycle that seek to develop demand for products, services, organizations, people, ideas, or causes (p. 410)

physical distribution broad range of activities concerned with efficient movement of finished products from the end of the production line to the consumer; includes customer service, transportation, materials handling, protective packaging, inventory control, order processing, warehouse site selection, and warehousing. Also known as logistics (p. 352)

place utility want-satisfying power created by marketers who have products available where consumers want to buy them (p. 277)

planned obsolescence deliberate production of an item with limited durability (p. 556)

planned shopping center group of retail stores planned, coordinated, and marketed as a unit to shoppers in a geographic trade area (p. 328)

planning press of anticipating the future and determining the courses of action necessary to achieve organizational objectives (p. 66)

point-of-purchase advertising displays and other promotions located in close proximity to where a buying decision is actually made (p. 422)

political and legal environment component of the marketing environment consisting of laws and interpretation of laws that require firms to operate under competitive conditions and to protect consumer rights (p. 36)

pollution spoiling or making unclean of natural resources (p. 556)

population (or universe) total group that the researcher wants to study. For a political campaign, the population might be eligible voters (p. 108)

positioning developing a marketing strategy aimed at a particular market segment and designed to achieve a desired position in the mind of the prospective buyer (p. 409)

POSLSQ acronym for unmarried persons of the opposite sex living together in the same quarters; U.S. Census Bureau designation of a household format whose numbers are increasing (p. 132)

possession utility *See* ownership utility.

posttesting assessment of an advertisement's effectiveness after it has been used (p. 420)

precall planning use of information collected during the prospecting and qualifying stages of the sales process and during previous contacts with the prospect to tailor the approach and presentation to match the needs of the consumer (p. 440)

premiums items given free or at low costs with the purchase of a specified good or service (p. 423)

presentation step in the personal sales process consisting of a description of a product's major features and the relating of them to a customer's problems or needs (p. 441)

pretesting assessment of an advertisement before it is actually used (p. 420)

price exchange value of a good or service (p. 464)

price flexibility pricing policy permitting variable prices for products and services (p. 505)

price lining *See* product line pricing.

pricing policy general guideline based upon pricing objectives and intended for use in specific pricing decisions (p. 504)

pricing strategy element of marketing decision making that deals with the methods of setting profitable and justified exchange values for goods and services (p. 16)

primary data information or statistics being collected for the first time during a marketing research study (p. 99)

Primary Metropolitan Statistical Areas (PMSAs) major urban areas within a larger Consolidated Metropolitan Statistical Area (CMSA). Long Island's Nassau and Suffolk counties are PMSAs within the larger New York CMSA (p. 127)

private brand brand name owned by a wholesaler or retailer (p. 256)

private carriers freight transporters who operate only for a particular firm and cannot solicit business from others (p. 357)

probability sample sample in which every member of the population has an equal chance of being selected (p. 108)

producers component of the organizational market consisting of industrial customers who purchase goods and services for the production of other goods and services (p. 188)

product bundle of physical, service, and symbolic attributes designed to produce consumer want satisfaction (p. 212)

product advertising nonpersonal selling of a good or service (p. 409)

production orientation business philosophy stressing efficiency in producing a quality product; attitude toward marketing is "a good product will sell itself" (p. 10)

product liability concept that manufacturers and marketers are responsible for injuries and damages caused by their products (p. 261)

product life cycle four stages through which a successful product passes: introduction, growth, maturity, and decline (p. 214)

product line various related goods offered by a firm (p. 240)

product-line pricing practice of marketing different lines of merchandise at a limited number of prices (p. 505)

product managers individuals in a manufacturing firm assigned a product or product line and given complete responsibility for determining objectives and establishing marketing strategies (p. 245)

product mix assortment of product lines and individual offerings available from a marketer (p. 240)

product positioning consumer's perception of a product's attributes, use, quality, and advantages and disadvantages (p. 243)

product segmentation dividing an industrial market into homogeneous groups on the basis of product specifications identified by industrial buyers (p. 138)

product strategy element of marketing decision making comprising activities involved in developing the right product or service for the firm's customers; involves package design, branding, trademarks, warranties, product life cycles, and new-product development (p. 15)

profit center any part of an organization to which revenue and controllable costs can be assigned (p. 509)

profit impact of market strategies (PIMS) project major research study that discovered a strong positive relationship between a firm's market share and its return on investment (p. 469)

profit maximization in pricing strategy, the point at which the additional revenue gained by increasing the price of a product equals the increase in total cost (p. 468)

promotion function of informing, persuading, and influencing the consumer's purchase decision (p. 378)

promotional allowances advertising or sales promotion funds provided by a manufacturer to other channel members in an attempt to integrate promotional strategy in the channel (p. 501)

promotional mix blending of personal selling and non-personal selling (including advertising, sales promotion, and public relations) by marketers in an attempt to accomplish promotional objectives (p. 381)

promotional price lower-than-normal price used as a temporary ingredient in a firm's marketing strategy (p. 506)

promotional strategy element of marketing decision making that involves appropriate blending of personal selling, advertising, and sales promotion for use in communicating with and seeking to persuade potential customers (p. 16)

prospecting step in the personal selling process involving the identification of potential customers (p. 440)

psychographics behavioral profiles developed from analyses of buyer activities, opinions, interests, and lifestyles that may be used to segment consumer markets (p. 406)

psychographic segmentation dividing a population into homogeneous groups on the basis of behavioral and lifestyle profiles developed by analyzing consumer activities, opinions, and interests (p. 135)

psychological pricing pricing policies based on the belief that certain prices or price ranges are more appealing than others to buyers (p. 504)

Public Health Cigarette Smoking Act (1971) federal legislation restricting tobacco advertising on radio and television (p. 42)

publicity stimulation of demand by placing commercially significant news or obtaining favorable media presentation that is not paid for by an identified sponsor (pp. 382, 424)

public relations communications by an organization with its various publics and its various relationships with them (pp. 382, 424)

public warehouse independently owned storage facility that stores and ships products for a rental fee (p. 305)

pulling strategy promotional effort by the producer of a product or service designed to stimulate final user demand; the consumer will then demand that retailers stock the product, thereby "pulling" it through the marketing channel (p. 386)

pure competition market structure characterized by homogeneous products in which there are so many buyers and sellers that none has a significant influence on price (p. 473)

Pure Food and Drug Act (1906) federal legislation that prohibits the adulteration and misbranding of foods and drugs in interstate commerce (p. 42)

pushing strategy promotional effort by the producer of a product or service aimed at members of the marketing channel and designed to motivate them to market it more actively to consumers, thereby "pushing" it through the marketing channel (p. 386)

qualifying step in the personal selling process in which the salesperson determines whether a prospect is actually a potential customer (p. 440)

quantity discounts price reductions granted for large volume purchases (p. 500)

quota See sales quota.

quota sample nonprobability sample that is selected in such a way as to assure that different segments or groups are represented in the total sample (p. 109)

rack jobber wholesaler who markets specialized lines of merchandise to retail stores and provides the services of merchandising and arrangement, pricing, maintenance, and stocking of display racks (p. 308)

raw materials industrial goods such as farm products (wheat, cotton, soybeans) and natural products (coal, lumber, iron ore) used in producing final products (p. 226)

rebates refunds for a portion of the purchase price, usually granted by the manufacturer of a product (p. 501)

reciprocity highly controversial practice of extending purchasing preference to suppliers who are also customers (p. 199)

recycling reprocessing of used materials for their reuse (p. 556)

reference groups groups with which an individual identifies to the point where the group dictates a standard of behavior for the individual (p. 155)

regional shopping center largest type of a planned cluster of retail stores, usually involving one or more major department stores and as many as 200 other stores. A center of this size typically is located in an area with at least 250,000 people within 30 minutes driving time of the center (p. 328)

reinforcement reduction in drive that results from an appropriate response (p. 170)

reminder advertising promotions used during the late maturity and decline stages of the product life cycle that seek to reinforce previous promotional activity by keeping the name of the product, service, organization, person, idea, or cause in front of the public (p. 410)

research design series of advanced decisions that, when taken together, comprise a master plan or model for conducting marketing research (p. 99)

response individual's reaction to cues and drive (p. 170)

retail advertising nonpersonal selling by stores that offer goods or services directly to the consuming public (p. 419)

retailer one who sells products or services to the ultimate consumer and not for resale (p. 276)

retail image consumer's perception of a retail store and the shopping experience it provides (p. 329)

retailing all activities involved in the sale of products and services to the ultimate consumer (p. 324)

reverse channel path goods follow from consumer to manufacturer, in an effort to recycle used products or by-products (p. 281)

Robinson-Patman Act (1936) federal legislation prohibiting price discrimination that is not based on a cost differential. The act also prohibits selling at an unreasonably low price to eliminate competition (p. 40)

roles behavior that members of a group expect of individuals who hold a specific position within the group (p. 155)

salary fixed compensation payments made on a periodic basis to employees, including some sales personnel (p. 450)

sales analysis in-depth evaluation of a firm's sales (p. 96)

sales branch establishment maintained by a manufacturer that serves as a warehouse for a particular sales territory, thereby duplicating the services of independent wholesalers. Sales branches carry inventory and process orders to customers from available stock (p. 305)

sales force composite qualitative sales forecasting method in which sales estimates are based upon the combined estimates of the firm's sales force (p. 80)

sales forecast estimate of company sales for a specified future period (p. 79)

sales management achievement of marketing and sales objectives through planning, organizing, staffing, motivating, compensating, and evaluating and controlling an effective sales force (p. 446)

sales maximization practice of setting the lowest acceptable profit level as a minimum and then seeking to enlarge sales within this framework. Under this policy, marketers believe that increased sales are more important than immediate high profits in the long run (p. 469)

sales office manufacturer's establishment that serves as a regional office for salespeople but does not carry inventory (p. 306)

sales orientation business philosophy assuming that consumers will resist purchasing nonessential products and services; attitude toward marketing is that creative advertising and personal selling are required to overcome consumer resistance and convince them to buy (p. 12)

sales promotion marketing activities (other than personal selling, advertising, and publicity) that stimulate consumer purchasing and dealer effectiveness; includes displays, trade shows and expositions, demonstrations, and various nonrecurrent selling efforts (pp. 382, 422)

sales quota level of expected sales for a territory, product, customer, or salesperson against which actual results can be compared (pp. 97, 450)

samples products that are distributed at no cost to consumers in an attempt to obtain future sales (p. 423)

scrambled merchandising practice of some retailers who carry dissimilar product lines in an attempt to generate added sales volume (p. 339)

secondary data previously published data (p. 99)

selective distribution market coverage policy under which a firm chooses only a limited number of retailers to handle its product line (p. 287)

selective perception idea that consumers "perceive by exception;" they are consciously aware of only those incoming stimuli they wish to perceive (p. 163)

self-concept mental conception of one's self comprised of four components: real self, self-image, looking-glass self, and ideal self (p. 171)

seller's market marketplace characterized by a shortage of goods and/or services (p. 12)

selling agent agent wholesaling intermediary responsible for the total marketing program of a firm's product line (p. 311)

selling up retail sales technique of convincing a customer to buy a higher-priced item than he or she originally intended to buy (p. 446)

services intangible tasks that satisfy consumer and industrial user needs when efficiently developed and distributed to chosen market segments (p. 228)

shaping process of applying a series of rewards and reinforcements so that more complex behavior can evolve over time (p. 170)

Sherman Antitrust Act (1890) federal antitrust legislation that prohibits restraint of trade and monopolization and subjects violators to civil suits as well as to criminal prosecution (p. 38)

shopping goods products purchased only after the consumer has made comparisons of competing goods in competing stores on bases such as price, quality, style, and color. Shopping goods can be classified as either homogeneous (consumer views them as essentially the same) or heterogeneous (consumer sees significant differences in quality and style) (p. 222)

shopping store establishment at which customers typically compare prices, assortments, and quality levels with those of competing outlets before making a purchase decision (p. 331)

simple random sample basic type of probability sample in which every item in the relevant universe has an equal opportunity of being selected (p. 108)

skimming pricing strategy pricing strategy involving the use of a relatively high price compared to the prices of competitive offerings (p. 494)

social class relatively permanent divisions of a society into which individuals or families are categorized on the basis of prestige and community status (p. 156)

social responsibility marketing philosophies, policies, procedures, and actions that have the advancement of society's welfare as one of their primary objectives (p. 555)

societal/cultural environment component of the marketing environment consisting of the relationship between the marketer and society and its culture (p. 50)

specialty advertising sales promotion technique that involves the use of articles such as key rings, calendars, and ballpoint pens that bear the advertiser's name, address, and advertising message (p. 422)

specialty goods products with perceived unique characteristics that cause the buyer to prize them and to make a special effort to obtain them (p. 223)

specifications written description of a product or a service needed by a firm. Prospective bidders use this description first to determine whether they can manufacture the product or deliver the service and then to prepare a bid (p. 200)

SSWD refers to single, separated, widowed, or divorced; a term applied to single-person households, an emerging market segment (p. 132)

stagflation situation in which an economy has both high unemployment and a rising price level (p. 46)

Standard Industrial Classification (SIC) numerical system developed by the U.S. government that subdivides the industrial marketplace into detailed product/service industries or market segments (p. 191)

status relative position of any individual member in a group (p. 155)

storage warehouse traditional warehouse where products are stored prior to shipment (p. 364)

straight rebuy recurring industrial purchase decision where an item that has performed satisfactorily is purchased again by a customer (p. 196)

strategic business unit (SBU) related product groupings or businesses within a multiproduct firm with specific managers, resources, objectives, and competitors; structured for optimal planning purposes (p. 76)

strategic planning process of determining an organization's primary objectives and allocating funds, then proceeding on a course of action designed to achieve those objectives (p. 67)

strategic window limited periods during which the "fit" between the key requirements of a market and the particular competencies of a firm is at an optimum (p. 70)

stratified sample probability sample that is constructed so that randomly selected subsamples of different groups are represented in the total sample (p. 108)

subcultures subgroups of a culture with their own distinguishing mode of behavior (p. 153)

subliminal perception receipt of information at a subconscious level of awareness (p. 166)

suboptimization condition in which individual objectives are accomplished at the expense of broader organizational objectives (p. 353)

suggestion selling form of retail selling that attempts to broaden the customer's original purchase with related items, special promotions, and holiday or seasonal merchandise (p. 446)

supermarket large-scale departmentalized retail store offering a variety of food products and various nonfood items. It typically operates on a self-service basis and emphasizes low prices and adequate parking (p. 332)

supplies regular expense items necessary in the daily operation of the firm but not part of the final product (p. 226). *See also* MRO items.

supply schedule of the amounts of a product or service that will be offered for sale at different prices during a specified time period (p. 473)

survey of buyer intentions qualitative sales forecasting method in which sample groups of present and potential consumers are surveyed concerning their purchase intentions (p. 81)

system organized group of parts or components linked together according to a plan to achieve specific objectives (p. 353)

tactical planning implementation of activities specified by the strategic plan that are necessary in the achievement of a firm's objectives (p. 67)

target return objectives short-run or long-run pricing objectives of achieving a specified return on either sales or investment (p. 468)

tariffs in international marketing, taxes levied on imported products (p. 526)

task-objective method promotional budget allocation method under which a firm defines its goals and then determines the amount of promotional spending needed to accomplish them (p. 391)

technological environment applications of knowledge based upon discoveries in science, inventions, and innovations to marketing (p. 46)

telephone selling promotional presentation involving the use of the telephone on an "outbound" basis by salespeople or an "inbound" basis by customers who initiate such calls to obtain information and place orders (p. 437)

teleshopping innovative method of retailing conducted through interactive cable television (p. 341)

test marketing process of selecting a specific city or television-coverage area considered reasonably typical of the total market and introducing the product with a marketing campaign in this area (p. 248)

time utility want-satisfying power created by marketers having products available when consumers want to buy them (p. 277)

trade discounts payments to a channel member or buyer for performing marketing functions; also known as a functional discount (p. 499)

trade fair periodic shows where manufacturers in a particular industry display wares for visiting retail and wholesale buyers (p. 306)

trade industries component of the organizational market consisting of retailers or wholesalers who purchase goods for resale to others (p. 188)

trade-ins credit allowances given for an old item when a customer purchases a new item (p. 500)

trademark brand that has been given legally protected status. Protection is granted solely to the brand's owner (p. 252)

trading stamps sales promotion technique involving special stamps that are given as a purchase premium in some retail establishments and can be collected and redeemed for cash or gifts at special redemption centers operated by the trading stamp company (p. 423)

transfer mechanism in marketing communications, the means of delivering a message (p. 379)

transfer price costs assessed when products are moved from one profit center in a firm to another center in the same firm (p. 509)

trend analysis quantitative sales forecasting method in which estimates of future sales are determined through statistical analyses of historical sales patterns (p. 81)

truck wholesaler limited-function merchant wholesaler who markets perishable food items. Also known as a truck jobber (p. 310)

truth-in-lending act (1968) federal legislation requiring disclosure of the annual interest rates on loans and credit purchases; formally known as Title I of the Consumer Credit Protection Act (1968) (p. 42)

tying agreement understanding between a marketing intermediary and a manufacturer that requires the intermediary to carry the manufacturer's full product line in exchange for an exclusive dealership (p. 289)

undifferentiated marketing marketing strategy employed by some organizations that produce only one product or service and market it to all customers using a single marketing mix (p. 72)

unfair trade laws state laws requiring sellers to maintain minimum prices for comparable merchandise (p. 41)

uniform delivered price system for handling transportation costs under which all buyers are quoted the same price (including transportation expenses) (p. 503)

unitizing combining as many packages as possible into one load, preferably on a pallet to produce faster product movement and reduce damage and pilferage (p. 367)

unit pricing pricing policy under which prices are stated in terms of a recognized unit of measurement or a standard numerical count (p. 505)

unit trains time- and money-saving service provided by railroads to large-volume customers, in which a train is loaded with the shipments of only one company and transports solely for that customer (p. 358)

Universal Product Code (UPC) special codes on packages read by optical scanners which can print the item name and price while simultaneously maintaining a sales and inventory record (p. 260)

utility want-satisfying power of a product or service (p. 6)

value added by manufacturing difference between the price charged for a manufactured good and the cost of the raw materials and other inputs (p. 189)

venture team organizational strategy for identifying and developing areas for new products by combining the management resources of technological innovation, capital, management, and marketing expertise (p. 246)

vertical marketing systems (VMS) professionally managed and centrally programmed marketing channel networks structured to achieve operating economy and maximum impact (p. 289)

warranty guarantee to the buyer that the manufacturer will replace a product or refund its purchase price if the product proves to be defective during a specified period of time (p. 212)

Webb-Pomerene Export Trade Act (1918) federal legislation that excludes voluntary export trade associations from restrictions of the Sherman Act, but only in their foreign dealings (pp. 38, 528)

wheel of retailing hypothesis stating that new types of retailers gain a competitive foothold by offering lower prices through reduction or elimination of services. Once established, they add more services, their prices gradually rise, and they are vulnerable to the emergence of a new low-price retailer with minimum services (p. 324)

Wheeler-Lea Act (1938) federal statute amending the FTC Act so as to ban deceptive or unfair business practices per se (p. 39)

wholesaler wholesaling intermediary who takes title to the goods handled. Also called jobber or distributor (p. 300)

wholesaling activities of those who sell to retailers, other wholesalers, and industrial users, but not in significant amounts to ultimate consumers (p. 276)

wholesaling intermediary broad term that describes not only wholesalers, but also agents and brokers who perform important wholesaling activities without taking title to the goods (p. 300)

Wool Products Labeling Act (1939) federal legislation requiring that the kind and percentage of each type of wool in a product be identified (p. 42)

zone pricing system for handling transportation costs under which the market is divided into geographic regions and a different price is set in each region (p. 503)

Name Index

Company Index

Subject Index

Key terms and the page number(s) on which they are defined appear in boldface type for ease in locating them.